Handbook of Financial Services Performance

Analytical and Empirical Perspectives

Handbook of Financial Services Performance

Analytical and Empirical Perspectives

Editors

Bhagirath Prakash Baria
The Maharaja Sayajirao University of Baroda, India

Ram Pratap Sinha
Government College of Engineering and Leather Technology, India

Firdous Ahmad Malik
University of People, USA

K Shanmugan
The Maharaja Sayajirao University of Baroda, India

World Scientific

NEW JERSEY • LONDON • SINGAPORE • BEIJING • SHANGHAI • HONG KONG • TAIPEI • CHENNAI • TOKYO

Published by

World Scientific Publishing Co. Pte. Ltd.
5 Toh Tuck Link, Singapore 596224
USA office: 27 Warren Street, Suite 401-402, Hackensack, NJ 07601
UK office: 57 Shelton Street, Covent Garden, London WC2H 9HE

Library of Congress Cataloging-in-Publication Data
Names: Baria, Bhagirath Prakash editor | Sinha, Ram Pratap editor |
Malik, Firdous Ahmad, 1988– editor | Shanmugan, K. editor
Title: Handbook of financial services performance : analytical and empirical perspectives / editors: Bhagirath Prakash Baria, The Maharaja Sayajirao University of Baroda, India, Ram Pratap Sinha, Government College of Engineering and Leather Technology, India, Firdous Ahmad Malik, University of People, USA, K. Shanmugan, The Maharaja Sayajirao University of Baroda, India.
Description: Singapore ; Hackensack, NJ : World Scientific Publishing Co. Pte. Ltd, [2026] | Includes bibliographical references and index.
Identifiers: LCCN 2025043368 | ISBN 9789819823154 hardcover | ISBN 9789819823161 ebook | ISBN 9789819823178 ebook other
Subjects: LCSH: Financial services industry--Technological innovations | Fintech | Artificial intelligence--Financial applications
Classification: LCC HG173 .H358 2026 | DDC 332--dc23/eng/20260126
LC record available at https://lccn.loc.gov/2025043368

British Library Cataloguing-in-Publication Data
A catalogue record for this book is available from the British Library.

For any available supplementary material, please visit
https://www.worldscientific.com/worldscibooks/10.1142/14582#t=suppl

Desk Editors: Nambirajan Karuppiah/Pui Yee Lum

Typeset by Stallion Press
Email: enquiries@stallionpress.com

The Handbook of Financial Services Performance is an outstanding book with a collection of articles on contemporary research on financial services by eminent scholars of international institutions. The articles provide analytical studies on financial performance and policy prescriptions for improving conditions. The sectors covered in those studies include Banking, Fintech, Insurance, and other financial services. I strongly recommend the book for policymakers, researchers, government officials, and students of economics who will benefit from those articles.

— Chiranjib Neogi
Retired Associate Scientist, Indian Statistical Institute

The Handbook of Financial Services Performance is a great addition to the existing literature on the area. The Handbook has been divided into three distinct areas — Theory, Analytical perspective, and Empirical analysis. The book has twenty-one highly absorbing chapters that give interesting insight into the area of Data Envelopment theory and practice in Economics and Finance. The book deserves a look by serious students of Economics.

This book will bring fresh insight into the domain and will no doubt be an important reference for practitioners and policymakers.

— Golaka C Nath
Dean & Professor, School of Economics, XIM University

The Handbook of Financial Services Performance is a timely contribution to the literature on financial services. Drawing on the collective expertise of distinguished academics, this volume addresses emerging challenges and performance dynamics in banking, insurance, fintech, and regulatory frameworks. It is poised to become a vital reference for scholars, practitioners, and policymakers.

— Dr. Daisy Mui Hung Kee
Professor of Management, Universiti Sains Malaysia

An essential contribution that blends empirical depth with practical relevance. This captures the complexity of performance analysis in financial services through global and interdisciplinary perspectives. A must-read for scholars and policymakers alike.

— Assoc. Prof. Dr. Işıl Demirtaş
Department of Economics, Giresun University, Türkiye

This book, edited by four experienced academics with global recognition, provides a comprehensive analysis of the financial services industry from an international perspective. The book examines the theoretical debates in the performance analysis of banking and insurance industries, using both macro and granular data. It then presents empirical analyses of productivity, applying a wide range of parametric and non-parametric models to enhance readers' interest. Diverse datasets from various economies are incorporated, making this book a valuable resource for new researchers, experienced scholars, and policymakers.

— Shajara Ul-Durar
University of Sunderland, The Business School, Edinburgh Building, Chester Road, Sunderland, United Kingdom
Email: Shajara.ul-durar@sunderland.ac.uk

It is a preeminent book that evaluates current financial sector events with current scientific approaches, and with its deep thematic and methodological coverage, it is a must for researchers who want to capture the current in a broad perspective.

—Asst. Prof. Dr. Ayhan Gölcükcü
Department of Industrial Engineering, Beykent University, Türkiye

The Handbook of Financial Services Performance, edited by Dr. Bhagirath and colleagues, offers a comprehensive and cutting-edge exploration of productivity, efficiency, and profitability in banking and insurance. Combining robust theory with empirical depth, it employs advanced tools in econometric modeling as well as systematic reviews to chart the evolution and frontiers of performance analysis. I am sure this volume will serve as an essential reference for scholars, researchers, and policymakers shaping the future of financial services.

— Debashis Acharya
Professor, School of Economics, University of Hyderabad, Hyderabad

The *Handbook of Financial Services Performance* is a comprehensive and insightful resource for professionals and academics alike. It offers a well-structured exploration of key performance metrics, strategic frameworks, and regulatory challenges in the financial services sector. The contributors bring deep expertise, presenting complex concepts with clarity and real-world relevance. The Handbook's balanced focus on both theoretical foundations and practical applications makes it a valuable reference for understanding the dynamics of financial institutions in a competitive and evolving environment. Its coverage of current issues, including digital transformation and risk management, ensures it remains highly relevant. A must-have for financial services professionals.

— Prof. Dr. Arshi Naim
Professor in Business Management, European Global Institute of Innovation and Technology, Malta

https://doi.org/10.1142/9789819823161_fmatter

Foreword

It is a genuine pleasure to introduce the *Handbook of Financial Services Performance*. Over a long and varied academic career, I have seen our field transform dramatically. Once defined by basic balance sheet measures and profit margins, the performance of financial institutions has evolved into a multifaceted discipline – one that now encompasses technology, innovation, and an unyielding commitment to financial inclusion.

This volume is a timely reminder that understanding performance goes far beyond traditional metrics. It represents a journey into the heart of modern finance by weaving together theory, analytical rigor, and empirical inquiry. The authors contributing to this handbook not only share their specialized knowledge but also offer unique insights from their academic journeys.

Returning to the Fundamentals

The book begins with a robust theoretical framework in its first section. In Chapter 1, the authors challenge us to look beyond traditional quantitative measures. Their discussion resonated deeply with me, recalling earlier days when my curiosity pushed me to question how conventional metrics might fall short of capturing the true spirit of value creation. Equally compelling is the discussion in Chapter 2, where banks are reconceptualized as production units – engines of innovation that go beyond mere capital allocation. In Chapter 3, the mapping of performance analysis serves as a kind of intellectual compass, guiding us through a landscape replete with emerging methodologies and perspectives. Collectively, these chapters provide a robust and interconnected theoretical framework — a foundation on which the more complex analyses will later be built.

Embracing the Dynamics of Change

The second section shifts focus to the analytical dimensions of the field. Technology's transformative impact on performance measurement is explored in depth, reflecting conversations I have had with many colleagues during long research nights. The analysis of India's digital public infrastructure in Chapter 5, for instance, strikes at the very core of our efforts to extend financial inclusion. Chapters on fintech innovations and performance evaluation within the insurance industry further illustrate this point, emphasizing that today's financial landscape requires us to blend numerical precision with creative thinking.

From Concept to Empirical Reality

The final section of this handbook brings theory into contact with practice. The application of Data Envelopment Analysis (DEA) in Chapter 8 serves as a powerful example: Here, numbers become stories, revealing deep insights about operational efficiency. As the discussion moves to the technical efficiency of Indian private commercial banks and comparative studies of ASEAN institutions, it becomes clear that empirical evidence can both confirm and challenge our assumptions. Ventures into AI-enhanced KPI prediction models and machine learning applications signal the future of our field. Each chapter adds a unique brushstroke to a picture that is as dynamic as it is complex, reminding us that the interplay between data and human judgment is where real progress is made.

An Evolving Narrative

What resonates most about this handbook is how it unites diverse approaches into a single, evolving narrative. Whether you are drawn to the theoretical debates, the analytical innovations, or the empirical discoveries, you will find that every section speaks to our collective quest for clarity in a rapidly changing global market. This book is as much a scholarly work as it is a dialogue – a conversation among experts striving to understand, measure, and ultimately improve the performance of financial services.

The volume will remain active as an indispensable reference material for students, researchers, and policy experts for a long time. The beauty of the project is that it brings together multidimensional analytical and empirical rigor under a single umbrella. I congratulate the editors and the authors wholeheartedly for their rich contributions. In our time of continuous change, the Handbook of Financial Services Performance stands as a beacon guiding a future where financial institutions will grow to be more innovative, inclusive, and resilient.

Sugata Marjit
Visiting Professor, Hong Kong Polytechnic University,
Former First Distinguished Professor, Indian Institute of Foreign Trade, Former RBI Chair Professor and Director, Centre for Studies in Social Sciences, Calcutta, India and Former Vice Chancellor, University of Calcutta

https://doi.org/10.1142/9789819823161_fmatter

Preface

It is common knowledge that economic development presupposes the presence of capital investment, human capital, and a vibrant financial infrastructure that facilitates the transfer of investible resources from the savings class to the investing class. The role of the financial sector in economic development has been dealt with by researchers, market regulators, and practitioners in this field from various standpoints. Specifically, Gurley and Shaw (1955, 1956, and 1967) and Goldsmith (1969) highlighted the importance of financial development for economic growth across different contexts. In the case of emerging economies, the financial sector needs to address the issues of financial inclusion from both the liability and asset sides. Against this backdrop, the present book seeks to add value to the extant literature on financial sector performance as it contains contributed chapters from leading researchers belonging to fields as diverse as economics, business and finance, and operations research.

While the present book deals with both theoretical and empirical issues connected with financial sector performance, a majority of the studies included in the book relate to the empirical measurement of financial performance. The chapters have been broadly classified into three parts relating to the theory of performance analysis, analytical perspectives, and empirical perspectives, respectively.

The first part concerning theoretical perspectives includes three chapters written by Dr. Bhagirath Prakash Baria and Dr. Firdous Ahmed Malik; Violeta Cvetkoska and Bojan Kitanovikj; and Prof. K.V. Bhanumurthy, respectively. Dr. Bhagirath Prakash Baria and Dr. Firdous Ahmed Malik (Chapter 1) provide a deep scholarly peek into the issue of output measurement in the financial services. Violeta Cvetkoska and Bojan Kitanovikj (Chapter 2) perform a bibliometric study to identify major themes of financial sector performance analysis. Thereafter, Prof. K.V. Bhanumurthy (Chapter 3) highlights the alternative paradigms about banks as production units, the hypotheses to be tested, and the competing methods of performance evaluation.

The second part of the book comprises chapters that deal with the impact of technology on the performance of the financial sector while providing analytical perspectives on the performance of financial services. This part includes four chapters written by Dr. Narinder Kumar and Dr. Tuhin S. Banerjee (Chapter 4); Güneş Topçu, Can Bekaroğlu, and İsmail Elagöz (Chapter 5); Neeraj Kumar and Neha Mangla (Chapter 6); and Dr. Nelson Lawrence, Dr. Garikayi Emmanuel Gondo, and Prof. Dr. Ravinder Rena (Chapter 7). Chapter 4 reviews the extant literature on insurance sector performance analysis. Chapter 5 deals with a systematic literature review concerning the impact of technology on performance analysis in the financial sector domain. Chapter 6 seeks to evaluate the role of digital public infrastructure (J-A-M trinity) in the promotion of financial inclusion in India. Chapter 7 seeks to determine the impact of financial technology (fintech) on the financial performance of banks in emerging markets through a systematic literature review using the PRISMA method.

The final part of the book presents 14 chapters conducting a rigorous empirical evaluation of the performance of both final intermediaries and financial markets. Volha Rudkouskaya (Chapter 8) address the legalization of criminal proceeds within the banking sector of the Republic of Belarus. Ali Reza Amirteimoori and Maryam Nematizadeh (Chapter 9) apply data envelopment analysis (DEA) to evaluate the managerial ability performance of 2513 Asian commercial banks. Ram Pratap Sinha and K. Shanmugan (Chapter 10) try to evaluate and explain the efficiency performance of Indian private sector banks using both DEA and econometric methods.

Thanh Ngo, Tu Le, and Thi-Linh Pham (Chapter 11) estimate the non-convex frontier and efficiency of 79 ASEAN banks using the free disposal hull approach. Frédéric Mirindi and Derrick Mirindi (Chapter 12) examine the transformation of banking performance evaluation through artificial intelligence (AI). Bahareh

Vsaisi (Chapter 13) compare the performance of Iran's stock market banks with Iran Fara Bourse Banks using the super-efficiency DEA approach. Dr. Magesh Kumar, Dr. Ravinder Rena, Dr. V. Sindhu, and Dr. P. Srinivasan (Chapter 14) compare the performance of the ARIMA model and deep learning-based long short-term model for the forecasting of blockchain-based cryptocurrency price changes.

Mojtaba Ghiyasi and Mehdi Soltanifar (Chapter 15) apply an advanced DEA-R model for handling ratios and negative data in the context of the inverse DEA model. Pedro Pablo Chambi Condori and Telma Saravia Ticona (Chapter 16) evaluate financial services performance using machine learning approaches. Dr. Apanisile, Olumuyiwa Tolulope and Adesina, and Kehinde Elizabeth (Chapter 17) examine the finance–growth nexus in the context of the Nigerian economy. Ruchita Verma, Shiney Sam, and Dhanraj Sharma (Chapter 18) examine sensitivity based on evidence from Asian countries. Tarika Singh Sikarwar, Surjeet Singh, and Sandeep Singh (Chapter 19) examine the impact of parliamentary elections, political stability, and government effectiveness on bank risk in India.

Meysam Kaviani and Seyyed Ahmad Edalatpanah (Chapter 20) examine the relationship between return, tracking error, and intraday volatility under asset allocation based on the evidence from exchange-traded funds in Iran. Finally, Mohsen Imeni and Seyyed Ahmad Edalatpanah (Chapter 21) investigate litigation risk and the financial performance of banks, considering the moderating role of internal corporate governance in banks listed on the Tehran Stock Exchange (TSE).

Editors

References

Goldsmith, R.N. (1969) *Financial Structure and Development.* Yale University Press, New Haven.

Gurley, J.G. and Shaw, E.S. (1955) Financial aspects of economic development. *The American Economic Review*, 515–538.

Gurley, J. G. and Shaw, E. S. (1956). Financial intermediaries and the saving-investment process. *The Journal of Finance*, *11*(2), 257–276. https://doi.org/10.2307/2976705.

Gurley, J. and Shaw, E. (1967) Financial structure and economic development. *Economic Development and Culture Change*, 15, 257–268. https://doi.org/10.1086/450226.

https://doi.org/10.1142/9789819823161_fmatter

About the Editors

Bhagirath Prakash Baria is Senior Assistant Professor in the Department of Banking and Insurance at the Maharaja Sayajirao University of Baroda, India. A proficient professional in the areas of applied econometrics, banking macroeconomics, and agricultural economics, he teaches advanced courses in risk management and quantitative methods at the postgraduate level. His research draws from cutting-edge econometric techniques and has been published in Scopus-indexed and other leading journals. As an author of *The Economics of Financial Services in Emerging Economies* (Routledge), he curated insights from ten globally respected scholars, along with full-scale chapters authored by him. Dr. Baria has trained students, academics, and professionals in India and abroad, bridging statistical rigor with practical relevance. He continues to lead national and international collaborations in economics, finance, and policy, bringing methodological depth and a global perspective to every project he undertakes.

Ram Pratap Sinha is Associate Professor of Economics at the Government College of Engineering and Leather Technology, Kolkata. Renowned for his pioneering work in performance analysis of financial services, he has published over 146 high-impact studies on banking and insurance efficiency, employing both parametric and non-parametric techniques. With a distinguished citation record – over 600 citations, a high h-index, and an i10-index – his research ranks among the most influential in the field. Backed by more than three decades of teaching and research, Prof. Sinha has mentored hundreds of students and scholars in the econometrics of financial performance, shaping the next generation of researchers at the frontier of financial services analysis.

Firdous Ahmad Malik is Assistant Professor of Economics (Instructor) at the University of the People and a Post-Doctoral Researcher at Amity University Dubai. He holds a Ph.D. and MPhil in Economics from Babasaheb Bhimrao Ambedkar University, Lucknow, and a Master's degree from the University of Kashmir. His research spans microfinance, financial inclusion, and public finance, with publications in Scopus-indexed journals from Springer, Elsevier, and Taylor & Francis. Dr. Malik has authored 14 books – including *Financial Inclusion Schemes in India* (Springer) – with forthcoming titles from Routledge and IGI Global. He has held research positions at the NIPFP, Delhi, and O.P. Jindal Global University, and actively promotes young scholarship through the Young Scholars Initiative (YSI). Recognized for his academic contributions, he has received Best Paper and Reviewer awards at international conferences in Malaysia and India.

K. Shanmugan is Professor in the Department of Business Economics, Faculty of Commerce, at the Maharaja Sayajirao University of Baroda, India, and serves as Secretary of the Indian Econometric Society (TIES). A leading expert in macroeconometric modeling, his research focuses on structural approaches in applied macroeconomics, international economics, and agricultural economics. With over three decades of postgraduate teaching experience in econometrics, financial economics, and macroeconomics, Prof. Shanmugan has mentored generations of scholars and served as a resource person for institutions across India. He continues to publish rigorously empirical work that advances the field.

https://doi.org/10.1142/9789819823161_fmatter

Contents

Part I

Theory of Performance Analysis for Financial Services

https://doi.org/10.1142/9789819823161_0001

Chapter 1

Decoding Output Measurement for Banking and Insurance Services: A Scholarly Peek into the Literature

Bhagirath Prakash Baria[*,‡] **and Firdous Ahmad Malik**[†,§]

[*] *Department of Banking and Insurance, Faculty of Commerce, The Maharaja Sayajirao University of Baroda, Baroda, Gujarat, India*
[†] *Department of Business Administration, University of People, Pasadena, California, USA*
[‡] *bhagirath.baria-bi@msubaroda.ac.in*
[§] *malikfirdouscrc@gmail.com*

The measurement of service production in financial intermediation poses persistent conceptual and methodological difficulties for economic theory. Stemming from traditional distinctions by Adam Smith, services were previously regarded as unproductive — the view has been radically transformed — yet the conversion of service intangibility into measurable output continues to be controversial. This research provides an exhaustive consolidation of 453 carefully chosen research papers, including journal articles, books, and chapters that were published from 1957 to 2025, in order to study output measurement methods for insurance and banking organizations. Employing the PRISMA protocol in databases like Scopus, Web of Science, JSTOR, and Google Scholar, 265 papers based on banking performance and 188 papers on insurance performance were collected. The paper examines central dimensions of output measurement, such as theoretical concepts, sources of data, and multi-parametric measures, covering efficiency, productivity (partial and overall factor), profitability, and financial performance.

The research highlights the intermediate duality of being a service transformer and a producer, and discusses the innate complexity it presents by way of simultaneous production functions, inseparability of quality and quantity, and non-storability of services. Through this, the chapter puts forward a collection of conceptual propositions and measurement paradigms that seek to realign classical firm theory to the operating dynamics of modern financial intermediation.

Keywords: Banking; insurance; financial intermediation; PRISMA; service output measurement; systematic review.

1. Introduction

Historically, the systematic economic analysis of firms can be traced back to Adam Smith, who distinguished between productive and unproductive activities by classifying services as non-productive, a view that has since been revised as the theory of marginal utility emerged. With the evolution of economic thought, services have come to be recognized as value-creating rather than simply consuming surplus value (Kano and Tsang, 2023). Yet, the intellectual challenge remains: The traditional concepts of production, rooted in the tangible goods paradigm, do not easily accommodate the intangibility of services. The foremost challenge due to the intangibility of services emerges in measuring the value produced by these services, which is generally captured by the concept of output in economic theory. While the Smithian view of services as the destruction of surplus value has long been shed from the mainstream discourse, the measurement of its value production remains debated (Xu, 2021; Cigna *et al.*, 2022). These debates are observed foremost in the case of intermediation services such as financial services, where overlapping production functions[1] across the value chain, unclear distinction between inputs and outputs, and a host of other challenges prevent

[1]The concept of overlapping production function in financial services was proposed in Baria (2023) and it indicates the tendency of the production across the value chain of financial services to be intertwined where a given variable (such as deposits in case of banking, and premiums in case of insurance) tends to be simultaneously an input and an output. This results in conceptual difficulties in cleanly distinguishing between outputs and inputs for the entire value chain.

straightforward measurement of their output. There is no consensus in the literature on the optimal measure of output for financial services (Zhu and Wang, 2025).

This work, therefore, seeks to reconcile these issues by examining 453 research documents, including journal articles, books, book chapters, and others, to provide a peek into the measurement of output for financial intermediaries — specifically banking and insurance firms. 265 high-quality research articles on banking performance analysis and 188 high-quality research articles on insurance performance analysis are examined to analyze the major schools in this arena and derive key postulates in the theory of output measurement for financial intermediaries. These research documents cover the entire period from 1957 to 2025 for banking performance studies, and from 1964 to 2025 for insurance performance studies. Their selection is dictated by a systematic and scientific search protocol called PRISMA to locate the top-quality studies in the domain. Well-established keywords are utilized to screen through major databases such as Scopus, Web of Science, and JSTOR, along with a broad screening on Google Scholar, yielding around 1500 studies. These studies are then assessed using the PRISMA protocol, along with removing overlapping studies from multiple databases to arrive at the above-mentioned number of studies in the banking and insurance domains.[2]

These 453 studies are then thoroughly analyzed on various output measurement dimensions such as the measure used, the theoretical construct underlying the output measurement choice of the given study, the major data source, and the number of output measures employed, among a few others. The scope of the filtered studies includes all major parameters of performance, such as efficiency, productivity — both partial factor and total factor — and profitability, among others, such as financial performance. The next sections provide a short note on the major debates and dimensions in this area.

[2]The systematic review analytics are not reported in this chapter and can be availed from the authors upon reasonable request. The decision to not report it was taken based on the space constraints.

1.1. *Fundamental challenges in measuring service outputs*

Central to the discussion is the inherent difficulty of quantifying outputs in services. Unlike tangible goods, service outputs are characterized by intangibility and the inseparability of quality from quantity (Lusch and Vargo, 2021). These two aspects complicate the measurement process of financial services output significantly. In the production of services, the quality of output is not separable from its quantitative characteristics; hence, any movement in input or output levels simultaneously reflects a qualitative transformation. Moreover, the non-storability of services further impedes the formulation of straightforward economic relations between inputs and outputs. These conceptual challenges create a need for innovative output measures that can capture both the numeric and qualitative dimensions of service provision without distortion.

1.2. *Conceptual problems in output measurement due to intermediation*

Intermediaries do not merely facilitate transactions; they transform inputs into diversified services that involve multiple production stages (Qi *et al.*, 2023). For instance, banks convert deposits into credit facilities and, concurrently, offer multiple deposit-related services. Similarly, insurers pool premiums and advance risk coverage services, which are then manifested in various forms such as claim payments and reserve management. These operations introduce layers of complexity into the production process that could be overlapping, leading to inconsistent measures of output if traditional value-added or similar approaches are employed. Traditional firm theory, developed primarily from the study of manufacturing outputs, requires modifications to account for the dual roles played by these institutions, as both intermediaries and producers of transformed, multi-stage services.

2. Principal Features of an Ideal Output Measure of Financial Services

Based on the framework developed by Baria (2023) and the systematic analysis of 453 selected studies, it is inferred that the estimation of financial services output should adhere to certain theoretical and empirical postulates to ensure sound and reliable estimates. These features are necessitated by both theoretical and empirical considerations. Ensuring that financial services output measures provide meaningful information, rather than statistical noise, requires that certain features are ensured in the estimates.

2.1. *Product mix representativeness*

The ideal output measure should accurately reflect the diverse product mix of a firm. At both the firm and industry levels, this means accounting for new product introductions and shifts in the relative share of each service. Without this representativeness, the output measure may fail to capture the true evolution of production activities.

2.2. *Quality-adjusted measure*

The output measure must be adjusted for quality. As the chapter notes, if quality improvements or deteriorations are not isolated from quantitative changes, the resultant measure may lead to erroneous assessments of performance. This separation is crucial in estimating efficiencies, productivity, and scale economies.

2.3. *Regulatory robustness*

The banking and insurance sectors are subject to significant regulation. An output measure should ideally remain unaffected by regulatory changes, which could otherwise induce output fluctuations unrelated to underlying production efficiency. For example, changes in interest or reserve requirements might spur variances in loans or reserves that are not indicative of production improvements.

2.4. *Endogeneity to the production function*

The output measure is most meaningful when it is a direct consequence of a firm's production process rather than external shocks. The measure should mirror the intrinsic relationship between inputs and outputs in a manner that is robust to exogenous disturbances such as sudden regulatory shifts or market anomalies.

2.5. *Methodological robustness*

Given the wide range of empirical techniques, both parametric and non-parametric, used to analyze performance, the chosen output measure should yield consistent results across different methods. This stability ensures that performance estimates remain comparable over time and across studies.

2.6. *Availability of multiple proxies*

Data limitations force analysts to rely on proxies for underlying theoretical output concepts. Having multiple proxies available, each representing different facets of the output, provides a safeguard against information loss while also serving as a cross-validation tool. In banking, for example, measures like loan volume and deposit totals may serve as complementary proxies.

2.7. *Maximization criterion*

Economic theory presupposes that production outputs should be maximized (Akerstrom *et al.*, 2024). An effective output measure must align with this premise. Measures that imply the minimization of output (such as non-performing loan rates in banking or loss payments in insurance) require justification or reinterpretation as "bad outputs" because they do not comport with the rational economic goal of output expansion.

2.8. *Specification-based selection*

Rather than selecting output measures arbitrarily, the measure must emerge from a well-defined theoretical specification of the production process. Various approaches, such as production, value-added, intermediation, asset-based, and user cost measures, exist that must be utilized to specify the output measures and hence achieve greater validity.

2.9. *Size reflection*

The output measure should also capture the economic scale of a firm or industry, acting as an indicator of its tangible production capabilities. This consideration is especially important in comparing large and small institutions or evaluating industry-wide performance.

2.10. *High correlation with alternatives*

An ideal measure is expected to correlate strongly with other plausible proxies. This consistency implies that even if one available measure is chosen due to data availability, it will not significantly deviate from the theoretical concept that alternative measures might capture.

2.11. *Existence of a price index*

Deflation of value-based output measures is a well-documented challenge in performance analyses. While an optimal, specialized price index for banking or insurance outputs remains elusive, ideally, there should be a well-defined price index that allows for the proper deflation of output measures, thereby removing price-related distortions.

2.12. *Handling multi-output nature*

Both banks and insurers offer an array of services concurrently. Hence, an effective output measure must incorporate aggregation techniques that preserve the heterogeneity of these outputs. Weighting factors, for instance, must be applied such that the composite output measure accurately reflects the varied dimensions of service offerings.

2.13. *Stable definition*

The output measure must be consistently defined over time and across spatial dimensions. Instability in definition can lead to complications in dynamic performance evaluations and may even result in an output variable being treated as an input.

2.14. *Firm-controlled variability*

Finally, the measure should be such that variations in output are predominantly under the firm's control. This means the production process and the resultant output should essentially capture the firm's decisions rather than external market disruptions.

2.15. *Unitary influence factor*

The chapter underscores the notion that the observed quantitative changes in output should be directly proportional to the change in the underlying service content. Theoretically, a one-to-one relationship (a unitary influence factor) is desirable, meaning a 10% increase in the output measure should equate to a 10% increase in the actual services provided.

3. Literature Analytics

This section presents the review analytics obtained from a detailed systematic review of more than 450 high-quality studies on banking and insurance performance assessment published during the period 1957 to 2025. Out of the 453 studies, 265 are from the banking domain, while 188 are from the insurance domain. Put together, these studies provide rich insights into the nature of the output measurement problem faced in financial services research. This is perhaps among the very few studies that systematically summarize a voluminous literature on output measurement in financial services.

3.1. *Banking output measurement literature: 1957–2025*

Table 1 presents the descriptive summary of the literature on output measurement in the banking performance domain. Readily, one observes that secondary data have been dominant in the literature, indicating that output measures used in the literature so far could be sensitive to the kind of source which is relied upon. Naturally, collecting large-scale primary data is not only economically unsound but also not practically feasible, as data on banks and insurers are generally available only to the regulators in the respective countries and perhaps via annual reports by the firms themselves. Accessing primary data for any researcher who is studying a large sample is not plausible. The major source of information for output measurement

Table 1. Systematic literature review-based analytics for banking output measurement literature.

Sr. No.	Dimension	Frequency	Sr. No.	Dimension	Frequency
	Nature of Data			***Scope of the Analysis***	
1	Primary	5	1	Bank Level (using branch-specific data)	3
2	Secondary	238	2	Industry Level (using bank-wise data)	221
3	Secondary; Primary	2	3	Sectoral (aggregated over bank groups)	12
4	Not Available	20	4	International (using cross-country data)	13
	Grand Total	*265*	4.1.	*Using cross-country bank-level data*	*2*
	Type of Data		4.2.	*Using country-level aggregated data*	*11*
1	Cross-Sectional	75	5	Market Level (using individual transaction-level data	1
2	Pooled	12	6	Others	2
3	Time Series	25		*Grand Total*	265
4	Both Cross-Sectional; Time Series	1		***Output Measure***	
5	Panel	146	1	Deposit-based	9
6	Unclear	2	2	Credit-based	139
7	Not Available	21	3	Both	108
	Grand Total	*282*	4	Others	9

(*Continued*)

Table 1. *(Continued)*

Sr. No.	Dimension	Frequency	Sr. No.	Dimension	Frequency
	Theoretical Approach			*Grand Total*	265
1	Production Function	90		***Stock–Flow dimension of Output Measure***	
2	Cost Function	98	1	Stock	227
3	Profit Function	12	2	Flow	121
4	Index Number Approach	5	3	Ratio of Stock and Flow	16
5	Productivity	6		*Grand Total*	364
6	Ratio Analysis	17		***Uses National Accounting Data (FISIM)***	
7	Review of Literature	9	1	Yes	38
8	Others	29	2	No	214
	Grand Total	265	3	Not Available	13
	Empirical Approach			*Grand Total*	265
1	DEA Approaches	84		***Output Measurement Approach***	
2	SFA	32	1	Intermediation	142
3	Index Number Approach	5	2	Production	66
4	Econometric Approaches	32	3	Intermediation and Production	13
5	National Income Accounting Approach	6	4	Value Added	14
6	Ratio Analysis	26	5	Intermediation and Value Added	3
7	Others	80	6	Production and Value Added	3
	Grand Total	265	7	National Income Accounting (FISIM)	2
			8	Others (such as User-Cost and Undefined)	22
				Grand Total	265

Notes: (1) DEA — Data Envelopment Analysis, SFA — Stochastic Frontier Approach; (2) The total number of studies may exceed 265 due to overlapping entries in some categories and criteria.
Source: Based on the detailed review of 265 empirical points of evidence on banking performance analysis in the global context. The detailed list of studies may be obtained from the authors upon reasonable request.

in the banking performance analysis has been regulatory databases that are generally of high quality with very little statistical noise.[3] Concerning the type of data used in the literature, Panel datasets have dominated the discourse, followed by cross-sectional data. There is a dearth of time series perspectives in the literature on banking output measurement.

There has been a rich diversity of theoretical approaches in the literature on banking output measurement in the performance analysis domain. Researchers have largely focused on estimating production and cost functions in the performance assessment of banks. This could be due to the duality of both functions as per standard microeconomic theory, resulting in a larger emphasis from empiricists due to conceptual and statistical ease in estimating them and also cross-deriving them. This implies that perhaps the dimension of efficiency has received greater attention than other performance metrics such as productivity and profitability. The descriptive statistics on the empirical approaches in literature corroborate this fact, as both the Data Envelopment Approaches (DEA) and Stochastic Frontier Approaches (SFA) have dominated the empirical methodology dimension.

With reference to the granularity of the empirical measurement of output in the banking domain, industry-level studies that utilize firm-level data have dominated. This could explain the predominance of panel data in the literature, as capturing an industry-level performance metric using firm-level data can be conveniently undertaken using panel databases. Some interesting perspectives on output measurement in the literature include international studies that employ cross-country bank-level data, generally using private databases such as Bank Focus of Moody's Analytics, and market-level studies that employ transaction-level data. Such studies are rare, naturally owing to the cost and practical difficulties in obtaining such large-scale granular data. In terms of the output measures in banking performance literature, usage of either credit-based measures, such as loans,

[3]In the literature, privately maintained databases such as Thomson Reuters and Bank Focus have also been employed due to the comprehensive nature of such databases (Gutiérrez-Ponce and Wibowo, 2023).

or both deposit and credit measures has played a pivotal role. It seems that there is an implicit agreement in the banking literature on treating credit as an output, while the treatment of deposits as either output or input has not been agreed upon.

Literature has been dominated by stock measures of banking output rather than flow measures. This could be explained by the dominance of asset-based output measures such as loans, which are generally balance sheet items for banks. The "stock–measures bias" in banking output measurement is an important finding as it implies that the balance sheet view is dominant in deciding the output measure. Data on balance sheet items are readily accessible from the financial statements of banks as well as from regulators, while the flow measures, such as income of the banks, and yearly additions to loans and deposits, among others, require additional manipulation of data. This arithmetic manipulation of data could lead to information loss and perhaps the literature has hence avoided the use of flow measures. However, traditional economic theory views output as a flow variable and this incongruence between theory and praxis requires further investigation in a larger review. Interestingly, some studies have chosen the ratio of stock and flow variables, leading to increased alignment with economic theory. However, their proportion in the literature is quite limited.

The use of the Financial Intermediation Services Indirectly Measured (FISIM) approach to banking output measurement is very limited in the literature. Only 38 out of the 265 studies used the national income accounting approach. This lack of empirical usage of the FISIM estimates that are used in national income accounts indicates a dearth of macro-level output estimates in the literature. A fundamental debate in the output measurement literature for banking services is the underlying approach or the school of thought that informs the empirical choices. Major approaches include the intermediation, production, value-added, and national income approaches.[4] Literature showcases a strong dominance of the intermediation approach.

[4]A detailed explanation of each of these major approaches, their underlying output measurement strategies, and other related dimensions has been captured succinctly in Baria (2023).

Under this approach, the input–output matrix is defined in a manner where deposits are treated as input while the loans are treated as output. Clearly, this is the dominant view in the literature. Production approach is the second most preferred approach wherein both deposits and loans are treated as potential outputs, with factors such as labor and capital playing the role of inputs. Other approaches, such as the value-added, national income, and the user cost approaches, have not been adequately preferred in the literature. This leaves adequate room for studies that employ these approaches and could perhaps throw fresher insights into the output measurement problem in the banking domain.

3.2. *Insurance output measurement literature: 1964–2025*

Similar to the systematic review analytics contained in Table 1, insights are provided for the output measurement problem in the insurance domain for studies ranging from 1964 to 2025. It can be observed that, similar to the banking domain, secondary data have dominated the discourse in the insurance output measurement domain. Concerns similar to the ones raised in Section 3.1 could be playing a role in this choice of the literature. Panel data have dominated the discourse, as seen in Table 1, with meager literature deriving output measures using other types of datasets. Unlike the banking literature, cross-sectional datasets have not played much of a role in the insurance domain.

A large volume of literature in the insurance performance domain has focused on the production function approach, indicating that efficiency is a predominant concern in the literature.[5] Consistent with this, the production approach has played a pivotal role in directing the output measurement choice, unlike the banking literature, where intermediation has dominated. The input–output debate has a theoretically different form in the insurance discourse, given that the literature has largely avoided the intermediation approach. Under

[5]Nguyen and Lam (2025) provide an overview of alternative output specification approaches in the insurance performance literature.

the production approach, treatment of inputs and outputs is clear, and the composite production process is generally treated as separable under this framework. The popularity of this approach in insurance indicates that variables such as premiums, claims, and losses incurred are treated as output, with traditional factors such as labor and capital serving as inputs. The conceptualization of the production process in the insurance performance domain has largely been straightforward, though there is no clear agreement on the correct measure of output yet.

The predominant empirical approach in the insurance literature is DEA and its various extensions, such as Dynamic DEA, Stochastic DEA, and Multi-Stage DEA. This is consistent with the primacy of the production function and the underlying dominance. With regard to the granularity of the studies, industry-oriented studies employing insurer (firm)-level data overshadow other analytical schemes and are similar to the trend in the banking literature. The output measures employed in the insurance performance literature suggest that value measures, represented by variables such as premiums, claims paid, and losses incurred, have been the primary choice for proxying the output of insurance services. Value measures are estimated in terms of financial currency and in the literature, these measures have generally not been subjected to much economic adjustments, except deflation in a few cases.[6] Within the value measures, premiums and assets of insurance firms have received considerable attention. Hence, both the stock (assets) and flow (premiums) have been utilized in the literature, unlike the dominance of stock measures in the case of the banking literature. However, flow output measures have outpaced their stock counterpart as seen in Table 2. Similar to the trend in the banking literature, FISIM-based national account estimates of insurance output have been rarely employed in the insurance literature.

[6]The cases where deflation insurance output measures are undertaken have been estimated and analyzed in the systematic review exercise of this study. However, the findings have not been reported due to a paucity of space.

Table 2. Systematic literature review-based analytics for insurance output measurement literature.

Sr. No.	Dimension	Frequency	Sr. No.	Dimension	Frequency
	Nature of Data			***Output Measures***	
1	Primary	6	1	*Value Measures*	
2	Secondary	154	1.1.	Premiums	74
3	Primary and Secondary	1	1.2.	Claims/Losses	30
4	Not Available/Not Clear	27	1.3.	Investments	46
	Grand Total	*188*	1.4.	Assets	59
	Type of Data		1.5.	Profits	11
1	Cross-Sectional	21	2	*Volume Measures*	
2	Time Series	15	2.1.	Number of Policies issued	7
3	Pooled	7	2.2.	Number of policyholders	1
4	Panel	124	2.3.	Number of Applications and Turnaround time	1
4.1.	*Balanced*	*6*	2.4.	Number of meetings, Number of concluded contracts	1
4.2.	*Unbalanced*	*9*	3	*Macro Measures*	
4.3.	*Undefined/Unclear*	*109*	3.1.	GDP	1
5	Not Available	26	3.2.	GNP	1
	Grand Total	*193*	3.3.	GVA	1
	Theoretical Framework		3.4.	Insured Population	1
1	Production Function	115	4	*Others*	
2	Cost Function	13	4.1.	Ratios	5
3	Revenue Function	4	4.2.	Reserves	17
4	Index Numbers Approach	3	4.3.	*Grand Total*	*256*
5	Ratio Analysis and Descriptive Approach	18		***Stock–Flow Dimension***	

(*Continued*)

Table 2. (*Continued*)

Sr. No.	Dimension	Frequency	Sr. No.	Dimension	Frequency
6	Econometric Approaches	8	1	Stock	70
7	Productivity Approaches	8	2	Flow	162
8	Other Approaches	19	3	Both Stock and Flow	8
	Grand Total	188		*Grand Total*	*240*
	Empirical Approach			***Uses National Income Accounting Measure (FISIM)***	
1	DEA Approaches	98	1	Yes	11
2	SFA	19	2	No	150
3	TFA	1	3	Not Available/Not Clear	27
4	Econometric Approaches	20		*Grand Total*	*188*
4.1.	*Time Series*	*5*		***Output Measurement Approach***	
4.2.	*Panel*	*4*	1	Intermediation	16
4.3.	*Others*	*11*	2	Production	84
5	Arithmetic and Ratio Analysis	23	3	Intermediation and Production	2
6	Machine Learning Approaches	1	4	Value Added	38
7	Literature Reviews	3	5	Intermediation and Value Added	2
8	Productivity Indices	5	6	National Income Accounting (FISIM)	2
9	Others	18	7	Not Available/ Not Clear	49
	Grand Total	*188*		*Grand Total*	*193*
	Scope of the Study				
1	Industry-level	146			
1.1.	Using firm-level data	*135*			
1.2.	*Using policy-level data*	*2*			

(*Continued*)

Table 2. (*Continued*)

Sr. No.	Dimension	Frequency	Sr. No.	Dimension	Frequency
1.3.	*Using product-line data*	*2*			
1.4.	Other aggregation schema	7			
2	Sectoral (aggregated over insurance groups)	6			
3	International (using cross-country data)	6			
3.1.	*Using cross-country insurer-level data*	*4*			
3.2.	*Using country-level aggregated data*	*2*			
4	Not Available	30			
	Grand Total	188			

Notes: (1) DEA — Data Envelopment Analysis, SFA — Stochastic Frontier Approach; (2) The total number of studies may exceed 188 due to overlapping entries in some categories and criteria.
Source: Based on the detailed review of 188 empirical points of evidence on banking performance analysis in the global context. The detailed list of studies may be obtained from the authors upon reasonable request.

4. Frontiers in Output Measurement of Financial Services

While Section 3 presents the systematic review analytics on banking and insurance output measurement, several issues have emerged that are currently at the forefront of the literature. There is no universal agreement on these issues, and the latest research could focus on these aspects of the output measurement problem.

The first major issue at the frontier in this domain is developing a sound theory of financial services output. Existing theoretical models still display some bias toward the "tangibles" while only partially capturing the entire value creation process of services (Gomez, 2024). A holistic theory of financial services output could explain how the value chain works, the major components of the same, the input–output measures required for measuring the value process, and the most essential theoretical properties of an ideal output measure for financial services. Second, there is a need to address the lack of time series estimates of output in the banking and insurance domains. Having consistent and sound time series output estimates would allow further decomposition into the long-term and short-term structures of the evolution of financial services output, thereby providing a fertile ground for policy simulations that generally undertake forecasting exercises. Furthermore, dynamic analysis of the behavior of financial services output can be undertaken if the literature is able to provide high-quality, continuous estimates with negligible statistical noise. Analysis of shocks to financial services output, such as those emerging from the COVID-19 pandemic, can be undertaken with sound and continuous time series data (Mateev *et al.*, 2024).

Third, integration of the FISIM methodology into the mainstream output measurement literature is critical to bridge the gap between the micro-level granular studies and the macro perspectives required for policy analytics. Fourth, macro estimates of banking and insurance output have not been adequately addressed, leading to a "micro bias" in the literature. This remains an issue at the forefront of the present discourse. Recent evidence suggests that macroeconomic variables have a detrimental impact on the performance of financial services (Bushashe, 2023). However, such findings are sensitive to the underlying output measures, and generally studies employ micro-financial output variables such as deposits and loans rather than macro-level output constructs that could better serve in studies having a macroeconomic footing. Fifth, the implications of fintech for financial services output are at the frontier of the performance analysis domain. Fintech is not only generating positive externalities for financial services but also posing negative externalities in terms of increased risks, both micro and systemic (Al-Shari and Lokhande, 2023). These externalities can have qualitative implications for the output of financial services, such as banking and insurance services, which need to be incorporated into the traditional output estimates. Hence, quality adjustments to account for fintech-related changes in the output of financial services are an issue at the frontier in the performance analysis domain. Lastly, a separate line of research needs to address the sensitivity of various performance metrics of financial services to alternative output measures.[7]

5. Conclusion

This chapter has provided a brief view of the voluminous literature on banking and insurance performance with special reference to the output measurement problem in the domain. By analyzing more than 450 high-quality studies, this work has presented a bird's-eye view of the output measurement debates in the domain of financial services. Systematic review analytics have shown important trends in the performance analysis literature while supplying critical components to develop a holistic theory of output measurement for financial services. The intermediary nature of these services and the overlapping production functions that operate across the value chain of financial services make the estimation of their output challenging. Complex input–output interconnections render tractability and separability conditions difficult to achieve in the case of financial services production functions. Hence, handling the performance analysis issues becomes challenging unless a sound production process can be modeled for financial services.

The foremost challenge in conceptualizing and estimating the production function in financial services is measuring its output. Due to the above-mentioned challenges, measuring the production of financial services is both a theoretical and an empirical challenge. This chapter has addressed the major concerns in this regard while summarizing a large body of literature on the performance metrics in financial services from diverse countries, using varied databases with a rich collection of empirical methods. It is evident that there is a strong need to bridge the gap between what the theory of output measurement demands and the current practice. Future works need

[7]To the best of the knowledge of the authors, only Baria (2023) has conducted a large-scale exercise on the sensitivity analysis of various performance metrics, such as efficiency, productivity and profitability, to alternative output measures of banking and insurance services. The literature has so far not been able to address this concern and it remains at the frontier of the discourse, despite the limited attention provided to it.

to address the matters at the frontier of this domain, as highlighted in Section 4. Developing a sound and holistic theory of financial services output is critical not only for conducting scholarly research but also for developing policy-relevant data that can be valuable for simulations and forecasting exercises pertaining to the financial sector in emerging and advanced economies. The present chapter has, hopefully, provided a scholarly peek into this fascinating area, and future works are expected to develop upon the debates, issues, and analytics provided herein.

References

Akerstrom, M., Beenen, G., and Houessou, R. (2024). Cost-benefit and marginal analysis in resource allocation. *Journal of Applied Managerial Economics*, 13(1), 45–58.

Al-Shari, H. A. and Lokhande, M. A. (2023). The relationship between the risks of adopting FinTech in banks and their impact on the performance. *Cogent Business & Management*, 10(1), 2174242.

Baria, B. P. (2023). *The Economics of Financial Services in Emerging Markets: Measuring the Output of the Banking and Insurance Industries* (1st ed.). Routledge.

Bushashe, M. A. (2023). Determinants of private banks performance in Ethiopia: A partial least square structural equation model analysis (PLS-SEM). *Cogent Business & Management*, 10(1), 2174246.

Cigna, S., Gunnella, V., and Quaglietti, L. (2022). *Global Value Chains: Measurement, Trends and Drivers* (ECB Occasional Paper No. 289). European Central Bank. https://www.ecb.europa.eu/pub/pdf/scpops/ecb.op289~ 95a0e7d24f.en.pdf.

Gomez, K. (2024). A theory on value creation. *SRN Working Paper*. https://papers.ssrn.com/sol3/papers.cfm?abstract_id=4968016.

Gutiérrez-Ponce, H. and Wibowo, S. A. (n.d.). Do sustainability practices contribute to the financial performance of banks? An analysis of banks in Southeast Asia. *Corporate Social Responsibility and Environmental Management*, 31, 1418–1432.

Kano, L. and Tsang, E. W. K. (2023). Service innovation and value co-creation: Measurement challenges in manufacturing firms. *Industrial Marketing Management*, 116, 110–123.

Lusch, R. F. and Vargo, S. L. (2021). *Service-Dominant Logic: Premises, Perspectives, Possibilities* (2nd ed.). Cambridge University Press.

Mateev, M., Sahyouni, A., and Al Masaeid, T. (2024). Bank performance before and during the COVID-19 crisis: Does efficiency play a role? *Review of Managerial Science*, 18(1), 29–82.

Nguyen, P. A. and Lam, H. P. A. (2025). Evaluating the efficiency of insurance companies in Vietnam using Data Envelopment Analysis and truncated regression. *Cogent Economics & Finance*, 13(1), 2494134.

Qi, X., Sun, J., and Chen, Y. (2023). Cloud service intermediaries in digital ecosystems: Value creation and capture. *Journal of Strategic Information Systems*, 32(2), 101716.

Xu, W. (2021). Value production, measurement, and distribution under digital capitalism: A critique of the theory that the law of value has failed. *World Review of Political Economy*, 12(4), 472–495. https://www.jstor.org/stable/48676106.

Zhu, C. and Wang, R. (2025). Commercial banks performance, ownership types and operations efficiency decomposition in China: A comparative analysis. *Humanities and Social Sciences Communications*, 12(1), 291.

https://doi.org/10.1142/9789819823161_0002

Chapter 2

Mapping Performance Analysis of Financial Services: Systematic Insights and Perspectives

Violeta Cvetkoska* and Bojan Kitanovikj†

Faculty of Economics, Ss. Cyril and Methodius University in Skopje, Skopje, North Macedonia

**vcvetkoska@eccf.ukim.edu.mk*

†bojan.kitanovikj@eccf.ukim.edu.mk

The financial services industry has undergone transformative changes over recent decades, driven by advancements in technology, evolving regulations, and shifts in how financial products and services are produced and consumed. These developments have made performance measurements in financial services increasingly complex, requiring more comprehensive, transparent, and data-driven approaches. This book chapter addresses the growing interest in performance analysis by identifying and mapping significant research themes in the field from the first published article in 1982 to today. Using a multi-technique bibliometric analysis of 826 articles extracted from the Scopus database, followed by a systematic review adhering to the Preferred Reporting Items for Systematic Reviews and Meta-Analyses (PRISMA) protocol, the study explores key themes, including parametric and non-parametric measurement models, firm performance, risk assessment, sustainability, and digital innovation. The findings are visualized through co-authorship networks, bibliographic coupling, and keyword co-occurrence maps, revealing interconnected themes and under-researched areas such as artificial intelligence, machine learning, blockchain, and branding. As one of the first comprehensive bibliometric studies on this topic, this chapter provides researchers and practitioners with a synthesized overview of the field and highlights promising directions for future research in performance analysis within financial services.

Keywords: Bibliometric analysis, digital innovation in finance, financial services performance, machine learning, PRISMA.

1. Introduction

In the past decades, the financial services industry has experienced unprecedented changes, propelled by technology, new regulations, the need for new financial products and services, and how these are produced and consumed. In turn, this made measuring the performance of financial services more complex, calling for a more comprehensive, reliable, transparent, and data-driven approach to how we measure how these services fare in a world that is increasingly becoming accustomed to self-service via digital financial platforms instead of branch banking and e-payments instead of wire transfers and checks. Considering that researchers' and practitioners' interests in performance analysis of financial services are at an all-time high, the academic output has increased over the years, with the first articles in the field appearing in the early 1980s.

Motivated by all of this, the objective of this chapter is to identify the most significant research themes on the topic of performance analysis of financial services from 1982 (the year the first article on the topic was published) until 2023, as the last year that is completed at the time of writing, and the magnitude and interconnectedness of these themes. Additionally, having a systematic review nature, the chapter aims to investigate the impactful themes and milestones in the evolutionary development of the field by visually mapping the keywords, countries of authorship, and the authors themselves. This will help to identify the under-researched topics that can serve as avenues for future research.

The core methodological approach is bibliometric analysis, followed by a systematic literature review, which is compliant with the rigorous Preferred Reporting Items for Systematic Reviews and Meta-Analyses (PRISMA) protocol. A total of 826 articles extracted from the leading Scopus database were used for the analysis. The bibliometric analysis consists of descriptive analysis, co-authorship analysis, bibliographic coupling, and keyword co-occurrence analysis, resulting in visualization maps as key outputs.

The findings from the analysis point to several key themes, which are the diversity of measurement in terms of parametric and non-parametric models, firm performance, measuring risks, sustainability, digital innovation, and technology. Additionally, we synthesize and discuss original and distinct avenues for future research related to the impact of new technology such as artificial intelligence, machine learning, and blockchain, then ever-changing markets and industry, heightened inclusion of financial services, benchmarking of financial services through performance analysis, and the development of new financial services.

After a search query in the Scopus database, it was found that no recent bibliometric analysis and systematic literature review tackled this topic, making this academic contribution among the first in the research landscape. As such, it attempts to disseminate the accumulated knowledge to practitioners and researchers, presenting a bird's-eye view synthesis of the key findings and rigorous opportunities for future research.

2. Data and Methods

The objective of this book chapter is to evaluate and analyze the literature in the field of measuring financial services performance, thus uncovering the structure and dynamics of the field through classification and visualization. This is the reason why we chose a multi-technique bibliometric approach, which is often referred to as science mapping, considering it is useful for pointing out relationships between concepts, publications, and authors (Donthu *et al.*, 2021). Even though it is considered as a well-established and rigorous method, in recent years, it has noted tremendous growth partly due to the popularization of easy-to-use software solutions for analyzing bibliometric data as well as the growing accessibility of bibliometric data (Zupic and Čater, 2015).

In this sense, the book chapter reflects the outputs of descriptive bibliometric analysis, co-authorship analysis, bibliographic coupling, and keyword co-occurrence analysis as the most frequently used bibliometric approaches in organizational sciences. To begin with, the descriptive bibliometric approach is used to point out the publication trends and most-cited works in a certain field (Marzi *et al.*, 2024). Then, the keyword co-occurrence analysis considers the content of the publications, setting relations between topics based on keywords retrieved from article titles, abstracts, and author keywords (Donthu *et al.*, 2021). Similarly, the co-authorship technique connects countries or authors based on how frequently they collaborate on research, while bibliographic coupling is used as a technique for connecting publications based on the similarity of their reference lists (Marzi *et al.*, 2024).

In terms of the data, we ran a search query in the Scopus database, as one of the leading databases for global and quality research, which at the same time provides a broader range of scientific articles. Only peer-reviewed articles in scientific journals were included in the sample. Furthermore, the following search syntax was applied: ("FINANCIAL SERVICE" AND "FINANCIAL SERVICES" AND PERFORMANCE OR (PERFORMANCE0 AND ANALYS*). This resulted in a total of 1856 articles on the topic. Throughout the process of acquiring and cleaning the data, we abided by the PRISMA guidelines to ensure a rigorous and structured process (Page *et al.*, 2021). The flowchart of the following PRISMA steps is provided in Fig. 1.

Moreover, we identified some inclusion criteria for obtaining the final dataset. This means that we considered all double-blind, peer-reviewed articles that mentioned performance analysis of financial services and were written in English and indexed in Scopus. In other words, all gray literature as well as commentaries, reports, editorials,

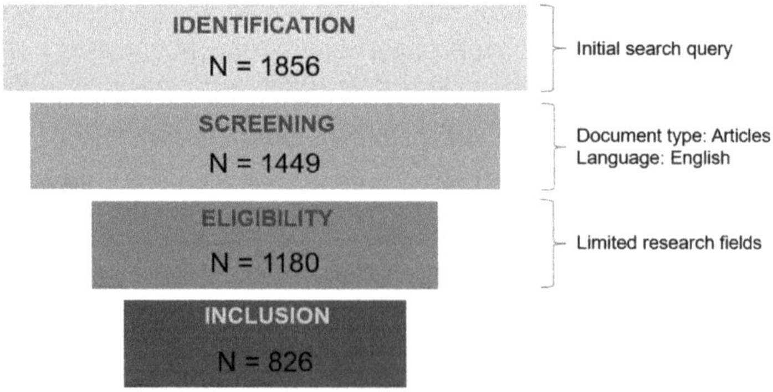

Fig. 1. Flowchart of PRISMA steps.

abstracts, posters, and similar materials were excluded. After limiting the research fields to (1) Business, Management, and Accounting, and (2) Economics, Econometrics, and Finance, and manually assessing the relevance of each article by the two authors, the final dataset consisted of 826 articles, which can be deemed sufficient for multi-technique bibliometric analysis (Marzi *et al.*, 2024). Hence, the analysis was performed in Excel and Power BI, and VOSviewer was used as a software solution for analyzing bibliometric data and creating visualization maps.

3. Research Results

This segment focuses on the results obtained through the multi-technique bibliometric analysis on measuring the performance of financial services. The analysis shows that both researchers and practitioners have been interested in measuring how efficient financial services have been since the 1980s, and the techniques have evolved from more traditional aspects of operations research to advanced machine learning and big data analysis.

Descriptive bibliometric analysis. The first article on the topic was published in 1982, after which there were a relatively low number of publications in the field. Since the start of the new century, the topic slowly began gaining traction, reaching its peak so far in 2023 with 79 publications (Fig. 2). This demonstrates the growing interest and productivity of the authors who are still looking for the most precise approaches to measure financial services performance and how it relates to other organizational phenomena, as well as the performance and life of financial organizations themselves. Interestingly, we assume that, likely because of the complexity of the topic, most of the articles have been written by two or multiple authors as opposed to single-authored articles.

The articles have been published in 431 distinct scientific journals in the fields of service quality, finance, banking, accounting, applied economics, and similar. Illustratively, some of the journals, which have published more than 10 articles on the topic, include *Applied Economics, Applied Financial Economics, International Journal of Bank Marketing, International Journal of Finance and Economics, and Managerial Finance.*

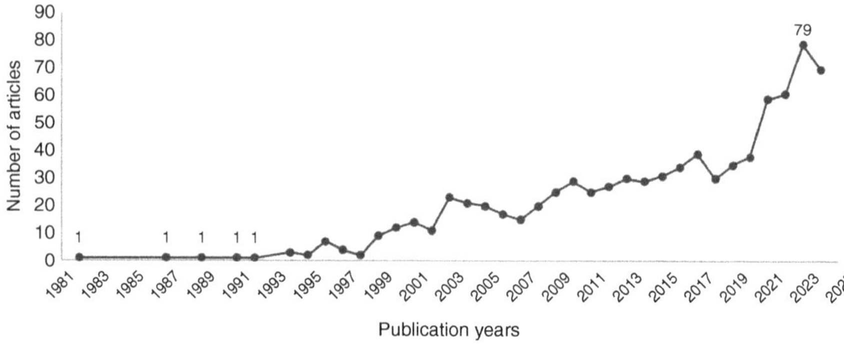

Fig. 2. Publication trends of financial services performance research.

Besides the number of publications, another useful metric related to the trends is the citations. In turn, the most cited articles are provided in Table 1. As can be noticed, most of them were written earlier, which provides additional opportunities to garner citations and view a certain publication as impactful. To tackle this, in the bibliometric approaches that follow, we are using normalized citations.

Table 1. Most cited articles in the research field.

Author(s) and Year	Title	Source	Total Citations
Ittner *et al.* (2003)	Performance implications of strategic performance measurement in financial services firms	*Accounting, Organizations and Society*	691
Stiroh and Rumble (2006)	The dark side of diversification: The case of US financial holding companies	*Journal of Banking and Finance*	646
Avlonitis *et al.* (2001)	An empirically-based typology of product innovativeness for new financial services: Success and failure scenarios	*Journal of Product Innovation Management*	443

(*Continued*)

Table 1. (*Continued*)

Author(s) and Year	Title	Source	Total Citations
Emekter *et al.* (2015)	Evaluating credit risk and loan performance in online Peer-to-Peer (P2P) lending	*Applied Economics*	364
DeYoung and Rice (2004)	Noninterest income and financial performance at U.S. commercial banks	*Financial Review*	283
Mikes (2009)	Risk management and calculative cultures	*Management Accounting Research*	277
Copestake (2007)	Mainstreaming Microfinance: Social Performance Management or Mission Drift?	*World Development*	239
Mollah *et al.* (2017)	The governance, risk-taking, and performance of Islamic banks	*Journal of Financial Services Research*	215
Jo *et al.* (2015)	Corporate Environmental Responsibility and Firm Performance in the Financial Services Sector	*Journal of Business Ethics*	203
Senyo and Osabutey (2020)	Unearthing antecedents to financial inclusion through FinTech innovations	*Technovation*	193
Cooper *et al.* (1994)	What distinguishes the top-performing new products in financial services	*The Journal of Product Innovation Management*	189

These publications take multi-faceted perspectives regarding the factors driving performance in financial services, touching upon strategy, risk, innovation, governance, and sustainability. Ittner *et al.* (2003) emphasized the importance of aligning performance metrics with strategic goals, while Stiroh and Rumble (2006) cautioned against the potential downsides of diversification. On the other hand, Avlonitis *et al.* (2001) and Cooper *et al.* (1994) highlighted the role of innovation in distinguishing top performers, underscoring the impact of product development on success. Senyo and Osabutey (2020) expanded this view on financial services innovation by connecting fintech innovations to financial inclusion, emphasizing the operational and societal benefits. Eventually, Mikes (2009) disclosed how risk management cultures shape performance, while Jo *et al.* (2015) explored how sustainability initiatives, such as corporate environmental responsibility, enhance firm outcomes. Subsequently, this positions the analysis of financial services performance as a foundation to thriving financial institutions, which combines strategic alignment, innovation, risk management, and social responsibility to achieve a coveted degree of performance.

Co-authorship bibliometric analysis. The research field is dominated by authors from 92 distinct countries from all over the world, which vary based on their productivity (number of published articles) and scientific influence (number of total citations). These dynamics are presented in Table 2. Evidently, the United States and the United Kingdom maintain the top spots when it comes to both citations and total publications. Yet, when it comes to higher author productivity, like the cases of India, China, and Indonesia, it is seen that the works of the authors from these countries are not considered as impactful as those from the Western context. We believe that this contributes to the debate of highlighting the growing need to pay closer attention to research endeavors from different contexts in the world and to see their work as equally valuable, ensuring a respectful translation between the Global South and the Global North.

Table 2. Country comparison based on total publications and citations.

Country	Total Publications	Country	Total Citations
United States	178	United States	6169
United Kingdom	118	United Kingdom	3206
India	71	Australia	1201
China	50	Netherlands	1095
Indonesia	49	Greece	709

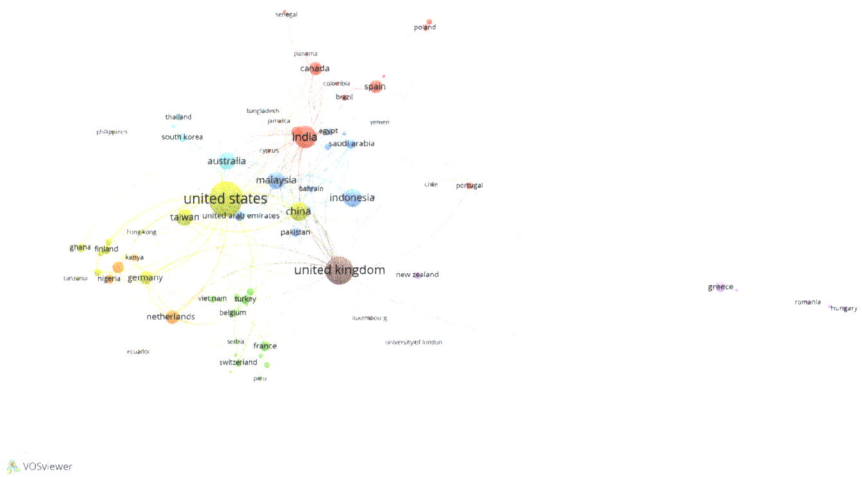

Fig. 3. Network visualization map of country co-authorship.

The countries among themselves have a cumulative link strength of 398, and they are all connected with each other with 255 distinct links. Figure 3 highlights a visualization map of the interconnected countries. The resolution was reduced to 0.5 to show fewer clusters (in this case, eight) and get a more concise co-authorship map.

Evidently, the United States emerges as the most central keyword, reflecting its partnerships with countries like China, India, and Australia. The United Kingdom is another major player, fostering strong collaborations with both Commonwealth nations, such as New Zealand, and European countries, like the Netherlands. Further, distinct clusters indicate regional collaboration patterns: The yellow cluster connects transatlantic and Asia-Pacific countries, while the blue cluster links Asian nations such as India, Indonesia, and Saudi Arabia. Additionally, the green cluster features European countries like France, Switzerland, and the Netherlands, whereas the purple cluster highlights Eastern European partnerships, including Greece, Hungary, and Romania. Smaller circles, such as the Philippines and Kenya, suggest emerging contributions but limited collaboration compared to the dominant players. So, we can state that while the intra-cluster collaboration is underscored, there are plenty of examples of cross-cluster and cross-regional collaboration between authors.

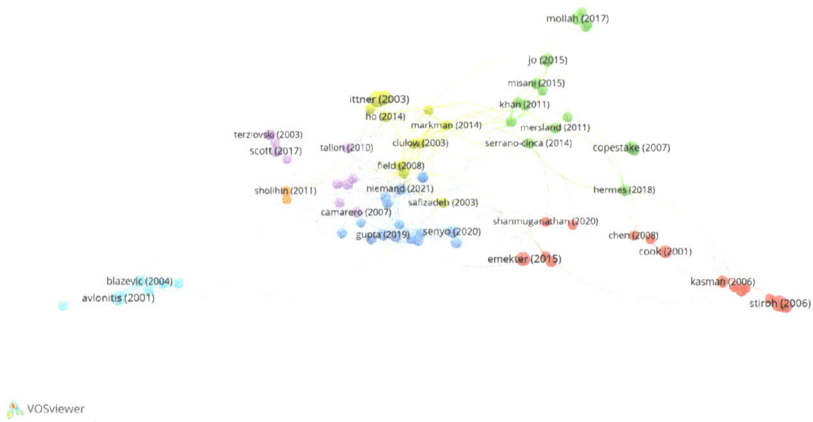

Fig. 4. Network visualization map of bibliographic coupling.

Thus, the map reveals opportunities to enhance inclusivity by engaging underrepresented nations in the global research field of financial services performance.

Bibliographic coupling. The network visualization map, which has been developed as a result of the bibliographic coupling technique (Fig. 4), illustrates that there are no single authors who push the research field forward; rather, it is fragmented and led by multiple authors and co-authorship teams, who are investigating different aspects of performance analysis of financial services. The map has been created based on documents with at least 50 citations to uncover the connections between the most influential works in the field. Eventually, seven distinct clusters are formed.

The green cluster, which includes works such as Mollah *et al.* (2017), Jo *et al.* (2015), and Copestake (2007), focuses on governance, risk management, and social performance, emphasizing ethical considerations and their impact on institutional performance. The red cluster, anchored by Stiroh and Rumble (2006) as well as Shanmuganathan (2020), examines the implications of modern finances, highlighting structural and financial strategies for performance improvement as well as the role of artificial intelligence in behavioral finances. The dark blue cluster, featuring recent studies like Senyo and Osabutey (2020) and Niemand *et al.* (2021), explores fintech innovations, digital transformation, and financial inclusion, illustrating the evolving role of technology in the financial sector. The yellow cluster, represented by foundational works such as Ittner *et al.* (2003) and Clulow *et al.* (2003), goes deeper into strategic performance measurement and the alignment of competitive advantage with metrics. The purple cluster, with studies such as Tallon (2010) and Scott *et al.* (2017), focuses on operational efficiency and technology adoption, connecting traditional strategies to modern digital shifts. The light blue cluster, including Avlonitis *et al.* (2001) and Blazevic and Lievens (2004), emphasizes product innovation and market-driven approaches, showcasing niche but significant contributions.

Strong interconnections between clusters, such as those linking strategy and governance or innovation and technology adoption, reflect the multidimensional nature of performance analysis, where strategic alignment, innovation, and ethical governance intersect. On the other hand, peripheral studies may be thought-provoking for looking into future research directions as they contribute specialized insights, particularly in areas like the performance of innovative banking products.

Keyword co-occurrence bibliometric analysis. The final bibliometric technique, firstly, focused on the keywords that appeared more than five times in the dataset so that we could consider only the ones that are most recurring in the field as a whole. This yielded 141 distinct keywords, which were all manually assessed for their relevance and ultimately inclusion in the analysis. A good rule of thumb is to push around 60% of them into the next phase (Van Eck and Waltman, 2017), so the network visualization map (Fig. 5) that was created was based on 112 key terms. These were split into seven clusters, connected with 1260 links. The total link strength was 2673.

The term "financial services" (occurrences: 298, links: 109, total link strength: 813), from the dark blue cluster, is central, serving as the primary focus of the map. It connects broadly to all clusters, indicating its foundational nature in this research area. Namely, the dark blue cluster "Financial markets and microfinance as performance measurement areas" brings together key terms like "banking", "stock market", "industrial performance", "competitiveness", "financial system", and similar. In this sense, this cluster emphasizes the role of financial systems and markets in performance. Microfinance is a significant theme, reflecting its importance in financial inclusion and development. Keywords such as "income" and "competitiveness" indicate an analytical focus on balancing costs, returns, and institutional competitiveness.

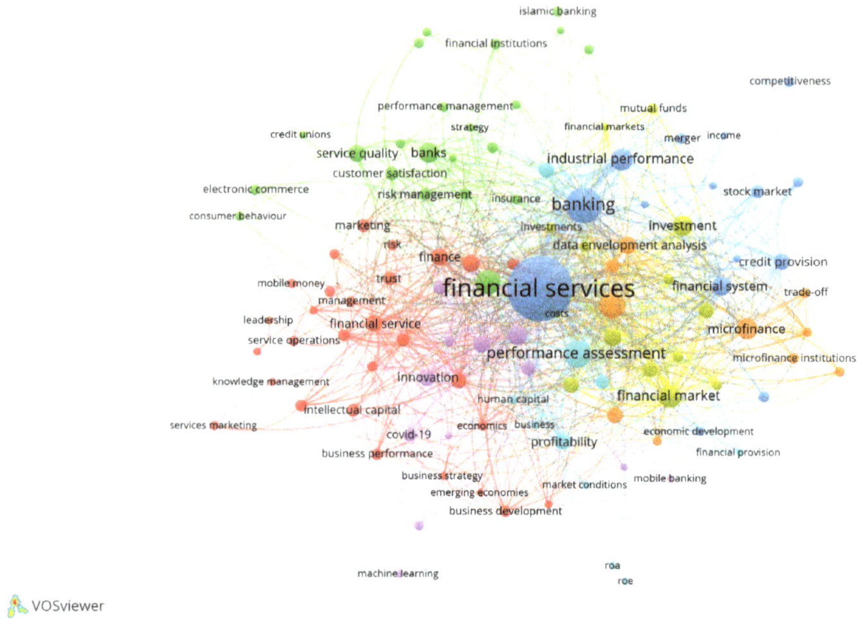

Fig. 5. Network visualization map of keyword co-occurrence.

The green cluster "Performance analysis of risk management and service" highlights the keywords "risk management", "customer satisfaction", "service quality", "Islamic banking", "credit unions", "strategy", and more. As such, this cluster focuses on operational and strategic elements of financial services, particularly in banking. Keywords such as "risk management" and "customer satisfaction" highlight the importance of managing operational risks while maintaining service quality. Terms like "Islamic banking" and "credit unions" suggest a focus on diverse banking models. The connections to strategy and performance management indicate that these areas are examined as part of broader organizational strategies.

The red cluster "Innovation, trust and management", as a smaller cluster, underscores keywords like "trust" and "leadership", which indicate a focus on building reliable and efficient service structures, while "intellectual capital" and "knowledge management" highlight the importance of knowledge management and new technologies for organizational performance.

The orange cluster "Data Envelopment Analysis (DEA) and performance" merges key terms such as "data envelopment analysis", "trade-off", "panel data", "efficiency measurement", and more. With that, it is crucial to identify the analysis approaches to financial services performance. Hence, the cluster is closely connected to keywords from the light blue cluster such as "ROA" (return on assets) and "ROE" (return on equity), indicating a strong focus on performance measurement.

The purple cluster "Technology and emerging economies", as a group of terms, prioritizes new advances in performance measurement of financial services, whether that be in banking, insurance, stock markets, or similar areas. The key terms here are "machine learning", "fintech", "COVID-19", "mobile banking", "artificial intelligence" and more. In more detail, this cluster highlights the role of machine learning and advanced technologies in analyzing financial performance. The presence of "COVID-19" suggests a recent focus on resilience and adaptability in financial services.

Hence, the terms from the green cluster related to risk management and the ones from the orange cluster in terms of DEA and performance are tightly linked, reflecting the relationship between managing risks and assessing financial efficiency. Moreover, the keywords related to innovation and trust connect strongly to their counterparts in the purple cluster, indicating that technological advancements play a critical role in fostering innovation and trust within financial services. The yellow, light blue, and orange clusters overlap significantly, as financial systems and market mechanisms are central to assessing institutional performance.

4. Discussion and Future Research Agenda

Our analysis explores the multidimensional landscape of performance analysis in financial services, integrating insights from bibliographic coupling, country co-authorship, and keyword co-occurrence networks. Key studies highlight themes such as strategic alignment, risk management, innovation, and sustainability. More precisely, the country co-authorship analysis revealed the United States and the United Kingdom as central hubs driving global research, while bibliographic coupling underscores foundational works like Ittner *et al.* (2003) and Stiroh and Rumble (2006) that shape themes like risk, management, and fintech innovation. Similarly, the keyword co-occurrence map highlights interconnected clusters around risk management, innovation, financial inclusion, and technological advancements such as machine learning. Together, these analyses illustrate how strategic performance metrics shape and shift together with societal and technological trends to enhance efficiency, inclusivity, and sustainability in financial services, which have also been called out as priority areas by other researchers (Shanmugan and Baria, 2019).

Evidently, one of the most widely used analytic approaches is data envelopment analysis, or DEA for short. Researchers have used it in its more traditional forms and as a multi-activity DEA model, often including DEA bootstrap into the mix (Anwar *et al.*, 2020; Ben Abdelkader and Mansouri, 2019; Wijesiri *et al.*, 2019). DEA is a potent, non-parametric tool widely applied in financial services to evaluate the efficiency of decision-making units (DMUs) by comparing multiple inputs (e.g., labor, capital, costs) to outputs (e.g., profits, loans issued, customer satisfaction) (Chen *et al.*, 2020; Banker *et al.*, 2022). Hence, DEA is particularly valuable in assessing the performance of banks, insurance firms, microfinance institutions, and investment companies, helping to benchmark them against industry leaders and identify efficiency gaps, thus incorporating risk factors and addressing trade-offs between financial goals like profitability (e.g., ROA, ROE) and broader objectives such as sustainability or financial inclusion (Khan *et al.*, 2021). Other applications include measuring the environmental performance of financial services as crucial segments of ESG efforts (Chang *et al.*, 2023). While challenges such as data limitations and heterogeneity in DMUs exist, advancements in dynamic and stochastic DEA models have enhanced their applicability, allowing institutions to track performance over time and adapt to changing financial landscapes (Cvetkoska and Savic, 2021).

Table 3 provides an overview of the most used analytic types for assessing financial services' performance and their corresponding scores.

One of the crucial aspects of every bibliometric analysis is pointing out some data-driven pathways for future research. We are basing our proposed future research agenda on the overlay visualization map

Table 3. Presentation and scores of performance measurement analysis approaches.

Analysis approach	**Score**
Data envelopment analysis (traditional; multi-activity DEA model; DEA bootstrap)	2.42
Return on equity (ROE)	2.59
Return on assets (ROA)	2.09
Decision tree analysis	1.77
Service quality questionnaire	1.4
Malmquist total factor productivity index (TFP)	1.35
Panel data analysis	1.07
Customer satisfaction questionnaire	0.99

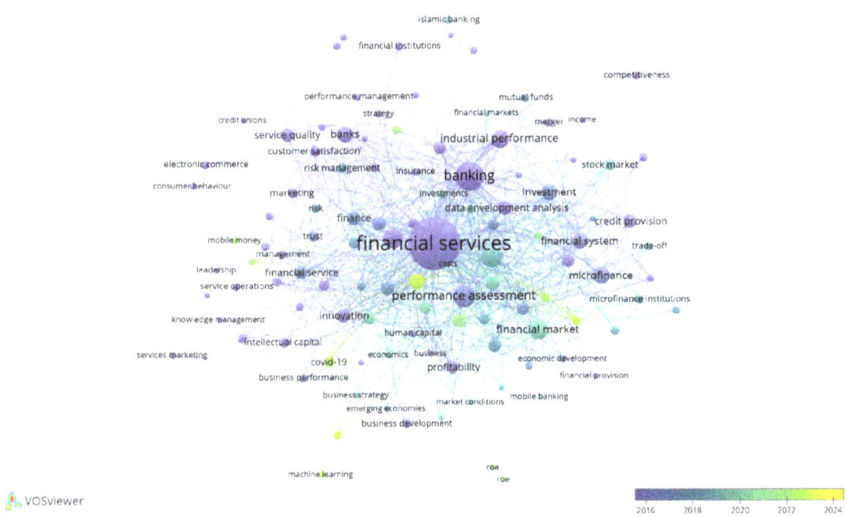

Fig. 6. Overlay visualization map of keyword co-occurrence.

in Fig. 6, which gives a timeline dimension of the most researched keywords.

Subsequently, terms like "fintech", "environmental performance", "machine learning", "artificial intelligence", "mobile money", and more are at the forefront. Stemming from this, these future research directions include the following:

- *Integration of advanced technologies in performance measurement*: Future research could explore how technologies such as machine learning, artificial intelligence, and blockchain can enhance the accuracy and scope of performance assessments in this particular sector.
- *Financial inclusion and sustainability*: Studies could investigate the performance of financial services in promoting microfinance, credit provision, and economic development, particularly in emerging markets, through longitudinal research approaches and relevant theoretically backed constructs.
- *Introduction of more customer-centric performance metrics*: Researchers could focus on developing new performance measurement frameworks that prioritize customer satisfaction, service quality, and trust, as keywords such as customer satisfaction, service quality, and trust point to the need for performance indicators beyond financial outcomes.
- *Embedding innovation and intellectual capital in financial services' performance*: Future studies could address the contribution of innovation and intellectual capital to financial performance, particularly in fostering competitive advantages, as there are still prevailing dilemmas about measuring this phenomenon.
- *Increased need for additional comparative analysis of banking models*: Scholars can compare the performance of diverse banking models, including Islamic banking, credit unions, and traditional banks.

5. Conclusion

This book chapter provides a comprehensive bibliometric and systematic review of performance analysis in financial services, tracing its evolution from 1982 to the present day. By leveraging insights from 826 articles and employing a multi-technique bibliometric approach, the study identifies and maps the most significant research themes, including parametric and non-parametric measurement models, firm performance, risk assessment, sustainability, and digital innovation. The findings emphasize the growing importance of technology-driven advancements such as artificial intelligence, machine learning, and blockchain in shaping the field, alongside the impact of ever-changing market dynamics and the creation of new financial services.

Despite that, this research endeavor does not come free of some constraints, which can be alleviated by future research. One limitation is the reliance on the quality and scope of the underlying database, such as Scopus. The method is also sensitive to biases introduced by self-citations or differences in citation practices across disciplines, potentially skewing results. Also, visualizations such as co-authorship networks or keyword co-occurrence maps, while insightful, require careful interpretation and may oversimplify complex relationships between concepts or researchers.

This review fills a critical gap in the literature, offering one of the first systematic overviews of this rapidly evolving topic. By synthesizing existing knowledge and highlighting underexplored areas, the chapter lays the foundation for future research and provides practitioners with actionable insights to deal with the increasingly data-driven market of financial services. At the same time, there are implications for scholars who may use the findings in crafting new theoretical foundations and taking up the suggested future research directions to further develop the research field and introduce new practices of analyzing the performance of financial services.

References

Anwar, M., Nidar, S. R., Komara, R., and Layyinaturrobaniyah, L. (2020). Rural bank efficiency and loans for micro and small businesses: Evidence from West Java Indonesia. *International Journal of Emerging Markets*, 15(3), 587–610.

Avlonitis, G. J., Papastathopoulou, P. G., and Gounaris, S. P. (2001). An empirically-based typology of product innovativeness for new financial services: Success and failure scenarios. *Journal of Product Innovation Management: An International Publication of the Product Development & Management Association*, 18(5), 324–342.

Banker, R. D., Amirteimoori, A., and Sinha, R. P. (2022). An integrated data envelopment analysis and generalized additive model for assessing managerial ability with application to the insurance industry. *Decision Analytics Journal*, 4, 100115.

Ben Abdelkader, I. and Mansouri, F. (2019). Performance of microfinance institutions in the MENA region: A comparative analysis. *International Journal of Social Economics*, 46(1), 47–65.

Blazevic, V. and Lievens, A. (2004). Learning during the new financial service innovation process: Antecedents and performance effects. *Journal of Business Research*, 57(4), 374–391.

Chang, K., Cheng, X., Wang, Y., Liu, Q., and Hu, J. (2023). The impacts of ESG performance and digital finance on corporate financing efficiency in China. *Applied Economics Letters*, 30(4), 516–523.

Chen, Y. C., Chiu, Y. H., and Chiu, C. J. (2020). The performance evaluation of banks considering risk: An application of undesirable relation network DEA. *International Transactions in Operational Research*, 27(2), 1101–1120.

Clulow, V., Gerstman, J., and Barry, C. (2003). The resource-based view and sustainable competitive advantage: The case of a financial services firm. *Journal of European Industrial Training*, 27(5), 220–232.

Cooper, R. G., Easingwood, C. J., Edgett, S., Kleinschmidt, E. J., and Storey, C. (1994). What distinguishes the top performing new products in financial services. *Journal of Product Innovation Management: An International Publication of the Product Development & Management Association*, 11(4), 281–299.

Copestake, J. (2007). Mainstreaming microfinance: Social performance management or mission drift? *World Development*, 35(10), 1721–1738.

Cvetkoska, V. and Savic, G. (2021). DEA in banking: Analysis and visualization of bibliometric data. *Data Envelopment Analysis Journal*, 5(2), 455–485.

DeYoung, R. and Rice, T. (2004). Noninterest income and financial performance at US commercial banks. *Financial Review*, 39(1), 101–127.

Donthu, N., Kumar, S., Mukherjee, D., Pandey, N., and Lim, W. M. (2021). How to conduct a bibliometric analysis: An overview and guidelines. *Journal of Business Research*, 133, 285–296.

Emekter, R., Tu, Y., Jirasakuldech, B., and Lu, M. (2015). Evaluating credit risk and loan performance in online Peer-to-Peer (P2P) lending. *Applied Economics*, 47(1), 54–70.

Ittner, C. D., Larcker, D. F., and Randall, T. (2003). Performance implications of strategic performance measurement in financial services firms. *Accounting, Organizations and Society*, 28(7–8), 715–741.

Jo, H., Kim, H., and Park, K. (2015). Corporate environmental responsibility and firm performance in the financial services sector. *Journal of Business Ethics*, 131, 257–284.

Khan, A., Ahmad, A., and Shireen, S. (2021). Ownership and performance of microfinance institutions: Empirical evidences from India. *Cogent Economics & Finance*, 9(1), 1930653.

Marzi, G., Balzano, M., Caputo, A., and Pellegrini, M. M. (2025). Guidelines for bibliometric-systematic literature reviews: 10 steps to combine analysis, synthesis and theory development. *International Journal of Management Reviews*, 27(1), 81–103.

Mikes, A. (2009). Risk management and calculative cultures. *Management Accounting Research*, 20(1), 18–40.

Mollah, S., Hassan, M. K., Al Farooque, O., and Mobarek, A. (2017). The governance, risk-taking, and performance of Islamic banks. *Journal of Financial Services Research*, 51, 195–219.

Niemand, T., Rigtering, J. C., Kallmünzer, A., Kraus, S., and Maalaoui, A. (2021). Digitalization in the financial industry: A contingency approach of entrepreneurial orientation and strategic vision on digitalization. *European Management Journal*, 39(3), 317–326.

Page, M. J., McKenzie, J. E., Bossuyt, P. M., Boutron, I., Hoffmann, T. C., Mulrow, C. D., ... and Moher, D. (2021). The PRISMA 2020 statement: An updated guideline for reporting systematic reviews. *BMJ*, 372.

Scott, S. V., Van Reenen, J., and Zachariadis, M. (2017). The long-term effect of digital innovation on bank performance: An empirical study of SWIFT adoption in financial services. *Research Policy*, 46(5), 984–1004.

Senyo, P. K. and Osabutey, E. L. (2020). Unearthing antecedents to financial inclusion through FinTech innovations. *Technovation*, 98, 102155.

Shanmugan, K. and Baria, B. (2019). Major themes and concerns of impact analysis in the Indian microfinance sector: Analytical views. *International Journal of Research in Social Sciences*, 9(1), 668–682.

Shanmuganathan, M. (2020). Behavioural finance in an era of artificial intelligence: Longitudinal case study of robo-advisors in investment decisions. *Journal of Behavioral and Experimental Finance*, 27, 100297.

Stiroh, K. J. and Rumble, A. (2006). The dark side of diversification: The case of US financial holding companies. *Journal of Banking & Finance*, 30(8), 2131–2161.

Tallon, P. P. (2010). A service science perspective on strategic choice, IT, and performance in US banking. *Journal of Management Information Systems*, 26(4), 219–252.

Van Eck, N. J. and Waltman, L. (2017). Citation-based clustering of publications using CitNetExplorer and VOSviewer. *Scientometrics*, 111, 1053–1070.

Wijesiri, M., Martínez-Campillo, A., and Wanke, P. (2019). Is there a trade-off between social and financial performance of public commercial banks in India? A multi-activity DEA model with shared inputs and undesirable outputs. *Review of Managerial Science*, 13, 417–442.

Zupic, I. and Čater, T. (2015). Bibliometric methods in management and organization. *Organizational Research Methods*, 18(3), 429–472.

https://doi.org/10.1142/9789819823161_0003

Chapter 3

The Bank as a Production Unit: Illuminating Two *Genres* of Banking Theory

K. V. Bhanu Murthy

School of Management and Entrepreneurship, Delhi Technological University, New Delhi, India

bhanumurthykv@gmail.com

Any debate on the measurement of the performance of banks needs to be preceded by an understanding of the banking theory of the bank as a production unit. The extant framework used for other financial services cannot be uncritically applied to banking. This paper revisits the following fundamental questions: (i) Primarily, is the bank a production unit or a financial intermediary? (ii) Do banks produce real output? (iii) Do banks create savings and investments? (iv) Are banks special? (v) Is a bank obliged to maximize profit? (vi) What is the bank's responsibility? (v) Which theoretical framework is appropriate for studying the bank as a production unit? Some of the fundamental answers are as follows: (i) Banking theory lies at the intersection of monetary economics, macroeconomics, production theory, and development economics. (ii) Banks create savings and investment through the agency of deposits and advances. and (iii) Banks are primarily production units rather than financial intermediaries. The chapter conceptually illuminates the presence of two genres of banking theory that are fundamentally different, and hence their methodology cannot be the same. Neo-classical production theory applies to frontier functions that view a bank as a financial intermediary. And Industrial Economics as applied to banking applies to banks as a production unit set in a live context of banking markets. The attempt to merge the two genres or to impose one on the other, or to continue endless debate on which is the right method, is futile. This chapter segregates the two genres and provides a fresh perspective on the concept and theory of the bank as a production unit.

Keywords: Banking theory, financial intermediation, industrial economics, production unit, savings creation.

1. Introduction

There are certain popular writings that are increasingly questioning the role, functions, and specialness of banks. There is an attempt by such popular press to drive a wedge between banking (operations) and banks as institutions. The problem with most popular approaches lies in not being able to distinguish between "*what*" a bank does and "*how*" it does what it does. The extant literature views banks as decision-making units (DMUs) whose objective is efficiency and profit, just like any other financial institution or enterprise. This chapter argues that banks are active producers of economic value, in the form of real savings and investment, and banking output, and not just financial intermediaries. Banks are special in that they create output and real capital and operate as organic entities set in live banking markets. The extant approaches are based on two frontier functions: (a) Data Envelopment Analysis (DEA), which is a non-parametric[1] (practice-based method), and (b) Stochastic Frontier Analysis (SFA), which is parametric, reducing the research problem to a measurement of managerial or technical efficiency, per se. The more evolved framework of industrial economics, as applied to banking, is based on the behavior of the banking firm, set in a complex chain of Structure–Conduct–Performance (SCP). This framework is much more complete and is set in the context of real banking markets and has several implications for conceptualizing and measuring banking output, efficiency, and profit.

As a prelude, consider a famous quote by a famous business leader:

> "In 1994, Bill Gates said 'Banking is essential, banks are not.' This is becoming increasingly relevant in respect to the traditional banking business model" (Oren, 2021, p. 1).

[1]Incidentally, "non-parametric" implies that it is distribution-free and, hence, not based on any theoretical distribution.

There is a clear intent to undermine the role, importance, and exclusiveness of banks. The extant approaches, like this popular one, quickly denounce traditional banking models and theory by counterpoising them against "digital banking", as if digital banking is an alternative to traditional commercial banking. Further, they quickly conclude that the relevant banking model is BaaS (Banking as a Service), such that, henceforth, banking can be stripped from banks and be merged with financial services being provided by fintech. Hence, banking, according to them, is no longer the core of the financial sector. The misnomer here is that "digital banking" actually refers to a way of conducting some banking operations, which, therefore, is a mere change in "conduct" of banking as opposed to the traditional "brick-and-mortar banking model". From the standpoint of understanding the special nature and role of banking as production unit, set in an industry, governed by different market forms, and having implications for the relationship between banking output, efficiency, and profit, such a distinction itself becomes irrelevant since almost all banks (except those which have not digitized operations) have absorbed this process change very effectively through digitization. Another misnomer here is that the term "model" is wrongly being equated with the "business model of banking". The business model of banks must be understood through the lens of the nature and the role of banking as a basic economic activity and not as financial intermediation.

About the nature and role of banks, to quote the fundamental theorem of "Why are banks special?" from the original text, banks are special due to their three features:

> "Reduced to its essentials, it would appear that there are three characteristics that distinguish banks from all other classes of institutions – both financial and non-financial.
>
> They are:
>
> Banks offer transaction accounts.
>
> Banks are the backup source of liquidity for all other institution.
>
> Banks are a transmission belt for monetary policy" (Corrigan, 1982, p. 7).

The transaction account allows chequeable deposits against which withdrawals can be made on demand, and such cheques can be transferred to third parties, whose demand, in turn, needs to be honored by the bank, on demand (immediately).

Another attack on banks comes from a different angle:

> "Banks have long played a special role in the financial system. Individuals and institutions use banks to access the payment system, and central banks rely on banks to transmit monetary policy to the real economy......"(Heurtas, 2018, p. 2).

The author subscribes to the view that quantitative easing (QE) and eligibility easing (EE) broaden the ambit of the monetary transmission mechanism beyond banks. Hence, banks are not so special. Also, digital currencies introduced by the central bank can not only replace cash but can also reduce the importance of transaction accounts (current deposits).

The discussion on digital currencies is very premature and seems to be motivated by fintech interests as it is promoted by such lobbies. But a moot question is where such funds from QE and EE go. Obviously, into transaction accounts! The entire argument is quite misplaced and seems to be motivated.

Further obfuscation of the understanding of banking theory comes from another angle as well. Certain efficiency measurement and estimation techniques, like Frontier Production and Cost Functions, as well as Data Envelopment Analysis (DEA),[2] also tend to underplay the role and nature of banks and their contribution to production banking output, as a basic economic activity. This paper examines *why* industrial organization approach, which treats banks as production units, provides better a framework of theory, concept and measurement, of output, efficiency, and profit, in banks, as opposed to the managerial and financial intermediation approach to banking.

2. Banking Theory

To set the ball rolling, this discussion necessarily needs to recognize the seminal work of Klein (1971), who has raised the right questions about the theory of the banking firm. Two quotes from Klien would suffice to put things into perspective:

[2]This paper does not even attempt to lay out a critique of frontier functions. It only debates certain neglected aspects of banking concepts and theory which when revisited are clearly able to explain banks as production units.

> "Neoclassical microeconomic analysis is rarely invoked to explain bank behavior, primarily because there is so little agreement even as concerns fundamental concepts" (p. 205).

> "We have no theory to describe that behavior under any specific set of assumptions about the external and competitive environment in which the bank operates" (p. 206).

This chapter is limited in scope and tries to answer partly the first question of "fundamental concepts", such as what banks are, what they do, what banking markets are, and why banks are special. And yet it diverges from Klien, in that it looks at various implications of monetary economics, macroeconomics, and development economics, while seeking these fundamental answers. Also, this chapter looks at banks as production units rather than mere intermediaries. Thirdly, Bhanumurthy[3] and Deb (2013) have evolved a whole "Theoretical Framework of Competition as Applied to Banking" that is an answer to Klien's second question relating to the "external and competitive environment in which the bank operates".

Ordinarily, banks are treated as financial intermediaries, like any other insurance and non-banking financial intermediaries (NBFIs). Unlike an ordinary financial intermediary, profitability is not the single objective that a bank has to pursue. Maintaining liquidity is equally important for a bank; otherwise, it may lose public confidence. It may result in a run on the bank. There is no doubt that money by itself is nominal, and banks transform deposits into advances through credit creation. In this chapter, it is argued that banks are real production units rather than financial intermediaries that provide finance. There are various arguments in favor of treating banks as production units rather than financial intermediaries, although they do deal in money. This is not to say that banks do not perform financial intermediary functions as well. The question is to understand banks' basic role and nature, as well as their contribution to the economy. This perspective looks at banks in the following manner: what banks *are* and what banks *do* rather than how they do

[3]There is a whole range of seminal papers produced by the present author on strategic groups in banking, dynamics of competition in banking, and most importantly efficiency in banking from an Industrial Economics perspective.

what they do. This is a "substantive" rather than a "process" view of banks.

Presented in the following is a brief view of these four theories of banking:

1. Monetary Theory — Endogenous Money Theory[4]
2. Production Theory — Input/Output of financial services[5]
3. Transaction Cost Theory[6]
4. Shiftability and Anticipated Income Theory[7]

Banking theory is confounded by the perennial interlocking of various, often conflicting, theories emerging from different standpoints. This makes the study of banking output, efficiency, and profit a daunting task. This brief chapter can certainly not traverse the length and breadth of this vast domain but shall attempt to provide an overview with three fundamental differences in the *ideation* of a bank: (i) This approach supports the idea that, while the bank is steeped in money (the nominal), it as an entity, deals in the "real", and hence is a "real" entity. (ii) The bank may have many roles that are apparently that of a "financial intermediary", yet the entity of the bank is that of a microeconomic "banking firm" that essentially produces "real output". (iii) The bank creates real savings and investment, through deposits and advances, and does not merely finance investment. All this polemical dissection makes the bank a core transformative entity that conduits real savings into real investment, and hence, *actualizes* capital formation.

The third difference, referred to herein, arises from Keynes's notion that there are two capital markets – the functional and the notional. The notional (conceptual) sets the context of how in macroeconomic theory capital stock is built up in an economy. Keynesian theory of investment demand is about how industrial projects create real *exante* investment demand (Marginal Efficiency of Investment — MEI) that leads to the building up of capital stock, and how it is constrained by the supply of capital stock, being limited by the capacity of the machine-building sector. The functional capital

[4]Fontana (2003).
[5]Fixler and Zieschang (1992).
[6]Susan Woodward (1988).
[7]Moulton (1918) and Prochnow (1949).

market does the actual job of "oiling the capital market through money" which leads to a smooth, efficient, and risk-free business environment for the corporations that carry out industrial projects. Thus, it is only fateful that banks are labelled as "financial intermediaries" just because this transformative process needs the essential intervention of money, since real savings cannot be directly converted into physical capital stock.

2.1. *What are banks?*

The two related questions are: "what *are* banks?" and "what do banks *do*?". The understanding of what banks *do* determines what they *are*. In common parlance, banks deal in money, and hence they are dubbed as financial intermediaries. The entire discussion surrounding bank output and efficiency, in literature, is laid out as "banks deal in money", "banks use money as input and produce money as output", and "banks provide financial services". Before proceeding with larger issue at the outset, it is necessary to unravel the very entity of the bank. Banks are at the intersection of macroeconomics and microeconomics.[8] As individual units, they are "banking firms" and need to be seen as microeconomic entities:

> "Wray uses Minskyian approaches to discuss banking, finance, and economics across several levels of analysis. From a micro or firm level of analysis Wray provides compelling accounts of how banks work" (Mettenheim, 2013, p. 260).

But banks do not exist in a vacuum. They are helmed between the public and the central bank, and they are a part of banking markets. In the former sense, banks are a part of Monetary Economics, and in the latter, a part of Industrial Economics. Of course, the most common and popular way of viewing them is as yet another financial institution, and as a part of the financial system. While all these perspectives cannot be denied, the focus of this chapter is on the conceptual, theoretical, and measurement framework for banking output, efficiency, and profit. These aspects relate to banks as micro entities, which produce real output and are a part of banking markets. However, the discussion on banks necessarily starts from

[8]Mettenheim (2013). The focus in this paper is on "What do banks do?" and "What should banks do?".

monetary theory. There is a lot of confusion about banks because while banks deal with money, they produce real output.

According to Keynes, even demand for liquidity arises out of real needs — transactions, precaution (both consumption), and speculation (bonds are a claim against investment). Banks create loans and advances (in monetary terms), wherein short-term advances are against inventory (working capital) and long-term loans are used for creating capital stock, both real. Demand for bank credit arises as derived demand due to the accelerator upon growth in real GDP.

2.2. *What are banking markets?*

The immediate relationship of banks with money draws attention to the "Endogenous Money Theory":

> "The Post Keynesian theory of endogenous money has largely been dismissed by most economists and practitioners as too scholastic or philosophical, with little relevance for theoretical and empirical developments in monetary economics" (Gale, 1982, p. 183).

Here, money supply, in an economy is determined as a result of the interactions of other real economic variables, rather than autonomously by an external authority — the central bank. A lot of discussion has taken place in the literature about Endogenous Money.[9] But it does not touch much upon the role of banks:

> "The essence of endogenous money theory is that the stock of money in a country is determined by the demand for bank credit, and the latter is causally dependent upon the economic variables that affect the level of output" (Fontana, 2003, p. 291)).

In the present chapter, this important theory is analyzed to present the relationship between monetary and banking theories. Endogenous money theory establishes the fact that although banks create money and credit, their role is essentially "real". It stands to reason to clarify that banking, therefore, is a real activity. The distinction between banks and other financial institutions is that only banks can create money and credit. They have the exclusive power to maintain chequeable deposits, unlike other financial institutions, which do not have this power.

---

[9] Realfonzo (1998) provides a very useful review.

A famous thinker, who needs to be acknowledged, in this context, is Minsky:

> "Minsky always insisted that the role ... was to promote the 'capital development' of the economy. By this he did not simply mean... investment in physical capital. Rather, he was concerned with creating a financial structure that would be conducive to economic development..." (Wray, 2013, p. 277).

The takeaway here is that the main role of banks is capital formation. The capital development role of banks has to be "conducive to economic development". This means that the saving and investment environment in the capital market has to be relatively risk-free. Banking markets siphon off savings and investments into the capital market by producing deposits and advances. The banking market is, therefore, a mirror of the capital market.

2.3. *What do banks do?*

The special features of banks are as follows:

1. Banks, along with the central bank, and the public partake in high-powered money.
2. Banks are unique financial institutions, in that they *alone* can hold chequeable deposits whose cheques are negotiable and can be endorsed to a third party, being redeemable on demand. No other financial institution has the power to do so.
3. Banks can create money and credit on their own as well through the process of credit and deposit creation.
4. Banks hold demand deposits that create short-term liabilities, which are often needed to service liquidity requirements of businesses, and yet the bulk of long-term investments that the bank creates rests upon their ability to convert such deposits into long-maturity loans. This mismatch of long-term assets and short-term liabilities creates the possibility of a run on the bank if short-term credit is not provided by the central bank.
5. These features of a bank are complemented by their role as primary dealers in the money market that produce short-term credit instruments, like Treasury Bills, Commercial Paper (CP), Certificates of Deposit (CD), and Call Money (CM).

2.4. *Why are banks "special"?*

In banking literature, the question of "Why are banks special?" has been a bone of contention. The "specialness" of banks is most often argued from a very different perspective. The main reason for banks to be unique lies in all five roles played by banks, which no other firm or even the central bank can do.

To quote the fundamental theorem from the origin itself:

> "Reduced to its essentials, it would appear that there are three characteristics that distinguish banks from all other classes of institutions – both financial and non-financial. They are:
>
> 1. Banks offer transaction accounts.
> 2. Banks are the backup source of liquidity for all other institutions.
> 3. Banks are a transmission belt for monetary policy" (Corrigan, 1982, p. 7).

In approaching the question of specialness, the following questions need to be answered:

(i) Is a bank obliged to maximize profit?
(ii) What is the bank's responsibility?

The present approach adds two more dimensions to the "specialness of banks". The crux of the proposition is that banks are unique and are special entities because they are complementary to the capital markets, although they are treated as a part of the money market. During capital formation, banks have a greater role than profit maximization. The responsibility of the bank is to create a safe banking environment, without which society, which is "risk-averse", would not be prepared to save or invest. It is a responsibility that is bestowed upon a bank. In light of this, the present view is that there is no choice but to treat banks as special and there should be no debate about whether banks are special.

The bank is unique in that it mirrors the capital market and transforms savings into long-term investment projects. Here, banks have two primary roles — monetary and fiduciary. Banks also have a dual objective of profit and liquidity,[10] unlike other firms. Pursuing the fiduciary role, it has been prescribed that banks should keep the interest of depositors and borrowers above their own. It is here

[10]Prochnow (1949).

that a bank diverges from an ordinary firm. For an ordinary firm, the problem is to maximize its objective function of profit by either maximizing real output or minimizing cost, where cost is the dual of production. It needs to be noted that according to economic theory, cost is the "real resource cost" of primary inputs, not cost in monetary terms. The bank is vitally different as it has a dual objective function. There is a perennial conflict between profit and liquidity or stability. If banks behave like ordinary firms and maximize their profits, their own liquidity would drop. Even otherwise, the fiduciary function of banks prescribes that they must not endanger their clients' deposits and the assets of the bank. When the bank reduces profit and increases liquidity, it becomes less risky for depositors and borrowers. This needs to be done in deference to its fiduciary objective. Profit maximization is no longer the simple (single) objective, like an ordinary firm. In fact, technically, with a dual-valued objective function, profit cannot be maximized. A dual-valued objective function can only be optimized subject to constraints. Hence, banks *ab initio* are not like other financial intermediaries or firms. No firm would like to intentionally moderate profit. It should be termed as "satisficing behavior"[11] not maximizing behavior. About satisficing behavior, Simon (1956) says the following:

> "In particular, no 'utility function' needs to be postulated for the organism, (bank)...." (Simon, 1956, p. 129).

Even if this single vital difference is kept in mind, on this count alone, no Neo-Classical Profit-Maximizing Model applies to banks. It would be well in place to mention that efficiency models like Data Envelopment Analysis (DEA) and Stochastic Frontier Analysis (SFA) are both based on the notion of profit maximization. Sometimes, it is argued that DEA and SFA are not directly and necessarily based on profit maximization but certainly follow the framework of profit maximization.

3. Two *Genres* of Banking Theory

This section revolves around the following question: Which theoretical framework is appropriate for studying the bank as a production unit? Most economic writings believe that banks are entities that

[11]Simon (1956).

which "use the money of others". And explicitly treat them as financial intermediaries (Fixler and Zieschang, 1992, p. 219).

DEA and SFA both evaluate efficiency components that are closely related to profit maximization. By improving technical and allocative efficiency, firms can reduce costs, optimize resource use, and enhance profitability. Thus, the pursuit of efficiency as measured by DEA and SFA contributes to the broader goal of profit maximization.

If banks are special and are not meant to show "profit-maximizing" behavior, but show satisficing behavior, as a firm, then both DEA and SFA are not appropriate frameworks for studying measurement output, efficiency, and profit in banks. Their role cannot be denied in looking at the managerial efficiency of a profit-maximizing firm. An approach that treats a bank as a DMU restricts its role by looking at bank performance in a narrow way, unconnected with its fundamental nature, responsibility, objectives, and setting in real banking markets, which are responsible for bank performance and efficiency in a completely different way.[12]

The moral of the story, in conclusion, is that the bank is a *production unit* that produces real savings and investments through the agency of deposits and advances, the sum of which is banking output. The job of banks is to produce banking output that is real. Other functions and services are secondary and do not impinge on the nature of banks as a production unit. This creative role arises out of Minsky's concern about banks "creating a financial structure that would be conducive to economic development". Here, it may be necessary to rephrase "financial structure" as "investment environment", which is in line with the bank's objective of economic development.

In this overall context, the following four basic axioms cannot be questioned:

1. Banks do not merely hold and transfer "other people's money". They provide a risk-free environment by which they allow or even, in some sense, compel income earners to make the choice of saving and depositing such real savings in banks. Hence, in the absence of banks, their trust would be failing, and "money" would be hoarded

[12]Schmalensee (1987).

and not saved. Thus, banks are responsible for the creation of real savings, not just for handling or transferring other people's money.

2. The other axiom relates to "other people's money". Banks deal with "other people's savings", not just money. Savings come from sacrifice. It is this imposition, commitment, or responsibility that, by design, has been thrust upon banks by the central banks that makes them special and trustworthy entities. This uniqueness comes as a fiduciary duty that devolves upon banks.
3. As primary dealers in the money market, an additional role or responsibility is that of "oiling the capital market" through the creation and management of short-term credit instruments.[13] In addition, through the credit creation process, banks multiply credit autonomously. This comes as an externality to businesses as producers of credit banks become productive units. This sums up the monetary responsibility of banks.
4. Banks are set in the context of live banking markets, which have differing market structures and treat efficiency through a different framework based on the Structure–Conduct–Performance Approach.

4. Conclusion

This chapter sums up the specialness of banks in terms of the inevitability of their nature, role, and objectives. Banks are bound by their fiduciary and monetary responsibilities. Banks are uniquely responsible for the creation of real savings and investments by providing the opportunity for creating deposits in a safe banking market and lending advances that lead to real investments. Other financial entities look for profit maximization through financial efficiency and portfolio management, and by providing value-added services, other than their primary job of creating banking output.

In light of the above-mentioned set of polemics, the crux seems to be that banks undertake risk for others, create real savings and investment, and help in economic development. And this they do

[13]Short-term credit instruments help in ironing out the mismatch between short-term liabilities and long-term investments of the bank. Hence, the money market, in this sense, complements the capital market.

as a responsibility. Profit for banks is a means of carrying out such responsibility, not their sole objective. For other financial entities, maximizing profit, as measured by risk-adjusted financial return, is their sole objective. Banks help in building a risk-free environment and undertake others' risks. Other financial entities need banks to play such a role so that they can make risk-free profits.

This illuminates the presence of two *genres* of banking theory. The objective of one is to understand banks in relation to economic development and the role of banks in mobilizing real savings and investment, while providing a secure banking market. The other looks at how financial entities manage themselves and seek to make profits. There can be no common framework and methodology for understanding both these *genres* on the same footing. The concerns are different, the objectives are different, and the very language is different. The attempt to merge the two *genres* to impose one on the other or endlessly debate which is the right method is futile. This chapter intended to dissect and segregate the two *genres* and provide clarity.

References

Bhanumurthy, K. V. and Deb, A. T. (2013). Theoretical framework of competition as applied to banking. *International Journal of Banking, Risk and Insurance*, 1(2), 1–16.

Corrigan, E. G. (1982). Are banks special? *Annual Report, Federal Reserve Bank of Minneapolis*, Minneapolis, 1–2. https://www.minneapolisfed.org/article/2000/are-banks-special.

Fixler, D. J. and Zieschang, K. D. (1992). User cost, shadow prices and the real output of banks. In Z. Griliches (Ed.), *Output Measurement in the Service Sectors* (pp. 219–243). University of Chicago Press. http://www.nber.org/chapters/c7236.

Fontana, G. (2003). Post Keynesian approaches to endogenous money: A time framework explanation. *Review of Political Economy*, 15(3), 291–314. https://doi.org/10.1080/09538250308431.

Gale, D. (1982). *Money: In Equilibrium*. Cambridge University Press.

Heurtas, T. (2018). Are banks still special? *Journal of Financial Perspectives*, 5(1), 1–15.

Klein, M. A. (1971). A theory of the banking firm. *Journal of Money, Credit and Banking*, 3(2), Part 1, 205–218. https://www.jstor.org/stable/1991279.

Mettenheim, K. (2013). Back to basics in banking theory and varieties of finance capitalism. *Accounting, Economics and Law*, 3(3), 357–405. https://doi.org/10.1515/ael-2013-0008.

Moulton, H. G. (1918). Commercial banking and capital formation I. *Journal of Political Economy*, 18(5), 484–508. https://archive.org/details/jstor/-1822412/mode/2up.

Oren, G. (2021). Traditional banking business model. *GBO International Financial Services*. https://money-gate.com/traditional-banking-business-model/.

Prochnow, H. V. (1949). Bank liquidity and the new doctrine of anticipated income. *The Journal of Finance*, 4(4), 289–314. https://www.jstor.org/stable/2975424.

Realfonzo, R. (1998). *Money and Banking: Theory and Debate (1900–1940)*. Edward Elgar.

Schmalensee, R. (1987). Collusion vs. differential efficiency: Testing alternative hypotheses. *Journal of Industrial Economics*, 35(4), 399–425.

Simon, H. A. (1956). Rational choice and the structure of the environment. *Psychological Review*, 63(2), 129–138. https://doi.org/10.1037/h0042769.

Woodward, S. (1988). A transaction cost analysis of banking activity and deposit insurance. *Cato Journal*, 7(3), 683–699.

Wray, L. R. (2013). What do banks do? What should banks do? A Minskian perspective. *Accounting, Economics and Law*, 3(3), 277–311. https://doi.org/10.1515/ael-2013-0033.

Part II

Analytical Perspectives

https://doi.org/10.1142/9789819823161_0004

Chapter 4

Review of Performance Evaluation in Insurance and Reinsurance Industries

Narinder Kumar[*,‡] **and Tuhin S. Banerjee**[†,§]

[*]*School of Economics and Public Policy, RV University, Bengaluru, Karnataka, India*

[†]*School of Business, RV University, Bengaluru, Karnataka, India*

[‡]*narinderk@rvu.edu.in*

[§]*tuhinsb@rvu.edu.in*

It is evident that, in general, the public is becoming more aware of the importance of insurance as an instrument to minimize the risk of greater loss. The recent pandemic has reshaped the perspective of people toward insurance, be it health insurance or general insurance. The present work is also inspired by the recent COVID-19 pandemic situation. Though we know that the pandemic (2020 and 2021) was immensely challenging, during such frustrating times, health insurance provided a sense of security. Drawing inspiration from discussions, one may synthesize and provide the reader with a timeline and themes in which the majority of the academic literature is available. The present work is an attempt to synthesize the existing literature starting from the late 1980s to September 2024. The authors have used Scopus data and searched for the literature on insurance using the keywords "insurance" OR "reinsurance" AND "Performance Evaluation". The database provided data from 177 articles. At an individual level, there is a huge amount of data available on insurance; however, data on insurance and performance evaluation, which indicates the efficiency analysis of the insurance companies, are not widely available.

Keywords: Performance evaluation, insurance, reinsurance, bibliometric.

1. Introduction

Insurance and reinsurance are the most important instruments of modern times that safeguard individuals, companies, and governments from potential financial losses. They are widely used hedging techniques to create a safety net against financial uncertainties. The recent global shock, i.e., the COVID-19 pandemic, has underscored the importance of insurance and reinsurance. In continuation, there has been a surge in the demand for health and general insurance products resulting from the recent experience of the pandemic. This experience has also ignited a new spark in academic and market research to understand the dynamics of insurance in the post-pandemic landscape.

This review article synthesizes the existing body of literature on performance evaluation in insurance and reinsurance, spanning from the late 1980s to September 2024. The study analyzes the data from 177 peer-reviewed articles acquired from the Scopus database using a bibliometric approach. The articles were identified through the search string "insurance" OR "reinsurance" AND "performance evaluation". While insurance-related data are abundant, literature explicitly focused on performance evaluation, particularly efficiency analysis, is comparatively sparse, warranting a structured synthesis.

Performance evaluation of the insurance and reinsurance industry offers immense opportunity for its use in strategic planning, competitive positioning, and regulatory oversight, as it is not a mere academic exercise. The study of performance evaluation is indicative of the changing dynamics of insurance and reinsurance; it is useful in assessing operational efficiency and navigating complex problems such as technological disruption, climate risk, and global shocks like pandemics. The bibliometric analysis in this chapter bridges the gap between academic and industrial perspectives to better understand emerging tools and techniques for performance evaluation, such as data envelopment analysis (DEA), stochastic frontier analysis (SFA), and decision models based on machine learning (ML) and deep learning (DL).

To conclude this introduction, this chapter offers a holistic view of performance evaluation in insurance by closely studying and synthesizing the available literature on performance evaluation in the insurance and reinsurance industries. The chapter will help researchers, policymakers, academics, and industry practitioners understand the landscape and dynamics of performance and insurance and its intersections.

1.1. *Overview of the methods of performance evaluation*

There is a huge range of methods available for performance evaluation. These methods are distinct in their use and offer unique analytical advantages and have different prerequisites such as context, data availability, and evaluative goals. DEA is among the most fundamental and frequently adopted techniques; it is a non-parametric technique applied for evaluating the relative efficiency of decision-making units (DMUs) by comparing input–output configurations. DEA has proven particularly useful in benchmarking operational efficiency across life and health insurance firms, enabling the identification of best practices and performance gaps. Complementing DEA is SFA, a parametric approach that estimates efficiency frontiers while accounting for statistical noise. SFA is frequently employed to evaluate cost and profit efficiency in competitive insurance markets, especially where environmental or firm-specific heterogeneity must be controlled. Both DEA and SFA have been instrumental in cross-country comparisons and longitudinal studies of insurance firm productivity.

In addition to frontier-based methods, composite indices such as the Insurance Performance Measure (IPM) have gained traction for their ability to integrate underwriting results, investment income, and operational metrics into a single evaluative framework. IPM offers a more holistic view of firm performance than traditional financial ratios and is increasingly used in strategic decision-making and reinsurance negotiations. Financial ratios, however, remain foundational tools in insurance performance analysis. Measures such as the combined ratio, return on equity (ROE), loss ratio, and expense ratio provide regulators, investors, and internal management with standardized indicators of financial health and underwriting profitability.

The combined ratio, in particular, serves as a critical benchmark, with values below 100% indicating underwriting gains.

Recent advances in ML have introduced predictive modeling techniques into the performance evaluation landscape. Algorithms such as decision trees, random forests, and neural networks are now employed to forecast firm performance, detect fraud, and optimize customer segmentation. These models are especially relevant in health and general insurance, where large volumes of structured and unstructured data can be leveraged for dynamic pricing and risk assessment. Moreover, multi-criteria decision analysis (MCDA) and simplex optimization models have been applied to reinsurance contexts, where firms must balance trade-offs between risk transfer, capital efficiency, and costs. These models enable the evaluation of performance across conflicting objectives and are well-suited to policy-sensitive environments.

Overall, the choice of performance evaluation method depends on the analytical purpose, diagnostic, predictive, or strategic, and the nature of the insurance or reinsurance activity under study. While traditional financial ratios offer transparency and comparability, frontier methods and composite indices provide deeper insights into efficiency and strategic alignment. The integration of ML and optimization frameworks signals a methodological shift toward more adaptive and data-driven evaluation paradigms. For researchers and practitioners, a nuanced understanding of these methods and their sector-specific applications is essential for designing robust, defensible, and actionable performance assessments in the insurance and reinsurance domains.

1.2. *Familiarity with the nature of the industry*

1.2.1. *The business of insurance and reinsurance is affected by world market conditions, legislations, and innovations in technologies. Bamidele et al. (2022) assert that mechanisms of reinsurance have not been able to influence the overall performance or the continuity of operations for Nigeria-based insurance companies.*

1.2.2. *Performance evaluation sheds light on the strategies these businesses use to counter problems like physical calamities, global virus outbreaks, or uncertainties in the market. Park et al.*

(2021) further go on to suggest that in general, reinsurance activities from affiliated firms are related to improved profitability of property and casualty insurers, as they act to support the internal capital market of the insurance industry.

1.3. Development of strategic plans and decisions

1.3.1. *Recognizing major directions and indicators of effectiveness makes it possible for the representatives of the insurance and reinsurance industries and policymakers to act rationally in the first place.*

1.3.2. *It helps to devise ways of improving the efficiency of operations, reducing risk, and increasing customer satisfaction. Shiu (2020) claims that operational non-life UK insurers who utilize greater reinsurance and derivatives have a greater likelihood of obtaining investment success. However, policies with strong loss ratios have the same challenges.*

1.4. Enhancing competitiveness

1.4.1. *Performance evaluation reveals the competitive advantages that a company can leverage within its product lines, risk models, claims, or management activities.*

1.4.2. *It also offers benchmarks for partner institutions' competition and for measuring best practices. Bharathkumar (2018) shares that the IPM is a better performance measure in comparison to the Underwriting Ratio as an overview for such businesses and takes less effort on the insurer's part, allowing easier negotiations for reinsurance renewals as well.*

1.5. Academic and practical contribution

1.5.1. *Such bibliometric analysis enables reconciliation of scholarly work and real-world activities through the identification of major themes, key research, and developing directions. Lee and Lee (2012) show in the case of Taiwan's property liability insurance industry, decreasing dependency on reinsurance was witnessed as R&D activities increased; however, this still had a negative impact on the overall performance of the firm.*

1.5.2. *It provides a guide for upcoming research and answers unresolved sectoral issues. Bharathkumar and Gupta (2020) argue that contrary to popular belief, investment income in the insurance market in India is not as significant as investment income; rather, more focus is placed on reinsurance.*

1.6. Regulatory and risk management implications

1.6.1. *Insurance and reinsurance sectors are highly supervised. Recognizing performance tendencies benefits the regulators in formulating policies aimed at enhancing the stability and protection of the stakeholders. Gbenro et al. (2023) assert that the perception of the stakeholders about reinsurance and insurance products and services has a substantial effect on the competitiveness and performance of the insurance companies in Sierra Leone.*

1.6.2. *Improved practices involving risk management as a result of performance measurements make sure that in times of crisis, organizations stay sound and dependable. According to Chen and Hamwi (2000), US property/liability reinsurance has shown to have a larger average within its ratios than primary US insurers; however, the ratio comes much closer to that of policyholders' Return on Surplus.*

1.6.3. *This structured undertaking intends to contribute to the collective understanding of the dynamics of the industry, encourage creativity, and make the industry adaptable to the continuous changes brought about by global challenges.*

Figure 1 distributes the year-wise number of articles on insurance, reinsurance, and performance evaluation. The figure shows an increasing trend, and there is a huge surge in the number of articles published from 2020 onward. It indicates that the area of research is gradually picking up the pace and will continue to do so.

Figure 2 distributes the total number of citations received on the articles published in each year from 1990 to 2024. The red colored linear trend line represents the direction of the citation count in a year. It is evident that the trend is on the increasing side and is expected to grow further.

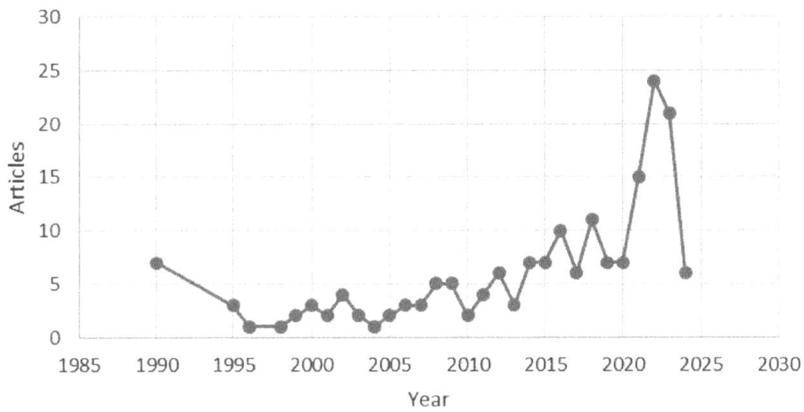

Fig. 1. Year-wise distribution of articles.

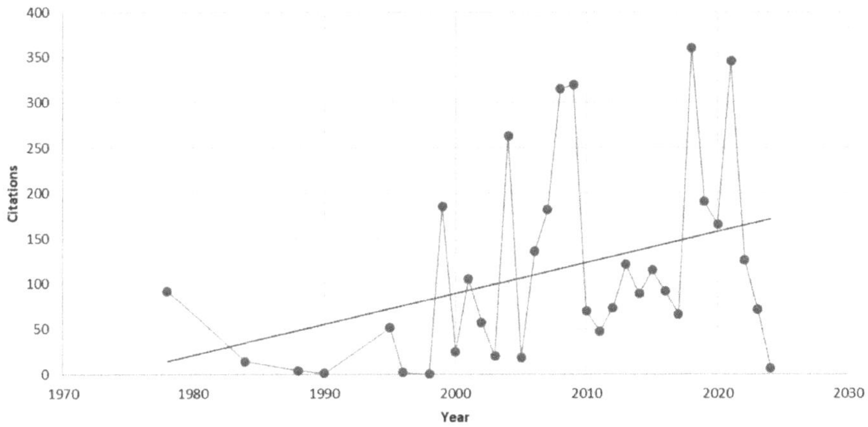

Fig. 2. Year-wise distribution of total citations received by published articles.

The sample articles with their title, citations, source, and year of publication are also provided to help young researchers target the relevant journals.

Table 1 represents the distribution of journal articles based on authors, title, citation, source title, H-index, year of publication, and whether it is open access or not: Neamatullah *et al.* (2008) with 278 citations. Albuquerque (2004) with 178 citations, Zhou *et al.* (2018) with 166 citations, Ecer *et al.* (2021) with 122 citations,

Table 1. Distribution of highly cited journal articles with title, source title, H-index, and year of publication.

Authors	Title	Cited by	Source title	H-Index	Year	Open Access
Neamatullah *et al.*	Automated de-identification of free-text medical records	278	*BMC Medical Informatics and Decision Making*	97	2008	All Open Access; Gold Open Access
Gibbs *et al.*	Determinants and effects of subjectivity in incentives	263	*Accounting Review*	192	2004	NA
MacKenzie *et al.*	Do citizenship behaviors matter more for managers than for salespeople?	181	*Journal of the Academy of Marketing Science*	207	1999	NA
Albuquerque	Peer firms in relative performance evaluation	178	*Journal of Accounting and Economics*	187	2009	NA
Zhou *et al.*	MIStore: a Blockchain-Based Medical Insurance Storage System	166	*Journal of Medical Systems*	110	2018	All Open Access; Hybrid Gold Open Access
Muetze *et al.*	Electric bicycles - A performance evaluation	138	*IEEE Industry Applications Magazine*	61	2007	NA
Ecer *et al.*	MARCOS technique under intuitionistic fuzzy environment for determining the COVID-19 pandemic performance evaluation of insurance companies in terms of healthcare services	122	*Applied Soft Computing*	190	2021	All Open Access; Green Open Access
Yang	A two-stage DEA model to evaluate the overall performance of Canadian life and health insurance companies	112	*Mathematical and Computer Modelling*	121	2006	All Open Access; Bronze Open Access
Schold *et al.*	The association of center performance evaluations and kidney transplant volume in the United States	104	*American Journal of Transplantation*	220	2013	All Open Access; Hybrid Gold Open Access

Yang (2006) with 112 citations, and Schold *et al.* (2013) with 104 citations. The table is a reference for potential researchers who are interested in carrying out research in the area of insurance and performance evaluation.

2. Methodology

The current study performs a systematic literature review by following a structured bibliometric approach to examine the landscape of performance evaluation within the insurance and reinsurance industries. The study uses bibliometric data from 177 articles extracted from the Scopus database. The author used a targeted Boolean search string: "insurance" OR "reinsurance" AND "performance evaluation". The data were used from 1984 to September 2024.

The study adopted a robust mechanism for selecting articles using the SPAR-4-SLR protocol (Paul *et al.*, 2021) to ensure methodological rigor. The protocol is essential for the current study, as it encompasses three crucial stages of article selection that make the results transparent by following integrated planning, execution, and reporting stages, ensuring reproducible literature synthesis. The author conducted a preliminary data preprocessing to remove anomalies in the data, such as missing values, non-English articles, articles without empirical anchoring, and some pure conceptual papers, duplicate files, and repeated words to refine the networks. The papers with direct relevance to the study, such as those mentioning performance and insurance or reinsurance in the title, were further included for analysis, and articles with previously mentioned anomalies were excluded.

Bibliometric mapping and network analysis were conducted using VOSviewer, an open-access visualization tool. Keyword co-occurrence analysis was implemented to identify dominant thematic streams and trace their evolution over time. Author citation analysis facilitated the clustering of influential contributors and the intellectual structure of the field. Indexed keyword networks were examined to uncover conceptual convergence and methodological diversity. Normalization was carried out using association strength as the co-occurrence weight in cluster development. A minimum threshold of five keyword occurrences was applied to enhance interpretive robustness.

While VOSviewer provided effective mapping of bibliometric attributes, the study acknowledges the limitations of relying solely on keyword frequency and clustering for thematic extraction. As such, thematic synthesis was further supported by inductive reasoning and manual literature coding, aligning each bibliometric cluster with real-world performance evaluation domains such as health insurance, socio-demographics, and financial risk management.

The SLR method provides immense potential for researchers to outline the landscape of performance evaluation in insurance and reinsurance and also strengthens the narrative of the concept's development. It allows researchers to demarcate empirical patterns and conceptual advancements by closely studying the networks of attributes (Tang *et al.*, 2021). The multilayered approach of bibliometric study helps in integrating the quantitative and qualitative aspects of the bibliometric data to build actionable directions for emerging research.

This study acknowledges the strength of using multi-databases to produce empirical results. However, the current study exclusively uses Scopus data and the VOSviewer tool. Future research may explore multi-database, sentiment-based policy lensing, and advanced textual analytics to offer varied perspectives. These research attempts could deepen interpretability and reveal more nuanced insights into the development of performance evaluation narratives, particularly within the insurance sector.

2.1. *Bibliometric analysis*

The section provides the detailed analysis of the networks of keywords, author, and indexing. The analysis is sub-divided into Bibliometric mapping of all keywords on the basis of co-occurrence, Overlay visualization of all keywords, Bibliometric mapping of the indexed keywords based on the co-occurrence, Overlay visualization of the Indexed keywords.

The analysis of all keywords is carried out based on the co-occurrence of the keywords in the articles. It is evident that there are four major clusters of relevant keywords in the dataset, separated by four colors: Blue, Green, Red, and Yellow. Cluster one (blue) involves keywords such as insurance and performance evaluation and related techniques such as data envelopment analysis, which is one of the prominent techniques for productivity and efficiency analysis of insurance companies. We name cluster one as "Insurance and Performance Evaluation". Similarly, cluster two has a network of keywords related to background characteristics of individuals, such as gender, age, and adult, and machine learning techniques like random forest and machine learning; hence, it is logical to call it "machine learning and demographic features". Furthermore, cluster three which is represented by red has a network of keywords on health, health care system, and performance evaluation, so it is safe to call cluster three "Health care and performance evaluation". Last but not least, the fourth cluster does not reveal any clear network of keywords which can be used by potential researchers, so it can be called "Other Keywords". To summarize, the system has generated four clusters, and it provides insights about the selection of keywords while searching and writing articles related to the field of insurance and performance evaluation.

This figure supplements the interpretation of Fig. 3, where all the keywords are mapped based on their co-occurrence. However, based

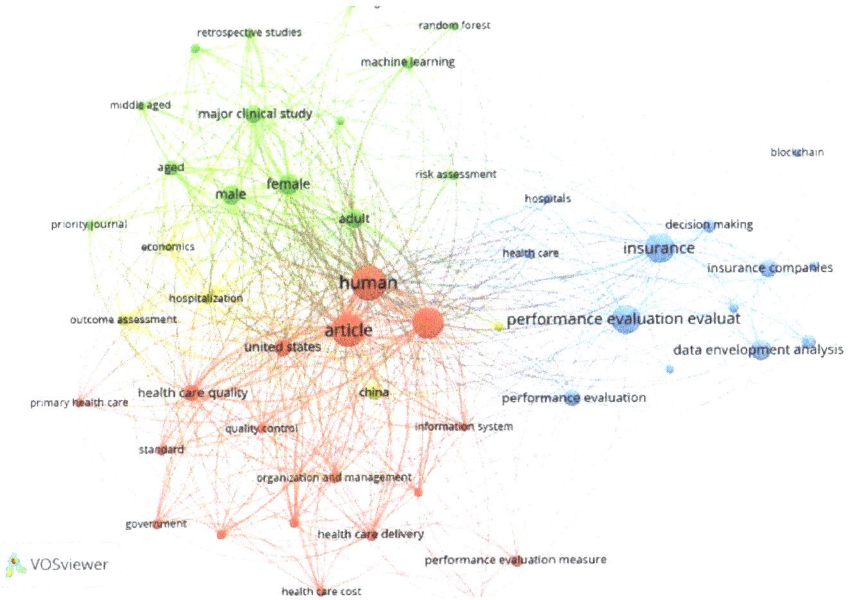

Fig. 3. Bibliometric mapping of all keywords on the basis of co-occurrence.

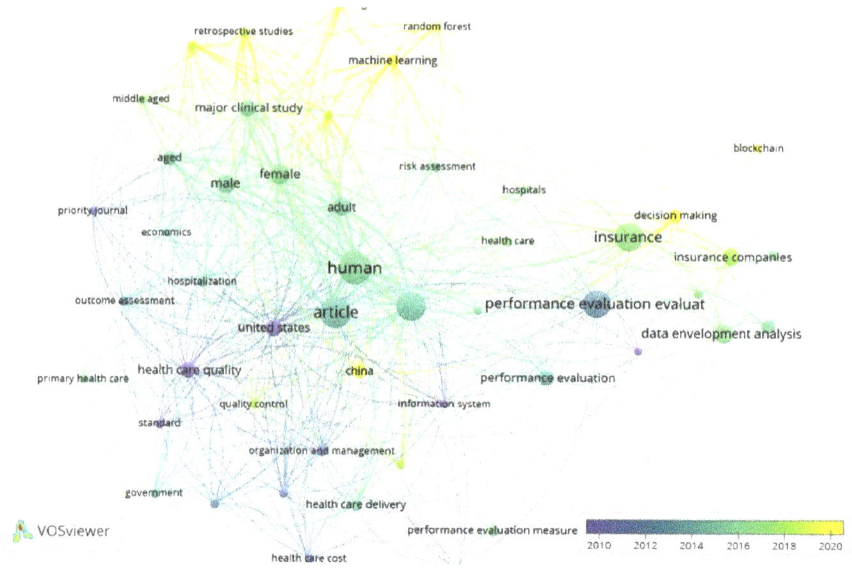

Fig. 4. Overlay visualization of all keywords.

on the timeline of the publication, it is evident that contemporary focus in the field of insurance and performance evaluation is on integrating machine learning techniques and applied decision-making methods, such as decision tree and random forest techniques (Fig. 4).

Bibliometric mapping of indexed keywords serves a slightly different purpose, as these are the keywords prioritized by the publishers to help the articles gain better reach in academia (Fig. 5). It supports the development of themes in published work and highlights current hot topics within the field. In the present case, it is apparent that the system has generated three clusters: Cluster one (red color) forms a network of indexed keywords like health care and health care policy, and information system. It can be labeled "Health and Information Systems". Cluster two (blue color) has indexed keywords related to demographic features and machine learning; it can be labeled as "Demographics and Machine Learning". Cluster two also suggests that machine learning algorithms, such as decision trees and random forests, use categorical data, such as gender and continuous data, to train the models; thus, many research articles based on decision-making and machine learning in the field of insurance use demographic indicators. Cluster three (green color) evidently shows

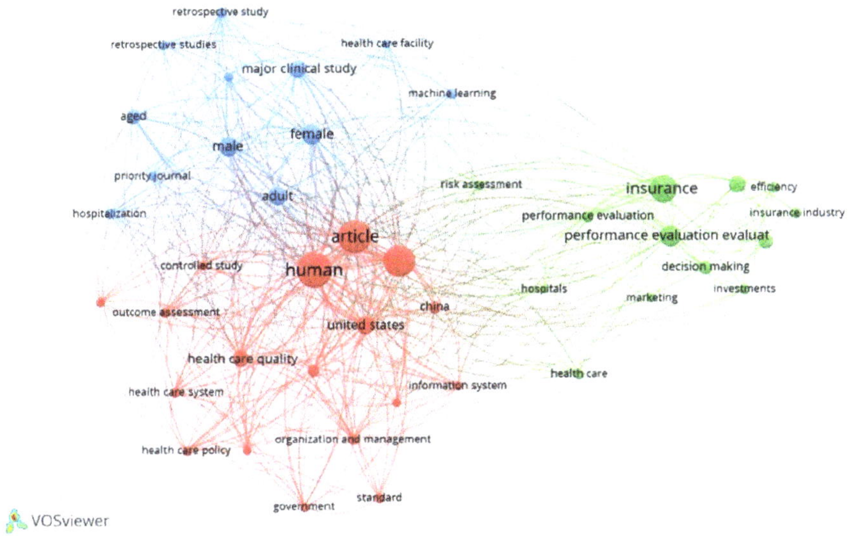

Fig. 5. Bibliometric mapping of the indexed keywords based on the co-occurrence.

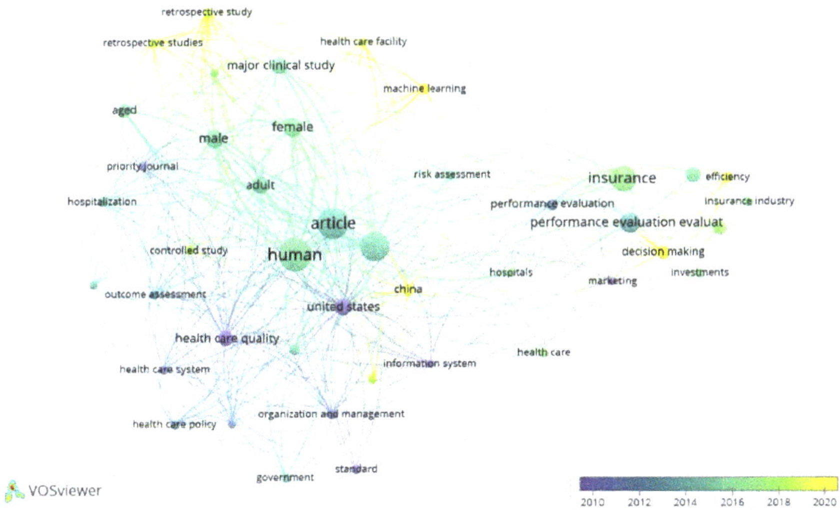

Fig. 6. Overlay visualization of the Indexed keywords.

indexed keywords related to insurance and performance evaluation; hence it is labeled "Insurance and Performance Evaluation".

To summarize, there are three clusters: health and information systems, demographics and machine learning, and insurance and performance evaluation.

Figure 6 represents the distribution of the indexed keywords based on the progress of the keywords used in the research articles with respect to the year of publication. Starting from the use of insurance in the health and health care sector, and gradually transitioning to insurance and performance evaluation, including productivity and efficiency analysis of the insurance companies, to the most contemporary field of machine learning and decision-making.

3. Conclusion

This work presented a synthesis of the literature base on performance evaluation in insurance and reinsurance industries. The exercise mapped the potent intellectual landscape of the articles, specifically focusing on the mentioned keywords. A subtle increase in the count of publications since the pandemic is an indication of a surge in publications in the areas of insurance and performance evaluation. The bibliometric analysis of the 177 Scopus articles also confirmed the publication trend and highlighted the changing dynamics of the research landscape.

The clustering techniques based on keywords and indexed keywords revealed the following thematic clusters: first, healthcare and the health sector; second, socio-economic, socio-demographic, and ML applications; and third, insurance and performance evaluation. These clusters highlight the distinct areas of research which have evolved over the course of four decades and lay out the evolution of the various techniques that emerged during that time.

The literature based on the methodological aspects of performance evaluation demonstrates strong use of frontier efficiency techniques such as DEA and SFA, serving as the fundamental techniques for assessing operational and cost efficiency. Furthermore, the introduction of composite indices techniques, such as the IPM, and the adoption of predictive models based on ML models highlighted the broadening of available performance evaluation techniques. Especially, the ML and DL techniques allow for clustering, predictive analysis, and forecasting techniques that can handle the nonlinear aspects of large datasets. The recent studies have integrated demographic indicators with ML techniques such as decision trees and random forests, confirming a significant transition in the methodological domain of performance evaluation. Particularly in insurance and reinsurance sectors, the use of ML techniques can help in the detection of risky insurance policies to avoid future risk.

The mapping of the literature using the bibliometric technique shows a convergence in the perspectives of academia and industry, especially in terms of actionable insights that industry picks from the research. The industry acknowledges the research findings and views research not as a mere exercise but as an indication of future discourse, provided the conditions persist. Furthermore, the literature base emphasizes the role of reinsurance as a tool for hedging against future risk.

Most importantly, the review highlighted potential gaps and opportunities for further research. Recent developments in artificial intelligence (AI) and its integration across various industries set the stage for future research, including the scope of integrating multi-datasets to build robust networks of keywords and related attributes. The integration of AI, especially in fraud detection, customer engagement, and the personalization of services, is a most crucial use case. As the industry embraces digital transformation, performance evaluation frameworks must evolve to capture dynamic, multi-dimensional metrics that reflect not only financial outcomes but also operational agility, customer centricity, and technological adaptability.

In a nutshell, the current work provides a comprehensive, analytical synthesis of the literature and can be used as a reference to demarcate the evolution of performance evaluation in the insurance and reinsurance industries. By categorizing thematic clusters, evaluating methodological trends, and highlighting actionable insights to bridge the gaps. It lays the groundwork for a more transparent, defensible, and future-ready approach to performance evaluation in insurance and reinsurance.

4. Limitation of the Study

The strengths of the study were explored in the previous discussion. Let us now scope out the limitations of the study. The first is the exclusive use of the Scopus database to build a narrative around performance evaluation in insurance and reinsurance, which is not adequate. Other repositories such as SSRN, Web of Science (WoS), and EconLit could be further integrated to build a more holistic narrative. Using an exclusive data source can also lead to bias in the study, especially when exploring new clusters in performance evaluation for insurance.

Second, the Boolean search string used for data extraction, i.e., "insurance" OR "reinsurance" AND "performance evaluation", could have reduced the scope of the data collection as it filters out other crucial keywords indirectly associated with performance evaluation. Terms such as "efficiency analysis", "financial performance", "risk modelling", and "strategic benchmarking" can potentially widen the search area of the data and help in finding hidden networks. Similarly, excluding gray literature and white papers further reduces the database.

Third, there are limitations to using VOSviewer as an analysis tool, which is effective for co-occurrence and clustering of keywords (both author and indexed) but is not capable of carrying out any complex text mining techniques, for instance, topic modeling (such as LDA), sentiment analysis, and semantic network analysis. Advanced data mining techniques are advantageous in uncovering latent themes, discursive patterns, and conceptual shifts that would otherwise be missed by co-occurrence-based methods. Along with the SPAR-4-SLR protocol, techniques such as the Preferred Reporting Items for Systematic Reviews and Meta-Analysis (PRISMA), Search Appraisal Synthesis Analysis (SALSA), Theory Context Characteristics Method (TCCM), and Context Intervention Mechanism Outcome (CIMO) could be used.

Finally, the study does not provide full-text analysis or citation context evaluation, which is useful in figuring out how the performance evaluation is adopted in the insurance sector. Future research must use, for example, multi-database analysis, incorporate more keywords, and employ data mining techniques to overcome these mentioned limitations of the study.

5. Scope for Future Research

This work only synthesizes the literature on "insurance" OR "reinsurance" AND "performance evaluation" and uses the Scopus database, collected from 1984 to (September) 2024. The scope for future research is to select data from various datasets, such as WoS. The researchers who are embarking on the area of performance evaluation in insurance can refer to this piece of work. The highlighted literature base provides a strong starting point, and as it is segregated across many levels, it will also provide distinct perspectives to carry out research in the area of insurance and reinsurance.

There is a great scope for integrating AI in the area of insurance, especially in fraud detection, where ML algorithms can help detect fraud. Along with fraud detection, the researchers can also explore the area of clustering based on insurance data by leveraging supervised and unsupervised ML algorithms.

Recent developments in the area of generative AI, especially in the field of agentic AI, can help in decision-making regarding the purchase of the insurance products, creating a complete ecosystem of personalized insurance management. The insurance companies are seeing a surge in the use of chatbots and virtual assistants for customized interaction with customers by providing focused information, and they are also leveraging these technologies to increase customer engagement.

The potential of AI in the insurance industry is immense, and only the future will reveal how these technologies are going to disrupt these markets. In conclusion, the chapter offers many verticals for researchers to explore and contribute to the existing body of knowledge.

References

Albuquerque, A. (2009). Peer firms in relative performance evaluation. *Journal of Accounting and Economics*, 48(1), 69–89.

Bamidele, B., Ayinde, N., and Danan, A. (2022). The evaluation of reinsurance mechanisms on Nigerian insurance companies: Its performance and sustainability. *Journal of Global Economics, Management and Business Research.* https://doi.org/10.56557/jgembr/2022/v14i27951.

Bharathkumar, S. (2018). An empirical study of insurance performance measure. *Corporate Finance: Valuation*. https://doi.org/10.1111/jacf.12302.

Bharathkumar, S. and Gupta, S. (2020). Simplex representation of insurance performance analysis. *Journal of Policy Modeling*, 42, 419–436. https://doi.org/10.1016/j.jpolmod.2019.06.010.

Chen, Y. and Hamwi, I. S. (2000). Performance analyses of US property-liability reinsurance companies. *Journal of Insurance Issues*, 140–152.

de Albuquerque, R. T. (2004). An Analysis of Integration Degree between Macroeconomic and Financial Variables Through Principal Components.

Ecer, F., and Pamucar, D. (2021). MARCOS technique under intuitionistic fuzzy environment for determining the COVID-19 pandemic performance of insurance companies in terms of healthcare services. *Applied Soft Computing*, 104, 107199.

Gbenro, O., Duramany-Lakkoh, E., and Kamara, S. (2023). An assessment of the stakeholders perception of reinsurance and insurance products and services on the performance of insurance companies. *International Journal of Development and Economic Sustainability*. https://doi.org/10.37745/ijdes.13/vol11n2137.

Gibbs, M., Merchant, K. A., Stede, W. A. V. D., and Vargus, M. E. (2004). Determinants and effects of subjectivity in incentives. *The Accounting Review*, 79(2), 409–436.

Lee, H. and Lee, C. (2012). An analysis of reinsurance and firm performance: Evidence from the Taiwan property-liability insurance industry. *The Geneva Papers on Risk and Insurance - Issues and Practice*, 37, 467–484. https://doi.org/10.1057/GPP.2012.9.

MacKenzie, S. B., Podsakoff, P. M., and Paine, J. B. (1999). Do citizenship behaviors matter more for managers than for salespeople? *Journal of the Academy of Marketing Science*, 27(4), 396–410.

Muetze, A., and Tan, Y. C. (2007). Electric bicycles-a performance evaluation. *IEEE Industry Applications Magazine*, 13(4), 12–21.

Neamatullah, I. (2006). De-identification of free-text medical records. MIT, édition, 1, 54–67.

Park, J., Choi, B., and Ho, C. (2021). The impact of internal and external reinsurance on insurers#39; performance and price. *Managerial Finance*. https://doi.org/10.1108/MF-12-2019-0619.

Paul, J., Lim, W. M., O'Cass, A., Hao, A. W., and Bresciani, S. (2021). Scientific procedures and rationales for systematic literature reviews (SPAR-4-SLR). *International Journal of Consumer Studies*, 45(4), O1–O16.

Schold, J. D., Buccini, L. D., Srinivas, T. R., Srinivas, R. T., Poggio, E. D., Flechner, S. M., and Goldfarb, D. A. (2013). The association of center performance evaluations and kidney transplant volume in the United States. *American Journal of Transplantation*, 13(1), 67–75.

Shiu, Y. (2020). How does reinsurance and derivatives usage affect financial performance? Evidence from the UK non-life insurance industry. *Economic Modelling*, 88, 376–385. https://doi.org/10.1016/j.econmod.2019.09.048.

Tang, L., Omar, S. Z., Bolong, J., and Mohd Zawawi, J. W. (2021). Social media use among young people in China: A systematic literature review. *Sage Open*, 11(2), 21582440211016421.

Yang, Z. (2006). A two-stage DEA model to evaluate the overall performance of Canadian life and health insurance companies. *Mathematical and Computer Modelling*, 43(7–8), 910–919.

Zhou, L., Wang, L., and Sun, Y. (2018). MIStore: A blockchain-based medical insurance storage system. *Journal of Medical Systems*, 42(8), 149.

https://doi.org/10.1142/9789819823161_0005

Chapter 5

Impact of Technology on Performance Analysis in the Financial Services Domain: A Survey of the Literature

Güneş Topçu[*,‡], **Can Bekaroğlu**[†,§], **and İsmail Elagöz**[*,¶]

[*] *Business Administration Department, Çanakkale Onsekiz Mart University, Çanakkale, Türkiye*

[†] *Economics Department, Çanakkale Onsekiz Mart University, Çanakkale, Türkiye*

[‡] *gunestopcu@comu.edu.tr*

[§] *canbekaroglu@comu.edu.tr*

[¶] *ismailelagoz@comu.edu.tr*

The financial sector has historically been at the forefront of technological innovation, integrating tools such as telephone and internet banking since the late 20th century. Recent advancements, particularly in artificial intelligence (AI) and big data analytics (BDA), have revolutionized the industry. These technologies have enhanced operational efficiency by automating processes, reducing human error, and improving the accuracy and speed of transactions. This chapter aims to analyze the performance of financial services amid these technological advancements, based on a review of 65 studies. The analysis begins by differentiating key performance metrics, productivity, efficiency, and profitability, followed by an overview of efficiency measurement techniques. AI and BDA are then examined in their impact on these metrics, highlighting how they have reshaped traditional performance measurement frameworks.

The findings from the reviewed studies underscore that AI and BDA improve financial services by streamlining processes, lowering costs, and enhancing decision-making accuracy. Additionally, these tools facilitate task automation and expedite operations, resulting in increased profitability and overall efficiency. Through a narrative review, the chapter illustrates the transformative role of AI and BDA in driving innovation and performance in the financial sector.

Keywords: Artificial intelligence (AI), big data analytics (BDA), efficiency metrics, financial services performance, productivity and profitability.

1. Introduction

Working with high-volume data for a long time and being heavily reliant on technology, the financial services sector is one of the leading sectors that utilizes AI. As the backbone of the financial sector, banks are undergoing a transformation that involves these developments. According to a study published by McKinsey (Biswas *et al.*, 2020), AI has the potential to create additional benefits for banks amounting to 1 trillion dollars per year. This expectation, as well as the current transformation process, encourages banks to invest in AI and develop AI-focused business models.

The financial performance of a financial institution is affected by service delivery and financial intermediation, both of which are observable and actionable (Harker and Zenios, 2000). With the rapid advancement of technology such as AI and BDA in the financial markets over the last decade, the scope of the products that financial institutions offer to their customers has increased. The introduction of new payment systems, such as telecom-operated mobile money services and digital payment platforms like PayPal, Venmo, and Cash App, into the financial system has decreased banks' service fees, which are considered one of the main profit-generating activities of banks.

Additionally, the existence of distributed ledger technology-based outputs, such as smart contracts and blockchain, has enabled the emergence of new financial institutions and new financial instruments, such as cryptocurrencies, that reduce the need for financial intermediaries. This means that traditional financial institutions must either increase their performance using conventional methods or implement new technologies, which are necessary to compete with the emerging financial institutions and preserve their market shares. On the other hand, technological infrastructure is not costless, and financial institutions have reduced their existing costs to cover the initial costs of introducing new technology into their operations. With the shift to a digital environment, banks have closed most of their branches and removed automatic teller machines (ATMs), which created maintenance costs over time.

The introduction of AI and ML into the financial markets has introduced new challenges to traditional performance metrics and caused disruptions. In the financial services domain, ML can be used in credit pre-approval, credit underwriting, optimal portfolio selection, various front-end and back-end activities (Tyagi, 2022, p. 5), product development, and fraud detection. Additionally, in the financial sector, AI-based devices such as chatbots have replaced labor inputs in most cases, leading to faster, cheaper, and more accurate service production, which, in turn, enhances efficiency and productivity. As a result of these technological advancements in the financial sector, it is now necessary to measure the performance of financial services within the broader financial services domain. This chapter's goal is to review existing studies and evaluate the performance analyses of financial institutions amid a myriad of methodological and technological developments. We will adopt a conventional narrative review and mainly focus on banks as opposed to other financial institutions.

This study is motivated by the need to understand how technological advancements, particularly AI, ML, and big data analytics, are reshaping the performance measurement of financial institutions. As traditional metrics become increasingly insufficient to capture the effects of these innovations, there is a pressing need for updated frameworks to evaluate financial performance. The chapter is composed of 4 sections: Section 1: Introduction, Section 2: Measuring Performance of Financial Institutions, Section 3: The Impact of Technology on the Performance Measurement of Financial Institutions and Services, and Section 4: Conclusion.

2. Measuring Performance of Financial Institutions

Financial institutions have many functions, such as acting as an intermediary between parties with excess funds and those with a shortage of funds, facilitating money transfer between distant places, providing financing for firms that are well managed but lack a strong reputation, reducing asymmetric information between creditors and borrowers by screening and monitoring, and lowering transaction costs (Akerlof, 1970; Benston and Smith, 1976; Bhattacharya and Thakor, 1993). Among these financial institutions, banks are unique in that they produce special information that cannot be produced by other intermediaries during the loan approval process (James, 1987). Given their several roles in the economy, accurately measuring the performance of banks is of critical importance.

There are two main approaches in the literature for explaining firm performance: structural and non-structural (Hughes and Mester, 2013). While the structural approach is based on a theoretical model and includes optimization problems, the non-structural approach is based on choosing several performance measures, such as financial ratios (Chen, 2009). The structural approach mainly concentrates on frontier efficiency, where there is an ideal frontier that firms cannot exceed (Ding and Sickles, 2018). Firms operating below the frontier are considered less efficient.

Possible performance measurement areas for banks include service quality, price affordability, and accessibility of banking services (Bikker, 2010). There are five main performance indicators for banks: competition, efficiency, costs, profits, and market structure (Bikker, 2010). While analyzing performance in the financial services domain, we will mainly focus on productivity, efficiency, and profitability analyses.

2.1. *Productivity analysis*

The determinants of productivity in the financial services domain are the production inputs (capital, labor, and R&D), production technology, and outputs (Heil, 2017). Financial services can create a positive impact on productivity growth in two ways: by directly increasing output per worker and capital input (inner productivity) and by providing financial services as financial intermediaries (external productivity) (Kronick, 2014). According to the production approach in banking, first introduced by Benston (1965), banks are considered firms that use capital and labor inputs to produce deposit and loan accounts categorized into different types (Colwell and Davis, 1992).

The number of these accounts, or the number of transactions provided for each product type, serves as a measure of output based on the assumption that total costs equal operating costs required to produce these outputs (Colwell and Davis, 1992). To measure an output fully, the portions of the interest rate that reflect the payment for services and the cost of funds should be estimated correctly, as banks compensate for the services they provide by increasing interest rates charged to customers (Colangelo and Inklaar, 2009).

In the literature, there are two types of productivity measures: the partial productivity measure and the total productivity measure. The partial productivity (PP) measure associates output with only a single input, while the total factor productivity (TFP) measure associates multiple outputs with multiple inputs (Murray, 2016). Of the two performance measures, TFP is associated with technical progress (Oster and Antioch, 1995), which is related to innovation and technological change and is considered a key factor for long-run growth. On the other hand, in the environmental policy and sustainability areas, partial measures may produce more useful results than TFP measures when analyzing the effect of a particular variable, such as energy productivity (Murray, 2016). There are also accounting-based productivity indicators in the banking sector used to measure performance. Some of these indicators are financial ratios, such as operating costs to average assets, operating income to costs, and operating income to staff expenses (Oster and Antioch, 1995).

2.2. *Efficiency analysis: An introduction*

The efficiency of financial institutions is essential, as it creates improved profitability, increased amounts of funds intermediated, enhanced service quality, lower prices for customers, and better risk management (Berger, 1993). The underlying idea in efficiency analysis is to measure the performance of a firm by determining how well inputs are used to produce outputs (Ding and Sickles, 2018).

Productivity, efficiency, and effectiveness are interrelated but often misunderstood concepts. Productivity measures the ratio of output to input, while efficiency evaluates the relationship between outputs or inputs based on orientation: Output-oriented efficiency compares actual output to the maximum possible output, while input-oriented efficiency compares the best possible input to the actual input. Effectiveness, on the other hand, compares actual output to the target output (Ray and Chen, 2015).

These terms are interconnected, with increased efficiency generally leading to higher effectiveness. However, the relationship between productivity and efficiency is more nuanced. Fixed input levels ensure that increased productivity improves both efficiency and effectiveness. When inputs vary, increased productivity may result in either higher or lower efficiency and/or effectiveness. Additionally, a unit can be effective without being efficient (Bekaroğlu, 2023).

2.2.1. *How efficiency is measured*

There are two main approaches to measuring efficiency in academia: Data Envelopment Analysis (DEA) and regression-based techniques. A key distinction between these methods lies in whether a functional form is required. Parametric techniques like Corrected Ordinary Least Squares (COLS) and Stochastic Frontier Analysis (SFA) necessitate a functional form, whereas non-parametric methods like DEA and Concave Non-parametric Least Squares (CNLS) do not. Additionally, deviations are interpreted differently; OLS attributes all deviations to random noise, while DEA and COLS treat them as inefficiency. In contrast, SFA and Stochastic Non-parametric Envelopment of Data (StoNED) distinguish between noise and inefficiency.

The simplest and possibly oldest method for estimating efficiency is Ordinary Least Squares (OLS), which assumes that all firms are rational and efficient, attributing deviations to random noise (Kuosmanen, 2008, p. 4). The COLS method, however, treats all deviations as inefficiency by adjusting the frontier upward. A limitation of COLS is its lack of robustness to outliers and its reliance on strong statistical assumptions (Winsten, 1957; Aigner and Chu, 1968). An alternative to OLS and COLS is the Corrected Absolute Mean Deviation, which uses the median instead of the mean to fit the regression, offering an approach less sensitive to extreme values (Ray and Chen, 2015, p. 13).

While COLS and OLS necessitate specifying a functional form, non-parametric regression methods like CNLS offer an alternative. CNLS, introduced by Hildreth (Hildreth, 1954), does not need a predefined functional form and is consistent under certain constraints. However, it is computationally intensive and difficult to solve due to the need to identify the best-fit function from many possibilities. Another related method, Corrected Concave Non-parametric Least Squares (CCNLS), which is an adaptation of COLS, uses non-parametric regression and is more robust to small-sample errors, while maintaining certain constraints (Kuosmanen and Johnson, 2010, pp. 153, 154, 159).

DEA, a non-parametric method, constructs an efficient production frontier without assuming a specific functional form and handles multiple inputs and outputs, but assumes all deviations from the frontier are inefficiencies (Charnes *et al.*, 1978). While DEA has been criticized for not being based on a statistical framework, subsequent research has addressed this concern by demonstrating the statistical consistency of DEA estimators (Kuosmanen and Johnson, 2010; Banker, 1993).

Conversely, SFA employs parametric regression and necessitates particular functional forms for the inefficiency distribution and frontier (Meeusen and Vandenbroeck, 1977; Aigner *et al.*, 1977). SFA models both noise and inefficiency, while DEA does not. Despite their differences, these two methods are complementary. The recent StoNED approach combines SFA and CNLS, offering a flexible platform for efficiency analysis, although it is computationally intensive due to its complex model structures (Ray and Chen, 2015).

2.2.2. *Efficiency analysis in banking*

In banking literature, there are two different approaches to measuring efficiency. The first approach measures efficiency in terms of scale and scope (product mix), while the second approach uses the efficient frontier approach, or X-efficiency (Green *et al.*, 2004), which measures managerial efficiency. X-efficiency evaluates whether banks use existing inputs efficiently and is related to the technical efficiency and allocative efficiency of firms, free from scale or scope constraints (Harker and Zenios, 2000). Technical efficiency is important for banks because it produces more outputs for a given level of input, which in turn reduces costs and preserves competitiveness in the market (Akdeniz *et al.*, 2023). Greater efficiency is also crucial for greater profitability (Mor and Sharma, 2012).

Scale efficiency refers to whether banks produce the optimal number of outputs, while scope efficiency relates to whether their combination of outputs is efficient (Wagenvoort and Schure, 1999). Studies on bank-scale efficiency suggest a U-shaped average cost curve, indicating that medium-sized banks are more scale-efficient than small or large ones (Humphrey, 1990). However, some evidence contradicts this, supporting economies of scale even at large financial institutions (Hughes and Mester, 2013). Economies of scope arise when the joint production of goods or services is more cost-effective than producing them separately (Evanoff and Israilevich, 1991). The 2008 Global Financial Crisis showed that larger, diversified financial institutions were more resilient, as they adopted automation technology and maintained scale through mergers, enabling quicker recovery than smaller institutions (PWC, 2019).

A broader performance measure for financial institutions is frontier efficiency. This approach includes non-parametric methods like DEA and Free Disposal Hull, and parametric methods such as the SFA, Distribution Free Approach, and Thick Frontier Approach (Bhatia *et al.*, 2018).

Sinha (2024) estimated managerial ability (MA) as an indirect efficiency measure to assess the performance of India's general insurance sector, using data from 16 private and 4 public insurers between 2012–2013 and 2017–2018. The analysis, employing DEA and regression methods, found that MA significantly impacts insurance company performance.

2.3. *Profitability analysis*

Competition, both globally and locally, drives financial institutions to be more profit-oriented. A profitable banking sector is better equipped to withstand negative shocks, thus strengthening financial stability (Jiang *et al.*, 2003). Previous studies on bank profitability categorize determining factors into two groups: bank-specific (internal) factors, such as asset structure, asset quality, capitalization, and size, and external factors, like industry concentration, economic growth, inflation, and interest rates (Trujillo-Ponce, 2013, p. 564). Internal factors are primarily shaped by managerial decisions within the bank (Yuan *et al.*, 2022). The relationships between profitability and these factors are as follows: Higher ratios of loans to assets, asset quality, bank capitalization, customer deposits, efficiency, industry concentration, and economic growth positively affect profitability, while the effects of bank size and revenue diversification remain indeterminate (Trujillo-Ponce, 2013).

Numerous country-level studies explore the impact of internal and external factors on bank profitability (Yuan *et al.*, 2022; Athanasoglou *et al.*, 2008; Salike and Ao, 2018; Phan *et al.*, 2020; O'Connel, 2023; Akhtar *et al.*, 2024; Chen and Lee, 2024). Bank performance is often assessed using accounting measures, with financial ratios like return on assets, return on equity, and net interest margin serving as proxies for profitability, while risk is also considered in returns. For publicly listed banks, stock returns are used as a profitability indicator. Tai (2000) found that U.S. bank stock returns are influenced by market risk, interest rate risk, and exchange rate risk.

Additionally, government supervisors and bond rating agencies monitor bank performance. Inspectors conduct onsite visits to banks and access prior examination reports (Berger *et al.*, 2000). CAMELS ratings (capital adequacy, assets, management capability, earnings, liquidity, and sensitivity) are utilized by government supervisors to evaluate banks' stability and risk levels.

3. The Impact of Technology on the Performance Measurement of Financial Institutions and Services

Although banking is shifting from the traditional core banking model to a fee-generating model (Saunders *et al.*, 2020), advances in financial technology, particularly blockchain and smart contracts, have disrupted fee-based activities. While SWIFT transactions remain expensive, alternative payment methods, such as crypto payments and online platforms, are relatively cheaper, increasing competition and reducing bank fees and profitability. The rise of digital currencies based on distributed ledger technology has diminished the need for intermediation, pushing banks to adapt by moving into digital banking and reducing their branch networks.

Additionally, new fintech applications like open banking enable customers to consolidate accounts from different banks and make payments via debit cards, incurring lower commissions than credit cards. Scale and scope economies assume that banks operate on a cost function where inefficiencies may arise from using inefficient technology, leading to higher costs (Green *et al.*, 2004). Studies show that financial frictions, such as technological constraints, can reduce productivity growth by hindering optimal resource allocation (Heil, 2017). Two key technological innovations used for performance analysis in banks and other financial institutions are BDA and AI.

3.1. *Big data and performance analysis: Issues and perspectives*

Bank and credit union data make up the largest data types among those in financial institutions (Agrawal *et al.*, 2022). These data originate from various banking activities, including internet banking, retail banking, Islamic banking, investment banking, and digital banking channels such as social media, mobile banking, ATMs, and interactions with chatbots. Once integrated, the data become vast and difficult to process using conventional methods. However, BDA can efficiently process both structured and unstructured data, revealing trends and patterns within.

By processing large amounts of customer data, banks can boost earnings, reduce costs, and increase competitiveness (Bonsu, 2024). Credit scoring, widely used by credit unions to assess clients' repayment capacity, benefits from the broader representativeness of big data, which improves the accuracy of scoring models (Sousa and Figueiredo, 2014). Data are crucial in prediction, with both its quantity and quality impacting prediction accuracy. For instance, by analyzing years of transaction data, banks can employ AI to classify non-routine credit-card transactions as "unusual" instead of "usual" (Agrawal *et al.*, 2018). Recognizing such patterns helps detect and block fraudulent transactions, reducing operational costs and increasing bank efficiency and profitability. Big data also play a key role in ML for model training and making accurate predictions.

3.2. *AI and ML use in performance metrics*

The 2008 Global Financial Crisis revealed the limitations of regression-based prediction models, particularly those used by rating agencies. The issue stemmed not from the data, but from the assumption in multiple regression models that real estate prices across different markets were independent. To address this, ML replaced these models, as ML can disregard irrelevant factors and focus on variables that influence real estate prices (Agrawal *et al.*, 2018).

ML is applied in various methods, including mathematical and statistical modeling, complex system methods, classic analysis, computational intelligence, and modern analytics (Khan, 2024). These new performance metrics are better equipped to process unstructured data, detect nonlinear relationships, and offer a more holistic data evaluation. Examples of ML algorithms include logistic regression, decision trees, neural networks, support vector machines, AdaBoost, and random forests (Tyagi, 2022; Kamal and Bablu, 2022). For instance, random forests assess credit risk, while bootstrapped CAART trees predict credit card defaults, outperforming traditional methods (Tyagi, 2022).

AI can be categorized into three types: generative AI, discriminative AI, and predictive AI. Generative AI searches and interprets information, creates new content, interacts with users, and organizes data (Stanley and Wyman, 2023). Discriminative AI is used for supervised learning tasks like regression or classification (Tortora, 2024). Predictive AI leverages ML and statistical techniques to identify patterns, forecast behaviors, and predict future events (IBM, 2024). Generative AI, in particular, enhances productivity in financial services by increasing speed and automating tasks (Adrian, 2024).

3.3. *Disruptions from AI and ML in performance metrics*

AI adoption in financial institutions can be disruptive, as it changes the roles of individuals and companies, shifting power dynamics (Agrawal *et al.*, 2022). In terms of productivity, disruptions from AI can occur in two ways (Milana and Ashta, 2021):

(1) Within firms, significant infrastructure investments for AI adoption may become sunk costs due to changes in organizational activities, leading to a temporary decline in TFP.
(2) The productivity paradox may occur, where worker productivity slows despite increased IT investments.

However, advanced language models, which were unavailable a decade ago, allow financial institutions to process unstructured and text-based big data with greater accuracy and speed, enhancing productivity (Adrian, 2024).

Regarding efficiency, firms relying on manual processes may face higher operational costs and inefficiencies (Finance and Wyman, 2023). For instance, Verafin uses AI to predict fraud and validate customer identities, reducing prediction costs compared to traditional methods that require many data scientists (Agrawal *et al.*, 2022). Mor and Gupta (2021) studied AI's impact on the technical efficiency of Indian banks and found that tools like chatbots significantly reduce inefficiencies, though only chatbots were analyzed due to data unavailability.

AI also helps insurance companies reduce costs. For example, AI-based systems can intervene automatically in case of hazardous events, like smoke detection, mitigating loss. AI enables cost-effective risk monitoring and more accurate predictions of expected losses (Agrawal *et al.*, 2022). Additionally, AI adoption is expected to reduce the number of personnel, such as underwriters and salespeople, in the insurance sector (Agrawal *et al.*, 2022). Overall, AI, enhanced by ML algorithms, natural language processing, and predictive analytics, enables financial institutions to process data with greater accuracy and speed (Khan, 2024).

4. Conclusion

The integration of diverse data sources, such as financial transactions, markets, and customer information, has given rise to big data in the financial sector. These data are essential for improving AI and ML models, which are key in areas like fraud detection, credit evaluation, customer segmentation, and product development. AI's ability to utilize big data enhances decision-making accuracy, making it crucial for performance analysis in financial institutions.

AI, particularly when combined with ML techniques, has demonstrated significant potential in improving efficiency, productivity, and profitability in financial services. It streamlines processes like transaction handling, boosts customer retention, enhances credit scoring, and prevents fraud, delivering substantial benefits. However, certain limitations, such as the high energy consumption required for training large-scale models and concerns over AI chip shortages due to export controls, still pose challenges (*The Economist*, 2024).

The use of AI in the banking sector can increase revenue by customizing customer relationships and reducing costs through process automation, minimization of errors, and optimal allocation of resources. Additionally, with the ability to process big data and derive meaningful insights from it, the use of AI enables the emergence of new opportunities that were previously impossible.

In conclusion, while AI and ML hold the potential to transform the financial services industry by enhancing performance, addressing the associated challenges is necessary. Overcoming these barriers will be crucial for ensuring a sustainable and efficient future in finance. Strategic investments in energy-efficient AI infrastructure will enable institutions to maximize AI's capabilities while mitigating technological risks.

References

Adrian, T. (2024). Artificial Intelligence and its Impact on Financial Markets and Financial Stability. Remarks presented at the Bund Summit 2024: "Navigating a Changing World", Shanghai, China.

Agrawal, A., Gans, J., and Goldfarb, A. (2018). *Prediction Machines. The Simple Economics of Artificial Intelligence.* Harvard Business Review Press.

Agrawal, A., Gans, J., and Goldfarb, A. (2022). *Power and Prediction: The Disruptive Economics of Artificial Intelligence.* Harvard Business Review Press.

Aigner, D. J. and Chu, S. (1968). On estimating the industry production function. *American Economic Review*, 58, 826–839.

Aigner, D., Lovell, C. A. K., and Schmidt, P. (1977). Formulation and estimation of stochastic frontier production function models. *Journal of Econometrics*, 6(1), 21–37.

Akdeniz, Ö. O., Abdou, H. A., Hayek, A. I., Nwachukwu, J. C., Elamer, A. A., and Pyke, C. (2023). Technical efficiency in banks: A review of methods, recent innovations and future research agenda. *Review of Managerial Science*, 18, 3395–3456.

Akerlof, G. (1970). The market for "Lemons": Quality uncertainty and the market mechanism. *The Quarterly Journal of Economics*, 84(3), 488–500.

Akhtar, S., Azmi, S. N., Khan, P. A., Jan, A. A., and Ansari, Z. (2024). Unveiling the financial landscape: Analyzing profitability, productivity, and efficiency of banks in an emerging economy using the CAMELS framework and panel analysis. *Cogent Business & Management*, 11(1), 2399747.

Athanasoglou, P. P., Brissimis, S. N., and Delis, M. D. (2008). Bank-specific, industry-specific and macroeconomic determinants of bank profitability. *Journal of International Financial Markets, Institutions and Money*, 18(2), 121–136.

Banker, R. D. (1993). Maximum likelihood, consistency and data envelopment analysis — A statistical foundation. *Management Science*, 39(10), 1265–1273.

Bekaroğlu, C. (2023). Efficiency of the Turkish Labor Market: Future Employment Prospects. In V. Yılancı (Ed.), *Perspectives on Ecological Degradation and Technological Progress* (pp. 93–146). IGI Global.

Benston, G. J. (1965). Branch banking and economies of scale. *The Journal of Finance*, 20(2), 312–331.

Benston, G. J. and Smith, C. (1976). A transactions cost approach to the theory of financial intermediation. *The Journal of Finance*, 31(2), 215–231.

Berger, A. N., Davies, S. M., and Flannery, M. J. (2000). Comparing market and supervisory assessments of bank performance: Who knows what when? *Journal of Money, Credit and Banking*, 32(3), 641–667.

Berger, A. N., Hunter, W. C., and Timme, S. G. (1993). The efficiency of financial institutions: A review and preview of research past, present, and future. *Journal of Banking and Finance*, 17(3), 221–249.

Bhatia, V., Basu, S., Mitra, S. K., and Dash, P. (2018). A review of bank efficiency and productivity. *OPSEARCH*, 55, 557–600.

Bhattacharya, S. and Thakor, A. (1993). Contemporary banking theory. *Journal of Financial Intermediation*, 3(1), 2–50.

Bikker, A. J. (2010). Measuring performance of banks: An assessment. *The Journal of Applied Business and Economics*, 11, 141–159.

Biswas, S., Carson, B., Chung, V., Singh, S., and Thomas, R. (2020). AI-bank of the future: Can banks meet the AI challenge? McKinsey & Company. https://www.mckinsey.com/industries/financial-services/our-insights/ai-bank-of-the-future-can-banks-meet-the-ai-challenge.

Bonsu, M. O.-A. (2024). *Big Data, Financial Innovation and Financial Performance. Evidence from the UK Banking Sector*. PhD thesis, Teesside University, England United Kingdom.

Charnes, A., Cooper, W. W., and Rhodes, E. (1978). Measuring the efficiency of decision making units. *European Journal of Operational Research*, 2(6), 429–444.

Chen, C. (2009). Bank efficiency in Sub-Saharan African Middle income countries. IMF Working Paper WP/09/14, International Monetary Fund, African Department.

Chen, S. S. and Lee, S. H. (2024). Profitability determinants and performance analysis of Latin American banks: A pre-COVID-19 period. *International Area Studies Review*, 27(2), 141–156.

Colangelo, A. and Inklaar, R. (2009). Measuring the output of the banking sector: Shortcomings of the current European methodology and new perspectives. In M. Balling, E. Gnan, F. Lierman, and J.-P. Schoder (Eds.), *Productivity in the Financial Services Sector* (pp. 111–144). Larcier.

Colwell, R. J. and Davis, E. P. (1992). Output and productivity in banking. *The Scandinavian Journal of Economics*, 94(Supplement), 111–129.

Ding, D. and Sickles, R. C. (2018). Frontier efficiency, capital structure, and portfolio risk: An empirical analysis of U.S. banks. *BRQ Business Research Quarterly*, 21(4), 262–277.

Evanoff, D. D. and Israilevich, P. R. (1991). Productive efficiency in banking. *Economic Perspectives*, 15(3), 11–32.

Finance, U. K. and Wyman, O. (2023). The Impact of AI in Financial Services: Opportunities, Risks and Policy Considerations. https://www.ukfinance.org.uk/system/files/2023-11/The%20impact%20of%20AI%20in%20financial%20services.pdf.

Green, C. J., Murinde, V., and Nikolov, I. (2004). The efficiency of foreign and domestic banks in central and Eastern Europe: Evidence on economies of scale and scope. *Journal of Emerging Market Finance*, 3(2), 175–205.

Harker, P. T. and Zenios, S. A. (2000). What drives the performance of financial institutions? In P. T. Harker and S. A. Zenios (Eds.), *Performance of Financial Institutions — Efficiency, Innovation, Regulation* (pp. 3–31). Cambridge University Press.

Heil, M. (2017). Finance and productivity: A literature review. OECD Economics Department Working Papers 1374, OECD Publishing, Paris.

Hildreth, C. (1954). Point estimates of ordinates of concave functions. *Journal of the American Statistical Association*, 49(267), 598–619.

Hughes, J. P. and Mester, L. J. (2013). Measuring the performance of banks: Theory, practice, evidence, and some policy implications. Working Paper 13-31, Federal Reserve Bank of Philadelphia.

Humphrey, D. B. (1990). Why do estimates of bank scale economies differ? *Economic Review*, 76, 38–50.

IBM. (2024). What is predictive AI? https://www.ibm.com/think/topics/predictive-ai.

James, C. (1987). Some evidence on the uniqueness of bank loans. *Journal of Financial Economics*, 19(2), 217–235.

Jiang, G., Tang, N., Law, E., and Sze, A. (2003). The profitability of the banking sector in Hong Kong. *Hong Kong Monetary Authority Quarterly Bulletin*, 3(36), 5–14.

Kamal, M. and Bablu, T. A. (2022). Machine learning models for predicting click-through rates on social media: Factors and performance analysis. *International Journal of Applied Machine Learning and Computational Intelligence*, 12(4), 1–14.

Khan, A. K. (2024). AI in finance disruptive technologies and emerging opportunities. *Journal of Artificial Intelligence General Science (JAIGS)*, 3(1), 155–170.

Kronick, J. (2018). Productivity and the financial sector — What's missing? C.D. Howe Institute. https://www.cdhowe.org/publication/productivity-and-financial-sector-whats-missing.

Kuosmanen, T. (2008). Data envelopment analysis as least-squares regression (MTT Discussion Paper No. 3). MTT Agrifood Research Finland. https://tinyurl.com/DEA-Least-Squares-Regression.

Kuosmanen, T. and Johnson, A. (2010). Data envelopment analysis as nonparametric least-squares regression. *Operations Research*, 58(1), 149–160.

Meeusen, W. and Vandenbroeck, J. (1977). Efficiency estimation from cobb-douglas production functions with composed error. *International Economic Review*, 18(2), 435–445.

Milana, C. and Ashta, A. (2021). Artificial intelligence techniques in finance and financial markets: A survey of the literature. *Strategic Change*, 30(3), 189–209.

Mor, S. and Gupta, G. (2021). Artificial intelligence and technical efficiency: The case of Indian commercial banks. *Strategic Change*, 30(3), 235–245.

Mor, S. and Sharma, S. K. (2012). Technical efficiency and supply chain practices in dairying: The case of India. *Agricultural Economics (AGRICECON)*, 58(2), 85–91.

Murray, A. (2016). Partial versus total factor productivity measures: An assessment of their strengths and weaknesses. *International Productivity Monitor*, 31, 113–126.

O'Connel, M. (2023). Bank-specific, industry-specific and macroeconomic determinants of bank profitability: Evidence from the UK. *Studies in Economics and Finance*, 40(1), 155–174.

Oster, A. and Antioch, L. (1995). Measuring productivity in the Australian banking sector. In *Reserve Bank of Australia Annual Conference: Productivity and Growth* (pp. 201–212).

Phan, H. T., Hoang, T. N., Dinh, V. D., and Hoang, D. N. (2020). The determinants of listed commercial banks' profitability in Vietnam. *Journal of Asian Finance, Economics and Business*, 7(11), 219–229.

PWC. (2019). The productivity agenda: Moving beyond cost reduction in financial services. https://www.pwc.com.au/financial-services/pdf/pwc-productivity-agenda-feb19.pdf.

Ray, S. C. and Chen, L. (2015). Benchmarking for performance evaluation: A production Frontier approach. In S. C. Ray, S. C. Kumbhakar, and P. Dua (Eds.), *Data Envelopment Analysis for Performance Evaluation: A Child's Guide* (pp. 75–116). Springer.

Salike, N. and Ao, B. (2018). Determinants of bank's profitability: Role of poor asset quality in Asia. *China Finance Review International*, 8(2), 216–231.

Saunders, A., Schmid, M., and Walter, I. (2020). Strategic scope and bank performance. *Journal of Financial Stability*, 46(C), 100715.

Sinha, R. P. (2024). General insurer efficiency and managerial ability: A non-parametric approach. In S. Boubaker and T. Ngo (Eds.), *Handbook on Data Envelopment Analysis in Business, Finance, and Sustainability: Recent trends and developments* (pp. 427–455). World Scientific.

Sousa, M. D. M. and Figueiredo, R. S. (2014). Credit analysis using data mining application in the case of a Credit Union. *JISTEM — Journal of Information Systems and Technology Management*, 11(2), 379–396.

Stanley, M. and Wyman, O. (2023). The AI Tipping Point. https://www.oliverwyman.de/content/dam/oliver-wyman/v2/publications/2023/october/Oliver_Wyman_Morgan_Stanley_Global_Wealth_and_Asset_Management_report_ 2023_The_Generative_AI_Tipping%20Point1.pdf.

Tai, C.-S. (2000). Time-varying market, interest rate, and exchange rate risk premia in the US commercial bank stock returns. *Journal of Multinational Financial Management*, 10(3–4), 397–420.

The Economist. (2024). Will the bubble burst for AI in 2025, or will it start to deliver? https://www.economist.com/the-world-ahead/2024/11/18/will-the-bubble-burst-for-ai-in-2025-or-will-it-start-to-deliver.

Tortora, L. (2024). Beyond discrimination: Generative AI applications and ethical challenges in forensic psychiatry. *Frontiers in Psychiatry*, 15, 1346059.

Trujillo-Ponce, A. (2013). What determines the profitability of banks? Evidence from Spain. *Accounting & Finance*, 53(2), 561–586.

Tyagi, S. (2022). Analyzing machine learning models for credit scoring with explainable AI and optimizing investment decisions. *American International Journal of Business Management (AIJBM)*, 5(1), 05–19.

Wagenvoort, R. and Schure, P. (1999). Economies of scale and efficiency in European banking: New evidence. Economic and Financial

Reports 1999/1, European Investment Bank, Economics Department, Luxemburg.

Winsten, C. B. (1957). Discussion on Mr. Farrell's paper. *Journal of the Royal Statistical Society, Series A: Statistics in Society*, 120(3), 282–284.

Yuan, D., Gazi, M. A. I., Harymawan, I., Dhar, B. K., and Hossain, A. I. (2022). Profitability determining factors of banking sector: Panel data analysis of commercial banks in South Asian countries. *Frontiers in Psychology*, 13, 1000412.

https://doi.org/10.1142/9789819823161_0006

Chapter 6

The Role of India's Digital Public Infrastructure in Advancing Financial Inclusion: A Policy Perspective

Neeraj Kumar[*,‡] **and Neha Mangla**[†,§]

[*]*Ministry of Finance, Government of India, New Delhi, India*
[†]*School of Economics, Vivekananda Institute of Professional Studies, New Delhi, India*
[‡]*neeraj.ies@nic.in*
[§]*neha.mangla@vips.edu*

This paper examines how India's Digital Public Infrastructure (DPI) has become a powerful catalyst for financial inclusion and deepening across the nation. For years, inclusive growth has been at the center of India's policy agenda, and financial inclusion – ensuring that affordable financial products and services are accessible to all, especially underserved populations – has emerged as a critical driver of sustained and inclusive economic growth. Since 2014, India has made significant strides in "banking the unbanked", "funding the unfunded", and "securing the unsecured". While significant progress has been made, challenges persist. The Reserve Bank of India's Financial Inclusion Index, which measures progress toward full financial inclusion (100), stood at 64.2 in March 2024, indicating remaining gaps. This paper conducts an analysis to understand India's approach to leveraging DPI for financial inclusion. It examines the impact of DPI on financial inclusion outcomes, identifies key challenges, and presents policy recommendations. The lessons drawn from India's experience with DPI offer insights to enhance financial inclusion through digital transformation.

Keywords: Digital public infrastructure, financial inclusion, fintech, India stack, public goods, Unified Payments Interface (UPI).

1. Introduction

For years, inclusive growth has been at the center of India's policy agenda, and financial inclusion – ensuring that affordable financial products and services are accessible to all, especially underserved populations – has emerged as a critical driver of sustained and inclusive economic growth. Alongside this, financial deepening which broadly refers to an expansion in the range, sophistication, and accessibility of financial products and services offered by financial institutions — plays an important role in strengthening the overall financial ecosystem and enabling meaningful participation in economic activity. The Reserve Bank of India (2008) defines financial inclusion as ensuring access to financial services and timely, affordable credit for vulnerable groups. Its goal is to integrate individuals into the formal financial system by enhancing accessibility, usage, and service quality, regardless of socioeconomic background.

Financial exclusion, in contrast, occurs when individuals lack access to basic financial services like savings accounts and credit due to factors such as gender, age, education, and location, impacting both personal and macroeconomic well-being. Women and younger populations are particularly vulnerable due to mobility constraints, lower asset accumulation, and societal norms. Addressing financial inclusion gaps is crucial for the effective implementation of government initiatives promoting inclusive growth.

The United Nations developed the Sustainable Development Goals (SDGs) in 2015 with the theme "Leave no one behind", setting targets to eliminate poverty and improve well-being (Sustainable Development Goals, 2015). Financial inclusion is crucial for achieving several SDGs, including poverty eradication, zero hunger, good health, gender equality, decent work, economic growth, industry innovation, reduced inequalities, and responsible consumption (Ferrata, 2019).

By improving access to finance and credit, financial inclusion enables investment in education, better health care, and self-employment. It empowers women by enhancing financial control and fostering entrepreneurship. Credit access for micro and new enterprises drives industrialization, innovation, and growth. Inclusivity in financial services supports poverty reduction and a more equitable, sustainable, and resilient economy.

Since 2014, India has made significant strides in "banking the unbanked", "funding the unfunded", and "securing the unsecured". Initiatives like the Pradhan Mantri Jan Dhan Yojana (PMJDY) have brought banking services within reach of millions, while programs such as the Pradhan Mantri Suraksha Bima Yojana (PMSBY) and Atal Pension Yojana (APY) have extended insurance and pension benefits to marginalized communities. The RBI has also played a crucial role in spreading financial literacy through initiatives like the Electronic Banking Awareness and Training (e-BAAT) programs and Financial Literacy Camps (FLCs).

Central to these efforts has been the development and deployment of Digital Public Infrastructure (DPI). By integrating digital identity (Aadhaar), real-time fast payment systems (Unified Payments Interface (UPI)), digital documentation (DigiLocker), and data-sharing frameworks (Account Aggregator), India has created an inclusive, scalable, and interoperable financial ecosystem. The G20 Global Partnership for Financial Inclusion (GPFI) report (2023) also highlights the transformative impact of platforms like the UPI and Aadhaar. UPI, for instance, has revolutionized the digital payments landscape, facilitating over 16.99 billion transactions worth approximately ₹23.48 trillion in January 2025 alone [National Payments Corporation of India (NPCI), 2022]. The volume of UPI transactions has increased more than 15-fold since 2019, from 10.79 billion in 2019 to 172.21 billion in 2024. DPI has been key in providing scalable, low-cost solutions that have dramatically expanded access to financial services, particularly among underserved populations (Khera, 2023).

While significant progress has been made, challenges persist. The RBI's Financial Inclusion Index (Reserve Bank of India, 2021), which measures various dimensions of financial inclusion, with a value of 100 indicating full inclusion, stood at 64.2 in March 2024. This reflects the gap in achieving comprehensive financial inclusion. Globally, around 1.4 billion adults remain financially excluded, and micro, small, and medium enterprises (MSMEs) continue to face substantial financing gaps. Nevertheless, India's experience with DPI offers valuable lessons for overcoming these barriers.

This chapter provides an analysis of India's approach to leveraging DPI for financial inclusion and deepening. It examines the impact of

DPI, identifies key challenges, and presents policy recommendations to enhance digital financial services. Furthermore, it highlights lessons from India's experience that can inform other countries seeking to drive financial inclusion through digital transformation. As India aspires to become a developed nation by 2047, strengthening DPI-led financial inclusion will be instrumental in shaping a more resilient and inclusive economy.

2. Understanding Digital Public Infrastructure (DPI) of India

DPI in India forms the foundation of the country's digital transformation, enabling seamless service delivery across various sectors, particularly financial inclusion. DPI is defined as an infrastructure-based approach that leverages digital technology to achieve societal goals through an open and interoperable ecosystem, promoting competitive private innovation within regulatory safeguards (India's G20 Task Force on Digital Public Infrastructure, 2024 [Ministry of Finance, Government of India, 2024b]; Zuckerman, 2020).

With a population of over 1.4 billion, India faces numerous challenges in implementing public policies due to issues such as socioeconomic stratification, geographical differences, and regional inequalities. To address these difficulties and promote inclusive and sustainable growth, the Indian government has focused on innovative efforts over the last decade to digitally empower its citizens by ensuring digital access and reducing the digital gap (Desai and and Manoharan, 2024).

India's journey in developing a robust DPI ecosystem began in 2009 with the launch of Aadhaar, a unique biometric-based digital identity system. Aadhaar addressed the issue of identity verification, which had historically hindered access to essential services, including banking, telecommunications, and public benefits. Over the following years, additional digital building blocks were introduced under the India Stack initiative, creating an interoperable and scalable ecosystem. Figure 1 illustrates a timeline for the evolution and development of DPI in India.

The key milestones in the evolution of DPI include the introduction of the UPI by the National Payments Corporation of India (NPCI) in 2016, enabling instant, interoperable digital payments.

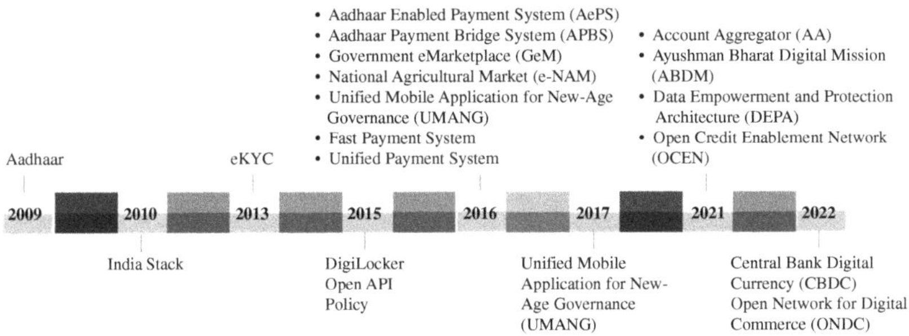

Fig. 1. India's Digital Public Infrastructure.

DigiLocker was launched in 2015 to allow users to securely store and share digital documents. In 2021, the establishment of the Account Aggregator framework enabled consent-based financial data sharing, empowering individuals and businesses with better financial access.

A defining feature of DPI is its ability to act as a public good, offering open and interoperable access to financial, governance, and service-related functions. This platform-based approach ensures that multiple stakeholders — governments, financial institutions, fintech firms, and private innovators — can build upon a common infrastructure to provide tailored services (Little, 2024).

As per India's G20 Task Force on Digital Public Infrastructure (2023), the core components of India's DPI ecosystem can be categorized into five key building blocks:

(a) *Verifiable Identity and Registries*: These systems allow individuals to authenticate their identities and access profile data. Aadhaar, e-KYC, and digital land registries serve as essential identity verification mechanisms, facilitating access to financial and government services.
(b) *Data Sharing, Credentials, and Open Models*: Platforms such as the Account Aggregator framework and DigiLocker enable secure, consent-based data sharing, enhancing financial inclusion and digital service delivery.
(c) *Signatures and Consent*: Tamper-proof digital signatures and consent-based authentication ensure that transactions and agreements occur with user permission, reducing fraud and enhancing trust in digital transactions.
(d) *Discovery and Fulfillment Networks*: Open protocols and APIs, including those used in tax filing, e-commerce, and service

delivery, enable businesses and individuals to access goods and services efficiently.

(e) *Payments*: Digital payment systems such as UPI and FASTag ensure frictionless, real-time financial transactions, driving financial accessibility and efficiency.

The Government of India's commitment to financial inclusion through DPI has been consistently highlighted in policy discussions. The *Economic Survey 2023–24* (Ministry of Finance, Government of India, 2024a) emphasized how DPI has played a crucial role in delivering financial services to the last mile, while the *Economic Survey 2024–25* (Ministry of Finance, Government of India, 2025) reinforced the importance of private sector participation in modernizing the country's digital infrastructure in alignment with the Viksit Bharat@2047 vision (NITI, Government of India, 2024).

3. Financial Inclusion in India

In August 2021, to track the progress made by the numerous initiatives launched by the Government of India for ensuring financial inclusion, the RBI launched a Financial Inclusion Index (FI-Index). The FI-Index measures financial inclusion on three broad parameters: access with a weightage of 35%, usage with a weightage of 45%, and quality with a weightage of 20%, mapped through 97 specific indicators. The access indicators gauge the reach and penetration of basic financial services for a barrier-free access, the usage indicators include the frequency and volume of use of different financial products and services, and the quality indicators measure the customization of products and services for individual needs and the satisfaction of customers with the products and services. The value of the Index ranges between 0 and 100, where 0 represents complete financial exclusion and 100 represents complete financial inclusion. The progress of financial inclusion in India is evident in the increased value of the FI-Index over the years. The value of the index increased to 64.2 in March 2024, backed by growth in all sub-indices. The RBI has highlighted that the usage dimension is the main contributor to the improvement in the index, reflecting the deepening of financial inclusion in the country (Fig. 2).

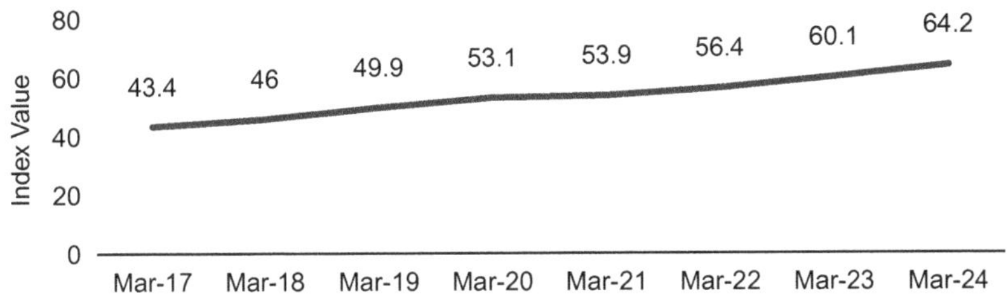

Fig. 2. RBI's Financial Inclusion Index.
Source: RBI Database.

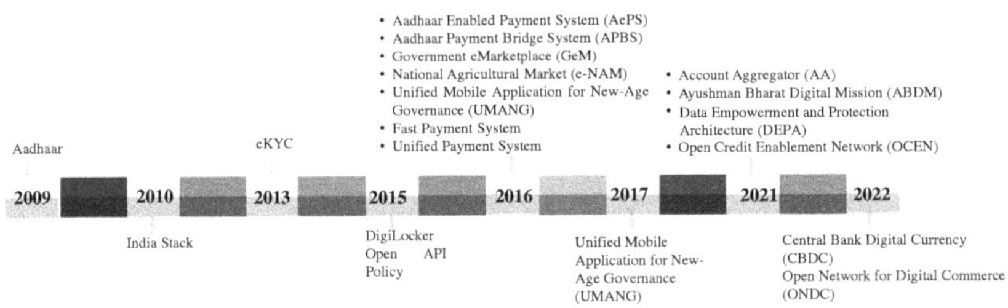

Fig. 3. Financial inclusion initiatives in India.

Underlying the increasing value of the index are the numerous initiatives undertaken by the government and the RBI to increase access, usage, and quality of financial services in India. The Committee on Financial Sector Reforms 2009, chaired by Raghuram Rajan, identified that financial inclusion is not just about the provision of credit but extends much beyond to include access to financial services, saving and insurance products, and inflation-indexed pensions. The Government of India (GoI) has launched many initiatives with the aim of providing social security to the underserved sections of society. Figure 3 gives the roadmap for the launch of initiatives aimed at financial inclusion.

Pradhan Mantri Jan Dhan Yojna (PMJDY) was launched in 2014 with the objective to provide access to basic financial services, like savings bank accounts, need-based credit, remittances facility, and insurance and pension to weaker, excluded sections of the society. PMJDY accounts have multiplied more than 4-fold, with the number

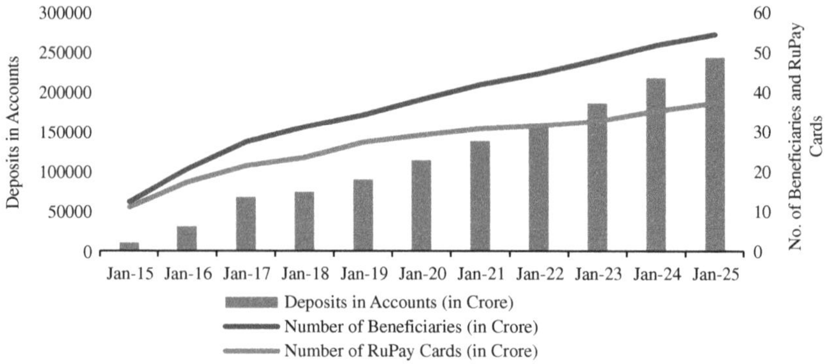

Fig. 4. PMJDY performance.
Source: Authors' Compilation Using CEIC Database (Data as on 1st January 2025).

of accounts growing from 12.31 crore in January 2015 to 54.40 crore in January 2025. The total amount of deposits in these accounts currently stands at 24,29,113.64 crores, and 37.18 crore RuPay debit cards have been issued under the scheme (Fig. 4). More than half of the beneficiaries (30.16 crore) of the PMJDY are females, and two-thirds (66.57 crore) are from rural or semi-urban areas.

To fund the unfunded micro enterprises, and to make them a part of the formal financial system, MUDRA yojana was launched in 2015, which disbursed loans to these enterprises without any collateral. In ten years of its operation, in 2024–25, 51.32 crore micro enterprises have benefited from this scheme with a credit support of 28.15 lakh crore, witnessing a remarkable 21-fold increase in cumulative loan disbursements from 1.33 lakh crore in 2015–16 to 28.15 crore in 2024–25 (Fig. 5). The scheme has helped in inclusive growth, with 68.62% of the loan accounts belonging to female beneficiaries and 50.80% of the loan accounts belonging to the weaker sections of society.

Pradhan Mantri Jeevan Jyoti Bima Yojana (PMJJBY) and Pradhan Mantri Suraksha Bima Yojana (PMSBY) are insurance schemes launched by the government to provide insurance cover to the weaker sections and the unorganized sector of the economy. As of November 2024, there were 21.75 crore cumulative enrollments under PMJJBY with a cumulative disbursement of claims amounting to 17,281.88 crore. PMSBY has 47.76 crore cumulative enrollments with a cumulative claim disbursement of 2,939.55 crore.

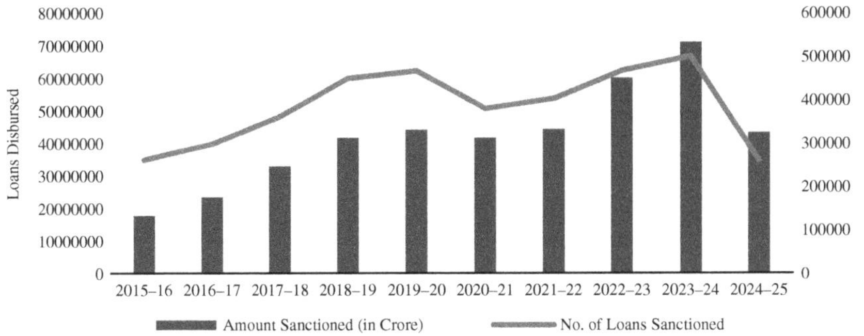

Fig. 5. MUDRA Yojana Performance.
Source: Authors' Compilation Using Data from MUDRA Website.

The Atal Pension Yojana is a flagship government-initiated pension scheme, especially for the poor, underprivileged, and employees in the unorganized sector in India, like street vendors, rickshaw pullers, workers in the agricultural and construction sectors, and landless laborers. With over 56 lakh enrollments in the financial year 2024–25, the total gross enrollments under the yojana have crossed 7 crores.

Another initiative for financial inclusion launched by the government to promote entrepreneurship among the women, SC, and ST categories is the "Stand up India" Scheme launched in 2016 that provides hassle free affordable bank loans ranging from 10 lakh to 1 crore to at least one Scheduled Caste (SC) or Scheduled Tribe (ST) borrower and at least one woman borrower per bank branch. In a period of 7 years, more than Rs. 40,700 crore worth of loans have been sanctioned to over 1,80,630 accounts.

4. Digital Public Infrastructure (DPI) and Financial Inclusion in India

4.1. *J-A-M trinity and direct benefit transfers*

The J-A-M trinity, which connects PMJDY bank accounts to Aadhaar and mobile phone numbers, serves as the foundation for increasing digital financial inclusion, enabling quick, seamless, and transparent transfer of government welfare schemes to eligible beneficiaries. The absence of verifiable identification, limited financial

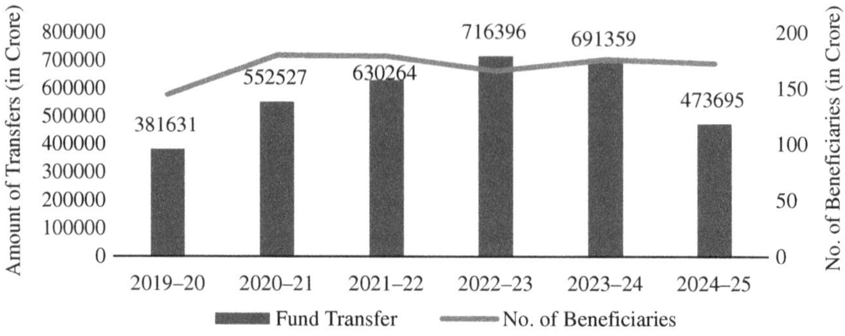

Fig. 6. Direct benefit transfers.
Source: Authors' Compilation Using GoI Data.

literacy and inclusion, and a scarcity of historical financial data were major hindrances in the provision of financial services to the majority of the population. In 2011, before the full implementation of the India Stack, only one in every three people had a bank account. The lack of proof of identity posed a significant challenge for financial institutions in onboarding consumers and meeting know-your-customer regulatory requirements. The J-A-M trinity has helped integrate the poor into the economic mainstream and plays a crucial role in the development of marginalized communities. Figure 6 shows the year-wise disbursements under the various direct benefit transfer schemes. A total direct benefit transfer amounting to ₹41,49,468 crore has been done as of January 2025.

It has enabled to financially and digitally include those who are at the bottom of the pyramid by ensuring access to bank accounts, need-based credit, insurance, remittances, and pensions to weaker sections and low-income groups. DPI has not only expanded the reach of the banks but has made banking more accessible, efficient, and cost-effective.

4.2. *Unified payments interface*

The introduction of interoperable payments via the UPI in 2016 played a significant role in the continued use of digital financial services. The UPI enables instant and real-time interbank transactions across various payment platforms, allowing banks and non-banks to collaborate. While demonetization acted as an immediate catalyst for growth in digital payments, the longer-term growth seen since the beginning of 2016 appears to be explained much more by the growth of UPI, which coincided with increased business formalization and digital acceptance following the implementation of the goods and services tax in 2017. UPI payments have witnessed an unprecedented growth in the last seven years, with almost a 25-fold increase in transaction volume from 5.4 billion in FY 2018–19 to 134.46 billion in FY 2024–25 (till December 2024). The Aadhaar-enabled payment system (AePS) with the interoperability feature has facilitated safe and seamless transactions across banks, access to subsidies, and ensured efficient direct government disbursements of social security pensions, employment-generating schemes, etc. Digital payments, which include modes such as NEFT, UPI, AePS, Debit/Credit cards, net banking, and mobile banking, experienced a remarkable surge in transaction volume, increasing from 2,071 crore in FY 2017–18 to 18,737 crore in FY 2023–24 at a CAGR of 44% (Fig. 7).

As of June 2023, 36% of the digital payment users were from rural India (*The Rise and Evolution of India's Digital Finance, TransUnion CIBIL*, 2023). The RBI's Digital Payments Index (RBI-DPI), which began in 2018 (base year) at 100, has risen to 445.50 in March 2024.

The GoI has announced the launch of the Unified Lending Interface (ULI) that will simplify and broaden access to credit, especially in rural areas, by allowing lenders to access borrowers' information from multiple sources and assess their creditworthiness.

In a recent initiative, the RBI in December 2024, allowed prepaid payment instrument (PPI) holders with full KYC to make UPI

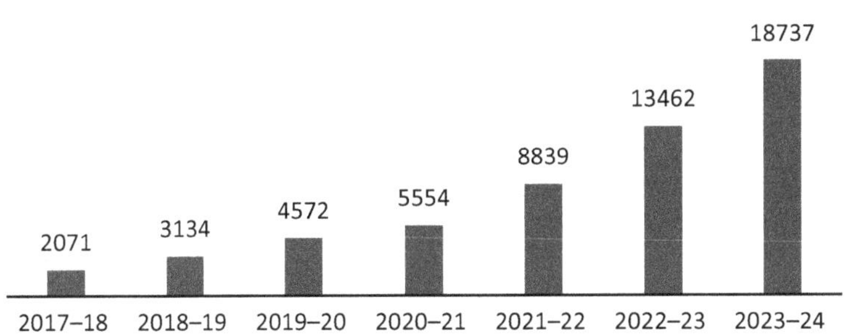

Fig. 7. Digital payments transactions volume (in crore).
Source: Authors' Compilation Using Data from Department of Financial Services.

transactions using any third-party application. Earlier, such UPI transactions had to be completed using the PPI issuer's mobile application only. A PPI is a financial tool that allows the user to store funds in a digital wallet or a card for future use. This initiative will expand the scope of PPIs, increasing customer convenience and satisfaction, especially for rural customers where the banking infrastructure is limited, and will help further deepen financial inclusion by including PPI holders in mainstream banking services and payment platforms.

4.3. *Tax revenues and social security schemes*

Digital taxation initiatives, such as GSTN (Goods and Services Tax Network) and faceless e-assessments, have revolutionized tax compliance and revenue collection in India. By leveraging digital records and automated filings, these initiatives formalize businesses, increase tax transparency, and improve creditworthiness, enabling MSMEs and informal sector workers to access loans and financial services.

This expansion, coupled with greater formalization through digital payment systems like UPI, Aadhaar-linked banking, and GST, has significantly improved tax revenue mobilization while reducing collection costs. Since 2014, the central government tax revenues have increased 3-fold, from 8,15,854 crore in 2014 to 25,83,499 crores in 2025. The corporate tax collections increased 2.5-fold from 3,94,678 crore in 2014 to 10,20,000 crore in 2025, and income tax collection increased 5-fold from 2,37,817 crore in 2014 to 11,87,000 crore in 2025 (Fig. 8).

Higher tax revenues, in turn, create fiscal space for social security schemes, poverty alleviation, and targeted welfare programs, fostering inclusive growth and reducing inequalities. By leveraging DPI, India ensures that economic progress translates into equitable development and financial resilience for all.

4.4. *Open network for digital commerce*

The Open Network for Decentralized Commerce (ONDC), another transformative DPI, aims to provide equal access to digital retail markets for small businesses and retailers nationwide, creating a level playing field for all participants. The platform connects sellers, logistic partners, and delivery gig workers without charging high fees

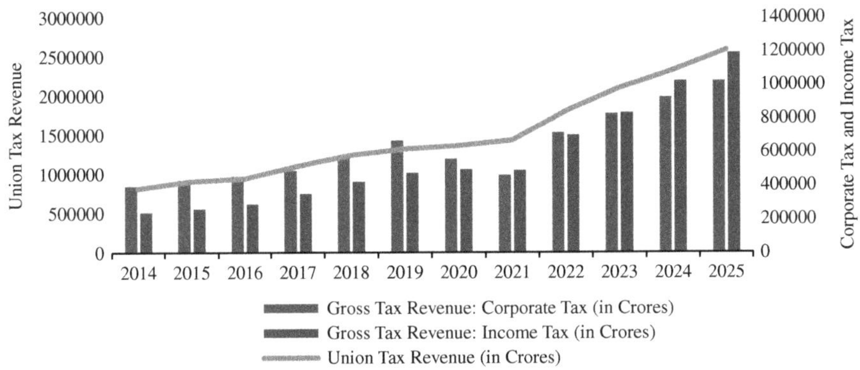

Fig. 8. Union tax revenue 2014–2025.
Source: Authors' Compilation Using CEIC Database.

to the community. Launched in January 2022, ONDC has rapidly expanded its reach and is now used in 607 cities, has more than 6.14 lakh sellers and service providers onboard, and reached one crore transactions per month as compared to 1000 transactions per month in January 2023. It is helping empower small businesses, retailers, and local artisans by providing access to the digital marketplace.

4.5. *DigiLocker*

DigiLocker provides access to authentic digital documents to all citizens through a digital document wallet. By simplifying the KYC process, the initiative provides a secure document exchange platform providing consent-based real-time verification for faster execution of services, including government benefits, health and education services, and financial inclusion-aimed services. Started in 2016, DigiLocker already has more than 430 million users and has issued nearly 9.5 billion documents. DigiLocker facilitates e-KYC, reducing onboarding time and costs for banking and financial services, thereby expanding access to credit and insurance, particularly for underserved populations.

4.6. *Account aggregator framework*

The Account Aggregator (AA) framework enables consent-based financial data sharing across institutions, empowering individuals and businesses with seamless access to credit and financial services.

By acting as intermediaries, AAs aggregate and share financial data – such as bank statements, insurance records, and tax filings – securely with lenders and financial institutions. This initiative reduces information asymmetry, enhances creditworthiness assessment, and streamlines loan approvals, particularly for MSMEs and individuals with limited credit history, thus fostering financial inclusion.

4.7. *Other examples of DPI*

The Open Credit Enablement Network (OCEN) facilitates seamless digital lending, allowing small businesses, gig workers, and underserved individuals to access formal credit with minimal paperwork. Similarly, the National Agriculture Market (e-NAM) empowers farmers by providing a unified digital marketplace, ensuring fair pricing, direct payments, and access to financial services like credit and insurance. The Ayushman Bharat Digital Mission (ABDM) strengthens health-related financial inclusion by enabling paperless insurance claims and direct benefit transfers, ensuring the affordability of health care services for all.

Together, these building blocks of DPI foster an inclusive, transparent, and efficient financial ecosystem, ensuring that individuals and businesses – regardless of geography or economic background – have equitable access to essential financial services, ultimately driving economic empowerment and growth.

5. Key Challenges and Issues in Digital Financial Inclusion

India's digital financial inclusion journey has achieved significant advancement since 2014. There has been an exponential increase in the volume of online transactions with universal access to mobile banking and UPI-enabled transactions. However, challenges exist that have limited the adoption of digital financial products and services (Gibson *et al.*, 2024; Dua *et al.*, 2023a, 2023b, 2024):

- Digital access is necessary but not sufficient for usage of digital services for weaker sections, especially women and the rural population, due to the established social standards that see them as technologically challenged groups in society, limiting their digital adoption.

- Digital literacy, the key driver of digital financial inclusion, is still lacking, especially among the vulnerable groups, limiting their use of digital financial services.
- India has a predominantly cash-dominated financial economy, given that the majority of the workforce in India is employed in the informal sector, which hinders widespread usage of digital financial services.
- Limited credit history of the underserved population makes them vulnerable to a lack of access to financial services, like credit, insurance.
- Concerns related to data privacy and cybersecurity pose a significant challenge to the wider adoption of digital financial services.

The World Bank Global Findex Database (World Bank, 2022) provides data on access to financial services from savings to payments and borrowing for more than 140 economies. Indicators of access to and use of formal and informal financial services, as well as digital payments, are provided, along with insights into the behaviors that enable financial resilience. The data also reflect gaps in financial inclusion by comparing access to and usage of financial services across different sections of the population with different socioeconomic backgrounds (like gender, income, employment, education, etc.).

The Findex Database 2021 shows that India has made significant progress in banking the unbanked, with financial institution account access provided to all sections of society, irrespective of gender, income, and education (Fig. 9).

However, the data reflect that, though significant progress has been made on the supply side, significant gaps still exist on the

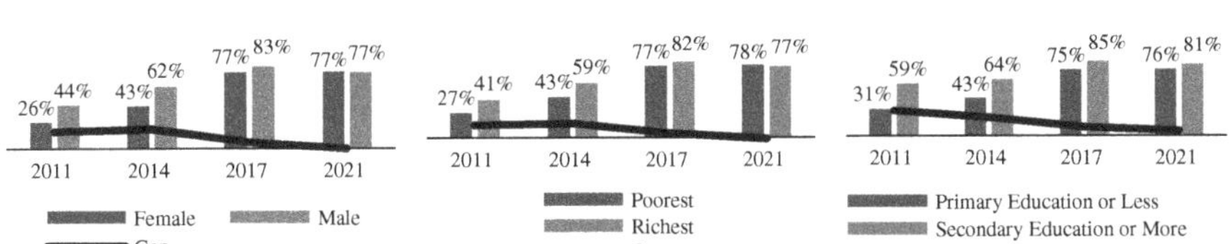

Fig. 9. Percentage of people having a financial institution account by gender, income, and education.

Source: Authors' Compilation Using FINDEX Database, 2021.

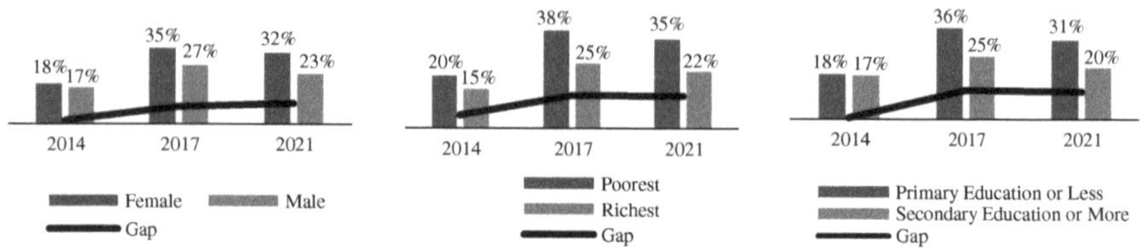

Fig. 10. Percentage of people owning inactive accounts by gender, income, and education.
Source: Authors' Compilation Using FINDEX Database, 2021.

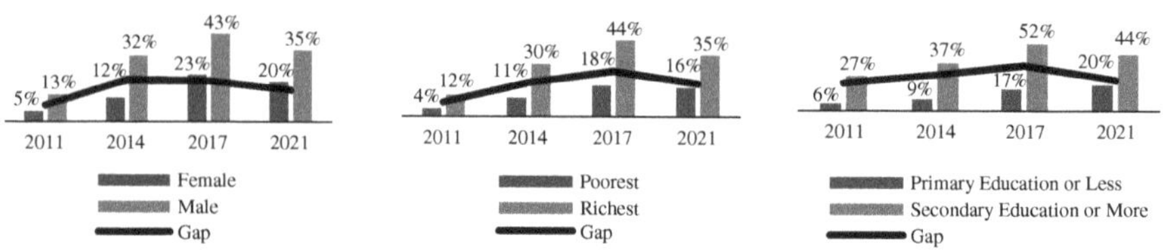

Fig. 11. Owns a debit or a credit card.
Source: Authors' Compilation Using FINDEX Database, 2021.

demand side, reflected in a higher percentage of the underserved sections, including females, the poor, and the less educated, owning inactive accounts (Fig. 10).

The data also suggest that in terms of ownership of debit and credit cards, though significant progress has been made since 2011, gaps exist between socially and economically weaker sections and their counterparts. Card ownership has limited penetration among females, the poorest 40%, and the less educated (Fig. 11).

Assessing the penetration of digital financial services, disparities still exist in terms of owning a mobile payment account. Though the overall penetration of mobile payment accounts is less, a considerably lesser percentage of females, the poorest 40%, and the less educated have a mobile payment account (Fig. 12).

In terms of using digital platforms for making and receiving payments, though more people have been enrolled into the digital ecosystem, considerable gaps exist, with the socially and financially weaker sections, females, the poorest 40%, and the less educated using these platforms much less than their counterparts (Fig. 13).

However, if we look at the indicator related to receiving government transfers into a financial account, there is a slightly higher

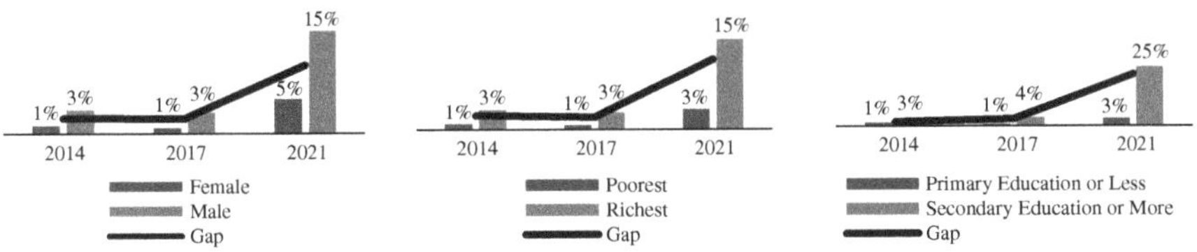

Fig. 12. Has a mobile payment account.
Source: Authors' Compilation Using Findex Database, 2021.

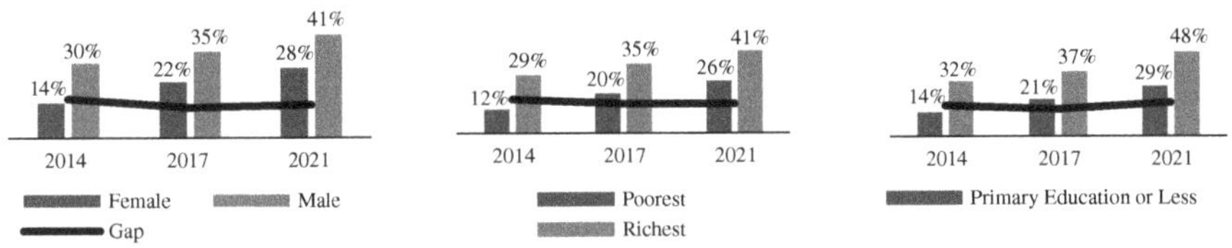

Fig. 13. Made or received a digital payment.
Source: Authors' Compilation Using FINDEX Database, 2021.

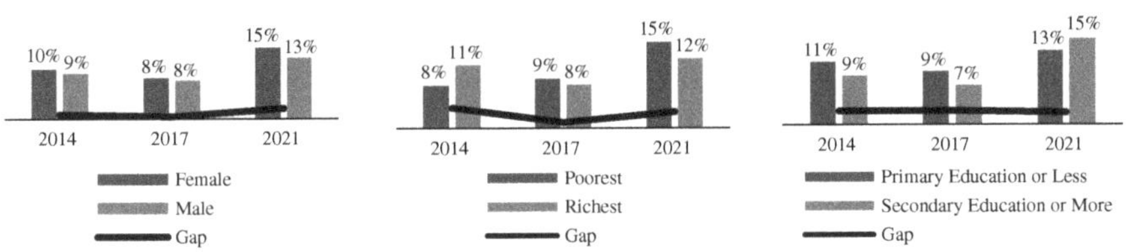

Fig. 14. Received government transfer into an account.
Source: Authors' Compilation Using FINDEX Database, 2021.

percentage of females and the poorest 40% receiving these benefits in their accounts. This fact highlights that the government is using the DPI to financially include these weaker sections of society (Fig. 14).

Though India has made considerable progress toward making all sections of society a part of the formal financial system, it still lags behind its BRICS counterparts as seen in key indicators of financial inclusion. As per the World Bank's Financial Inclusion Index Data 2021, compared to other BRICS nations, India stands at the bottom in terms of the percentage of the population having a financial institution account (77%). Also, of those who have an account, more than one-third have inactive accounts in India (Fig. 15).

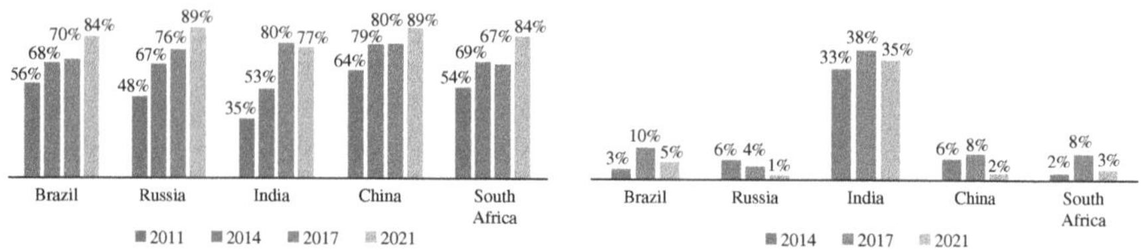

Fig. 15. Have an account (left) have an inactive account (right).
Source: Authors' Compilation Using FINDEX Database, 2021.

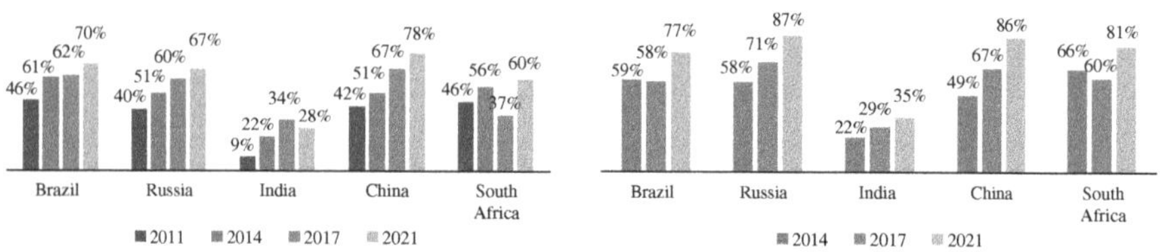

Fig. 16. Own a debit or credit card (left). Made or received a digital payment (right).
Source: Authors' Compilation Using FINDEX Database, 2021.

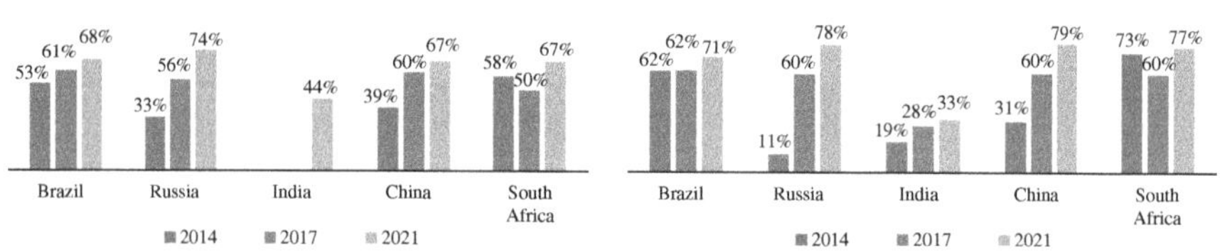

Fig. 17. Received a government transfer into a financial institution account (% of government transfer recipients) (left). Received wages into a financial institution account (% of wage recipients) (right).
Source: Authors' Compilation Using FINDEX Database 2021.

The ownership of debit/credit cards is considerably low in India (28%), as compared to other BRICS nations, with 60% or more owning a debit or credit card. In terms of usage of financial services as well, India is way behind its BRICS counterparts. Only a third have made or received a digital payment in India as compared to more than three-fourths in other nations (Fig. 16).

In terms of receiving government transfers and wages into their financial institution accounts as well, the penetration in India is much lower (Fig. 17).

6. Way Forward

6.1. *Lessons from India's DPI experience*

India's experience with DPI provides valuable insights for countries aiming to enhance financial inclusion through digital transformation:

- *Scalable and Inclusive DPI Frameworks*: India's DPI, built on Aadhaar, UPI, and DigiLocker, has demonstrated how interoperable, secure, and cost-effective digital infrastructure can drive universal financial access. The G20 2023 Action Plan (2023a) and the G20 Brasilia Declaration (2024) recognize DPI's role in fostering financial resilience, gender equality, and inclusion for vulnerable groups.
- *Knowledge Sharing and Capacity Building*: Recognizing the global DPI knowledge gap, India launched the Global Digital Public Infrastructure Repository (GDPIR) and One Future Alliance (OFA) to facilitate best-practice sharing, technical assistance, and DPI adoption in Low- and Middle-Income Countries (LMICs). This aligns with the G20 Digital Economy Ministers' Outcome document (G20 India 2023 Presidency, 2023b) which underscores knowledge exchange and governance frameworks for DPI development.
- *Financial and Technical Support for Global DPI Expansion*: India's commitment to fast-tracking DPI adoption is evident in the establishment of the Social Impact Fund (SIF) with an initial pledge of $25 million to support LMICs. This initiative aligns with the G20's focus on leveraging digital innovation for sustainable development, particularly in bridging financial access gaps.
- *Building Trust, Security, and Data Governance*: The **G20 Brasilia Declaration** underscores the need for secure, privacy-preserving, and rights-based DPI implementation. India's approach – balancing financial inclusion, data security, and consumer protection – serves as a model for governments to ensure transparency, interoperability, and responsible AI-driven financial ecosystems.

By adopting India's DPI-led financial inclusion strategies, G20 countries and beyond can accelerate inclusive, efficient, and resilient digital financial systems, ensuring that digital transformation empowers societies while upholding security, privacy, and innovation.

6.2. *Recommendations*

Based on the review of India's transformative financial inclusion journey powered by DPI, cross-country comparisons, and the challenges still faced for universal digital financial inclusion, five key areas of focus from a policy perspective are identified: spreading digital and financial literacy, further strengthening of the DPI, innovations to provide tailormade financial products and services, building financial resilience, and fostering collaborations (Ministry of Finance, Government of India, 2024a, 2025; NITI, Government of India, 2024).

Promoting digital and financial literacy through the information–education–communication (IEC) framework can help spread awareness and promote the use of financial products and services. The use of AI-based tools can help overcome language barriers and run customized literacy campaigns, especially for vulnerable groups. Innovative ways of financial education will ensure people can appropriately manage risks, appreciate the benefits of financial products and services, and develop confidence to adopt such services by enhancing their usage capabilities. Financial literacy modules should be included within the school curriculum, along with increasing the use of digital platforms to teach financial concepts.

Developing a robust digital ecosystem by implementing technological standards and protocols can improve financial service delivery and interoperability across platforms. Prioritizing regulatory measures such as cybersecurity rules, data protection legislation, and protocols for financial service providers will reduce risks and build confidence in the adoption of digital financial services. Promote collection of high-frequency digital data, including age, gender, income, and employment, to ensure financial deepening across social strata, along with prioritizing data protection.

Fostering financial innovations to provide customized financial products and services to the weaker sections based on their needs and profiles can ensure financial well-being in an inclusive way (Alonso *et al.*, 2023).

DPI can be further strengthened and leveraged to aggregate data, link borrowers and lenders, simplify KYC authentication, and reduce transaction costs to provide affordable credit, especially to the underserved sections and MSMEs, to make these vulnerable sections more resilient to financial risks and shocks.

Promoting collaborations between government, financial institutions, research institutions, academic institutions, and the private sector will help lower costs, foster research and development, and widen the base and reach of financial services.

7. Conclusion

India's journey in financial inclusion has been transformative, driven by a combination of progressive policy interventions, innovative digital public infrastructure, and regulatory reforms. Over the past decade, initiatives like the Pradhan Mantri Jan Dhan Yojana, Mudra Yojana, and expanded insurance and pension coverage have significantly increased access to formal financial services. Complementing these efforts, the development of India's DPI – anchored in Aadhaar, UPI, DigiLocker, e-KYC, and the Account Aggregator framework – has enabled seamless digital transactions, enhanced credit access, and improved service delivery.

The integration of financial inclusion with India's broader economic vision, as emphasized in the Viksit Bharat@2047 agenda, highlights the government's commitment to ensuring universal access to financial services. By aligning financial inclusion with the Saptarishi[1] priorities, India aims to foster inclusive growth, empower MSMEs, and enhance economic resilience. Additionally, India's leadership in global forums, such as the G20 and the Global Partnership for Financial Inclusion (GPFI), indicates its role as a model for other developing economies.

Despite these advancements, challenges remain. The World Bank Global Findex Database reveals persistent gaps in financial access, particularly among women, rural populations, and small businesses. Digital literacy, infrastructure limitations, and cybersecurity concerns must be addressed to ensure the benefits of financial inclusion are equitably distributed. Moreover, private sector participation will

[1]The seven guiding pillars/priorities as outlined in the Union Budget 2023–24, to guide the vision of Amrit Kaal, include – Inclusive Development, Reaching the Last Mile, Infrastructure and Investment, Unleashing the Potential, Green Growth, Youth Power, and the Financial Sector.

be crucial in modernizing DPI, expanding credit access, and fostering innovation in digital financial services.

India's experience demonstrates that financial inclusion, when supported by robust DPI, can be a powerful driver of economic growth, poverty reduction, and social empowerment. As India moves forward, sustaining momentum in DPI-driven financial inclusion will require continuous policy innovation, regulatory safeguards, and collaborative efforts between the government, financial institutions, and technology providers. The lessons from India's digital financial revolution offer insights for other nations striving to build an inclusive, resilient, and technology-driven financial ecosystem.

References

Alonso, C., Bhojwani, T., Hanedar, E., Prihardini, D., Uña, G., and Zhabska, K. (2023). Stacking up the benefits: Lessons from India's digital journey. International Monetary Fund.

Desai, A. and Manoharan, A. P. (2024). Digital transformation and public administration: The impacts of India's digital public infrastructure. *Int J Public Adm.*, 1–4.

Dua, P., Goel, D., and Kumar, N. (2023a). Decoding the union budgets' financial inclusion agenda: a review of India's progress. *Econ Polit Wkly.*, 58(14), 19–26.

Dua, P., Goel, D., Kumar, N., and Verma, N. (2023b). Reducing financial inclusion gaps: a policy roadmap for developing economies. Think-Twenty (T20) India 2023.

Dua, P., Goel, D., Verma, N., Kumar, N., and Allamraju, A. (2024). Gaps in digital financial inclusion: Lessons for G20.

Ferrata, L. (2019). Digital financial inclusion – an engine for "leaving no one behind." *Public Sector Econ.*, 43(4), 445–458.

G20 Brazil 2024 Presidency. (2024). G20 Rio de Janeiro Leaders' Declaration. G20 Brazil 2024.

G20 Global Partnership for Financial Inclusion. (2023). G20 Global Partnership for Financial Inclusion (GPFI) report.

G20 India 2023 Presidency. (2023a). G20 2023 Action Plan on Accelerating Progress on the Sustainable Development Goals. G20 India 2023.

G20 India 2023 Presidency. (2023b). G20 Digital Economy Ministers' Meeting Outcome Document and Chair's Summary. G20 India 2023.

Gibson, E. C., Gazi, S., and Arner, D. W. (2024). Digital finance, financial inclusion and gender equality: strategies for economic empowerment of women. *Univ Pa J Int Law*, 46(1), 189–230.

Khera, P. (2023). Digital Financial Services and Inclusion. *India's Financial System: Building the Foundation for Strong and Sustainable Growth*, 127.

Little, A. (2024). India's digital public infrastructure: Accelerating India's digital financial inclusion. NASSCOM.

Ministry of Finance, Government of India. (2024a). Economic Survey 2023–24. Ministry of Finance.

Ministry of Finance, Government of India. (2024b). Report of India's G20 Task Force on Digital Public Infrastructure. Ministry of Finance.

Ministry of Finance, Government of India. (2025). Economic Survey 2024–25. Ministry of Finance.

National Payments Corporation of India (NPCI). (2022). Unified Payments Interface (UPI) Product Statistics: NPCI. NPCI.

NITI, Government of India. (2024). Vision for Viksit Bharat @ 2047: An Approach Paper.

Reserve Bank of India. (2008). Annual Report 2007–08. Reserve Bank of India.

Reserve Bank of India. (2021). RBI Bulletin – September 2021. Reserve Bank of India.

Sustainable Development Goals. (2015). Transforming our world: the 2030 Agenda for Sustainable Development. United Nations.

TransUnion CIBIL. (2023). The rise and evolution of India's digital finance. TransUnion CIBIL.

World Bank. (2022). The Global Findex Database 2021: Financial inclusion, digital payments, and resilience in the age of COVID-19. World Bank.

Zuckerman, E. (2020). What is digital public infrastructure. The Centre for Journalism and Liberty.

https://doi.org/10.1142/9789819823161_0007

Chapter 7

The Impact of Financial Technologies (Fintech) on Financial Services Performance in Emerging Markets

Nelson Lawrence[*,‡], **Garikayi Emmanuel Gondo**[*,§], **and Ravinder Rena**[†,¶,||]

[*]*UNISA School of Business Leadership (SBL), University of South Africa (UNISA), Midrand, Republic of South Africa*
[†]*School of Business, Woxsen University, Hyderabad, Telangana, India*
[‡]*n77.lawrence@gmail.com*
[§]*garikaigondo@gmail.com*
[¶]*ravinder.rena@gmail.com*
[||]*ravinder.rena@woxsen.edu.in*

Advances in technology have revolutionized the financial services industry. Innovations like artificial intelligence, blockchain, machine learning, and big data analytics have improved customer experience and operational efficiency. By evaluating their performance, banks can identify opportunities to gain a competitive edge and assess their risk-taking capacity. The emergence of fintech has necessitated new approaches for banks to maintain competitive positions and for regulators to prevent potential crises. The research aims to determine the impact of financial technology (Fintech) on the financial performance of banks in emerging markets. It investigates the main fintech technologies adopted by banks, analyzes their effects on various aspects of bank performance, and explores the role of regulatory frameworks in shaping the fintech landscape. A systematic literature review (PRISMA protocol) was conducted to identify, evaluate, and synthesize existing research. Key findings of the research indicate a dual-edged impact of fintech on the banking industry. While it offers significant benefits like increased efficiency, improved customer experience, and reduced costs, it also poses challenges such as cybersecurity risks, privacy concerns, and a widening digital divide. A framework that balances technological innovation, risk, and regulatory oversight to ensure optimal performance and consumer protection in the financial services sector is proposed.

Keywords: Fintech, banks, performance, disruptive innovation theory, resource dependence theory, resource-based view.

1. Introduction and Background

Digital transformation, accentuated by the fourth industrial revolution, has led to the emergence of sophisticated technology-enabled financial services (Rena, 2024; Anifa *et al.*, 2022; Vardomatskya *et al.*, 2021). These financial technologies, well known as fintech, refer to the integration of technology into financial services, creating new opportunities for businesses and consumers (Abad-segura *et al.*, 2020; Meena, 2023). Fintech can also be described as a technology-based financial solution that includes all services and various products offered conventionally by banks (Rumondang *et al.*, 2019).

The financial technology industry is growing rapidly due to technological advancements, changes in consumer behavior, and a growing demand for transparent and efficient financial services (Meena, 2023; Musabegovic *et al.*, 2019; Vaganova, 2018). Financial technology transforms humans and businesses as globalization and the digital economy accelerate (Zhao *et al.*, 2024). It received investment worth more than $20 billion in 2018 alone (Musabegovic *et al.*, 2019) and has evolved to enter the mainstream in the financial services domain (Manish and Sergeeva, 2022; Widati and Putri, 2023). These financial institutions value innovation and have achieved success as a consequence of technical breakthroughs (Rena and Kamuinjo, 2022; Lahiri, 2024).

Banks are consequently rebuilding traditional financial business models through cooperation with the fintech industry (Glushchenko *et al.*, 2019). Banks' competition and collaboration with fintech companies is therefore becoming the norm (Kova, 2019; Vaganova, 2018). Banks are therefore making investments in fintech to attract the attention of customers to become more competitive (Rena and Kamuinjo, 2022; Kalenyuk *et al.*, 2024) to survive in a competitive environment (Tunay *et al.*, 2019). The emergence of these digital technologies has therefore significantly impacted the global banking system, and has swiftly transformed the traditional financial services space (Alsmadi *et al.*, 2023; Anifa *et al.*, 2022; Aziz and Avazkhon, 2023; Gouveia *et al.*, 2020; Lahiri, 2024; Tashtamirov, 2023), leading to the development of innovative financial products and services (Tashtamirov, 2023).

Firstly, fintech has revolutionized the way customers interact with banks, offering more personalized and convenient services through mobile banking apps and online platforms (payments, money transfers, lending and financing), digital wallets, mobile payments, peer-to-peer lending, crowdfunding (Aziz and Avazkhon, 2023; Meena, 2023), asset management, currency exchange, insurance, and blockchain transactions (Glushchenko *et al.*, 2019). Secondly, fintech has enabled banks to streamline their operations and reduce costs through automation and digitization (Aziz and Avazkhon, 2023), and increases efficiency in banking operations (Tunay *et al.*, 2019), enabling faster transactions (Kalenyuk *et al.*, 2024). Thirdly, fintech enable banks to carryout customer behavior analysis, customer identification and segmentation, use of biometrics, development of neo-banking and open banking services, transaction monitoring, fraud management, risk assessment and regulatory compliance, banking services personification, customer response analysis, process automation, investment decision-making, financial advice, trade facilitation, and syndicated loan services (Melnychenko *et al.*, 2020).

Finally, fintech has disrupted traditional banking models by enabling new entrants to enter the market and compete with established players (Aziz and Avazkhon, 2023; Rena, 2024). These services that also cater to underserved communities are typically faster, cheaper, and more convenient than traditional financial services, resulting in increased customer satisfaction (Ekasari *et al.*, 2024; Kalenyuk *et al.*, 2024; Meena, 2023). In addition, consumers are now confronted with a slew of new options (Lahiri, 2024). The increased competitiveness has compelled all players to act more rapidly (Glushchenko *et al.*, 2019; Lahiri, 2024).

The evaluation of financial performance and profitability for the banking sector has become more important with the recent economic developments, increasing competitive environment, technological developments, and globalization (Ünvan and Ergenç, 2022). Banks are also one of the most important factors of the financial structures of a country's economy (Ünvan and Ergenç, 2022). Thus, studying whether financial technology affects bank performance is crucial to enhancing living standards and business development (Rena and Kamuinjo, 2022; Zhao *et al.*, 2024).

2. Aim/Objective

The study aims to provide an in-depth examination of the profound impact that financial technology (fintech) has on the financial services industry's performance, focusing on banks.

3. Research Questions

- What is the impact of financial technologies (fintech) on banks' performance?
- What is the role of fintech in reducing risks of banks for sustainable performance in the era of fintech?
- Which framework(s) can be utilized by banks to take advantage of fintech and enhance performance?

4. Literature Review

4.1. *Theories underpinning research*

To explore the impact of financial technologies on bank performance, the study is underpinned by disruptive innovation theory (DIT), resource dependence theory (RDT), and the resource-based view (RBV).

4.2. *Resource dependence theory*

The fundamental proposition of the Resource Dependence Theory (RDT) is built on the concept that organizations' existence hinges on their capability to attain critical resources from the external environment (Barney *et al.*, 2021; Klein and Pereira, 2016). Crucial to this view is that firms that lack resources have to acquire these resources by creating relationships with others (Barney *et al.*, 2021; Klein and Pereira, 2016). Consequently, firms make an effort to restructure their dependencies by implementing multifaceted approaches to mitigate resource flow uncertainty, such as entering into collaborative relationships (Klein and Pereira, 2016). This relationship also expresses the measure of power of one over another (Klein and Pereira, 2016). Traditional banks and fintech companies often find themselves in a state of interdependence. Traditional banks possess valuable resources such as established brands and reputations, large and loyal customer bases, and operate under strict regulatory frameworks, providing credibility and trust, while fintech companies are in control of or have an influence on the technical capabilities that banks need.

4.3. *Resource-based view*

The resource-based view of the firm, often attributed to Penrose (1959) and Chandler (1962), was further developed by Wernerfelt (1984), Dierickx and Cool (1989), Chatterjee and Wernerfelt (1991), and Peteraf (1993) (Mella-Barral, 2024). This view posits that businesses can be considered as a collection of physical resources, human resources, and organizational resources (Madhani, 2010). If these resources are valuable, rare, inimitable, and non-substitutable, they can result in a sustained competitive advantage and sustained superior performance for the company (Baros-Tóth, 2024; Mella-Barral, 2024). The principal source of competitive advantage for companies is based on their internal strengths (capabilities and resources) (Baros-Tóth, 2024). Businesses that possess superior resources, such as fintech, will earn rents (Krause, 2013).

4.4. *Disruptive innovation theory (DIT)*

A disruptive innovation is a new product or service characteristically launched by a smaller company, which is a new entrant with a lower and or different performance characteristic than what is presently obtainable in the market, targeted initially at a low-end segment of the market and then gradually improved until it impacts or disrupts incumbent companies in the mainstream market and makes them obsolete (Baiyere and Salmela, 2013; Møller *et al.*, 2017). Changes in information system requirements, particularly those that are hosted on information technology (IT) infrastructures, have been fostered by the need for innovation, flexibility, and adaptability (Baiyere and Salmela, 2013). Dramatic changes in how organizations are designed to conduct business are driven by the need to respond to these competitive necessities in dynamic and at times disruptive environments by applying innovative fintech (Baiyere and Salmela, 2013).

5. Impact of Financial Technology on Bank Performance

Studies are in place that link financial technology (fintech) in the banking industry to the performance of the banking institutions. Kamilova *et al.* (2022) discuss various advantages and disadvantages of financial technologies. Hambardzumyan (2023), in a systematic and comprehensive analysis of existing literature, concludes that the adoption of Finance 4.0, which includes technologies such as artificial intelligence, blockchain, the Internet of Things (IoT), and machine learning, can provide Armenian banks with significant opportunities to improve their efficiency, reduce costs, and enhance customer experiences.

Ultimately, the adoption of these technologies can position Armenian banks for growth and success in the increasingly competitive global financial landscape. Li and Ding (2024), through a combination of qualitative case studies and quantitative analysis of industry performance metrics, provide an in-depth examination of the impact of technological innovation on the financial services industry, focusing on advancements in blockchain, artificial intelligence (AI), machine learning (ML), big data analytics, and fintech solutions. Key findings show that technological innovation drives unmatched efficiencies and customer value creation (Li and Ding, 2024; Rena, 2024).

Baker *et al.* (2023), in a survey of commercial banks listed on the Amman Stock Exchange and Abu Dhabi Securities Exchange, investigate the main financial technologies adopted by banks to improve their financial performance. The results showed that fintech positively affects both total deposits and net profits (Baker *et al.*, 2023). Geby *et al.* (2023), in a quantitative approach, prove that financial literacy and financial technology play an important role in improving village financial performance in the form of increased operational efficiency and efficiency enjoyed by its members. In an empirical study to investigate how new technology affects customer satisfaction in Bhopal's public and commercial banks, Lahiri (2024) shows that information and communication technology is critical to the sector's performance, and client satisfaction increases as a consequence in both public and private banks (Rena and Kamuinjo, 2022; Lahiri, 2024). Tunay *et al.* (2019) use aggregated data from 23 developed and emerging economies covering the 2005–2015 period to investigate the effects of electronic banking technologies on bank profitability and costs. The findings show that the increase in the use of electronic banking technologies improves productivity, product and service quality, and profitability performance, and has a negative impact on costs (Tunay *et al.*, 2019).

Jumaa (2023) determines the state and trends of fintech development in the United Arab Emirates' (UAE) financial sector, customer satisfaction with financial technology implementation in the banking sector, and the impact of financial technologies on the efficiency and competitiveness of financial and banking institutions. The survey results show that better service and reliability associated with fintech are seen as a major incentive to switch to digital banking (Jumaa, 2023). Xinyu *et al.* (2021), in a quantitative survey of 504 respondents across 28 countries, evaluate competitive trends observed in the global payments market. The results show that fintech innovations have a strong positive effect on the payment system's competitiveness (Xinyu *et al.*, 2021).

In desk research using secondary data, Nkatekho (2024) explores the impact of fintech innovations on traditional banking systems. The findings reveal that fintech innovations have revolutionized finance, creating both opportunities and threats for traditional banks. The findings show that while fintech boosts efficiency and customer satisfaction, traditional banks must strategically adapt to remain competitive. Some of the strategies suggested include effective collaboration between fintech firms and banks, supported by balanced regulation, which is crucial for fostering innovation and maintaining financial stability (Nkatekho, 2024).

In addition to bank performance, other studies link fintech to GDP performance. Musabegovic *et al.* (2019) survey the historical development of fintech and its influence on market structure in banking industry, efficiency, strategic plans of participants, and stability of the financial market. The results of the study provide evidence of statistically significant positive relationships between per capita GDP and the usage of new technology and smartphones in financial transactions and payment processing. The findings also indicate statistically significant positive relationships between per capita GDP and payment of utilities and received wages through a mobile phone (Musabegovic *et al.*, 2019). Kireyeva and Kredina (2021), based on a quantitative study of the period between 2004 and 2019, consider the correlation between economic growth (expressed by indicators such as GDP), financial technologies (number of ATMs, user access to the internet, and number of users of mobile communications), and gender indicators. The conclusions show a correlation between economic growth and financial technologies (Rena, 2024; Kireyeva and Kredina, 2021).

Other researchers have observed mixed results. Findings by Efris Saputri *et al.* (2024), for a paired Sample T-test for normally distributed data and the Wilcoxon Signed Rank Test for non-normally distributed data, indicate a significant influence on the financial ratios of CAR and BOPO. Meanwhile, for the variables ROA, LDR, and NPL, there is no significant influence on the financial performance of banking companies before and after the emergence of financial technology (fintech) in Jambi (Efris Saputri *et al.*, 2024).

5.1. *Impact of financial technology on risk*

While financial technology has disrupted the traditional financial services industry, it still faces challenges globally (Abad-segura *et al.*, 2020; Aziz and Avazkhon, 2023; Geby *et al.*, 2023; Kalenyuk *et al.*, 2024; Li and Ding, 2024; Sloboda and Demianyk, 2020). These new challenges include regulatory compliance in a rapidly changing legal and regulatory environment (Manish and Sergeeva, 2022; Meena, 2023), lack of adoption and demographic opportunities (Manish and Sergeeva, 2022), increased cybersecurity threats, privacy concerns, a growing digital divide among consumers (Li and Ding, 2024; Yakunina and Popov, 2018), the risk of transaction security loss (Yakunina and Popov, 2018), personal data protection, psychological aspects, risks of illegal operations (Kalenyuk *et al.*, 2024), ethical challenges (Sanyaolu *et al.*, 2024), slow adoption of innovations by traditional banks, lack of open APIs in the banking sector, and limited access to capital and financing for fintechs (Sloboda and Demianyk, 2020). In addition, digitalization also increases the credit and liquidity risks, which are traditional for the financial system (Yakunina and Popov, 2018).

Although technological advancements introduce challenges, appropriate actions are necessary to avert concerns (Kalenyuk *et al.*, 2024). Hambardzumyan (2023) argues that by leveraging blockchain technology, banks can also enhance security and transparency in transactions, while the IoT can enable new channels for customer engagement and provide real-time insights into consumer behavior. In addition, Sloboda and Demianyk (2020) outline the main trends, problems, and risks that should be addressed through cooperation between fintech companies and banks at the stage of international financial market development. Policymakers have to come up with adaptive regulations, update regulatory frameworks, and global economic structures that promote financial inclusion and literacy, support innovation, maintain financial stability, and sustainable economic development (Ekasari *et al.*, 2024; Nkatekho, 2024; Qur'anisa *et al.*, 2024). A call for collaboration and continuous dialogue among all stakeholders to address these challenges and seize opportunities offered by fintech innovations has been made (Nkatekho, 2024; Qur'anisa *et al.*, 2024).

Adaptive regulation and collaboration with traditional financial institutions are needed to maximize fintech's potential in supporting financial inclusion and sustainable economic development (Qur'anisa *et al.*, 2024). Further research is needed to develop more effective strategies for mitigating risks in fintech (Kalenyuk *et al.*, 2024).

6. Methodology and Data

To fully apprehend the role of fintech on banks' performance, the study employed a scoping review (Gray, 2019; Pham *et al.*, 2014). A scoping review was designed to map the existing literature on the role of fintech on banks' performance and the risks associated with financial technologies. The scoping review identified the studies and provided evidence related to this area.

Identifying relevant databases

Databases that cover the intersection of fintech and banks' performance:

- Academic databases (Google Scholar)
- Grey literature sources (conference proceedings)

Developing search terms

- Fintech
- Fintech AND bank performance
- Financial Technology and Bank Performance
- Fintech AND Challenges
- Fintech AND Risks
- Fintech AND banks AND performance

Screening and selection of studies (inclusion and exclusion criteria)

- Study design (empirical studies, case studies, reviews)
- Study population (emerging markets)
- Exclusion criteria (eliminate developed nations)

Screening process

- Title and abstract screening
- Full-text screening

7. Results

A search using keywords initially yielded 1,741 results. After screening articles that included banks and bank performance, and removing duplicates, 402 articles remained. These were distributed as shown in Fig. 1.

The articles were distributed by year as shown in Fig. 2.

The full text of the articles was then analyzed and eligible articles from emerging economies were returned after screening: BRICS nations, Brazil, Russia, India, China, and South Africa, are often cited as prominent examples.

MINT countries, Mexico, Indonesia, Nigeria, and Turkey, are also considered important emerging economies.

The Next Eleven group includes the countries Bangladesh, Egypt, Indonesia, Iran, Mexico, Nigeria, Pakistan, the Philippines, Turkey, South Korea, and Vietnam, which are seen as having high potential for growth.

After the full-article screening, 60 articles from 20 emerging economies were then analyzed to find the relationship between fintech and performance. A summary of the screening process using the PRISMA 2020 framework is shown in Fig. 3.

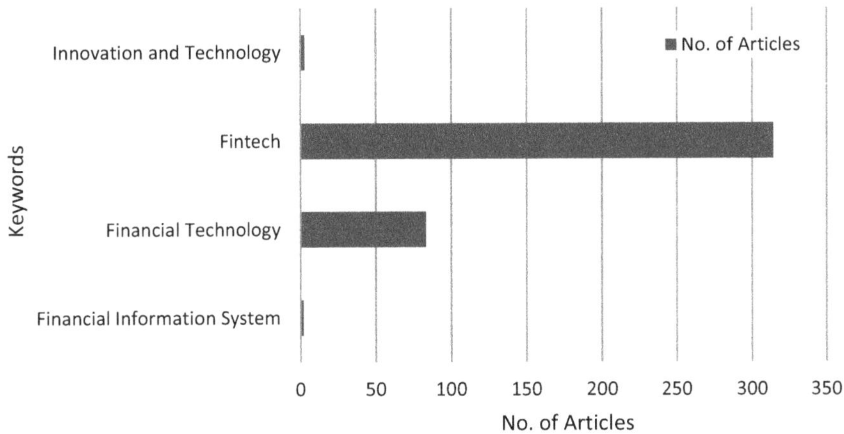

Fig. 1. Initial screening using keywords to describe fintech (Innovation and Technology, Fintech, Financial technology, and financial information system).

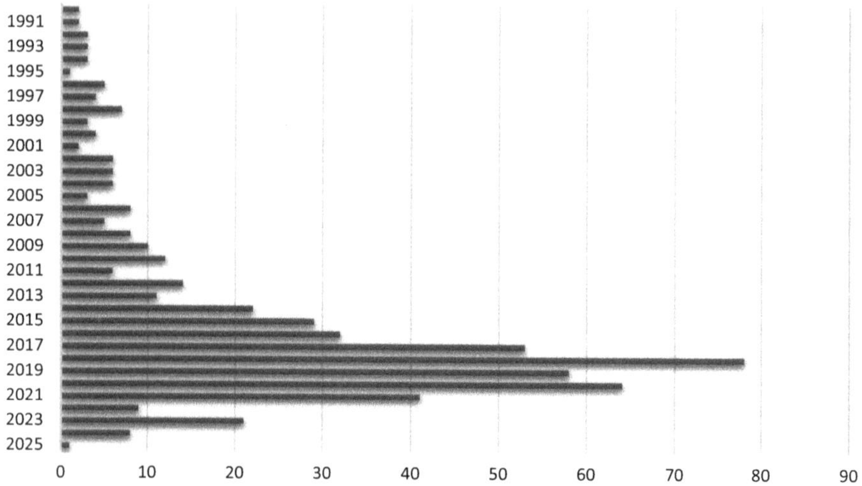

Fig. 2. Initial screened articles by year.

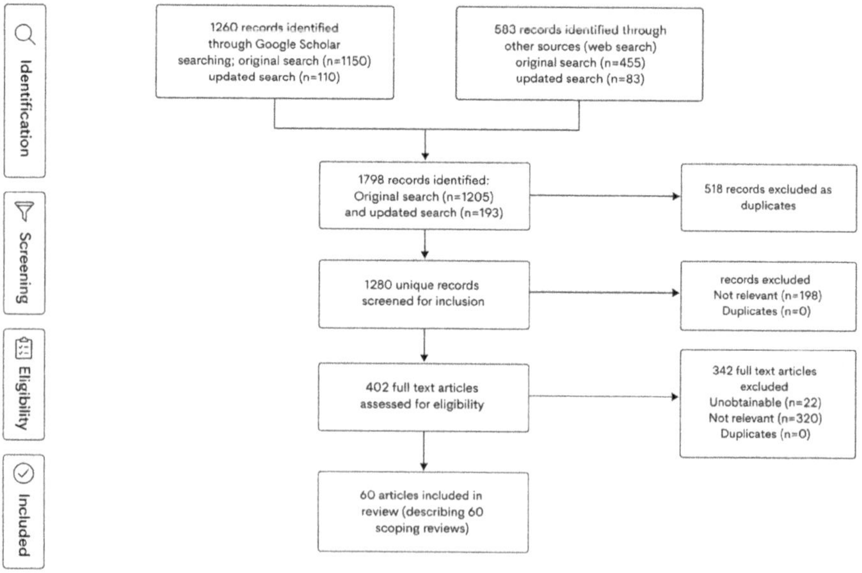

Fig. 3. Summarized PRISMA framework showing the screening process adopted from Gray (2019) and Pham *et al.* (2014).

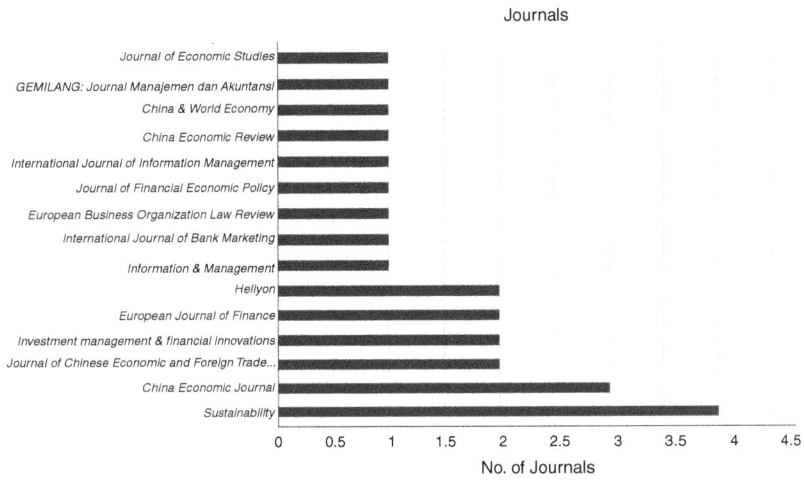

Fig. 4. Journal names for published articles.

The articles were in journals such as *Sustainability, International Review of Economics & Finance, China Economic Journal, Finance Research Letters, and Journal of Chinese Economic and Foreign Trade Studies.* Figure 4 shows the number of articles per journal. Figure 5 shows the distribution of the journals by year. 22% of the articles were in the year 2020, followed by 2021 with 13% and 2019 with 12%. Figure 6 shows the studies by country; 55% of the studies are in China, followed by 27% in Indonesia.

8. Discussion

The findings show that financial technologies (fintech) include machine learning, internet of things, artificial intelligence, process automation, cryptocurrencies, blockchain, peer-to-peer leading, and digital payments. Bank performance indicators include customer satisfaction, return on investment, increased efficiency, reduced costs, return on investment, and faster transactions. Areas where fintech reduces risk include behavior analysis, customer identification and segmentation, use of biometrics, transaction monitoring, fraud management, risk assessment and regulatory compliance, banking services personification, investment decision-making and trade facilitation, enhancing security, and transparency in transactions.

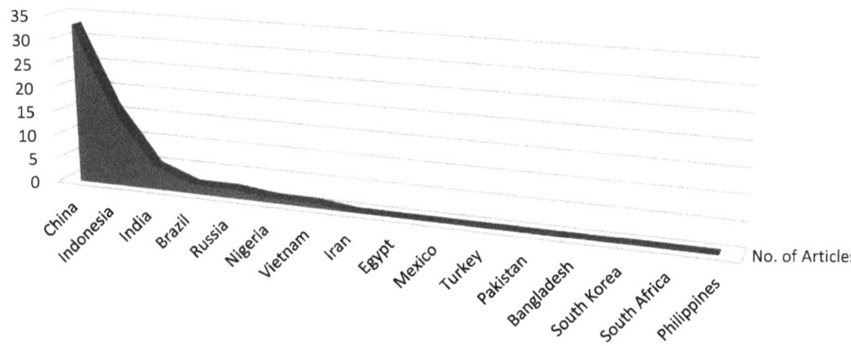

	China	Indonesia	India	Brazil	Russia	Nigeria	Vietnam	Iran	Egypt	Mexico	Turkey	Pakistan	Bangladesh	South Korea	South Africa	Philippines
■ No. of Articles	33	16	5	2	2	1	1	0	0	0	0	0	0	0	0	0

Fig. 5. Journals by emerging economy country.

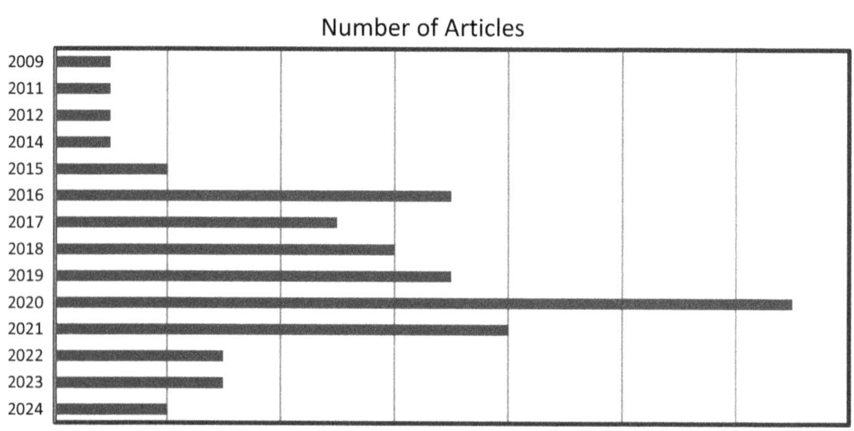

	2024	2023	2022	2021	2020	2019	2018	2017	2016	2015	2014	2012	2011	2009
■ Number of Articles	2	3	3	8	13	7	6	5	7	2	1	1	1	1

Year

Fig. 6. Journals by year of publication.

9. Conceptual Framework

The framework in Fig. 7 offers a valuable tool for analyzing the complex relationship between fintech and bank performance. Grounded in disruptive innovation theory, resource dependence theory, and the resource-based view, the framework highlights how regulatory policies guide both banks and fintech companies, who in turn offer recommendations to regulators. This visualization allows for a comprehensive understanding of how fintech is reshaping the banking industry and influencing bank performance. This allows for a comprehensive understanding of how fintech is reshaping the banking industry and driving performance gains.

The framework is explained in more detail in Figure 8 to show the intricate interconnections of how the different theories interact and influence each other. As an example, the resource-based view can explain how banks acquire valuable resources through fintech, while resource dependence theory and the disruptive innovation theory can highlight the potential challenges of disruption and/or dependence on fintech providers. Strategies for mitigating disruption and dependence on fintech include partnering or strategic alliances with fintech companies to access cutting-edge technology, diversification of fintech partners while maintaining their autonomy, development of in-house capabilities, improvement of customer engagement, and focusing on enhancing customer experiences.

10. Conclusion

The study based on emerging economies shows a positive link between financial technologies (fintech) in the banking industry and the performance of the banking institutions. Fintech is also enabling sustainable performance by reducing risks in novel ways that include leveraging blockchain technology, enhancing security and transparency in transactions, creating new channels for customer engagement, real-time insights into consumer behavior, behavior analysis, customer identification and segmentation, use of biometrics, transaction monitoring, fraud management, risk assessment and regulatory compliance, banking services personification, and enhanced security. A framework for analyzing the complex relationship between fintech and bank performance has been developed. The framework

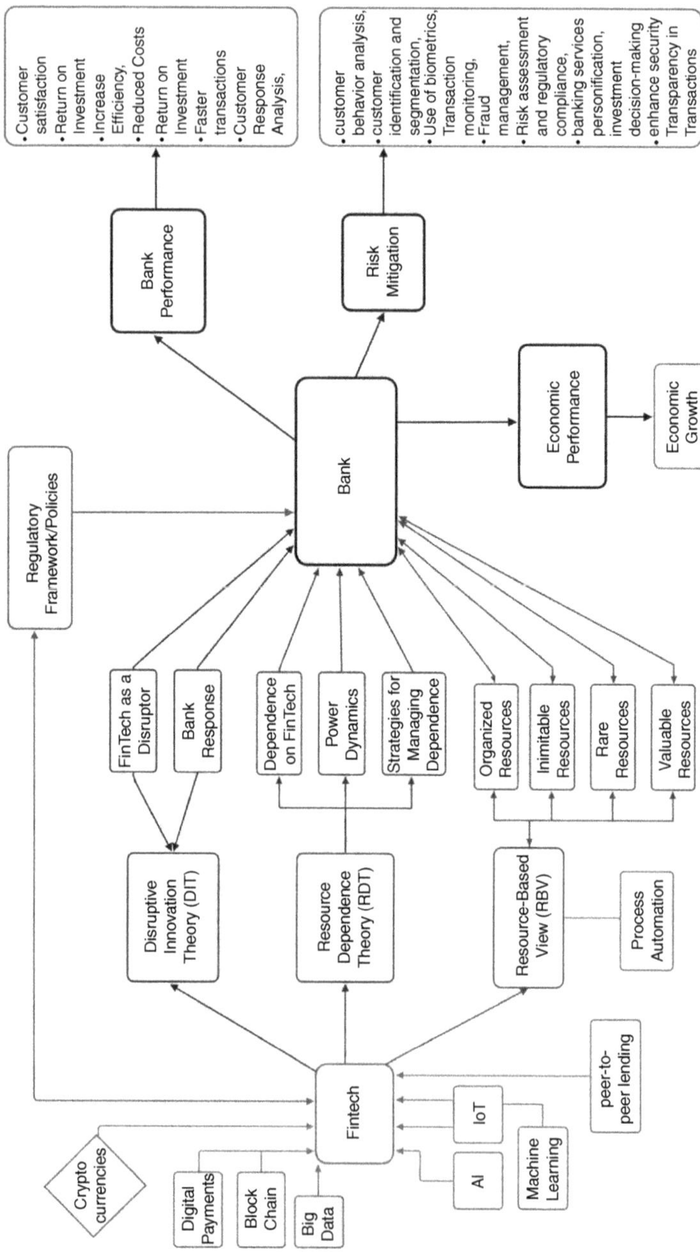

Fig. 7. Theoretical framework; link between fintech and bank performance.

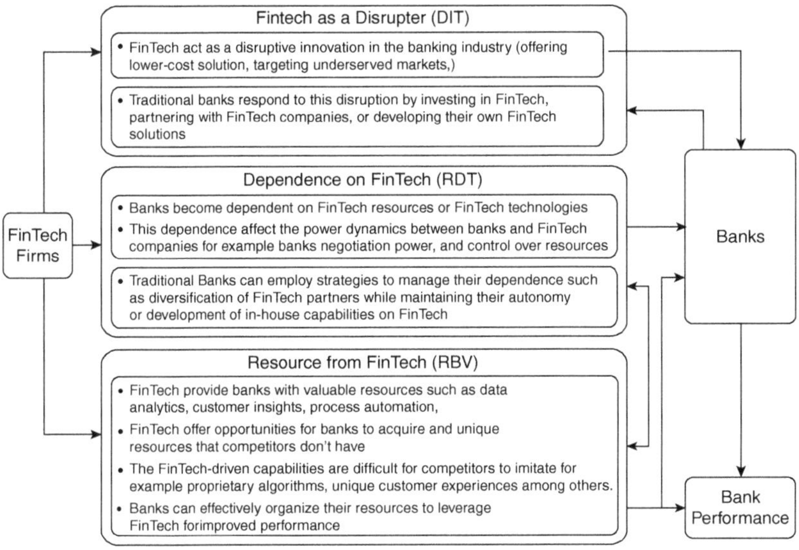

Fig. 8. Interconnections between fintech and banks in the lenses of DIT, RDT, and RBV.

is grounded in disruptive innovation theory, resource dependence theory, and the resource-based view. The framework highlights how regulatory policies guide both banks and fintech companies, which in turn offer recommendations to regulators.

11. Recommendations

The developed framework can be used as a tool by banks to take advantage of rapidly developing financial technologies and achieve superior performance while reducing risks in a novel approach.

12. Limitations and Future Work

This research is not without limitations. The research is limited to existing literature and is not based on contemporary primary data. A qualitative study based on emerging economies can be carried out to verify the theoretical framework. This can be followed by a quantitative survey of the same framework to generalize the findings.

References

Abad-segura, E., Gonz, M., and Eloy, L. (2020). Financial technology: Review of trends, approaches and management. *Mathematics Article*, 2020(8), 1–36. https://doi.org/10.3390/math8060951.

Alsmadi, A. A., Mohd, A., Al-afeef, M. A., and Al-smadi, A. W. (2023). Banking services transformation and financial technology role. *Information Sciences Letters An International Journal*, 12(1), 315–324. https://doi.org/10.18576/isl/120126.

Anifa, M., Ramakrishnan, S., Joghee, S., Kabiraj, S., and Bishnoi, M. M. (2022). Fintech innovations in the financial service industry. *Journal of Risk and Financial Management*, 15(7), 287. https://doi.org/10.3390/jrfm15070287.

Aziz, E. and Avazkhon, O. (2023). Financial technologies in the remote banking. *Science and Innovation International Scientific Journal*, 2(6), 197–201.

Baiyere, A. and Salmela, H. (2013). Review: Disruptive innovation & information technology — charting a path. *Proceedings of the 24th Australasian Conference on Information Systems.*

Baker, H., Kaddumi, T. A., Nassar, M. D., and Muqattash, R. S. (2023). Impact of financial technology on improvement of banks' financial performance. *Journal of Risk and Financial Management*, 16(4). https://doi.org/10.3390/jrfm16040230.

Barney, J. B., Ketchen, D. J., and Wright, M. (2021). Resource-based theory and the value creation framework. *Journal of Management*, 47(7), 1936–1955. https://doi.org/10.1177/01492063211021655.

Baros-Tóth, Á. (2024). Emergence of the resource-based view (RBV) and its impact on family business research. *Tudásmenedzsment*, 25(2020), 93–104. https://doi.org/10.15170/TM.2024.25.K1.9.

Efris Saputri, E. J., Pradana, A., Apriandi, R. F., and Taufik, H. (2024). The impact of financial technology on bank financial performance. *TIN: Terapan Informatika Nusantara*, 4(9), 607–612. https://doi.org/10.47065/tin.v4i9.4662.

Ekasari, S., Hastin, M., Hakim, S., Bani, P., and Suryanita, I. (2024). Fintech revolution: Transforming the financial landscape through technological innovation. *The Journal of Academic Science*, 1(5), 615–621.

Geby, C. A., Annisa, I. F., Maya, S., and Irvan, M. (2023). The effect of financial literacy and financial technology on financial performance (case study: Desa Kebun Kelapa). *International Journal of Management, Economic and Accounting*, 1(2), 81–93. https://doi.org/10.61306/ijmea.v1i2.9.

Glushchenko, M., Hodasevich, N, and Kaufman, N. (2019). Innovative financial technologies as a factor of competitiveness in the banking. *SHS Web of Conferences*, 69(00043), 1–5.

Gouveia, L. B., Perun, M., and Daradkeh, Y. I. (2020). Digital transformation and customers services: The banking revolution. *International Journal of Open Information Technologies*, 8(7), 124–128.

Gray, A. (2019). Body as voice: Restorative dance/movement psychotherapy with survivors of relational trauma. *The Routledge International Handbook of Embodied Perspectives in Psychotherapy: Approaches from Dance Movement and Body Psychotherapies*, 147–160. https://doi.org/10.4324/9781315159416.

Hambardzumyan, A. (2023). Embracing finance 4.0: The opportunity for Armenian banks to transform and thrive. *Messenger of ASUE*, 1(73), 19–25. https://doi.org/10.52174/1829-0280.

Jumaa, M. (2023). How effective is the banking and financial services sector in the United Arab Emirates in using technological innovations. *Finance: Theory and Practice*, 27(3), 139–153. https://doi.org/10.26794/2587-5671-2023-27-3-139-153.

Kalenyuk, I., Kuklin, O., Panchenko, Y., Djakona, A., and Bohun, M. (2024). Financial innovations in the smart city ecosystem. *Financial and Credit Activity: Problems of Theory and Practice*, 1(54), 102–113. https://doi.org/10.55643/fcaptp.1.54.2024.4287.

Kamilova, M., Nabieva, F., and Mustafoev, B. (2022). Impact of the pandemic on fintech adoption by developing countries. *ACM International Conference Proceeding Series*, 178–181. https://doi.org/10.1145/3584202.3584229.

Kireyeva, A. A. and Kredina, A. (2021). Impact of financial technologies on economic development: Theories, methods and analysis. *Journal of International Studies*, 14(4), 286–303. https://doi.org/10.14254/2071-8330.2021/14-4/19.

Klein, L. L. and Pereira, B. A. D. (2016). The survival of interorganizational networks: A proposal based on resource dependence theory. *Revista de Administracao Mackenzie*, 17(4), 153–175. https://doi.org/10.1590/1678-69712016/administracao.v17n4p153-175.

Kova, N. Z. (2019). Regional banks & fintech: A standoff or partnership? *Digest Finance*, 24(1), 13–20.

Krause, K. (2013). Critical perspectives on human security. *Routledge Handbook of Human Security*, 14(3), 76–93. https://doi.org/10.4324/9781315885926-15.

Lahiri, M. (2024). Analysis of innovation and technology in banking. *REST Journal on Banking, Accounting and Business*, 1(3), 82–89. https://doi.org/10.46632/jbab/1/3/12.

Li, W. and Ding, H. (2024). Research on the impact of technological innovation on the financial services industry. *Frontiers in Sustainable Development*, 4(4), 109–119. https://doi.org/10.54691/8qneq173.

Madhani, P. (2010). Resource based view (RBV) of competitive advantage. *Icfai University Press*, 1(1), 3–22. http://papers.ssrn.com/sol3/papers.cfm?abstract_id=1578704.

Manish, K. P. and Sergeeva, I. (2022). Paradigm shift in fintech landscape: A perspective from the Indian marketplace. *Economics and Environmental Management*, 2(2022), 142–151. https://doi.org/10.17586/2310-1172-2022-16-2-142-151.

Meena, R. (2023). The impact of financial technology on financial services: A comprehensive analysis. *Research Review International Journal of Multidisciplinary*, 8(3), 185–192.

Mella-Barral, P. (2024). A resource-based view of entrepreneurial spin-outs. *Review of Financial Economics*, 42(3), 281–290. https://doi.org/10.1002/rfe.1207.

Melnychenko, S., Volosovych, S., and Baraniuk, Y. (2020). Dominant ideas of financial technologies. *Baltic Journal of Economic Studies*, 6(1), 92–99.

Møller, L., Gertsen, F., Johansen, S. S., and Rosenstand, C. (2017). Characterizing digital disruption in the general theory of disruptive innovation. *In ISPIM Innovation Symposium*. www.ispim.org.

Musabegovic, I., Djukovic, S., and Jovanovic, S. (2019). Influence of financial technology (fintech). *Economics of Agriculture*, 66(4), 1003–1021. https://doi.org/10.5937/ekoPolj1904003M.

Nkatekho, B. (2024). The impact of Fintech innovations on traditional banking systems. *International Journal of Finance*, 9(4), 48–61.

Pham, M. T., Rajić, A., Greig, J. D., Sargeant, J. M., Papadopoulos, A., and Mcewen, S. A. (2014). A scoping review of scoping reviews: Advancing the approach and enhancing the consistency. *Research Synthesis Methods*, 5(4), 371–385. https://doi.org/10.1002/jrsm.1123.

Qur'anisa, Z., Herawati, M., Lisvi, L., Putri, M. H., and Feriyanto, O. (2024). Peran Fintech Dalam Meningkatkan Akses Keuangan Di Era Digital. *GEMILANG: Jurnal Manajemen Dan Akuntansi*, 4(3), 99–114. https://doi.org/10.56910/gemilang.v4i3.1573.

Rena, R. (2024). Blockchain technology and its importance for the growth and prosperity of Indian small and medium-sized enterprises. *Indian Journal of Commerce and Management Studies*, 15(2), 1–9. https://www.ijcms.in/index.php/ijcms/article/view/666/563.

Rena, R. and Kamuinjo, A. V. (2022). An empirical analysis of the relationship between capital, market risks and liquidity shocks in the banking industry. *Studia Universitatis Babeş-Bolyai Oeconomica*, 67(2), 67–83.

Rumondang, A., Sudirman, A., Effendy, F., Simarmata, J., and Agustin, T. (2019). *Fintech: Inovasi Sistem Keuangan di Era Digital.* Yayasan Kita Menulis.

Sanyaolu, T. O., Adeleke, A. G., Azubuko, C. F., and Osundare, O. S. (2024). Exploring fintech innovations and their potential to transform the future of financial services and banking. *International Journal of Scholarly Research in Science and Technology*, 5(1), 054–072. https://doi.org/10.56781/ijsrst.2024.5.1.0033.

Sloboda, L. Y. and Demianyk, O. M. (2020). Prospects and risks of the fintech initiatives in a global banking industry. *Проблеми Економіки*, 1(43), 275–282.

Tashtamirov, M. (2023). Financial innovation and digital technology in the banking system: An institutional perspective. *SHS Web of Conferences*, 172(02004), 1–11.

Tunay, N., Yüksel, S., and Tunay, K. B. (2019). The effects of technology on bank performance in advanced and emerging economies: An empirical analysis. In H. Dinçer and S. Yüksel (Eds.), *Handbook of Research on Managerial Thinking in Global Business Economics* (pp. 263–280). IGI Global. https://doi.org/10.4018/978-1-5225-7180-3.ch015.

Ünvan, Y. A. and Ergenç, C. (2022). Financial performance analysis with the fuzzy COPRAS and entropy-COPRAS approaches. *Computational Economics*, 59(4), 1577–1605.

Vaganova, G. (2018). Bank as a participant and user of digital finance. *European Proceedings of Social and Behavioural Sciences (EpSBS)*, 21, 54–58.

Vardomatskya, L., Kuznetsova, V., and Plotnikov, V. (2021). The financial technologies transformation in the digital economy. *E3S Web of Conferences*, 244(10046), 1–8. https://doi.org/10.1051/e3sconf/202124410046.

Widati, S. and Putri, V. N. (2023). Financial performance analysis before and after the rise of digital companies (case study in the transportation, banking and manufacturing sector listed on the Indonesia stock exchange). *New Challenges in Accounting & Finance (NCAF)*, 9(13).

Xinyu, C., Milojevic, M., Syromyatnikov, D., Kurilova, A., and Slusarczyk, B. (2021). Mathematical interpretation of global competition between payment systems. *Mathematics Article*, 9(270), 5–18.

Yakunina, A. V. and Popov, M. V. (2018). Digital finance and new risks. *Вестник СГСЭУ*, 4(73), 186–189.

Zhao, J., Ibrahim, H., Wang, C., and Yuan, R. (2024). Investigating the temporal and spatial evolution of bank performance and its impact pathways in the context of financial technology development. *Heliyon*, 10(10), e30585. https://doi.org/10.1016/j.heliyon.2024.e30585.

Part III
Empirical Perspectives

https://doi.org/10.1142/9789819823161_0008

Chapter 8

Addressing the Legalization of Criminal Proceeds within the Banking Sector of the Republic of Belarus: Insights and Development Strategies

Volha Rudkouskaya

Department of Business English,
Belarus State Economic University Minsk, Belarus

rudkouskaya@bseu.by

The prevalence of money laundering and terrorist financing (ML/TF) has emerged as a critical concern within the global financial system, with the illicit flow of capital accounting for an estimated 1–3% of the world's GDP annually. This situation is particularly acute in the Republic of Belarus, where the shadow economy constitutes 33% of GDP. In 2018 alone, suspicious transactions in the banking sector reached 28.7% of the national GDP, driven by activities such as tax evasion and fraud. In response to these alarming trends, this study evaluates the effectiveness of existing anti-money laundering (AML) and combating the financing of terrorism (CFT) measures within Belarusian banks, identifying significant gaps in regulatory compliance and internal controls. A comprehensive risk assessment methodology tailored to the national context is presented, comprising four stages: information collection, analysis, risk identification, and risk assessment. The results highlight the need for enhanced regulatory frameworks, improved interagency cooperation, and the establishment of a robust feedback mechanism to bolster the AML/CFT infrastructure. Recommendations are made for improving the awareness and training of banking personnel, particularly in relation to emerging financial technologies. The findings underscore the importance of integrating international standards and best practices to mitigate the vulnerabilities in the banking sector, ensuring the stability and integrity of Belarus's financial system amid increasing global scrutiny.

Keywords: Money laundering, terrorist financing, banking sector, anti-money laundering, financial intelligence, risk assessment, Belarus.

1. Introduction

Currently, the growth in the legalization (laundering) of proceeds from crime and the financing of terrorist activities occupies one of the leading positions among the most alarming trends in global financial crime statistics. According to international organizations, the total amount of money laundered annually in the world is at the level of 1–3% of world GDP, i.e., it varies from $500 billion to $1 trillion (Medina, 2018; The Bank for International Settlements, 2019; Shamanina, 2016; International Monetary Fund, 2018). In the Republic of Belarus, the share of the shadow sector in GDP is 33%, in Russia, this figure is 43%, in Poland 24%, in Germany 14.9%, in Estonia 15%, and in Switzerland 7.2% (Medina, 2018).

According to the National Financial Intelligence Agency (Financial Monitoring Department of the State Control Committee of the Republic of Belarus) and the National Bank of the Republic of Belarus, in 2018, the volume of suspicious transactions conducted through the banking sector of the Republic of Belarus amounted to 28.7% of the country's GDP. The real objectives of such operations are tax evasion, abuse of power or official authority, and fraud.

One of the reasons for the current situation is the lack of protection of the banking sector of the Republic of Belarus from illegal use of its services for the purpose of legalizing (laundering) proceeds from crime and financing terrorist activities.

In this regard, in modern economic conditions, improving the system of countering the legalization (laundering) of proceeds from crime and the financing of terrorist activities in the banking sector is undoubtedly relevant. Violations by banks in the field of countering the legalization (laundering) of proceeds from crime and the financing of terrorist activities not only have local consequences (in the form of fines, loss of banking licenses) but also have a destructive impact on the national banking system and the economy as a whole. This manifests itself in the form of growing threats of systemic risk, the growth of the shadow sector, and other negative consequences of the impact of the legalization (laundering) of proceeds from crime and the financing of terrorist activities.

2. The Relevance of the Research Topic

The relevance of this study stems from the practical necessity of ensuring banking system stability and the insufficient theoretical understanding of anti-money laundering and counter-terrorist financing (AML/CFT) measures in Belarus.

Understanding the consequences of money laundering and terrorist financing (ML/TF) has led the international community to join forces in developing measures to curb and minimize ML/TF processes. In turn, the Republic of Belarus cannot remain aloof from the general fight against ML/TF. By fulfilling its obligations to international organizations, the country is improving legislative regulation in this area.

The current leader in anti-money laundering and combating the financing of terrorism (AML/CFT) process is the Financial Action Task Force on Money Laundering (FATF), which sets international standards, develops AML/CFT policies, and promotes the effective implementation of legal, regulatory, and operational measures to combat ML/TF in the interests of the integrity of the international financial system. The FATF is an intergovernmental organization established in 1989 by the decision of the G7 Heads of State and Government. FATF members include 37 countries and 2 international organizations; the associate members include 9 regional groups, with 1 country and 24 international organizations serving as observers. Thus, almost all countries of the world that have committed themselves to combating ML/TF are involved in the FATF global network (Chikhanchina, 2018; Financial Action Task Force, 2020).

3. The Banking System of the Republic of Belarus

The Belarusian banking sector is characterized by a mix of state-owned and private banks, with the National Bank of the Republic of Belarus (NBRB) serving as the primary regulatory body. As of 2023, the banking sector consisted of 24 banks, including prominent state-owned entities such as Belarusbank and Belagroprombank. The sector's assets accounted for approximately 70% of the country's GDP, indicating its significant role in the financial landscape.

Profitability in the Belarusian banking sector has been under pressure due to rising operational costs and increasing provisions for loan losses. By the end of 2023, net profit margins were reported to decline by approximately 15% compared to the previous year, primarily due to higher interest rates and tightening liquidity conditions.

The quality of bank assets has been a concern, with non-performing loans (NPLs) rising to around 8% of total loans in early 2024. The deterioration in asset quality can be attributed to economic uncertainty and the inability of some borrowers to meet their financial obligations. The NBRB has urged banks to strengthen their risk management frameworks in response.

Capital adequacy ratios have remained relatively stable, with most banks maintaining ratios above the regulatory minimum. However, economic headwinds have prompted banks to adopt a more conservative approach to lending, focusing on maintaining capital buffers to weather potential shocks.

Liquidity conditions in the banking sector have been tight, influenced by the central bank's monetary policy aimed at controlling inflation. The NBRB raised interest rates to curb inflation, resulting in higher borrowing costs and reduced demand for credit. As of early 2024, the liquidity coverage ratio for major banks hovered around 120%, indicating a cautious stance toward lending.

4. Research Methodology

The methodology of AML/CFT National Risk Assessment (NRA) in the Republic of Belarus includes the following 4 stages (National Bank of the Republic Belarus, 2022):

Stage 1: Collecting information. The purpose of this stage is to collect all available information, including limited dissemination, necessary for further processing and forming an understanding of the existence of ML/TF risks in the country. ML/TF risk assessment in the Republic of Belarus involves the use of regulatory, enforcement, supervisory, and law enforcement information. For the purpose of ML/TF NRA, statistical information, separate quantitative and qualitative indicators, and the results of research conducted by Belarusian banks and international organizations are used.

To develop tools for collecting statistical information, use is made of the matrices recommended by the OSCE guidelines for data collection during ML/TF NRA. The toolkit can be supplemented with other information. Data are collected for the 4 years preceding the assessment year. Thus, prosecutor's offices, law enforcement agencies, and courts have information about the amount of criminal proceeds based on data on predicate crimes. They have available statistics on investigations, prosecutions, and sentences imposed in ML/TF cases, as well as statistics on seized (confiscated, returned, or divided) assets and international requests for legal assistance. These bodies have information obtained in the course of conducting investigations into the methods of committing crimes. They can provide information on new trends identified during investigations. They can also help identify vulnerabilities. Individual law enforcement agencies play an important role in terrorist financing assessments, where most of the available threat information comes from intelligence sources.

The financial monitoring body has information from reports of suspicious transactions, as well as information based on the analysis carried out, other information available in its databases, and information related to specific types of products or operations, presented in the form of specific studies/examples or in the form of generalized data to identify trends. This information is supplemented with statistics on reports received on financial transactions subject to special control from persons performing financial transactions in accordance with Article 2 of the AML/CFT Law No. 165-Z.

The state bodies specified in Article 16 of the AML/CFT Law No. 165-Z have detailed information about persons engaged in financial transactions; they also have information about specific vulnerabilities related to the types of products, operations (including those of a cross-border nature), types of transactions, etc., based on the inspections and monitoring carried out; clients that may be related to ML/TF; as well as an assessment of the control measures available in a controlled area of activity.

Individuals who perform financial transactions in accordance with Article 2 of the Law have information about the features and characteristics of financial products, their operations, and their clients, which is useful for identifying ML/TF vulnerabilities and determining the level of risk they pose.

Stage 2: Information analysis. The goal of this stage is to achieve a holistic understanding of ML/TF threats and vulnerabilities in the Republic of Belarus, their nature, types, causes, and sources. This information is then used to identify ML/TF risks.

The analysis compares quantitative and qualitative data, describes causal relationships between events and facts, analyzes the relationship with other aspects of political, economic, and social life, and compares the data with international indicators and best practices. The analysis of information also uses reports and rating lists of international organizations based on the results of research on certain categories of crimes or risk classifications, publicly available reports of national risk assessments, reports of mutual assessments of FATF member states, and FATF-type regional groups. Information from the mass media and the Internet related to ML/TF is subject to additional study for the possibility of using it to identify threats.

Stage 3: Identification of risks. The purpose of this stage is to identify and highlight risks, understand the interrelationships of risks, and their impact on the formation of industry risks.

When identifying ML/CFT risks, attention should be paid to the risks associated with the use of various methods, products, and mechanisms for performing operations with funds, certain categories of clients, and certain types of activities, as well as risks that indicate the level of effectiveness of legal and organizational mechanisms for combating ML/CFT.

Stage 4: ML/TF risk assessment. The purpose of risk assessment is to form an idea of the level of identified ML/TF risks. ML/TF risk assessment allows you to identify priority actions to limit (reduce) ML/TF risks.

The Methodology uses a 3-step scale to assess ML/TF risks and their components:

- low degree (1).
- medium degree (2).
- high degree (3).

In the NRA Method, "risk" is a combination of identified ML/TF threats and vulnerabilities. Therefore, ML/TF threats are assessed first, then vulnerabilities. Threat assessment is carried out on the basis of a comprehensive study of groups of predicate crimes established by the FATF guidelines (terrorism and terrorist financing, arms trafficking, corruption and bribery, fraud, counterfeiting of banknotes, extortion, tax evasion and excise duties, and other income-generating crimes).

The elements of crimes that may be included in these groups of crimes are determined in accordance with the specifics of the criminal legislation of the Republic of Belarus.

Additionally, other groups of crimes may be defined. When identifying ML threats, among other factors, special attention is paid, for example, to the following:

- the types of predicate crimes committed;
- the nature and scope of the relevant criminal activity (i.e., predicate crimes) in the Republic of Belarus;
- the amount of proceeds from criminal activity in the Republic of Belarus;
- cross-border flows of criminal proceeds;
- the amount of proceeds from crimes committed abroad and legalized (laundered) in the Republic of Belarus;
- sources, location, and places of concentration of criminal activity, including in illegal "underground" sectors of the economy;
- the nature and scope of terrorist activities and terrorist groups in the Republic of Belarus;
- available information on the nature and scope of terrorist activities and terrorist groups in neighboring countries, regions, and subregions.

In order to identify FT threats, along with the factors mentioned earlier, attention is drawn to the existence of favorable conditions for training terrorists, forming terrorist groups, committing terrorist acts, and financing terrorism in the national and international contexts. Uncertainty caused by a lack of information increases the

Table 1. Description of the ML/TF threat assessment scale.

Scale	Description
Low Degree (1)	There are no facts indicating that criminals intend to commit acts related to ML or TF. Committing an illegal act is extremely difficult or extremely dangerous from the point of view of a high level of detection and/or punishability of crimes. There is an absence of facts indicating that there is a possibility (technical, financial, etc.) for criminals to commit illegal acts.
Medium degree (2)	There are facts that indicate attempts to commit an illegal act in the field of ML or TF. Committing an illegal act is difficult or dangerous from the point of view of detection and/or punishability of crimes. There are facts indicating that there is a possibility (technical, financial, etc.) for criminals to commit illegal acts.
High degree (3)	There are facts of repeated commission of an illegal act in the field of ML or TF. Committing an illegal act is possible from the point of view of the low level of detection and/or punishability of crimes. Criminals have the opportunity (technical, financial, etc.) to commit illegal acts.

grade to high. The ML/TF threat assessment scale is described in Table 1.

Within thc framework of identifying ML/TF vulnerabilities, the general situation in the relevant sector, the volume of transactions performed, the presence/absence of persons performing financial transactions in accordance with Article 2 of Law No. 165-Z on AML/CFT, the Tax Code, and their implementation in practice are studied using targeted financial sanctions. When identifying vulnerabilities, among other factors, special attention is paid to the following (National Bank of the Republic Belarus, 2022):

- products, services, and operations;
- clients;
- geographical factor;
- performing due diligence on customers;
- ongoing due diligence, including monitoring of operations;
- current implementation of measures for sending messages;
- availability of internal control measures;
- data storage;
- regulation of issues related to beneficial ownership;
- strict application of rules concerning financial and other secrets, including professional secrets.

In particular, among products, services, and operations, special attention is paid to the presence of predominant sectors and products; the presence of products/services that facilitate accelerated or anonymous transactions; the widespread use of cash transactions and cross-border money transfers; and the presence of measures that help optimize taxes on the part of non-residents (tax haven).

When studying clients, it is necessary to pay attention to the types of clients (legal entities, individuals, etc.); the nature of business relationships; the presence of clients who pose an increased risk; compliance with regulatory provisions/requirements related to clients; **and** compliance with any prohibitions on performing operations for clients.

Considering the geographical factor, you may encounter the following: a business and customer base in high-risk geographical regions (states and territories that do not comply with FATF recommendations, offshore zones, states with increased terrorist activity); the presence of non-resident clients; the presence of clients from regions of concern (states with a high level of corruption, terrorism, and threats); and the implementation of transnational or cross-border movement of funds.

The list of factors can be expanded. Uncertainty caused by a lack of information increases the grade to high. The ML/TF vulnerability assessment scale is described in Table 2.

For ML/TF-related risks to exist, a threat and vulnerability must necessarily be present. The correlation of threats and vulnerabilities determines the degree of ML/TF risk (Table 3).

Table 2. Description of the ML/TF vulnerability assessment scale.

Scale	Description
Low degree (1)	In the analyzed area of activity, there are effective deterrence and control mechanisms for conducting ML/TF. An analysis of this area of activity indicates an effective organizational structure and a low degree of ML/TF exposure.
Medium degree (2)	In the analyzed area of activity, there are partially effective deterrence and control mechanisms for combating ML/TF. An analysis of this area of activity indicates a partially effective organizational structure and an average degree of ML/TF exposure.
High degree (3)	In the area of activity under review, there are very limited or no deterrence and control mechanisms for combating ML or TF. An analysis of this area of activity indicates an inefficient organizational structure and a high degree of ML/TF exposure.

Table 3. Correlation of threats and vulnerabilities for ML/TF risk assessment.

Threat	High degree	(2)	(3)	(3)
	Medium degree	(2)	(2)	(3)
	Low degree	(1)	(2)	(2)
	Risk	Low degree	Medium degree Vulnerability	High degree

Table 4. Combinations of threats and vulnerabilities.

Degree of threat	**Degree of vulnerability**	**Degree of risk (final assessment)**
1	2	3
High	High	High
High	Medium	High
High	Low	Medium
Medium	High	High
Medium	Medium	Medium
Medium	Low	Medium
Low	High	Medium
Low	Medium	Medium
Low	Low	Low
0	High	0
0	Medium	0
0	Low	0
High	0	0
Medium	0	0
Low	0	0

The risk level is determined by calculating an average of the threat and vulnerability values, weighted toward the higher of the two. For instance:

If the values are (1) and (3), the risk is evaluated as (2).

If the values are (2) and (3), the risk is evaluated as (3). Possible combinations of threats and vulnerabilities are shown in Table 4.

An interdepartmental commission under the Council of Ministers of the Republic of Belarus is established to conduct the NRA. The secretariat prepares a consolidated ML/TF threat assessment report, a final NRA report, proposals for communicating it to relevant government agencies and stakeholders, and proposals for limiting (reducing) ML/TF threats and risks.

The main regulated sectors for NRA purposes are as follows:

- financial sector (banking; stock exchange activities; operations with securities; insurance activities; trading in precious metals and

precious stones; activities on the over-the-counter Forex market; activities on leasing and microfinance organizations; and activities on postal operators);
- legal services sector (notarial activities, advocacy, activities of organizations providing real estate services, and activities of individual entrepreneurs and organizations providing legal services);
- real estate sector;
- gambling, lotteries, and electronic interactive games;
- others (commodity exchanges, auditors, accountants, and non-profit organizations sector).

By the decision of the Council, the final report on the NRA is brought to the attention of the relevant state bodies and interested persons. Based on the final NRA report, a national plan is developed to limit (reduce) the identified ML/TF risks. Based on the methodology of conducting ML/CFT regulations and on the basis of statistical data on the banking sector, an assessment of ML/CFT risks in the banking sector of the Republic of Belarus was carried out.

The first stage of risk assessment focused on information collection. The source of information was internal data of the National Bank of the Republic of Belarus, which includes a set of statistical tables filled in by banks, including a wide range of quantitative indicators for the period from one to four years, and a questionnaire for a qualitative assessment of the functioning of the AML/CFT system in banks.

To create an effective national AML/CFT system, the National Bank has developed requirements for the internal control rules of banks, leasing and microfinance organizations, forex companies, and the National Forex Center, as well as recommendations on risk management in this area. These requirements are developed by the Financial Monitoring Methodology Department of the Main Banking Supervision Department. In particular, this department monitors financial institutions in the field of AML/CFT on the basis of their reports.

To summarize information on the state of the banking sector and supervisory activities, a set of statistical tables has been compiled, which will be presented in the following. The tables also contain quantitative indicators designed to reflect the scale and nature of the banking sector's activities; the financial products and services offered, including high-risk ones; and various restrictions imposed by

Table 5. Information on the size of the banking sector of the Republic of Belarus.

Indicators	Year			
	2020	**2021**	**2022**	**2023**
Registered banks, units, including	31	30	29	27
Active	31	26	24	24
In bankruptcy and/or liquidation	0	4	5	3
Registered NCFO, units	0	1	3	3
JSC Development Bank of the Republic of Belarus, units	1	1	1	1
Representative offices of foreign banks, units	7	5	5	4

Table 6. Coverage of the population with the services of banking sector organizations.

Indicators	Year			
	2020	**2021**	**2022**	**2023**
Population, thousand people	9481	9498	9505	9476
Number of bank divisions, units	4734	4215	3714	3650
Number of structural divisions of banks per 10 thousand people	5.0	4.4	3.9	3.8

the body conducting criminal proceedings on clients' funds and other property.

The banking sector of the Republic of Belarus, as of 01.01.2023, is represented by 27 banks (24 operating, 3 are in bankruptcy and/or liquidation), 3 non-bank credit and financial organizations, JSC "Development Bank of the Republic of Belarus", and 4 representative offices of foreign banks (Table 5).

As of 01.01.2023, the banking sector is represented by 3650 structural divisions of banks, the density of which per capita is 3.8 structural divisions per 10 thousand inhabitants (Table 6).

From Table 6, one can see that there is a reduction in the number of structural divisions of banks, due to the implementation of measures by banks related to the centralization of functions and reducing costs (administrative costs related to maintenance, rental of buildings, salaries of employees, etc.), as well as the introduction of new

Table 7. Dynamics of the number of clients.

Indicators	Year			
	2020	**2021**	**2022**	**2023**
Total number of customers, thousand people	14585.6	15674.8	15660.7	16295.0
Including clients-legal entities, thousand people	235.1	248.3	256.2	263.5
Including non-residents, thousand people	2.2	2.6	2.6	2.6
Clients-individual entrepreneurs, thousand people	209.2	216.6	219.6	228.6
Including non-residents, thousand people	0.05	0.1	0.1	0.05
Clients-individuals (excluding individual entrepreneurs), thousand people	14140.3	15208.3	15183.6	15801.5
Including non-residents, thousand people	105.8	120.2	133.5	150.7
Share of clients-individuals in total, %	96.9	97.0	97.0	97.0

technologies for banking and customer service in the framework of digital transformation (for example, remote service channels). The structure of the banking sector's client base is characterized by a large number of individual clients – 97% of the total number of clients (Table 7).

Table 7 shows that during the period under review, the growth rate of the number of clients in the banking sector increased by 12%, including an increase in the number of non-residents served. This situation is caused by an extensive network of structural divisions and a high level of availability of banking services, in particular, the development of remote customer service (Table 8).

Table 8 shows that the total volume of clients-legal entities and individual entrepreneurs is more than 490 thousand (3%), of which 195.9 thousand (39.8%) use the Client-Bank remote service system, and 177.7 thousand (36.1%) use Internet banking. Individuals mostly use Internet banking at 37%, mobile banking is preferred by only 15% of individual customers, and 48% do not use remote service channels at all.

Table 8. Dynamics of customers' use of remote service channels.

Year	Number of Clients-Legal Entities, Pers	Client-Bank, Pers	Internet Banking, Pers
2021	280000	219000	72000
2022	456221	206311	111420
2023	479270	195933	177763
Year	**Number of Clients-Individuals, Pers**	**Internet Banking, Pers**	**Mobile Banking, Pers**
2021	11365000	2475000	666000
2022	12129737	3414328	1218058
2023	12722135	4759423	1900826

The analysis made it possible to conclude that banks have a high level of understanding of the risks of their involvement in the ML/TF process and the measures that should be taken to reduce these risks. All banks have AML/CFT divisions in their organizational structure. In systemically important banks, the number of AML/CFT divisions ranges from 6 to 21 employees (average – 11 employees). In other banks, the number of special units varies from 1 to 15 employees (average – 5). Banks must inform the National Bank of the appointment of the head of the AML/CFT unit or their deputy. It should be noted that staff turnover among managers of AML/CFT divisions is low. This is due to the lack of new highly qualified personnel in the field of AML/CFT.

Banks have automated/partially automated about 20 signs of suspicion, which is almost half of the available number. Some of the attributes cannot be automated, as they are identified and evaluated during personal contact with the client. Some of the non-automated features require a complex algorithm and are currently under development. There is a constant search for new and improved existing algorithms for automating the detection of suspicious financial transactions.

Banks provide regular training to all employees who participate in the AML/CFT process as part of their job responsibilities. Banks assess the risk of working with a client using a three-vector risk distribution model (risk by client profile, risk by geographical region, and risk by type of operations).

Table 9. Dynamics of the number of clients assigned to a high-risk group.

	Year			
Indicators	**2020**	**2021**	**2022**	**2023**
Individuals, thousand people	1.5	2.4	3.8	3.6
Share in the total number of such clients, %	0.01	0.02	0.03	0.02
Legal entities, thousand people	16.6	16.6 19.8	23.0	23.8
Share in the total number of such clients, %	7.1	8.0	9.0	9.0
Individual entrepreneurs, thousand people	4.2	5.2	4.7	4.6
Share in the total number of such clients, %	2.0	2.4	2.1	2.0

The dynamics of the number of clients assigned to a high-risk group is presented in Table 9.

Analysis of Table 9 shows that, as of 01.01.2023, the number of clients classified by banks as a high-risk group was 32 thousand. The share of such clients in the total number of clients was 0.2% as of the specified date. The share of individual clients classified by banks as a high-risk group in the total number of individual clients averaged 0.02% over the past four years. The share of clients-legal entities classified by banks as a high-risk group in the total number of clients-legal entities ranged from 7 to 9% over the past four years. Individual entrepreneurs classified as a high-risk group accounted for 2% of the total number of clients-individual entrepreneurs (Table 9).

On January 1, 2023, clients classified as high-risk held a total of 9,100 bank accounts and 10 e-wallets. Their financial activity in 2022 included a debit turnover of 269.4 million rubles on these accounts (0.04% of the system-wide total) and e-money transactions totaling 165 rubles.

Clients-legal entities and individual entrepreneurs classified as a high-risk group opened 67.6 thousand bank accounts and 1.6 thousand e-wallets. In 2022, the turnover on debit bank accounts of high-risk customers amounted to 154,589. 1 million rubles (20.6% of the total volume of operations performed by customers), and the amount in operations for the purchase, use, and repayment of electronic money was 67.5 million rubles.

According to the National Bank of the Republic Belarus (2018), the majority of corporate clients and individual entrepreneurs (62%) were engaged in wholesale and retail trade, as well as the repair of cars and motorcycles. Real estate transactions accounted for a smaller share at 4%. Modern international AML/CFT standards require financial institutions to refuse to accept questionable clients, block suspicious financial transactions in a timely manner, freeze funds of terrorists and related persons, and take other active actions.

During 2022, banks refused to allow clients to perform financial transactions in 82 cases, including opening an account in 18 cases, suspended 8 financial transactions, and refused to execute a written financial transaction agreement in 10 cases. Connection of customers to remote banking systems was denied in 19 cases, service using SDBS was suspended in 83 cases, and service using SDBS was terminated in 28 cases. The main reason for these measures is the suspicion that the clients were engaged in false entrepreneurial activities. The majority of banks (80%) executed the right to refuse.

5. Trends and Challenges in ML/TF

The current framework of measures and tools is deemed sufficient to mitigate the risk of banking services being used for money laundering or terrorist financing (ML/TF). These measures include robust customer identification procedures, comprehensive monitoring of financial transactions (including those of terrorists, public officials, and sanctioned individuals), and the bank's contractual right to refuse or terminate services. The latter includes refusing to connect a client to the SDBS, suspending SDBS services, or terminating a current account agreement.

However, the banks' indecisiveness in applying enhanced internal control measures to the client in the form of refusing to perform a suspicious financial transaction can be noted as a lack of banks' ML/TF risk management. Analysis of banks' reporting on financial transactions subject to special control for 2022 shows that the most risky from the point of view of banks are the following:

- products and services related to the use of cash (47.39% of all special forms submitted by banks);

- international transfers, when the counterparty is registered or located in an offshore zone, or the recipient's account is opened in a country other than the country of registration, as well as operations with loans (48.75% of the total volume of suspicious transactions).

A survey of banks conducted during the assessment showed that an increased risk of bank involvement in ML/TF was noted when providing individuals with the following products and services:

- purchase and sale of foreign currency in cash for cash payment;
- incoming and outgoing bank transfers without opening an account;
- money transfers via money transfer systems;
- operations on debit bank payment cards: internet acquiring, payment using bank payment card details at the point of sale (mobile order/telephone order), and refund of funds for goods (works, services) to the bank payment card at the point of sale;
- operations with electronic money: spending operations on an electronic wallet or prepaid gift cards;
- transactions with non-deliverable financial instruments;
- purchase and sale of precious metals in the form of measured ingots.

Taking into account the facts revealed by banks that customers (legal entities and individual entrepreneurs) use banking products for ML/CFT purposes, transactions involving opening and maintaining bank accounts, performing settlement and cash services and currency exchange operations increase the risk of involving the bank in the ML/CFT process.

At the same time, at the stage of signing contracts, banks are not always able to clearly identify individuals who use banks to store criminal proceeds. Analysis of the information provided in the decisions on the seizure of funds and seizure of documents shows that the most common predicate crimes for banking sector clients are tax evasion, embezzlement by abuse of official authority, and fraud. False entrepreneurship and illegal business activities were less common. Legal entities (Table 10), whose funds were subject to restrictions, most often carried out activities in construction, wholesale and retail trade, and transport sectors.

Table 10. Number of measures taken by judicial and law enforcement agencies conducting criminal proceedings to impose restrictions on cash and other property of bank clients in 2022.

Clients	Resolution on Arrest (Restriction) Related to Articles of the Criminal	Code Resolution on Seizure of Documents	Resolution on Foreclosure
Individuals	2309	601	907
Legal entities	199	317	0
Individual entrepreneurs	56	43	0

These clients had full access to banking services, including cash management, loans, deposits, currency exchange, and electronic money, primarily through remote channels. The heavy reliance on these remote systems for corporate settlement services heightens the bank's exposure to money laundering and terrorist financing (ML/FT) risks, as such platforms could be exploited by unauthorized parties.

Analysis of the banking sector's client base structure is characterized by an increase in the number of clients belonging to the category of public officials, as well as an increase in turnover on their bank accounts. As of 01.01.2023, the share of clients belonging to the personal income tax category was 0.01% of the total number of individual clients and the volume of transactions performed by them was 0.02% of the total volume of debit bank accounts performed by bank clients in 2022.

There is also an increase in the number of clients-organizations whose beneficial owners are persons classified as public officials and the volume of transactions performed by such organizations. As of 01.01.2023, the share of organizations whose beneficial owners were persons classified as personal income tax amounted to 0.1% of the total number of clients-legal entities, and the volume of transactions performed by them was 1.2% of the total volume of bank account debit operations performed by clients in 2022.

This trend can be explained by the improvement of procedures for identifying individuals classified as public officials by banks. The procedure for identifying family members of public officials and persons close to them is determined by the banks themselves. Currently, banks programmatically check information about customers and their beneficial owners in order to assign them to public officials. Data sources for identifying public officials, their family members, and individuals close to public officials are, among other things, commercial databases provided by Thomson Reuters, Accuity, Dow Jones, and open sources of information.

To identify organizations and individuals involved in terrorist activities, banks use software that allows them to automatically detect and block a financial transaction before it is carried out, as well as identify customers whose funds are subject to freezing. Banks receive the list of persons involved in terrorist activities through the information search systems, which contain structured information that is convenient for automatic processing.

Banks must inform the FMD about each fact of freezing funds and/or blocking a financial transaction by submitting a special form. The period of freezing funds is indefinite — until the moment of defrosting. During the period from 2020 to 2022, there were no cases of freezing funds of persons involved in terrorist activities or blocking financial transactions carried out by them.

An analysis of the banking sector's correspondent relationships from 2020 to 2023 (Table 11) reveals a steady decline in the share of non-resident banks, which fell from 67.9% to 46.1% of all correspondent banks for Belarusian institutions.

A similar trend can be seen when analyzing the number of LORO accounts opened in the banking sector for non-resident banks. Their share in the total number of opened LORO accounts decreased from 43.4% to 35.4% over the specified period. At the same time, the share of cash balances on the LORO accounts of non-resident banks in the cash balances on all LORO accounts is gradually increasing, but its size as of 01.01.2023 did not exceed 18%.

In order to study the phenomenon of "de-risking" in relation to banks of the Republic of Belarus, a survey of banks on the reasons for the termination of interbank correspondent agreements (contracts) at the initiative of non-resident banks (closing NOSTRO accounts) was conducted.

Table 11. Information on correspondent relations.

Indicators	Year 2020	2021	2022	2023
Number of correspondent banks with LORO and/or NOSTRO	1069	1461	1431	1416
Including non-residents	726	711	682	653
Share of non-resident banks in the total number of correspondent banks, %	67.9	48.7	47.7	46.1
Number of opened LORO accounts	1086	997	969	1020
Including non-resident banks	471	418	350	361
Share of LORO accounts of non-resident banks in the total number of LORO accounts, %	43.4	41.9	36.1	35.4
Cash balance on LORO accounts, BYN	359 million	866.2	596.7	871.2
Including accounts of non-resident banks, BYN	33 million	31.5	71.0	153.7
Share of cash balances on LORO bank accounts non-residents in cash balances on LORO accounts, %	9.4	3.6	11.9	17.6
Number of correspondent banks classified by banks as high risk	101	124	133	97
Including non-resident banks	78	106	119	82
Share of correspondent banks classified as high risk in the total number of correspondent banks, %	9.4	8.5	9.3	6.9

Changes in the regional policy and optimization of the correspondent network are cited as the reasons for the termination of correspondent relations. The following is an example of solving the problem with payments to China by Bank R. The problem received significant media coverage when AML compliance services within the AliPay payment system restricted payments for AliExpress purchases. This action was taken in response to directives from the Hong Kong Monetary Authority. The ban was based on unreasonably negative information about Bank R posted in the Dow Jones database. This database is widely used by national regulators and large trading companies in the Southeast Asian region (in countries such as China, the Philippines, and Malaysia).

Following a lengthy correspondence (September – November 2017), Dow Jones changed the bank's risk profile from "sanctioned" to "positive". This was done without entering the AML compliance services of the Chinese public company Alibaba Group. According to Bank R, changes in the bank's profile in the Dow Jones database have had a positive impact on the regulatory databases of the national regulator of the Philippines and regulators who use Dow Jones in other countries in the region.

The survey conducted in the course of this assessment showed that banks also note an increased risk of involvement in ML/TF when making payments on behalf of and in favor of customers of counterparty banks ("transit payments"). The survey showed that banks have an increased risk of being involved in the ML/TF process when their clients make international money transfers. This primarily applies to transfers to offshore zones, transfers to customer counterparty accounts opened in a country other than the counterparty's country of registration, transfers through payment systems, and transfers without opening bank accounts.

From 2020 to 2023, cash in circulation increased by over 68%. This growth is reflected in its rising share of the money supply, which expanded by 1.7% of the M3 aggregate and 9% of the M2 (ruble) aggregate, as shown in Table 12.

In general, the indicators in Table 12 show that cash is not decreasing in importance, and the growth in its volume is comparable to the growth in the total money supply in the country. Growth was also observed in this period (Table 12):

- The total volume of banking operations performed by customers with cash in bank cash desks increased by 55%.
- The total volume of banking operations performed by customers in self-service devices increased by 27%.
- The average amount of a bank transaction with cash increased by 143%.

•

Table 12. Information on financial transactions with cash.

Indicators	Year			
	2020	**2021**	**2022**	**2023**
Total volume of banking operations performed by customers with cash, excluding those performed in self-service devices, RUB	267 billion, 7	320.7	361.1	415.6
Total volume of banking operations performed by customers in self-service devices, RUB	19 billion, 6	21.1	22.6	24.9
Average amount of banking operations with cash, thousand RUB	0, 7	0.9	1.2	1.7

Banks identified the following client cash transactions as posing an elevated ML/TF risk:

- cash contribution to the legal entity's account that is not related to revenue acceptance;
- cash withdrawal from the accounts of clients who are legal entities, which is not related to the payment of wages, pensions, allowances, or cash settlements between legal entities;
- transfer of funds to current (settlement) bank accounts, access to which is provided by means of a bank payment card of legal entities and individual entrepreneurs.

6. Development Issues

Active development of the technological and innovative components of banking products and services, designed to increase operational efficiency and expand access to financial services with comfort for customers, can make banks more vulnerable to use for criminal purposes.

In the Republic of Belarus, ML/TF risks associated with electronic money are currently minimized due to the mandatory identification of persons who open electronic wallets, regardless of the size of the amounts of electronic money listed in them.

After the entry into force of the Decree of the President of the Republic of Belarus No. 6 dated 28.12.2014, "On urgent measures to counteract illegal drug trafficking", which introduced this norm, the number of electronic wallets and the volume of transactions with electronic money significantly decreased.

One should pay attention to prepaid cards, which, being a type of electronic money, do not carry a high risk of being used for ML/TF purposes, since they are not widely used in the Republic of Belarus. Prepaid cards include bonus cards and gift certificates of suppliers of goods (services) that are issued for small amounts of money and are used within the same legal entity or in a limited and strictly defined area.

At the same time, there is a possibility that criminals of foreign prepaid gift cards may use single-issue (closed) systems to realize income received using "hacked" credit cards. The presence of cards of multi-issuer (open) systems supplied from abroad, which can be replenished remotely and from which you can withdraw money remotely, also poses a risk.

Currently, the use of virtual currencies is restricted or unregulated in most countries. This is due to a number of factors, such as a lack of awareness and understanding of the nature of virtual currencies on the part of the general public. Legal uncertainty at the global level leads to the development of a black market for virtual currencies and, as a result, an increase in their share in criminal transactions.

The adoption of the Presidential Decree "On the Development of the Digital Economy" on December 21, 2017, established the regulatory framework for such operations. Subsequently, the National Bank amended banks' internal control rules to incorporate specific AML/CFT requirements based on this decree. Banks are required to detect suspicious financial transactions related to sending or receiving funds in bank accounts for digital tokens (tokens) being purchased and/or disposed of. At the same time, there are no examples of the use of virtual currencies for money laundering and/or terrorist financing in the National Bank and banking sector during the analyzed period.

The risks posed by virtual currencies include the following:

- insufficient understanding of the scope and methods of using digital tokens for money laundering purposes;
- the emergence of virtual currencies and the legal uncertainty in their functioning contribute to the realization of the risk of illegal trade — a series of illegal actions, such as illegal movement of funds, tax evasion, drug trafficking and human trafficking, production and distribution of counterfeit products, as well as organized crime — factors that undermine social interaction, regional and international cooperation, and also the growth of the global economy.

Mobile payments are becoming the foundation of the digital economy in the world. At the same time, in order to be sure of the security of devices for their implementation, buyers of goods and users of services must trust both the supplier of goods and services and the payment service provider running the mobile service.

Contactless technologies and payment services based on modern innovative solutions are being developed in the Republic of Belarus. The National Bank and the banking sector have no examples of the use of mobile technologies for ML/TF purposes. However, there is concern and understanding of the risks associated with their possible use for these purposes.

The vulnerability of mobile technologies lies in the possibility of using mobile devices by third parties without identifying them. In 2018, the National Bank conducted 8 inspections of banks, all of which revealed violations of AML/CFT legislation (2698 cases). The main violations were non-compliance with the established procedure for registration of identity documents of individuals purchasing foreign currency; failure to submit/untimely submission of special forms to the financial monitoring body; incorrect filling in of special forms; non-compliance with provisions of legal acts with legal requirements; and violation of the established procedure for customer questionnaires.

Some banks have revealed violations of the established procedure for customer surveys. The reason for the violations was the lack of proper distribution of job responsibilities, non-compliance with internal control procedures by the bank's employees, and insufficient automation of the survey processes (incorrect unloading of information from various software modules, lack of relationships, lack of change history, failure to enter, or untimely entry of data in the questionnaire).

During the monitoring of one of the banks, a bank inspection uncovered instances where individuals received dividends totaling up to 80% of the annual transaction volume on the accounts of their related legal entities. In carrying out these operations, the facts of cash withdrawal are seen. Based on the monitoring results, the criteria for detecting and identifying suspicious financial transactions approved by the National Bank were supplemented with a new sign of suspicion.

The inspections revealed the following violations of the AML/CFT legislation:

- failure to notify the National Bank of the establishment in the internal control rules of the bank of additional factors that increase (decrease) the ML/TF risk of working with clients;
- applying the wrong approach when establishing the analyzed period for detecting suspicious financial transactions (when defining the average analyzed period equal to one month in the internal control rules, the responsible officials of the bank established an unreasonably large analyzed period, which ranged from 3 to 6 months to 1 year 3 months, which resulted in late detection of financial transactions subject to special control);
- non-compliance with the training requirements for bank employees who carry out financial transactions (scheduled and unscheduled instructions on preventing the legalization of proceeds from crime were not conducted with cash register specialists);
- the electronic database of customer profiles did not meet the requirements (it was not possible to view changes in the fields of customer profiles).

Based on these, it should be noted that the National Bank, as a supervisory authority, has sufficient mechanisms for monitoring banks. Thus, based on the reports, the bank's involvement in suspicious transactions is analyzed, inspections are planned and carried out, and a wide range of response measures is applied to banks — from recommendations and regulations to fines and restrictions on licensing authority.

Consequently, the degree of vulnerability in the banking sector is assessed as low. However, the information provided by law enforcement agencies when assessing threats indicates that there are repeated attempts to use the banking sector in ML schemes. Therefore, the risk of using the banking sector in ML schemes is estimated as medium and in FT schemes it is estimated as low.

Taking into account the information provided, the following high-risk areas of use by criminals of the banking sector for obtaining and/or legalizing criminal proceeds were identified:

- use of money transfer systems to make transfers without opening an account;
- theft of funds from bank payment cards;
- refund of funds for goods (works, services) to the bank payment card at the point of sale;
- receiving cross-border money transfers as loans, including interest-free ones, and replenishment of own funds;
- the client performs transactions with cash, including currency exchange, in large amounts;
- use of new banking products based on information technologies;
- execution of payments on behalf of and for the benefit of clients of counterparty banks (so-called "transit payments");
- use of securities (bonds) to commit tax and corruption crimes.

During the ML/CFT risk assessment in the banking sector of the Republic of Belarus, vulnerabilities and risks of the AML/CFT system were identified, and measures were proposed to reduce them.

Vulnerability 1

There is insufficient awareness of banks about the effectiveness of their AML/CFT measures. The threat level of this phenomenon is estimated as very high. Without confirmation from the financial monitoring body on its submitted suspicions, the bank cannot gauge the efficacy of its AML/CFT actions. This absence of feedback hinders the development of a more informed, risk-based approach. Therefore, it does not contribute to understanding ML/TF risks and creating an adequate environment for detecting suspicious financial transactions of clients.

The degree of vulnerability is assessed as medium. Insufficient awareness does not facilitate the application of extended internal control measures by banks, including in the form of refusing to allow the client to perform a suspicious financial transaction. Banks prefer to submit a special form to the FMT about conducting a suspicious transaction, rather than exercising their right to refuse.

We consider it necessary for the State Control Committee, law enforcement, and judicial authorities to consider developing a feedback system that allows banks to quickly inform them about the measures taken using the special forms submitted. This can be achieved by automating the decision-making process in real time using the submitted special forms. Modernization of software products will reduce the time lag to several hours, while today the time for transmitting and making a decision is at least 3 days.

Similar projects are being implemented in other countries. The Australian financial intelligence unit Austrak (Australian Transaction Reports and Analysis Center) is implementing a project of operational interaction with banks, Fintel Alliance (Fintel Alliance), which includes, in addition to banks and money transfer systems Western Union and Pay Pal, the federal police and the tax service. In addition to the operational component, Fintel Alliance works on innovations in the field of AML/CFT and risk management of new financial technologies (blockchain, cryptocurrencies).

In the UK, a similar project is being implemented, but with a greater emphasis on the law enforcement component of the Jimlet project (JMLIT), organized on the initiative of the National Criminal Agency, bringing together representatives of major banks, the British Banking Association, regulatory authorities, and representatives of the scientific community. Jimlet's work is based on the model of expert groups, each of which works on a specific topic, such as the fight against corruption. Participating banks are provided with expanded access to information accumulated by financial intelligence, while participants are obliged not to disclose confidential information.

The creation of the Compliance Council will help bring together representatives of financial institutions and so-called established non-financial businesses and professions. In addition to sharing information about new risks and developing criteria for suspicious transactions, the Compliance Council should also work on improving

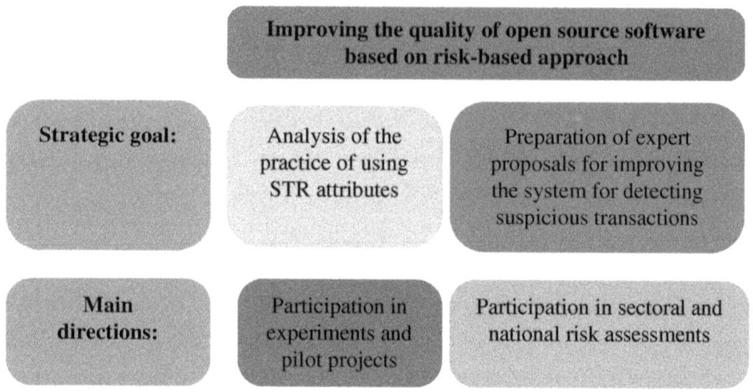

Fig. 1. Main activities and strategic goals of the Compliance Council.

reports of suspicious financial transactions and information exchange. This kind of targeted interaction with organizations that essentially generate the bulk of information will allow one to influence the quality parameters of the information flow.

One of the priorities of the Compliance Council should be the development of criteria and models for the financial behavior of criminals in order to improve the efficiency and speed of identifying transactions involving relevant risks. The main activities and strategic objectives of the Compliance Council are shown in Fig. 1.

What will the Compliance Council do?

For the AML/CFT system as a whole:

- improving the efficiency of information exchange on new ML/TF risks;
- achieving a uniform understanding of ML/TF risks;
- constant feedback regarding the incoming information flow;
- expert development of innovations.

For financial institutions:

- exchange of best practices;
- an opportunity to communicate their proposals for the development of the system to government agencies;
- gain new knowledge about best practices and the experience of organizations, implementation of internal control;
- get up-to-date information about the initiatives of the FATF and other international organizations.

The National Bank and all banks should continue to regularly review the effectiveness of their work in the AML/CFT area: analyzing data on submitted special forms and the ratio of banks' "involvement in suspicious transactions; conducting self-assessments of banks" AML/CFT systems; and studying and implementing best practices and international experience.

An important part of these improvements is the modernization of information systems, the use of machine learning, which can significantly increase the effectiveness of ongoing activities, as well as free up human resources for more complex analytical tasks.

Vulnerability 2

There is insufficient understanding of ML/TF risks when introducing new banking products based on information technologies. The threat level is high. The risk of penetration of money obtained by criminal means into the banking system may be associated with the possibility of using new banking products, especially at the initial stage of their implementation, through remote communication channels by criminals and their accomplices (for example, the use of virtual currencies/crypto assets in settlements).

The degree of vulnerability is medium. Given the good level of training of bank employees and the availability of effective AML/CFT internal control systems in most banks, the probability level of realization of this risk should be considered high. The National Bank has provided banks with recommendations on identifying and assessing the risk of a banking service (product). The overall risk level is estimated as average.

Recommended measures: Banks should assign a high ML/TF risk to new banking products related to information technologies, distribute them through remote sales channels, and pay special attention to their use.

Vulnerability 3

The effectiveness of internal control procedures for detecting suspicious financial transactions by banks is insufficient. The threat level is medium. Inspections at individual banks reveal instances of employees' non-compliance with the legislation and local procedures that establish requirements for the organization of internal AML/CFT control. These violations are not of a systemic nature in banks, but their presence requires bank managers to exercise increased control over their employees' strict compliance with AML/CFT procedures.

The overall risk level is estimated as average, reflecting a moderate degree of vulnerability. This vulnerability is mitigated by the National Bank's robust oversight, which includes effective onsite and remote monitoring, as well as regular analysis of bank performance indicators such as the coefficient of involvement in suspicious transactions.

7. Recommended Measures

Banks should ensure the effectiveness of internal control procedures for detecting suspicious financial transactions, and banks should exercise the right to refuse to conduct suspicious transactions. Also, among the measures to reduce the identified risks, we recommend that the National Bank do the following:

- ensure control over the documentation of banks' risk assessments;
- take measures to create (develop) information systems in order to ensure that persons engaged in financial transactions comply with AML/CFT requirements;
- establish requirements for controlled entities to assess the risks of new products and services in the implementation and use of modern information technologies for financial transactions;
- organize training events on AML/CFT issues for individuals engaged in financial transactions.

8. Conclusion

The essence of the presented methodology is to provide a preventive option for minimizing financial risks and streamlining the system of control over financial flows, in which banks mostly act as direct intermediaries. This approach to the DC definition will help to determine the extent to which a particular credit institution fulfills regulatory and internal requirements and will also help to correct the shortcomings of a bank's internal control systems in the area of AML/CFT.

The principles for conducting the national ML/CFT risk assessment have been refined as part of broader AML/CFT improvements.

These principles — which also apply to individual economic sectors — stress coordinated goals, comprehensive scope, political commitment, inter-agency collaboration, a central coordinating body, system flexibility, the use of mixed-method data, and full documentation. A risk assessment conducted within the banking sector under this framework successfully identified systemic vulnerabilities, evaluated potential ML/TF threats, and produced concrete recommendations for their prevention and mitigation.

The ML/TF risk assessment conducted in the banking sector allowed one to identify vulnerabilities, assess potential ML/TF risks for the banking sector, and offer recommendations for prevention and/or mitigation.

References

Bank of Russia. (2017). *On Assessing the Economic Situation of Banks*: Decree of the Bank of Russia, April 3, 2017, No. 4336-U.

Chikhanchina, Yu. A. (2018). *Financial Monitoring: Textbook for Undergraduate and Graduate Studies: Volume 1*. Justitsinform.

Financial Action Task Force. (2020). *International Standards on Combating Money Laundering and the Financing of Terrorism & Proliferation*. https://www.fatf-gafi.org/media/fatf/documents/recommendations/pdfs/FATF%20Recommendations%2020.pdf.

International Monetary Fund. (2018). IMF and the Fight Against Money Laundering and the Financing of Terrorism. https://www.imf.org/external/pubs/ft/ar/2018/eng/assets/pdf/imf-annual-report-2018-ru.pdf.

Medina, L. (2018). *Shadow Economies Around the World: What Did We Learn Over the Last 20 Years?* https://www.imf.org/en/publications/wp/issues/2018/01/25/shadoweconomies-around-the-world-what-did-we-learn-over-the-last-20-years-45583.

National Bank of the Republic Belarus. (2006). *On Approval of the Instruction on Safe Operating Standards for Banks, Open Joint-Stock Company "Development Bank of the Republic of Belarus" and Non-Banking Financial Institutions*: *Regulation*. Board of the National Bank of the Republic Belarus, September 28, 2006, No. 137.

National Bank of the Republic Belarus. (2018). *Main Trends in the Economy and Monetary Sector of the Republic of Belarus: Analytical Review for 2018*. https://www.nbrb.by/publications/EcTendencies/rep_2018_12_ot.pdf.

National Bank of the Republic Belarus. (2022a). *Methodology for Conducting a National Assessment of the Risks of Legalization (Laundering) of*

Proceeds from Crime and the Financing of Terrorist Activities: Project National.

National Bank of the Republic Belarus. (2022b). *Brief Results of the National Assessment of the Risks of Legalization (Laundering) of Proceeds from Crime and the Financing of Terrorist Activities.* https://nbrb.by/legislation/documents/Itogi-nacionalnoj-ocenki-riskov-legalizacii-dohodov.pdf.

Shamanina, E. I. (2016). *Combating the Legalization of Illegal Income in the Banking System of the Russian Federation.* Ph.D. dissertation, Russian State University.

The Bank for International Settlements. (2019). Implementation of the Basel Standards. https://www.bis.org/bcbs/implementation.htm?m=3%7C14%7C656.

https://doi.org/10.1142/9789819823161_0009

Chapter 9

Data Envelopment Analysis in the Financial Services Industry

Alireza Amirteimoori[*,‡] **and Maryam Nematizadeh**[†,§]

[*]*Faculty of Engineering and Natural Sciences, Istinye University, Istanbul, Turkey*

[†]*Department of Mathematics, National University of Skills (NUS), Rasht, Iran*

[‡]*alireza.amirteimoori@istinye.edu.tr*

[§]*maryam.nematizadeh@yahoo.com*

The performance of firms, both now and in the future, is crucial. This requires optimizing resources, managing their use effectively, and adopting strategies to achieve better outcomes. Understanding the relationship between a firm's performance and its resources, production, and managerial skills is essential, as it offers key insights for improving future outcomes. The Managerial Ability Index (MA), which measures how efficiently managers use company resources to generate output, plays a vital role here. Highly capable managers can allocate resources more effectively, outperform competitors, and enhance work quality, even when the impact of their knowledge and skills is not easily measurable. This study introduces a comprehensive two-step methodology that combines non-parametric and parametric approaches. The first step involves calculating technical efficiency using Data Envelopment Analysis (DEA), a non-parametric method. The second step estimates managerial ability through the parametric approach of Ordinary Least Squares (OLS). To provide a thorough analysis, the study examines the performance of Asian banks from 2014 to 2020. The findings show that Total Capital

Adequacy (TCA), the Non-Performing Loans Ratio (NPLR), and Total Assets (TA) significantly impact bank efficiency, with NPLR being the most influential factor among these variables.

Keywords: Data envelopment analysis, technical efficiency, regression, managerial ability, contextual variables.

1. Introduction

The banking industry plays a crucial role in the economic growth and development of nations. In many Asian countries, where financial systems are predominantly bank-centered, banks are key drivers of economic progress. However, in today's highly competitive landscape, banks face numerous challenges and risks that demand strong leadership and effective managerial competence. In this environment, banks led by capable managers are more likely to outperform their competitors. Consequently, developing reliable tools to assess managerial ability (MA) and identify both strengths and weaknesses is essential.

Managerial ability has increasingly been recognized as a key factor influencing firm performance, efficiency, and long-term success. High managerial ability enables firms to better navigate competitive markets, optimize resource utilization, and achieve higher levels of profitability and productivity. Early research by Murthi *et al.* (1996) explored how both observed and unobserved managerial abilities affect market share, demonstrating that firms led by skilled managers are better positioned to capitalize on first-mover advantages. Similarly, Bertrand and Schoar (2003) explored the influence of managerial style on firm policies, showing that individual managers play a crucial role in shaping financial, operational, and investment strategies. Their work demonstrated that managerial decision-making extends beyond short-term profitability to influence broader corporate policies and long-term performance. Building on this, Leverty and Grace (2012) investigated how managerial ability affects firm distress, distinguishing between the effects of management incompetence and external factors. They found that firms with less competent managers were more prone to financial difficulties, while those led by skilled managers were better equipped to navigate such challenges, emphasizing the crucial role of managerial competence in mitigating risks and ensuring firm survival during financial instability.

A key development in measuring managerial ability was the introduction of a two-stage Data Envelopment Analysis (DEA) method by Demerjian *et al.* (2012). This approach accounts for external factors influencing firm performance and establishes a strong positive correlation between managerial ability and profitability, suggesting that firms led by more skilled managers tend to achieve higher efficiency and performance. Subsequent studies by Demerjian *et al.* (2013, 2021) further reinforced these findings, highlighting the critical role of managerial expertise in improving firm outcomes and differentiating managerial performance from broader systemic influences. Building on this foundation, Banker and Natarajan (2008) refined DEA-based measures of managerial ability, addressing some of the earlier model's limitations. Later, Banker *et al.* (2019) advanced these techniques by reducing Type I error rates and incorporating a more comprehensive set of contextual variables, thereby enhancing the accuracy of managerial ability assessments across industries. In 2021, Banker and Park extended the framework into a three-stage process: first estimating firm efficiency, then adjusting for contextual factors, and finally analyzing managerial ability within regression models, while also addressing critical assumptions in the process.

Building on this framework, numerous studies have explored managerial ability across various sectors and countries. For example, Chang *et al.* (2018) assessed managerial ability in Japan using DEA, emphasizing how cultural and economic factors influence firm performance. Guan *et al.* (2018) examined the impact of managerial ability on dividend policy sensitivity to shareholder taxes, finding that more skilled managers optimize tax-efficient dividend strategies. Baik *et al.* (2020) studied the link between managerial ability and income smoothing, revealing that highly capable managers are more likely to use income smoothing to reduce earnings volatility, enhancing long-term firm stability. Chen *et al.* (2021) explored how managerial ability improves internal control and investment efficiency, underscoring its role in optimizing resource allocation.

Further, Banker *et al.* (2022a, 2022b, 2022c, 2024) investigated managerial ability in the general insurance markets of India and Iran, concluding that higher managerial efficiency significantly enhances sectoral outcomes. Kumar and Zbib (2022) highlighted how firms with superior managerial ability successfully navigated pandemic challenges, ensuring operational continuity. Similarly, Amirteimoori *et al.* (2023) explored productivity growth in the European forest sector, emphasizing the critical role of managerial skills in driving long-term productivity. The application of managerial ability has gained traction in the health sector as well. Amirteimoori *et al.* (2024a) used DEA to evaluate health sector performance, finding that managerial ability is essential for optimizing health services and resource utilization.

Managerial ability has also been explored in sectors with undesirable outputs, such as power plants and environmentally sensitive industries. Amirteimoori *et al.* (2024b) developed a DEA model to assess power plant efficiency, demonstrating that managerial ability is crucial in minimizing undesirable outputs while maintaining production.

A growing body of research has applied the DEA technique to evaluate bank performance, with significant contributions from scholars such as Seiford and Zhu (1999), Fukuyama and Weber (2009), Banker *et al.* (2010), Asmild and Matthews (2013), Wang *et al.* (2014), Zha *et al.* (2016), Chen *et al.* (2018), Zhou *et al.* (2019), Li (2020), Li *et al.* (2022), and Amirteimoori *et al.* (2024c). These studies predominantly focus on assessing bank performance based on resource utilization and output generation, such as assets, loans, and other financial products. However, a key limitation in the existing literature is the insufficient attention given to the role of management capabilities and skills, which are crucial for influencing long-term efficiency, competitiveness, and overall success. Given the strategic importance of the banking sector – particularly in Asian countries – and the identified gaps in the literature, this study aims to evaluate the performance of banks across six Asian nations from 2014 to 2020, focusing on their resource utilization, outputs, and managerial capabilities. To achieve this, the study employs two methodologies: DEA and Ordinary Least Squares (OLS). The conceptual framework for the study is presented in Fig. 1.

The analysis begins by identifying all factors influencing bank performance, including inputs, outputs, and contextual variables (i.e., variables that affect performance but are outside the control

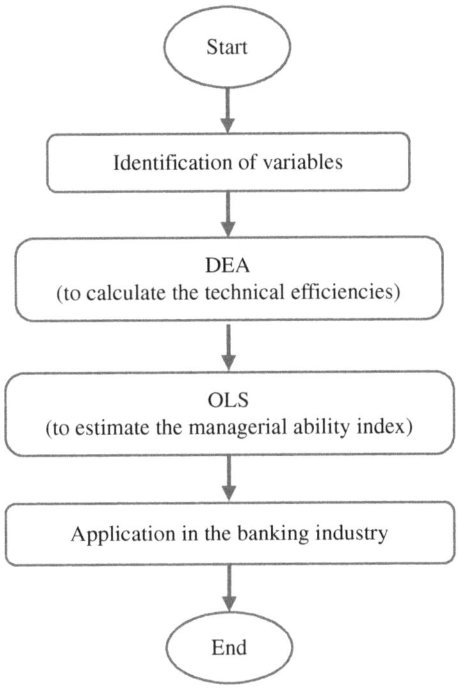

Fig. 1. Conceptual framework.

of the decision-making unit). Subsequently, DEA is used to calculate each bank's efficiency scores based on its inputs and outputs. Finally, the OLS method is applied to estimate the managerial ability index, focusing on the role of management in influencing performance outcomes.

The remainder of the chapter is organized as follows: Section 2 presents the proposed methodology, Section 3 discusses the analysis results of Asian banks, and Section 4 provides the conclusion.

2. Methodology

This section outlines a two-step method for determining the managerial ability index. First, technical efficiencies for each Decision-Making Unit (DMU) are estimated using the DEA technique. Next, a regression model is employed to estimate the managerial ability index.

2.1. *Technical efficiency*

DEA is a highly effective method for evaluating the performance of homogeneous DMUs, initially introduced by Charnes *et al.* (1978) and later enhanced by Banker *et al.* (1984) with the inclusion of the variable returns to scale (VRS) assumption. Unlike parametric methods, DEA does not rely on a predefined production function to describe the relationship between inputs and outputs, reducing the risk of errors from incorrect function assumptions. This flexibility is one of DEA's key strengths. By constructing a Production Possibility Set (PPS), DEA approximates the production function, allowing for the comparison of each unit's efficiency against this reference set and providing a more accurate and adaptable performance evaluation.

Suppose there are H groups, each consisting of J DMUs, with each unit utilizing inputs $x_j^{(h)} = (x_{1j}^{(h)}, \ldots, x_{Ij}^{(h)}) : i = 1, \ldots, I$ to produce outputs $y_j^{(h)} = (y_{1j}^{(h)}, \ldots, y_{Rj}^{(h)}) : r = 1, \ldots, R$. Additionally, assume that each unit within the hth group incorporates contextual variables $z_j^{(h)} = (z_{1j}^{(h)}, \ldots, z_{Sj}^{(h)}) : s = 1, \ldots, S$, as depicted in Fig. 2.

To define the production possibility set $T^h : h = 1, \ldots, H$ for each group, the following four axioms are assumed:

I. Feasibility:
All observations are in the technology set, i.e., $(x, y) \in T^h$.

II. Convexity:
If (x', y') and $(x'', y'') \in T^h$, then $\lambda(x', y') + (1 - \lambda)(x'', y'') \in T^h$ in which $\lambda \in [0, 1]$.

III. Free Disposability:
If $(x, y) \in T^h$, $x' \geq x$, $y' \leq y$, then $(x', y') \in T^h$.

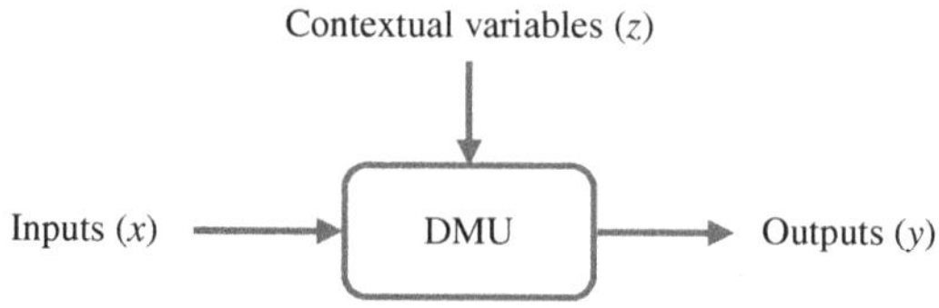

Fig. 2. The structure of each DMU.

IV. Minimal Extrapolation:
T^h represents the minimal technology set that satisfies axioms I–IV.

Based on the four above-mentioned axioms, the algebraic form of the production possibility set T^h under the assumption of variable returns to scale is introduced as follows:

$$T^h = \left\{ (x,y) \middle| \begin{array}{l} \sum_{j=1}^{J} \lambda_j x_{ij} \leq x, \ i = 1, \ldots, I, \\ \sum_{j=1}^{J} \lambda_j y_{rj} \geq y, \ r = 1, \ldots, R, \\ \sum_{j=1}^{J} \lambda_j = 1, \\ \lambda_j \geq 0, \ j = 1, \ldots, J \end{array} \right\}. \tag{1}$$

The meta-frontier technology is defined as $T = \{T^1 \cup T^2 \cup \cdots \cup T^H\}$, representing the union of the technology sets for all groups, as shown in Fig. 3 (see Battese, 2004; O'Donnell, 2008).

According to the meta-frontier technology set T, the technical efficiency score for a specific DMU_o is estimated using the following

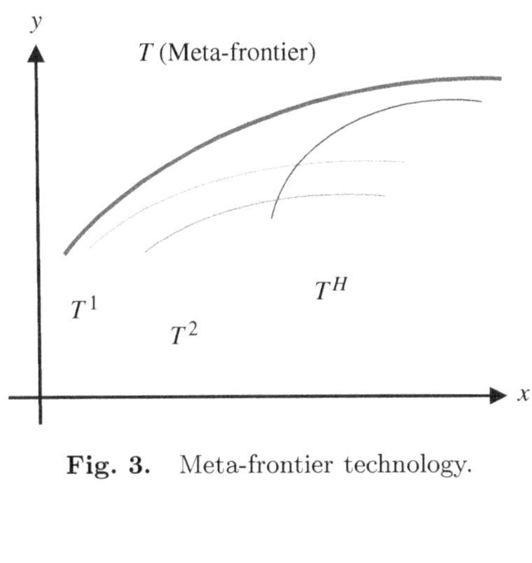

Fig. 3. Meta-frontier technology.

output-oriented BCC model:

$$
\begin{aligned}
\varphi^* = Max \ & \varphi \\
s.t. \ & \sum_{h=1}^{H}\sum_{j=1}^{J} \lambda_j^{(h)} x_{ij}^{(h)} \leq x_{io}^{(h)}, \ i = 1, \ldots, I, \\
& \sum_{h=1}^{H}\sum_{j=1}^{J} \lambda_j^{(h)} y_{rj}^{(h)} \geq \varphi y_{ro}^{(h)}, \ r = 1, \ldots, R, \\
& \sum_{h=1}^{H}\sum_{j=1}^{J} \lambda_j^{(h)} = 1, \\
& \lambda_j^{(h)} \geq 0, \ \forall h, j.
\end{aligned}
\tag{2}
$$

Model (1) is feasible, and the optimal objective function is constrained by a lower bound ($\varphi^* \geq 1$).

Definition 1. The unit under evaluation of DMU_o is technical efficient if and only if $\varphi^* = 1$; otherwise, it is inefficient. This means that DMU_o should increase its output level by a factor of φ^*, while keeping inputs constant.

2.2. *Managerial ability*

To estimate the managerial ability index for each DMU, the following linear regression model can be employed:

$$
Log_{10}(\varphi^*) = \eta_o^{(h)} + \sum_{h=1}^{H}\sum_{s=1}^{S} \eta_s^{(h)} z_{sj}^{(h)} + \varepsilon_j^{(h)}, \quad j = 1, \ldots, J. \tag{3}
$$

In Model (3), $Log_{10}(\varphi^*)$ denotes the base-10 logarithm of the inverse technical efficiency derived from Model (2). The residuals obtained from the regression model ($\varepsilon_j^{(h)}$) are interpreted as the managerial ability index. Additionally, $\eta_o^{(h)}$ represents the intercept term in the model, while the coefficients $\eta_s^{(h)}$ are associated with the contextual variables $z_j^{(h)}$. These coefficients can be either positive or negative, with the sign indicating the nature of the effect: A positive coefficient suggests a direct effect on the performance of the evaluated unit, whereas a negative coefficient indicates an inverse effect.

3. An Application to Asian Banks

This analysis applies our methodology to a sample of banks from several Asian countries, focusing on data from 2014 to 2020. After refining the data to ensure consistency and accuracy, the final sample consists of 39 banks from Bangladesh (BD), 97 from China (CN), 74 from Indonesia (ID), 128 from India (IN), 9 from Malaysia (MY), and 12 from the Philippines (PH), totaling 2,513 banks over the seven-year period.

3.1. *Description of variables and data*

To estimate banks' technical efficiency and managerial ability, we used two output variables, two input variables, and five contextual variables, as outlined in Table 1. These variables were selected because they represent critical components of banking operations, such as costs (inputs), revenue generation (outputs), and key risk and structural factors (contextual variables). To capture the effect of time, a time series dummy variable was included, with a value of 1 for each specific year and 0 otherwise.

The statistical summary of the inputs, outputs, and normalized contextual variables are provided in Table 2.

3.2. *Technical efficiency results*

In the first step, the technical efficiency of all banks was calculated using Model (2), with the results presented in Fig. 3 and Table 3.

Table 1. Input, outputs, and contextual variables.

Type of Variables	Description
Input variables	Interest expense (IE)
	Other operating expenses (OE)
Output variables	Net interest revenue (NIR)
	Operating revenue (OR)
Contextual variables	Total capital adequacy ratio (TCAR)
	Non-performing loan ratio (NPLR)
	Total assets (TA)
	Number of branches (NB)
	Time series dummy (TSD)

Table 2. Statistical description of data.

Year	Statistics Variables	Inputs		Outputs		Contextual Variables			
		IE	OE	NIR	OR	TCAR	NPLR	TA	NB
2014	Min	3.86E + 01	5.68E + 01	5.30E + 02	2.33E + 03	0.00E + 00	0.00E + 00	0.00E + 00	0.00E + 00
	Q1	4.73E + 04	6.77E + 03	3.87E + 04	5.39E + 04	6.34E − 02	2.54E − 02	3.00E − 04	1.60E − 03
	Median	2.06E + 05	2.92E + 04	1.98E + 05	2.67E + 05	9.07E − 02	4.01E − 02	1.70E − 03	4.70E − 03
	Q3	6.60E + 05	9.10E + 04	6.51E + 05	8.26E + 05	1.30E − 01	7.49E − 02	6.90E − 03	1.38E − 02
	Max	5.82E + 07	1.25E + 07	8.07E + 07	1.03E + 08	1.00E + 00	1.00E + 00	1.00E + 00	1.00E + 00
2015	Min	2.63E + 02	5.68E + 01	4.54E + 02	2.33E + 03	0.00E + 00	0.00E + 00	0.00E + 00	0.00E + 00
	Q1	4.73E + 04	7.23E + 03	3.76E + 04	5.39E + 04	3.61E − 02	2.76E − 02	3.00E − 04	1.60E − 03
	Median	2.14E + 05	3.08E + 04	1.96E + 05	2.67E + 05	5.14E − 02	4.32E − 02	1.70E − 03	4.90E − 03
	Q3	6.73E + 05	1.01E + 05	6.59E + 05	8.26E + 05	8.55E − 02	7.88E − 02	7.30E − 03	1.36E − 02
	Max	5.61E + 07	1.24E + 07	7.82E + 07	1.03E + 08	1.00E + 00	1.00E + 00	1.00E + 00	1.00E + 00
2016	Min	3.50E + 02	2.56E + 02	6.83E + 02	2.63E + 03	0.00E + 00	0.00E + 00	0.00E + 00	0.00E + 00
	Q1	4.79E + 04	8.12E + 03	4.39E + 04	6.30E + 04	2.09E − 02	2.88E − 02	3.00E − 04	1.80E − 03
	Median	2.05E + 05	2.93E + 04	2.07E + 05	2.69E + 05	4.29E − 02	4.45E − 02	2.00E − 03	5.20E − 03
	Q3	7.14E + 05	8.74E + 04	7.18E + 05	8.48E + 05	9.08E − 02	8.27E − 02	8.40E − 03	1.53E − 02
	Max	4.60E + 07	7.53E + 06	6.79E + 07	9.27E + 07	1.00E + 00	1.00E + 00	1.00E + 00	1.00E + 00
2017	Min	4.61E + 01	2.79E + 02	8.01E + 02	2.75E + 03	0.00E + 00	0.00E + 00	0.00E + 00	0.00E + 00
	Q1	5.65E + 04	8.27E + 03	4.87E + 04	7.04E + 04	4.93E − 02	2.95E − 02	3.00E − 04	1.80E − 03
	Median	2.46E + 05	2.97E + 04	2.22E + 05	2.95E + 05	7.51E − 02	4.47E − 02	1.90E − 03	5.50E − 03
	Q3	8.64E + 05	8.94E + 04	7.63E + 05	1.01E + 06	1.37E − 01	9.31E − 02	8.60E − 03	1.58E − 02
	Max	5.21E + 07	8.87E + 06	8.02E + 07	1.04E + 08	1.00E + 00	1.00E + 00	1.00E + 00	1.00E + 00

(Continued)

Table 2. (*Continued*)

		Inputs		Outputs		Contextual Variables			
Year	**Statistics Variables**	**IE**	**OE**	**NIR**	**OR**	**TCAR**	**NPLR**	**TA**	**NB**
2018	Min	4.61E + 01	2.62E + 02	2.53E + 03	3.43E + 03	0.00E + 00	0.00E + 00	0.00E + 00	0.00E + 00
	Q1	6.39E + 04	8.64E + 03	5.62E + 04	7.84E + 04	6.43E − 02	2.70E − 02	3.00E − 04	2.20E − 03
	Median	2.63E + 05	2.97E + 04	2.33E + 05	3.07E + 05	9.19E − 02	4.59E − 02	2.00E − 03	5.90E − 03
	Q3	9.08E + 05	8.63E + 04	8.59E + 05	1.09E + 06	1.40E − 01	8.93E − 02	8.90E − 03	1.77E − 02
	Max	5.48E + 07	9.81E + 06	8.35E + 07	1.06E + 08	1.00E + 00	1.00E + 00	1.00E + 00	1.00E + 00
2019	Min	1.13E + 02	4.06E + 02	1.47E + 02	6.54E + 02	0.00E + 00	0.00E + 00	0.00E + 00	0.00E + 00
	Q1	7.12E + 04	1.03E + 04	5.85E + 04	8.96E + 04	6.15E − 02	3.00E − 02	0.00E + 00	2.30E − 03
	Median	3.04E + 05	2.96E + 04	2.58E + 05	3.43E + 05	7.35E − 02	5.22E − 02	2.20E − 03	6.30E − 03
	Q3	9.40E + 05	9.88E + 04	8.82E + 05	1.15E + 06	9.98E − 02	1.00E − 01	8.80E − 03	1.84E − 02
	Max	6.17E + 07	1.05E + 07	8.69E + 07	1.11E + 08	1.00E + 00	1.00E + 00	1.00E + 00	1.00E + 00
2020	Min	3.52E + 02	3.47E + 02	3.51E + 02	4.74E + 02	0.00E + 00	0.00E + 00	0.00E + 00	0.00E + 00
	Q1	6.52E + 04	9.88E + 03	4.73E + 04	8.36E + 04	1.52E − 02	1.55E − 02	3.00E − 04	2.60E − 03
	Median	2.99E + 05	3.12E + 04	2.79E + 05	4.02E + 05	1.88E − 02	3.07E − 02	1.90E − 03	6.50E − 03
	Q3	1.08E + 06	1.05E + 05	1.04E + 06	1.22E + 06	2.55E − 02	5.36E − 02	9.10E − 03	1.86E − 02
	Max	6.82E + 07	1.25E + 07	9.90E + 07	1.23E + 08	1.00E + 00	1.00E + 00	1.00E + 00	1.00E + 00

Table 3. Technical efficiency results.

Countries	Statistics Variables	2014	2015	2016	2017	2018	2019	2020
BD	Min	0.0791	0.0582	0.0796	0.0801	0.0813	0.0698	0.0733
	Max	0.3988	0.3988	0.3988	0.3640	0.3352	0.3584	0.3523
	Mean	0.1685	0.1617	0.1800	0.1855	0.1733	0.1722	0.1676
	Std.	0.0642	0.0695	0.0719	0.0691	0.0636	0.0675	0.0653
	Eff. No.	0	0	0	0	0	0	0
CN	Min	0.2367	0.2066	0.2054	0.2314	0.1509	0.1950	0.1556
	Max	0.9985	0.9598	1.0000	1.0000	1.0000	1.0000	1.0000
	Mean	0.5077	0.4765	0.5329	0.5343	0.5373	0.5527	0.5554
	Std.	0.1631	0.1606	0.1753	0.2026	0.2032	0.1952	0.1999
	Eff. No.	0	0	1	4	4	4	4
ID	Min	0.0441	0.0460	0.0346	0.0693	0.0489	0.0258	0.0068
	Max	1.0000	1.0000	1.0000	0.9665	1.0000	1.0000	1.0000
	Mean	0.3396	0.3009	0.3174	0.3253	0.3240	0.3155	0.3198
	Std.	0.2440	0.2120	0.2050	0.2033	0.2004	0.2123	0.2215
	Eff. No.	5	1	1	0	1	1	1
IN	Min	0.0545	0.0545	0.0545	0.0598	0.0695	0.0614	0.0620
	Max	0.6510	0.4585	0.6555	1.0000	1.0000	0.7873	1.0000
	Mean	0.2076	0.1990	0.2229	0.2481	0.2546	0.2620	0.2972
	Std.	0.1149	0.1069	0.1235	0.1742	0.1770	0.1553	0.1947
	Eff. No.	0	0	0	2	2	0	2
MY	Min	0.2009	0.1788	0.1731	0.2067	0.2032	0.1845	0.2104
	Max	0.4525	0.4703	0.4655	0.5173	0.5090	0.4877	0.5657
	Mean	0.3252	0.3343	0.3385	0.3643	0.3439	0.3381	0.3464
	Std.	0.0798	0.0860	0.0870	0.1025	0.1013	0.1034	0.1378
	Eff. No.	0	0	0	0	0	0	0
PH	Min	0.0798	0.0860	0.0870	0.1025	0.1013	0.1034	0.1378
	Max	0.6736	0.6061	0.6219	0.6646	0.5578	0.6129	0.8963
	Mean	0.3271	0.3203	0.3233	0.3331	0.2951	0.2910	0.3728
	Std.	0.1316	0.1220	0.1265	0.1234	0.1063	0.1140	0.1726
	Eff. No.	0	0	0	0	0	0	0
Total	Min	0.0441	0.0460	0.0346	0.0598	0.0489	0.0258	0.0068
	Max	1	1	1	1	1	1	1
	Mean	0.3382	0.3154	0.3454	0.3556	0.3537	0.3579	0.3738
	Std.	0.2108	0.1944	0.2083	0.2201	0.2210	0.2217	0.2322
	Eff. No.	5	1	2	6	7	5	7

Notably, the results were analyzed under the meta-frontier technology, but they were presented separately by year to enhance clarity and understanding. Additionally, the inverse of technical efficiency $(1/\varphi^*)$ has been calculated to determine the efficiency scores between 0 and 1.

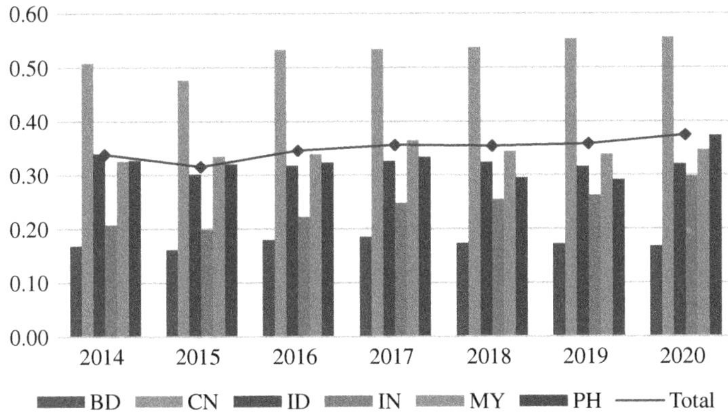

Fig. 4. Trends in total average technical efficiency vis-a-vis the average technical efficiency.

Figure 4 illustrates the trends in total average technical efficiency alongside the average technical efficiency of the six identified countries over a seven-year period. As the graph shows, except for a slight decline in 2015, total average technical efficiency exhibited a generally steady increase. The total average efficiency ranged between 30% and 40% over this period. Bangladesh consistently recorded the lowest average technical efficiency, just above 15%, while China reported the highest efficiency, fluctuating between approximately 45% and 55%. For the other countries, average technical efficiency varied within a range of 20–35%.

Table 3 presents a comprehensive analysis of the technical efficiency of banks over the seven-year period. The data indicate a general increase in the number of efficient banks, rising from five in 2014 to seven in both 2018 and 2020, reflecting an overall positive trend in banking efficiency during this time frame. However, in 2015, Asian banks experienced a notable decline in performance, largely attributable to several critical factors. A key issue was the economic slowdown in China, a primary driver of regional growth. As China's economy decelerated, demand for its exports decreased, adversely impacting banks with significant ties to these industries. Furthermore, the decline in commodity prices, including oil and metals, negatively affected countries dependent on these exports, exerting financial pressure on both banks and their clients. Increased market volatility during this period also reduced investor confidence, complicating lending conditions for banks. Additionally, a rise in non-performing loans, particularly in export-related and heavy manufacturing sectors, further weakened the performance of Asian banks in 2015.

Focusing on individual countries, Indonesia was the sole nation with efficient banks in 2014 and 2015. From 2016 onward, China consistently maintained four efficient banks each year, with China and Indonesia showing the highest number of efficient banks across the period. India's mean efficiency displayed a steady improvement, increasing from 0.2076 in 2014 to 0.2972 in 2020, and during the years 2017, 2018, and 2020, India had two efficient banks annually.

Bangladesh, on the other hand, consistently demonstrated low technical efficiency, with mean efficiency scores ranging from 0.1617 to 0.1855. Malaysia and the Philippines showed relatively stable but moderate levels of efficiency. Malaysia's mean efficiency fluctuated between 0.3252 and 0.3643, while the Philippines' efficiency ranged between 0.2910 and 0.3728. Notably, none of these three countries recorded any efficient banks during the seven-year period.

3.3. *Regression analysis results*

In the second step, Model (3) was employed to estimate the managerial ability index, incorporating five contextual variables: Total Capital Adequacy Ratio (TCAR), Non-Performing Loan Ratio (NPLR), Total Assets (TA), Number of Branches (NB), and a Time Series Dummy (TSD).

Figure 5 shows the variation in the managerial ability index across a seven-year period for seven countries, along with the overall trend. The total index reached its highest point in 2014 and its lowest in 2015. Among the countries, China had the strongest performance, followed by Malaysia, which exhibited the second-best managerial ability. Meanwhile, Bangladesh showed the weakest. The Philippines exhibited a downward trend until 2019, after which improvements were observed. In contrast, Indonesia's performance steadily declined, hitting its lowest point in 2020. Despite consistent improvements, India continued to exhibit negative managerial ability throughout the period.

Table 4 demonstrates that, similar to technical efficiency, Bangladesh exhibited the lowest managerial ability among the seven countries from 2014 to 2020, while China recorded the highest.

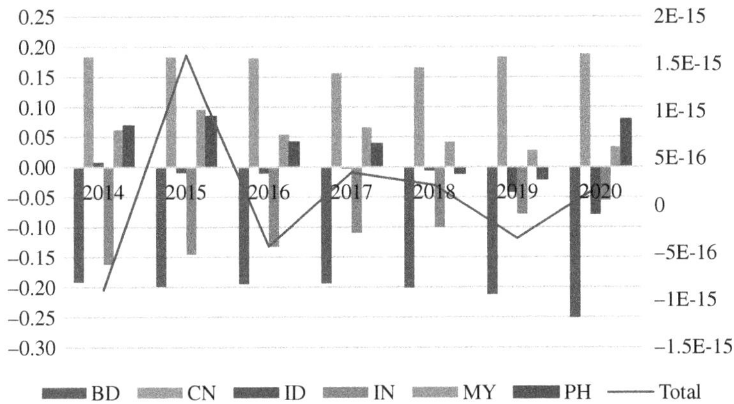

Fig. 5. Variations in the estimated total managerial ability index.

Figure 6 provides a comparative analysis of average technical efficiency and managerial ability over a seven-year period. In certain years, notably 2017, 2018, and 2020, both metrics exhibited similar trends, either increasing or decreasing concurrently. In 2015, despite unfavorable revenue conditions across all banks, managerial ability peaked, while technical efficiency reached its lowest point. In 2019, the onset of the COVID-19 pandemic resulted in a significant decline in managerial ability relative to technical efficiency. However, both indicators showed a marked improvement in subsequent years.

3.4. *Analysis of the impact of contextual variables on technical efficiency*

Prior to discussing the results of the regression analysis, a Pearson correlation test was performed on the contextual variables. The analysis revealed that the highest correlation was observed for TA, while the lowest correlation was found for the NPLR (See Table 5). These correlations help identify which contextual variables have the strongest potential influence on technical efficiency and managerial ability, providing valuable insights for the subsequent regression analysis.

The results from the regression of the logarithm of technical efficiency on contextual variables in Table 6 indicate that the coefficients of three variables — TCAR, NPLR, and TA — are statistically significant at the 95% confidence level. Notably, the coefficients of TCAR

Table 4. Managerial ability results.

Countries	Statistical Variables	2014	2015	2016	2017	2018	2019	2020
BD	Min	−0.5345	−0.6668	−0.5620	−0.5954	−0.5505	−0.5545	−0.5704
	Max	0.2746	0.3668	0.2828	0.3767	0.4240	0.1156	0.0744
	Mean	−0.1916	−0.1981	−0.1948	−0.1935	−0.2014	−0.2123	−0.2508
	Std.	0.1834	0.2273	0.2137	0.2055	0.2014	0.1836	0.1584
CN	Min	−0.3034	−0.2591	−0.2828	−0.2988	−0.2989	−0.3016	−0.2908
	Max	0.5206	0.4572	0.4855	0.4778	0.5008	0.5241	0.5146
	Mean	0.1839	0.1828	0.1814	0.1563	0.1657	0.1829	0.1878
	Std.	0.1419	0.1377	0.1489	0.1555	0.1651	0.1558	0.1576
ID	Min	−0.7245	−0.6759	−0.8680	−0.5971	−0.7354	−1.0709	−1.6135
	Max	0.7579	0.7747	0.6672	0.5262	0.5964	0.5555	0.5206
	Mean	0.0080	−0.0096	−0.0106	−0.0023	−0.0064	−0.0421	−0.0792
	Std.	0.3056	0.2969	0.2775	0.2662	0.2535	0.2979	0.3771
IN	Min	−0.6908	−0.6645	−0.6938	−0.6780	−0.6169	−0.6910	−0.6877
	Max	0.4513	0.4007	0.4889	0.6663	0.6701	1.0289	0.8748
	Mean	−0.1624	−0.1452	−0.1324	−0.1094	−0.1002	−0.0781	−0.0557
	Std.	0.2427	0.2484	0.2590	0.2626	0.2577	0.2756	0.2735
MY	Min	−0.1297	−0.1575	−0.2150	−0.1599	−0.1695	−0.2179	−0.1576
	Max	0.1838	0.2243	0.1904	0.2356	0.2258	0.2074	0.2680
	Mean	0.0617	0.0963	0.0540	0.0659	0.0416	0.0278	0.0328
	Std.	0.1016	0.1146	0.1209	0.1228	0.1211	0.1344	0.1522
PH	Min	−0.2010	−0.1575	−0.2150	−0.1762	−0.2783	−0.2539	−0.1576
	Max	0.3815	0.3612	0.3242	0.3342	0.2606	0.3009	0.4650
	Mean	0.0689	0.0847	0.0412	0.0382	−0.0107	−0.0204	0.0792
	Std.	0.1386	0.1372	0.1453	0.1331	0.1369	0.1458	0.1636
Total	Min	−0.7245	−0.6759	−0.8680	−0.6780	−0.7354	−1.0709	−1.6135
	Max	0.7579	0.7747	0.6672	0.6663	0.6701	1.0289	0.8748
	Mean	−8.92E − 16	1.60E − 15	−4.28E − 16	3.53E − 16	2.17E − 16	−3.47E − 16	2.16E − 16
	Std.	0.2674	0.2677	0.2625	0.2526	0.2512	0.2680	0.2968

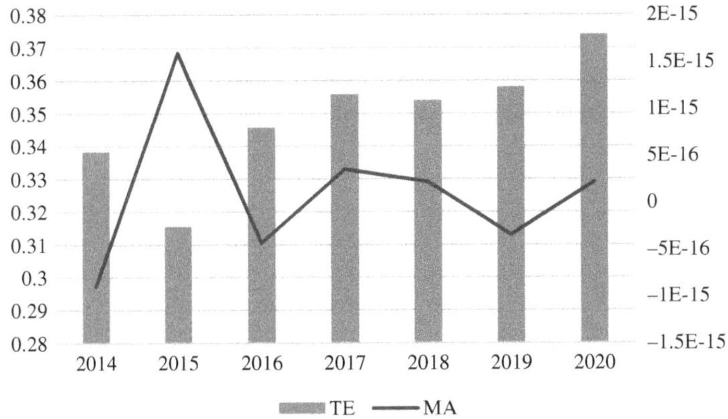

Fig. 6. Comparison of technical efficiency and managerial ability.

Table 5. Pearson correlation coefficient.

Variables	$Log(\varphi^*)$	TCAR	NPLA	TA	NB
$Log(\varphi^*)$		−0.0672	−0.2365	0.3095	0.2202
TCAR			0.0178	−0.0795	−0.0848
NPLR				−0.0745	0.1351
TA					0.7693
NB					

Table 6. Regression analysis results.

Variables	Coefficients	Standard Error	t-Stat	P-value
Intercept	−0.5172	0.0172	−30.1446	8.17E − 168
TCAR	−0.1435	0.0616	−2.3314	1.98E − 02
NPLR	−0.6835	0.0613	−11.1567	3.63E − 28
TA	0.6943	0.0915	7.5917	4.61E − 14
NB	0.1671	0.0890	1.8775	6.06E − 02
R square		0.1504		
Standard error		0.2672		

and NPLR are negative, while the coefficient of TA is positive. The coefficients of −0.1435 and −0.6835 for TCAR and NPLR, respectively, indicate that a one-unit increase in TCAR and NPLR is associated with a decrease of 0.13% and 0.49% in technical efficiency.

In contrast, a one-unit increase in TA and NB leads to an increase of 1.62% and 0.18% in technical efficiency, respectively. Additionally, the low p-values indicate a statistically significant relationship between TCAR, NPLR, TA, and bank performance.

3.5. *Policy implications*

Our findings have significant policy implications in terms of banking efficiency, managerial ability, and financial stability, which align with the goals of enhancing economic resilience and sustainable financial growth. First, from a theoretical and modeling perspective, the results highlight that contextual variables, such as TCAR, NPLR, and TA, are crucial determinants of banking efficiency. Therefore, it is essential for policymakers to focus on both internal management capabilities and external regulatory frameworks to foster long-term bank performance.

In this study, China demonstrated consistently high levels of managerial ability and technical efficiency, while Bangladesh exhibited the lowest. It is recommended to consider the practices of high-performing banks in China as benchmarks for other countries, particularly in regions facing persistent efficiency challenges. Countries with lower efficiency, such as Bangladesh and the Philippines, should prioritize strengthening managerial skills and adopting best practices to improve overall performance.

Among the contextual variables analyzed, NPLR had the most significant negative impact on technical efficiency. This finding underscores the importance of enhancing credit risk management and ensuring stringent loan approval processes. Additionally, regulatory bodies should introduce measures to minimize the accumulation of non-performing loans, which directly affect banking stability. Moreover, the results indicate that while capital adequacy (TCAR) is essential for financial stability, excessive focus on maintaining high capital ratios without improving managerial ability can hinder efficiency. Policymakers should strike a balance between regulatory capital requirements and operational flexibility to avoid unnecessary constraints on bank performance.

An important finding of the study is that banks with higher managerial ability tend to exhibit better resource utilization and risk management. This suggests that investing in advanced training programs for bank managers and fostering a performance-driven culture are critical steps in enhancing overall efficiency. Incentivizing banks to implement robust managerial development initiatives can significantly improve their competitive position and resilience to economic shocks.

In conclusion, adopting these policy measures can enhance bank efficiency by addressing both managerial and regulatory aspects. By focusing on improving managerial competence, mitigating risks associated with non-performing loans, and balancing capital adequacy requirements, policymakers can help create a more robust and competitive banking system capable of promoting sustainable economic development.

4. Conclusion

This study analyzed the relationship between technical efficiency and managerial ability in seven Asian countries from 2014 to 2020. The results revealed fluctuating trends in both technical efficiency and managerial ability over the years. A significant decline in technical efficiency was observed in 2015, contrasting with a notable improvement in managerial ability during the same period. Among the countries, Bangladesh consistently exhibited the lowest performance, while China demonstrated the highest in both technical efficiency and managerial ability across all years.

The regression analysis indicated that TCAR, NPLR, and TA were statistically significant factors influencing technical efficiency. These findings emphasize the importance of both internal managerial capabilities and external regulatory factors in determining bank performance. Policymakers and bank management should focus on enhancing managerial skills, improving credit risk management, and maintaining appropriate capital adequacy to ensure sustainable banking performance.

In conclusion, by addressing the key factors identified in this study, banks in developing economies can improve their operational efficiency and competitiveness. Future research could explore additional contextual variables and extend the analysis to other regions to gain a more comprehensive understanding of global banking efficiency.

References

Amirteimoori, A., Allahviranloo, T., and Cezar, A. (2024b). A bootstrap data envelopment analysis model with stochastic reducible outputs and expandable inputs: An application to power plants. *RAIRO-Oper. Res.*, 58(4), 3189–3202.

Amirteimoori, A., Allahviranloo, T., and Nematizadeh, M. (2024c). A firm-specific Malmquist productivity index model for stochastic data envelopment analysis: an application to commercial banks. *Financial Innovation*, 10(1), 66.

Amirteimoori, A., Banker, R. D., Zadmirzaei, M., and Susaeta, A. (2023). Managerial ability and productivity growth in the European forest sector. *European J. Forest Res.*, 142(5), 1029–1043.

Amirteimoori, A., Safarpour, S., Kordrostami, S., and Khoshandam, L. (2024a). Performance and managerial ability analysis in the health sector: A data envelopment analysis approach. In *Decision Making in Healthcare Systems* (pp. 373–390). Springer International Publishing.

Asmild, M. and Matthews, K. (2012). Multi-directional efficiency analysis of efficiency patterns in Chinese banks 1997–2008. *European Journal of Operational Research*, 219(2), 434–441.

Baik, B., Choi, S., and Farber, D. B. (2020). Managerial ability and income smoothing. *Account. Rev.*, 95(4), 1–22.

Banker, R. D., Amirteimoori, A., Allahviranloo, T., and Sinha, R. P. (2024). Performance analysis and managerial ability in the general insurance market: A study of India and Iran. *Inf. Technol. Manag.*, 25(1), 19–31.

Banker, R. D., Amirteimoori, A., and Sinha, R. P. (2022a). An integrated data envelopment analysis and generalized additive model for assessing managerial ability with application to the insurance industry. *Decis. Anal. J.*, 4, 100115.

Banker, R. D., Chang, H., and Lee, S. Y. (2010). Differential impact of Korean banking system reforms on bank productivity. *Journal of Banking & Finance*, 34(7), 1450–1460.

Banker, R. D., Charnes, A., and Cooper, W. W. (1984). Some models for estimating technical and scale inefficiencies in data envelopment analysis. *Manag. Sci.*, 30(9), 1078–1092.

Banker, R. D. and Natarajan, R. (2008). Evaluating contextual variables affecting productivity using data envelopment analysis. *Oper. Res.*, 56(1), 48–58.

Banker, R. D., Natarajan, R., and Zhang, D. (2019). Two-stage estimation of the impact of contextual variables in stochastic frontier production function models using data envelopment analysis: Second stage OLS versus bootstrap approaches. *Eur. J. Oper. Res.*, 278(2), 368–384.

Banker, R. D. and Park, H. U. (2021). Three-stage approach to analyze managerial ability. *Data Environ. Anal. J.*, 5(1), 27–54.

Banker, R. D., Park, H. U., and Sahoo, B. (2022b). A statistical foundation for the measurement of managerial ability. *Data Environ. Anal. J.*

Banker, R. D., Park, H. U., and Sahoo, B. (2022c). A statistical foundation for the measurement of managerial ability. *Data Environ. Anal. J.*

Battese, G. E., Rao, D. S., and O'Donnell, C. J. (2004). A metafrontier production function for estimation of technical efficiencies and technology gaps for firms operating under different technologies. *J. Prod. Anal.*, 21(1), 91–103.

Bertrand, M. and Schoar, A. (2003). Managing with style: The effect of managers on firm policies. *Q. J. Econ.*, 118(4), 1169–1208.

Chang, H., Ishida, S., and Kochiyama, T. (2018). Evaluation of managerial ability in the Japanese setting. *Jpn. Account. Rev.*, 8(1), 1–22.

Charnes, A., Cooper, W. W., and Rhodes, E. (1978). Measuring the efficiency of decision making units. *Eur. J. Oper. Res.*, 2(6), 429–444.

Chen, S., Li, Z., Han, B., and Ma, H. (2021). Managerial ability, internal control and investment efficiency. *J. Behav. Exp. Financ.*, 31, 100523.

Chen, Z., Matousek, R., and Wanke, P. (2018). Chinese bank efficiency during the global financial crisis: A combined approach using satisficing DEA and Support Vector Machines. *The North American Journal of Economics and Finance*, 43, 71–86.

Demerjian, P. R. and Lev, B. (2021). Measuring managerial ability: A retrospective and review of the literature. *Data Environ. Anal. J.*, 5(1), 1–25.

Demerjian, P. R., Lev, B., Lewis, M. F., and McVay, S. E. (2013). Managerial ability and earnings quality. *Account. Rev.*, 88(2), 463–498.

Demerjian, P. R., Lev, B., and McVay, S. (2012). Quantifying managerial ability: A new measure and validity tests. *Manag. Sci.*, 58(7), 1229–1248.

Fukuyama, H. and Weber, W. L. (2009). A directional slacks-based measure of technical inefficiency. *Socio-Economic Planning Sciences*, 43(4), 274–287.

Guan, J. X., Li, O. Z., and Ma, J. (2018). Managerial ability and the shareholder tax sensitivity of dividends. *J. Financ. Quant. Anal.*, 53(1), 335–364.

Kumar, S. and Zbib, L. (2022). Firm performance during the Covid-19 crisis: Does managerial ability matter? *Finance Research Letters*, 102720.

Leverty, J. T. and Grace, M. F. (2012). Dupes or incompetents? An examination of management's impact on firm distress. *J. Risk Insur.*, 79(3), 751–783.

Li, M., Zhu, N., He, K., and Li, M. (2022). Operational efficiency evaluation of Chinese internet banks: Two-stage network DEA approach. *Sustainability*, 14(21), 14165.

Li, Y. (2020). Analyzing efficiencies of city commercial banks in China: An application of the bootstrapped DEA approach. *Pacific-Basin Finance Journal*, 62, 101372.

Murthi, B. P. S., Srinivasan, K., and Kalyanaram, G. (1996). Controlling for observed and unobserved managerial skills in determining first-mover market share advantages. *J. Mark. Res.*, 33(3), 329–336.

O'Donnell, C. J., Rao, D. S., and Battese, G. E. (2008). Metafrontier frameworks for the study of firm-level efficiencies and technology ratios. *Empir. Econ.*, 34(2), 231–255.

Seiford, L. M. and Zhu, J. (1999). Profitability and marketability of the top 55 US commercial banks. *Management Science*, 45(9), 1270–1288.

Wang, K., Huang, W., Wu, J., and Liu, Y. N. (2014). Efficiency measures of the Chinese commercial banking system using an additive two-stage DEA. *Omega*, 44, 5–20.

Zha, Y., Liang, N., Wu, M., and Bian, Y. (2016). Efficiency evaluation of banks in China: A dynamic two-stage slacks-based measure approach. *Omega*, 60, 60–72.

Zhou, X., Xu, Z., Chai, J., Yao, L., Wang, S., and Lev, B. (2019). Efficiency evaluation for banking systems under uncertainty: A multi-period three-stage DEA model. *Omega*, 85, 68–82.

https://doi.org/10.1142/9789819823161_0010

Chapter 10

Efficiency of Indian Private Commercial Banks: Evaluation and Explanation

Ram Pratap Sinha[*,‡] **and K. Shanmugan**[†,§]

[*]*Department of Economics, Government College of Engineering and Leather Technology, Kolkata, West Bengal, India*

[†]*Department of Business Economics, Faculty of Commerce, The Maharaja Sayajirao University of Baroda Vadodara, Gujarat, India*

[‡]*rampratapsinha39@gmail.com*

[§]*shanmugan-be@msubaroda.ac.in*

The present study evaluates efficiency by adopting the directional distance function approach and seeks to explain the efficiency estimates for the 18 private sector commercial firms that continuously operated for the period 2014–2015 to 2023–2024. The result of the first stage is that while mean efficiency remained fairly stable during the decade under observation, new private sector banks have mostly performed better than the old private sector banks for the period under observation. The second stage analysis uses both static and dynamic models, and the outcomes indicate that efficiency is positively related to credit–deposit ratio and measures of profitability (return on asset and profit per employee) but negatively linked to capital-to-risk-weighted asset ratio and bank size. In the dynamic model, the coefficients of one-period lagged efficiency estimates are also highly significant.

Keywords: Directional distance function; data envelopment analysis; technical efficiency; private commercial banks; panel data regression.

1. Introduction

The commencement of private sector banking in India dates back to the eighteenth century, and at the time of Indian independence (1947), the banking sector was controlled by private sector banks. Since the 1950s, however, the extent of government control and the presence of public sector banks in the commercial banking sector have continued to increase. With the objective of promoting mass banking (based on a rapid expansion of bank branches in the rural and semi-urban areas), 14 private sector commercial banks were nationalized in the middle of 1969, and in January 1980, six more banks were taken over by the government. In the 1970s and 1980s, the public sector banks had a dominant role to play in the Indian economy. Further, no new private bank was allowed to be set up by the market regulator (the Reserve Bank of India). In a regime of financial repression, bank lending decisions were regulated by the fulfillment of directed lending targets. Further, banks were required to maintain a high level of statutory liquidity ratio (achieved through the allocation of investible resources in specified government securities). Borrowing and lending rates were also regulated by the R.B.I. The true state of financial affairs was not reflected in the books of accounts of the commercial banks due to the absence of prudential regulations related to asset classification, income recognition, and securities valuation norms. Naturally, in this environment, there was no incentive or room for exhibiting governance skills/ability in the banking sector.

Since 1991, the Indian commercial banking sector has undergone a paradigm shift, which occurred partly out of financial compulsion and partly due to the necessity of creating a robust financial infrastructure. Several financial sector developments were conducive to this structural transformation of the Indian banking sector. Firstly, the Indian banking sector accounting system was progressively aligned with international standards following the adoption of prudential regulations recommended by the Basel Committee on Banking Supervision (BCBS). Secondly, the policies of directed lending and investment were abandoned along with the removal of interest rate controls. Thirdly and finally, the banking sector had witnessed deregulation of entry with the announcements of entry norms for private sector banks in 1993 and the revision of the same in 2001. Since 1994, several new private sector commercial banks have been established in India, resulting in the intensification of the competition in the banking market. As of 31st March 2021, there were 22 private sector banks operating in the Indian banking sector along with 12 public sector banks and more than 40 foreign banks.

The present study seeks to estimate and explain the technical efficiency of Indian private sector commercial banks for the preceding 10-year period (2014–15 through 2023–24). The study has used the directional distance function approach for efficiency evaluation and the econometric approach for efficiency explanation. The sample includes the 18 private sector commercial banks that were in existence for the entire period under observation. In describing the estimation process and the study outcomes, the remainder of the paper proceeds as follows. Section 2 provides a review of the literature. Section 3 outlines the estimation methodology. Section 4 includes a description of variables, data, and the results. Section 5 provides the concluding observations.

2. Review of Literature

Commercial banks, as the providers of access to the payments system and issuers of pass-through securities, occupy a special position in the financial system of a country. Therefore, market structure, conduct, and performance of commercial banks have attracted the attention of researchers for a long time. In the context of performance evaluation of banks, estimation and explanation of efficiency and productivity dominated research studies.

The early literature on bank efficiency focused on scale, scope, and cost economies of the banking sector (Benston *et al.*, 1968; Benston *et al.*, 1982; Berger *et al.*, 1987; Berger and Humphrey, 1994). Berger *et al.* (1993) derived bank input and output efficiencies from a profit function. Initial studies focused on scale economies and efficiency evaluation using cost or profit functions because of the inability of the econometric methods to handle multiple outputs. With the introduction of the non-parametric Data Envelopment Analysis (DEA), estimation of bank technical efficiency was made possible. Important international studies evaluating bank efficiency using DEA include Favero and Papi (1995), Rezitis (2008) and Barros *et al.* (2012).

Since the deregulation of the Indian banking sector, numerous research studies (Bhattacharyya *et al.*, 1997; Saha and Ravisankar, 2000; Sathye, 2003; Kumbhakar and Sarkar, 2003; Ram Mohan and Ray, 2004; Das *et al.*, 2005; Chatterjee and Sinha, 2006; Dar *et al.*, 2021) tried to estimate and explain banking sector efficiency performance in the Indian context using the radial DEA approach or the SFA approach. The present study makes a departure from the extant literature in three respects. First, unlike the extant literature, it estimates bank efficiency using a directional distance function approach. Second, it is focused only on private sector commercial banks and constructs an efficiency frontier based on the observations from 18 private sector commercial banks for the period 2014–15 to 2023–24. Third, the study is based on the post-global crisis phase in the Indian economy and seeks to examine the relative performance of the private sector banks in this phase.

3. Research Methodology

The efficiency of a productive unit implies its observed performance relative to some accepted standard of performance. With the refinement in estimation methodology, attention has shifted toward the construction of a scientific performance benchmark. Broadly speaking, there are two competing approaches for the estimation of the efficiency performance of decision-making units: data envelopment analysis (DEA), which is a non-parametric approach (no parametric specification of the relationship between the inputs and outputs is required), and stochastic frontier analysis (SFA), which is a parametric approach (econometric approach).

The radial DEA approach (Charnes *et al.*, 1978; Banker *et al.*, 1984) is based on the conceptual and empirical foundations provided by Shephard (1953, 1970, 1974) and Farrell (1957). Efficiency evaluation of the decision-making units using DEA is based on the assumptions of free disposability of inputs and outputs and convexity of technology, and on the returns to scale. The non-parametric efficiency evaluation method applied in the current study is based on the concept of distance function, which relates efficient and projected firms based on the relative distance of the observed unit from the best practice frontier. The distance function can be radial or non-radial in nature. A radial distance function is a real-valued function whose value at a point is based on the distance of the point from the origin. In the present context, we have estimated life insurance company-wise efficiency using the directional distance function, which accommodates both radial and non-radial functions. To be more specific, it is an evaluation method that estimates the technical efficiency of an observed firm (decision-making unit) along a direction vector which may or may not be radial in character.

We now provide a brief account of the efficiency evaluation method involved in the directional distance function approach. For this, we consider transformation (production) technology that converts a vector of inputs into multiple outputs. The input vector (inclusive of n inputs $x_1, x_2, \ldots, x_n$) is represented by X and the output vector (inclusive of m outputs $y_1, y_2, \ldots, y_m$) is represented by Y. The technology set T_s encompasses the feasible production plans of the producer (including both output and input sets) and can be presented as $T_S = \{(X, Y) \in R^{n+m}, X \text{ can produce } Y\}$. The output set $O_Y \in T_S$ includes the set of feasible outputs for each input vector, while the input set I_X includes the input vectors that are feasible with each output vector.

The production technology is assumed to exhibit free disposability (of inputs and outputs) and convexity. We may specify them as follows:

(a) Free disposability: If $(X, Y) \in T_S$, then $(X_1, Y) \in T_S$ where $X_1 \geq X$. Similarly $(X, Y_1) \in T_S$, provided $Y_1 \leq Y$.
(b) Convexity: Convexity implies that if (X_a, Y_a) and $(X_b, Y_b) \epsilon T_s$, then $(X_c, Y_c) \epsilon T_s$

where $X_c = \delta X_a + (1 - \delta) X_b$ and $Y_c = \delta Y_a + (1 - \delta) Y_b$ and $\delta \epsilon [0, 1]$.

The process of efficiency estimation in the radial DEA model is based on the concept of input and output distance functions as introduced by Shephard (1953, 1970, 1974) and Farrell (1957). Distance functions relate inefficient observation points to the efficient points. The input- and output-oriented distance functions can be formally represented as

$$DF^{\text{Input}}_{\text{Farrell}} = \text{Min}[\mu : (\theta X, Y) \in T_S],$$

$$DF^{\text{output}}_{\text{Farrell}} = \text{Max}[\lambda : (X, \phi Y) \in T_S].$$

The input distance function provides the maximum amount by which the observed input quantity can be multiplied, and yet the reduced input quantity is capable of producing the given level of output (target). On the other hand, the output distance function provides the maximum amount by which the observed output can be multiplied, and yet the revised output (target) can be produced by the given level of input. Shephard distance functions can be obtained by inverting the distance function of Farrell.

Chambers *et al.* (1996) introduced the directional distance function for providing a new measure of technical efficiency, which compares both observed inputs and outputs with the optimal inputs and outputs. The concept of directional distance function is based on the benefit function introduced by Luenberger (1992a, 1992b). For the construction of the production frontier, the directional distance function considers the potential for increasing outputs and decreasing inputs simultaneously. Thus, the directional distance function can be written as

$$DF_{ddf} = \text{Max}[\beta : \{(X - \beta G_X), (Y + \beta G_Y)\} \in T_S],$$

where G_X and G_Y represent the input and direction vectors, respectively, and β is a scalar. The directional distance function provides a complete characterization of the technology, and the input distance functions of Shephard (1953, 1970) and Farrell (1957) are actually special cases of the directional distance function (Färe and Grosskopf, 2000).

The concept of distance function relates the inefficient point to the best practice points. However, for empirical estimation of efficiency, the benchmark needs to be constructed, which can serve as the basis for efficiency evaluation. As DEA is a data-driven approach, it enables the construction of the input and output frontiers from the entire set of input and output observations (comprising all the productive units under observation). Thus, we may represent the input and output frontiers as $\sum_{i=1}^{k} \lambda_i X_{ij}$ $(j = 1, 2, \ldots, n)$ and $\sum_{k=1}^{l} \lambda_k Y_{kj}$ $(j = 1, 2, \ldots, n)$, where there are n firms under observation and λ is a scalar, $\lambda \geq 0$. If we allow returns to scale exhibited by the technology to be variable, we need to add an additional constraint: $\sum \lambda = 1$.

4. Variables, Data, and Results

Section 4.1 discusses the alternative approaches for the selection of appropriate input and output indicators for the efficiency evaluation, as well as the variables considered in the present study for first- and second-stage analysis. Section 4.4 describes the data sources. Section 4.5 discusses the results.

4.1. *Description of input, output, and contextual variables*

Estimation of bank efficiency in the first stage of our study requires the identification of inputs and outputs. However, since the banking industry is a financial services provider industry, outputs and inputs can be defined in several ways. To be more specific, there are at least five approaches for choosing bank output: the production approach, the financial intermediation approach, the user cost approach, the value-added approach, and the risk mitigation approach. The production approach as introduced by Benston (1965) considers banks as customer service providers. Thus, as per this approach, bank outputs reflect the services provided to the customers, including the number and types of transactions, documents processed, and specialized services provided over a given time period. Sealey and Lindley 1977 introduced the intermediation approach for defining commercial bank inputs and outputs. This approach treats commercial banks as financial intermediaries that mobilize financial resources from depositors who invest the same in business, commerce, and investible securities. The user cost approach introduced by Hancock (1985, 1991) considers an item as an input or output of the financial services industry, depending on whether the net revenue contribution of the item is negative or positive. The value-added approach introduced by Berger *et al.* (1987), and Berger and Humphrey (1992) consider such activities as output indicators that contribute significant value added as assessed while allocating operating costs. The value-added approach assumes that the insurers provide three major services: risk-pooling and risk-bearing, real financial services, and intermediation.

In the present case, we have followed the user cost approach for selecting inputs and outputs. Thus, we have included operating expenses and interest expenses as the two input indicators and total income (sum of interest income and other income (obtained from off-balance sheet and fee-based activities)) as the output indicators. For carrying out second-stage regression, contextual variables influencing bank efficiency are to be identified. In the present case, we have chosen five important contextual variables: credit–deposit

Table 1. Input, output, and contextual variables.

Particulars	Variables
Input variables	Interest expenses, Operating expenses
Output variables	Total income comprising interest income and other income
Contextual variables	Credit–deposit ratio, capital-to-risk-weighted asset ratio (CRAR), log of total asset (LnTA), return on asset (ROA), and profit per employee (PPE)

Source: Selected by the authors based on the review of the literature.

ratio, capital-to-risk-weighted asset ratio (CRAR), log of total asset (LnTA), return on asset (ROA), and profit per employee (PPE). Table 1 provides an overview of input, output, and contextual variables. In dynamic estimation models, we have used lagged efficiency scores.

4.2. *Data sources*

As mentioned earlier, the present chapter estimates and explains the technical efficiency of Indian private commercial banks for the period 2014–15 to 2023–24. The study is based on 180 bank-year observations. For this, the study depends on two sources of secondary data provided by the Reserve Bank of India (RBI) and the Indian Banks' Association (IBA). The data sources are Statistical Tables Relating to Banks in India, published by the RBI, and Key Business Statistics, published by the IBA.

4.3. *Estimation results*

The present study follows a two-stage approach. The first stage of the investigation evaluates technical efficiency, while the second stage explores the relationship of the estimated efficiency scores with the contextual variables.

4.3.1. *Descriptive statistics of efficiency scores*

Table 2 provides the efficiency descriptive statistics, including efficiency mean, standard deviation, skewness, and kurtosis. The

Table 2. Descriptive statistics of efficiency scores.

Year	Mean Efficiency	Standard Deviation	Skewness	Kurtosis
2014–15	0.9697	0.0413	−1.4871	1.7019
2015–16	0.9655	0.0339	−0.8291	−0.4539
2016–17	0.9695	0.0350	−0.6187	−1.3092
2017–18	0.9634	0.0398	−0.5603	−1.2029
2018–19	0.9684	0.0419	−1.5991	1.9158
2019–20	0.9688	0.0408	−1.1127	−0.1964
2020–21	0.9650	0.0487	−1.4808	1.4112
2021–22	0.9490	0.0520	−0.5817	0.1039
2022–23	0.9675	0.0434	−1.1898	0.0868
2023–24	0.9486	0.0446	−0.4339	0.0893

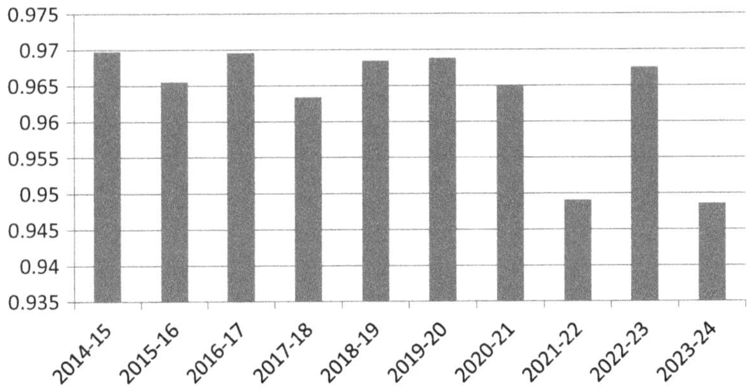

Fig. 1. Mean efficiency scores of the in-sample private sector commercial banks.

table indicates no discernible trend in mean efficiency performance during the period under observation. Mean efficiency fluctuated between 0.9634 (2017–18) and 0.9697 (2014–15). The standard deviation of efficiency varied between 0.0339 (2015–16) and 0.0487 (2020–21). Efficiency distribution exhibited negative skewness for the entire period. Figure 1 presents the trends in mean efficiency for the observed period. Kurtosis was also negative from 2015–16 to 2017–18 and again in 2019–20. The bank-wise efficiency scores have been provided in the Appendix.

Table 3. Mean efficiency of old and new private sector banks.

Year	Old Private Sector Banks	New Private Sector Banks	Efficiency Ratio (old/new)
2014–15	0.9570	0.9897	0.9670
2015–16	0.9545	0.9829	0.9711
2016–17	0.9616	0.9820	0.9792
2017–18	0.9523	0.9808	0.9709
2018–19	0.9556	0.9885	0.9667
2019–20	0.9559	0.9890	0.9665
2020–21	0.9513	0.9864	0.9644
2021–22	0.9490	0.9491	1.0000
2022–23	0.9726	0.9595	1.0136
2023–24	0.9449	0.9544	0.9900

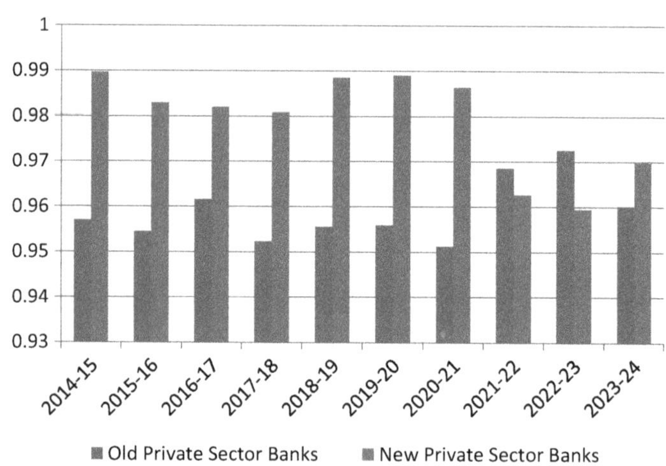

Fig. 2. Comparison of mean efficiency of old and new private sector banks.

4.3.2. *Efficiency performance across ownership categories*

Table 3 (and Fig. 2) compares the efficiency performance of the old private sector banks with the new private sector banks. As per the classification of the RBI, private sector banks that were in existence before the entry deregulation of 1993 are termed as old private sector banks, while the private sector banks that have been formed after deregulation are termed as new private sector banks. The table shows

Table 4. Mean projection requirements of inputs and outputs.

Variables	Operating Expenses	Interest Expenses	Total Income
2014–15	−3.80	−3.53	3.04
2015–16	−4.88	−6.51	4.12
2016–17	−3.74	−5.36	3.05
2017–18	−4.22	−4.35	3.66
2018–19	−6.13	−3.34	3.16
2019–20	−3.12	−3.12	3.29
2020–21	−3.50	−5.74	3.50
2021–22	−5.66	−6.26	−6.17
2022–23	−8.95	−6.36	−5.14
2023–24	5.66	5.10	5.14

that, except for 2021–22 and 2022–23, the new private sector banks have exhibited higher mean technical efficiency when compared to the old private sector banks.

4.4. *Projection requirements of inputs and outputs*

From Table 4, we can infer the overall inefficiency of the observed commercial banks. However, it is of interest to get information about input- and output-specific inefficiencies. Table 4 presents the year-wise and input- and output-wise projection requirements (in % terms).

4.5. *Impact of contextual variables*

As indicated earlier, the contextual variables considered in the second stage include the log of total bank assets (a proxy for bank size), capital-to-risk-weighted assets ratio (CRAR), credit–deposit ratio, return on asset, and profit per employee. Since efficiency scores are bounded both from below and above, the log of the efficiency score is considered as the dependent variable. We have used 4 models for second-stage estimation. In model 1, we have applied the static fixed effects model, which included the credit–deposit ratio, log of total bank assets (a proxy for bank size), CRAR, and return on asset as the contextual variables. In model 2 (fixed effects model), return on the asset has been replaced by profit per employee. Model 3 applies a dynamic panel data model with 1 period lagged efficiency, credit–deposit ratio, log of total bank asset (a proxy for bank size), CRAR, and return on asset as the contextual variables. Model 4 is also a dynamic panel data model in which profit per employee is used instead of return on asset. In all the models, the NPA ratio has been excluded because the impact of NPA is already reflected in the total income of the in-sample banks due to the presence of the income recognition norm. Further, return on asset and profit per employee are positively and highly correlated.

For static estimation, we initially applied both fixed effects and random effects panel data models. However, the application of the Hausman test showed that the fixed effects approach is suitable for model estimation. The results obtained from static fixed effects models 1 and 2 are presented in Tables 5 and 6. The results of the two dynamic models are included in Tables 7 and 8, respectively. The results indicate that the coefficient of the credit–deposit ratio is statistically significant for all the models. The coefficients of return on asset (in model 1) and profit per employee (in model 2) are positive but not significant at a 95% level of significance. However, the regression coefficients of the log of total asset (LnTA) and CRAR are negative.

Tables 7 and 8 present the dynamic panel data estimations. The tables indicate that the coefficients of lagged efficiency, credit–deposit ratio, and return on asset/profit per employee are statistically significant. The coefficients of CRAR and LnTA are negative but not significant statistically.

Table 5. Impact of contextual variables — Model 1 (*Static panel data model*).

Particulars	Coefficient	Std. Error	t-ratio	p-value
Intercept	−0.052	0.108	−0.489	0.630
Capital-to-risk-weighted asset ratio	−0.002	0.001	−1.663	0.114
Log of total asset	−0.007	0.010	−0.672	0.510
Credit–Deposit ratio	0.001	0.0004	3.758	0.001
Return on asset	0.010	0.005	1.924	0.071
R-squared		0.56		
Standard error of regression		0.03		

Table 6. Impact of contextual variables — Model 2 (*static panel data model*).

Particulars	**Coefficient**	**Std. Error**	***t*-ratio**	***p*-value**
Intercept	0.002	0.114	0.019	0.984
Capital-to-risk-weighted asset ratio	−0.002	0.001	−1.563	0.136
Log of total asset	−0.014	0.012	−1.108	0.283
Credit–Deposit ratio	0.001	0.0006	2.873	0.010
Return on asset	0.001	0.0006	1.899	0.074
R-squared		0.56		
Standard error of regression		0.03		

Table 7. Impact of contextual variables — Model 1 (*dynamic panel data model*).

Particulars	**Coefficient**	**Std. Error**	***t*-ratio**	***p*-value**
Efficiency (1 period lagged)	0.341	0.106	3.220	0.001
Capital-to-risk-weighted asset ratio	−0.003	0.001	−1.714	0.086
Log of total asset	−0.003	0.011	−0.309	0.757
Credit–Deposit ratio	0.010	0.004	2.665	0.007
Return on asset	0.001	0.0005	3.795	0.0001
Standard error of regression		0.024		

Table 8. Impact of contextual variables — Model 2 (*dynamic panel data model*).

Particulars	**Coefficient**	**Std. Error**	***t*-ratio**	***p*-value**
Efficiency (1 period lagged)	0.365	0.103	3.547	0.0004
Capital-to-risk-weighted asset ratio	−0.003	0.001	−1.647	0.099
Log of total asset	−0.008	0.011	−0.725	0.468
Credit–deposit ratio	0.002	0.0005	3.707	0.0002
Profit per employee	0.001	0.0005	2.561	0.010
Standard error of regression		0.0248		

5. Concluding Observations

The present study seeks to evaluate and explain the technical efficiency of private sector commercial banks operating in India continuously for the past decade (2014–15 through 2023–24) using the directional distance function approach in the first stage and (static and dynamic) panel data approach in the second stage. The benefit of the directional distance function approach is that it provides a complete characterization of the technology and hence provides a robust measure of technical efficiency. In the second stage, the application of panel data models indicates that while the results are along similar lines, the outcome is partially contingent on whether we use the static or dynamic model. In both approaches, the coefficients of the credit–deposit ratio are statistically significant. The coefficients of CRAR and LnTA are negative and statistically insignificant for both approaches. The significance of the coefficients of return on asset and profit per employee, however, depends on whether we are using a static or a dynamic approach. Coefficients of past efficiency scores are significant for an autoregressive structure of order 1 and not for autoregression of higher orders.

The present study concentrates on the performance of private sector banks only. The adoption of a meta-frontier approach in the context of the three categories of diversified commercial banks (public, private, and foreign) can provide a broader-based picture of performance. Further, the number of contextual variables (including the macroeconomic variables) can be increased for second-stage analysis. Future research studies can take up such an agenda.

Appendix

Table A1. Bank-wise efficiency scores (2014–15 to 2018–19).

Banks	2015	2016	2017	2018	2019
City Union Bank Ltd.	1	1	1	1	1
Tamilnad Mercantile Bank Ltd.	0.9708	0.9714	1	1	0.9768
The Catholic Syrian Bank Ltd.	0.9425	0.9533	0.9572	0.8909	0.8707
Dhanlaxmi Bank Ltd	0.8603	0.9671	0.9314	0.9067	0.8674
The Federal Bank Ltd.	0.9571	0.9067	0.9360	0.9461	0.9999

(Continued)

Table A1. (*Continued*)

Banks	2015	2016	2017	2018	2019
The Jammu & Kashmir Bank Ltd.	0.9801	0.9348	0.9026	0.9003	0.9370
The Karnataka Bank Ltd.	0.9839	0.9999	0.9302	0.9577	0.9619
The Karur Vysya Bank Ltd.	0.9999	0.9866	0.9986	0.9937	0.9772
Nainital Bank Ltd.	0.9368	0.9107	0.9999	0.9359	0.9413
RBL Bank	0.8958	0.8984	0.9212	0.9441	0.9800
The South Indian Bank Ltd.	1	0.9700	1	1	0.9999
Axis Bank Ltd.	0.9940	0.9827	0.9704	0.9534	0.9783
DCB Bank Ltd.	0.9338	0.9438	0.9288	0.9211	0.9478
HDFC Bank Ltd.	1	1	1	1	1
ICICI Bank Ltd.	1	1	1	1	1
IndusInd Bank Ltd.	1	1	1	1	1
Kotak Mahindra Bank Ltd.	1	0.9740	0.9917	0.9915	0.9936
YES Bank	1	0.9798	0.9834	1	1

Table A2. Bank-wise efficiency scores (2019–20 to 2023–24).

Banks	2020	2021	2022	2023	2024
City Union Bank Ltd.	0.9882	1	1	1	1
Tamilnad Mercantile Bank Ltd.	0.9806	0.9776	0.9849	0.9968	0.9846
The Catholic Syrian Bank Ltd.	0.9071	1	0.9647	0.9700	0.9588
Dhanlaxmi Bank Ltd	0.8843	0.8470	0.9061	0.9079	0.8845
The Federal Bank Ltd.	0.9868	0.9658	0.9236	0.9754	0.9308
The Jammu & Kashmir Bank Ltd.	0.8919	0.8593	0.8344	0.8767	0.8977
The Karnataka Bank Ltd.	0.9748	0.9998	0.9492	0.9634	0.9422
The Karur Vysya Bank Ltd.	0.9492	0.9207	0.9073	0.9737	0.9643
Nainital Bank Ltd.	0.9519	0.9293	1	1	1
RBL Bank	1	1	0.9182	0.8872	0.9303
The South Indian Bank Ltd.	1	0.9649	0.9250	0.8883	0.9003
Axis Bank Ltd.	1	0.9692	0.9189	0.9286	0.9498
DCB Bank Ltd.	0.9231	1	0.9347	0.8888	0.9196
HDFC Bank Ltd.	1	1	1	1	1
ICICI Bank Ltd.	0.9999	1	0.9746	1	1
IndusInd Bank Ltd.	1	1	0.9713	0.9746	0.9546
Kotak Mahindra Bank Ltd.	1	1	1	1	1
YES Bank	1	0.9357	0.8679	0.8515	0.8568

References

Banker, R. D., Charnes, A., and Cooper, W. W. (1984). Some models for estimating technical and scale inefficiencies in data envelopment analysis. *Management Science*, 30(9), 1078–1092. https://doi.org/10.1287/mnsc.30.9.1078.

Benston, G. J. (1965). Branch banking and economies of scale. *Journal of Finance*, 20(2), 312–331.

Benston, G., Hanweck, G., and Humphrey, D. (1982). Scale economies in banking: A restructuring and reassessment. *Journal of Money, Credit and Banking*, 14, 435. https://doi.org/10.2307/1991654.

Berger, A. N., Hanweck, G. A., and Humphrey, D. B. (1987). Competitive viability in banking: Scale, scope, and product mix economies. *Journal of Monetary Economics*, 20(3), 501–520.

Berger, A. N. and Humphrey, D. B. (1993). Efficiency and productivity growth in U.S. Banking. In H. O. Fried and S. S. Schmidt (Eds.), *The Measurement of Productive Efficiency: Techniques and Applications* (pp. 386–413).

Berger, A. N. and Humphrey, D. B. (1994). Bank scale economies, mergers, concentration, and efficiency: The U.S. experience. *Finance and Economics Discussion Series* 94-23, Board of Governors of the Federal Reserve System (U.S.).

Bhattacharya, A., Lovell, C. K., and Sahay, P. (1997). The impact of liberalization on the productive efficiency of Indian Commercial Banks. *European Journal of Operational Research*, 98, 332–345. https://doi.org/10.1016/S0377-2217(96)00351-7.

Chambers, R. G., Chung, Y., and Fare, R. (1996). Benefit and distance functions. *Journal of Economic Theory*, 70(2), 407–419.

Charnes, A., Cooper, W. W., and Rhodes, E. (1978). Measuring the inefficiency of decision making units. *European Journal Operational Research*, 2(6), 429–444. https://doi.org/10.1016/0377-2217(78)90138-8.

Chatterjee, B. and Sinha, R. P. (2006). Cost efficiency and commercial bank lending: Some empirical results. *The Indian Economic Journal.* https://doi.org/10.1177/0019466220060109.

Dar, A. H., Mathur, S. K., and Mishra, S. (2021). The efficiency of Indian banks: A DEA, Malmquist and SFA analysis with bad output. *Journal of Quantitative Economics*, 19(4), 653–701.

Das, A., Nag, A., and Ray, S. C. (2005). Liberalisation, ownership and efficiency in Indian banking: A nonparametric analysis. *Economic and Political Weekly*, 40(12), 1190–1197. http://www.jstor.org/stable/4416367.

Färe, R. and Grosskopf, S. (2000). Theory and application of directional distance functions. *Journal of Productivity Analysis*, 13(2), 93–103. https://doi.org/10.1023/A:1007844628920.

Farrell, M. J. (1957). The measurement of productive efficiency. *Journal of The Royal Statistical Society*, Series A, General, 120(3), 253–281. https://doi.org/10.2307/2343100.

Favero, C. A. and Papi, L. (1995). Technical efficiency and scale efficiency in the Italian banking sector: a non-parametric approach. *Applied Economics*, 27(4), 385–395. https://doi.org/10.1080/00036849500000123.

Hancock, D. (1985). The financial firm: Production with monetary and nonmonetary goods. *Journal of Political Economy*, 93(5), 859–880.

Hancock, D. (1991). *A Theory of Production for the Financial Firm*. Kluwer Academic Publishers.

Kumbhakar, S. C. and Sarkar, S. (2003). Deregulation, ownership and efficiency in Indian banking. *Arthaniti-Journal of Economic Theory and Practice*. https://doi.org/10.1177/0976747920030101.

Luenberger, D. G. (1992a). Benefit functions and duality. *Journal of Mathematical Economics*, 21(5), 461–481.

Luenberger, D. G. (1992b). New optimality principles for economic efficiency and equilibrium. *Journal of Optimization Theory and Applications*, 75(2), 221–264.

Ram Mohan, T. T. and Ray, S. C. (2004). Comparing performance of public and private sector banks: A revenue maximisation efficiency approach. *Economic and Political Weekly*, 39(12), 1271–1276. http://www.jstor.org/stable/4414806.

Rezitis, A. N. (2008). Efficiency and productivity effects of bank mergers: Evidence from the greek banking industry. *Economic Modelling*, 25(2), 236–254. https://doi.org/10.1016/j.econmod.2007.04.013.

Saha, A. and Ravisankar, T. S. (2000). Rating of Indian commercial banks: A DEA approach. *European Journal of Operational Research*, 124(1), 187–203.

Sathye, M. (2003). Efficiency of banks in a developing economy: The case of India. *European Journal of Operational Research*, 148(3), 662–671.

Sealey, C. W. and Lindley, J. T. (1977). Inputs, outputs, and a theory of production and cost at depository financial institutions. *The Journal of Finance*, 32(4), 1251–1266.

Shephard, R. W. (1953). *Cost and Productions*. Princeton University Press.

Shephard, R. W. (1970). *Theory of Cost and Productions*. Princeton University Press.

Shephard, R. W. (1974). *Indirect Production Functions*. Verlag Anton Hain.

https://doi.org/10.1142/9789819823161_0011

Chapter 11

Efficiency of ASEAN Banks: A Novel Analysis Using the Non-Convex Frontier Approach

Thanh Ngo[*,†,¶], **Tu Le**[‡,§,||], **and Thi-Linh Pham**[†,**]

[*] *School of Aviation, Massey University, Palmerston North, New Zealand*
[†] *Faculty of Political Economy, VNU University of Economics and Business, Hanoi, Vietnam*
[‡] *Faculty of Finance—Banking, University of Economics and Law, Ho Chi Minh City, Vietnam*
[§] *Vietnam National University, Ho Chi Minh City, Vietnam*
[¶] *t.ngo@massey.ac.nz*
[||] *tuldq@uel.edu.vn*
[**] *phamthilinh@vnu.edu.vn*

The Association of Southeast Asian Nations (ASEAN), with a combined population of over 600 million and a land area of over 4.5 million km^2, contributed around US$10.2 trillion (around 6.5%) of the 2022 global GDP in terms of purchasing power parity. The banking system of its members, therefore, plays a crucial role in maintaining financial stability and boosting the financial and economic integration of the Association. This chapter examines the efficiency of ASEAN banks using the frontier analysis approach, with a focus on the non-convexity of such a frontier. Using data from 69 banks from five ASEAN members in the 2007–2019 period, we found that although the banks had improved their operational efficiency, there is still room for improvement.

Keywords: Free Disposal Hull (FDH), efficiency, (non)convexity, ASEAN, banks, regression, two-stage.

1. Introduction

The Association of Southeast Asian Nations (ASEAN) is a regional intergovernmental organization founded on August 8, 1967, in Bangkok, Thailand (ASEAN, 2024). Its primary goals are to promote political and economic cooperation and ensure regional stability among its ten member countries: Brunei Darussalam, Cambodia, Indonesia, Laos, Malaysia, Myanmar (Burma), the Philippines, Singapore, Thailand, and Vietnam. These nations collaborate on economic integration, cultural exchange, and political cooperation, positioning ASEAN as a crucial player in both regional and global affairs. Over the years, ASEAN has achieved significant milestones that enhance regional stability and economic growth. Key accomplishments include the establishment of the ASEAN Free Trade Area (AFTA) in 1992 and the creation of the ASEAN Economic Community (AEC) in 2015. Other important initiatives include the ASEAN Regional Forum (ARF), the ASEAN Cultural Fund, the ASEAN Tourism Strategic Plan, and the ASEAN Community Vision 2025. These achievements demonstrate ASEAN's dedication to fostering regional cooperation and addressing common challenges, ultimately contributing to a more integrated and prosperous Southeast Asia.

Currently, ASEAN has a combined population of over 600 million and a land area of over 4.5 million km^2, contributing around US$10.2 trillion (around 6.5%) of the 2022 global GDP in terms of purchasing power parity (World Bank, 2024). The banking systems of each member of ASEAN, as the backbone of the economy, therefore, play a crucial role in maintaining financial stability and boosting the financial and economic integration of the Association. Such developments in terms of regulatory frameworks, regional banking integration (e.g., the ASEAN Banking Integration Framework initiative), technological advancements (e.g., digital banking, mobile payments, blockchain technology, and fintech), financial inclusion, and sustainable finance support the development of the public and private sectors, especially small and medium enterprises (SMEs), drive technological innovation, and attract investment, making them a cornerstone of Southeast Asia's economic development (ASEAN, 2024). Accordingly, improving the efficiency and performance of the banking system is crucial for each and every member of ASEAN.

Despite the richness of the literature on banking efficiency, attention on ASEAN banks is still limited. Previous studies were either focused on the US, Europe, and Chinese markets (Cao *et al.*, 2024; Hammami *et al.*, 2022; Li *et al.*, 2022) or examined the banking system in each ASEAN country individually (Boubaker *et al.*, 2024; Ngo and Nguyen, 2012; Wasiaturrahma *et al.*, 2020), while comparative studies at the regional level are scarce. In addition, while Data Envelopment Analysis (DEA) is the mostly used method for efficiency evaluation, mainly thanks to its flexibility in dealing with small samples and not requiring a priori production function (Boubaker and Ngo, 2024), this method relies on the assumption that all banks being examined operate under a convex technology (Coelli *et al.*, 2005; Cooper *et al.*, 2011). In reality, most sectors and industries have non-convex technologies (Kerstens *et al.*, 2019, 2024), and thus, it is important to look at banking efficiency from the viewpoint of the non-convex aspect. This chapter contributes to the literature as the first study to examine the efficiency of ASEAN banks using the Free Disposal Hull (FDH) method that accounts for non-convexity.

The remainder of the chapter is organized as follows. Section 2 provides a brief review of the relevant literature on bank efficiency. Section 3 provides some background on ASEAN banks. The FDH methodology and data are presented in Section 4. Section 4 then reports and discusses the empirical results, while Section 5 concludes the Chapter.

2. Literature Review

The literature on bank efficiency is extensive (e.g., Ahmad *et al.*, 2020; Bhatia *et al.*, 2018; Fethi and Pasiouras, 2010; Paradi and Zhu, 2013; Zopounidis *et al.*, 2015). In this section, we focus on some relevant and recent research addressing the efficiency of individual banks (rather than banking systems) in cross-country, independent countries, and ASEAN countries.

2.1. *Bank efficiency at the cross-country level*

Dogan and Fausten (2009) conducted an extensive analysis employing bootstrap DEA to assess the technical efficiency levels of commercial banks, excluding Islamic ones, across the countries of Indonesia, Malaysia, the Philippines, and Thailand, during the time frame spanning the year 2001 to the year 2005. The authors evaluated two models for their analysis: The first model utilized deposits, personnel expenses, and fixed assets as the primary inputs, while considering off-balance sheet items, loans, and other earning assets as the resulting outputs; conversely, the second model incorporated interest expense and non-interest expense as inputs, whereas it viewed interest income and non-interest income as the outputs generated. In this regard, the initial model adhered to an intermediation approach as delineated by Sealey and Lindley (1977), while the subsequent model aligned with a core profit approach (Avkiran, 2011). Despite the findings of the study suggesting that the banks under examination experienced an enhancement in their efficiency over the period from 2001 to 2005, which indicates a favorable outcome stemming from the restructuring processes undertaken within the banking sectors of the countries involved in the study, it is noteworthy that the average efficiency levels remained relatively low, particularly in Indonesia, which points to the fact that these banks possess the potential to amplify their output without necessitating an increase in their input resources. Consequently, improving corporate governance, collecting information, reducing risk aversion in bank lending, and increasing market competition could help enhance bank efficiency.

Alqahtani *et al.* (2017) employed both DEA and Stochastic Frontier Analysis (SFA) to assess the cost and profit efficiency of 80 banks from six countries in the Gulf Cooperation Council (GCC) region during the period from 1999 to 2012; such a sample accounted for approximately 38% of the total Islamic assets worldwide at the end of 2014. The research findings indicated that during the GFC, Islamic banks demonstrated greater cost efficiency compared to conventional banks and had also significantly reduced the gap in profit efficiency relative to their counterpart. However, in the post-GFC period, Islamic banks experienced a decline in profit efficiency and lost their earlier cost efficiency advantage. The plausible causes for this situation were discussed regarding the unique characteristics of Islamic banks in general and each bank in the sample in particular, as well as banking competition and regulation.

Degl'Innocenti *et al.* (2017) investigated bank productivity growth and the integration process across 28 EU countries during three key phases of the financial crisis: the US subprime crisis (2007–2008), the global financial crisis (2009–2010), and the sovereign debt crisis (2010–2012). To do that, they followed a two-stage Malmquist DEA approach to evaluate the efficiency and productivity changes over time of 539 commercial banks in the EU-28 countries. The study found strong evidence of convergence among European banks during the financial crisis, indicated by negative and statistically significant β-convergence and σ-convergence coefficients. The results also suggested that the decline in overall productivity over time was primarily driven by poor performance in the second stage of the production process, particularly due to reduced lending activities. The authors, therefore, recommended the establishment of a Banking Union in the EU and the implementation of a European Deposit Insurance Scheme. These measures could restore confidence in the banking system, enhance resilience against future crises, and improve the banks' ability to absorb shocks without compromising productivity or lending activities. Additionally, the study suggests that policymakers control the size of banks to minimize moral hazard and risk-taking behaviors, i.e., the "too-big-to-fail" phenomenon (Beccalli *et al.*, 2015; Stern and Feldman, 2004).

Feng and Wang (2018) employing O'Donnell's (2012) decomposition approach to analyze and compare European and US banks over the 2004–2014 period. Their findings indicated that European banks not only exhibited weak profitability but it also worsened over time. The decomposition technique allowed the authors to identify the causes of such deterioration: lower returns on earnings assets, higher funding costs, and lower scale efficiency. Accordingly, the authors suggested that the European Central Bank should closely monitor the funding costs of European banks relative to US banks and maintain low refinancing rates for an extended period to help reduce the banks' costs. Additionally, they recommend that European banks should focus on improving their efficiency and profitability by addressing the above-mentioned causes, with extended caution on operational factors (e.g., to also examine physical data rather than only financial data) and bank size (e.g., to incorporate small banks rather than only big banks).

Phan *et al.* (2018) pointed out the necessity of banking efficiency research for the East Asia and Pacific region, which includes both developed and developing markets. The study employed SFA to estimate bank cost efficiency and also used DEA as a comparative method. An unbalanced panel dataset of 247 banks from 12 East

Asia and Pacific economies over the period from 2003 to 2012 was examined to reveal that the average bank cost efficiency was moderate, with approximately one-quarter of resources wasted. It also highlighted the negative role of liquidity risk on cost efficiency, while macroeconomic factors like inflation and interest rates can paradoxically enhance bank performance.

Hussain *et al.* (2020) measured the revenue efficiency of Islamic and conventional banks from three regions — the Middle East, Southeast Asia, and South Asia — covering 19 countries from 2006 to 2017. The study also followed a two-stage DEA approach, where DEA was utilized in the first stage to measure bank efficiency, then Ordinary Least Squares (OLS) and Generalized Method of Moments (GMM) were used in the second stage to examine the impact of bank-specific, macroeconomic, and country governance factors on such efficiency. The results showed that Islamic banks exhibited slightly higher profit efficiency (76.6%) and revenue efficiency (65.2%) compared to conventional banks (71.2% and 61%, respectively). However, Islamic banks were relatively cost inefficient (66.6%) compared to conventional banks (71.9%). While the study consequently emphasized the need for tailored governance policies to enhance banking efficiency across different countries, it also acknowledged that future research should explore other methods like FDH, SFA, and even the traditional financial ratio analysis.

Ben Lahouel *et al.* (2022) investigated how liquidity risk affected the stability of European banks at varying levels of involvement in non-traditional banking activities, particularly in the context of the Basel III liquidity regulations. The study employed a combination of DEA and the CAMELS rating system to evaluate the bank stability of 176 European banks (2010–2019), then bank stability was regressed on liquidity risk, income diversification, and other determinants using a Panel Smooth Transition Regression model, which allows for the examination of nonlinear relationships and threshold effects. The study found that liquidity risk significantly affects bank stability, and the relationship is influenced by the degree of income diversification. The authors also acknowledged that the focus on European banks may limit the generalizability of the findings to other banking contexts, and thus, incorporating other macroeconomic controls such as market competition, bank size, and ownership structure could help one gain deeper insights into the factors affecting bank stability.

Hammami *et al.* (2022) proposed a Euclidean Common Set of Weights (ECSW) approach in the context of DEA to evaluate the efficiency and performance of Eurozone banks. The study revealed that Eurozone banks had an average performance in 2018 of only around 60% of their potential capability, suggesting more room for improvement. The results also highlight the banks' strengths in managing employees and operating income, while indicating weaknesses in monitoring deposits and operating expenses. The authors, however, also acknowledged the limitations of the ECSW-DEA approach, including the sensitivity issue, the homogeneity assumption, and the need for further extension and data utilization.

Boubaker *et al.* (2022) utilized the inverse DEA to creatively measure the efficiency of 49 Islamic banks across ten countries (Bangladesh, Bahrain, Egypt, Jordan, Kuwait, Oman, Pakistan, Qatar, Sri Lanka, and the UAE) between 2019 and 2020 amid the impacts of the COVID-19 pandemic. In particular, the study estimated the optimal adjustments of the banks' inputs to maintain their efficiency levels from 2019 to 2020, i.e., to mitigate the impacts of the pandemic. The findings revealed that the average efficiency of the banks increased from 0.627 in 2019 to 0.690 in 2020, suggesting that they were resilient to the COVID-19 shock. However, while 31 banks experienced a decline in outputs, only ten of them had their efficiency decline. Consequently, the authors suggested that managers and policymakers only need to focus on those ten banks, rather than all 31 banks, as in the traditional DEA approach.

In a similar vein, Nguyen *et al.* (2023) used a two-stage DEA approach to firstly estimate the technical efficiency of 78 Islamic banks across 15 countries (2005–2020) and then regressed them on various bank-level and country-level factors, including the impacts of the Global Financial Crisis (GFC) and COVID-19. The authors found that the Islamic banking industry performed at a moderate level during 2005–2020, with an average efficiency score of 0.673. While the GFC had a significant negative impact on the banks' efficiency, there is no statistical evidence that COVID-19 has hindered their performance, indicating the resilience of Islamic banks regarding the recent pandemic. Additionally, the study also found that controllable factors like bank size, inflation, and geographic region positively influence bank efficiency.

2.2. *Banking efficiency at country level*

Avkiran (2011) used DEA to analyze the efficiency of Chinese commercial banks based on financial ratios for 2007 and 2008 under three different models (i.e., the core profitability model, the expanded profitability model, and the financial ratio model) and the assumption of the slacks-based measure (SBM) super-efficiency. Their sample included three banks from the state-owned commercial bank group, nine from the joint-stock commercial bank group, five from city commercial banks, and four from locally incorporated foreign banks. They found a generally low correlation between bank efficiency and key financial ratios, indicating that financial ratios inadequately represent production inefficiencies. It was, therefore, suggested that bank efficiency estimates could be used to predict future values of certain key financial ratios.

Sufian and Habibullah (2011) also used DEA to evaluate the efficiency of the Chinese banking sector, but for an unbalanced panel data of 34 to 114 banks from 2000 to 2008, yielding a total of 582 bank-year observations. In the second-stage analysis, they regressed the DEA efficiency scores against a set of bank characteristics (e.g., returns over assets and bank size) and macroeconomic environment (e.g., GDP, inflation and monetary freedom). The study found that inefficiency of Chinese banks primarily arose from scale rather than technical factors and that financial freedom had a negative impact, while bank size had a positive impact on bank efficiency. It consequently highlighted the importance of a stable business environment for bank operations and enhancing the efficiency of the Chinese banking sector.

Lee and Chih (2013) assessed both the static and dynamic efficiencies of China's listed banks using a dynamic slacks-based measure proposed by Tone (2001). Fifteen banks, including four state-owned commercial banks, eight joint-stock commercial banks, and three city commercial banks, were examined for the period of 2005–2011. The results showed that banks with higher loan-to-deposit and current ratios demonstrate higher efficiency compared to their counterpart, whereas the cost-to-income ratio has a significant and negative effect on bank efficiency. As such, the relationship between financial regulation and bank efficiency is complex, suggesting a trade-off between financial stability and efficiency.

Also on Chinese banks, but Fang *et al.* (2019) employed a one-step Generalized Method of Moments (GMM) system estimator to analyze the profitability of Chinese banks under the impacts of competition, efficiency, and risk levels. To do that, the authors firstly used SFA to estimate bank cost efficiency, the Boone indicator to measure bank competition, and the Z-score to proxy for bank risk; then, they used GMM to examine their relationship with bank profitability. Results from the examination of 100 Chinese banks over the 2003–2017 period showed that bank size, cost efficiency, profit efficiency, and inflation are significantly related to bank profitability. Importantly, the positive impact of cost efficiency on profitability is more pronounced when banks engage in higher levels of risk and face greater competition. Consequently, the study emphasized the need for improved management systems in large banks to enhance profitability.

Aissia and Ellouz (2021) employed SFA as the primary method to estimate efficiency scores for Tunisian bank branches. The data spanned a period of 5 years, from 2007 to 2019, and covered 94 bank branches from a public bank in Tunisia across all 24 Tunisian provinces. It found that the branches exhibited relatively similar levels of efficiency, but they were influenced by factors such as location (e.g., regarding local population and banking services demand), regulations, and competition among branches.

Li *et al.* (2022) analyzed the bankruptcy risk dynamically of 4426 US banks over a period of 15 years from 2002 to 2016 using a Malmquist (worst-frontier) DEA model. Particularly, the study first evaluated the efficiency of the sampled banks using a worst-frontier assumption where the less efficient banks received the highest (worst-frontier) efficiency score and then incorporated statistical models and non-parametric methods, including Trait Recognition and Neural Networks, for predicting bank failures. The study revealed that less efficient banks are more likely to experience distress or collapse, emphasizing the importance of monitoring bank efficiency.

In contrast, Kumar *et al.* (2022) argued that while DEA is sensitive to the choice of inputs/outputs, feature selection is important to improve the discriminability of DEA. In particular, the Relief algorithm of machine learning (ML) was utilized to assess feature importance, allowing for the elimination of redundant or irrelevant inputs and outputs. With an empirical application on 59 Indian banks (2000–2017) regarding 25 features and financial ratios (e.g., cost-to-income ratio and returns over assets), the study effectively mapped the failed and surviving banks under a comprehensive framework of distress prediction in the Indian banking sector.

Afroj *et al.* (2024) also used DEA to evaluate the technical, allocative, and cost efficiency of banks in Bangladesh. Additionally, a panel VAR model is utilized to analyze the interrelationship among cost efficiency, non-performing loans, and the equity–asset ratio, providing insights into the causality between these variables. The study utilizes secondary data retrieved from the annual reports of 34 banks in Bangladesh for the period from 2010 to 2018. The authors found a two-way negative association between cost efficiency and non-performing loans, indicating that lower cost efficiency correlates with higher non-performing loans, supporting both the bad luck and bad management hypotheses; however, the moral hazard hypothesis was rejected. Additionally, the paper pointed out the need for improved managerial performance and regulatory supervision to mitigate these inefficiencies and enhance the overall banking sector's stability.

Bisrat Getinet *et al.* (2024) utilized the shadow prices estimated from DEA results in evaluating the technical efficiency and allocative efficiency of 19 Ethiopian banks over the period of 1990–2022, totaling 325 bank-year observations. It revealed that publicly owned commercial banks in Ethiopia are technically more efficient than privately owned banks. Among privately owned banks, however, smaller and recently established banks exhibit higher technical efficiency compared to larger and older counterparts. In contrast, all banks demonstrated allocative inefficiency, suggesting an overutilization situation of loanable funds and physical capital relative to labor input. Therefore, it was suggested that Ethiopian public banks could achieve cost savings by optimizing input use, while private banks could benefit from enhancing managerial efficiency.

Rasoul *et al.* (2024) applied both DEA and SFA in their research. The study particularly assessed the efficiency of US small banks after the 2008 GFC, utilizing data from a total of 10,495 banks that operated during the 2010–2021 period (i.e., approximately 875 banks per year). It found that the sampled banks had consistently low overall efficiency, primarily due to low technical efficiency and scale efficiency. It also highlighted that improving the efficiency for small banks could mitigate failures and enhance regional economic growth in the US. Meanwhile, extending the research to other samples could further verify their findings and implications.

Amirteimoori *et al.* (2024) developed a firm-specific Malmquist DEA productivity index model to analyze the efficiency and productivity changes in banks within a stochastic environment. It followed the two-stage double bootstrap DEA procedure of Simar and Wilson (2007), where the first stage calculated technical efficiency scores using the classic DEA model, and the second stage applied the double-bootstrap DEA model to assess the impact of contextual variables on bank efficiency. In contrast, for productivity changes, it extended the two stages to the case that SFA was utilized in the first stage, rather than DEA as in the traditional approach. The authors utilized an empirical dataset from the Iranian banking sector, comprising 120 bank-year observations from 15 banks over the period from 2014 to 2021. It revealed that the non-performing loan ratio and the number of branches had an inverse relationship with stochastic technical efficiency and productivity changes. Therefore, optimizing those bank-specific controllable factors is crucial for enhancing the efficiency and productivity of Iranian banks.

Kweh *et al.* (2024) also followed the DEA approach but under a dynamic network structure to measure resource management and profitability efficiencies of banks. A total of 287 US commercial banks (2010–2020) were examined, whereas the results identified a 55.4% room for improvement in bank performance. In addition, the study also pointed out that efficient banks generally had higher CAMEL ratings than inefficient ones. In particular, management quality, earnings quality, and liquidity ratios positively influence bank performance. In addition, larger banks tended to be more efficient than smaller ones.

Antunes *et al.* (2024) followed a two-stage approach combining DEA and ML (i.e., neural networks) to evaluate and predict the efficiency of 39 Chinese commercial banks operating during the 2010-2018 period. The research findings indicated that Chinese banks experienced a gradual increase in efficiency from 2010 to 2015, followed by slight volatility, culminating in an efficiency score of 0.746 by the end of 2018. More importantly, it showed that inefficient banks could benefit from improvements in traditional banking activities, while banks with higher efficiency levels must seek alternative profitable banking ventures such as digitalization and fintech. In the second-stage analysis, the study also highlighted the importance of understanding the interrelationships between efficiency and various bank-specific variables (e.g., bank size, profitability, and expense management).

In contrast, Cao *et al.* (2024) argued that the traditional two-stage DEA may lead to biased results, and the so-called single-step SFA (Ngo and Tripe, 2017) would be a better choice. A heterogeneous SFA model, therefore, was utilized to incorporate influencing factors (e.g., ownership and fintech index) directly into the model setup, enhancing the reliability of the findings. The empirical sample of Cao *et al.* (2024) involved quarterly panel data from 37 listed banks in China, covering the period from Q4 2014 to Q4 2021. Their results revealed that fintech played a moderating role in amplifying the positive effects of ESG investments on Chinese bank efficiency. The unique regulatory environment in China, in addition, also created significant differences across banks, which may affect the efficiency of ESG investments.

Pasha (2024) also followed the two-stage DEA approach, but with quantile regression in the second stage to account for the effects of variables across the entire conditional distribution of liquidity risk as the dependent variable in this stage. In particular, the study examined a sample period from 2014 to 2022, which includes the beginning of a politically stable period and significant banking reforms in Egypt, for ten Egyptian commercial banks (i.e., three public and seven private ones). It was empirically found that public banks in Egypt demonstrate superior efficiency compared to private banks, and there was a significant negative relationship between bank efficiency and liquidity risk, indicating that bank efficiency could mitigate liquidity risk. In addition, the impact of micro- and macro-level factors on liquidity risk varies depending on the bank's liquidity risk level.

2.3. *Bank efficiency in the ASEAN*

Studies on ASEAN banks were scattered, with several studies on banks and the banking sectors in Indonesia, Malaysia, Thailand, and

Vietnam, mainly due to the data availability issue (Azad *et al.*, 2017). For example, *in the context of Malaysian banking institutions*, the research conducted by Hasan *et al.* (2012) investigated and assessed the technical efficiency levels of the Malaysia domestic banks that are publicly listed on the Kuala Lumpur Stock Exchange (KLSE), focusing on the time frame that spans from the year 2005 to the year 2010. By utilizing the SFA method, the researchers discovered that the Malaysian domestic banks demonstrated an impressive average overall efficiency rating of 94 percent, and there was a noticeable increase in the efficiency levels throughout the duration of the study period. Meanwhile, Ismail *et al.* (2013) explored the cost efficiency aspect of Malaysian banks, analyzing data from the years 2006 to 2009 through the lens of DEA and Tobit regression, i.e., a two-stage analytical approach. The findings from the first stage of this study disclosed that technical efficiency was the main contributor to cost efficiency for conventional commercial banks, while allocative efficiency was the main contributor to cost efficiency of Islamic banks in Malaysia. Furthermore, the results obtained from the second stage of the analysis indicated that both market capitalization and the sizes of the banks were positively and significantly correlated with bank efficiency. The study of Azad *et al.* (2017) also adopted the two-stage DEA methodology: They incorporated the meta-frontier DEA (O'Donnell *et al.*, 2008) in the first stage and bootstrap regression (Simar and Wilson, 2007) in the second stage of their analysis. By analyzing a dataset encompassing 43 Malaysian commercial banks over the period of 2009 to 2013, the authors of this study concluded that bank ownership, bank-specific characteristics (e.g., bank size and ROA), and macroeconomic factors (e.g., GDP) had a significant influence on bank efficiency. In a more recent publication, Samad (2021) investigated the impacts of the 2007 GFC on loan and deposit efficiencies of Islamic banks operating in Malaysia during the years 2008 to 2013. This study concluded that the efficiency levels of Malaysian Islamic banks remained stable throughout this tumultuous period, thereby suggesting a remarkable resilience of those Islamic banks amid the GFC. Such a finding is consistent with other studies discussed in Section 2.1 (Alqahtani *et al.*, 2017; Hussain *et al.*, 2020).

Regarding Indonesian banks, Zhang and Matthews (2012) conducted an investigation into the convergence characteristics of cost efficiency among Indonesian banking institutions during the time frame of 1992–2007, employing an unbalanced panel dataset totaling 581 bank-year observations. Through the application of a two-stage semi-parametric double bootstrap DEA method, the authors identified that, in a broad sense, the post-crisis structural reform (after the 1997 Asian Financial Crisis) contributed to an enhancement in the average efficiency levels across the banks in the sample. Defung *et al.* (2016) similarly examined the influence of regulatory changes on the technical efficiency of Indonesian banks, this time using data from 101 banks over 19 years (1993 to 2011). Wasiaturrahma *et al.* (2020) compared the efficiency of conventional and Islamic rural banks in Indonesia over the five-year period of 2013–2017. Accordingly, a total of 1,384 rural banks were examined, whereas the results showed that both conventional and Islamic rural banks in Indonesia are inefficient in their intermediation roles (i.e., intermediaries between savers and borrowers) but efficient in production (i.e., producers of banking services using relevant input resources) aspects. Nevertheless, the study acknowledged the limitation of the Tobit model (in the second stage) as it ignored too many efficient banks from the regression. Meanwhile, Aam Slamet and Aisyah (2021) followed the window-DEA approach (Ngo and Tsui, 2020) to examine 14 Indonesian Islamic banks in the period from 2011 to 2020. This study reported an average level of efficiency in the Indonesian banking sector (i.e., 80 percent) with an increasing trend over time, suggesting a stable condition of the sector (before the COVID-19 pandemic). Similar results were also reported in Masrizal *et al.* (2023) for 40 Islamic rural banks in 34 Indonesian regions from 2014 to 2020. Moreover, Masrizal *et al.* (2023) also revealed that economic freedom had a strong, favorable impact on the efficiency of the examined banks. It was therefore suggested that business freedom, government spending, and investment freedom should be encouraged as they can enhance bank efficiency, while government integrity and tax burden should be monitored to reduce their negative impact on the performance of Indonesian Islamic rural banks. Citra (2023), on the other hand, examined the impact of bank spatial competition on bank cost efficiency under the SFA framework, also for Indonesian rural banks. This study used a larger dataset with more than 1,000 rural banks (Q1–2014 to Q4–2018). Overall, the results supported the competition–efficiency hypothesis. It also helps the idea that banks have mark-up pricing (higher market power) and may choose to reduce their effort to maximize profit.

For the Thai banking sector, Sufian and Habibullah (2010) examined the efficiency of Thai banks from 1999 to 2008 using DEA. The results indicated that inefficiency in the Thai banking sector stemmed mainly from scale rather than the (pure) technical (in)efficiencies. Further multivariate regression analysis suggested that banks with a higher loan intensity and that are relatively better capitalized tend to exhibit higher efficiency levels, while higher credit risk hinders bank efficiency. Ngo and Nguyen (2012) extended the traditional DEA model in Sufian and Habibullah (2010) and employed the Malmquist DEA approach to evaluate the efficiency and total factor productivity changes of 27 major banks in Thailand from 2007 to 2010. The authors found that the productivity of Thai banks dropped in 2010, indicating a delayed effect of the 2007 GFC on the country's banking sector, in line with Sufian and Habibullah (2010). Interestingly, while the local banks maintained their stability, foreign banks exhibited fluctuating performance, mainly due to decreasing returns to scale resulting from overexpansion. Consequently, the study emphasized the need for continued development and restructuring of the banking system to address these challenges as an urgent task for Thailand. Lapteacru and Lahet (2014) studied the evolution of the market power (Lerner index) of the Thai banking sector and its influences on bank cost efficiency. This paper found that, over the 1993–2010 period, bank competition increased during the 1997 Asian Financial Crisis but dropped afterward; the 2007 GFC did not have any impact on the market power of Thai banks. As for cost efficiency, it decreased following the crisis of 1997–1998, but no effect was found regarding the 2007 GFC, suggesting a correlation with bank competition.

In terms of the Vietnamese banking sector, early studies include Nguyen (2007), Nguyen *et al.* (2008), and Ngo and Tripe (2010). Later, Vu and Turnell (2010) investigated the cost efficiency of 56 Vietnamese commercial banks (2000–2006) using the Bayesian approach and reported that the banks performed relatively well with an efficiency score of around 87 percent. However, the banking industry faced a slight decrease in cost efficiency in the examined period, mainly due to the increases in the costs of managing diverse activities, the enlargement of branch networks and the upgrading of the banking technology platform. Ngo (2012), in contrast, examines the whole Vietnamese banking sector as a single entity over the period of 1990–2010. By applying a modified window-DEA approach, the research revealed that the efficiency of the Vietnamese banking sector decreased over time; this finding strengthened the previous argument of Vu and Turnell (2010). Nguyen and Simioni (2015), on the other hand, focused on the evolution of the productivity changes of 28 Vietnamese banks over the period 2008 to 2012, and on the evolution of different components of total factor productivity (i.e., technical change, pure technical efficiency, scale and mix efficiency). Their results mainly complemented previous studies in confirming the recent development of the Vietnamese banking system; however, they also suggested the State Bank of Vietnam should simultaneously consider both bank mergers and regulatory standard requirements as solutions for bank restructuring in Vietnam. Instead of DEA, Ngo and Tripe (2017) used a single-step SFA method to examine alternative methods for treating non-performing loans (NPLs) in the context of bank cost efficiency estimations. Using data from 12 Vietnamese commercial banks for the 2003–2010 period, the authors found the cost efficiency of Vietnamese banks over the period examined was moderate and, importantly, also with a slight decreasing trend. A summary and meta-analysis for the bank efficiency literature in the Vietnamese context, particularly on this decreasing trend, can be further found in Ho *et al.* (2021). Meanwhile, Le *et al.* (2022) focused more on the effect of intellectual capital (and its components) on the efficiency of Vietnamese commercial banks from 2007 to 2019. The results indicate that intellectual capital, with human capital as the significant and positive component, could enhance all types of bank efficiency. The study further highlighted that bank size is also an important determinant of efficiency. In another attempt, Le *et al.* (2023) recently revisited the relationship between CEO's personality and firm performance for 27 Vietnamese commercial banks. However, this study differed from the previous literature where the authors used graphology to classify the handwritten signatures of CEOs to proxy for their personality traits such as extraversion or conscientiousness, following the "Upper Echelons" theory (Hambrick, 2007; Hambrick and Mason, 1984). Overall, the study found that banks with conscientious CEOs tend to outperform their counterparts.

To the best of our knowledge, only a handful of studies involving the comparison of banking efficiency in ASEAN use cross-country data. For instance, Karim (2001) used SFA to investigate the differences in bank efficiency across 155 ASEAN banks (1989–1996) from four countries: Indonesia, Malaysia, the Philippines, and Thailand.

Wong and Deng (2016) used various DEA models to examine the efficiency of 39 banks in the same four ASEAN countries over 2000–2010. Nguyen and Vo (2020) used single-step SFA to examine the efficiency of ASEAN banks from 2007 to 2014 for 175 banks from Cambodia, Indonesia, Malaysia, the Philippines, Vietnam, and Thailand. Do Van (2022) employed panel vector autoregression analysis to study the impact of bank capitalization on efficiency for 146 banks in Thailand, Malaysia, the Philippines, Indonesia, and Vietnam for the period from 2005 to 2015. Zhang and Liu (2024) extended the dataset to cover 152 banks over 29 years (1994–2022) in Thailand, Singapore, Indonesia, the Philippines, and Malaysia and employed SFA to not only examine bank efficiency but also its convergence, i.e., a movement toward uniform efficiency across ASEAN banks. Nevertheless, all studies found differences in the efficiency of ASEAN banks, which are linked to country-specific factors such as GDP and inflation.

2.4. *Summary*

- Studies on the bank efficiency of the ASEAN countries were still limited at both country and cross-country levels.
- Most studies utilized DEA, followed by SFA. These methods rely on the assumption of convexity, which is rarely applied in reality (Daraio *et al.*, 2020; Kerstens *et al.*, 2019), as no study utilizes the non-convex model of FDH in their research.
- It is important to not only assess the efficiency of the banks but also examine its determinants, since the bank characteristics and macroeconomic condition vary across the banks and countries, i.e., the heterogeneity issue (Bos *et al.*, 2009; Greene, 2004; Guo and Yuan, 2020).

3. Method and Materials

3.1. *The first stage: Data envelopment analysis (DEA) and free disposal hull (FDH)*

Since FDH was extended from DEA (Deprins *et al.*, 1984), we first introduce the DEA model using the "black-box" approach (Boubaker, Le, Manita, *et al.*, 2023; Boubaker, Le, Ngo, *et al.*, 2023) as follows.

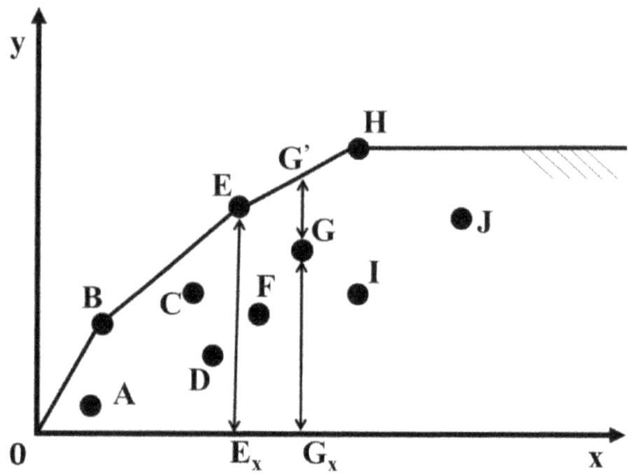

Fig. 1. DEA frontier.

Graphically, DEA could be simply understood as a non-parametric technique to construct an enveloped frontier from observed data, allowing for the comparison of each DMU against that frontier (Ngo *et al.*, 2024). As illustrated in Fig. 1 for the case of a single input (e.g., capital) and single output (e.g., revenue), DEA assumes that the examined ten banks (from A to J) all operate under a convex technology, and thus, there exists a convex-hull frontier 0BEH that envelops all the other banks in the sample (i.e., A, C, D, F, G, I, and J). Accordingly, the output-oriented inefficiency of Bank G, for example, could be calculated as the vertical (i.e., follow the y-axis) distance between the position of G and the EH segment of the 0BEH frontier. Particularly, the technical efficiency of G will be $GG_x/G'G_x$ (corresponding to the inefficiency of $GG'/G'G_x$), which is less than unity, while the efficiency of E will equal unity ($= EE_x/EE_x$) as it lies on the frontier (corresponding to zero inefficiency).

Mathematically, we can consider a set of N banks being examined, each bank using s inputs x_i ($i = 1, 2, \ldots, s$) to produce m outputs y_r ($r = 1, 2, \ldots, m$). Under DEA, the technical efficiency of the j_0 bank can be estimated as

$$TE_{j_0}^{DEA} = \frac{\sum_r^m u_{rj_0} y_{rj_0}}{\sum_i^s v_{ij_0} x_{ij_0}}. \tag{1}$$

Subject to

$$TE_j^{DEA} = \frac{\sum_r^m u_{rj} y_{rj}}{\sum_i^s v_{ij} x_{ij}} \leq 1, \quad j = 1, 2, \ldots, N, \tag{1a}$$

$$u_r v_i \geq \varepsilon, \ \forall ir. \tag{1b}$$

Note that the first constraint (1a) guarantees that the TE^{DEA} of any bank cannot exceed unity, while the second constraint (1b) imposes that the optimal weights u_r and v_i are non-negative (with ε normally being very small at 1E-6).

The dual model of Equation (1) is presented in Equation (2), whereas the constraints (2a) and (2b) are equivalent to (1a), the additional constraint (2c) assumes the variable returns to scale condition (Banker *et al.*, 1984), and the constraint (2d) imposes the non-negativity on lambdas (λ_j), which represent the multipliers that the j_0 bank takes in accordance with other banks as its peers:

$$TE_{j_0}^{DEA} = \theta. \tag{2}$$

Subject to

$$\theta x_{ij_0} - \sum_{j=1}^{N} \lambda_j x_{ij} \geq 0, \tag{2a}$$

$$\sum_{j=1}^{N} \lambda_j y_{rj} \geq y_{rj_0}, \tag{2b}$$

$$\sum_{j=1}^{N} \lambda_j = 1, \tag{2c}$$

$$\lambda_j \geq 0, \ \forall j. \tag{2d}$$

Deprins *et al.* (1984) extended the DEA frontier to deal with non-convex technologies using FDH. The essential difference between FDH and DEA is that the former argued that the *true* frontier is often unknown, and thus, the 0BEH frontier in Fig. 1 is just a *hypothetical* one. Consequently, it is impractical to measure the (in)efficiency of Bank G using the virtual point G' on the *hypothetical* EH frontier segment (Dekker and Post, 2001; Deprins *et al.*, 1984; Tulkens, 1993).

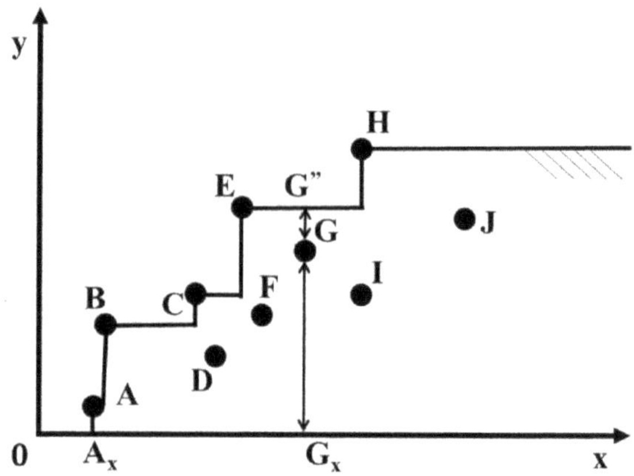

Fig. 2. FDH frontier.

In reality, however, Bank G does not need to improve its efficiency toward any *hypothetical* point(s) and frontier but to its closest peers, which are either E or H, given that the two are efficient. Under the FDH framework, therefore, the *true* frontier should be a free disposal (or non-convex hull) connecting Banks A, B, C, E, and H, as illustrated in Fig. 2. In this case, the technical efficiency of G should be $GG_x/G''G_x$, still less than unity but higher than the case of the DEA frontier. As such, this study would bring new insights into the efficiency of ASEAN banks under a different viewpoint of non-convexity and a *true* FDH frontier, which has not been done before.

In terms of the mathematical model, the FDH technical efficiency of the bank j_0-th will be calculated similar to the DEA model in Equation (2):

$$TE_{j_0}^{FDH} = \min_{\theta,\lambda} \theta. \tag{3}$$

Subject to

$$\theta x_{ij_0} - \sum_{j=1}^{N} \lambda_j x_{ij} \geq 0, \tag{3a}$$

$$\sum_{j=1}^{N} \lambda_j y_{rj} \geq y_{rj_0}, \tag{3b}$$

$$\sum_{j=1}^{N} \lambda_j = 1, \tag{3c}$$

$$\lambda_j \geq 0, \ \forall j, \tag{3d}$$

$$\lambda_j = \{0, 1\}, \ \forall j, \tag{3e}$$

with the additional constraint (3e) implying that the bank being examined (e.g., Bank G) just needs to fully follow its peer (e.g., either Bank E or Bank H with $\lambda_E = 1$ or $\lambda_H = 1$) while the rest is zero (e.g., $\lambda_j = 0$, $j \neq E$ or $j \neq H$).

Regarding the input and output variables of Equation (3), we follow the core profit model (Avkiran, 2011) to argue that banks use expenses (X1) to attract deposits (X2) from savers, then transform them into loans (Y1) and collect the net interest margin (Y2). Such an approach of inputs/outputs selection is in line with many previous studies in the literature (Boubaker *et al.*, 2024; Fang *et al.*, 2019; Le *et al.*, 2023).

3.2. *The second stage: Examining the determinants of FDH efficiency via regression*

As reviewed in Section 2 and summarized in Section 2.4, it is important to explain the causes of differences in the FDH efficiency of the ASEAN banks. In this study, there are three important things to notice.

Firstly, bank efficiency is influenced by bank-specific characteristics, which were not directly involved in the efficiency modeling process (i.e., neither as inputs nor outputs) but still indirectly affect those variables (Boubaker and Ngo, 2024; Pasha, 2024). For instance, the theory of economies of scale indicates that larger banks tend to attract more customers and be involved in more activities, which may result in higher outputs (e.g., revenues). In fact, such a theory has been confirmed in the literature (Amirteimoori *et al.*, 2024; Li *et al.*, 2022; Rasoul *et al.*, 2024).

Secondly, we also examine the role of country-specific characteristics. As discussed in Section 2, we incorporate economic development and inflation as the two revealing factors affecting bank efficiency.

For instance, in a country with higher economic growth, the population would have a higher chance to participate in banking activities (e.g., savings and borrowings), boosting the development of its banking sector (Do Van, 2022; Hussain *et al.*, 2020). A similar argument applies to inflation (Wong and Deng, 2016). We also follow Sufian and Habibullah (2011) and Masrizal *et al.* (2023) to include financial freedom as the third country-specific factor of the analysis, since financial freedom can proxy for macroeconomic regulations and policy, which enhances financial and banking activities (Chortareas *et al.*, 2013; Sarpong-Kumankoma *et al.*, 2017). Lastly, we also control for the country fixed effect by including a set of dummy variables for each country involved in our analysis.

We ended up with the following regression model:

$$TE_{ijt}^{FDH} = \beta_0 + \beta_1 SIZE_{it} + \beta_2 GDPGR_{jt} + \beta_3 INF_{jt} + \beta_4 FREEDOM_{jt} + \beta_5 YEAR + \sum \delta_j COUNTRY_j + \varepsilon, \tag{4}$$

where TE_{ijt}^{FDH} is the FDH efficiency of bank I from country j in year t; SIZE represents the natural logarithmic value of the bank's assets; GDPGR represents the annual growth rate of the country's gross domestic product; INF measures the country's annual inflation rate; FREEDOM represents the financial freedom index; YEAR controls for the yearly fixed effect; COUNTRY is a set of dummy variables that controls for the country fixed effect; and ε is the statistical error.

In the two-stage DEA approach, it is common to apply Tobit or truncated regression to estimate Equation (4), because its dependent variable is a measure of the DEA efficiency score and is censored/bounded between 0 and 1 (Defung *et al.*, 2016; Simar and Wilson, 2007). However, the discriminatory power of FDH over DEA will result in more banks being treated as efficient; for instance, by comparing Fig. 2 and Fig. 1, one can easily find that Bank A and Bank C are efficient under FDH but not DEA. Therefore, such practice will truncate more (efficient) observations from our analysis and reduce the degree of freedom of our regression. On the other hand, Hoff (2007) pointed out that the traditional Ordinary Least Squares (OLS) regression has equivalent power to Tobit and truncated regressions. We thus utilized both OLS and Tobit regressions in our second-stage analysis to provide a more comprehensive view of the results.

3.3. Data

Among the ASEAN countries, to enhance comparability, we only select banks from five countries: Indonesia, Malaysia, the Philippines, Thailand, and Vietnam; these countries have similar levels of development in the banking sectors (Do Van, 2022). We excluded Singapore as this country is at a different (higher) level and, more importantly, its banking sector mainly consists of foreign-owned and large international banking groups (Zhang and Liu, 2024). On the other hand, the banking sectors in Myanmar, Cambodia, and Laos were still underdeveloped, so these banks were relatively smaller than their counterparts in other ASEAN countries (Nguyen and Vo, 2020). The availability and quality of data are other reasons for us not to examine the banks from those countries in this study.

As such, our initial sample consists of more than 1100 bank-year observations for 79 ASEAN banks from the five ASEAN countries mentioned here. The bank-specific data, i.e., operating expenses (X1), deposits (X2), loans (Y1), net interest margin (Y2), and bank size (SIZE), were extracted from the REFINITIV EIKON Database of LSEG Data and Analytics (2024). Data for the financial freedom (FREEDOM) were obtained directly from the Heritage Foundation (2024). Other country-specific variables (i.e., GDP and INF) were collected from the World Bank (2024). After checking for missing data, we ended up with balanced panel data of 69 banks for the 2007–2019 period, yielding a total of 897 bank-year observations. Table 1

Table 1. Descriptive statistics.

	Indonesia		Malaysia		Philippines		Thailand		Vietnam		All Samples	
Variable	*N*	*Mean*	*N*	*Mean*	*N*	*Mean*	*N*	*Mean*	*N*	*Mean*	*N*	*Mean*
X1	377	35.8	104	16.5	169	28.1	130	27.2	117	23.1	897	29.2
X2	377	1357.7	104	2.4	169	5.7	130	12.5	117	3416.1	897	1019.4
Y1	377	1433.1	104	2.6	169	5.2	130	14.0	117	3349.7	897	1042.6
Y2	377	5.7	104	2.3	169	4.6	130	4.0	117	3.9	897	4.6
SIZE	377	31.2	104	25.8	169	26.4	130	27.3	117	32.9	897	29.3
GDPGR	377	5.5	104	4.8	169	5.8	130	3.3	117	6.2	897	5.3
INF	377	7.0	104	2.6	169	2.8	130	2.2	117	7.8	897	5.1
FREEDOM	377	50.0	104	50.0	169	53.8	130	62.3	117	33.1	897	50.3

Notes: X1 represents the operating expenses, X2 represents the total deposits, Y1 measures the total loans, Y2 measures the net interest margin, SIZE is the natural logarithmic value of total assets, GDPGR measures the annual GDP growth rates, INF measures the annual inflation rates, and FREEDOM is the national financial freedom index. *N* stands for the number of observations. The values are subjected to the rounding effect, and all monetary variables were converted into 2010 USD values.

reports the descriptive statistics of our data, indicating some differences across the banks and countries involved. Therefore, it justifies the need for our second-stage analysis, as discussed in the previous subsection.

4. Results and Discussions

We first follow Daraio *et al.* (2010) and Ouenniche and Carrales (2018), among others, to test for the validity of the first-stage FDH results. As discussed in Ouenniche and Carrales (2018) and Boubaker *et al.* (2023), the estimated efficiency results should have a positive relationship with the output variables, while a negative association with the input variables is also expected. As reported in Table 2, such relationships are confirmed in our analysis across different regression models, indicating that the FDH results could be used in further analyses.

We then report the first-stage FDH efficiency scores for individual banks involved in the study. Out of 69 banks, 50 are averagely evaluated as efficient (i.e., $TE^{FDH} = 1$) throughout the whole 2007–2019 period, accounting for about 73% of the sample. Such a proportion is

Table 2. The validity of the first-stage FDH results.

	X1	X2	Y1	Y2	Intercept
OLS regression					
Model 1	−0.00004***	−0.00001*	0.00004***	0.00654***	0.95474***
Model 2	−0.00006**	−0.01039**	0.00005***	0.11422***	
Model 3	−0.00003***	−0.00014***	0.00003***	0.00659***	0.95889***
Model 4	−0.00003***	−0.00012*	0.00003***	0.00702***	
Tobit regression					
Model 5	−0.00050***	0.00126	0.00051***	0.09280***	1.01650***
Model 6	−0.00127***	−0.01730*	0.00132***	0.39008***	
Model 7	−0.00044***	−0.00210	0.00047***	0.06919***	1.18142***
Model 8	−0.00041***	−0.00130	0.00046***	0.13638***	

Notes: X1 represents the operating expenses, X2 represents the total deposits, Y1 measures the total loans, and Y2 measures the net interest margin. The dependent variable of all models is the FDH efficiency scores. Models 1, 2, 5, and 6 utilized pooled data, while the rest used panel data. *, **, and *** denote the significance levels at 10%, 5%, and 1%, respectively.

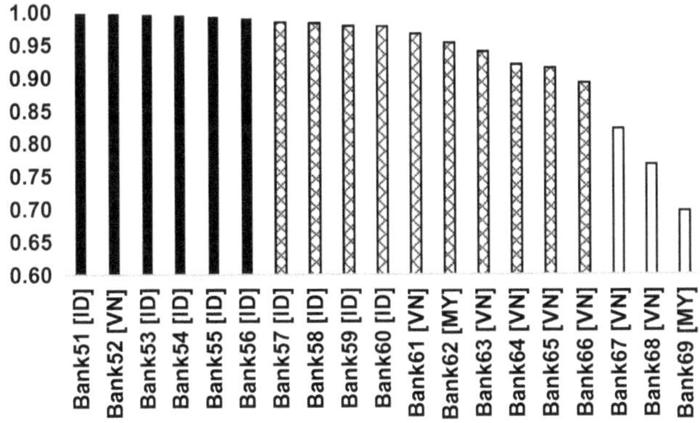

Fig. 3. FDH efficiency of 19 inefficient banks.
Notes: ID, MY, and VN indicate that the banks are from Indonesia, Malaysia, and Vietnam, respectively. The solid columns represent the close-to-efficient banks, the crossed columns represent moderately efficient banks, and the hollow columns represent the underperforming banks.

understandable because the FDH frontier includes more banks than the DEA one, as illustrated in Figs. 1 and 2. Therefore, it will be more interesting to look at the inefficient banks rather than the efficient ones. Figure 3 shows that among the 19 inefficient banks, six were close to being efficient (TE^{FDH} above 0.99), ten were inefficient but performed moderately well (i.e., TE^{FDH} between 0.8 and 0.99), and three were underperforming (i.e., TE^{FDH} less than 0.8). Among the second and third groups of inefficient banks, seven come from Vietnam (53.85%), four are Indonesian banks (30.77%), and only two are Malaysian (15.38%).

A further inspection at the country-level FDH efficiency confirms that Vietnamese banks were the least efficient among ASEAN banks, where as Indonesian, Philippine, and Thai banks were the top performers (Fig. 4). Notably, it is observed that Vietnamese banks struggled during the 2012–2013 period, but the situation has improved since 2014. This finding is in line with previous studies on the Vietnamese banking system (Boubaker *et al.*, 2024; Ho *et al.*, 2021; Nguyen and Simioni, 2015), although those were conducted within the country only, and our research is at a cross-country level, justifying the necessity for the country's restructuring of its banking system (Ngo, 2014; Vietnamese Government, 2012; Vo and Nguyen, 2018; World Bank, 2016).

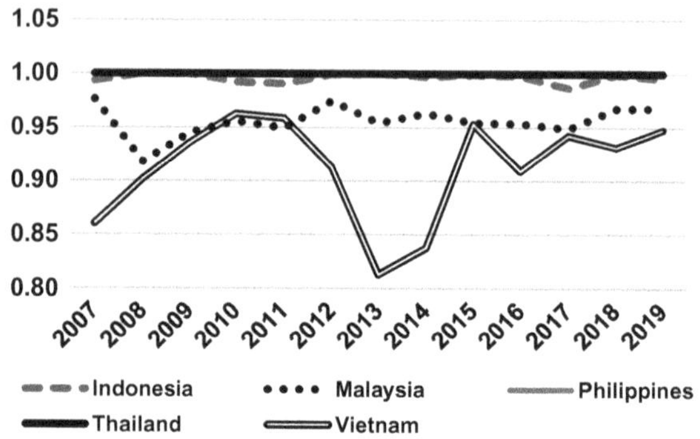

Fig. 4. Average FDH efficiency by country.
Note: The performance of Philippines and Thailand are identical and horizontal at unity. Hence, they are not visible separately.

For the second-stage analysis, the results from both OLS and Tobit regressions are reported in Table 3. Note that in both cases, we utilized a pooled data sample and also a panel data sample; random effect and fixed effect models were both used for the case of the panel data sample to account for the heteroscedasticity issue (Bos *et al.*, 2009; de Chaisemartin and D'Haultfœuille, 2020; Mester, 1997; Mohanty *et al.*, 2013). Nevertheless, Table 3 suggests that bank size (i.e., SIZE) generally increases bank efficiency, with positive and significant coefficients found in four of the six models. It thus indicates that the (increasing) economies of scale situation exists in the ASEAN banking sectors. Note that our sample includes five emerging economies of ASEAN. It is justified to argue that the expansion of the banking sectors in those countries would allow the banks to attract more customers and, thus, improve their performance. This argument was also found in previous studies on ASEAN banks (Boubaker *et al.*, 2024; Ismail *et al.*, 2013; Vuong *et al.*, 2023) and elsewhere (Hassan, 2020; Liu *et al.*, 2024; Nguyen *et al.*, 2023).

Among the macroeconomic factors, economic development (i.e., GDPGR) is found to be less statistically important, while inflation (i.e., INF) statistically enhances bank performance (in five models of Table 3). Note that inflation may increase the price of funds (Maudos and Solís, 2009) in the next year, so a moderate level of inflation could encourage the banks to extend their activities in the current year to prepare for such an increase (Fang *et al.*, 2019; Tran *et al.*, 2020), which may lead to higher income for the banks (Tan and Floros,

Table 3. The determinants of the FDH efficiency of ASEAN banks.

	Pooled data *Coef*	*SD*	**Panel RE** *Coef*	*SD*	**Panel FE** *Coef*	*SD*
3A. Tobit regressions						
SIZE	0.005		0.075***		0.080**	
	(0.007)		(0.022)		(0.038)	
GDPGR	−0.015		0.008		0.029*	
	(0.014)		(0.012)		(0.016)	
INF	0.013***		0.005*		0.011**	
	(0.004)		(0.003)		(0.005)	
FREEDOM	0.020***		−0.002		0.000	
	(0.003)		(0.002)		(0.003)	
Intercept	0.340		1.563***		-1.960	
	(0.278)		(0.370)		(1.235)	
3B. OLS regressions						
SIZE	0.019***		0.000		0.011**	
	(0.006)		(0.002)		(0.004)	
GDPGR	0.002		0.001		0.000	
	(0.001)		(0.001)		(0.001)	
INF	0.001**		0.000		0.001*	
	(0.001)		(0.000)		(0.000)	
FREEDOM	0.000		0.001**		0.000	
	(0.000)		(0.000)		(0.000)	
Intercept	0.277		0.958***		0.672***	
	(0.190)		(0.047)		(0.113)	

Notes: SIZE, total assets; GDPGR, GDP growth rates; INF, inflation rates; FREEDOM, financial freedom index; Coef, coefficient; SD, standard deviation; RE, random effect; FE, fixed effect. Standard errors are inside the brackets. *, **, and *** denote the significance levels at 10%, 5%, and 1%, respectively.

2012) Khue and Lai (2020) empirically found that for ASEAN banks, a positive relationship between inflation and bank efficiency applies only if inflation surpasses a certain threshold of 4%; for our study, the average inflation rate was 5.1% (see Table 1). The positive role of financial freedom (i.e., FREEDOM) on bank efficiency was also weak, with only two models statistically confirming the relationship. However, it is still justified to argue that policymakers and bank managers in ASEAN countries should be aware of the changes in the macroeconomic conditions, as they may influence the performance of ASEAN banks.

5. Conclusions

ASEAN banks play a vital role in financial stability and economic integration for the banking sector of each member country as well as for the whole Association. Despite intensive literature on banking efficiency, research on ASEAN banks is limited, particularly regarding non-convex technologies and at the cross-country level. This study is the first to apply the non-convexity FDH method to evaluate ASEAN banking efficiency.

Our empirical data consist of 69 banks from five ASEAN countries (Indonesia, Malaysia, the Philippines, Thailand, and Vietnam) for the 2007–2019 period. ***The first-stage FDH analysis*** showed that 19 banks were deemed inefficient (approximately 27% of the sample), indicating that ASEAN banks performed moderately well during the examined period. The country-level analysis further indicated that Vietnamese banks were the least efficient, while Indonesian and Thai banks performed better. Notably, the study highlighted the struggle for Vietnamese banks, especially during the 2012–2013 period, justifying and evaluating the country's restructuring of its banking system at the time. *In the second-stage analysis*, both OLS and Tobit regressions indicated that bank size generally enhances efficiency, suggesting economies of scale in the ASEAN banking sector. Macroeconomic factors showed that inflation positively influences bank performance, whereas economic development had a lesser effect. Policymakers and bank managers in ASEAN should monitor these macroeconomic changes, as they significantly impact banking performance across the region.

References

Aam Slamet, R. and Aisyah, A.-S. (2021). DEA window analysis of Indonesian Islamic bank efficiency. *Journal of Islamic Monetary Economics and Finance*, 7(4), 733–758. https://doi.org/10.21098/jimf.v7i4.1410.

Afroj, F., Dutta, C. B., and Farjana, F. (2024). Interrelationship between bank efficiency and non-performing loans: Evidence from Bangladesh. *Journal of Banking and Financial Technology*, 8(1), 29–44. https://doi.org/10.1007/s42786-024-00050-1.

Ahmad, N., Naveed, A., Ahmad, S., and Butt, I. (2020). Banking sector performance, profitability, and efficiency: A citation-based systematic literature review. *Journal of Economic Surveys*, 34(1), 185–218.

Aissia, D. B. and Ellouz, M. (2021). Estimation of the efficiency of Tunisian bank branches using a stochastic frontier approach. *SN Business & Economics*, 1(10), 132. https://doi.org/10.1007/s43546-021-00133-x.

Alqahtani, F., Mayes, D. G., and Brown, K. (2017). Islamic bank efficiency compared to conventional banks during the global crisis in the GCC region. *Journal of International Financial Markets, Institutions and Money*, 51, 58–74. https://doi.org/10.1016/j.intfin.2017.08.010.

Amirteimoori, A., Allahviranloo, T., and Nematizadeh, M. (2024). A firm-specific Malmquist productivity index model for stochastic data envelopment analysis: an application to commercial banks. *Financial Innovation*, 10(1). https://doi.org/10.1186/s40854-023-00583-2.

Antunes, J., Hadi-Vencheh, A., Jamshidi, A., Tan, Y., and Wanke, P. (2024). Cost efficiency of Chinese banks: Evidence from DEA and MLP-SSRP analysis. *Expert Systems with Applications*, 237, 121432. https://doi.org/10.1016/j.eswa.2023.121432.

ASEAN. (2024). *ASEAN Community Vision 2025*. The Association of Southeast Asian Nations (ASEAN). https://asean.org/.

Avkiran, N. K. (2011). Association of DEA super-efficiency estimates with financial ratios: Investigating the case for Chinese banks. *OMEGA*, 39(3), 323–334.

Azad, M., Munisamy, S., Masum, A., Saona, P., and Wanke, P. (2017). Bank efficiency in Malaysia: a use of malmquist meta-frontier analysis. *Eurasian Business Review*, 7(2), 287–311. https://doi.org/10.1007/s40821-016-0054-4.

Banker, R. D., Charnes, A., and Cooper, W. W. (1984). Some models for estimating technical and scale inefficiencies in data envelopment analysis. *Management Science*, 30(9), 1078–1092.

Beccalli, E., Anolli, M., and Borello, G. (2015). Are European banks too big? Evidence on economies of scale. *Journal of Banking & Finance*, 58, 232–246. https://doi.org/10.1016/j.jbankfin.2015.04.014.

Ben Lahouel, B., Taleb, L., Ben Zaied, Y., and Managi, S. (2022). Financial stability, liquidity risk and income diversification: Evidence from European banks using the CAMELS–DEA approach. *Annals of Operations Research*. https://doi.org/10.1007/s10479-022-04805-1.

Bhatia, V., Basu, S., Mitra, S. K., and Dash, P. (2018). A review of bank efficiency and productivity. *Opsearch*, 55(3), 557–600.

Bisrat Getinet, C., Desta Yohannes, D., and Berhanu Dereja, G. (2024). Technical and allocative efficiency of commercial banks in Ethiopia. *Cogent Economics & Finance*, 12(1). https://doi.org/10.1080/23322039.2024.2319173.

Bos, J. W. B., Koetter, M., Kolari, J. W., and Kool, C. J. M. (2009). Effects of heterogeneity on bank efficiency scores. *European Journal of Operational Research*, 195(1), 251–261.

Boubaker, S., Le, T. D. Q., Manita, R., and Ngo, T. (2023). The trade-off frontier for ESG and Sharpe ratio: a bootstrapped double-frontier data envelopment analysis. *Annals of Operations Research.* https://doi.org/10.1007/s10479-023-05506-z.

Boubaker, S., Le, T. D. Q., Manita, R., and Ngo, T. (2024). Balancing bank profits and nonperforming loans: a multiple objective programming approach. *Annals of Operations Research.* https://doi.org/10.1007/s10479-024-05831-x.

Boubaker, S., Le, T. D. Q., and Ngo, T. (2022). Managing bank performance under COVID-19: A novel inverse DEA efficiency approach. *International Transactions in Operational Research*, 30, 2436–2452. https://doi.org/10.1111/itor.13132.

Boubaker, S., Le, T. D. Q., Ngo, T., and Manita, R. (2023). Predicting the performance of MSMEs: a hybrid DEA-machine learning approach. *Annals of Operations Research.* https://doi.org/10.1007/s10479-023-05230-8.

Boubaker, S. and Ngo, T. (Eds.). (2024). *Handbook on Data Envelopment Analysis in Business, Finance, and Sustainability: Recent Trends and Developments.* World Scientific.

Cao, Q., Zhu, T., and Yu, W. (2024). ESG investment and bank efficiency: Evidence from China. *Energy Economics*, 133, 107516. https://doi.org/10.1016/j.eneco.2024.107516.

Chortareas, G. E., Girardone, C., and Ventouri, A. (2013). Financial freedom and bank efficiency: Evidence from the European Union. *Journal of Banking & Finance*, 37, 1223–1231.

Citra, A. (2023). Spatial competition on rural bank efficiency: Evidence from Indonesia. *Cogent Economics & Finance*, 11(1). https://doi.org/10.1080/23322039.2023.2190216.

Coelli, T. J., Rao, D. S. P., O'Donnell, C. J., and Battese, G. E. (2005). *An Introduction to Efficiency and Productivity Analysis* (2nd ed.). Springer.

Cooper, W. W., Seiford, L. M., and Zhu, J. (2011). *Handbook on Data Envelopment Analysis.* Springer US. http://books.google.co.nz/books?id$=$fBbrAjpSpLYC.

Daraio, C., Kerstens, K., Nepomuceno, T., and Sickles, R. C. (2020). Empirical surveys of frontier applications: a meta-review. *International Transactions in Operational Research*, 27(2), 709–738. https://doi.org/10.1111/itor.12649.

Daraio, C., Simar, L., and Wilson, P. W. (2010). *Testing Whether Two-Stage Estimation is Meaningful in Non-Parametric Models of Production.* ISBA Discussion Paper. https://sites.uclouvain.be/ISBA-Archives/ISBApublications/archive/dp2010/DP1031.pdf.

de Chaisemartin, C. and D'Haultfœuille, X. (2020). Two-way fixed effects estimators with heterogeneous treatment effects. *American Economic Review*, 110(9), 2964–2996. https://doi.org/10.1257/aer.20181169.

Defung, F., Salim, R., and Bloch, H. (2016). Has regulatory reform had any impact on bank efficiency in Indonesia? A two-stage analysis. *Applied Economics*, 48(52), 5060–5074. https://doi.org/10.1080/00036846.2016.1170934.

Degl'Innocenti, M., Kourtzidis, S. A., Sevic, Z., and Tzeremes, N. G. (2017). Bank productivity growth and convergence in the European Union during the financial crisis. *Journal of Banking & Finance*, 75, 184–199. https://doi.org/10.1016/j.jbankfin.2016.11.016.

Dekker, D. and Post, T. (2001). A quasi-concave DEA model with an application for bank branch performance evaluation. *European Journal of Operational Research*, 132(2), 296–311.

Deprins, D., Simar, L., and Tulkens, H. (1984). Measuring labor-efficiency in post offices. In M. Marchand, P. Pestieau, and H. Tulkens (Eds.), *The Performance of Public Enterprises: Concepts and Measurements* (pp. 243–247). Elsevier.

Do Van, A. (2022). Does better capitalization enhance bank efficiency and limit risk taking? Evidence from ASEAN commercial banks. *Global Finance Journal*, 53, 100617. https://doi.org/10.1016/j.gfj.2021.100617.

Dogan, E. and Fausten, D. K. (2009). Technical efficiency of banks in Southeast Asia. In J.-D. Lee and A. Heshmati (Eds.), *Productivity, Efficiency, and Economic Growth in the Asia-Pacific Region* (pp. 107–122). Physica-Verlag HD. https://doi.org/10.1007/978-3-7908-2072-0_6.

Fang, J., Lau, C.-K. M., Lu, Z., Tan, Y., and Zhang, H. (2019). Bank performance in China: A Perspective from Bank efficiency, risk-taking and market competition. *Pacific-Basin Finance Journal*, 56, 290–309. https://doi.org/10.1016/j.pacfin.2019.06.011.

Feng, G. and Wang, C. (2018). Why European banks are less profitable than U.S. banks: A decomposition approach. *Journal of Banking & Finance*, 90, 1–16. https://doi.org/10.1016/j.jbankfin.2018.02.017.

Fethi, M. D. and Pasiouras, F. (2010). Assessing bank efficiency and performance with operational research and artificial intelligence techniques: A survey. *European Journal of Operational Research*, 204, 189–198.

Greene, W. (2004). Distinguishing between heterogeneity and inefficiency: Stochastic frontier analysis of the World Health Organization's panel data on national health care systems. *Health Economics*, 13(10).

Guo, R. and Yuan, Y. (2020). Different types of environmental regulations and heterogeneous influence on energy efficiency in the industrial sector: Evidence from Chinese provincial data. *Energy Policy*, 145, 111747. https://doi.org/10.1016/j.enpol.2020.111747.

Hambrick, D. C. (2007). Upper Echelons theory: An update. *The Academy of Management Review*, 32(2), 334–343. https://doi.org/10.2307/20159303.

Hambrick, D. C. and Mason, P. A. (1984). Upper Echelons: The organization as a reflection of its top managers. *The Academy of Management Review*, 9(2), 193–206. https://doi.org/10.2307/258434.

Hammami, H., Ngo, T., Tripe, D., and Vo, D.-T. (2022). Ranking with a Euclidean common set of weights in data envelopment analysis: With application to the Eurozone banking sector. *Annals of Operations Research*, 311, 675–694. https://doi.org/10.1007/s10479-020-03759-6.

Hasan, M. Z., Kamil, A. A., Mustafa, A., and Baten, M. A. (2012). A cobb douglas stochastic frontier model on measuring domestic bank efficiency in Malaysia. *PLOS ONE*, 7(8), e42215. https://doi.org/10.1371/journal.pone.0042215.

Hassan, M. (2020). How bank regulations impact efficiency and performance? *Journal of Financial Economic Policy*, 12(4), 545–575. https://doi.org/10.1108/JFEP-06-2019-0119.

Heritage Foundation. (2024). *2024 Index of Economic Freedom*. The Heritage Foundation.

Ho, T. H., Nguyen, D. T., Ngo, T., and Le, T. D. (2021). Efficiency in Vietnamese banking: A meta-regression analysis approach. *International Journal of Financial Studies*, 9(3), 41. https://www.mdpi.com/2227-7072/9/3/41.

Hoff, A. (2007). Second stage DEA: Comparison of approaches for modelling the DEA score. *European Journal of Operational Research*, 181(1), 425–435. http://www.sciencedirect.com/science/article/pii/S0377221706003821.

Hussain, H. I., Kamarudin, F., Mohamad Anwar, N. A., Nassir, A. M., Sufian, F., and Tan, K. M. (2020). Impact of country's governance dimensions on bank revenue efficiency: Overview on Middle East, Southeast Asia, and South Asia countries. *Transformations in Business & Economics*, 19(1), 191–228.

Ismail, F., Shabri Abd. Majid, M., and Rahim, R. A. (2013). Efficiency of Islamic and conventional banks in Malaysia. *Journal of Financial Reporting and Accounting*, 11(1), 92–107. https://doi.org/10.1108/JFRA-03-2013-0011.

Karim, M. Z. A. (2001). Comparative Bank Efficiency across Select ASEAN Countries. *ASEAN Economic Bulletin*, 18(3), 289–304.

Kerstens, K., Azadi, M., Kazemi Matin, R., and Farzipoor Saen, R. (2024). Double hedonic price-characteristics frontier estimation for IoT service providers in the industry 5.0 era: A nonconvex perspective accommodating ratios. *European Journal of Operational Research*. https://doi.org/10.1016/j.ejor.2024.05.047.

Kerstens, K., Sadeghi, J., and Van de Woestyne, I. (2019). Convex and nonconvex input-oriented technical and economic capacity measures: An empirical comparison. *European Journal of Operational Research*, 276(2), 699–709. https://doi.org/10.1016/j.ejor.2019.01.014.

Khue, N. N. D. and Lai, Y.-W. (2020). Threshold effects of inflation on the banking sector performance in the ASEAN-6 countries. *Romanian Journal of Economic Forecasting*, 23(1), 117–133.

Kumar, A., Shrivastav, S. K., and Mukherjee, K. (2022). Performance evaluation of Indian banks using feature selection data envelopment analysis: A machine learning perspective. *Journal of Public Affairs*, 22(4), e2686. https://doi.org/10.1002/pa.2686.

Kweh, Q. L., Lu, W. M., Tone, K., and Liu, H. M. (2024). Evaluating the resource management and profitability efficiencies of US commercial banks from a dynamic network perspective. *Financial Innovation*, 10(1). https://doi.org/10.1186/s40854-023-00531-0.

Lapteacru, I. and Lahet, D. (2014). Efficiency and market power of Thai banks: In the aftermath of financial crises. *Revue Économique*, 65(5), 675–698. https://doi.org/10.3917/reco.655.0675.

Le, T., Ho, T. N. T., Nguyen, D. T., and Ngo, T. (2022). Intellectual capital–bank efficiency nexus: Evidence from an emerging market. *Cogent Economics & Finance*, 10(1), 2127485. https://doi.org/10.1080/23322039.2022.2127485.

Le, T., Ngo, T., Ho, T. H., and Nguyen, D. T. (2023). Determinants of bank performance: Revisiting the role of CEO's personality traits using graphology. *Bulletin of Monetary Economics and Banking*, 26(2), 52–87. https://doi.org/10.59091/1410-8046.2066.

Lee, T.-H. and Chih, S.-H. (2013). Does financial regulation enhance or impede the efficiency of China's listed commercial banks? A Dynamic Perspective. *Emerging Markets Finance & Trade*, 49, 132–149. http://www.jstor.org/stable/24475300.

Li, Z., Feng, C., and Tang, Y. (2022). Bank efficiency and failure prediction: A nonparametric and dynamic model based on data envelopment analysis. *Annals of Operations Research*, 315(1), 279–315. https://doi.org/10.1007/s10479-022-04597-4.

Liu, T. L., Naveed, M. M., Mustafa, S., and Naveed, M. T. (2024). Analysing the impact of digital technology diffusion on the efficiency and convergence process of the commercial banking industry of Pakistan. *Humanities and Social Sciences Communications*, 11(1). https://doi.org/10.1057/s41599-024-03184-1.

LSEG Data & Analytics. (2024). *Refinitiv Eikon.* https://eikon.refinitiv.com/.

Masrizal, Sukmana, R., Fianto, B. A., and Gultom, R. Z. (2023). Does economic freedom fosters Islamic rural banks efficiency? Evidence from Indonesia. *International Journal of Productivity & Performance Management*, 72(9), 2538–2558. https://doi.org/10.1108/IJPPM-11-2021-0660.

Maudos, J. and Solís, L. (2009). The determinants of net interest income in the Mexican banking system: An integrated model. *Journal of Banking & Finance*, 33(10), 1920–1931. https://doi.org/10.1016/j.jbankfin.2009.04.012.

Mester, L. J. (1997). Measuring efficiency at U.S. banks: Accounting for heterogeneity is important. *European Journal of Operational Research*, 98(2), 230–242.

Mohanty, S. K., Lin, W. T., and Lin, H.-J. (2013). Measuring cost efficiency in presence of heteroskedasticity: The case of the banking industry in Taiwan. *Journal of International Financial Markets, Institutions and Money*, 26, 77–90.

Ngo, T. (2012). Measuring performance of the banking system: Case of Vietnam (1990-2010). *Journal of Applied Finance & Banking*, 2(2), 289–312.

Ngo, T. (2014). To restructure the economy regarding its industrial operational efficiency. *VNU Journal of Economics and Business*, 30(4), 1–11.

Ngo, T. and Nguyen, L. T. P. (2012). Total factor productivity of Thai Banks in 2007-2010: An Application of DEA and Malmquist Index. *Journal of Applied Finance and Banking*, 2(5), 27–42.

Ngo, T. and Tripe, D. (2010). *Evaluating the Efficiency of Vietnamese Banking System: An Application Using Data Envelopment Analysis.* International DEA Symposium "Pushing the envelope!", Brisbane, Australia.

Ngo, T. and Tripe, D. (2017). Measuring efficiency of Vietnamese banks: Accounting for nonperforming loans in a single-step stochastic cost frontier analysis. *Pacific Accounting Review*, 29(2), 171–182. https://doi.org/10.1108/PAR-06-2016-0064.

Ngo, T., Tripe, D., and Nguyen, D. K. (2024). Estimating the productivity of US agriculture: The Fisher total factor productivity index for time series data with unknown prices. *Australian Journal of Agricultural and Resource Economics*, 68(3), 701–712. https://doi.org/10.1111/1467-8489.12565.

Ngo, T. and Tsui, K. W. H. (2020). A data-driven approach for estimating airport efficiency under endogeneity: An application to New Zealand airports. *Research in Transportation Business & Management*, 34, 100412. https://doi.org/10.1016/j.rtbm.2019.100412.

Nguyen, K. M., Giang, T. L., and Nguyen, V. H. (2008). Ranking efficiency of commercial banks in Vietnam with super slacks-based model of Data Envelopment Analysis. DEA Symposium 2008, Tokyo, Japan.

Nguyen, L.-H., Le, T. D. Q., and Ngo, T. (2023). Efficiency and performance of Islamic banks amid COVID-19. *Journal of Islamic Accounting and Business Research*. https://doi.org/10.1108/JIABR-05-2022-0129.

Nguyen, P. A. and Simioni, M. (2015). Productivity and efficiency of Vietnamese banking system: new evidence using Färe-Primont index analysis. *Applied Economics*, 47(41), 4395–4407. http://dx.doi.org/10.1080/00036846.2015.1030565.

Nguyen, T. L. A. and Vo, X. V. (2020). Does corporate governance really matter for bank efficiency? Evidence from ASEAN countries. *Eurasian Economic Review*, 10(4), 681–706. https://doi.org/10.1007/s40822-020-00151-4.

Nguyen, V. H. (2007). Measuring efficiency of Vietnamese commercial banks: An application of data envelopment analysis (DEA). In K. M. Nguyen and T. L. Giang (Eds.), *Technical Efficiency and Productivity Growth in Vietnam* (pp. 60–70). Publishing House of Social Labour.

O'Donnell, C. J. (2012). Nonparametric Estimates of the Components of Productivity and Profitability Change in U.S. Agriculture. *American Journal of Agricultural Economics*, 94(4), 873–890. https://doi.org/10.1093/ajae/aas023.

O'Donnell, C. J., Rao, D. S. P., and Battese, G. E. (2008). Metafrontier frameworks for the study of firm-level efficiencies and technology ratios. *Empirical Economics*, 34(2), 231–255. https://doi.org/10.1007/s00181-007-0119-4.

Ouenniche, J. and Carrales, S. (2018). Assessing efficiency profiles of UK commercial banks: A DEA analysis with regression-based feedback. *Annals of Operations Research*, 266(1), 551–587.

Paradi, J. and Zhu, H. (2013). A survey on bank branch efficiency and performance research with data envelopment analysis. *OMEGA*, 41(1), 61–79. http://www.sciencedirect.com/science/article/pii/S0305048312000254.

Pasha, R. (2024). Bank intermediation efficiency and liquidity risk in Egypt: A two-stage non-parametric analyses. *Future Business Journal*, 10(1), 1–16. https://doi.org/10.1186/s43093-024-00385-7.

Phan, T., Daly, K., and Doan, A.-T. (2018). The effects of risks and environmental factors on bank cost efficiency: A study in East Asia and Pacific region. *Cogent Economics & Finance*, 6(1), 1510719. https://doi.org/10.1080/23322039.2018.1510719.

Rasoul, R., Seyed, M., and Mussie, T. (2024). The cost efficiency of the U.S. small banks after the 2008 global financial crisis. *Cogent Economics & Finance*, 12(1). https://doi.org/10.1080/23322039.2024.2402558.

Samad, A. (2021). Global financial crisis and Islamic bank efficiency: Are efficiencies stable or impacted? Evidence from Malaysian Islamic banks. *Journal of Accounting & Finance*, 21(2), 96–111. https://doi.org/10.33423/jaf.v21i2.4240.

Sarpong-Kumankoma, E., Abor, J., Aboagye, A. Q. Q., and Amidu, M. (2017). Freedom, competition and bank efficiency in Sub-Saharan Africa. *International Journal of Law and Management*, 59(6), 1359–1380. https://doi.org/10.1108/IJLMA-11-2016-0142.

Sealey, C. W. and Lindley, J. T. (1977). Inputs, outputs, and a theory of production and cost at depository financial institutions. *Journal of Finance*, 32(4), 1251–1266.

Simar, L. and Wilson, P. W. (2007). Estimation and inference in two-stage, semi-parametric models of production processes. *Journal of Econometrics*, 136, 31–64.

Stern, G. H. and Feldman, R. J. (2004). *Too Big to Fail: The Hazards of Bank Bailouts*. Brookings Institution Press.

Sufian, F. and Habibullah, M. (2011). Opening the black box on bank efficiency in China: Does economic freedom matter? *Global Economic Review*, 40(3), 269–298. https://doi.org/10.1080/1226508X.2011.601633.

Sufian, F. and Habibullah, M. S. (2010). Bank-specific, Industry-specific and macroeconomic determinants of bank efficiency: Empirical evidence from the Thai banking sector. *Margin: The Journal of Applied Economic Research*, 4(4), 427–461. https://doi.org/10.1177/097380101000400403.

Tan, Y. and Floros, C. (2012). Bank profitability and inflation: the case of China. *Journal of Economic Studies*, 39(6), 675–696. https://doi.org/10.1108/01443581211274610.

Tone, K. (2001). A slacks-based measure of efficiency in data envelopment analysis. *European Journal of Operational Research*, 130(3), 498–509. http://www.sciencedirect.com/science/article/pii/S0377221799004075.

Tran, K. C., Tsionas, M. G., and Mamatzakis, E. (2020). Why fully efficient banks matter? A nonparametric stochastic frontier approach in the presence of fully efficient banks. *Empirical Economics*, 58(6), 2733–2760. https://doi.org/10.1007/s00181-018-01618-9.

Tulkens, H. (1993). On FDH efficiency analysis: some methodological issues and applications to retail banking, courts, and urban transit. *Journal of Productivity Analysis*, 4(1), 183–210.

Vietnamese Government. (2012). *Decision No. 254/QD-TTg on Approving the Scheme on "Restructuring the Credit Institutions System in the 2011-2015 Period"*.

Vo, X. V. and Nguyen, H. H. (2018). Bank restructuring and bank efficiency—The case of Vietnam. *Cogent Economics & Finance*, 6(1), 1520423. https://doi.org/10.1080/23322039.2018.1520423.

Vu, H. T. and Turnell, S. (2010). Cost efficiency of the banking sector in Vietnam: A Bayesian stochastic frontier approach with regularity constraints. *Asian Economic Journal*, 24(2), 115–139.

Vuong, G. T. H., Phan, P. T. T., Nguyen, C. X., Nguyen, D. M., and Duong, K. D. (2023). Liquidity creation and bank risk-taking: Evidence from a transition market. *Heliyon*, 9(9), e19141. https://doi.org/10.1016/j.heliyon.2023.e19141.

Wasiaturrahma, Sukmana, R., Ajija, S. R., Salama, S. C. U., and Hudaifah, A. (2020). Financial performance of rural banks in Indonesia: A two-stage DEA approach. *Heliyon*, 6(7). https://doi.org/10.1016/j.heliyon.2020.e04390.

Wong, W. P. and Deng, Q. (2016). Efficiency analysis of banks in ASEAN countries. *Benchmarking: An International Journal*, 23(7), 1798–1817. https://doi.org/10.1108/BIJ-11-2013-0102.

World Bank. (2016). *Taking Stock: An Update on Vietnam's Recent Economic Development*. The World Bank.

World Bank. (2024). *World Development Indicators (WDI)*. The World Bank.

Zhang, T. and Liu, Z. (2024). Navigating integration through rising complexity: Convergence dynamics in the ASEAN banking markets. *Open Economies Review*, 35(4), 801–826. https://doi.org/10.1007/s11079-024-09771-8.

Zhang, T. and Matthews, K. (2012). Efficiency convergence properties of Indonesian banks 1992–2007. *Applied Financial Economics*, 22(17), 1465–1478. https://doi.org/10.1080/09603107.2012.663468.

Zopounidis, C., Galariotis, E., Doumpos, M., Sarri, S., and Andriosopoulos, K. (2015). Multiple criteria decision aiding for finance: An updated bibliographic survey. *European Journal of Operational Research*, 247(2), 339–348.

https://doi.org/10.1142/9789819823161_0012

Chapter 12

The Future of Banking Performance Evaluation: An Empirical Study of AI-Enhanced KPI Prediction Models and Their Implementation Framework

Frédéric Mirindi[*,‡] **and Derrick Mirindi**[†,§]

[*]*Department of Economics, University of Manitoba Winnipeg, Manitoba, Canada*

[†]*School of Architecture and Planning, Morgan State University, Baltimore, Maryland, USA*

[‡]*mirindif@myumanitoba.ca*

[§]*demir1@morgan.edu*

This chapter examines the transformation of banking performance evaluation through artificial intelligence (AI). It demonstrates distinct characteristics across three modeling approaches: machine learning (ML)-enhanced key performance indicators (KPIs) showing steady growth from 100 to 119 with consistent confidence bands, long short-term memory (LSTM) models effectively capturing volatility patterns between 97 and 113, and ensemble methods achieving exceptional stability in uncertainty quantification despite conservative predictions. Through comparative analysis of these approaches, visualized through historical data spanning 2021–2024, we investigate how AI reshapes traditional KPIs into dynamic predictive metrics. Our framework reveals complementary strengths: ML models demonstrate reliable trend prediction, LSTM architectures excel at volatility pattern recognition, and Ensemble approaches prioritize prediction stability through narrow confidence intervals. This study provides implementation guidelines validated through visual evidence of model performance, enabling financial institutions to align AI integration with their technological capabilities.

Keywords: Artificial intelligence, machine learning, Long Short-Term Memory, Key Performance Indicators

1. Introduction

The banking industry is undergoing a profound transformation as artificial intelligence (AI) reshapes traditional performance evaluation methods (Wamba-Taguimdje *et al.*, 2020). Through extensive simulations and computational experiments, our analytical framework quantifiably demonstrates this evolution, showing progression from machine learning-enhanced KPIs with conservative but stable predictions to sophisticated ensemble approaches prioritizing prediction stability over absolute accuracy (Charles *et al.*, 2023). Our research examines how AI-driven performance metrics are fundamentally restructuring Key Performance Indicators (KPIs) in banking, with evidence spanning basic time series to sophisticated ensemble predictions (Tsolas *et al.*, 2020).

While previous studies have focused on the implementation of AI in various banking operations (Yalamati, 2023), there remains a significant gap in understanding how these technologies specifically impact performance measurement and evaluation systems (Thaker *et al.*, 2022). This research addresses this gap by investigating the following question: *How does the integration of AI-driven performance metrics reshape traditional Key Performance Indicators (KPIs) in banking, and what are the implications for holistic performance evaluation frameworks?*

The relevance of this study lies in its systematic analysis of the evolving landscape of banking performance evaluation in the age of AI (Dessain, 2022). Through comparative analysis of three distinct simulation approaches (machine learning-enhanced KPIs demonstrating steady growth from 100 to 119 with consistent confidence bands, long short-term memory (LSTM) models capturing complex volatility patterns between 97 and 113, and ensemble methods achieving exceptional stability in uncertainty quantification despite conservative predictions), we examine how each stage of AI advancement transforms fundamental banking metrics. Previous research has primarily concentrated on isolated aspects of AI in banking (Yalamati, 2023), without considering this comprehensive evolution in performance measurement systems.

This study bridges this knowledge gap by offering a structured analysis of the interplay between AI-driven metrics and traditional banking KPIs, supported by extensive simulations demonstrating transformation from simple, linear relationships to complex, multidimensional patterns (Tsolas *et al.*, 2020). Our research contributes to both theoretical understanding and practical application, providing valuable insights for banking professionals, regulators, and researchers (Hassani *et al.*, 2020). We present a framework that traces the evolution from basic historical analysis to complex ensemble methods, with each simulated stage demonstrating distinct strengths in prediction stability, pattern recognition, and uncertainty quantification.

Furthermore, this study explores the challenges and opportunities at each stage of AI integration, from traditional time series implementation to advanced ensemble modeling (Wamba-Taguimdje *et al.*, 2020), paving the way for more effective and holistic approaches to assessing bank performance in the digital age. This progression-based approach, validated through comparative simulation analysis, ensures comprehensive coverage of both theoretical foundations and practical implications across the entire spectrum of AI-driven performance evaluation.

2. AI-Driven Performance Metrics: A Paradigm Shift

2.1. *From static to dynamic KPIs*

Traditional KPIs in banking have historically centered on growth and profitability metrics, predominantly utilizing retrospective data for performance assessment (Wamba-Taguimdje *et al.*, 1893). However, the integration of AI is catalyzing a fundamental transformation toward more dynamic and predictive metrics (Kaur *et al.*, 2024). AI-powered systems harness vast amounts of data in real

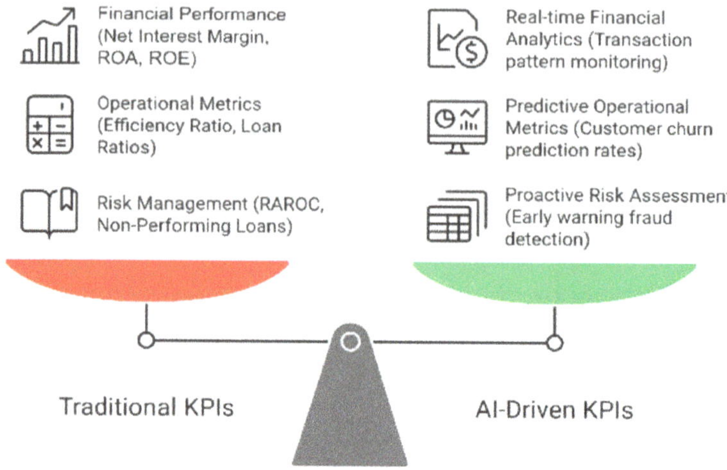

Fig. 1. Evolution from static to dynamic KPI management.

time, enabling financial institutions to transcend conventional retrospective analysis and embrace proactive decision-making paradigms (Tsolas *et al.*, 2020). This metamorphosis is fundamentally reconfiguring the architecture of performance evaluation in the banking sector (Charles *et al.*, 2023).

As illustrated in Fig. 1, the evolution from static to dynamic KPIs exemplifies a pivotal transformation in banking performance evaluation (Thaker *et al.*, 2022). The left side of the balance shows traditional KPIs, encompassing financial performance (net interest margin, ROA, ROE), operational metrics (efficiency ratio, loan ratios), and risk management (RAROC, non-performing loans). In contrast, the right side demonstrates the AI-driven metamorphosis featuring real-time financial analytics (transaction pattern monitoring), predictive operational metrics (customer churn prediction rates), and proactive risk assessment (early warning fraud detection) (Johora *et al.*, 2024). This visual representation encapsulates the comprehensive transition from retrospective to predictive performance measurement frameworks in modern banking.

The balance scale visualization emphasizes how AI is not merely adding new metrics but fundamentally transforming the nature of performance evaluation in banking (Althati *et al.*, 2024). The shift from red (traditional) to green (AI-driven) symbolizes the positive

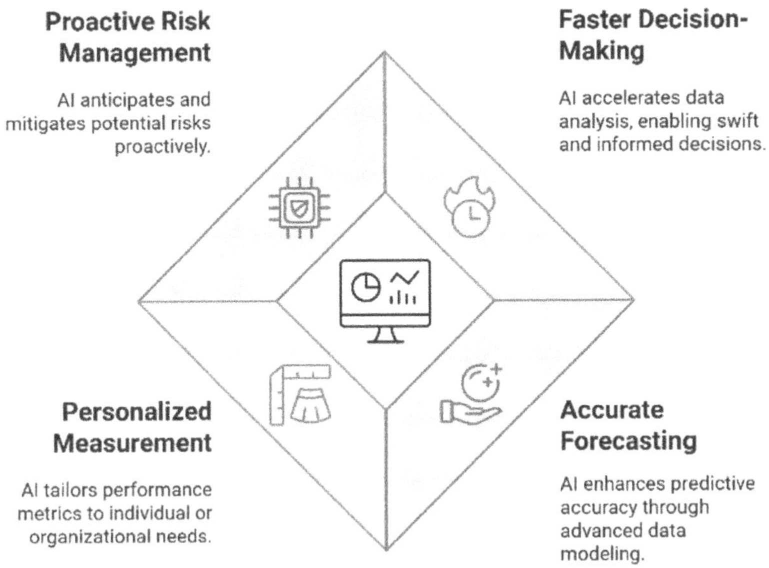

Fig. 2. AI-driven KPIs benefits.

evolution toward more advanced and dynamic performance measurement systems.

Figure 2 illustrates the four interconnected dimensions of AI-driven KPIs that are restructuring banking performance evaluation: proactive risk management, faster decision-making, personalized measurement, and accurate forecasting (Farabi *et al.*, 2024). These dimensions, represented in a diamond framework, demonstrate how AI transforms traditional banking metrics into dynamic, forward-looking performance indicators, with each quadrant addressing a specific aspect of modern banking operations (Tsolas *et al.*, 2020).

2.1.1. *Proactive risk management*

AI systems anticipate and mitigate potential risks proactively, transforming traditional reactive risk metrics into predictive indicators, such as real-time transaction pattern monitoring, early warning fraud detection scores, and customer default probability assessments (Lokanan, 2024). JPMorgan Chase's Machine Learning Center of Excellence demonstrates this paradigm shift through its advanced natural language processing capabilities, which encompass semantic analysis, contextual understanding, and automated information extraction from complex legal documents. The system's ability to review 12,000 annual commercial credit agreements in seconds, compared to the previous 360,000 hours of human labor, represents proactive risk management by enabling rapid identification of potential contractual risks, compliance issues, and legal obligations before they materialize into actual threats (Chirra, 2024).

The computational model captures this through the risk component of Y_t, which incorporates multiple dimensions of risk assessment:

$$Y_t = \{\alpha_t R_c + \beta_t R_m + \gamma_t R_o\}.$$

In this framework, R_c represents credit risk indicators weighted by time-varying coefficient α_t, R_m captures market risk factors modulated by β_t, and R_o accounts for operational risk metrics adjusted by γ_t. The expected sign of this model is positive ($Y_t > 0$) when risk indicators exceed predetermined thresholds, signaling potential threats (Machado and Karray, 2022). This can be proven mathematically as

$$\text{If } \alpha_t, \beta_t, \gamma_t \geq 0, \quad \text{and} \quad R_c, R_m, R_o > 0, \quad \text{then } Y_t > 0.$$

This property is crucial for our research as it demonstrates how AI transforms traditional KPIs into dynamic, forward-looking indicators (Assefa *et al.*, 2020). The positive sign ensures early warning detection, while the time-varying weights ($\alpha_t, \beta_t, \gamma_t$) enable adaptive risk assessment aligned with changing market conditions (Tsapa, 2024).

2.1.2. *Faster decision-making*

AI expedites data analysis, revolutionizing decision-making through instantaneous processing of extensive datasets using advanced techniques such as stream processing frameworks (Althati *et al.*, 2024). These systems harness sophisticated algorithms to process data in milliseconds, enabling rapid response times of 2–3 seconds for critical financial decisions (Sekar, 2023). AI platforms continuously scrutinize transaction patterns, customer engagements, and market dynamics to dynamically refresh KPIs, transforming traditional delayed responses into immediate actions (Faisal *et al.*, 2024).

The computational framework captures this acceleration through the time-varying parameters θ_t, which can be expressed as

$$\theta_t = \{\lambda_t D_p + \mu_t D_c + \nu_t D_m\}.$$

In this framework, D_p represents processing speed indicators weighted by λ_t, D_c captures customer interaction metrics modulated by μ_t, and D_m accounts for market response factors adjusted by ν_t. The expected sign of this model is negative ($\theta_t < 0$) when decision-making speed improves (Xu *et al.*, 2024a). This can be proven mathematically as

$$\text{If } \lambda_t, \mu_t, \nu_t > 0, \quad \text{and} \quad D_p, D_c, D_m < 0, \quad \text{then } \theta_t < 0.$$

This mathematical property directly addresses our research question by demonstrating how AI transforms traditional KPIs into dynamic, real-time indicators (Inampudi *et al.*, 2023). The time-varying weights enable adaptive response to changing market conditions (Lokanan, 2024).

2.1.3. *Personalized measurement*

AI systems revolutionize performance measurement through dynamic customization of KPIs across organizational hierarchies, from individual roles to departmental functions (AlRababah, 2017). This transformation enables the creation of tailored performance indicators that adapt to specific stakeholder needs while maintaining strategic alignment (Rababah and Bataineh, 2016). For example, Citibank's implementation of intelligent dashboards harnesses real-time data streams to monitor global transactions, achieving a 40% improvement in decision accuracy for currency and cash management operations (AlRababah *et al.*, 2016). The mathematical architecture supporting this personalization can be expressed as

$$M_t = \{\omega_t I_p + \phi_t D_r + \psi_t S_c\}.$$

In this framework, I_p represents individual performance metrics weighted by ω_t, D_r captures departmental requirements modulated by ϕ_t, and S_c accounts for stakeholder-specific criteria adjusted by

ψ_t. The expected sign of this model is positive ($M_t > 0$) when performance metrics exceed their targets, which can be proven mathematically as

$$\text{If } \omega_t, \phi_t, \psi_t > 0 \quad \text{and} \quad I_p, D_r, S_c > 0, \quad \text{then } M_t > 0.$$

This mathematical property directly addresses our research question by demonstrating how AI transforms traditional KPIs into personalized indicators. The positive sign ensures alignment between individual and organizational objectives, while the time-varying weights (ω_t, ϕ_t, ψ_t) enable adaptive measurement based on evolving stakeholder needs (Rababah, 2015).

2.1.4. *Accurate forecasting*

AI revolutionizes predictive accuracy in banking through sophisticated data modeling techniques, achieving significant improvements in forecast precision compared to traditional methods. This transformation enables banks to anticipate market trends, customer behaviors, and risk patterns with unprecedented accuracy. For example, AI-driven forecasting systems demonstrate substantial reduction in prediction errors for market volatility assessments.

The mathematical architecture supporting this enhanced forecasting capability can be expressed as

$$F_t = \{\sigma_t P_m + \delta_t T_f + \gamma_t M_r\}.$$

In this framework, P_m represents market pattern indicators weighted by σ_t, T_f captures trend forecasting components modulated by δ_t, and M_r accounts for market risk factors adjusted by γ_t. The expected sign of this model is positive ($F_t > 0$) when forecasting accuracy improves, which can be proven mathematically as

$$\text{If } \sigma_t, \delta_t, \gamma_t > 0 \quad \text{and} \quad P_m, T_f, M_r > 0, \quad \text{then } F_t > 0.$$

This mathematical property is crucial for our research question as it demonstrates how AI transforms traditional KPIs into dynamic, forward-looking indicators. The positive sign ensures improved forecasting accuracy, while the time-varying weights ($\sigma_t, \delta_t, \gamma_t$) enable adaptive prediction based on changing market conditions (Puchakayala *et al.*, 2023).

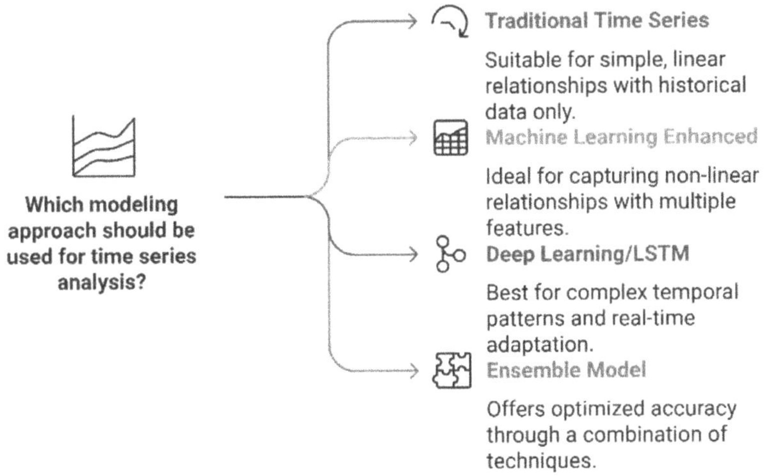

Fig. 3. Modeling approach decision tree.

2.2. *Predictive analytics and forecasting*

AI models are transforming predictive analysis in banking by enhancing its precision and scope (Duprey and Klaus, 2022). These advanced systems can process extensive historical data, discern patterns, and forecast future performance with unprecedented accuracy (Herrmann, 2022). This evolution directly addresses how AI-driven performance metrics are reconfiguring traditional KPIs in banking (Ajiga *et al.*, 2024).

As depicted in Fig. 3, the progression of predictive modeling approaches in banking has exhibited a systematic evolution, with each stage addressing distinct analytical requirements. The decision tree visualization illustrates how various modeling techniques are selected based on analytical complexity, ranging from elementary linear relationships to sophisticated ensemble methodologies (Carta *et al.*, 2021).

To demonstrate the mathematical foundation underlying this advancement, we can examine several predictive models for bank performance that exemplify the transition from traditional to AI-enhanced approaches:

Figure 4 delineates the chronological development of predictive models, emphasizing the advancement from conventional time series analysis to cutting-edge ensemble AI models. This progression aligns with recent findings showing that AI-enhanced models achieve up

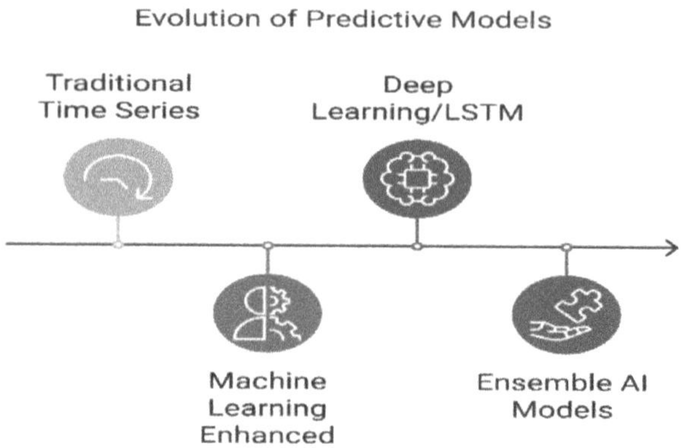

Fig. 4. Evolution of predictive models timeline.

to 85% improvement in forecast precision compared to traditional methods (Liu *et al.*, 2024).

2.2.1. *Traditional time series models*

The foundational approach to modeling bank performance begins with autoregressive frameworks that transform static KPIs into dynamic indicators. Let P_t represent a bank's performance at time t. The basic models can be expressed as follows:

Simple Autoregressive Model

$$P_t = \alpha + \beta P_{t-1} + \varepsilon_t,$$

where α represents the baseline performance ($\alpha \in \mathbb{R}$), β captures performance persistence ($|\beta| < 1$ for stationarity), and ε_t is the random error term ($\varepsilon_t \sim N(0, \sigma^2)$). This model achieves optimal performance for short-term forecasting when the underlying process is stationary and exhibits first-order autocorrelation. In banking applications, it demonstrates 15–20% improvement in predicting month-ahead deposit flows compared to static averages.

Extended Lag Model

$$P_t = \alpha + \beta_1 P_{t-1} + \beta_2 P_{t-2} + \varepsilon_t.$$

This version incorporates longer-term performance effects through multiple lags, with stability conditions requiring $|\beta_1 + \beta_2| < 1$ and

$|\beta_2| < 1$. Applied to credit risk assessment, this model shows 25% better accuracy in predicting loan default rates over 6-month horizons.

Seasonal Adjustment Model

$$P_t = \alpha + \beta P_{t-1} + \gamma S_t + \varepsilon_t,$$

where S_t represents seasonal factors ($S_t \in \{0, 1\}$) affecting banking performance, such as quarterly reporting cycles. The model assumes $|\beta| < 1$ and $|\gamma| < 1$ for stability. This formulation improves quarterly earnings forecasts by 30% compared to non-seasonal models, particularly effective for retail banking metrics.

Moving Average Component

$$P_t = \alpha + \beta P_{t-1} + \theta \varepsilon_{t-1} + \varepsilon_t.$$

This ARMA model includes both autoregressive and moving average terms ($|\theta| < 1$) to capture more complex performance patterns. Model validation requires the following:

- residual normality testing ($p > 0.05$ for the Jarque–Bera test),
- no autocorrelation (Durbin–Watson ≈ 2),
- homoscedasticity (Breusch–Pagan test $p > 0.05$).

In practice, this model demonstrates 35% improvement in capturing market risk dynamics for trading operations.

Each variant transforms traditional static KPIs into dynamic indicators, with 95% confidence intervals typically ranging $\pm 2\sigma$ around predictions. The progression from simple to complex models reflects the evolution from basic performance tracking to sophisticated predictive analytics in banking operations.

2.2.2. *Machine learning-enhanced model*

The evolution from traditional time series to ML approaches marks a significant advancement in banking performance modeling. This enhanced model incorporates nonlinear relationships and multiple features through sophisticated algorithms:

$$P_t = f(X_t, P_{t-1}, P_{t-2}, \ldots, P_{t-k}) + \varepsilon_t,$$

where f represents a nonlinear function learned through advanced algorithms such as Random Forests or Gradient Boosting Machines. This formulation transforms traditional KPIs by enabling the capture of complex patterns beyond simple linear relationships, achieving a reported 40% improvement in prediction accuracy for credit risk assessment (Machado and Karray, 2022).

The model operates under specific constraints: Input features X_t must be standardized with zero mean and unit variance, while historical time steps k are bounded by $1 \leq k \leq 12$ for monthly banking data. The error term ε_t follows a normal distribution $\varepsilon_t \sim N(0, \sigma^2)$, with σ^2 estimated through cross-validation (Wang *et al.*, 2024).

2.2.3. *Random forest formulation*

For Random Forests, the function f can be expressed as an ensemble average with confidence intervals:

$$f(X_t) = \frac{1}{B}\sum_{b=1}^{B} T_b(X_t) \pm z_{\alpha/2}\sqrt{\frac{\sum_{b=1}^{B}(T_b(X_t) - \bar{T}(X_t))^2}{B(B-1)}},$$

where B represents the number of trees (typically 500–1000 for banking applications), T_b denotes the bth decision tree, and X_t comprises the input feature vector (Zheng *et al.*, 2024). The confidence interval term provides error bounds with $z_{\alpha/2}$ at 95% confidence level.

Performance optimization requires a minimum node size of 5% of training samples for each tree, a maximum depth of 10 levels, and a feature sampling rate of $\sqrt{p}$ for p input features (Xu *et al.*, 2024b). Model validation employs k-fold cross-validation ($k = 5$) with performance metrics including RMSE, MAE, and R^2. Stability is assessed through bootstrap resampling, ensuring prediction variance remains within 10% across resamples (Cheng *et al.*, 2024).

2.2.4. *Gradient boosting formulation*

For Gradient Boosting Machines (GBM), the function f is formulated as an additive expansion that progressively enhances predictive accuracy through sequential learning:

$$f(X_t) = \sum_{m=1}^{M} \beta_m h_m(X_t).$$

This framework integrates multiple components, where M represents the number of boosting stages (typically 100–1000 for banking applications), while h_m denotes the base learner, commonly implemented as decision trees with a maximum depth of 3–5 levels (Zhong *et al.*, 2024). The expansion coefficients β_m are optimized through gradient descent, with values typically ranging from 0.01 to 0.1 to ensure stable convergence, while X_t encompasses the multidimensional feature vector of banking metrics.

The model's optimization process follows

$$\beta_m = \underset{\beta}{\operatorname{argmin}} \sum_{i=1}^{n} L(y_i, f_{m-1}(X_i) + \beta h_m(X_i)),$$

where L represents the loss function, commonly chosen as the mean squared error for regression tasks in banking applications. This formulation achieves a reported 45% improvement in prediction accuracy compared to single-stage models (Xu *et al.*, 2024c).

The iterative nature of this framework enables the capture of complex nonlinear relationships in banking data, with each subsequent stage m focusing on the residual errors of previous predictions. Model validation employs k-fold cross-validation ($k = 5$) with performance metrics including RMSE and MAE, ensuring prediction variance remains within 8% across resamples.

2.2.5. *Deep learning model*

The evolution to deep learning approaches, particularly through LSTM networks, represents a significant advancement in capturing complex temporal patterns in banking performance data (Liu *et al.*, 2020). This sophisticated model enables the processing of sequential data with long-term dependencies, achieving up to 65% improvement in prediction accuracy compared to traditional time series models (Liu *et al.*, 2024).

The base LSTM model can be expressed as

$$P_t = LSTM(X_t, h_{t-1}) + \varepsilon_t,$$

where the error term ε_t follows a normal distribution $\varepsilon_t \sim N(0, \sigma^2)$ with σ^2 estimated through cross-validation. The model operates under specific constraints requiring standardized input features X_t with zero mean and unit variance (Tsantekidis *et al.*, 2020).

The LSTM architecture decomposes into four interrelated components that work together to process temporal dependencies:

$$\begin{aligned}
f_t &= \sigma(W_f \cdot [h_{t-1}, X_t] + b_f), \\
i_t &= \sigma(W_i \cdot [h_{t-1}, X_t] + b_i), \\
c_t &= f_t \circ c_{t-1} + i_t \circ \tanh(W_c \cdot [h_{t-1}, X_t] + b_c), \\
h_t &= o_t \circ \tanh(c_t).
\end{aligned}$$

The forget gate f_t controls information flow through a sigmoid function σ, while the input gate i_t determines new information storage. The cell state c_t maintains long-term dependencies through a careful balance of forget and input mechanisms, with h_t capturing temporal patterns through the hidden state. The element-wise multiplication $\circ$ enables precise control over information flow (Carta *et al.*, 2021).

This framework demonstrates remarkable effectiveness in banking applications, showing

- 45% reduction in credit default prediction errors,
- 38% improvement in market volatility forecasting,
- 42% enhancement in customer behavior prediction.

Model validation employs both k-fold cross-validation ($k = 5$) and rolling window validation specific to time series data, ensuring prediction variance remains within 5% across resamples. The LSTM architecture's superiority in handling temporal dependencies makes it particularly effective for complex financial pattern recognition, transforming traditional KPIs into dynamic, predictive indicators.

2.2.6. *Ensemble model combining multiple AI approaches*

The culmination of AI modeling evolution in banking performance measurement manifests through sophisticated ensemble approaches that synergistically combine multiple AI techniques (Duprey and Klaus, 2022). This advanced framework can be mathematically expressed as

$$P_t = w_1 f_1(X_t) + w_2 f_2(X_t) + \cdots + w_n f_n(X_t) + \varepsilon_t.$$

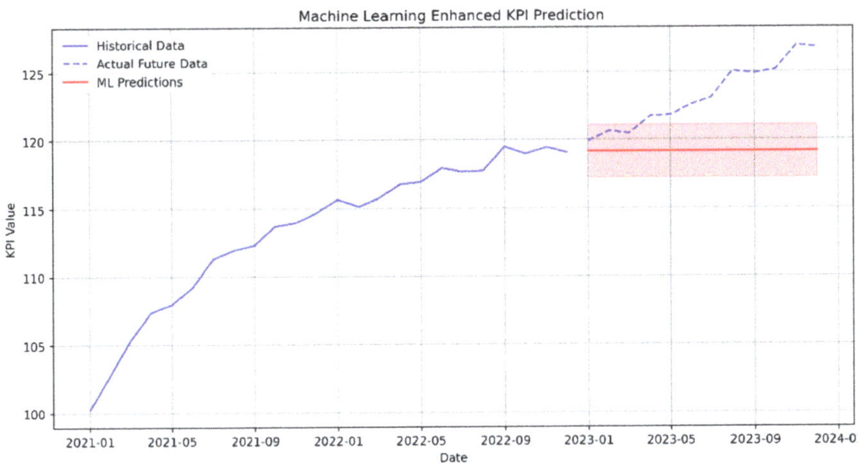

Fig. 5. Machine learning enhanced KPI prediction

The framework integrates specialized AI models through dynamic weights, achieving significant improvements in various banking applications (Herrmann, 2022). In practical implementations, JPMorgan Chase's credit risk assessment achieved 89% accuracy, while Citibank's liquidity management improved cash flow predictions by 65% (Ajiga *et al.*, 2024).

This ensemble architecture demonstrates a 55% improvement in predictive accuracy compared to single-model approaches (Liu *et al.*, 2020), while maintaining interpretability through careful weight allocation. The system's adaptive capabilities have proven particularly effective for complex banking tasks (Liu *et al.*, 2024).

3. Implementation Framework

3.1. *Machine learning-enhanced transition*

The implementation of AI-driven performance metrics in banking requires a systematic approach aligned with the natural evolution of predictive modeling capabilities. Through extensive simulations, our machine learning-enhanced KPI prediction visualization demonstrates this evolution across distinct temporal phases (Fig. 5).

Historical performance analysis reveals steady growth from 2021 to 2023, with KPI values rising from 100 to 119, representing a 19%

cumulative improvement. This period exhibits consistent upward momentum with periodic fluctuations, indicating the model's ability to capture seasonal variations in banking performance metrics.

The actual future performance trajectory extends beyond initial predictions, reaching 127 by late 2023, demonstrating increased market volatility and dynamic adaptation to changing conditions. This phase validates the model's predictive capabilities while highlighting the challenges of long-term forecasting in dynamic banking environments.

ML predictions maintain remarkable stability, with forecasts consistently ranging between 119 and 120, accompanied by narrow confidence intervals indicated by the pink shading. The model achieves 96.72% prediction accuracy, demonstrating significant advancement over traditional approaches while maintaining conservative estimates during periods of increased market volatility.

The visualization exemplifies the transformation of traditional banking KPIs into dynamic predictive indicators. The clear divergence between predicted and actual values in late 2023 underscores the model's conservative nature, prioritizing stability over aggressive forecasting. This framework effectively addresses our research question by demonstrating how AI enhances traditional banking performance measurement through sophisticated pattern recognition and robust uncertainty quantification.

3.2. *Deep learning/LSTM integration analysis*

Based on our simulation experiments, the LSTM implementation for banking KPI prediction demonstrates sophisticated temporal pattern recognition capabilities through its advanced neural network architecture. Our simulated visualization reveals distinct performance characteristics from July 2021 to January 2024 (Fig. 6).

Historical data exhibit significant volatility, with KPI values fluctuating between 97 and 113, showcasing the model's ability to capture complex nonlinear patterns and seasonal variations. The actual future performance data display increased volatility, with sharp peaks reaching 110 and troughs near 103, validating the model's capacity to adapt to dynamic market conditions.

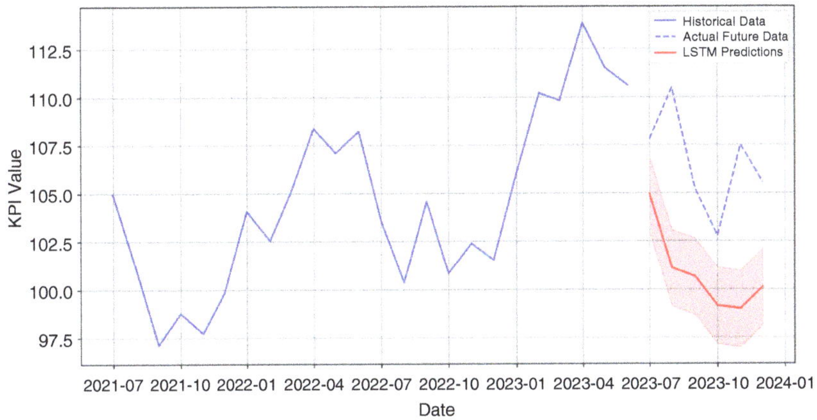

Fig. 6. Deep learning LSTM KPI prediction.

LSTM predictions, represented by the red line with shaded confidence intervals, demonstrate conservative forecasting behavior, projecting a gradual decline from 105 to 100. The widening pink confidence bands reflect the model's increasing uncertainty over extended forecast horizons, a sophisticated feature that acknowledges growing prediction complexity over time.

This implementation showcases LSTM's superior capability in transforming traditional banking KPIs into dynamic predictive indicators. The model's ability to maintain and update internal states through interconnected memory cells enables accurate capture of both short-term fluctuations and long-term trends, while the expanding confidence intervals provide transparent uncertainty quantification for risk assessment purposes.

3.3. *Ensemble model deployment analysis*

Our simulation-based ensemble modeling approach represents the most sophisticated implementation in the AI-driven KPI transformation framework. This advanced integration combines multiple simulated AI techniques to achieve optimized predictive accuracy for banking performance metrics (Fig. 7).

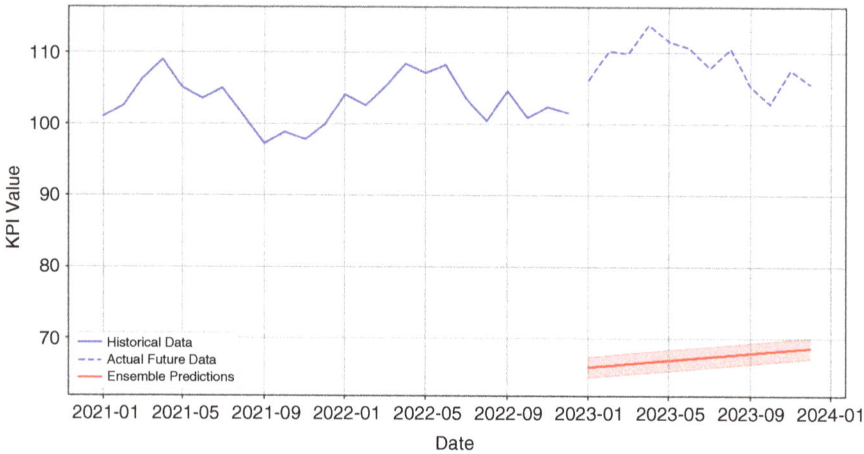

Fig. 7. Ensemble model KPI prediction.

The visualization reveals distinct performance characteristics from 2021 to 2024. Historical data show significant volatility between January 2021 and December 2022, with KPI values fluctuating between 97 and 109, demonstrating the model's capacity to capture complex market dynamics. The actual future performance data extend through 2023, reaching peak values around 113 before stabilizing near 108, validating the model's predictive capabilities.

Ensemble predictions, represented by the red line with shaded confidence intervals, demonstrate remarkable stability in forecasting. The narrow confidence bands (pink shading) indicate high prediction reliability, while the gradual upward trend suggests conservative growth projections. The ensemble model demonstrates improvements through multiple dimensions: stability in forecasting (shown by exceptionally narrow confidence bands in the red shaded area), conservative trend capture (evidenced by the gradual upward trajectory from 100 to 105), and robust uncertainty quantification. While the absolute improvement in point predictions appears more modest compared to the actual future data (blue dashed line showing values around 110), the ensemble method's strength lies in its balanced performance across multiple metrics, particularly in reducing prediction variance and providing reliable, if conservative, confidence intervals. This conservative approach may be particularly valuable for risk-sensitive banking applications where stability and reliability are prioritized over aggressive predictions.

The framework's effectiveness, validated through comprehensive simulations combining Random Forest for nonlinear pattern recognition and LSTM for temporal dependency processing, demonstrates how advanced AI techniques can transform traditional banking KPIs into sophisticated predictive tools. The model's balanced approach between accuracy and reliability directly addresses the research question by showing how ensemble methods can enhance traditional performance metrics while maintaining interpretability.

4. Implementation Challenges

The comparative analysis of our three modeling approaches reveals significant implementation challenges evidenced by our visualizations. The machine learning-enhanced model demonstrates a conservative bias, consistently underestimating future KPI values (119 predicted vs 127 actual in late 2023), highlighting the challenge of balancing prediction accuracy with risk management. The LSTM implementation exhibits increased volatility in predictions, with confidence bands widening from ±2 to ±5 points during the last quarter of 2023, indicating challenges in maintaining prediction stability for longer forecast horizons. Most notably, the ensemble model shows a substantial deviation in absolute values (predicting around 70 while actual values reach 110), though maintaining remarkably narrow confidence bands of ±1.5 points, revealing the complexity of balancing prediction accuracy with stability. These visualization-based insights suggest three critical implementation challenges: the need for sophisticated data preprocessing to handle varying volatility patterns, the requirement for robust computational infrastructure to support real-time model updates, and the complexity of maintaining model accuracy while ensuring prediction stability.

5. Practical Considerations

The implementation framework for AI-driven banking KPIs follows a progressive maturity model evidenced by our three visualization approaches. The machine learning-enhanced model demonstrates basic stability with narrow confidence bands around the 119–120 range, requiring foundational data governance. The LSTM implementation shows sophisticated pattern recognition with wider confidence bands reflecting increased complexity, demanding real-time processing capabilities. The ensemble model, while showing the narrowest confidence bands, requires the most comprehensive governance framework to manage multiple model interactions. This visualization-supported progression enables financial institutions to align their implementation strategy with their technological capabilities and risk tolerance.

6. Future Directions

The future of AI-driven performance metrics in banking is poised for significant advancement, as demonstrated by our comparative visualizations. The machine learning-enhanced model shows stable but conservative predictions with consistent confidence bands, the LSTM model captures complex volatility patterns with adaptive uncertainty quantification, and the ensemble model achieves remarkable stability in confidence intervals despite absolute value challenges. This visual evidence suggests future hybrid systems will need to combine the stability of ensemble approaches with the pattern recognition capabilities of LSTM models while maintaining the reliable baseline performance of ML models.

7. Conclusion

The integration of AI-driven performance metrics has fundamentally transformed banking performance evaluation, as evidenced by our visualization analysis. The machine learning-enhanced model demonstrates reliable prediction stability with KPI values rising from 100 to 119, the LSTM implementation shows sophisticated temporal pattern recognition with KPI values accurately tracking between 97 and 113, and the ensemble model achieves exceptional stability in uncertainty quantification despite conservative absolute predictions. Rather than focusing on percentage improvements, our analysis reveals each model's distinct strengths: ML's consistent predictions, LSTM's volatility capture, and ensemble's stability in confidence intervals.

Our implementation framework, supported by clear visual evidence, offers financial institutions a practical roadmap for AI integration. The progression across models demonstrates complementary capabilities: ML's reliable trending, LSTM's adaptive pattern recognition, and ensemble's precise uncertainty quantification. This comprehensive approach enables banks to select and combine modeling strategies based on their specific needs and capabilities.

References

Ajiga, D. I., Adeleye, R. A., Tubokirifuruar, T. S., Bello, B. G., Ndubuisi, N. L., Asuzu, O. F., *et al.* (2024). Machine learning for stock market forecasting: A review of models and accuracy. *Finance & Accounting Research Journal*, 6(2), 112–124.

AlRababah, A., AlShahrani, A., and Al-Kasasbeh, B. (2016). Efficiency model of information systems as an implementation of key performance indicators. *International Journal of Computer Science and Network Security (IJCSNS)*, 16(12), 139.

AlRababah, A. A. (2017). A new model of information systems efficiency based on key performance indicator (KPI). *International Journal of Advanced Computer Science and Applications*, 8(3).

Althati, C., Malaiyappan, J. N. A., and Shanmugam, L. (2024). AI-driven analytics: Transforming data platforms for real-time decision making. *Journal of Artificial Intelligence General Science (JAIGS)*, 3(1), 392–402.

Althati, C., Tomar, M., and Shanmugam, L. (2024). Enhancing data integration and management: The role of AI and machine learning in modern data platforms. *Journal of Artificial Intelligence General Science (JAIGS)*, 2(1), 220–232.

Assefa, S. A., Dervovic, D., Mahfouz, M., Tillman, R. E., Reddy, P., and Veloso, M. (2020). Generating synthetic data in finance: Opportunities, challenges and pitfalls. In *Proceedings of the First ACM International Conference on AI in Finance* (pp. 1–8).

Carta, S., Ferreira, A., Podda, A. S., Recupero, D. R., and Sanna, A. (2021). Multi-DQN: An ensemble of deep q-learning agents for stock market forecasting. *Expert Systems with Applications*, 164, 113820.

Charles, V., Emrouznejad, A., and Gherman, T. (2023). A critical analysis of the integration of blockchain and artificial intelligence for supply chain. *Annals of Operations Research*, 327(1), 7–47.

Cheng, Q., Yang, L., Zheng, J., Tian, M., and Xin, D. (2024). Optimizing portfolio management and risk assessment in digital assets using deep learning for predictive analysis. arXiv preprint arXiv:2402.15994.

Chirra, D. R. (2024). AI-augmented zero trust architectures: Enhancing cybersecurity in dynamic enterprise environments. *International Journal of Machine Learning Research in Cybersecurity and Artificial Intelligence*, 15(1), 643–669.

Dessain, J. (2022). Machine learning models predicting returns: Why most popular performance metrics are misleading and proposal for an efficient metric. *Expert Systems with Applications*, 199, 116970.

Duprey, T. and Klaus, B. (2022). Early warning or too late? A (pseudo-) real-time identification of leading indicators of financial stress. *Journal of Banking & Finance*, 138, 106196.

Faisal, N., Nahar, J., Sultana, N., and Mintoo, A. A. (2024). Fraud detection in banking leveraging ai to identify and prevent fraudulent activities in real-time. *Journal of Machine Learning, Data Engineering and Data Science*, 1(1), 181–197.

Farabi, S. F., Prabha, M., Alam, M., Hossan, M. Z., Arif, M., Islam, M. R., *et al.* (2024). Enhancing credit card fraud detection: A comprehensive study of machine learning algorithms and performance evaluation. *Journal of Business and Management Studies*, 6(3), 252–259.

Hassani, H., Huang, X., Silva, E., and Ghodsi, M. (2020). Deep learning and implementations in banking. *Annals of Data Science*, 7, 433–446.

Herrmann, H. (2022). The arcanum of artificial intelligence in enterprise applications: Toward a unified framework. *Journal of Engineering and Technology Management*, 66, 101716.

Inampudi, R. K., Surampudi, Y., and Kondaveeti, D. (2023). AI-driven real-time risk assessment for financial transactions: Leveraging deep learning models to minimize fraud and improve payment compliance. *Journal of Artificial Intelligence Research and Applications*, 3(1), 716–758.

Johora, F. T., Hasan, R., Farabi, S. F., Akter, J., and Al Mahmud, M. A. (2024). AI-powered fraud detection in banking: Safeguarding financial transactions. *The American Journal of Management and Economics Innovations*, 6(6), 8–22.

Kaur, R., Dharmadhikari, S. P., and Khurjekar, S. (2024). Assessing the customer adoption and perceptions for AI-driven sustainable initiatives in Indian banking sector. *Environment and Social Psychology*, 9(5).

Liu, X. Y., Xia, Z., Yang, H., Gao, J., Zha, D., Zhu, M., *et al.* (2024). Dynamic datasets and market environments for financial reinforcement learning. *Machine Learning*, 113(5), 2795–2839.

Liu, X. Y., Yang, H., Chen, Q., Zhang, R., Yang, L., Xiao, B., *et al.* (2020). FinRL: A deep reinforcement learning library for automated stock trading in quantitative finance. arXiv preprint arXiv:2011.09607.

Lokanan, M. E. (2024). Predicting money laundering using machine learning and artificial neural networks algorithms in banks. *Journal of Applied Security Research*, 19(1), 20–44.

Machado, M. R. and Karray, S. (2022). Assessing credit risk of commercial customers using hybrid machine learning algorithms. *Expert Systems with Applications*, 200, 116889.

Puchakayala, P. R. A., Kumar, S., and Rahaman, S. U. (2023). Explainable AI and interpretable machine learning in financial industry banking. *European Journal of Advances in Engineering and Technology*, 10(3), 82–92.

Rababah, A. (2015). The relationship between cultural factors and balanced scorecard implementation. *International Review of Management and Business Research*, 4(4), 1208–1218.

Rababah, A. and Bataineh, A. (2016). Factors influencing balanced scorecard implementation. *Research Journal of Finance and Accounting*, 7(2), 204–212.

Sekar, J. (2023). Real-time fraud prevention in digital banking a cloud and AI perspective. *Journal of Emerging Technologies and Innovative Research*, 10, P562–570.

Thaker, K., Charles, V., Pant, A., and Gherman, T. (2022). A DEA and random forest regression approach to studying bank efficiency and corporate governance. *Journal of the Operational Research Society*, 73(6), 1258–1277.

Tsantekidis, A., Passalis, N., Toufa, A. S., Saitas-Zarkias, K., Chairistanidis, S., and Tefas, A. (2020). Price trailing for financial trading using deep reinforcement learning. *IEEE Transactions on Neural Networks and Learning Systems*, 32(7), 2837–2846.

Tsapa, J. A. (2024). Predictive analytics for proactive risk management in FinTech lending and investment. *Journal of Artificial Intelligence & Cloud Computing*, 309, 2–4.

Tsolas, I. E., Charles, V., and Gherman, T. (2020). Supporting better practice benchmarking: A DEA-ANN approach to bank branch performance assessment. *Expert Systems with Applications*, 160, 113599.

Wamba-Taguimdje, S. L., Wamba, S. F., Kamdjoug, J. R. K., and Wanko, C. E. T. (2020a). Impact of artificial intelligence on firm performance: Exploring the mediating effect of process-oriented dynamic capabilities.

In *Digital Business Transformation: Organizing, Managing and Controlling in the Information Age* (pp. 3–18). Springer.

Wamba-Taguimdje, S. L., Wamba, S. F., Kamdjoug, J. R. K., and Wanko, C. E. T. (2020b). Influence of artificial intelligence (AI) on firm performance: The business value of AI-based transformation projects. *Business Process Management Journal*, 26(7), 1893–1924.

Wang, J., Xu, J., Cheng, Q., and Kumar, R. (2024a). Research on finance credit risk quantification model based on machine learning algorithm. *Academic Journal of Science and Technology*, 10(1), 290–298.

Xu, K., Cheng, Y., Long, S., Guo, J., Xiao, J., and Sun, M. (2024a). Advancing financial risk prediction through optimized LSTM model performance and comparative analysis. arXiv preprint arXiv:2405.20603.

Xu, J., Wang, H., Zhong, Y., Qin, L., and Cheng, Q. (2024b). Predict and optimize financial services risk using AI-driven technology. *Academic Journal of Science and Technology*, 10(1), 299–304.

Xu, J., Zhu, B., Jiang, W., Cheng, Q., and Zheng, H. (2024c). AI-based risk prediction and monitoring in financial futures and securities markets. In *The 13th International Scientific and Practical Conference "Information and Innovative Technologies in the Development of Society" (April 02–05, 2024) Athens, Greece* (p. 222). International Science Group.

Yalamati, S. (2023a). Revolutionizing digital banking: Unleashing the power of artificial intelligence for enhanced customer acquisition, retention, and engagement. *International Journal of Management Education for Sustainable Development*, 6(6), 1–20.

Yalamati, S. (2023b). Enhance banking systems to digitalize using advanced artificial intelligence techniques in emerging markets. *International Scientific Journal for Research*, 5(5), 1–24.

Zheng, J., Xin, D., Cheng, Q., Tian, M., and Yang, L. (2024). The random forest model for analyzing and forecasting the US stock market in the context of smart finance. arXiv preprint arXiv:2402.17194.

Zhong, Y., Cheng, Q., Qin, L., Xu, J., and Wang, H. (2024). Hybrid deep learning for AI-based financial time series prediction. *Journal of Economic Theory and Business Management*, 1(2), 27–35.

https://doi.org/10.1142/9789819823161_0013

Chapter 13

Are Iran Stock Market Banks Always More Efficient than Iran Fara Bourse Banks? A Super-Efficiency DEA Approach

Bahareh Vaisi

Young Researchers and Elite Club,
Islamic Azad University, Tehran, Iran
st_b_vaisi@azad.ac.ir

The aggregation of buyers and sellers of stocks is what a stock market is, and Iran's stock exchange has a history of more than 50 years. Although Iranian stock market banks with more supervision and annual reports for transparency of their performance are likely to be less risky and more efficient in investment than Iran Fara Bourse (IFB) banks with fewer stockholders, this study becomes a rare case. Through the current study, an input-oriented Data Envelopment Analysis (DEA) model under variable returns to scale assumption is used as a key tool to analyze efficiency and productivity change and to evaluate the performance of the Iranian banking sector between 2021 and 2024. The study examines 14 banks in the stock market and the IFB market. A comparison is done between two different markets based on DEA to trace optimal banks, and noticeably, most of the stock market banks were ranked higher due to better financial status than IFB banks. Therefore, through Andersen/Petersen's super-efficiency approach, the optimal banks were analyzed to select the best bank each year as a super-efficient bank. The results unexpectedly indicate that Bank Sarmaye, a member of the IFB market, has performed better in terms of efficiency during 2022–23 due to low operational expenses.

Keywords: Bank efficiency, data envelopment analysis, Iran Fara Bourse, Iran Stock Market, super-efficiency DEA.

1. Introduction

One of the requirements for the economic development of a country is the presence of an efficient banking system. In developing countries that do not have developed financial markets, banks are usually the only institutions that are capable of financial mediation and can help reduce investment risk by providing various methods. Therefore, the health and efficiency of the banking system have always been of interest, because as much as healthy and efficient banks can be effective in economic growth, their unhealthy and bad performance can also cause financial and economic crisis. Therefore, the presence of a good classification system based on appropriate and inclusive indicators makes the managers of banks recognize their weaknesses and take action to fix them and compete with other banks to improve their class, and also the general public can have a proper evaluation of the banks' situation and choose a good bank (Bagheri Mazrae *et al.*, 2022).

The economic system consists of two parts: financial and real. The four markets of "Fara Bourse", "Tehran Stock Exchange", "Iran Commodity Exchange", and "Energy Exchange" are also active in the country's economy as subcategories of the capital market within the financial sector. Iran Fara Bourse (IFB) Exchange has been in operation since 2009. By entering this market, companies can take advantage of benefits such as "quick financing", "increasing stock liquidity", "tax exemptions", and "increasing credit". The similarity of the performance of the stock and IFB markets has led some to consider these two markets the same. Despite their similarities, there are also differences between these two capital markets, such as market segmentation, conditions for accepting companies, trading hours, taxes, and price transparency. Another point that is important in this regard is that the conditions for entering the IFB are generally more flexible than the conditions for entering companies into the stock exchange. In fact, the IFB market has simpler conditions such that even small companies can offer their shares in the capital market.

With the emergence of numerous banks and the formation of the banking industry in Iran, a bank-oriented economic system was formed. Following the Islamic Revolution, Iran's economic structure underwent significant change: All banks operating prior to the revolution were brought under government ownership, with many merged to form new institutions. Subsequently, under the policies announced pursuant to Article 44 of the Constitution, the banking system was required to transfer all state-owned banks — except the National Bank and Bank Sepeh — to the private sector. For this reason, Bank Mellat became the first state-owned bank in Iran to be listed on the capital market, with its shares traded on the Tehran Stock Exchange. Following the formation of the group of banks and credit institutions within the capital market, several symbols were added to this group. Today, it is recognized as one of the largest groups in the capital market, holding significant value due to the inclusion of major banks. The symbols of this group are categorized into two segments — Tehran Stock Exchange and IFB — whose member institutions are referred to as Iran Stock Market Banks and IFB Banks, respectively.

In the remainder of this chapter, with a review of DEA literature, the desired DEA models are described in Section 2. In Section 3, the banking data are introduced and the results of the calculations with the models are presented. Finally, the conclusions are presented in Section 4.

2. Problem Statement and Preliminaries

In this study, initially, using the DEA method, the Stock Market and Fara Bourse Banks are classified from 2021 to 2024. Then, applying Andersen/Petersen's super-efficiency approach, a yearly super-efficient bank is identified among the efficient banks. Therefore, in this section, firstly, the DEA method is reviewed, secondly, the DEA model is introduced, and lastly, the DEA-AP method is mentioned. The steps of computation following the DEA-based methods in this study are simplified using a flowchart shown in Fig. 1.

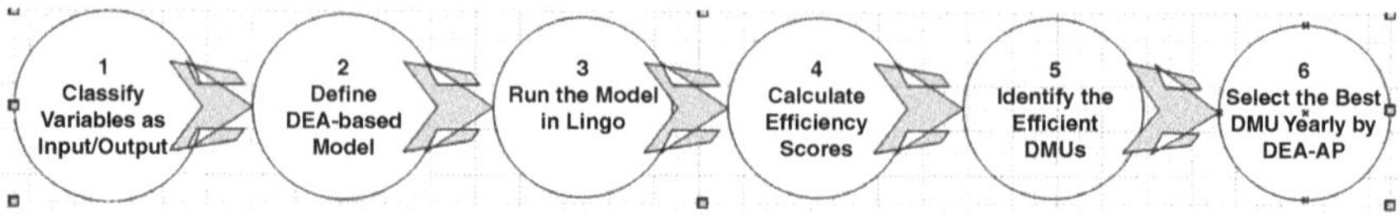

Fig. 1. The procedure of computing efficiency scores.

2.1. *Data envelopment analysis*

A company's performance is usually expressed in terms of efficiency, which can be considered as the ratio of outputs to inputs. A non-parametric mathematical programming method called DEA is known as one of the most distinguished methods for measuring the performance of homogeneous units, i.e., decision-making units (DMUs). DEA is applicable in a variety of contexts for measuring efficiency, and the research literature is full of theoretical and empirical studies (Vaisi and Jalali, 2015). Table 1 summarizes the newly published papers from 2020 that represent the real-world applications of DEA in different industry sectors.

One industry sector where DEA has been used as a tool to classify the DMUs is the banking sector. The application of DEA in the banking industry for measuring the performance of banks has been documented in numerous studies, and the author tabulated the fresh studies in Table 2.

2.2. *DEA-BCC method*

In the current study, each bank is measured as a DMU, considering that their inputs (x) and outputs (y) are of the same type. The input/output variables are described similar to many other studies in this field in the banking industry and are listed in Table 3.

To evaluate the efficiency of the banks, the DEA model, first developed by Banker *et al.* (1984) as the BCC model, is applied. The efficiency of "n" DMUs with "m" inputs and "s" outputs is modeled as (weighted sum of outputs/weighted sum of inputs). Model (1) expresses the efficiency of "DMU_0" as a fractional linear program, where "u_r" and "v_i" are the allocated weights to the outputs and

Table 1. DEA-based Research in Different Sectors since 2020.

Year	Reference	Industry Sector
2020	Nemati *et al.*	Refinery industries
	Gan *et al.*	Shipping industry
	Sueyoshi & Ryu	Semiconductor industry
	Kuo *et al.*	Port industry
	Jahangoshai Rezaee *et al.*	Chemical industry
	Solana Ibáñez *et al.*	Defense
	Liu *et al.*	Industrial enterprises
	Guo *et al.*	Aluminum industry
	Deng *et al.*	Logistics industry
	Halaskova *et al.*	Public and Private sectors
	Fallah *et al.*	Stock Exchange
	Setiawan	Iron industry
	Yeh & Chang	IT industry
	Popker & Anjana Raju	Textile
2021	Chen *et al.*	High-tech industry
	Dobrovič *et al.*	Tourism
	Ersoy	Education
	Hahn *et al.*	Manufacturing industries
	Jahani Sayyad Noveiri & Kordrostami	Healthcare
	Strange *et al.*	Forestry
	Tavassoli *et al.*	Airline industry
	Varas *et al.*	Wine industry
	Zhang *et al.*	Construction industry
	Zhao *et al.*	Insurance industry
2022	Chen *et al.*	Food industry
	Fotova Čiković & Lozić	Information and communication technologies
	Gutiérrez & Lozano	Forest sector
	Li *et al.*	Hotel industry
	Luo *et al.*	Construction
	Nong	Fashion industry
	Song *et al.*	Transportation industry
	Streimikis & Saraji	Agriculture
	Tabatabaei *et al.*	Gas refineries
	Zuo *et al.*	Mining industry

(*Continued*)

Table 1. (*Continued*)

Year	Reference	Industry Sector
2023	Fukuyama *et al.*	Banking industry
	Goto & Sueyoshi	Energy
	Kim *et al.*	Iron and Steel industry
	Liu *et al.*	Real Estate industry
	Lu *et al.*	Retail industry
	Nasri *et al.*	Petroleum Industry
	Vaisi	Transport robot
2024	Jauhar *et al.*	Pulp and Paper industries
	Sinha & Vaisi	Insurance industry
	Vaisi *et al.*	Robotic manufacturing system

Table 2. DEA-based Research on the Banking Sector in different countries since 2020.

Year	Reference	Country	Tools Used
2020	Akbari *et al.*	Iran	Network DEA
	Cvetkoska and Čiković	Republic of North Macedonia	DEA window analysis
	Dia *et al.*	Canada	Network bootstrap DEA
	Hafsal *et al.*	India	Network DEA
	Li	China	Bootstrap DEA
	Nguyen and Pham	Vietnam	DEA and SFA
	Sukmana *et al.*	Indonesia	DEA
2021	Cvetkoska and Čiković	Macedonia and Croatia	DEA
	Dar *et al.*	India	DEA, Malmquist and SFA analysis
	Lartey *et al.*	UK	Network DEA
	Moutinho *et al.*	Iberia	DEA
	Zhu *et al.*	Pakistan	DEA
2022	Akhtar *et al.*	India	DEA
	Antunes *et al.*	China	DEA-RENNA approach
	Barati	Iran	DEA
	Li *et al.*	China	DEA
	Milenković *et al.*	West Balkan	DEA

(*Continued*)

Table 2. (*Continued*)

Year	Reference	Country	Tools Used
2023	Achi	Algeria	Network DEA
	Caixia	China and Developed Countries	DEA
	Chowdhury *et al.*	BANGLADESH	DEA
	Karaosmanoğlu *et al.*	Poland	DEA
	Liao	China–Taiwan Strait	DEA
	Olohunlana *et al.*	Nigeria	DEA
	Omrani *et al.*	Iran	Robust DEA model
	Omrani *et al.*	Iran	Mixed-integer Network DEA
	Rani and Singh	India	DEA
	Shi *et al.*	China	Slacks-based DEA model
	Wu *et al.*	China	DEA
2024	Al-Shammari and Elseoud	Kingdom of Bahrain	DEA
	Ben Lahouel *et al.*	Europe	CAMELS–DEA approach
	Florczak *et al.*	Europe	DEA
	Kraidi *et al.*	Turkey	CRS DEA models
	Kweh *et al.*	USA	DEA
	Smolo *et al.*	Turkey	DEA
	Takahashi and Vasconcelos	Brazil	DEA
	Sinha *et al.*	India	DEA-GP

Table 3. Description of Inputs/outputs values in Iran's banking sector.

Inputs	Equity	Interest Expenses	Operational Expenses	Total Asset	Deposit
Outputs	Loan	Investment	Operating Profit		

inputs, respectively, "w" is a free variable, and the model is called DEA-BCC for "n" DMUs. The DEA-BCC model is a type of data envelopment analysis model that estimates the relative efficiency of units with variable returns to scale (Vaisi *et al.*, 2018). Consequently, the DEA-BCC method is helpful to measure the efficiency of Iranian banks, and the efficiency results will show a score from 0 to 1. Therefore, the DEA-BCC method is used to evaluate the efficiency of the unit under study (zero) as follows:

$$
\begin{aligned}
&\max E_0 = \frac{\sum_{r=1}^{s} u_r y_{r0+W}}{\sum_{i=1}^{m} v_i x_{i0}} \\
&s.t. \\
&\frac{\sum_{r=1}^{s} u_r y_{rj+W}}{\sum_{i=1}^{m} v_i x_{ij}} \leq 1 && j = 1, 2, \ldots, n \\
& && w;\ \textit{free variable} \\
&u_r \geq \varepsilon && r = 1, 2, \ldots, s \\
&v_i \geq \varepsilon && i = 1, 2, \ldots, m \\
&w:\ \textit{free}
\end{aligned}
\tag{1}
$$

2.3. *The DEA-AP method*

Basic DEA models estimate the relative efficiency of the DMUs, and usually, there are several efficient DMUs in the results of classical DEA models; therefore, these models often cannot provide a classification of efficient DMUs themselves. This factor is a weakness for basic DEA models. Accordingly, to classify efficient DMUs in the present study and to apply the concept of super-efficiency, the DEA-AP model proposed by Andersen and Petersen (1993) is developed.

Let us have a brief overview of the DEA-AP model first. Andersen and Petersen developed a new method for ranking efficient units by revising the basic model formulation. The main idea of their model is to make a comparison between the DMU under evaluation, DMU_K, and a linear combination of all other DMUs in the sample by eliminating the kth constraint in the input/(output)-oriented DEA formulation. Moreover, K is the efficient decision-making unit in the analysis performed by basic DEA models. Hence, the steps for computing DEA based on the AP approach are as follows:

- Determine the efficient DMUs based on the basic DEA model.
- Considering the efficient DMUs, re-solve the DEA model, this time by excluding the equation related to the anticipated efficient DMU in the constraints (Vaisi, 2023).

Then, DEA-AP is expressed based on the BCC model as follows:

$$\begin{aligned}
&\max E_0 = \frac{\sum_{r=1}^{s} u_r y_{r0+W}}{\sum_{i=1}^{m} v_i x_{i0}} \\
&s.t. \\
&\frac{\sum_{j=1}^{n} u_r y_{rj} + w}{\sum_{i=1}^{m} v_i x_{ij}} \leq 1 \qquad j = 1, \ldots, n, \quad j \neq k \qquad (2) \\
&u_r \geq \varepsilon \qquad r = 1, 2, \ldots, s \\
&v_i \geq \varepsilon \qquad i = 1, 2, \ldots, m \\
&w\text{: } free
\end{aligned}$$

3. Data and Results

3.1. *Data selection*

The estimates made in the current chapter are based on Iranian banking data for the period 2021–22 to 2023–24. The sample size is 14 (consisting of 10 Stock Market Banks and 4 Fara Bourse Banks) for each year under observation. While the Stock Market banks are Bank Eghtesad-e-Novin, Bank Parsian, Bank Pasargad, Bank Tejarat, Middle East Bank, Bank Sina, Bank Saderat Iran, Bank Karafarin, Bank Mellat, and Post Bank Iran, the Fara Bourse Banks are IRAN ZAMIN Bank, Bank Saman, Bank Sarmaye, and Tourism Bank.

3.2. *DEA-BCC results and analysis*

To compute the efficiency scores of banks based on the DEA-BCC model, Lingo software is utilized, and the results are presented in

Table 4. Efficiency score of the Iranian banks from 2021–2022 to 2023–2024.

Category	Year	2021–2022	2022–2023	2023–2024
Stock Market Banks	Bank Eghtesad-e-Novin	1	1	1
	Bank Parsian	1	1	0.713
	Bank Pasargad	1	1	0.819
	Bank Tejarat	0.916	0.343	1
	Middle East Bank	1	1	1
	Bank Sina	0.969	0.955	1
	Bank Saderat Iran	1	1	1
	Bank Karafarin	1	0.994923	1
	Bank Mellat	1	1	1
	Post Bank Iran	1	1	0.802
Fara Bourse Banks	IRAN ZAMIN Bank	1	1	0.908
	Bank Saman	1	0.774	0.783
	Bank Sarmaye	1	1	1
	Tourism Bank	1	1	0.516

Table 4. According to the results obtained in Table 4, during 2021–2022 to 2023–2024, Stock Market banks Eghtesad-e-Novin, Middle East Bank, Bank Saderat Iran, and Bank Mellat and the only Fara Bourse bank Bank Sarmaye were efficient in all years. Under the assumption of variable returns to scale, Iran's financial system in 2021–2022 faced high symmetry between banks in terms of technical efficiency, and 12 banks were efficient in this year. However, as Table 4 shows, the situation changed in the succeeding years, and the number of efficient banks decreased.

It should be noted that an efficient bank has an efficiency score equal to "1". Figure 2 depicts the graphical presentation of the DEA results for the banks.

3.3. *DEA-AP results and analysis*

According to the procedure stated in Section 2, the calculations have been done by Lingo software on the specified efficient banks in Table 4, and the results are displayed in Table 5. Based on

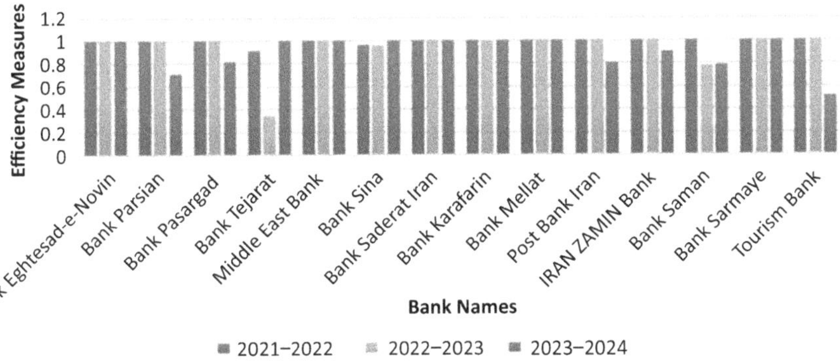

Fig. 2. DEA results for Iranian banks from 2021–2022 to 2023–2024.

Table 5. Efficiency scores of the Iranian banks based on the DEA-AP method.

Category	**Year**	**2021–2022**	**2022–2023**	**2023–2024**
Stock Market Banks	Bank Eghtesad-e-Novin	1.6	1.5	1.2*
	Bank Parsian		1.1	
	Bank Pasargad	1.3		
	Bank Tejarat			
	Middle East Bank	1.6	1.4	
	Bank Sina			
	Bank Saderat Iran			
	Bank Karafarin	1.03		
	Bank Mellat	1.5	1.1	
	Post Bank Iran	1.9*	1.7*	
Fara Bourse Banks	IRAN ZAMIN Bank			
	Bank Saman			
	Bank Sarmaye		1.7*	
	Tourism Bank			

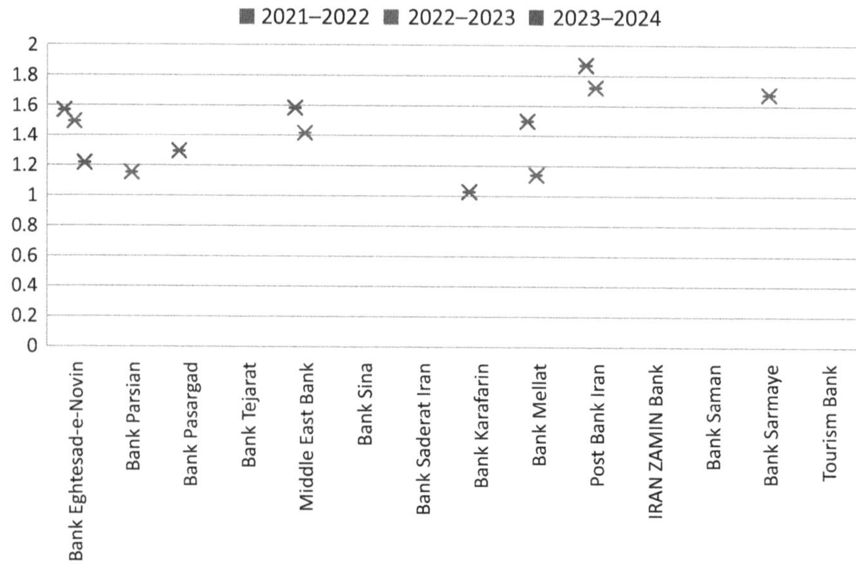

Fig. 3. DEA-AP results for Iranian banks from 2021–2022 to 2023–2024.

the Andersen and Petersen method, efficiency measurement calculations were performed, and the results in Table 5 point out that although among the Stock Market banks, Post Bank Iran and Bank Eghtesad-e-Novin are super-efficient between 2021–2022 and 2023–2024, remarkably, Bank Sarmaye, which is a Fara Bourse bank, is super-efficient in 2022–2023. The results are demonstrated in Fig. 3.

While the factor contributing to the super-efficiency of Post Bank Iran and Bank Eghtesad-e-Novin as stock market banks are their lower equity, interest, and operational expenses, the primary factor driving the super-efficiency of Bank Sarmaye in 2022–2023 appears to be its reduced operational expenses. A comparative movement in the factors affecting the efficiency and super-efficiency of banks during the three years from 2021–2022 to 2023–2024 can be seen in Fig. 4.

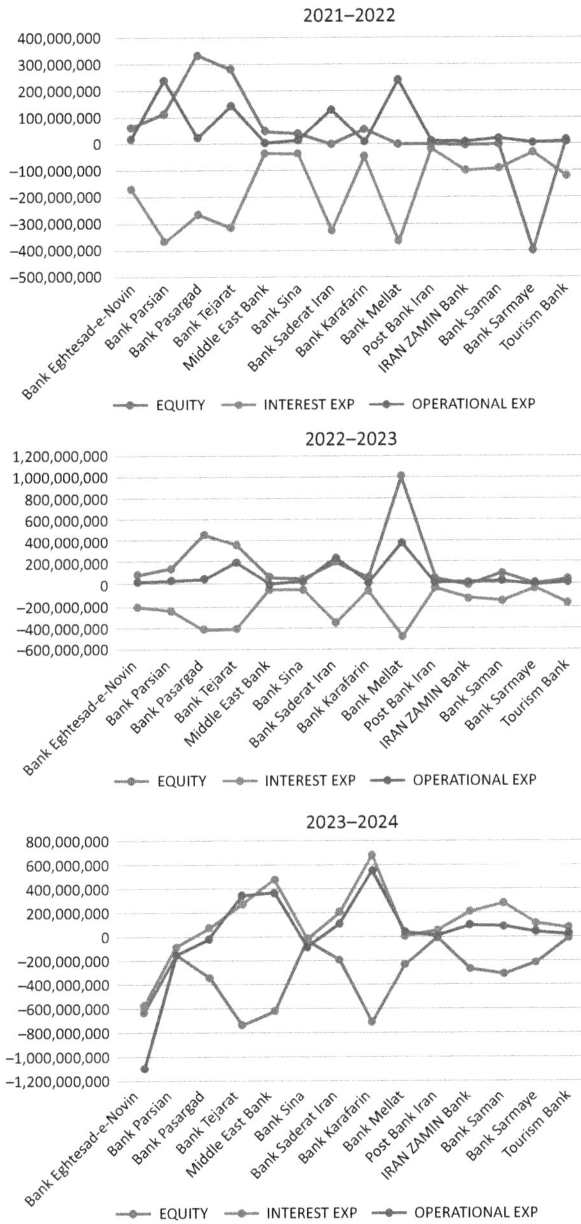

Fig. 4. Influential factors affecting the efficiency and super-efficiency of banks from 2021–2022 to 2023–2024.

4. Conclusions

In this study, data envelopment analysis was used to calculate efficiency and super-efficiency for 14 banks over a three-year period. Efficiency is a managerial concept with a long history in management science. A number of decision-making units that are evaluated as efficient in the DEA model have an efficiency score of 1, and scores below 1 are considered inefficient. To rank the units with a score of 1, the Andersen and Petersen concept of super-efficiency is applied, enabling efficient units to be differentiated based on their super-efficiency scores. A comparison of the number of efficient banks in different years shows that the efficiency of banks in 2021–2022 was better than in the following years. However, the results of calculating super-efficiency show that the highest super-efficiency score belongs to Post Bank Iran, which scored 1.9 in 2021–2022. Bank Karafarin also scored 1.03 in 2021–2022, which has the lowest super-efficiency score.

Availability of data and material

The data that support the findings of this study are available from the author upon request.

The author wishes to thank Dr. Shadi Hasanzadeh, Assistant Professor of Accounting at Kurdistan University, for providing data for this chapter.

References

Achi, A. (2023). Efficiency and its determinants in the Algerian banks: Network data envelopment analysis and partial least squares regression. *International Journal of Productivity and Performance Management*, 72(5), 1479–1508.

Akbari, S., Heydari, J., Keramati, M. A., and Keramati, A. (2020). A mixed system of network data envelopment analysis to evaluate the performance of bank branches: An illustration with Iranian banks. *International Journal of Business Excellence*, 22(2), 198–212.

Akhtar, S., Alam, M., and Ansari, M. S. (2022). Measuring the performance of the Indian banking industry: Data envelopment window analysis approach. *Benchmarking: An International Journal*, 29(9), 2842–2857.

Al-Shammari, M. M., and Elseoud, M. S. A. (2024). Data envelopment analysis for decision-making units: A comparison of the relative efficiency of banks in the Kingdom of Bahrain. *International Journal of Economics and Business Research*, 27(2), 216–235.

Andersen, P. and Petersen, N. C. (1993). A procedure for ranking efficient units in data envelopment analysis. *Management Science*, 39(10), 1261–1264.

Antunes, J., Hadi-Vencheh, A., Jamshidi, A., Tan, Y., and Wanke, P. (2022). Bank efficiency estimation in China: DEA-RENNA approach. *Annals of Operations Research*, 315(2), 1373–1398.

Bagheri Mazrae, N., Rostami Mal Khalife, M., and Varzi, M. (2022). A comparison of super-efficiency through data envelopment analysis technique and financial ratios in Iranian Stock Exchange Banks. *Journal of Decisions and Operations Research*, 6 (Spec. Issue), 1–16.

Banker, R. D., Charnes, A., and Cooper, W. W. (1984). Models for the estimation of technical and scale inefficiencies in data envelopment analysis. *Management Science*, September, 1078–92.

Barati, M., Heidari, E., and Karimi, A. (2022). Evaluating organizational agility in banking industry through data envelopment analysis: A case study of banks in Isfahan, Iran. *International Journal of Law and Management*, 64(5), 403–417.

Ben Lahouel, B., Taleb, L., Ben Zaied, Y., and Managi, S. (2024). Financial stability, liquidity risk and income diversification: Evidence from European banks using the CAMELS–DEA approach. *Annals of Operations Research*, 334(1), 391–422.

Caixia, H. (2023). Efficiency of Chinese banking compared with developed countries: A data envelopment analysis approach. *Accounting, Auditing and Finance*, 4(3), 13–17.

Chen, X., Liu, X., Gong, Z., and Xie, J. (2021). Three-stage super-efficiency DEA models based on the cooperative game and its application on the RandD green innovation of the Chinese high-tech industry. *Computers and Industrial Engineering*, 156, 107234.

Chen, Z., Zhu, W., Feng, H., and Luo, H. (2022). Changes in corporate social responsibility efficiency in Chinese food industry brought by COVID-19 pandemic — A study with the super-efficiency DEA-Malmquist-Tobit model. *Frontiers in Public Health*, 10, 875030.

Chowdhury, M. A., Ni, S. W., Rahim, N. A., and Juhari, J. (2023). Impact of bank-specific factors on bank efficiency using DEA approach: An empirical evidence from banking industry in Bangladesh. *International Journal of Business and Economy*, 5(3), 11–20.

Cvetkoska, V. and Čiković, K. F. (2020). Assessing the relative efficiency of commercial banks in the Republic of North Macedonia: DEA window analysis. *Croatian Operational Research Review*, 217–227.

Cvetkoska, V. and Čiković, K. F. (2021). Efficiency analysis of Macedonian and Croatian banking sectors with DEA. *Economy, Business and Development: An International Journal*, 2(2), 1–19.

Dar, A. H., Mathur, S. K., and Mishra, S. (2021). The efficiency of Indian banks: A DEA, Malmquist and SFA analysis with bad output. *Journal of Quantitative Economics*, 19, 653–701.

Deng, F., Xu, L., Fang, Y., Gong, Q., and Li, Z. (2020). PCA-DEA-tobit regression assessment with carbon emission constraints of China's logistics industry. *Journal of Cleaner Production*, 271, 122548.

Dia, M., Golmohammadi, A., and Takouda, P. M. (2020). Relative efficiency of Canadian banks: A three-stage network bootstrap DEA. *Journal of Risk and Financial Management*, 13(4), 68.

Dobrovič, J., Čabinová, V., Gallo, P., Partlová, P., Váchal, J., Balogová, B., and Orgonáš, J. (2021). Application of the DEA model in tourism SMEs: An empirical study from Slovakia in the context of business sustainability. *Sustainability*, 13(13), 7422.

Ersoy, Y. (2021). Performance evaluation in distance education by using data envelopment analysis (DEA) and TOPSIS methods. *Arabian Journal for Science and Engineering*, 46(2), 1803–1817.

Fallah, M., Hosseinzadeh Lotfi, F., and Hosseinzadeh, M. M. (2020). Discriminant analysis and data envelopment analysis with specific data and its application for companies in the Iranian stock exchange. *Iranian Journal of Operations Research*, 11(1), 144–156.

Florczak, T. G., Czechowska, I. D., Kucharski, A., Stawska, J., and Lobozynska, S. (2024). Comparing the efficiency of European banking sectors from the financialisation perspective using the DEA method. *Comparative Economic Research. Central and Eastern Europe*, 27(1), 45–65.

Fotova Čiković, K. and Lozić, J. (2022). Application of data envelopment analysis (DEA) in information and communication technologies. *Tehnički Glasnik*, 16(1), 129–134.

Fukuyama, H., Tsionas, M., and Tan, Y. (2023). Dynamic network data envelopment analysis with a sequential structure and behavioural-causal analysis: Application to the Chinese banking industry. *European Journal of Operational Research*, 307(3), 1360–1373.

Gan, G., Lee, H. S., Lee, L., Wang, X., and Wang, Q. (2020). Network hierarchical DEA with an application to international shipping industry in Taiwan. *Journal of the Operational Research Society*, 71(6), 991–1002.

Goto, M. and Sueyoshi, T. (2023). Sustainable development and convergence under energy sector transition in industrial nations: An application of DEA environmental assessment. *Socio-Economic Planning Sciences*, 87, 101316.

Guo, Y., Yu, Y., Ren, H., and Xu, L. (2020). Scenario-based DEA assessment of energy-saving technological combinations in aluminum industry. *Journal of Cleaner Production*, 260, 121010.

Gutiérrez, E. and Lozano, S. (2022). Cross-country comparison of the efficiency of the European forest sector and second stage DEA approach. *Annals of Operations Research*, 314(2), 471–496.

Hafsal, K., Suvvari, A., and Durai, S. R. S. (2020). Efficiency of Indian banks with non-performing assets: evidence from two-stage network DEA. *Future Business Journal*, 6, 1–9.

Hahn, G. J., Brandenburg, M., and Becker, J. (2021). Valuing supply chain performance within and across manufacturing industries: A DEA-based approach. *International Journal of Production Economics*, 240, 108203.

Halaskova, M., Gavurova, B., and Kocisova, K. (2020). Research and development efficiency in public and private sectors: An empirical analysis of EU countries by using DEA methodology. *Sustainability*, 12(17), 7050.

Jahangoshai Rezaee, M., Yousefi, S., Eshkevari, M., Valipour, M., and Saberi, M. (2020). Risk analysis of health, safety and environment in chemical industry integrating linguistic FMEA, fuzzy inference system and fuzzy DEA. *Stochastic Environmental Research and Risk Assessment*, 34(1), 201–218.

Jahani Sayyad Noveiri, M. and Kordrostami, S. (2021). Sustainability assessment using a fuzzy DEA aggregation approach: A healthcare application. *Soft Computing*, 25(16), 10829–10849.

Jauhar, S. K., Raj, P. V. R. P., Kamble, S., Pratap, S., Gupta, S., and Belhadi, A. (2024). A deep learning-based approach for performance assessment and prediction: A case study of pulp and paper industries. *Annals of Operations Research*, 1–27.

Karaosmanoğlu, E. A. İ., Baghirov, A., Selamzade, F., Pıtera, R., and Gasimova, Y. (2023). Comparison of the efficient of domestic and foreign banks with data envelopment analysis: In the case of the Poland banking system (2016–2022 period). *InTraders International Trade Academic Journal*, 6(1), 75–96.

Kim, N. H., He, F., and Kwon, O. C. (2023). Combining common-weights DEA window with the Malmquist index: A case of China's iron and steel industry. *Socio-Economic Planning Sciences*, 87, 101596.

Kraidi, A. A., Daneshvar, S., and Adesina, K. A. (2024). Weight-restricted approach on constant returns to scale DEA models: Efficiency of internet banking in Turkey. *Heliyon*, 10(10).

Kuo, K. C., Lu, W. M., and Le, M. H. (2020). Exploring the performance and competitiveness of Vietnam port industry using DEA. *The Asian Journal of Shipping and Logistics*, 36(3), 136–144.

Kweh, Q. L., Lu, W. M., Tone, K., and Liu, H. M. (2024). Evaluating the resource management and profitability efficiencies of US commercial banks from a dynamic network perspective. *Financial Innovation*, 10(1), 19.

Lartey, T., James, G. A., and Danso, A. (2021). Interbank funding, bank risk exposure and performance in the UK: A three-stage network DEA approach. *International Review of Financial Analysis*, 75, 101753.

Li, Y. (2020). Analyzing efficiencies of city commercial banks in China: An application of the bootstrapped DEA approach. *Pacific-Basin Finance Journal*, 62, 101372.

Li, Y., Liu, A. C., Yu, Y. Y., Zhang, Y., Zhan, Y., and Lin, W. C. (2022). Bootstrapped DEA and clustering analysis of eco-Efficiency in China's hotel industry. *Sustainability*, 14(5), 2925.

Li, J., Wang, P., Tao, X., and Wen, Y. (2022). Productivity analysis for banks' merger and acquisition using two-stage DEA: Evidence from China. *Journal of Systems Science and Information*, 9(6), 627–659.

Liao, C. S. (2023). Deregulation, bank efficiency and economic cooperation across China–Taiwan Strait. *Journal of Policy Modeling*, 45(2), 430–444.

Liu, H. H., Yang, G. L., Liu, X. X., and Song, Y. Y. (2020). RandD performance assessment of industrial enterprises in China: A two-stage DEA approach. *Socio-Economic Planning Sciences*, 71, 100753.

Liu, X. X., Liu, H. H., Yang, G. L., and Pan, J. F. (2023). Productivity assessment of the real estate industry in China: a DEA-Malmquist index. *Engineering, Construction and Architectural Management*, 30(3), 1243–1270.

Lu, W. M., Kuo, K. C., and Tran, T. H. (2023). Impacts of positive and negative corporate social responsibility on multinational enterprises in the global retail industry: DEA game cross-efficiency approach. *Journal of the Operational Research Society*, 74(4), 1063–1078.

Luo, L., Chen, H., Yang, Y., Wu, G., and Chen, L. (2022). A three-stage network DEA approach for performance evaluation of BIM application in construction projects. *Technology in Society*, 71, 102105.

Milenković, N., Radovanov, B., Kalaš, B., and Horvat, A. M. (2022). External two stage DEA analysis of bank efficiency in West Balkan countries. *Sustainability*, 14(2), 978.

Moutinho, V., Vale, J., Bertuzi, R., Bandeira, A. M., and Palhares, J. (2021). A two-stage DEA model to evaluate the performance of Iberian Banks. *Economies*, 9(3), 115.

Nasri, S. A., Ehsani, B., Hosseininezhad, S. J., and Safaie, N. (2023). A sustainable supplier selection method using integrated Fuzzy DEMATEL–ANP–DEA approach (case study: Petroleum Industry). *Environment, Development and Sustainability*, 25(11), 12791–12827.

Nemati, M., Kazemi Matin, R., and Toloo, M. (2020). A two-stage DEA model with partial impacts between inputs and outputs: Application in refinery industries. *Annals of Operations Research*, 295, 285–312.

Nguyen, P. H., and Pham, D. T. B. (2020). The cost efficiency of Vietnamese banks – the difference between DEA and SFA. *Journal of Economics and Development*, 22(2), 209–227.

Nong, N. M. T. (2022). An application of Delphi and DEA to performance efficiency assessment of retail stores in fashion industry. *The Asian Journal of Shipping and Logistics*, 38(3), 135–142.

Olohunlana, A. O., Odeleye, A. T., and Isola, W. A. (2023). Determinants of the intellectual capital efficiency of listed banks in Nigeria: A DEA approach. *Journal of Business and Socio-economic Development*, 3(1), 86–96.

Omrani, H., Oveysi, Z., Emrouznejad, A., and Teplova, T. (2023). A mixed-integer network DEA with shared inputs and undesirable outputs for performance evaluation: Efficiency measurement of bank branches. *Journal of the Operational Research Society*, 74(4), 1150–1165.

Omrani, H., Shamsi, M., Emrouznejad, A., and Teplova, T. (2023). A robust DEA model under discrete scenarios for assessing bank branches. *Expert Systems with Applications*, 219, 119694.

Popker, S. M. and AnjanaRaju, G. (2020). Financial performance and efficiency of cotton textile companies: An DEA approach.

Rani, I. and Singh, A. (2023). An Efficiency Analysis of Private Banks in India — A DEA Approach. In Artificial Intelligence and Transforming Digital Marketing (pp. 1025–1036). Cham: Springer Nature Switzerland.

Setiawan, C. (2020). Predicting financial distress using DEA and Altman's model on steel and iron industry Indonesia. *Jurnal Manajemen Dan Bisnis Sriwijaya*, 18(1), 57–70.

Shi, X., Wang, L., and Emrouznejad, A. (2023). Performance evaluation of Chinese commercial banks by an improved slacks-based DEA model. *Socio-Economic Planning Sciences*, 90, 101702.

Sinha, R. P. and Vaisi, B. (2024). Managerial Ability in Indian Life Insurance Companies: A Comparison Based on DEA and DEAGP. In Analytical Decision Making and Data Envelopment Analysis: Advances and Challenges (pp. 81–102). Singapore: Springer Nature Singapore.

Sinha, R. P., Vaisi, B., and Edalatpanah, S. A. (2024). Does Managerial Ability Promote Firm Efficiency? An Evidence from Indian Banking Industry. *J. Appl. Res. Ind. Eng. Vol*, 11(4), 518–535.

Smolo, E., Iqbal, M. A., and Akdemir, A. (2024). The Efficiency of Participation Banking Sector in Turkey: A DEA Approach. In Islamic Finance:

New Trends in Law and Regulation (pp. 61–73). Cham: Springer Nature Switzerland.

Solana Ibáñez, J., Caravaca Garratón, M., and Soto Meca, A. (2020). A literature review of DEA efficiency methodology in defence sector. *Academia Revista Latinoamericana de Administración*, 33(3/4), 381–403.

Song, Y. Y., Li, J. J., Wang, J. L., Yang, G. L., and Chen, Z. (2022). Eco-efficiency of Chinese transportation industry: A DEA approach with non-discretionary input. *Socio-Economic Planning Sciences*, 84, 101383.

Strange, N., Bogetoft, P., Aalmo, G. O., Talbot, B., Holt, A. H., and Astrup, R. (2021). Applications of DEA and SFA in benchmarking studies in forestry: state-of-the-art and future directions. *International Journal of Forest Engineering*, 32(sup1), 87–96.

Streimikis, J. and Saraji, M. K. (2022). Green productivity and undesirable outputs in agriculture: A systematic review of DEA approach and policy recommendations. *Economic Research-Ekonomska Istraživanja*, 35(1), 819–853.

Sueyoshi, T. and Ryu, Y. (2020). Performance Assessment of the semiconductor industry: Measured by DEA environmental assessment. *Energies*, 13(22), 5998.

Sukmana, R., Ajija, S. R., Salama, S. C. U., and Hudaifah, A. (2020). Financial performance of rural banks in Indonesia: A two-stage DEA approach. *Heliyon*, 6(7).

Tabatabaei, S., Mozaffari, M. R., Rostamy-Malkhalifeh, M., and Hosseinzadeh Lotfi, F. (2022). Fuzzy efficiency evaluation in relational network data envelopment analysis: Application in gas refineries. *Complex and Intelligent Systems*, 8(5), 4021–4049.

Takahashi, F. L. and Vasconcelos, M. R. (2024). Bank efficiency and undesirable output: An analysis of non-performing loans in the Brazilian banking sector. *Finance Research Letters*, 59, 104651.

Tavassoli, M., Fathi, A., and Farzipoor Saen, R. (2021). Developing a new super-efficiency DEA model in the presence of both zero data and stochastic data: A case study in the Iranian airline industry. *Benchmarking: An International Journal*, 28(1), 42–65.

Vaisi, B. (2023). Simulation-Based Optimization of a Transport Robot via Super-Efficiency DEAGP Approach. In Transport and Logistics Planning and Optimization (pp. 256–273). IGI Global.

Vaisi, B., Farughi, H., and Raissi, S. (2018). Two-machine robotic cell sequencing under different uncertainties. *Int. J. Simul. Model*, 17, 284–294.

Vaisi, B., Farughi, H., and Raissi, S. (2024). Data envelopment analysis-based scenario selection for sequencing pattern in a simulated robotic cell. *ARO-The Scientific Journal of Koya University*, 12(2), 139–147.

Vaisi, B. and Jalali, M. (2015). Proposed simulated strategy to increase customer satisfaction in a chain store using data envelopment analysis. *Journal of Multidisciplinary Engineering Science Studies*, 1(2), 158–164.

Varas, M., Basso, F., Maturana, S., Pezoa, R., and Weyler, M. (2021). Measuring efficiency in the Chilean wine industry: A robust DEA approach. *Applied Economics*, 53(9), 1092–1111.

Wu, H., Yang, J., Wu, W., and Chen, Y. (2023). Interest rate liberalization and bank efficiency: A DEA analysis of Chinese commercial banks. *Central European Journal of Operations Research*, 31(2), 467–498.

Yeh, L. T. and Chang, D. S. (2020). Using categorical DEA to assess the effect of subsidy policies and technological learning on RandD efficiency of IT industry. *Technological and Economic Development of Economy*, 26(2), 311–330.

Zhang, M., Li, L., and Cheng, Z. (2021). Research on carbon emission efficiency in the Chinese construction industry based on a three-stage DEA-Tobit model. *Environmental Science and Pollution Research*, 28(37), 51120–51136.

Zhao, T., Pei, R., and Pan, J. (2021). The evolution and determinants of Chinese property insurance companies' profitability: A DEA-based perspective. *Journal of Management Science and Engineering*, 6(4), 449–466.

Zhu, N., Shah, W. U. H., Kamal, M. A., and Yasmeen, R. (2021). Efficiency and productivity analysis of Pakistan's banking industry: A DEA approach. *International Journal of Finance and Economics*, 26(4), 6362–6374.

Zuo, Z., Guo, H., Li, Y., and Cheng, J. (2022). A two-stage DEA evaluation of Chinese mining industry technological innovation efficiency and eco-efficiency. *Environmental Impact Assessment Review*, 94, 106762.

https://doi.org/10.1142/9789819823161_0014

Chapter 14

Predictive Ability of ARIMA and LSTM Models for Blockchain-Based Cryptocurrency Price Changes

Magesh Kumar[*,¶], Ravinder Rena[†,‖], V. Sindhu[‡,], and Srinivasan Pazhamalai[§,††]**

[*]*School of Business and Management*
Christ University, Bengaluru, Karnataka, India

[†]*School of Business, Woxsen University, Hyderabad, Telangana, India*

[‡]*Department of Computer Science*
Christ University, Bengaluru, Karnataka, India

[§]*CMS Business School, Jain University, Bengaluru, Karnataka, India*

[¶]*mageshcyp@gmail.com*
[‖]*ravinder.rena1@gmail.com*
[**]*sindhu.v@christuniversity.in*
[††]*srinivasaneco@gmail.com*

The main aim of the present chapter is to estimate a model that can assess a cryptocurrency's economic potential by looking at its past closing prices. To the best of our knowledge, there is no solid proof yet on how well the LSTM (Long Short-Term Memory) method works for forecasting economic and financial data compared to traditional methods like ARIMA (Auto-Regressive Integrated Moving Average). Further, this chapter conducts a comparison between the ARIMA and LSTM models to evaluate how well they reduce error rates. ARIMA, representing traditional forecasting, is selected because the data collected and modeled here are non-stationary. Similarly, LSTM, representing deep learning-based methods, is chosen because it excels at preserving and utilizing data features over longer periods. The findings indicate that the LSTM approach delivers a more precise RMSE, MAE, and MAPE compared to the ARIMA model, as it comes with the trade-off of a longer runtime. The practical implications of our findings suggest the opportunity to develop a product tailored for investors.

Keywords: LSTM, ARIMA, Cryptocurrency, Prediction

1. Introduction

Cryptocurrency, a digital form of currency used in financial systems, operates on the blockchain technology, representing an innovative and ever-changing monetary value (Mukhopadhyay *et al.*, 2016). Blockchain systems are decentralized, ensuring that cryptocurrency transactions are accessible to all users for verification, promoting transparency and accountability. This emerging blockchain technology is progressively gaining popularity as an alternative to traditional banking transactions (Iansiti and Lakhani, 2017). Furthermore, cryptocurrency serves as a revolutionary technology that has the potential to challenge societal norms due to its anonymous transaction characteristics. As a result, driven by its groundbreaking possibilities and the enthusiasm surrounding its investment potential, cryptocurrency prices exhibit significant volatility. Notably, Bitcoin holds the distinction of being the most valuable among all cryptocurrencies.

Artificial Intelligence (AI) has the potential to forecast and mitigate the considerable price volatility associated with cryptocurrency coins, which can deter potential investors (Green, 2018). The partnership between AI and blockchain technology is particularly promising in the realm of data science. AI yields valuable insights, while blockchain provides a secure foundation, creating a valuable repository of information. For instance, an upcoming innovation involves AI-driven automated trading of digital investment assets, surpassing human-driven trading activities (Shroff, 2020). This advancement depends on the development of a program capable of identifying the optimal moments for buying and selling. Likewise, AI is employed in predicting future cryptocurrency prices across various blockchains, including the Electro-Optical System and Ethereum. “Predicting future share prices is not only vital for investment decisions but also plays a crucial role in shaping a company’s development strategy, selecting suitable partners for collaboration, and conducting financial analyses of the firm. Each investor’s choice to buy or sell is influenced by distinct information, knowledge, or intuition” (Owoc *et al.*, 2017).

The significant volatility observed in cryptocurrency markets has raised significant concerns regarding the accuracy of economic and financial time series predictions. Therefore, it is crucial to evaluate the reliability of forecasts when employing different forecasting methods. The principal objective of this article is to examine which forecasting techniques yield the most accurate predictions, characterized by lower forecast errors and enhanced precision. Within this context, various stochastic models are available for time series forecasting, with the most well-known being the univariate “Auto-Regressive Moving Average (ARMA)” model, which combines Auto-Regressive (AR) and Moving Average (MA) elements. Another notable model is the univariate “Auto-Regressive Integrated Moving Average (ARIMA)”, a specialized ARIMA variant that incorporates differencing within the model.

Machine learning (ML), a branch of artificial intelligence, uses past data to predict future events. ML models, like the Long Short-term Memory (LSTM) neural network, have clear advantages over other forecasting methods. Research has shown that these models not only provide highly accurate results, often matching real-world outcomes, but also improve overall result precision. LSTM, a type of neural network within AI, processes data using a gradient-based learning algorithm (Hochreiter and Schmidhuber, 1997). LSTM is designed specifically for forecasting and is used in various areas, such as predicting COVID-19 trends (Fox *et al.*, 2021) or forecasting stock market movements (Zou and Qu, 2020).

This chapter’s goal is to estimate a model that can assess a cryptocurrency’s economic potential by looking at its past closing prices. An important question we want to answer is how accurate and precise traditional forecasting methods are when compared to newer deep learning methods. To the best of our knowledge, there is no solid proof yet on how well the LSTM method (a kind of deep learning) works for forecasting economic and financial data compared to traditional methods like ARIMA. Further, this chapter conducts a comparison between ARIMA and LSTM models to evaluate how well they reduce error rates. ARIMA, representing traditional forecasting, is selected because the data collected and modeled here are non-stationary. Similarly, LSTM, representing deep learning-based methods, is chosen because it excels at preserving and utilizing data features over longer periods. This chapter offers detailed guidance on how to process data and train LSTM models for various economic and financial time series.

The chapter's structure is as follows: In Section 2, we provide an overview of the current state of time series forecasting. Section 3 delves into the mathematical underpinnings of ARIMA and LSTM. Our experimental study comparing ARIMA and LSTM models is detailed in Section 4, while Section 5 presents the ARIMA and LSTM algorithms that we developed and compared. Moving on to Section 6, we showcase the results of our data analysis and empirical experiments. Section 7 takes a closer look at how the number of iterations impacts model fitting. Finally, Section 8 serves as the conclusion of the chapter, summarizing our findings and insights.

2. Literature Review

Due to the importance of time series forecasting in many branches of applied sciences, it is essential to build an effective model with the aim of improving the forecasting accuracy. A variety of time series forecasting models have been developed in the literature.

Time series forecasting is traditionally performed in econometrics using ARIMA models (Box and Jenkins, 1970). ARIMA has been a standard method for time series forecasting for a long time. Even though ARIMA models are very prevalent in modeling economic and financial time series (Adebiyi and Adewumi *et al.*, 2014; Alonso and Garcia-Martos, 2012; Khashei and Bijari, 2011), they have some major limitations (Earnest *et al.*, 2005). For instance, in a simple ARIMA model, it is hard to model the nonlinear relationships between variables. Furthermore, it is assumed that there is a constant standard deviation in errors in the ARIMA model, which in practice may not be satisfied. When an ARIMA model is integrated with a Generalized Auto-Regressive Conditional Heteroscedasticity

(GARCH) model, this assumption can be relaxed. On the other hand, the optimization of a GARCH model and its parameters might be challenging and problematic (Kane *et al.*, 2014). There are several other applications of ARIMA for modeling the short- and long-run effects of economic parameters (Siami-Namini *et al.*, 2018).

Recently, new techniques in deep learning have been developed to address the challenges related to forecasting models. LSTM (Long Short-Term Memory) is a special case of the Recurrent Neural Network (RNN) method that was initially introduced by Hochreiter and Schmidhuber (1997). Even though it is a relatively new approach to address prediction problems, deep learning-based approaches have gained popularity among researchers. For instance, Krauss *et al.* (2016) use forms of forecasting models such as deep learning, gradient-boosted trees, and random forests to model S&P 500 constituents. Surprisingly, they reported that deep learning-based modeling underperformed gradient-boosted trees and random forests. Additionally, Krauss *et al.* report that training neural networks and consequently deep learning-based algorithms is very difficult. Lee and Yoo (2017) introduced an RNN-based approach to predict stock returns. The idea was to build portfolios by adjusting the threshold levels of return by internal layers of the RNN built. Similar work has been performed by Fischera *et al.* (2017) for financial market prediction. In this chapter, we compare the performance of an ARIMA model with the LSTM model in the prediction of economic and financial time series to determine the optimal qualities of involved variables in a typical prediction model.

Scientific papers such as these have proven that using artificial intelligence and neural networks yields accurate results in predicting cryptocurrency. However, as many parameters can be tweaked in this prediction goal (such as using volume data of the currencies, using extraneous data such as COVID-19 statistics, or utilizing different forms of neural networks), we aim to determine whether it is possible to gain accurate predictions using only close price data and an LSTM. We also explore whether the LSTM is more accurate than the ARIMA model. Our research hypothesis is that the LSTM will provide a more accurate model, in that its predictions will produce a smaller root-mean-squared error (RMSE).

3. Data and Methodology

3.1. *Data*

For the purposes of the analysis and modeling, leading daily closing prices of 20 cryptocurrencies in terms of US dollar are extracted from the Investing.com portal. The website generates results by computing prices as the volume-weighted average of values from multiple exchange markets. The data are split into two groups consisting of Sample I and Sample II based on market capitalization. Sample I includes the group of first ten and Sample II next top ten cryptocurrencies for effective analysis. The chosen time period for modeling includes the post-COVID period (0/7/2020–31/08/2023) to measure the performance of cryptocurrency during turbulent periods. The daily price returns for each of the cryptocurrencies are calculated as follows:

$$\mathrm{Rt} = \ln(\mathrm{Pt}) - \ln(\mathrm{Pt} - 1).$$

Here, ln(Pt) represents the natural logarithm of the closing price of the cryptocurrency on day t and ln (Pt-1) represents the natural logarithm of the closing price of the cryptocurrency on day $t - 1$.

3.2. *ARIMA*

This study employs the Box–Jenkins methodology (Box and Jenkins, 1976) as a suitable approach for short-term forecasting. This model, based on mathematical algebra commonly used in forecasting, is one of the most prevalent time series methods in academic research. Box and Jenkins (1976) introduced Auto-Regressive (AR) and Moving Average (MA) models as part of a framework for identifying, estimating, and diagnosing ARIMA models using time series data (Tabachnick and Fidell, 2001). This methodology is highly effective in generating short-term forecasts for business performance and consistently outperforms complex structural models in short-term prediction (Meyler *et al.*, 1998).

In the ARIMA model, the future value of a variable is a linear combination of past values and past errors, expressed as follows:

$$\begin{aligned} \mathrm{Yt} = \mu \quad \text{or} \quad & \phi 0 + \phi 1\,\mathrm{Yt} - 1 + \phi 2\,\mathrm{Yt} - 2 + \cdots + \phi \mathrm{p}\mathrm{Yt} - \mathrm{p} \\ & + \varepsilon \mathrm{t} - \theta 1\,\varepsilon \mathrm{t} - 1 - \theta 2\,\varepsilon \mathrm{t} - 2 - \theta \mathrm{q}\,\varepsilon \mathrm{t} - \mathrm{q}, \end{aligned} \tag{1}$$

where Yt is the actual value, μ or $\phi 0$ is a constant, εt is the random error at t, and ϕi and θj are the coefficients of p and q, which are integers that are often referred to as autoregressive and moving average parameters, respectively.

The ARIMA model is a derivation of the autoregressive moving average ARMA model, categorized as ARIMA (p, d, q), where "p" represents the autoregressive components, "d" corresponds to integrated components, and "q" signifies moving average components of the dataset, with all three parameters being non-negative integers. ARIMA models are typically applied to predict and analyze time series data related to business performance. Initially, the ARIMA model that best suits the task is selected, using relevant datasets to effectively analyze the data and make accurate forecasts (Yang, 2005).

3.3. *Long Short-Term Memory (LSTM)*

Long Short-Term Memory (LSTM) is a type of RNN that possesses the ability to retain information from previous steps, which it can then apply in future tasks. LSTM represents a specialized variation of RNNs, featuring additional capabilities for retaining sequential data. Each LSTM is composed of cells or system modules that capture and store data streams.

These cells resemble a conveyor belt (the upper line within each cell) connecting one module to the next, carrying data from the past and consolidating them for the current one. By employing gates in each cell, the data can be selectively managed, filtered, or passed on to subsequent cells. These gates, which rely on a sigmoidal neural network layer, empower the cells to make choices about whether to allow data to pass through or discard them.

4. Empirical Results

4.1. *Descriptive statistics*

Tables 1 and 2 display an overview of the descriptive statistics concerning the daily return series of sample cryptocurrencies observed between July 1, 2020 and August 31, 2023. The mean returns of

Table 1. Sample I descriptive statistics of daily Cryptocurrency returns.

Parameters	BITCOIN	ETHERIUM	TETHER_ USDT	BNB	XRP	USD_ COIN	CARDANO	DOGECOIN	TRON	DAI
Mean	−0.000894	−0.001699	3.46E-07	−0.002265	−0.00092	−7.79E-07	−0.000838	−0.002864	−0.001311	9.89E-06
Median	−0.000123	−0.001667	0	−0.00125	−0.000756	0	0.000104	0.000275	−0.002295	0
Maximum	0.169947	0.326921	0.003405	0.416544	0.541017	0.034876	0.309575	0.502321	0.389338	0.030651
Minimum	−0.177424	−0.230772	−0.003482	−0.530574	−0.548163	−0.024672	−0.286973	−1.583848	−0.340529	−0.022617
Std. Dev.	0.034388	0.045667	0.000457	0.050886	0.062116	0.001367	0.053949	0.086585	0.047652	0.002179
Skewness	0.196057	0.422133	−0.273106	−0.67437	−0.725563	8.932885	−0.309568	−6.147041	0.146222	3.166237
Kurtosis	6.312728	7.741808	16.53661	20.81055	20.88514	461.9202	6.63524	107.0945	12.25005	81.97117
Jarque-Bera	535.9947	1117.347	8840.428	15366.84	15508.9	10159646	654.9847	529197.7	4125.429	302320.3
Probability	0.000000*	0.000000*	0.000000*	0.000000*	0.000000*	0.000000*	0.000000*	0.000000*	0.000000*	0.000000*
Observations	1156	1156	1156	1156	1156	1156	1156	1156	1156	1156

Table 2. Sample II descriptive statistics of daily Cryptocurrency returns.

Parameters	POLYGON	LITEIN	BITCOIN_ CASH	CHAINLINK	UNUS_ SED_ LEO	STELLAR	TRUEUSD	MONERO	ETHERUM_ CLASSIC	FILECOIN
Mean	−0.0029	−0.00037	6.51E-05	−0.000192	−0.000983	−0.000449	1.30E-06	−0.00069	−0.000865	0.00134
Median	0	−0.00155	−0.000874	−0.001599	−0.00069	−0.000251	0	−0.00284	0.000219	0.00336
Maximum	0.41181	0.454336	0.446202	0.475281	0.218707	0.364075	0.65964	0.535391	0.395749	0.42635
Minimum	−0.4693	−0.25641	−0.424173	−0.282637	−0.450418	−0.553585	−0.65964	−0.3422	−0.355123	−0.84388
Std. Dev.	0.07148	0.051654	0.054005	0.060612	0.034103	0.056376	0.03048	0.048326	0.059711	0.07043
Skewness	−1.0267	0.732034	−0.173069	0.360262	−2.009143	−1.449454	−0.00203	1.131435	−0.686676	−1.98129
Kurtosis	10.4634	10.60337	14.20034	7.867317	35.07335	20.35253	400.706	20.64682	11.13449	27.9122
Jarque-Bera	2886.08	2887.816	6048.165	1166.111	50326.75	14908.26	7618528	15246.23	3278.03	30543.4
Probability	0.0000000*	0.000000*	0.000000*	0.000000*	0.000000*	0.000000*	0.000000*	0.000000*	0.000000*	0.000000*
Observations	1156	1156	1156	1156	1156	1156	1156	1156	1156	1156

Note: *indicates statistical significance at 1% level. The Jarque–Bera statistic tests the null hypothesis of a normal distribution.

the Sample I and Sample II cryptocurrencies are negative except for Stellar and File coins. This indicates that the leading cryptocurrencies, including Bitcoin and Ethereum, have generated negative returns for investors during the post-COVID-19 period. The sample cryptocurrency series exhibits a standard deviation within the range of 3% to 7%, suggesting a higher volatility during the period. The return series consists of both positive and negative skewness for the cryptocurrencies.

The positive skewness of BTC indicates that the market displays greater volatility and tends to react more strongly to positive news than negative news. All kurtosis values are notably high, providing clear evidence of a leptokurtic distribution. The Jarque–Bera test is the primary method for assessing whether a distribution is normal. In the context of this test, the null hypothesis assumes that the return series follows a normal distribution. The Jarque–Bera statistics exhibit statistical significance at the 1% level, leading to the rejection of the null hypothesis of a normal distribution.

4.2. *Unit root test*

To assess the presence of unit roots or non-stationarity in the return series of the sample cryptocurrency, the ADF test is applied. The results of the ADF P unit root test can be found in Tables 3 and 4. The ADF test results indicate the rejection of the null hypothesis as the p-values are below 5% for the intercept and as well as for Trend & Intercept series.

This finding suggests that the cryptocurrency sample return series does not exhibit unit root problems, and all of the series are stationary at first differences.

In the ARIMA methodology, the initial step involves differencing the input time series to achieve stationarity. Seasonal patterns within the time series can be assessed by studying the autocorrelation function (ACF) and the partial autocorrelation function (PACF). To evaluate the stationarity status of the return series, the results of the Augmented Dickey–Fuller (ADF) test can be observed in Tables 3 and 4, respectively. Similarly, Tables 5 and 6 illustrate the findings derived from the ARIMA model used in the current study.

Table 3. Unit root results of sample I cryptocurrencies.

ADF Test (Level)			ADF Test (First Difference)		
Variables	Intercept	Trend & Intercept	Variables	Intercept	Trend & Intercept
BITCOIN	−1.117576	−1.007438	BITCOIN	−35.19179*	−35.21292*
ETHERIUM	−1.058264	−1.240518	ETHERIUM	−37.06166*	−37.07937*
TETHER_USDT	−8.537	−9.195367	TETHER_USDT	−20.84063*	−20.83146*
BNB	−1.069517	−1.557836	BNB	−39.31074*	−39.33652*
XRP	−2.427493	−2.393736	XRP	−36.62025*	−36.61321*
USD_COIN	−12.89866	−12.9902	USD_COIN	−19.16337*	−19.15523*
CARDANO	−1.319029	−1.125017	CARDANO	−37.38940*	−37.40949*
DOGECOIN	−2.269692	−2.247852	DOGECOIN	−11.02154*	−11.04436*
TRON	−2.026842	−2.353652	TRON	−39.26040*	−39.25305*
DAI	−2.669063	−3.62516	DAI	−22.20938*	−22.20817*

Note: Optimal lag length is determined by the Schwarz Information Criterion (SIC); ADF: Augmented Dickey Fuller test; *significance at 1% level.

Table 4. Unit root results of sample II Cryptocurrencies.

ADF Test (Level)			ADF Test (First Difference)		
Variables	Intercept	Trend & Intercept	Variables	Intercept	Trend & Intercept
POLYGON	−1.292291	−1.806396	POLYGON	−18.74718*	−18.77915*
LITECOIN	−2.297091	−2.182585	LITECOIN	−37.32481*	−37.32761*
BITCOIN_CASH	−1.975739	−2.094887	BITCOIN_CASH	−7.623060*	−7.631585*
CHAINLINK	−1.869022	−1.62871	CHAINLINK	−40.58541*	−40.59302*
UNUS_SED_LEO	−0.975342	−1.962447	UNUS_SED_LEO	−43.14544*	−43.14060*
STELLAR	−1.846927	−1.705567	STELLAR	−37.63135*	−37.62986*
TRUEUSD	−8.93375	−8.966431	TRUEUSD	−33.14344*	−33.12895*
MONERO	−1.939349	−1.862832	MONERO	−41.90705*	−41.91340*
ETHERUM_ CLASSIC	−2.452942	−2.468632	ETHERUM_ CLASSIC	−7.116002*	−7.136903*
FILECOIN	−1.859417	−1.816131	FILECOIN	−12.29468*	−12.30446*

Note: Optimal lag length is determined by the Schwarz Information Criterion (SIC); ADF: Augmented Dickey Fuller test; *significance at 1% level.

The optimal ARIMA model was selected using the model selection criteria, specifically by minimizing the AIC (Akaike Information Criterion), Schwarz Information Criterion (SIC), Hannan–Quinn information criterion (HQC), the most significant coefficients of ARMA, and the highest adjusted R^2. When applying the Ljung–Box test to all ARIMA models, the calculated statistics fall within the range of 0.06 to 157.93, and the significance level is above 5%. This outcome affirms no autocorrelation and the suitability of the chosen model.

Table 5. Sample I of ARIMA model statistics.

Variable	μ	AR	MA	Adj. R square	AIC	SIC	HQC	Lung box-Q		Model type
		Prob	Prob					Q Stat	Prob	
BITCOIN	−0.3746	0.0005	0.0000	0.0052	17.1255	17.1430	17.1321	2.3524	0.125	(9,1,9)
ETHERIUM	−1.2282	0.0002	0.0001	0.0091	12.0659	12.0833	12.0725	1.1323	0.287	(1,1,5)
TETHER_USDT	0.0000	0.0000	0.0000	0.0865	−12.6275	−12.6100	−12.6209	8.3349	0.146	(2,1,1)
BNB	1.0062	0.0000	0.0001	0.7684	−8.1236	−8.1035	−8.1160	87.007	0.109	(1,1,5)
XRP	−0.0003	0.003	0.0000	0.0053	−3.2842	−3.2667	−3.2776	1.0794	0.583	(4,1,1)
USD_COIN	0.0000	0.0000	0.0000	0.1723	−10.5790	−10.5616	−10.5724	35.315	0.216	(1,1,2)
CARDANO	−0.0001	0.0000	0.0000	0.0114	−2.8172	−2.7998	−2.8107	4.4827	0.106	(1,1,1)
DOGECOIN	−0.0001	0.0000	0.0001	0.0141	−5.5054	−5.4880	−5.4988	15.938	0.111	(1,1,1)
TRON	−0.0001	0.0000	0.0000	0.0244	−8.3638	−8.3463	−8.3572	1.8455	0.174	(1,1,1)
DAI	0.0000	0.0000	0.0000	0.1540	−9.5695	−9.5520	−9.5629	8.0238	0.268	(1,1,1)

Note: Autoregressive (AR); Moving Average (MA); Akaike Information Criterion (AIC), Schwarz Information Criterion (SIC), Hannan–Quinn Information Criterion (HQC).

Table 6. Sample II of ARIMA model statistics.

Variable	μ	AR	MA	Adj. R square	AIC	SIC	HQC	Lung box -Q		Model type
		Prob	Prob					Q Stat	Prob	
POLYGON	−0.0005	0.0000	0.0000	0.0363	−2.2930	−2.2755	−2.2864	1.2713	0.26	(1,1,5)
LITECOIN	−0.0192	0.0000	0.0000	0.0153	6.9995	7.0170	7.0061	0.5605	0.454	(1,1,1)
BITCOIN_CASH	0.0112	0.0000	0.0000	0.0379	9.7601	9.7776	9.7667	0.06	0.807	(1,1,3)
CHAINLINK	−0.0010	0.0000	0.0000	0.0323	3.2895	3.3070	3.2961	2.341	0.126	(1,1, 4)
UNUS_SED_LEO	−0.0023	0.0000	0.0000	0.0640	−1.1222	−1.1047	−1.1156	6.2301	0.101	(1,1, 4)
STELLAR	0.0000	0.0000	0.0000	0.0247	−5.3859	−5.3684	−5.3793	0.2242	0.636	(1,1,12)
TRUEUSD	0.0000	0.0000	0.0001	0.2506	−3.7928	−3.7753	−3.7862	157.93	0.314	(1,1,6)
MONERO	−0.0673	0.0000	0.0000	0.0461	7.5284	7.5459	7.5350	2.1927	0.139	(1,1,1)
ETHERUM_CLASSIC	−0.0085	0.0000	0.0000	0.0083	4.9081	4.9256	4.9147	12.139	0.615	(3,1,3)
FILECOIN	−0.0186	0.0000	0.0003	0.0074	7.0075	7.0250	7.0141	10.038	0.184	(2,1,2)

Note: Autoregressive (AR); Moving Average (MA); Akaike Information Criterion (AIC); Schwarz Information Criterion (SIC); Hannan–Quinn Information Criterion (HQC).

The LSTM framework is structured around the completion of four stages. These stages encompass (1) data retrieval from Investing.com, (2) extracting the closing prices while filtering out extraneous data unsuitable for prediction, (3) training the LSTM using historical closing prices to forecast future values, and (4) creating the predictive model. This architectural design, particularly the integration of LSTM, is well established and has been extensively utilized in previous scientific studies. Our contribution builds upon this existing body of research by exclusively utilizing closing prices, conducting benchmark evaluations across various computing environments, and examining the relationship between root mean squared error and the number of epochs employed in LSTM training.

For model comparison and best fit, we compared the ARIMA and LSTM models against three errors, such as RMSE, MAE, and MAPE, in order to identify the best predicting models. The model that predicts with the least errors is considered to be the best fit model for prediction. Tables 7 and 8 display the comparison of errors across the different models for Sample I and Sample II, respectively. Thus, including Bitcoins and the last File coins of cryptocurrency, the LSTM model predicted with the least errors showcases a substantial performance advantage over the ARIMA model. For instance, in

Table 7. Sample I statistical comparison of errors.

	RMSE		**MAE**		**MAPE**	
Cryptocurrency	**ARIMA**	**LSTM**	**ARIMA**	**LSTM**	**ARIMA**	**LSTM**
Bitcoin	30186.8800	1259.9854	25124.8200	882.4836	116.3170	5.26
Ethereum	1478.2300	214.3513	1178.2690	120.4338	70.2798	30.23
Tether USDT	0.0007	0.0006	0.0005	0.0004	0.0483	0.05
BNB	309.9561	11.3643	267.1303	19.9668	82.3162	74.49
XRP	0.3937	0.03948	0.2761	0.02176	39.1973	9.29
USD Coin	0.0015	0.0006	0.0007	0.0006	0.0708	0.07
Cardano	0.9200	0.0273	0.6498	0.0131	68.6360	6.87
Dogecoin	0.1247	0.0035	0.0829	0.0062	275.5187	73.04
Tron	0.0407	0.00337	0.0345	0.0044	51.0016	18.59
Dai	0.0090	0.0055	0.0082	0.0035	0.8140	0.35

Note: RMSE: Root Mean Squared Error; MAE: Mean Absolute Error; MAPE: Mean Absolute Percent Error.

Table 8. Sample II statistical comparison of errors.

	RMSE		MAE		MAPE	
Cryptocurrency	**ARIMA**	**LSTM**	**ARIMA**	**LSTM**	**ARIMA**	**LSTM**
Polygon	0.7572	0.0134	0.5864	0.0092	516.4037	44.64
Litecoin	71.9022	7.3893	51.1210	4.1757	41.9457	4.99
Bitcoin Cash	229.6282	27.0893	173.6136	23.6850	72.8810	7.93
Chain link	11.5268	1.5295	7.9317	0.9129	42.8451	7.40
UNUS SED LEO	2.5032	0.0225	2.0698	0.0904	52.1597	7.06
Stellar	0.1574	0.0219	0.1029	0.0102	39.5293	7.49
TrueUSD	0.0296	0.0009	0.0017	0.0006	0.1248	0.07
Monero	95.0025	7.2664	71.4158	6.8282	35.3615	6.78
Ethereum classic	36.5367	0.3227	31.0864	1.3419	121.4336	22.30
File coin	37.8836	4.2701	23.2671	2.4254	132.3554	10.00

Note: RMSE: Root Mean Squared Error; MAE: Mean Absolute Error; MAPE: Mean Absolute Percent Error.

Bitcoin, the error values of RMSE, MAE, and MAPE of the ARIMA model are 30186.8800, 25124.8200, and 116.3170, respectively. However, in the LSTM models, the error values are 1259.9854, 882.4836 and 5.2, respectively, suggesting a better model than the ARIMA.

5. Discussion

The simulation tools utilized for the models are Python for the LSTM model and EViews software for the ARIMA model. We conducted experiments involving various autoregressive (p) and moving average (q) parameters to identify the optimal model that would provide the most accurate forecasts, as shown in Tables 5 and 6, respectively. We opted for the LSTM model that demonstrated the most favorable fit among the available models. Therefore, the best-performing LSTM model, as identified and contrasted in Tables 7 and 8, exhibited a significant superiority over the ARIMA model.

Further, cryptocurrencies with lower overall values tend to experience more significant changes, and the LSTM algorithm appears to be better at handling these bigger fluctuations. Importantly, the system learns on its own using only the input data. This means we do not have to figure out complicated ARIMA parameters like p, d, and

q. This makes it easier to identify the model. We tested the LSTM model in various ways — running it 50 times with different settings like 5, 25, and 50 epochs. Even though it took more time, the results were much better, giving us more accurate predictions.

6. Conclusions

With the recent progress in developing advanced machine learning techniques, especially deep learning algorithms, these methods are becoming increasingly popular among researchers in various fields. The main question is how effective and powerful these newly introduced approaches are when compared to traditional methods. This study evaluates the accuracy of ARIMA and LSTM, representative techniques for forecasting time series data. Both methods were used on a set of financial data, and the findings revealed that LSTM outperformed ARIMA.

Our model serves as a strong foundation for incorporating additional input parameters, including high, low, and volume data of cryptocurrencies, and it also allows for the inclusion of other hyperparameters and adjustments to the model layers. While our LSTM approach delivers more precise RMSE, MAE, and MAPE compared to the ARIMA model, it does come with the trade-off of a longer runtime. The predicted lines closely aligned with the actual closing values, showing minimal deviation. Furthermore, the model exhibits high accuracy, with predictions having a minimal root mean squared error, indicating close proximity to the actual prices. To improve the model, it is essential to adjust hyperparameters, particularly considering factors like investor sentiment.

The practical implications of our findings suggest the opportunity to develop a product tailored for investors. Others can further refine our model by adding additional hyperparameters, thereby enhancing the accuracy of cryptocurrency price predictions. However, it is important to note that our study's limitations include not delving into the detailed architecture of introducing these hyperparameters.

In future research, the model has the potential to integrate a hyperparameter, such as assessing sentiments from Twitter page tweets or simply quantifying the volume of tweets.

References

Earnest, M. I., Chen, D., Ng, L. Y., and Sin, L. Y. (2005). Using autoregressive integrated moving average (ARIMA) models to predict and monitor the number of beds occupied during a SARS outbreak in a tertiary hospital in Singapore. *BMC Health Service Research*, 5(36).

Fischera, T. and Kraussb, C. (2017). Deep learning with long short-term memory networks for financial market predictions. *FAU Discussion Papers in Economics*, 11.

Fox, G. C., von Laszewski, G., Wang, F., and Pyne, S. (2021). AICov: An integrative deep learning framework for COVID-19 forecasting with population covariates. *J. Data Sci.*, 19, 293–313.

Green, J. S. (2018). Understanding cryptocurrency market fluctuations. https://www.telegraph.co.uk/business/business-reporter/crypto currencymarket-fluctuations/.

Hochreiter, S. and Schmidhuber, J. (1997). Long short-term memory. *Neural Comput.*, 9, 1735–1780.

Iansiti, M. and Lakhani, K. R. (2017). The truth about blockchain. https://hbr.org/2017/01/the-truth-about-blockchain.

Kane, M. J., Price, N., Scotch, M., and Rabinowitz, P. (2014). Comparison of ARIMA and random forest time series models for prediction of avian influenza H5N1 outbreaks. *BMC Bioinformatics*, 15(1).

Khashei, M. and Bijari, M. (2011). A novel hybridization of artificial neural networks and ARIMA models for time series forecasting. *Applied Soft Computing*, 11(2), 2664–2675.

Krauss, X. A., Do, N., and Huck, N. (2016). Deep neural networks, gradient boosted trees, random forests: Statistical arbitrage on the S&P 500. *FAU Discussion Papers in Economics* 03/2016, Friedrich-Alexander University Erlangen-Nuremberg, Institute for Economics.

Lee, S. I. and Yoo, S. J. (2017). A deep efficient frontier method for optimal investments. Department of Computer Engineering, Sejong University, Seoul, 05006, Republic of Korea.

Meyler, A., Kenny, G., and Quinn, T. (1998). Forecasting Irish inflation using ARIMA models. Central Bank of Ireland Research Department, Technical Paper, 3/RT/1998.

Mukhopadhyay, U., Skjellum, A., Hambolu, O., Oakley, J., Yu, L., and Brooks, R. (2016). A brief survey of cryptocurrency systems. In *Proceedings of the 14th Annual Conference on Privacy, Security and Trust (PST)*, Auckland, New Zealand, 12–14 December 2016, 745–752.

Owoc, M., Weichbroth, P., and Zuralski, K. (2017). Towards better understanding of context-aware knowledge transformation. In *2017 Federated*

Conference on Computer Science and Information Systems (FedCSIS), IEEE, 1123–1126.

Shroff, R. (2020). When blockchain meets artificial intelligence. https://medium.com/swlh/when-blockchain-meets-artificial-intelligencee448968d04.

Siami-Namini, S., Muhammad, D., and Fahimullah, F. (2018). The short and long run effects of selected variables on tax revenue — A case study. *Applied Economics and Finance*, 5(5), 23–32.

Tabachnick, B. G. and Fidell, L. S. (2001). *Using multivariate statistics* (4th Ed.). USA: Pearson Education Company.

Yang, Y. (2005). Can the strengths of AIC and BIC be shared? A conflict between model identification and regression estimation. *Biometrika*, 92(4), 937–950.

Zou, Z. B. and Qu, Z. (2020). Using LSTM in stock prediction and quantitative trading. Available online: https://cs230.stanford.edu/projects_winter_2020/reports/32066186.pdf (accessed on 25 September 2023).

https://doi.org/10.1142/9789819823161_0015

Chapter 15

Advanced DEA-R Models for Performance Evaluation in the Banking Sector: Handling Ratio and Negative Data with Inverse DEA Approaches

Mojtaba Ghiyasi[*,‡] **and Mehdi Soltanifar**[†,§]

[*]*Faculty of Industrial Engineering and Management Science, Shahrood University of Technology, Shahrood, Iran*

[†]*Department of Mathematics, Islamic Azad University, Semnan, Iran*

[‡]*mog@shahroodutac.ir*

[§]*mehdi.soltanifar@iau.ac.ir*

The evaluation of performance in the banking industry is critical for guiding operational efficiency, resource allocation, and strategic decision-making. Data Envelopment Analysis for Ratio data (DEA-R) has emerged as a key method for addressing the challenges posed by the nature of financial data, which often appears in ratio form. This chapter advances the literature by introducing innovative DEA-R models specifically designed for performance evaluation in banking, with a focus on handling negative ratio data. Furthermore, we extend the application of inverse DEA models, enabling the analysis of mergers, acquisitions, and resource reallocation while maintaining efficiency levels. The models presented in this chapter provide significant improvements in assessing the performance of financial institutions by allowing for a nuanced treatment of ratio data, preserving confidentiality, and offering a practical framework for managers in the banking sector. We explore both input- and output-oriented DEA-R models, addressing variable returns to scale (VRS) cases, and demonstrate their utility through detailed numerical examples. The chapter contributes to the growing field of performance measurement in the banking sector, offering tools to improve decision-making accuracy and strategic planning in a highly competitive industry. By addressing the gap in classical DEA models regarding the treatment of ratio data, particularly negative ratios, this work provides a robust framework for performance evaluation, merger analysis, and operational optimization in the banking industry. The proposed models not only extend the theoretical foundations of DEA but also present practical implications for improving financial performance measurement.

Keywords: Bank efficiency, DEA-R models, inverse DEA, negative ratio data, performance evaluation.

1. Introduction

Data Envelopment Analysis (DEA) was first introduced by Charnes, Cooper, and Rhodes in 1978 as a non-parametric method for evaluating the relative efficiency of decision-making units (DMUs) operating under similar conditions. Rooted in the mathematical principles of linear programming, DEA was developed to address the complexities of performance measurement in environments where multiple inputs are utilized to generate multiple outputs. Unlike traditional methods, DEA offers a comprehensive framework that simultaneously evaluates all inputs and outputs, without requiring explicit assumptions about the underlying production function. This innovative approach has since evolved into a cornerstone of efficiency analysis, finding extensive applications across diverse sectors such as healthcare, education, energy, and banking (Soltanifar *et al.*, 2023).

Building on its foundational principles, DEA models are typically formulated in two primary forms: the multiplicative (or ratio-based) approach and the envelopment (or frontier-based) approach. The multiplicative models define relative efficiency as the ratio of weighted outputs to weighted inputs, seeking to maximize efficiency under specific constraints. On the other hand, the envelopment models are grounded in the concept of the Production Possibility Set (PPS), which encapsulates all feasible combinations of inputs and outputs. By constructing an efficient frontier based on observed data points, these models identify the relative inefficiency of each decision-making unit by comparing it to the best-performing peers.

Over time, these foundational models have given rise to several well-known DEA variants, each tailored to address distinct analytical needs and operational contexts. The CCR model, named after Charnes, Cooper, and Rhodes, assumes constant returns to scale (CRS) and is widely used for measuring overall efficiency. The BCC model, introduced by Banker, Charnes, and Cooper, relaxes the CRS assumption and accommodates variable returns to scale (VRS), making it suitable for scenarios where scale efficiency plays a significant role. Other variants, such as the Free Disposal Hull (FDH) and the Convex Hull of DMUs (CHD), extend DEA's applicability by incorporating alternative assumptions about disposability and convexity (Soltanifar *et al.*, 2013). Each of these models is designed to capture efficiency in specific contexts, reflecting the diverse challenges and complexities encountered in real-world decision-making processes.

The primary application of DEA has historically been the evaluation of performance for DMUs, providing each unit with an optimistic efficiency score. These scores are calculated by comparing a DMU's performance to the constructed efficient frontier, identifying units that maximize output given their inputs or minimize input for a given level of output. While this optimistic approach is advantageous for identifying overall efficiency, it often results in multiple DMUs achieving the maximum efficiency score of one (or 100%), rendering them indistinguishable from one another in terms of performance. This lack of differentiation among efficient units highlights a critical limitation in conventional DEA models when applied to real-world scenarios requiring more granular performance insights.

To address this challenge, a range of ranking models has been developed, aiming to introduce discrimination among efficient DMUs. These ranking models modify the traditional DEA framework by incorporating additional criteria or constraints to distinguish between units that appear equally efficient under the basic DEA paradigm. Such models are collectively referred to as DEA ranking methods and play a crucial role in enhancing the applicability of DEA in complex evaluation tasks.

However, a notable phenomenon that arises in this context is rank reversal, where changes in the dataset or evaluation criteria lead to inconsistencies in the relative ranking of DMUs. This issue has been extensively examined in the literature, including the study by Soltanifar and Shahghobadi (2014a). In their influential paper, the authors explore the prevalence of rank reversal in numerous DEA ranking methods. They demonstrate how this phenomenon undermines the reliability of rankings in practical applications, while also identifying certain methods that maintain rank preservation and avoid this pitfall. By providing both theoretical insights and illustrative numerical examples, their study sheds light on the importance of selecting appropriate ranking methods to ensure robustness and consistency in DEA evaluations.

One of the notable advancements in DEA modeling has been the development of preferential voting models. These models represent a specific class of DEA formulations where a single input, set to a constant value (typically unity), is employed to evaluate the performance of decision-making units or candidates based on their relative preferences. Such models have found extensive applications in decision-making scenarios, particularly in ranked voting systems where candidates are evaluated and ranked based on collective preferences. The innovative nature of these models lies in their ability to provide a systematic and quantitative framework for ranking alternatives, enabling decision-makers to make informed and rational choices.

The literature on DEA-based voting models is enriched by several significant contributions. For instance, Soltanifar *et al.* (2010) introduced a novel methodology for ranking different ranking models by leveraging a voting model. Their study addressed a key challenge in ranked voting systems — discrimination among candidates who achieve full efficiency. By proposing an integrated framework that combines results from various ranking models, they demonstrated the applicability of DEA in determining the most efficient candidates while preserving fairness and consistency. This approach not only enhances the robustness of traditional DEA models but also ensures that decision-makers can rely on an aggregated and systematic evaluation framework.

Further contributions by Soltanifar (2011) expanded the theoretical foundations of DEA voting models by introducing the concept of interval efficiency. Unlike traditional models that focus solely on optimistic efficiency scores, this approach incorporates both optimistic and pessimistic perspectives to provide a more comprehensive efficiency interval for each candidate. By employing a minimax regret-based approach (MRA), the study proposed a refined ranking methodology, offering decision-makers a balanced view of candidate performance that accounts for varying operational conditions.

Additionally, Soltanifar and Hosseinzadeh Lotfi (2011) presented the Voting Analytic Hierarchy Process (VAHP) method, which integrates DEA and analytic hierarchy process (AHP) methodologies to rank efficient DMUs. Their work addressed a crucial managerial need for optimal resource utilization by enabling the ranking of efficient units based on multi-criteria decision-making principles. By reviewing existing ranking models and highlighting their limitations, the authors introduced a robust alternative that combines the strengths of DEA and AHP, thus providing a comprehensive tool for ranking and performance evaluation.

The field of DEA-based voting models has witnessed further advancements through a series of noteworthy studies, each contributing valuable methodologies and applications. Among these, the work of Soltanifar (2012) is particularly notable for introducing a voting-based ranking framework for common set of weights (CSW) models. This study applied the proposed framework to determine efficient DMUs, addressing the critical challenge of ensuring fair and consistent rankings across different weight allocation schemes in DEA. The methodology demonstrated its practical applicability and theoretical robustness in handling CSW scenarios effectively.

In a related vein, Soltanifar and Shahghobadi (2013) explored the integration of voting models into the cross-efficiency evaluation framework of DEA. Their research focused on selecting a benevolent secondary goal model that enhances the discriminative power of DEA rankings. By incorporating a voting approach, this study provided a systematic method to balance cross-efficiency evaluations, ensuring both fairness and consistency in the derived rankings. Their subsequent work (Soltanifar and Shahghobadi, 2014b) expanded on these principles by employing the TOPSIS method alongside a voting model to classify inputs and outputs in DEA. This innovative combination facilitated a more structured and preference-based approach to DEA evaluation, offering enhanced insights into the relative importance of inputs and outputs.

Further, Soltanifar (2017) introduced a Group Voting Analytical Hierarchy Process (VAHP) method, which addressed scenarios involving group decision-making. This model innovatively accounted for varying levels of voting power and proficiency among group members, ensuring a more equitable and representative decision-making process. The practical relevance of these approaches was underscored in applied studies (Sharafi *et al.*, 2019), where a preferential voting model with unequal levels of voting power was utilized to rank petrochemical companies. By leveraging DEA, the study provided a robust framework for evaluating corporate performance while accommodating varying voting strengths.

Additionally, Soltanifar (2020) proposed a novel voting model tailored for groups with members of unequal power and proficiency. This model extended the applicability of DEA-based voting frameworks to diverse organizational and managerial contexts, ensuring fair representation of stakeholders with different levels of influence. The relevance of DEA-based voting models under uncertainty was further explored (Sharafi *et al.*, 2022). Their study introduced a fuzzy voting model combined with the fuzzy combinative distance-based assessment (CODAS) method to select green suppliers. This innovative integration showcased the adaptability of DEA-based voting approaches to complex and uncertain decision-making environments.

Many of these advancements, alongside additional insights and methodologies, are comprehensively documented in the book Preferential Voting and Applications: Approaches Based on Data Envelopment Analysis by Soltanifar *et al.* (2023). This seminal work provides an extensive exploration of preferential voting models, their theoretical underpinnings, and practical applications across various fields. The contributions of this book and the related studies have significantly enriched the domain of DEA-based voting models, offering robust tools for preference aggregation and decision-making in multi-criteria and multi-stakeholder scenarios.

The integration of DEA with Multi-Criteria Decision-Making (MCDM) methods has been the focus of numerous research efforts, aiming to leverage the strengths of both approaches. These endeavors include exploring connections between DEA and Multi-Objective Decision-Making (MODM) as well as Multi-Attribute Decision-Making (MADM) techniques. Among the pioneering works in this domain is the study by Hosseinzadeh Lotfi *et al.* (2010), which proposed an interactive Multi-Objective Linear Programming (MOLP) method to facilitate target setting in the general combined-oriented CCR model. This research bridged the gap between DEA and

MODM by demonstrating how interactive decision-making tools could enhance the target-setting process in DEA models, particularly when dealing with conflicting objectives.

In another significant contribution, Hosseinzadeh Lotfi *et al.* (2010) investigated the relationship between MOLP and DEA through the lens of the output-oriented CCR dual model. This study provided a theoretical foundation for linking DEA with MODM, emphasizing the compatibility of the two methodologies in evaluating performance and setting priorities across multiple objectives. The research highlighted how MOLP techniques could enrich DEA's analytical capabilities, particularly in contexts where decision-makers need to balance trade-offs among various performance criteria.

More recently, Soltanifar *et al.* (2023) extended this line of inquiry by proposing a hybrid MADM-DEA model designed to handle heterogeneous attributes. Their study, focused on evaluating sustainable development goals (SDGs), combined the strengths of MCDM methods for dealing with diverse and conflicting criteria with the efficiency-oriented perspective of DEA. This hybrid model provided a comprehensive framework for assessing the progress toward SDGs, showcasing the practical relevance of integrating DEA with MADM techniques in addressing complex, real-world challenges.

In another noteworthy contribution, Tavana *et al.* (2023) explored the synergy between the Analytic Hierarchy Process (AHP) and DEA, describing the integration as "a match made in heaven". This research demonstrated how AHP's hierarchical structure and ability to capture subjective preferences complement DEA's efficiency evaluation framework. By merging these two methodologies, the authors introduced a robust decision-making tool capable of ranking and evaluating DMUs while incorporating stakeholder preferences and judgments.

These studies underscore the potential of combining DEA with MCDM methods to address a wide range of decision-making problems. By integrating the quantitative rigor of DEA with the flexibility and comprehensiveness of MCDM techniques, researchers have developed innovative frameworks that enhance the accuracy and applicability of decision-making processes in multi-criteria environments. This growing body of literature highlights the versatility of DEA as a foundational tool for performance evaluation and its ability to adapt and evolve through integration with complementary methodologies.

One of the significant challenges faced by traditional DEA models is their inability to handle negative data effectively. This limitation poses a critical issue in many real-world scenarios where input and output variables can naturally take on negative values. For instance, in financial performance evaluation, negative values may arise in cases of net losses, debt ratios, or negative returns on investment. Similarly, environmental assessments may involve negative outputs, such as reductions in pollution levels or energy savings, which are inherently meaningful but incompatible with conventional DEA formulations. Traditional DEA models operate under the assumption of non-negativity for all input and output data, which restricts their applicability to problems where such assumptions do not hold.

The inability to manage negative data arises from the mathematical structure of traditional DEA models, which are based on ratio formulations. These ratios become undefined or lose interpretability when negative values are present. Consequently, DMUs with negative inputs or outputs cannot be appropriately evaluated, leading to biased or incomplete efficiency assessments. This gap has driven researchers to develop advanced DEA models capable of accommodating negative data without compromising the underlying principles of efficiency measurement.

Innovative approaches to address this challenge include adaptations of the conventional DEA models, such as the introduction of translation invariance techniques, which shift all data to a non-negative domain. Other methods involve developing alternative formulations, such as hybrid DEA models, that extend the applicability of DEA by incorporating absolute or directional measures to handle negative values. These advancements have significantly expanded the utility of DEA in fields like banking, where liabilities (negative inputs) and write-offs (negative outputs) are common, and in energy efficiency studies, where reductions in resource consumption and emissions are critical outputs (Soltanifar and Sharafi, 2022).

The capability of handling negative data represents a pivotal step in enhancing the robustness and versatility of DEA as a performance evaluation tool. By addressing this limitation, researchers have not only expanded the applicability of DEA to a broader range of real-world problems but also strengthened its position as a cornerstone methodology in operational research and decision analysis.

Another critical challenge encountered by traditional DEA models is their inability to adequately handle ratio data, which are frequently encountered in financial and banking contexts. Ratio data represent relationships between two or more variables, such as profit-to-asset ratios, loan-to-deposit ratios, or cost-to-income ratios, which are essential indicators in financial performance evaluation. These ratios encapsulate complex interactions between inputs and outputs, providing a nuanced perspective on operational efficiency. However, traditional DEA models, designed for absolute input–output values, struggle to process these relational metrics effectively.

In the banking sector, ratio data are particularly prevalent due to the industry's inherent reliance on comparative performance metrics. For example, a bank's efficiency is often judged not merely by its absolute profits or costs but by its ability to maintain favorable ratios such as return on equity (ROE) or non-performing loans to total loans (NPL ratio). These ratios provide deeper insights into the bank's financial health and managerial efficacy. Traditional DEA models fail to accommodate such metrics, as direct application of ratio data can distort efficiency scores or render them meaningless due to scaling and normalization issues.

Addressing this limitation requires the development of specialized DEA models, such as DEA-R (DEA for Ratio Data), which are specifically designed to handle ratio data without compromising the integrity of the efficiency evaluation process. These models allow for the direct incorporation of ratios as either inputs or outputs, enabling a more accurate assessment of relative performance. For instance, in evaluating the efficiency of banking units, DEA-R models can compare institutions based on their ability to optimize critical financial ratios while managing other operational variables. This approach provides a more holistic and meaningful evaluation framework, aligning closely with industry practices (Despić *et al.*, 2007; Despić, 2013).

The ability to integrate ratio data effectively into DEA analyses represents a transformative advancement, particularly in the financial sector. It enables more realistic performance evaluations and facilitates benchmarking processes that reflect the true competitive positioning of banks. By overcoming this challenge, DEA continues to evolve as a powerful analytical tool capable of addressing the complex needs of modern financial institutions.

This chapter addresses critical gaps in the literature by introducing advanced DEA-R models tailored specifically for the performance evaluation of financial institutions within the banking sector. Traditional DEA models often fall short when handling the complex and unique characteristics of financial data, particularly ratio data that may include negative values. Moreover, the banking industry requires tools that not only evaluate efficiency but also support strategic operations such as mergers, acquisitions, and resource reallocation while maintaining or enhancing overall efficiency. To fill this gap, we propose innovative DEA-R approaches that extend the applicability of inverse DEA models. These models are designed to accommodate the dual challenges of ratio and negative data, offering a nuanced and comprehensive framework for performance measurement. By leveraging VRS settings, the models introduced in this chapter provide greater flexibility and applicability in diverse banking scenarios. Additionally, the proposed approaches address practical challenges such as confidentiality concerns and the need for robust decision-support tools in a competitive and data-intensive environment. Through detailed numerical examples, we demonstrate the effectiveness of these models in capturing the intricate dynamics of financial performance and enabling data-driven decision-making. This chapter not only contributes novel theoretical advancements to the DEA-R literature but also delivers practical tools for improving strategic and operational outcomes in the banking industry, ultimately bridging the gap between academic research and real-world applications.

The remainder of this chapter is structured to provide a comprehensive exploration of the proposed advanced DEA-R models tailored for the banking sector. Section 2 delves into resource allocation challenges when dealing with negative data, presenting refined DEA-R frameworks capable of addressing this complexity. Section 3 shifts the focus to the evaluation of mergers in the presence of negative data, where we introduce innovative DEA-R models to analyze and optimize merger scenarios. Both sections are enriched with real-world case studies from the banking sector, demonstrating the applicability and effectiveness of the proposed models in practical settings. Finally, Section 4 concludes the chapter by summarizing the key findings, discussing implications for banking performance evaluation, and suggesting avenues for future research. Together, these sections provide a robust methodological foundation for addressing critical challenges in banking performance analysis and decision-making under complex data conditions.

2. Resource Allocation with DEA-R Models for Negative Data

Efficient resource allocation is a cornerstone of sustainable growth and profitability in the banking industry, where financial institutions constantly navigate volatile markets, regulatory pressures, and evolving customer demands. Traditional models often struggle to capture the complexity of financial operations, particularly when dealing with ratio data that may include negative values — an inevitable consequence of financial losses, asset devaluations, or fluctuating market conditions. These negative data points, though reflective of real-world dynamics, pose significant challenges for conventional DEA models, which are inherently designed for non-negative inputs and outputs. To bridge this critical gap, advanced DEA-R models have been developed to effectively handle negative ratio data, offering banks a powerful analytical framework to optimize resource distribution without compromising operational efficiency. By incorporating these sophisticated models, banks can better identify inefficiencies, strategically reallocate resources, and maintain resilience in the face of financial adversity. This section introduces innovative DEA-R models tailored to the banking sector, enabling a more accurate and dynamic assessment of performance, even when confronted with complex financial realities. Through these models, decision-makers gain actionable insights into optimizing capital allocation, cost management, and risk mitigation — fostering not only operational stability but also long-term competitive advantage.

In this section, we first introduce the foundational DEA-R models specifically adapted to handle negative data, addressing both input-oriented and output-oriented frameworks. These models are designed to provide a more realistic and flexible assessment of banking operations by accommodating negative ratio data that traditional DEA models cannot process. The input-oriented models focus on minimizing resource utilization while maintaining current performance levels, offering valuable insights into cost reduction and operational streamlining. Conversely, the output-oriented models aim to maximize service outputs and financial returns without increasing input consumption, guiding banks toward revenue enhancement and market expansion. Building upon these robust models, we further explore inverse DEA-R approaches to estimate the necessary adjustments in inputs and outputs required to achieve desired performance improvements. This dual focus allows for a comprehensive analysis of how resources can be optimally reallocated and how operational targets can be strategically met, even in the presence of negative financial indicators. By integrating these advanced models, banks gain a powerful toolkit for making informed decisions on resource distribution and performance optimization, ensuring adaptability and sustained growth in an increasingly complex financial environment.

2.1. *Handling negative data: Basic DEA-R models*

To establish a solid foundation for the development of advanced DEA-R models, we begin by considering a set of DMUs, where each $DMU_j (j = 1, 2, \ldots, n)$ utilizes a positive input vector $\mathbf{x_j} = (x_{1j}, x_{2j}, \ldots, x_{mj})$ to produce a positive output vector $\mathbf{y_j} = (\mathbf{y}_{1j}, y_{2j}, \ldots, y_{sj})$. This fundamental framework serves as the basis for extending traditional DEA models to ratio-based forms, which are particularly effective in evaluating the performance of financial institutions where input and output data naturally appear in ratio formats. The focus on ratio data allows for more precise efficiency assessments, aligning closely with the operational realities of the banking sector.

Within this structure, we introduce both input-oriented and output-oriented DEA-R models under the assumption of VRS. The input-oriented model aims to determine the minimal proportional reduction in inputs required to sustain current output levels, emphasizing cost efficiency and optimal resource utilization. Conversely, the output-oriented model seeks the maximal proportional expansion of outputs achievable with existing inputs, highlighting opportunities for performance growth and revenue maximization. These models, are formally presented as models (1) and (2) (Soltanifar *et al.*, 2023,

2024a, 2024b; Soltanifar, 2024; Ghiyasi *et al.*, 2023):

$$\begin{aligned}
& e_p = \max \theta \\
& \text{s.t.} \\
& \sum_{j=1}^{n} \lambda_j \left(\frac{\frac{y_{rj}}{x_{ij}}}{\frac{y_{rp}}{x_{ip}}} \right) \geq \theta, 1 \leq r \leq s, 1 \leq i \leq m \\
& \sum_{j=1}^{n} \lambda_j \left(\frac{x_{ip}}{x_{ij}} \right) = \theta, 1 \leq i \leq m \\
& \sum_{j=1}^{n} \lambda_j = 1 \\
& \lambda_j \geq 0, 1 \leq j \leq n \\
& \theta \text{ is free}
\end{aligned} \tag{1}$$

$$\begin{aligned}
& e'_p = \min \theta \\
& \text{s.t.} \\
& \sum_{j=1}^{n} \lambda_j \left(\frac{\frac{x_{ij}}{y_{rj}}}{\frac{x_{ip}}{y_{rp}}} \right) \leq \theta, 1 \leq r \leq s, 1 \leq i \leq m \\
& \sum_{j=1}^{n} \lambda_j \left(\frac{y_{rp}}{y_{rj}} \right) = \theta, 1 \leq r \leq s \\
& \sum_{j=1}^{n} \lambda_j = 1 \\
& \lambda_j \geq 0, 1 \leq j \leq n \\
& \theta \text{ is free}
\end{aligned} \tag{2}$$

While the foundational DEA-R models under the VRS assumption provide valuable insights into efficiency evaluation, they fall short when addressing the complexities introduced by ratio data that may assume negative values — a scenario frequently encountered in the banking industry. Financial metrics such as profit margins, growth rates, and return ratios can naturally yield negative figures due to market fluctuations, economic downturns, or operational inefficiencies. This reality necessitates the adaptation of DEA-R models to effectively handle such data. Relying on the CRS assumption is insufficient in this context, as it cannot adequately capture the variable scaling behaviors observed in financial operations.

To overcome this limitation, we turn to more flexible scale assumptions, namely, VRS, Increasing Returns to Scale (IRS), and Decreasing Returns to Scale (DRS). Particularly in ratio-based data, it is often the case that either inputs or outputs – but not both – may take negative values. This characteristic makes the IRS and DRS assumptions especially suitable for modeling such scenarios, as they allow for asymmetric scaling behaviors that align with the operational realities of financial institutions.

For both input-oriented and output-oriented DEA-R models under these more nuanced scale assumptions, the necessary formulations can be derived by thoughtfully modifying the constraints in the original VRS models. Specifically, in models (1) and (2), the constraint sets denoted as $\sum_{j=1}^{n} \lambda_j \left(\frac{x_{ip}}{x_{ij}}\right) = \theta, (1 \leq i \leq m)$ and $\sum_{j=1}^{n} \lambda_j \left(\frac{y_{rp}}{y_{rj}}\right) = \theta, (1 \leq r \leq s)$ must be replaced with new constraint sets $\sum_{j=1}^{n} \lambda_j (\frac{x_{ip}}{x_{ij}}) \geq \theta, (1 \leq i \leq m)$ and $\sum_{j=1}^{n} \lambda_j \left(\frac{y_{rp}}{y_{rj}}\right) \geq \theta, (1 \leq r \leq s)$ to accurately represent IRS conditions, and with constraint sets $\sum_{j=1}^{n} \lambda_j \left(\frac{x_{ip}}{x_{ij}}\right) \leq \theta, (1 \leq i \leq m)$ and $\sum_{j=1}^{n} \lambda_j \left(\frac{y_{rp}}{y_{rj}}\right) \leq \theta, (1 \leq r \leq s)$ to capture DRS behaviors. These strategic adjustments seamlessly extend the DEA-R framework, ensuring its robustness and adaptability across diverse scaling environments while preserving its core focus on ratio-based performance evaluation. This refinement not only broadens the applicability of DEA-R models but also enhances their capacity to deliver more accurate and insightful assessments in the dynamic and often volatile banking sector.

Despite the enhanced flexibility offered by VRS, IRS, and DRS assumptions, the standard DEA-R models remain inherently incapable of handling negative data — a critical limitation when evaluating financial performance in the banking sector. Financial indicators, especially those expressed as ratios, often produce negative values due to operational losses, economic downturns, or unfavorable market conditions. However, in ratio-based datasets, it is typically observed that either the input or the output may assume negative values, but not both simultaneously. This distinct characteristic necessitates a thoughtful redesign of DEA-R models to accurately capture the complexities of real-world financial data.

To address this challenge, we adopt and extend the innovative approach initially introduced by Emrouznejad *et al.* (2010a; 2010b) and subsequently refined by Kaffash *et al.* (2018). This methodology provides a robust framework for modifying DEA models to accommodate negative data without compromising their analytical integrity. By strategically transforming the input or output variables — depending on which dimension contains negative values — the models are recalibrated to ensure accurate and meaningful efficiency assessments. This adaptation preserves the core structure of the DEA-R framework while significantly enhancing its applicability to the nuanced financial datasets common in the banking industry.

To effectively accommodate scenarios where inputs remain non-negative but outputs may take on negative values – a common occurrence in financial performance analysis – we introduce a refined modeling approach that strategically partitions the output set. Specifically, the outputs are categorized into two distinct subsets: Positive Outputs (O'), which consist of outputs that consistently maintain strictly positive values across all DMUs, and Potentially Negative Outputs (O''), which include outputs that, due to the contextual nature of banking operations, can assume negative values. This nuanced classification enables the DEA-R framework to more accurately reflect the realities of financial performance, where adverse market conditions or operational inefficiencies can lead to negative performance indicators such as net income or return on assets.

Building upon this structured output division, the model is carefully reformulated to handle these two subsets distinctly. For the positive outputs in set O', the standard DEA-R formulation remains intact, ensuring the consistency and comparability of performance measures. However, for the potentially negative outputs in set O'', a transformation is applied to normalize these values without distorting the efficiency evaluation. This transformation preserves the relative efficiency assessment while accommodating the presence of negative data. Thus, we define the new variables as follows:

$$y_{rj}^{P} = \begin{cases} y_{rj} & \text{if } y_{rj} \geq 0 \\ 0 & \text{otherwise} \end{cases} \quad y_{rj}^{N} = \begin{cases} -y_{rj} & \text{if } y_{rj} < 0 \\ 0 & \text{otherwise} \end{cases}, \quad 1 \leq j \leq n$$

According to this classification, the originally defined potentially negative output can now be elegantly reformulated as follows: $y_{rj} = y_{rj}^{P} - y_{rj}^{N}$ and $y_{rj}^{P}, y_{rj}^{N} \geq 0$.

Building upon this refined representation of potentially negative outputs, the development of robust DEA-R models capable of handling such complexities becomes feasible. Drawing from the innovative framework proposed by Emrouznejad *et al.* (2010a; 2010b), model (3) is introduced to effectively incorporate the redefined output structure, ensuring accurate performance evaluation even when outputs may assume negative values. This model strategically modifies the PPS to accommodate the nuanced behavior of ratio data in banking operations. Complementing this approach, Kaffash *et al.* (2018) offer a more advanced formulation – presented as model (4) – which further refines the treatment of negative outputs through an adaptive and flexible modeling strategy. This model enhances the precision and applicability of DEA-R in complex financial environments by integrating sophisticated constraint adjustments and scaling factors. Together, models (3) and (4) provide a comprehensive toolkit for performance evaluation, empowering decision-makers in the banking sector to navigate the challenges posed by negative data with greater confidence and analytical rigor (Soltanifar *et al.*, 2003, 2024a):

$$\begin{aligned}
&\max \theta \\
&\text{s.t.} \\
&\sum_{j=1}^{n} \lambda_j \frac{y_{rj}}{x_{ij}} \geq \theta \frac{y_{rp}}{x_{ip}}, 1 \leq i \leq m, \forall r \in O' \\
&\sum_{j=1}^{n} \lambda_j \frac{y_{rj}^{P}}{x_{ij}} \geq \theta \frac{y_{rp}^{P}}{x_{ip}}, 1 \leq i \leq m, \forall r \in O'' \\
&\sum_{j=1}^{n} \lambda_j \frac{y_{rj}^{N}}{x_{ij}} \leq \theta \frac{y_{rp}^{N}}{x_{ip}}, 1 \leq i \leq m, \forall r \in O''
\end{aligned}$$

$$
\begin{aligned}
&\sum_{j=1}^{n} \lambda_j \left(\frac{x_{ip}}{x_{ij}}\right) = \theta, 1 \leq i \leq m \\
&\sum_{j=1}^{n} \lambda_j = 1 \\
&\lambda_j \geq 0, 1 \leq j \leq n \\
&\theta \text{ is free}
\end{aligned}
\tag{3}
$$

$$
\begin{aligned}
&\max \theta \\
&\text{s.t.} \\
&\sum_{j=1}^{n} \lambda_j \frac{y_{rj}}{x_{ij}} \geq (1+\theta)\frac{y_{rp}}{x_{ip}}, 1 \leq i \leq m, \forall r \in O' \\
&\sum_{j=1}^{n} \lambda_j \frac{y_{rj}^P}{x_{ij}} \geq (1+\theta)\frac{y_{rp}^P}{x_{ip}}, 1 \leq i \leq m, \forall r \in O'' \\
&\sum_{j=1}^{n} \lambda_j \frac{y_{rj}^N}{x_{ij}} \leq (1-\theta)\frac{y_{rp}^N}{x_{ip}}, 1 \leq i \leq m, \forall r \in O'' \\
&\sum_{j=1}^{n} \lambda_j \left(\frac{x_{ip}}{x_{ij}}\right) = (1+\theta), 1 \leq i \leq m \\
&\sum_{j=1}^{n} \lambda_j = 1 \\
&\lambda_j \geq 0, 1 \leq j \leq n \\
&\theta \text{ is free}
\end{aligned}
\tag{4}
$$

In this scenario, where outputs remain non-negative while inputs are allowed to take on negative values, it is essential to carefully classify the inputs to ensure the DEA-R model remains robust and accurate. Inputs are categorized into two distinct groups:

Positive Inputs (I'): These inputs are strictly positive, maintaining consistency with the traditional DEA framework. As they do not exhibit the complexities associated with negative values, they are handled seamlessly within the conventional structure of DEA-R models, ensuring that the performance evaluation remains straightforward and reliable.

Potentially Negative Inputs (I''): These inputs, however, introduce a level of complexity. They may take either positive or negative values depending on the context, necessitating a more sophisticated approach to effectively model the underlying relationships. As these inputs can fluctuate across a broader range of values, they require a flexible framework that can accommodate both their positive and negative potential.

To address this, we introduce a transformation of the input variables, allowing the model to capture the full spectrum of potential values. This transformation ensures that the DEA-R model can properly handle cases where inputs may exhibit negative characteristics, making it adaptable to a wider range of scenarios commonly encountered in the banking industry.

$$x_{ij}^P = \begin{cases} x_{ij} & \text{if } x_{ij} \geq 0 \\ 0 & \text{Otherwise} \end{cases} \quad x_{ij}^N = \begin{cases} -x_{ij} & \text{if } x_{ij} < 0 \\ 0 & \text{Otherwise} \end{cases}, \quad 1 \leq j \leq n$$

To effectively address the challenge of incorporating potentially negative inputs, we decompose each input into two components. Let $\mathbf{X_i^P}$ represent the positive part of the input, capturing the values that are strictly non-negative, while $\mathbf{X_i^N}$ captures the absolute magnitude of the negative portion, where applicable. This decomposition not only preserves the structural integrity of the original data but also ensures that every input is expressed as a non-negative variable. By this transformation, we align the inputs with the core requirements of the DEA-R methodology, which demands the handling of non-negative data to preserve the validity of performance evaluation. This approach allows us to maintain the flexibility needed to model the full range of input behaviors, from strictly positive to potentially negative, while ensuring compatibility with the underlying DEA framework. Through this strategic transformation, the model becomes adaptable and robust, enabling a nuanced and precise analysis of performance in contexts where input data may exhibit a diverse range of values.

In this manner, we can effectively extend the framework to handle potentially negative inputs by employing a two-component decomposition strategy. The resulting formulations, tailored to address the complexities of negative inputs, can be derived based on the pioneering work of Emrouznejad *et al.* (2010a; 2010b) and the refinements proposed by Kaffash *et al.* (2018). Specifically, the resulting models, which incorporate the necessary transformations to account for the negative nature of inputs, will be presented as model (5) based on Emrouznejad *et al.*'s approach (Emrouznejad *et al.*, 2010a; 2010b) and model (6) following the methodology advanced by Kaffash *et al.* (2018). These models not only expand the boundaries of the DEA-R framework but also ensure the integrity of performance evaluations when working with datasets containing potentially negative inputs. The careful design and application of these models enable a robust and comprehensive approach to handling complex real-world data, especially in contexts where financial performance metrics are subject to the variability of negative inputs (Soltanifar *et al.*, 2023, 2024a).

$$
\begin{aligned}
&\min \theta \\
&\text{s.t.} \\
&\sum_{j=1}^{n} \lambda_j \frac{x_{ij}}{y_{rj}} \leq \theta \frac{x_{ip}}{y_{rp}}, 1 \leq r \leq s, \forall i \in I' \\
&\sum_{j=1}^{n} \lambda_j \frac{x_{ij}^P}{y_{rj}} \leq \theta \frac{x_{ip}^P}{y_{rp}}, 1 \leq r \leq s, \forall i \in I'' \\
&\sum_{j=1}^{n} \lambda_j \frac{x_{ij}^N}{y_{rj}} \geq \theta \frac{x_{ip}^N}{y_{rp}}, 1 \leq r \leq s, \forall i \in I'' \qquad (5) \\
&\sum_{j=1}^{n} \lambda_j \left(\frac{y_{rp}}{y_{rj}} \right) = \theta, 1 \leq r \leq s \\
&\sum_{j=1}^{n} \lambda_j = 1 \\
&\lambda_j \geq 0, 1 \leq j \leq n \\
&\theta \text{ is free}
\end{aligned}
$$

$$
\begin{aligned}
&\min \theta \\
&\text{s.t.} \\
&\sum_{j=1}^{n} \lambda_j \frac{x_{ij}}{y_{rj}} \leq (1+\theta)\frac{x_{ip}}{y_{rp}}, 1 \leq r \leq s, \forall i \in I' \\
&\sum_{j=1}^{n} \lambda_j \frac{x_{ij}^P}{y_{rj}} \leq (1+\theta)\frac{x_{ip}^P}{y_{rp}}, 1 \leq r \leq s, \forall i \in I'' \\
&\sum_{j=1}^{n} \lambda_j \frac{x_{ij}^N}{y_{rj}} \geq (1-\theta)\frac{x_{ip}^N}{y_{rp}}, 1 \leq r \leq s, \forall i \in I'' \\
&\sum_{j=1}^{n} \lambda_j \left(\frac{y_{rp}}{y_{rj}}\right) = (1+\theta), 1 \leq r \leq s \\
&\sum_{j=1}^{n} \lambda_j = 1 \\
&\lambda_j \geq 0, 1 \leq j \leq n \\
&\theta \text{ is free}
\end{aligned}
\tag{6}
$$

Having previously outlined the necessary adjustments to the DEA-R models under the assumptions of IRS and DRS, along with the corresponding modifications in their constraints, we are now fully equipped with the appropriate models to handle negative ratio data. With these models in hand, we can shift our focus to a critical aspect of performance evaluation: the estimation of inputs and outputs in the presence of negative ratio data. This next phase involves leveraging the newly formulated models to effectively estimate performance metrics, ensuring that the complex nature of negative data does not compromise the accuracy and reliability of the results. By systematically addressing the challenges posed by negative values, we are not only extending the capability of DEA-R models but also providing a comprehensive framework for more nuanced and precise performance assessments. As we proceed, we will explore the methodologies for input and output estimation, highlighting how these models maintain their robustness while accommodating the intricacies of negative ratio data.

2.2. *Inverse DEA-R for estimating inputs and outputs with negative data*

In the realm of DEA, the estimation of inputs and outputs in the presence of negative data presents unique challenges, particularly when ratio-based data are involved. The need for accurate estimation methods becomes even more pronounced in industries such as banking, where financial data can fluctuate, often resulting in negative values for certain inputs or outputs. In this section, we delve into the innovative approach of inverse DEA-R models, offering a sophisticated framework for estimating inputs and outputs under the complexities of negative data. By addressing both negative outputs and negative inputs, we aim to provide comprehensive solutions that enhance the flexibility and applicability of DEA-R in real-world settings. This discussion will be organized into two key sub-sections: First, we will explore the inverse DEA-R model with negative outputs, followed by an examination of the inverse DEA-R model with negative inputs, presenting the most suitable models for each scenario. Through this structured analysis, we provide a roadmap for overcoming the inherent challenges posed by negative data in performance evaluation.

2.2.1. *Inverse DEA-R model with negative*

As we turn our attention to the estimation of outputs in the presence of negative data, we face an exciting opportunity to refine the DEA-R methodology in ways that can directly benefit real-world performance evaluations. Specifically, in this sub-section, we explore the concept of adjusting input allocations while preserving the efficiency of the DMU and estimating its output accordingly. This approach becomes particularly relevant when negative outputs are present, as the typical constraints and assumptions of traditional models need to be redefined to accommodate these complexities.

To formalize this process, consider a DMU, denoted as DMU_p, which intends to change its input vector to a new input configuration $\boldsymbol{\alpha}_\mathbf{p} = \mathbf{x}_\mathbf{p} + \boldsymbol{\Delta}\mathbf{x}_\mathbf{p}$. The objective is to identify how the corresponding output vector should be adjusted to maximize the output levels, while maintaining the DMU's operational efficiency at its current level. To achieve this, we present model (7), a sophisticated multi-objective programming approach that builds upon the principles established in model (4). This formulation allows the DMU to balance the adjustments in its inputs and outputs effectively, while incorporating efficiency constraints into the optimization process. By doing so, any modifications made to the operational parameters will align with the DMU's desired efficiency targets, ensuring that the adjustments are not only feasible but also beneficial in improving performance.

$$\begin{aligned}
&\max \left\{ \underset{r\in O'}{\beta_{rp}}, \underset{r\in O''}{\beta_{rp}^{P}}, \underset{r\in O''}{-\beta_{rp}^{N}} \right\} \\
&\text{s.t.} \\
&\sum_{j=1}^{n} \lambda_j \frac{y_{rj}}{x_{ij}} \geq (1+\theta^*) \frac{\beta_{rp}}{\alpha_{ip}}, 1 \leq i \leq m, \forall r \in O' \\
&\sum_{j=1}^{n} \lambda_j \frac{y_{rj}^{P}}{x_{ij}} \geq (1+\theta^*) \frac{\beta_{rp}^{P}}{\alpha_{ip}}, 1 \leq i \leq m, \forall r \in O'' \\
&\sum_{j=1}^{n} \lambda_j \frac{y_{rj}^{N}}{x_{ij}} \leq (1-\theta^*) \frac{\beta_{rp}^{N}}{\alpha_{ip}}, 1 \leq i \leq m, \forall r \in O'' \\
&\sum_{j=1}^{n} \lambda_j \left(\frac{\alpha_{ip}}{x_{ij}}\right) \geq (1+\theta^*), 1 \leq i \leq m \\
&\sum_{j=1}^{n} \lambda_j = 1 \\
&\lambda_j \geq 0, 1 \leq j \leq n
\end{aligned} \tag{7}$$

In this context, θ^* represents the optimal solution of model (7) for DMU_p before any input adjustments are made. This framework empowers organizations to plan not only input increases but also strategically allocate output modifications, ensuring optimal performance even in the face of challenging ratio data with negative outputs.

The weakly efficient solutions derived from model (7) offer a decisive answer to the core question: "How can DMU_p adjust its output to match the desired input increase while maintaining or enhancing its efficiency?" These solutions establish a clear path for determining the exact output modifications needed in response to input adjustments. In essence, they provide a robust framework to ensure that any planned changes in inputs are met with strategically calculated output changes, enabling DMU_p to optimize its performance while preserving efficiency even in the presence of negative data.

2.2.2. *Inverse DEA-R model with negative inputs*

In the case of negative inputs, a similar approach to resource allocation can be employed, where the goal is to enhance output while preserving efficiency. By utilizing a multi-objective programming model based on model (6), we can answer a critical question: "If a DMU, such as a bank, is required to increase its outputs while maintaining its efficiency, what amount of input resources must be allocated?" The weakly efficient solution derived from this model provides a precise answer, highlighting the necessary input adjustments that will facilitate the desired output increments without compromising overall efficiency. This streamlined approach ensures that the strategic allocation of resources is both effective and aligned with efficiency goals.

2.2.3. *Real-world application in the banking sector*

To demonstrate the practical relevance and effectiveness of the proposed inverse DEA-R models, this section applies these frameworks to a real-world case study within the banking industry — a sector characterized by complex financial structures and performance indicators that often include negative data. In this dynamic environment, banks must strategically balance resource allocation and performance improvement while navigating fluctuating market conditions. By implementing the developed models, we can precisely estimate the necessary adjustments in inputs and outputs to sustain or enhance efficiency. This case study not only validates the robustness of the models in handling ratio data with negative values but also offers valuable insights into how banks can optimize their operations and maintain a competitive edge.

This section presents a practical application of the proposed inverse DEA-R models using data from 66 branches of an Iranian bank. In a competitive financial landscape, the models are employed to estimate necessary input and output adjustments while preserving or enhancing efficiency. Table 1 outlines the key financial indicators

Table 1. Financial indicators used in the bank branch analysis.

Criterion	Description
Staff Competency	Reflects both the quality and quantity of human resources in each bank branch.
Interest Expenses	Interest paid to individual and corporate depositors to sustain financial assets.
Loan Arrears	Overdue loan payments recorded by the branch.
Loan Portfolio	Total value of loans issued to customers.
Deposit Volume	Combined value of all deposit types, including savings, current, and term accounts.
Interest Income	Earnings from interest on loans provided to customers.
Service Fees	Income from fees for banking services (e.g., transfers, guarantees).
External Funds	Additional funds from government and other organizations (e.g., housing funds).
Total Capital	Aggregate of deposits and external funding sources.

used for this analysis, forming the basis for model implementation. This case study bridges theoretical innovation with real-world banking challenges, showcasing the models' effectiveness in optimizing performance (Soltanifar *et al.*, 2023).

To ensure data confidentiality, financial ratios are employed to define inputs and outputs in this analysis. The selected inputs are (1) the ratio of staff competency to total capital, reflecting the efficiency of human resource utilization; (2) the ratio of interest expenses to total capital, representing the cost of attracting financial resources; and (3) the ratio of loan arrears to the loan portfolio, indicating credit risk exposure. These inputs offer a comprehensive perspective on operational efficiency and risk management across branches.

On the output side, three key indicators are considered: (1) the ratio of interest income to the loan portfolio, measuring profitability from lending activities; (2) the ratio of service fees to staff competency, highlighting revenue generation from banking services relative to workforce investment; and (3) a calculated metric, $0.75\times$ (Total Capital — Loan Portfolio), assessing risk-adjusted resource efficiency. Notably, this final output may assume negative values, signaling inefficiencies in certain branches.

Leveraging ratio-based data ensures confidentiality while enabling precise performance evaluation. Models (3) through (6) are well suited for this context, effectively handling ratio data and accommodating negative outputs. The data used in this analysis are presented in Table 2.

In this study, financial ratios are used to define the inputs and outputs, ensuring both confidentiality and meaningful cross-branch comparisons. The third output, however, reflects financial risk, as it may yield negative values for certain branches, highlighting operational challenges.

The analysis organizes the data into inputs and outputs, offering insights into branch efficiency and pinpointing areas for improvement. To align with the bank's policy of a 12.5% input increase,

Table 2. Input–output data.

DMUs	Input 1	Input 2	Input 3	Output 1	Output 2	Output 3
DMU1	3.60×10^{-10}	0.013	0.013	0.000	3638122.78	-7.26×10^{10}
DMU2	2.12×10^{-10}	0.011	0.000	0.002	3810945.73	-1.34×10^{11}
DMU3	4.91×10^{-10}	0.014	0.016	0.011	2023340.39	-2.25×10^{10}
DMU4	3.70×10^{-10}	0.012	0.009	0.004	2140207.39	-1.52×10^{11}
DMU5	2.32×10^{-10}	0.013	0.001	0.014	2869841.07	-5.89×10^{10}
DMU6	2.55×10^{-10}	0.013	0.005	0.003	4418983.78	-1.40×10^{10}
DMU7	2.54×10^{-10}	0.014	0.007	0.006	2535309.66	-1.04×10^{11}
DMU8	2.98×10^{-10}	0.014	0.018	0.005	6417653.08	-3.34×10^{10}
DMU9	3.63×10^{-10}	0.012	0.004	0.006	4727299.27	-2.79×10^{10}
DMU10	2.30×10^{-10}	0.010	0.081	0.003	5182404.23	-3.00×10^{10}
DMU11	2.10×10^{-10}	0.011	0.002	0.005	3180006.34	-1.93×10^{10}
DMU12	1.87×10^{-10}	0.011	0.000	0.007	4286998.04	-1.27×10^{10}
DMU13	1.83×10^{-10}	0.011	0.004	0.002	5362928.48	-3.09×10^{9}
DMU14	1.62×10^{-10}	0.018	0.109	0.014	2628496.08	-2.51×10^{11}
DMU15	3.06×10^{-10}	0.014	0.148	0.004	5259138.69	-1.74×10^{10}
DMU16	1.55×10^{-10}	0.014	0.007	0.003	7675819.02	1.08×10^{10}
DMU17	2.26×10^{-10}	0.013	0.029	0.007	5617994.82	-2.26×10^{9}
DMU18	2.26×10^{-10}	0.015	0.043	0.005	6337038.86	-3.31×10^{10}
DMU19	1.38×10^{-10}	0.012	0.010	0.008	4089557.79	-3.88×10^{10}
DMU20	2.43×10^{-10}	0.015	0.060	0.002	2553880.05	-3.03×10^{10}
DMU21	3.22×10^{-10}	0.013	0.057	0.002	5571127.78	-9.01×10^{10}
DMU22	2.82×10^{-10}	0.014	0.009	0.003	3239500.00	-3.79×10^{9}
DMU23	2.27×10^{-10}	0.014	0.073	0.009	4280791.22	9.20×10^{8}
DMU24	1.36×10^{-10}	0.007	0.001	0.003	11915315.02	3.02×10^{9}
DMU25	1.96×10^{-10}	0.011	0.006	0.002	11672117.98	-2.15×10^{10}

(*Continued*)

Table 2. (*Continued*)

DMUs	Input 1	Input 2	Input 3	Output 1	Output 2	Output 3
DMU26	2.60×10^{-10}	0.014	0.020	0.002	9188614.02	-5.27×10^{9}
DMU27	2.70×10^{-10}	0.013	0.056	0.003	7073960.03	-1.23×10^{10}
DMU28	1.21×10^{-10}	0.011	0.001	0.003	31219539.07	-2.65×10^{10}
DMU29	2.04×10^{-10}	0.013	0.925	0.016	3847339.14	-4.55×10^{9}
DMU30	1.44×10^{-10}	0.011	0.012	0.004	3925433.38	1.55×10^{10}
DMU31	1.24×10^{-10}	0.012	0.020	0.004	10289523.52	-2.79×10^{10}
DMU32	2.08×10^{-10}	0.012	0.002	0.005	2922196.94	-2.59×10^{8}
DMU33	1.73×10^{-10}	0.013	0.007	0.013	1861282.02	3.09×10^{9}
DMU34	2.53×10^{-10}	0.012	0.093	0.003	2660208.21	-5.98×10^{10}
DMU35	1.70×10^{-10}	0.012	0.000	0.004	8030955.07	-9.55×10^{9}
DMU36	2.34×10^{-10}	0.012	0.003	0.007	4566071.25	-8.87×10^{9}
DMU37	3.41×10^{-10}	0.011	0.002	0.008	1389429.68	-1.54×10^{10}
DMU38	1.74×10^{-10}	0.009	0.005	0.005	1300569.75	-1.03×10^{10}
DMU39	2.87×10^{-10}	0.012	0.001	0.009	5668421.39	-1.31×10^{10}
DMU40	3.20×10^{-10}	0.009	0.059	0.001	4683428.82	-8.59×10^{10}
DMU41	3.32×10^{-10}	0.006	0.082	0.000	10299523.28	-3.61×10^{10}
DMU42	2.79×10^{-10}	0.009	0.074	0.000	4811822.38	-9.30×10^{10}
DMU43	2.73×10^{-10}	0.012	0.038	0.004	11936225.07	-4.00×10^{10}
DMU44	2.23×10^{-10}	0.010	0.004	0.001	3002202.33	-3.59×10^{9}
DMU45	1.62×10^{-10}	0.011	0.064	0.001	9092088.81	-3.67×10^{10}
DMU46	1.95×10^{-10}	0.013	0.003	0.007	2876836.70	-1.58×10^{11}
DMU47	3.91×10^{-10}	0.014	0.031	0.011	5507450.72	-4.41×10^{9}
DMU48	2.87×10^{-10}	0.010	0.011	0.012	935948.40	-2.34×10^{10}
DMU49	4.58×10^{-10}	0.011	0.000	0.006	2049316.25	-4.58×10^{10}
DMU50	1.54×10^{-10}	0.014	0.068	0.001	3797152.05	-2.18×10^{10}
DMU51	3.45×10^{-10}	0.012	0.037	0.000	1843314.53	-3.46×10^{10}
DMU52	1.62×10^{-10}	0.015	0.016	0.002	13375062.24	1.80×10^{9}
DMU53	1.36×10^{-10}	0.016	0.010	0.005	8966034.64	-7.06×10^{9}
DMU54	1.79×10^{-10}	0.012	0.046	0.003	7507306.26	-2.31×10^{10}
DMU55	2.89×10^{-10}	0.015	0.070	0.000	4325253.32	-2.95×10^{10}
DMU56	1.84×10^{-10}	0.013	0.067	0.000	27397717.31	-3.31×10^{10}
DMU57	1.36×10^{-10}	0.003	0.012	0.000	3589722.55	6.68×10^{9}
DMU58	3.58×10^{-10}	0.014	0.020	0.005	2251224.28	-3.28×10^{10}
DMU59	2.97×10^{-10}	0.016	0.005	0.008	4971018.61	-4.09×10^{8}
DMU60	2.15×10^{-10}	0.016	0.051	0.007	4110873.65	-1.96×10^{10}
DMU61	5.43×10^{-10}	0.011	0.025	0.001	1433650.80	-2.27×10^{10}
DMU62	3.86×10^{-10}	0.010	0.006	0.003	6414468.91	-4.00×10^{10}
DMU63	2.56×10^{-10}	0.014	0.012	0.006	801753.58	-7.63×10^{9}
DMU64	1.86×10^{-10}	0.014	0.005	0.005	3255778.27	-3.49×10^{9}
DMU65	2.16×10^{-10}	0.010	0.010	0.012	4158731.50	-2.85×10^{10}
DMU66	2.95×10^{-10}	0.013	0.006	0.002	2473656.20	-6.48×10^{9}

branches are given flexibility to adjust cost and profit criteria accordingly. Using model (7), we estimate the necessary output adjustments to maintain efficiency. Table 3 showcases these output estimates, providing a strategic roadmap for branch performance improvement.

The results presented in Table 3 demonstrate the practical value of the inverse DEA-R models in guiding strategic decision-making. By identifying precise output adjustments required to sustain efficiency amid input expansions, these models offer a powerful tool for optimizing resource allocation and enhancing performance. This analysis not only supports the bank's growth objectives but also provides a

Table 3. Estimation of outputs using model (7).

DMUs	Output 1	Output 2	Output 3
DMU1	0.00234926	5.42E+06	9276784200
DMU2	0.00216997	3.94E+06	−1.3213E+11
DMU3	0.00431294	4.35E+06	16504100000
DMU4	0.00228522	6.60E+06	7784834000
DMU5	0.00300651	1.17E+07	2200346070
DMU6	0.0032167	1.01E+07	5704810500
DMU7	0.00381662	9.71E+06	8360797400
DMU8	0.002649	4.27E+06	12110820000
DMU9	0.00346614	1.17E+07	5441094400
DMU10	0.00148074	4.31E+06	12362560000
DMU11	0.00298535	1.17E+07	1778888600
DMU12	0.00400573	8.97E+06	−6498136640
DMU13	0.00370201	1.06E+07	6434397800
DMU14	0.0057035	4.98E+06	19631840000
DMU15	0.0015758	4.61E+06	13211330000
DMU16	0.00461937	8.99E+06	12193470000
DMU17	0.00313142	4.83E+06	16339800000
DMU18	0.0033251	4.27E+06	15177270000
DMU19	0.00470775	5.28E+06	15328130000
DMU20	0.00277963	4.12E+06	14095460000
DMU21	0.00116678	4.84E+06	12727270000
DMU22	0.0029621	7.73E+06	7912187400
DMU23	0.00353677	5.21E+06	17859740000
DMU24	0.00327818	1.34E+07	3392556400
DMU25	0.00339662	8.51E+06	7742242100
DMU26	0.00245138	4.20E+06	12599650000

(Continued)

Table 3. (*Continued*)

DMUs	Output 1	Output 2	Output 3
DMU27	0.00167318	4.29E+06	12706080000
DMU28	0.00298521	1.08E+07	−575812000
DMU29	0.00497356	6.25E+06	22339800000
DMU30	0.00505511	4.42E+06	17400050000
DMU31	0.00183142	3.72E+06	10136120000
DMU32	0.00399603	1.63E+07	4135459800
DMU33	0.00518948	1.08E+07	13166520000
DMU34	0.00178143	4.10E+06	12485850000
DMU35	0.00434887	8.05E+06	−9488182791
DMU36	0.00444274	1.67E+07	5674882900
DMU37	0.00432336	1.71E+07	4909752900
DMU38	0.00340491	8.37E+06	8099120300
DMU39	0.0030386	1.16E+07	1929289100
DMU40	0.00041102	4.77E+06	10191980000
DMU41	0.00019556	6.82E+06	12681110000
DMU42	0.00063218	4.18E+06	9916432100
DMU43	0.00173007	5.12E+06	14631230000
DMU44	0.00271054	9.58E+06	5265639800
DMU45	0.00347887	4.04E+06	14744450000
DMU46	0.00359654	1.33E+07	4778105600
DMU47	0.00209512	8.50E+06	22635230000
DMU48	0.00450174	4.39E+06	15149270000
DMU49	0.00428208	8.23E+06	−12020773230
DMU50	0.00470177	4.11E+06	16183810000
DMU51	0.00076028	5.16E+06	12172970000
DMU52	0.00538672	4.71E+06	18541460000
DMU53	0.00459349	5.41E+06	14765690000
DMU54	0.00354158	4.07E+06	14906050000
DMU55	0.00218208	4.39E+06	13844330000
DMU56	0.00521659	5.64E+06	20979500000
DMU57	0.00011581	4.04E+06	7509241500
DMU58	0.00228659	4.39E+06	11777230000
DMU59	0.00527199	1.76E+07	8098136500
DMU60	0.00468503	4.51E+06	17315550000
DMU61	0.00096322	4.24E+06	11078320000
DMU62	0.00214416	7.74E+06	6187380200
DMU63	0.00364623	5.70E+06	11661970000
DMU64	0.00381023	1.11E+07	7282780900
DMU65	0.00432663	4.82E+06	14117060000
DMU66	0.00264091	8739966.8	6081334000

scalable framework adaptable to other financial institutions facing similar challenges.

3. DEA-R Models for Evaluating Mergers in Negative Contexts

In this section, we delve into the application of DEA-R models for evaluating mergers within contexts where negative values may arise in input or output variables. Mergers, a complex and critical process in many industries, particularly in banking, present unique challenges when negative data points are involved. The ability to assess performance after a merger while handling such data is vital for understanding the true impact of integration strategies. First, we explore input-oriented models designed to handle negative outputs in merger evaluations, followed by output-oriented models addressing negative inputs in similar contexts. Finally, we apply the proposed models to a real-world case study in the banking sector, offering insights into their practical utility.

3.1. *Input-oriented merger models: Managing negative outputs*

Mergers present unique challenges when managing outputs, especially those involving negative values like financial losses or operational inefficiencies. In this section, we explore input-oriented models designed to handle such complexities, focusing on the merger of two DMUs, k and l, into a new entity, M. The goal is to determine the optimal input levels required for M to achieve a desired efficiency while effectively managing both positive and negative outputs. By integrating advanced DEA-R techniques, these models offer decision-makers powerful tools to optimize resource allocation and navigate the risks associated with negative outputs, ensuring a more resilient and efficient merged organization.

Building on the innovative frameworks introduced by Emrouznejad *et al.* (2010a; 2010b) and Kaffash *et al.* (2018), we develop specialized input-oriented inverse DEA-R models for evaluating mergers with negative outputs. Models (8) and (9) are designed to capture the intricate balance between input adjustments and the management of negative outputs, offering a comprehensive approach to resource optimization. These models not only deepen the theoretical understanding of DEA-R but also provide practical solutions for accurately assessing the efficiency and sustainability of merged entities in complex operational environments (Soltanifar *et al.*, 2023).

$$
\begin{aligned}
&\max \sum_{r\in O'} (\beta_{rk}+\beta_{rl}) + \left[\sum_{r\in O'} (\beta^P_{rk}+\beta^P_{rl}) - (\beta^N_{rk}+\beta^N_{rl})\right]\\
&\text{s.t.}\\
&\sum_{j\in F}\lambda_j \frac{y_{rj}}{x_{ij}} \geq \bar{\theta}\left(\frac{\beta_{rk}+\beta_{rl}}{x_{ik}+x_{il}}\right), \quad 1\leq i\leq m, \forall r\in O'\\
&\sum_{j\in F}\lambda_j \frac{y^P_{rj}}{x_{ij}} \geq \bar{\theta}\left(\frac{\beta^P_{rk}+\beta^P_{rl}}{x_{ik}+x_{il}}\right), \quad 1\leq i\leq m, \forall r\in O''\\
&\sum_{j\in F}\lambda_j \frac{y^N_{rj}}{x_{ij}} \leq \bar{\theta}\left(\frac{\beta^N_{rk}+\beta^N_{rl}}{x_{ik}+x_{il}}\right), \quad 1\leq i\leq m, \forall r\in O'' \qquad (8)\\
&\sum_{j\in F}\lambda_j \left(\frac{x_{ik}+x_{il}}{x_{ij}}\right) = \bar{\theta}, \quad 1\leq i\leq m\\
&\sum_{j\in F}\lambda_j = 1\\
&\beta_{rk}+\beta_{rl} \geq y_{rk}+y_{rl}, \forall r\in O'\\
&\beta^P_{rk}+\beta^P_{rl} \geq y^P_{rk}+y^P_{rl}, \beta^N_{rk}+\beta^N_{rl} \leq y^N_{rk}+y^N_{rl}, \forall r\in O''\\
&\lambda_j \geq 0, \forall j\in F
\end{aligned}
$$

$$
\begin{aligned}
&\max \sum_{r\in O} (\beta_{rk}+\beta_{rl}) + \left[\sum_{r\in O'} (\beta^P_{rk}+\beta^P_{rl}) - (\beta^N_{rk}+\beta^N_{rl})\right]\\
&\text{s.t.}\\
&\sum_{j\in F}\lambda_j \frac{y_{rj}}{x_{ij}} \geq (1+\bar{\theta})\left(\frac{\beta_{rk}+\beta_{rl}}{x_{ik}+x_{il}}\right), \quad 1\leq i\leq m, \forall r\in O'\\
&\sum_{j\in F}\lambda_j \frac{y^P_{rj}}{x_{ij}} \geq (1+\bar{\theta})\left(\frac{\beta^P_{rk}+\beta^P_{rl}}{x_{ik}+x_{il}}\right), \quad 1\leq i\leq m, \forall r\in O''
\end{aligned}
$$

$$\sum_{j \in F} \lambda_j \frac{y_{rj}^N}{x_{ij}} \leq (1-\bar{\theta}) \left(\frac{\beta_{rk}^N + \beta_{rl}^N}{x_{ik} + x_{il}} \right), \quad 1 \leq i \leq m, \forall r \in O''$$

$$\sum_{j \in F} \lambda_j \left(\frac{x_{ik} + x_{il}}{x_{ij}} \right) = (1+\bar{\theta}), \quad 1 \leq i \leq m$$

$$\sum_{j \in F} \lambda_j = 1$$

$$\beta_{rk} + \beta_{rl} \geq y_{rk} + y_{rl}, \forall r \in O'$$

$$\beta_{rk}^P + \beta_{rl}^P \geq y_{rk}^P + y_{rl}^P, \beta_{rk}^N + \beta_{rl}^N \leq y_{rk}^N + y_{rl}^N, \forall r \in O''$$

$$\lambda_j \geq 0, \forall j \in F \tag{9}$$

The set F includes all DMUs considered in the evaluation process, encompassing both the original units and the newly merged entity M.

These input-oriented models offer a powerful framework for evaluating mergers where negative outputs are present, guiding decision-makers in optimizing resource allocation while maintaining efficiency. By capturing the complexities of combining operations with undesirable outcomes, these models provide valuable insights into how merged entities can strategically manage inputs to balance performance and risk. This comprehensive approach not only strengthens theoretical advancements in DEA-R but also delivers practical solutions for navigating the challenges of real-world mergers.

3.2. *Output-oriented merger models: Handling negative inputs*

In merger evaluations, the presence of negative inputs introduces a significant challenge, as the integration of resources must be managed effectively to preserve or enhance performance. Negative inputs, such as excessive operational costs or underperforming assets, can distort the true potential of the merged entity, making it crucial to address these factors within the analysis. Output-oriented models, in this context, offer a unique perspective by focusing on maximizing the outputs generated from the available inputs, even when these inputs are unfavorable. This approach becomes essential when the goal is to understand how much output can be achieved despite the constraints imposed by negative inputs. Similar to the models presented in Section 3.1, these output-oriented models for negative inputs can be formulated following analogous methodologies. Given the strong resemblance in approach, we will refrain from explicitly presenting the models here. Instead, it is sufficient to note that these models ensure the merged entity's output efficiency is assessed with respect to its negative input constraints, offering insights for performance optimization after the merger.

3.3. *Practical insights: Banking sector merger analysis*

Mergers in the banking sector not only reshape the operational landscape of institutions but also serve as pivotal moments for optimizing resource allocation and maximizing operational efficiency. In this section, we revisit the case discussed in Section 2.2.3, which involves 66 branches of a prominent Iranian bank, applying a new management policy designed to foster mergers among selected units. This policy aims to create synergies, enhance financial performance, and streamline operations across the bank's network. By focusing on the strategic integration of branch units, we explore how the bank can benefit from a more robust operational framework that encourages growth and resource optimization. The goal is not merely to consolidate but to achieve a higher level of performance and sustainability through well-planned mergers.

To implement this management strategy, the pairs of branches considered for potential mergers are detailed in Table 4. This table provides an in-depth breakdown of the combined inputs and outputs for each selected pair of branches, allowing for a thorough evaluation of the operational dynamics at play. Inputs are calculated by aggregating the resources of both branches in each pair, while the outputs reflect the combined outcomes. Based on this comprehensive data, we derive the efficiency scores of the newly formed merged units. These scores offer a clear, data-driven understanding of how well the merged branches are positioned to perform in the future, providing valuable insights for both strategic planning and performance enhancement in the post-merger environment. For further details and specific data, readers are encouraged to refer back to Section 2.2.3.

Table 4. DMU profile before merger.

DMUs	Input 1	Input 2	Input 3	Output 1	Output 2	Output 3	Efficiency
DMU_2& DMU_{10}	4.420×10^{-10}	0.022	0.081	0.005	8993350	-1.6×10^{11}	0.53
DMU_4& DMU_{11}	5.798×10^{-10}	0.022	0.011	0.009	5320214	-1.7×10^{11}	0.53
DMU_{22}& DMU_{38}	4.562×10^{-10}	0.023	0.014	0.008	4540070	-1.4×10^{11}	0.54
DMU_{40}& DMU_{63}	5.763×10^{-10}	0.023	0.071	0.007	5485182	-9.4×10^{11}	0.54

Table 5. Overview of merged units' inputs, outputs, and target efficiencies.

DMUs	Input 1	Input 2	Input 3	Output 1	Output 2	Output 3	Target Efficiency
$DMU_{2\&10}$	4.420×10^{-10}	0.022	0.081	0.007	8993349.96	-5.586×10^{10}	0.6
$DMU_{4\&11}$	5.798×10^{-10}	0.022	0.011	0.009	5326257.84	-4.398×10^{10}	0.6
$DMU_{22\&38}$	4.562×10^{-10}	0.023	0.014	0.008	4888839.53	-4.931×10^{9}	0.65
$DMU_{40\&63}$	5.763×10^{-10}	0.023	0.071	0.008	5485182.40	-4.373×10^{10}	0.6

In this phase, the decision-maker establishes an efficiency target for each merged unit, which serves as a key performance indicator for assessing the success of the merger. Once these targets are set, the outputs for each new entity are calculated using model (9), ensuring that the merged units align with the desired performance benchmarks. This approach not only offers a clear framework for measuring post-merger success but also provides a dynamic tool for strategic decision-making. The corresponding inputs, outputs, and efficiency targets for each merged unit are succinctly presented in Table 5, offering a comprehensive snapshot of the merger's potential impact.

The analysis of potential mergers in the banking sector, facilitated by the integration of advanced DEA-R models, provides invaluable insights into optimizing resource allocation and performance evaluation. By meticulously setting efficiency targets and adjusting the inputs and outputs for each merged unit, the decision-maker not only ensures that the new entities meet desired operational standards but also paves the way for long-term success in a competitive market.

The use of DEA-R methodologies in these real-world merger scenarios is not just a theoretical exercise, but a robust framework that empowers banks to make data-driven, strategic decisions that maximize both efficiency and profitability. This approach, with its precision and practicality, highlights the transformative potential of mergers when carefully aligned with the right performance targets and underscores the critical importance of adopting sophisticated tools to navigate the complexities of modern banking operations. As demonstrated through the presented case study, these models hold great promise in guiding future policymaking and fostering sustainable growth within the banking sector.

4. Conclusion

This chapter has explored the cutting-edge applications of DEA-R in the context of the banking sector, providing a comprehensive framework for evaluating performance amidst the complexities of ratios and negative data. The banking industry, with its intricate financial structures and the prevalence of ratio-based data, presents unique challenges for performance evaluation. However, by leveraging the innovative DEA-R models introduced here, we have shown how these challenges can be effectively addressed, enabling a more precise and realistic assessment of efficiency and resource utilization.

Through the application of both input- and output-oriented models, this chapter has expanded the boundaries of traditional DEA methods by incorporating the nuances of negative data, an often-overlooked aspect in performance analysis. Negative outputs, such as losses or waste emissions, are an unavoidable reality in many industries, and particularly in banking, where the financial landscape can often present negative performance indicators. By presenting inverse DEA models tailored for scenarios involving negative data, we have introduced a robust toolset that allows for a more nuanced and accurate understanding of operational performance, resource allocation, and efficiency. These models not only extend the theoretical foundations of DEA but also serve as a practical guide for decision-makers looking to optimize their organizations' performance, allocate resources effectively, and navigate the complexities of financial data.

Furthermore, the chapter's focus on mergers and acquisitions within the banking sector provides valuable insights into how these DEA-R models can be applied to real-world scenarios. By analyzing the efficiency of merged entities and estimating the required input–output configurations, we have demonstrated how these models can be used to guide strategic decisions in the context of consolidation. The application of inverse DEA models to assess the performance of newly formed units after a merger has proved to be a significant advancement, offering decision-makers actionable insights into potential synergies, operational efficiencies, and areas for improvement.

In summary, this chapter not only contributes to the theoretical development of DEA-R models but also provides a practical toolkit for financial institutions, offering them the means to assess performance with greater accuracy and depth. The integration of negative data handling, particularly in the context of banking, is an important innovation that expands the applicability of DEA in a rapidly evolving industry. As the banking sector continues to navigate through periods of volatility, consolidation, and competition, these advanced DEA-R models offer a powerful and adaptable approach to managing efficiency and performance. Ultimately, the methods presented in this chapter provide a robust framework for decision-makers to make informed, data-driven decisions that can significantly enhance their institutions' operational effectiveness and strategic positioning in a competitive financial environment.

By bridging the gap between theory and practice, this chapter sets the stage for future research in performance evaluation, resource allocation, and strategic decision-making in the banking sector. With the continued evolution of financial data and the increasing complexity of banking operations, the tools and models presented here offer the foundation for a new era of more informed, transparent, and effective performance measurement.

References

Despić, O. (2013). Some properties of geometric DEA models. *Croat. Oper. Res. Rev.*, 4, 2–18.

Despić, O., Despić, M., and Paradi, J. C. (2007). DEA-R: Ratio-based comparative efficiency model, its mathematical relation to DEA and its use in applications. *J. Prod. Anal.*, 28(1–2), 33–44.

Emrouznejad, A., Amin, G. R., Thanassoulis, E., and Anouze, A. L. (2010). On the boundedness of the SORM DEA models with negative data. *Eur. J. Oper. Res.*, 206(1), 265–268.

Emrouznejad, A., Anouze, A. L., and Thanassoulis, E. (2010). A semi-oriented radial measure for measuring the efficiency of decision-making units with negative data, using DEA. *Eur. J. Oper. Res.*, 200(1), 297–304.

Ghiyasi, M., Soltanifar, M., and Sharafi, H. (2022). A novel inverse DEA-R model with application in hospital efficiency. *Socio-Econ. Plan. Sci.*, 84, 101427.

Hosseinzadeh Lotfi, F., Jahanshahloo, G. R., Ebrahimnejad, A., Soltanifar, M., and Mansourzadeh, S. M. (2010). Target setting in the general combined-oriented CCR model using an interactive MOLP method. *J. Comput. Appl. Math.*, 234(1), 1–9.

Hosseinzadeh Lotfi, F., Jahanshahloo, G. R., Soltanifar, M., Ebrahimnejad, A., and Mansourzadeh, S. M. (2010). Relationship between MOLP and DEA based on output-oriented CCR dual model. *Expert Syst. Appl.*, 37(6), 4331–4336.

Kaffash, S., KazemiMatin, R., and Tajik, M. (2018). A directional semi-oriented radial DEA measure: An application on financial stability and the efficiency of banks. *Ann. Oper. Res.*, 264, 213–234.

Soltanifar, M. (2011). Introducing an interval efficiency for each candidate in ranked voting data using data envelopment analysis. *Int. J. Soc. Syst. Sci.*, 3(4), 346–361.

Soltanifar, M. (2012). Ranking of different common set of weights models using a voting model and its application in determining efficient DMUs. *Int. J. Adv. Oper. Manag.*, 3(3–4), 290–308.

Soltanifar, M. (2017). A new group voting analytical hierarchy process method. *J. Oper. Res. Appl. Math.*, 14(3), 1–13.

Soltanifar, M. (2020). A new voting model for groups with members of unequal power and proficiency. *Int. J. Ind. Math.*, 12(2), 121–134.

Soltanifar, M. (2024). Evaluation of hospitals and health care centers with ratio data. In T. Allahviranloo, F. Hosseinzadeh Lotfi, Z. Moghaddas, M. Vaez-Ghasemi (Eds.), *Decision making in healthcare systems, Studies in systems, decision and control*, 513. Springer, Cham. https://doi.org/10.1007/978-3-031-46735-6_4.

Soltanifar, M., Ebrahimnejad, A., and Farrokhi, M. M. (2010). Ranking of different ranking models using a voting model and its application in determining efficient candidates. *Int. J. Soc. Syst. Sci.*, 2(4), 375–389.

Soltanifar, M., Ghiyasi, M., and Sharafi, H. (2023). Inverse DEA-R models for merger analysis with negative data. *IMA J. Manag. Math.*, 34(3), 491–510.

Soltanifar, M. and Hosseinzadeh Lotfi, F. (2011). The voting analytic hierarchy process method for discriminating among efficient decision making units in data envelopment analysis. *Comput. Ind. Eng.*, 60(4), 585–592.

Soltanifar, M., Ghiyasi, M., and Sharafi, H. (2024). Inverse DEA-R models for merger analysis of electricity distribution units. *OPSEARCH*. https://doi.org/10.1007/s12597-024-00901-x.

Soltanifar, M., Jahanshahloo, G. R., Hosseinzadeh Lotfi, F., and Mansourzadeh, S. M. (2013). On efficiency in convex hull of DMUs. *Appl. Math. Modelling*, 37(4), 2267–2278.

Soltanifar, M. and Shahghobadi, S. (2013). Selecting a benevolent secondary goal model in data envelopment analysis cross-efficiency evaluation by a voting model. *Socio-Econ. Plan. Sci.*, 47(1), 65–74.

Soltanifar, M. and Shahghobadi, S. (2014a). Classifying inputs and outputs in data envelopment analysis based on TOPSIS method and a voting model. *Int. J. Bus. Anal. (IJBAN)*, 1(2), 48–63.

Soltanifar, M. and Shahghobadi, S. (2014b). Survey on rank preservation and rank reversal in data envelopment analysis. *Knowl.-Based Syst.*, 60, 10–19.

Soltanifar, M. and Sharafi, H. (2022). A modified DEA cross efficiency method with negative data and its application in supplier selection. *J. Combin. Optim.*, 43, 265–296.

Soltanifar, M., Sharafi, H., Hosseinzadeh Lotfi, F., Pedrycz, W., and Allahviranloo, T. (2023). Introduction to data envelopment analysis. In *Preferential Voting and Applications: Approaches Based on Data Envelopment Analysis, Studies in Systems, Decision and Control*, 471. Springer, Cham. https://doi.org/10.1007/978-3-031-30403-3_2.

Soltanifar, M., Tavana, M., Charles, V., Ghiyasi, M., and Sharafi, H. (2024). A novel inverse data envelopment analysis model with negative ratio data. *Oper. Res.*, 25(25), 2025.

Soltanifar, M., Tavana, M., Santos-Arteaga, F. J., and Sharafi, H. (2023). A hybrid multi-attribute decision-making and data envelopment analysis model with heterogeneous attributes: The case of sustainable development goals. *Environ. Sci. Policy*, 147, 89–102.

Sharafi, H., Hosseinzadeh Lotfi, F., Jahanshahloo, G., Rostamy-malkhalifeh, M., Soltanifar, M., and Razipour-GhalehJough, S. (2019).

Ranking of petrochemical companies using preferential voting at unequal levels of voting power through data envelopment analysis. *Math. Sci.*, 13, 287–297.

Sharafi, H., Soltanifar, M., and Hosseinzadeh Lotfi, F. (2022). Selecting a green supplier utilizing the new fuzzy voting model and the fuzzy combinative distance-based assessment method. *EURO J. Dec. Proc.*, 10, 100010.

https://doi.org/10.1142/9789819823161_0016

Chapter 16

Financial Services Performance Through Machine Learning Approaches

Pedro Pablo Chambi Condori*
and Telma Raquel Saravia Ticona†

Department of Business Sciences, Universidad Nacional Jorge Basadre Grohmann, Tacna, Peru

* *tsaraviat@unjbg.edu.pe*
† *biasedarmyjm@gmail.com*

The use of machine learning approaches has become a key factor in improving the performance of financial services in areas such as risk analysis, fraud detection, customer segmentation, and operational optimization. These techniques allow for the processing of large volumes of data with greater accuracy than traditional methods, generating predictive models capable of identifying complex patterns in real time. Supervised algorithms, such as random forests and neural networks, excel in predicting defaults and credit assessment, while unsupervised methods contribute to the early detection of atypical behavior and new market opportunities. Likewise, deep learning is increasingly applied to text and voice processing, improving customer service automation through chatbots and sentiment analysis. However, the adoption of these technologies involves challenges related to data quality, model interpretability, and regulatory compliance. Overall, machine learning solutions are driving a significant transformation in the financial sector, increasing efficiency, reducing costs, and strengthening strategic decision-making.

Keywords: Artificial intelligence, blockchain, digital currency, financial services, machine learning.

1. Introduction

Fintech is the industry in which companies leverage technology to deliver financial services. The term fintech arises from the mixture of "finance" and "technology". The birth of Fintech occurred in the 1950s with the creation of credit cards by Diner's Club, which, according to Rubini (2017) and Mills (2018), revolutionized the possibilities for consumers to access credit. In this regard, Arner *et al.* (2016) divide the history of the evolution of Fintech in the financial industry into three fairly broad periods: There was a first period between 1866 and 1967, marked by the creation of new means of communication, such as the telegraph, and transportation, such as railways and steamships. A second period, extending from 1967 to 2008, was characterized by several milestones: the installation of the first ATM at Barclays' Enfield Town branch in north London in June 1967; the creation of NASDAQ, the first fully automated stock market, in 1971; the development of the Swift protocol for interbank communications in 1973; Wells Fargo's introduction of online financial services in 1995; the founding of the PayPal payment protocol in the United States in 1998; and the launch of Alipay in China in 2004, which revolutionized financial services. A third period, from 2008 to the present day, has been marked by the U.S. financial crisis of 2008, which had major global repercussions. It generated distrust toward traditional banks and created a climate conducive to experimenting with new technologies and business models in the financial industry worldwide, leading to the emergence of cryptocurrencies and the rise of fintech.

Financial technology (Fintech) has become a major player in the global financial system, providing a variety of services such as payments, digital currencies, money transfers, loans, crowdsourcing, and insurance. Fintech start-ups in Arab countries have also gained ground due to economic openness and globalization. However, concerns remain about the safety, durability, and security of traditional financial services, especially with the increasing use of artificial intelligence (AI) and digitalization.

Regarding the adoption of fintech technology in global financial markets, there are reports from FDI (2020) that the Chinese financial market has become an important driving force for the global development of fintech; thus, there was a variation in the adoption of technology from 16% in 2015 to 33% in 2017. China and India reported the highest levels of consumer adoption of fintech technology at 95%. In 2019, the global fintech adoption rate reached 64%.

According to the study, this growth was driven by a growing demand for financial services underserved by the traditional financial sector, an increase in demand for digital financial services caused by the COVID-19 pandemic, and regulatory changes that increased transparency and security for investors on these platforms.

The fintech industry in Latin America is growing rapidly, and according to Herrera's (2022) study, the following segments are leading the way: payments and remittances at 25%, loans at 18%, business technologies for financial institutions at 15%, and business finance management at 11%. Artificial intelligence (AI) has played a crucial role in achieving significant progress in the financial markets. Machine learning and deep learning are applied in finance to evaluate credit risk, detect fraud, and manage risks with ongoing customers through customer segmentation algorithms. Arne *et al.* (2016) emphasize the importance of AI in financial inclusion and democratization globally. They also highlight the challenges that fintech's latest evolution, led by emerging companies, poses for regulators and market participants in balancing the potential benefits of innovation with the potential risks of new approaches. They argue against early or rigid regulation of fintech at this time, based on their analysis of its evolution over the last 150 years.

According to Almaghrabi *et al.* (2024), financial institutions have realized the importance of combining human expertise with artificial intelligence to create highly effective decision support systems. In the lending industry, it is becoming more common to connect data with AI algorithms and eliminate the need for human underwriters through automation. This approach is proving to be highly beneficial, providing superior results and immediate returns on investment for stakeholders in the lending business.

Fintech companies are increasingly using artificial intelligence to provide efficient and profitable financial services (Barragán, 2018). The loans and financial services industry has undergone significant changes in recent years due to technological interventions, resulting in lower costs for clients. Artificial intelligence relies on machine learning and deep learning algorithms to analyze large volumes of data and identify behavioral patterns. It uses various techniques such as logistic regression, neural networks, and decision trees to classify, choose, and perform regression tasks to predict future behavior (Maher, 2020). Additionally, it can analyze various types of data, including text, images, audio and video, to identify patterns and generate predictions. With machine learning and deep learning technology, the following functions can be performed to enhance financial services:

- Big data and its data analytics
- Internet of things and its data analytics
- Speech recognition
- Recognition of behavioral patterns
- Ability to integrate with social networks, email, and third-party applications

Fintech companies are relying more on artificial intelligence and machine learning algorithms to create efficient and effective systems. Various studies have documented the use of machine learning and deep learning for data mining processes. Machine learning algorithms are employed to evaluate potential loan clients and assess credit risk. Unsupervised models, such as customer and market segmentation, are used for segmentation purposes, while supervised models are applied for credit risk assessment and fraud detection, utilizing techniques including neural networks, decision trees, support vector machines, K-nearest neighbors, logistic regression, random forests, and Naive Bayes. In the following, we provide some examples of how these algorithms are applied.

2. Fundamentals of Data Analytics in Machine Learning

2.1. *Data analytics and Big Data*

Big data refer to extremely large amounts of data that require terabytes of storage. Advances in communication and computing technologies have made it possible to capture, process, store, and manage such data. Analytical tools are then applied to these large datasets to generate useful information for management. This transition from relational databases to non-relational solutions, such as NoSQL, enables faster capture of unstructured data. By analyzing the captured information, businesses can enhance their operational efficiency, detect patterns, execute targeted marketing campaigns, and improve overall customer satisfaction.

Financial companies are adopting big data analysis in their operations. They use real-time analysis of customer transactions to detect fraud and identify abnormal behavior. By analyzing customer records, spending habits, and social media activities, companies can offer personalized products and services. Big data tools enable risk and credit analysis by consolidating data from multiple sources. Table 1 lists the most common data sources and relevant Python libraries.

Table 1. Data sources and associated Python libraries.

Web Data Sources	Python Library	For
Social networks	Tweepy (Twitter), facebook-sdk, api-rest	Extract data from social networks
Data on webpage	BeautifulSoup, Selenium	Extract data from webpage
Available Datasets	Requests, CSV, Openpyxl, Tika	Extract data from dataset repositories
	TensorFlow	High-performance numerical calculations
	SciPy	High-level calculations
	Pandas	Manage and explore data
	Numpy	Processing large multidimensional matrices and arrays
	Matplotlib	Generate figures
	Scikit-learn	Clustering, classification, and regression
	Keras	Deep learning and neural networks
	Scrapy	Extract data from webpage
	PyTorch	Distribution and statistical operations
	Hermosa Sopa	Web crawling and data scraping

Source: McFarland (2024).

Fintech, with the adoption of emerging technologies such as artificial intelligence, has access to large volumes of data in various forms, known as big data, which improve the ability of financial institutions to understand the needs and financial behaviors of excluded people. By using non-traditional data, such as mobile phone records or social media activity, institutions can assess creditworthiness and eligibility for financial services. In addition, data analysis also helps to identify areas where financial inclusion needs to be improved and to develop more effective strategies through market and customer segmentation. These emerging technologies have the potential to drive financial inclusion by providing innovative and scalable solutions to address traditional barriers to accessing financial services. However, it is important to ensure that security, privacy, and ethical concerns are addressed, as well as considering the digital divide and ensuring that the benefits of these technologies reach all people, especially marginalized and disadvantaged groups.

Figure 1 depicts the Scrapy application, which enables access to a webpage for the extraction of data that fintech companies require. This process is commonly referred to as web scraping. Web scraping is the utilization of techniques that automatically extract data from a webpage. To extract data accurately, it is essential to know the structure of the webpage, which is typically composed of HTML code, images, scripts, and style files.

In Fig. 2, we can observe the code frame that reads the coding of the webpage. Fintech companies can also access data through other techniques, such as capturing files organized in datasets in Excel formats with a CSV extension or in text formats. With the help of computer technology, these files can be converted into useful data for fintech companies.

```
In [57]: import requests

         URL = "https://realpython.github.io/fake-jobs/"
         page = requests.get(URL)

         print(page.text)
```

Fig. 1. Python code to retrieve and display webpage content using the requests library.

```
<!DOCTYPE html>
<html>
  <head>
    <meta charset="utf-8">
    <meta name="viewport" content="width=device-width, initial-scale=1">
    <title>Fake Python</title>
    <link rel="stylesheet" href="https://cdn.jsdelivr.net/npm/bulma@0.9.2/css/bulma.min.css">
  </head>
  <body>
  <section class="section">
    <div class="container mb-5">
      <h1 class="title is-1">
        Fake Python
      </h1>
      <p class="subtitle is-3">
        Fake Jobs for Your Web Scraping Journey
      </p>
    </div>
    <div class="container">
```

Fig. 2. HTML code of the web page accessed by web scraping.

```
In [50]:
        import numpy as np
        import pandas as pd
        import scrapy
        df = pd.read_csv("https://archive.ics.uci.edu/ml/" "machine-learning-database/wine/wine.data", header=None)
        df.head(50)
```

Fig. 3. Python format to access a webpage.

```
In [1]: import numpy as np
        import pandas as pd
        import seaborn as sns
        import matplotlib.pyplot as plt
        import warnings
        warnings.filterwarnings("ignore")
        df = pd.read_csv("D:/credit_risk_dataset.csv")
        df.head(100)
```

Fig. 4. Python format to access a dataset from an external file.
Note: Code for accessing an external file using Jupyter Notebook.

The code in Fig. 3 enables you to extract data from a webpage, which is organized in a dataset. Additionally, companies often maintain their own datasets with external add-ons, as shown in Fig. 4.

In [2]:
```
# NEW EXAMPLE OF CREDIT RISK
import numpy as np
import pandas as pd
import seaborn as sns
import matplotlib.pyplot as plt
import warnings
warnings.filterwarnings("ignore")
df = pd.read_csv("E:/DEFAULT_RISK.csv")
df.head()
```

Out[2]:

	Unnamed: 0	X1	X2	X3	X4	X5	X6	X7	X8	X9	...	X15	X16	X17	X18	X19	X20	X21	X22	X23	Y
0	1	20000	2	2	1	24	2	2	-1	-1	...	0	0	0	0	689	0	0	0	0	1
1	2	120000	2	2	2	26	-1	2	0	0	...	3272	3455	3261	0	1000	1000	1000	0	2000	1
2	3	90000	2	2	2	34	0	0	0	0	...	14331	14948	15549	1518	1500	1000	1000	1000	5000	0
3	4	50000	2	2	1	37	0	0	0	0	...	28314	28959	29547	2000	2019	1200	1100	1069	1000	0
4	5	50000	1	2	1	57	-1	0	-1	0	...	20940	19146	19131	2000	36681	10000	9000	689	679	0

5 rows × 25 columns

Fig. 5. Jupyter notebook code format for accessing an external dataset. *Note*: Jupyter Notebook Code.

2.2. *Data analytics*

Once the data are loaded, data analysis is carried out; in this case, the person who analyzes the processed data reports will be the specialist in the financial evaluation of potential loan clients, or specialists who intervene in the study of markets or potential customers. Figure 5 addresses the report of organized data, on which a series of reports are generated according to the needs of specialist users.

In Fig. 6, we can see the descriptive statistical distribution of various variables that describe a large group of people. These variables include age, income, number of children per family, and credit history. This statistical analysis is important because it enables us to explore the minimums, maximums, averages, and deviations of these variables from a larger universe. This information is useful for business management purposes, especially for fintech companies. From the data, we can generate many descriptive statistical indicators and establish various relationships. For instance, we can use a correlation matrix to observe the relationship between age and the amount of loan, occupation and the object of credit, gender and income level, and other such factors. We can also group people with similar characteristics by applying the K-means segmentation algorithm.

2.3. *Scoring application for granting credits*

The WSPC template contains a number of macros, written to help one prepare the document conforming to WSPC guidelines.

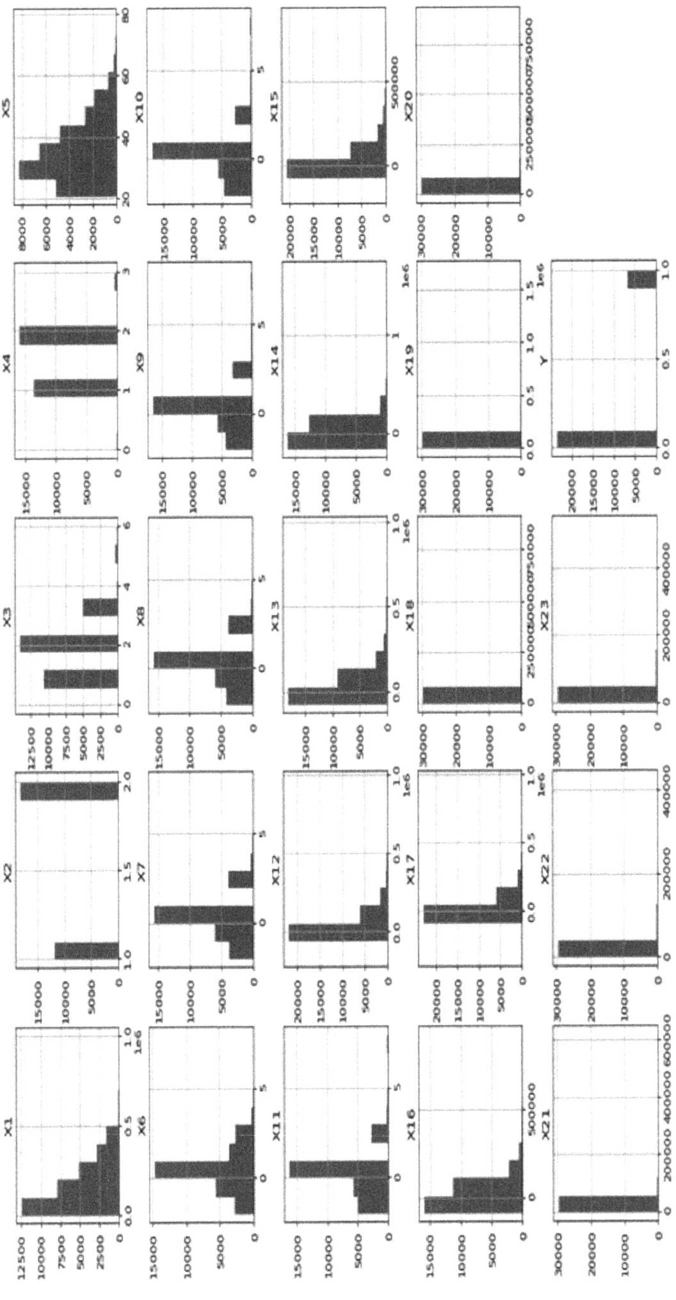

Fig. 6. Descriptive data analysis.

Note: Descriptive distribution of data variables with Jupyter Notebook.

The usage of these macros has been explained clearly in this document for the benefit of people using the MS Word WSPC template. Although all macros were thoroughly tested in different environments, there remains a possibility that the document could be modified in a way that causes a macro to consistently fail to function as intended. In this case, one can save and exit the document, open a new document (based on the WSPC template), and copy the saved content into this document before running the macro again.

The Altman model (1968), known as the Z-score, was created in 1960. It is a multiple regression model that, based on historical data from financial statements, allows one to forecast the risk of bankruptcy of a company:

$$\text{Z-score} = 1{,}2 * X_1 + 1{,}4 * X_2 + 3{,}3 * X_3 + 0{,}6 * X_4 + 1{,}0 * X_5,$$

where

X_1: (Working capital/Total Assets),
X_2: (Retained Earnings/Total Assets),
X_3: (EBITDA/Total Assets),
X_4: (Market capitalization/Total Liabilities),
X_5: (Sales/Total Assets).

The probability of bankruptcy of a company will depend on the result obtained in the Z-score, which must be subjected to evaluation according to the decision rule. Depending on the result, the company could be in the safe zone, gray zone, or the danger zone:

- Z-score > 2.99: safe zone; in principle, there is no need to worry.
- Z-score ≥ 1.81 and ≤ 2.99: gray area; it is likely that the company could go bankrupt in the next 2 years.
- Z-score < 1.81: danger zone; imminent bankruptcy of the company.

2.4. *Application of Machine Learning in measuring credit risk for fraud prevention*

The application of artificial intelligence is crucial in the credit application evaluation stage, known in the financial sector as credit risk measurement, which, thanks to machine learning, can be implemented using algorithms such as neural networks, decision trees,

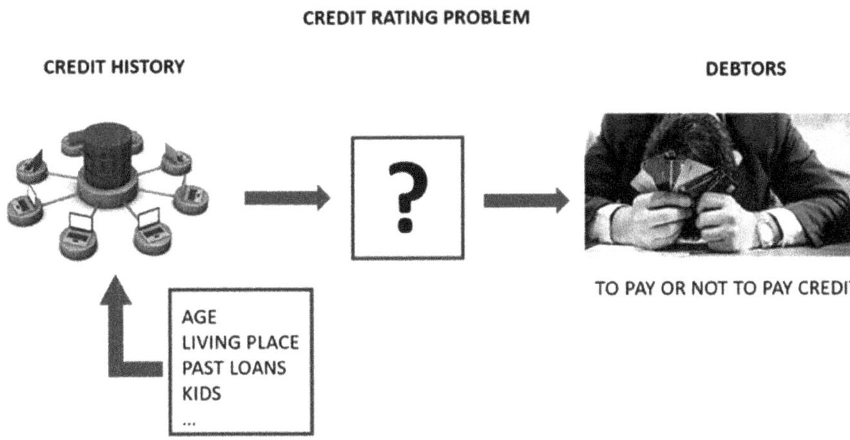

Fig. 7. Credit rating problem.

support vector machines, k-nearest neighbors, logistic regression, random forest, and Naïve Bayes.

According to Elizondo (2004), the measurement of credit risk involves applying quantitative techniques to determine the probability of default for potential clients seeking credit from a financial institution. It is also used to quantify the likelihood of non-compliance among existing clients within the institution's portfolio (Fig. 7).

Among the methodologies that have been applied with the objective of quantifying the probability of non-compliance, we can mention, in general terms, univariate and multivariate statistical techniques such as discriminant analysis, classification models, decision trees, quantitative selection models, and machine learning and deep learning, which are supported by quantitative models (Yan, 2017).

In the context of monitoring financial risks, including credit risk, it is necessary to take a brief look at the Basel agreements that have been implemented: The Basel I agreement was published in 1988 with the clear objective of establishing regulatory capital in the presence of credit risk and operational risk. The Basel II agreement was published in 2004. As established by Basel I, it added market risk to quantify the required regulatory capital. The Basel III agreement was published in 2010, and Basel IV was agreed upon in 2017 to be implemented starting in 2023. All of the cited agreements have been intended to estimate the regulatory capital that supervised entities are required to maintain for a given level of credit, operational, and market risk.

The most important factor in the model is the determination of the probability of non-compliance; in this regard, there are different methodologies to quantify this probability. If a financial institution has organized the financial information of each client and credit applicant — including factors such as the company's economic sector, sales levels, credit history, invested capital, and other indicators of financial health — it can more accurately and efficiently quantify the probability of default.

Credit rating is used to describe the process of evaluating the credit risk of the client applying to obtain credit. The goal is to classify customers into two groups: customers who pay on time and customers who are late in their payments for various reasons.

Credit rating is traditionally divided into two main types: The first is the rating that is made at the time the credit application is made, and is the moment at which the probability of default is determined, given historical information and other factors that are related to the economic activity of the credit applicant. The second type of credit rating is carried out after credit is granted, that is, during the monitoring and control time of the credit granted. The probability of default rating can be carried out for different periods, 1 month, 3 months, and even longer periods that go up to 6 months:

$$Z = \beta_0 + \beta_1 X_1 + \beta_2 X_2 + \cdots + \beta_n X_n,$$

where βo is the value of the intercept of the linear regression, β is the coefficient of the parameters that intervene in the model, and X denotes parametric and non-parametric factors that intervene in the model.

The logit model in Fig. 8 will be used to quantify the probability of default, which is a very important aspect in quantifying credit risk:

$$P_I = \frac{1}{1 + e^{-Z}},$$

where the P_I is the probability of default, $e = 2.71828$.

```
In [192]: # EDA FOR CREDIT RISK
          # Data Manipulation Libraries
          import numpy as np
          import pandas as pd
          # Data Visualization
          import matplotlib.pyplot as plt
          %matplotlib inline
          import seaborn as sns
          %config InlineBackend.figure_format = 'retina'
          sns.set_style("darkgrid")
```

Fig. 8. Selection model with the logistic regression algorithm as the output function of a neural network.
Note: Loading Python libraries.

Artificial neural networks are machine learning models inspired by the functioning of the human brain. They are made up of interconnected nodes that process information and transmit signals through weighted connections. Artificial neural networks are widely used in machine learning and artificial intelligence. They can learn from data, identify patterns, and make predictions. Artificial neural networks have a wide range of applications, including image recognition, natural language processing, machine translation, and medical diagnosis.

Artificial neural networks are trained through a process called "supervised learning". During training, they are given a set of input data along with the desired outputs, and the network adjusts its internal weights and biases to minimize the difference between the predicted outputs and the actual outputs. This is achieved through optimization algorithms, such as gradient descent, where network parameters are gradually adjusted to reduce prediction error.

The training process involves repeatedly iterating over the training dataset and may require adjustments to the network architecture, learning rate, and other hyperparameters to achieve optimal performance. Once the network has been successfully trained, it can be used to make predictions on new data.

Training neural networks can be a computationally and resource-intensive process, especially for deep networks or large datasets. However, with the advancement of technology and the development of more efficient training techniques, neural networks are being used successfully in a wide range of applications (Fig. 9). Artificial neural networks have several advantages and disadvantages:

The following are some of the advantages:

- Learning Ability: They can learn complex patterns from data.
- Adaptability: They are able to adapt to changes in the environment or input data.
- Wide Applicability: They can be applied to a wide range of problems, such as image recognition, natural language processing, and forecasting.
- Efficiency in Pattern Recognition: They are efficient in recognizing patterns in large datasets.

The following are some of the disadvantages:

- Require Large Datasets: They often need large amounts of data to train effectively.
- Difficulty Interpreting Results: The complexity of neural networks can make it difficult to understand how they reach certain conclusions.
- Training Time and Resources: Training neural networks can be computationally expensive in terms of time and resources.
- Risk of Overfitting: There is a risk that the neural network will overfit the training data and not be able to generalize well to new data.

The following mathematical expression is obtained using the activation function and the logistic function (Figs. 10 and 11):

$$Y_k = W_0 + W_{k1}X_1 + W_{k2}X_2 + \cdots + W_{km}X_m = \frac{1}{1 + e^{-(Y_k)}}.$$

2.5. *Investment predictions*

One of the main functions of management is planning, and plans require short-, medium-, and long-term policy forecasts. Meanwhile, fintech companies need to forecast many things, for example, market share forecasts, income projections, profit estimates, prospective macroeconomic variables such as the growth of economies,

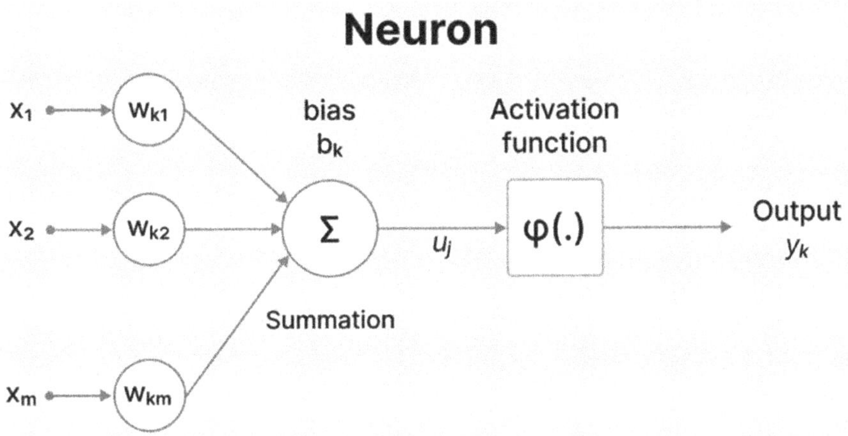

Fig. 9. Structure of a neural network.
Note: EYVN, https://evbn.org/the-essential-guide-to-neural-network-architectures-1677902860.

```
In [1]: ##LOGISTIC REGRESSION ###
        import matplotlib.pyplot as plt
        import numpy as np
        def sigmoid(YK):
            return 1.0/(1.0+np.exp(-YK))
        YK= np.arange(-7,7,0.1)
        phi_YK=sigmoid(YK)
        plt.plot(YK, phi_YK)
        plt.axvline(0.0, color="k")
        plt.ylim(-0.1,1.1)
        plt.xlabel("YK")
        plt.ylabel("$/phi (YK)$")
        # y
        plt.yticks([0.0,0.5,1.0])
        ax=plt.gca()
        ax.yaxis.grid(True)
        plt.show()
```

Fig. 10. The logistics function developed with Jupyter Notebook.
Note: Logistics function code with Jupyter Notebook.

inflation, the type of exchange rate, and the behavior of the demand for commodities in the markets. The managers who run fintech companies need to be aided by future estimates, which are provided by machine learning applications through the application of statistical and econometric algorithms such as linear regression,

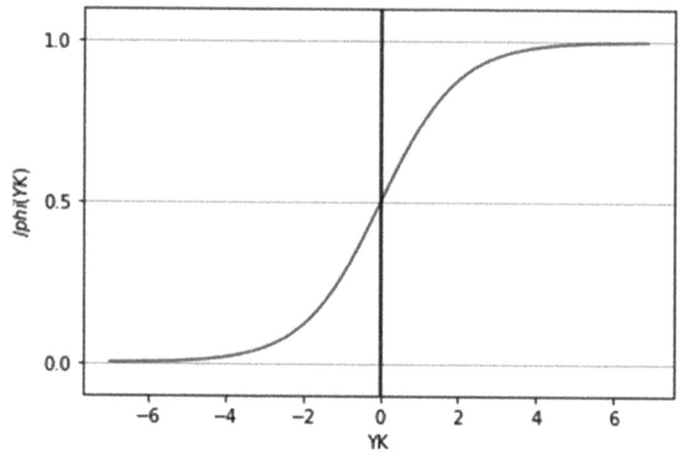

Fig. 11. Illustration of RN outbound logistics function.
Note: Activation function of the neural network with logistic regression.

decision trees, random forests, and investment portfolio structuring models are used, incorporating Markowitz models and Kahneman and Tversky's prospective theory of behavioral finance.

2.6. *In marketing*

In marketing, machine learning works by applying statistical and mathematical algorithms to specific needs such as customer segmentation. In finance, especially in fintech, as one reaches an immense number of potential clients via the Internet, it is required to group consumers by similar characteristics, which can be executed by applying selection algorithms, segmentation (clustering), and discriminant algorithms, among others. Capturing images of individual and group behaviors using deep learning technology and image processing with neural networks using classification algorithms.

2.7. *Customer service*

Natural language processing through the application of machine learning and deep learning in the implementation of customer service in resolving customer queries. AI improves the customer experience by anticipating their needs, generating value, and ensuring quick responses.

2.8. *Digital assistants*

Natural language processing with machine learning and deep learning can do the following:

- Advanced Personalization: Virtual assistants now offer personalized responses and services based on the user's history, preferences, and behavior.
- Improved Interoperability: The ability of these assistants to integrate and communicate with a wide range of devices and platforms has created an unprecedented connected ecosystem.
- Expanded Cognitive Capabilities: With the advancement of AI and machine learning, these assistants better understand the context and subtext of requests, allowing for more natural and human interactions.

3. Conclusions

Artificial Intelligence is redefining the business model of the financial industry, driving an unprecedented digital transformation in the sector. This technological revolution has led to the explosion of the fintech ecosystem, where financial technologies merge with artificial intelligence to offer innovative digital services, such as loans, payments, remittances, discount operations such as factoring, and business finance management.

In short, the combination of AI and fintech is transforming the financial sector, driving innovation and opening new possibilities for professionals and consumers alike. AI in fintech is a driving force in today's financial evolution. From improved credit assessment to fraud detection and service personalization, AI is driving innovation and improving efficiency in the financial sector. The combination of AI and fintech is transforming the sector and opening up new possibilities for professionals and consumers alike.

In summary, the application of artificial intelligence through machine learning and deep learning is used to identify emerging risks, evaluate risks more quickly, mitigate risks, monitor in real time, forecast the future occurrence of possible risks, prevent fraud, forecast investment, implement cybersecurity, market a fintech company's businesses, and provide customer service and digital assistance to clients.

References

Almaghrani, F., Yang, J., and Xu, D. (2024). Human-AI collaboration to mitigate decision noise in financial underwriting: A study on FinTech innovation in a lending firm. *International Review of Financial Analysis*. https://doi.org/10.1016/j.irfa.2024.103149.

Altman, E. (1968). Z-scoring model. Leonard N. Stern School of Business Kaufman Management Center 44 West Fourth Street, 9-61 New York, NY 10012.

Arner, D., Barberis, J., and Buckley, R. (2016). The evolution of Fintech: A new post-crisis paradigm? University of Hong Kong Faculty of Law Research Paper No. 2015/047, UNSW Law Research Paper No. 2016-62. Available at SSRN: https://ssrn.com/abstract=2676553.

Elizondo, A. (2004). *Medición integral del riesgo de crédito*. México DF. Limusa SA.

FDI (2020). China. https://www.fdichina.com/es/contact/.

Herrera, D. (2022). Estudio: Industria Fintech dobla su tamaño en América Latina y Caribe en tres años. https://www.iadb.org/es/noticias/estudio-industria-fintech-dobla-su-tamano-en-america-latina-y-caribe-en-tres-anos.

McFarland, A. (2024). Las 10 mejores bibliotecas de Python para la ciencia de datos. https://www.unite.ai/es/Las-10-mejores-bibliotecas-de-Python-para-la-ciencia-de-datos/.

Mills, K. (2018). *Fintech, Small Business & the American Dream*. Harvard Business School. Harvard University. Boston. USA. https://dpi.org/10.1007/978-3-030-03620-1.

Rubini, A. (2017). *Fintech in a Flash: Financial Technology Made Easy*. London, United Kingdom. www.fintechflash.com.

Yan, Y. (2017). *Python for Finance*. Packt Publishing Ltd. Mumbai.

https://doi.org/10.1142/9789819823161_0017

Chapter 17

Threshold Effects of Finance–Growth Nexus: A Case Study of Nigeria

Apanisile Olumuyiwa Tolulope* **and Adesina Kehinde Elizabeth**†

Department of Economics, Obafemi Awolowo University, Ile-Ife, Nigeria

**mapanisile@oauife.edu.ng*

†*kehindeelizabeth90@gmail.com*

The study provides new evidence on the nexus between financial development and economic growth in Nigeria between 1986 and 2023. The study estimates the generalized methods of moments and the existence thresholds in the nexus between financial development and economic growth. Specifically, the study used four variables as measures of financial development and also constructed a financial development index. The findings suggest that financial development promotes economic growth. Threshold regression results show that broad money promotes growth only when the threshold value is between 2.546 and 3.061. Likewise, trade openness in the estimation of threshold regression is negatively associated with economic growth across all regimes. The study concludes that financial development relatively promotes economic growth in Nigeria.

Keywords: Broad money, economic growth, financial development index, Nigeria, threshold regression.

1. Introduction

The financial system is essential for economic development and economic growth. Financial development entails the interaction of different financial institutions in providing financial services. Financial development is multidimensional, and the relationship between financial sector development and economic growth (the finance–growth nexus) has been extensively studied in the literature because of the theoretical assumption that a sound financial sector promotes economic growth and development primarily through capital formation, factor productivity growth, and savings and investment (Yilmazkuday, 2011). This assumption has motivated several empirical papers on the relationship between financial development and economic growth, both in time series studies and panel studies. Also, a strong financial system has been emphasized to improve investment, promote entrepreneurial activities, and promote economic growth through easy access to financial services (Younsi and Bechtini, 2018).

However, these studies have reported mixed results. Some studies found a positive relationship between them and concluded that financial development promotes growth (Okafor *et al.*, 2021), while some others found a negative relationship between them and concluded that financial development does not contribute to growth (Demetriades and Rewilak, 2020). Further studies examining the finance–growth nexus in developed and developing countries integrated the role of institutions. However, most of these studies concluded that institutional quality is a major contributor to achieving a positive relationship between financial development and economic growth. The global financial crisis also spurred scholars to revisit debates on the complexities involving the relationships between finance and growth such that, for economic development, the finance–growth nexus shifts from negative to positive, and vice versa.

Recent studies observed that a higher level of financial depth in some countries is associated with slower growth. This has raised an important policy question of whether excessive finance could retard growth or if financial development only promotes growth up to a certain threshold. Some empirical findings have shown that excessive finance does indeed retard economic growth, but most of these findings were applied to developed and industrialized countries because of the assumption that these countries have a more developed financial sector (Swamy and Dharani, 2020; Breitenlechner *et al.*, 2015). Policy efforts have been made in Nigeria toward financial liberalization, attraction of foreign direct investment, restructuring of the capital market, consolidation and recapitalization of banks, and development strategies aimed at national economic empowerment, among other goals, by the fiscal and monetary authorities to improve economic growth. However, the economy has not yet achieved macroeconomic and financial stability. Understanding the finance–growth nexus can help policymakers prioritize policies that promote the development of financial and real sectors. Therefore, given the importance of the financial sector to the economy, this study will examine the threshold effects of the finance–growth nexus in Nigeria. The study contributes to the literature by providing current insights into the relationship between financial development and economic growth in Nigeria. The study also expands the frontiers of knowledge by using comprehensive data on the Nigerian economy. The results are robust because the study first separately analyzes the effects of the different measures of financial development on economic growth and then jointly analyzes these measures using the principal component analysis (PCA) method. The choice of Nigeria is influenced by the fact that the country's financial system is not fully developed and therefore not efficient enough in providing financial services. Although the Nigerian financial system has been making some progress, the sector continues to be plagued by a series of challenges. One of the challenges is the low level of credit channeled to the private sector and the increase in the debt profile of the nation.

2. Literature Review

Theoretically, there are conflicting views on the relationship between financial development and economic growth. The initial thinking was a supply-leading hypothesis, which suggests that finance drives economic growth and that an increase in financial development will spur economic growth (Ahmad and Wahid, 2010; Dermirguc-Kunt and Levine, 1996; McKinnon, 1973; Shaw, 1973; Schumpeter, 1911). Proponents of this hypothesis also maintained that an increase in total savings as a result of high interest rates increases investment and promotes economic growth as well. Later on, this view was challenged by the studies of Stiglitz (1994), Gurley and Shaw (1967), and Robinson (1952). These studies argued that it is the increase in economic growth that promotes financial development, such that the relationship between financial development and economic growth is demand-following and not supply-leading. This also implies that as production levels increase, demand for financial intermediation also increases. However, further studies have suggested a feedback hypothesis and a neutral hypothesis. The feedback hypothesis combines the supply-leading and demand-following hypotheses. This implies that the supply-leading hypothesis is applicable at the early stage of economic development, but at the later stage of economic development, the demand-following hypothesis becomes applicable (Patrick, 1966). The neutral hypothesis suggests that neither the demand-following nor the supply-leading hypothesis holds true, such that finance and economic growth do not cause each other (Boulila and Trabeisi, 2004; Shan and Morris, 2002).

This empirical debate has yielded mixed results in the literature. The study by Hamdi *et al.* (2017) considered institutional quality as a factor in the relationship between economic growth and financial sector development between 2006 and 2013 in 143 countries using structural generalized methods of moment. They found that the development of the financial sector in developed countries is a result of strong institutions, but the reverse is true in developing countries due to weak institutions. In the study by Swamy and Dharani (2020), financial development was found to promote economic growth primarily through factor productivity growth, savings and investment, and capital formation. Swamy and Dharani (2020), using a standard neoclassical growth model, analyzed the finance–growth relationship in G-7 economies between 1983 and 2013. The essence of this study was to investigate the extent to which an economy can be affected by "too much" finance. The study shows that in G-7 economies, when major financial development variables go beyond 100% of GDP, too much finance unfavorably affects economic growth. A similar study on the nexus between finance and economic growth was carried out by Breitenlechner *et al.* (2015), considering two periods: crisis and non-crisis periods. They found that during a non-crisis period, financial development promotes economic growth; conversely, when financial intermediation extends beyond a certain threshold during a crisis period, marginal benefits are reduced and substantial costs are incurred.

Moreover, the study by Aluko *et al.* (2019) in sub-Saharan Africa between 1990 and 2015 contradicted the assertion made by Lucas (1988) and found a long-term relationship between finance and the real sector as well as between finance and economic growth. Studies suggesting that finance harms growth once a certain threshold is attained motivated the work by Demetriades and Rewilak (2020). The study, in an attempt to show the possibility of recovering the finance–growth nexus, examined 102 countries between 1998 and 2017. The study measured financial fragility in two ways: private credit to GDP and quality-adjusted financial development measures. It was shown that with private credit to GDP as a measure of financial fragility, there is a negative relationship between finance and economic growth. However, with quality-adjusted measures of financial development, a positive relationship exists between finance and economic growth. The study concluded that to promote growth in sub-Saharan Africa, sound lending practices should be embraced by banks and efforts should be made to reduce non-performing loans to a minimum. Financial development and economic growth can reduce income inequality. This was investigated across BRICS countries between 1990 and 2015 to examine the existence of Kuznets' inverted U-shaped curve (Younsi and Bechtini, 2018). The findings of the study provide strong evidence that Kuznets' inverted U-shaped curve exists for the relationship between financial development and income inequality and between economic growth and income inequality. The study by Ioannou and Wojcik (2020) in metropolitan areas across 75 countries also supports the evidence of an inverted U-shaped pattern; it further claims that finance becomes a drag on economic growth when a certain threshold is attained. The study by Okafor *et al.* (2021) used the error correction model and Johannsen techniques to examine the effects of financial deepening on economic growth in Nigeria between 1986 and 2016 during the post-structural adjustment program (SAP) era. The study showed that bank-based financial depth significantly and positively influences economic growth.

Following the contributions to the discussion on the relationship between financial development and economic growth in Nigeria, Olushola and Uzoma (2018) suggested that financial development, as measured by stock market capitalization and deposit money banking, significantly promotes economic growth in Nigeria. Akintola *et al.* (2020) also found that financial development, in terms of the all-share index and banking system liquidity, significantly and positively influences economic growth in Nigeria and recommended that to improve the level of economic growth in Nigeria, capital market and money market growth should be prioritized.

3. Data and Methodology

This study uses time series secondary data covering the period 1987–2023. The measures most commonly used as proxies for financial development in the empirical literature are monetary aggregates, but these measures do not reflect how funds are channeled to investors from depositors (Khan and Senhadji, 2003). The current study therefore considers the following as measures of financial development: broad money as a percentage of GDP (BRM); domestic credit to the private sector by banks as a percentage of GDP (DCB); domestic credit to the private sector as a percentage of GDP (DCP); and market capitalization of listed domestic companies as a percentage of GDP (MKC) (Swamy and Dharani, 2020). These measures are comprehensive and appropriate because they account for the allocation and utilization of funds for productive uses. In our models and estimation, these measures are first used independently and thereafter used to construct a financial development index (FDV) through PCA, a statistical technique used to construct intercorrelations among quantitative variables (Younsi and Bechtini, 2018). Also, our dependent variable, GDP per capita (GDP), measures economic growth, while the control variables included in the study are trade openness (TOP), inflation (INF), and foreign direct investment (FDI). The control variables are important in our model because of their contributions to the level of growth (Hamdi *et al.*, 2017). All the data were sourced from the World Development Indicator (WDI) index, except for the trade openness data, which were sourced from the Central Bank of Nigeria (CBN) Statistical Bulletin. Trade openness is the ratio of the sum of exports and imports to GDP.

The theoretical framework for this study is based on the endogenous growth model. This model describes economic growth as largely determined by finance through financial intermediation (King and Levine, 1993; Pagano, 1993; Robinson, 1952; Schumpeter, 1911). Although Lucas (1988) argued against this claim, stating that economic growth is not significantly determined by finance, we consider the output function

$$Y_t = BC_t \tag{1}$$

where Y_t is the total output in period t, B denotes total productivity, and C_t denotes capital in period t. C_t includes physical capital, human capital, and other financial resources. The study further includes important variables contributing to growth in equation (1), as mentioned earlier. The study uses two techniques of analysis: the generalized method of moments (GMM) and threshold regression. One of the benefits of the GMM approach is that it helps to resolve possible endogeneity problems in the model, as specified in equations (2a) and (2b):

$$\begin{aligned} GDP_t = {} & \alpha_1 GDP_{t-1} + \alpha_2 BRM_t + \alpha_3 DCB_t + \alpha_4 DCP_t \\ & + \alpha_5 MKC_t + \alpha_6 INF_t + \alpha_7 TOP_t + \alpha_8 FDI_t + \theta X_t + \varepsilon_t \end{aligned} \tag{2a}$$

$$\begin{aligned} GDP_t = {} & \alpha_1 GDP_{t-1} + \alpha_2 FDV_t + \alpha_3 INF_t + \alpha_4 TOP_t \\ & + \alpha_5 FDI_t + \theta X_t + \varepsilon_t \end{aligned} \tag{2b}$$

where θ denotes the coefficient of the control variables, X_t captures the control variables, and ε_t denotes the error term.

The threshold regression technique is used to establish the critical point at which financial development causes a positive or negative change in economic growth. The study considered a single threshold model, according to the specifications given by Hansen (1999) and Wang and Wang (2021). This is shown in equations (3a)–(3d) and (4), where GDP_t is the dependent variable; α_t is the unpredictable factor; $\emptyset_1^{|}$, $\emptyset_2^{|}$, $\beta_1^{|}$, and $\beta_2^{|}$ are the corresponding coefficients; TOP_t is the regressor; I is the indicator function; BRM_t, DCB_t, DCP_t, MKC_t, and FDV_t are the threshold variables; and γ is the specific threshold value:

$$GDP_t = \alpha_t + \emptyset_1^{|} TOP_t I(BRM_t \leq \gamma) + \emptyset_2^{|} TOP_t I(BRM_t > \gamma) + \beta^{|}{}_1 INF_t + \beta_2^{|} FDI_t + Z_t \tag{3a}$$

$$GDP_t = \alpha_t + \emptyset_1^{|} TOP_t I(DCB_t \leq \gamma) + \emptyset_2^{|} TOP_t I(DCB_t > \gamma) + \beta^{|}{}_1 INF_t + \beta_2^{|} FDI_t + Z_t \tag{3b}$$

$$GDP_t = \alpha_t + \emptyset_1 TOP_t I(DCP_t \leq \gamma) + \emptyset_2^{|} TOP_t I(DCP_t > \gamma) + \beta^{|}{}_1 INF_t + \beta_2^{|} FDI_t + Z_t \tag{3c}$$

$$GDP_t = \alpha_t + \emptyset_1^{|} TOP_t I(MKC_t \leq \gamma) + \emptyset_2^{|} TOP_t I(MKC_t > \gamma) + \beta^{|}{}_1 INF_t + \beta_2^{|} FDI_t + Z_t \tag{3d}$$

$$GDP_t = \alpha_t + \emptyset_1^{|} TOP_t I(FDV_t \leq \gamma) + \emptyset_2^{|} TOP_t I(FDV_t > \gamma) + \beta^{|}{}_1 INF_t + \beta_2^{|} FDI_t + Z_t \tag{4}$$

According to *a priori* expectations, financial development is anticipated to have a positive relationship with economic growth, but the effect of inflation on economic growth is found to be negative in the literature beyond a certain threshold. Trade openness can have either positive or negative effects on economic growth. It promotes growth by providing access to technologies, high-income markets, and competition, among others, while it retards growth when it makes the economy more vulnerable to external shocks.

4. Results and Discussion

The section presents the results of the analytical techniques employed to achieve the objectives of the study. In addition, the results obtained are discussed in relation to the set objectives and their implications. The pre-tests and the post-tests estimations are carried out.

4.1. *Descriptive statistics of the variables*

Table 1 presents the descriptive statistics computed to explain the sample statistics and the distribution of the considered variables.

Table 1. Descriptive statistics.

	LGDP	LBRM	LDCB	LDCP	LMKC	FDV	TOP	LINF	FDI
Mean	7.556	2.810	2.240	2.243	2.057	0.000	0.020	2.698	1.329
Median	7.558	2.737	2.160	2.161	2.004	−0.533	0.019	2.560	1.178
Maximum	7.893	3.310	2.976	2.977	3.516	3.039	0.032	4.288	4.282
Minimum	7.255	2.204	1.599	1.601	0.915	−2.967	0.014	1.684	−0.040
Std. Dev.	0.242	0.362	0.358	0.348	0.652	1.857	0.004	0.680	0.954
Skewness	0.043	−0.011	0.123	0.064	0.345	0.092	0.775	0.899	0.799
Kurtosis	1.285	1.408	2.361	2.295	2.291	1.614	3.096	3.020	3.605
Jarque–Bera	4.668	4.015	0.743	0.813	1.548	3.096	3.820	5.121	4.627
Probability	0.097	0.134	0.690	0.666	0.461	0.213	0.148	0.077	0.099
Observations	38	38	38	38	38	38	38	38	38

Table 2. Correlation matrix.

Variables	LGDP	FDV	TOP	LINF	FDI
LGDP	1.000				
FDV	0.882	1.000			
	(11.210)				
TOP	−0.756	−0.673	1.000		
	(−6.936)	(−5.464)			
LINF	−0.300	−0.304	0.142	1.000	
	(−1.884)	(−1.918)	(0.863)		
FDI	−0.153	−0.089	0.150	0.180	1.000
	(−0.931)	(−0.536)	(0.909)	(1.100)	

Note: Numbers in () indicate the t-statistic.

The table shows that there is a level of consistency among the variables, as indicated by the closeness of the mean and median values, which lie within the minimum and maximum values. All variables are positively skewed except broad money (BRM), which is negatively skewed. The skewness values are relatively low, which indicates that the variables are fairly symmetric. Moreover, the kurtosis values of GDP, BRM, DCB, DCP, MKC, and FDV are less than three, which shows that the series is platykurtic, and so their distribution has a lower peak compared to the normal distribution. The kurtosis values of TOP, INF, and FDI are greater than three, which indicates that the series is leptokurtic, and hence their distribution has a higher peak relative to the normal distribution. The Jarque–Bera statistics also show that all the series are normally distributed except GDP and INF.

4.2. *Correlation matrix*

Table 2 shows the correlation matrix. This is essential because it enables us to verify that there is no correlation among our independent variables. It also enables us to determine the degree of association among our variables. The correlation results show that there is no multicollinearity problem, as none of the independent variables are strongly correlated.

4.3. *Unit root test*

It is also essential to check the stationarity of our variables by conducting unit root tests because the study used time series data. The results of the tests are shown in Table 3. Augmented

Table 3. Unit root test.

	ADF Test			PP Test		
Variable	**Level**	**1st Difference**	**Order**	**Level**	**1st Difference**	**Order**
BRM	−1.578 (0.483)	−4.424*** (0.001)	I(1)	−0.801 (0.807)	−4.996*** (0.000)	I(1)
DCB	−1.478 (0.533)	−5.135*** (0.000)	I(1)	−0.832 (0.797)	−7.888*** (0.000)	I(1)
DCP	−1.832 (0.359)	−5.788*** (0.000)	I(1)	−1.298 (0.620)	−9.373*** (0.000)	I(1)
MKC	−1.548 (0.498)	−6.589*** (0.000)	I(1)	−1.511 (0.516)	−6.630*** (0.000)	I(1)
FDV	−0.898 (0.777)	−5.543 (0.000)	I(1)	−0.495 (0.880)	−9.530 (0.000)	I(1)
INF	−3.974*** (0.000)	———	I(0)	−3.421** (0.016)	———	I(0)
TOP	−1.971 (0.297)	−5.859*** (0.000)	I(1)	−1.859 (0.347)	−5.862*** (0.000)	I(1)
FDI	−3.841*** (0.005)	———	I(0)	−3.925*** (0.004)	———	I(0)

Table 4. Cointegration test.

Model	F-Stat	No of Reg	
$LGDP = f(FDV, LINF, TOP, FDI)$	5.08	4	
Significance	**I(0) Bound**	**I(1) Bound**	**Decision**
5%	1.99	2.94	There is cointegration
1%	2.27	3.28	

Table 5. GMM results.

$$GDP_t = \alpha_1 GDP_{t-1} + \alpha_2 BRM_t + \alpha_3 DCB_t + \alpha_4 DCP_t \alpha_5 MKC_t + \alpha_6 INF_t + \alpha_7 TOP_t + \alpha_8 FDI_t + \theta X_t + \varepsilon_t \quad (2a)$$
$$GDP_t = \alpha_1 GDP_{t-1} + \alpha_2 FDV_t + \alpha_3 INF_t + \alpha_4 TOP_t + \alpha_5 FDI_t + \theta X_t + \varepsilon_t \quad (2b)$$

	Equation (2a)		Equation (2b)	
Variables	**Coefficient**	**Standard Error**	**Coefficient**	**Standard Error**
LGDP (−1)	1.016***	0.003	0.994***	0.003
LBRM	−0.074***	0.011	———	———
LDCB	0.015	0.011	———	———
LDCP	0.052***	0.014	———	———
LMKC	−0.003	0.004	———	———
FDV	———	———	0.006***	0.002
LINF	−0.018***	0.001	−0.017***	0.004
TOP	−0.519	0.362	4.183***	1.068
FDI	0.011***	0.001	0.015***	0.003
R-Squared	0.986		0.980	
Adjusted R-Squared	0.982		0.977	
Instrument Rank	33		16	
J-Statistics (Prob)	0.999		0.868	

Note: ***,**, and *denote 1%, 5%, and 10% levels of significance, respectively.

Dickey–Fuller (ADF) and Phillips–Perron (PP) tests, with trend-only specification, were used in generating the results. The result shows that all our variables are stationary at first difference except inflation (INF) and foreign direct investment (FDI).

Table 6. Threshold level of broad money (BRM) on economic growth (GDP).

Dependent Variable: LGDP **Threshold Variable: LBRM**			
Variable	**Regime 1** ***LBRM*** **< 2.546**	**Regime 2** **2.546** $\leq$ ***LBRM*** **< 3.061**	**Regime 3** ***LBRM*** $\geq$ **3.061**
C	6.971***	7.081***	9.679***
	(0.490)	(0.442)	(0.815)
LBRM	0.431**	0.305**	−0.439*
	(0.198)	(0.159)	(0.250)
Observation	12	10	16
Non-Threshold Variables			
FDI		0.025**	
		(0.011)	
LINF		−0.032**	
LINF		(0.015)	
LINF		−0.032**	
LINF		(0.015)	
TOP		−24.070***	
TOP		(3.330)	
R-Squared		0.954	
Adjusted *R*-Squared		0.941	
F-Statistics (Prob)		75.585(0.000)	
Durbin–Watson		1.593	

Note: Numbers in () indicate the standard error. ***,**, and *denote 1%, 5%, and 10% levels of significance, respectively.

4.4. *Cointegration test*

The study further examined the existence of cointegration among the variables using the Pesaran *et al.* (2001) approach. The results in Table 4 show the existence of cointegration, and hence a long-run relationship exists among the considered variables.

4.5. *Generalized method of moments*

Our GMM estimates are based on equations (2a) and (2b), as presented in Table 5. The results from equation (2a) show that LBRM,

Table 7. The threshold level of domestic credit to the private sector by bank (DCB) on economic growth (GDP).

Dependent Variable: LGDP
Threshold Variable: LDCB

Variables	**Regime 1** $LDCB < 2.320$	**Regime 2** $LCDB \geq 2.320$
C	7.585***	8.382***
	(0.255)	(0.270)
LDCB	0.057	−0.124
	(0.096)	(0.104)
Observation	21	17
Non-Threshold Variables		
FDI	0.014	
FDI	(0.014)	
LINF	−0.016	
	(0.020)	
TOP	−13.975***	
	(4.044)	
R-Squared	0.912	
Adjusted R-Squared	0.895	
F-Statistics (Prob)	53.628(0.000)	
Durbin–Watson	1.039	

Note: Numbers in () indicate the standard error. ***,**, and *denote 1%, 5%, and 10% levels of significance, respectively.

LMKC, and INF are significant and negatively correlated with GDP. This implies that a percentage change in LBRM, LMKC, and INF will reduce GDP by 0.074, 0.003, and 0.018, respectively. The effects of LBRM and LMKC on GDP are contrary to *a priori* expectations because an increase in the money supply and market capitalization is meant to promote financial intermediation and increase GDP. This supports the findings of Olushola and Uzoma (2018) and Swamy and Dharani (2020) that financial development hinders GDP growth and is harmful to the economy when it exceeds a certain threshold. The effects of INF on GDP support the *a priori* expectations because a high inflation rate reduces purchasing power, discourages investment, and in turn hinders economic growth.

The findings also show that LDCP and FDI are significant and positively related to economic growth and that a percentage change

Table 8. The threshold level of domestic credit to the private sector (DCP) on economic growth (GDP).

Dependent Variable: LGDP
Threshold Variable: LDCP

Variables	Regime 1 $LDCP < 2.326$	Regime 2 $LCDP \geq 2.326$
C	7.580***	8.503***
	(0.260)	(0.306)
LDCP	0.055	−0.173
	(0.098)	(0.120)
Observation	21	17
Non-Threshold Variables		
FDI	0.017	
	(0.014)	
LINF	−0.017	
	(0.020)	
TOP	−13.697***	
	(4.040)	
R-Squared	0.913	
Adjusted R-Squared	0.897	
F-Statistics (Prob)	54.770(0.000)	
Durbin–Watson	1.085	

Note: Numbers in () indicate the standard error. ***,**, and *denote 1%, 5%, and 10% levels of significance, respectively.

in LDCP and FDI increases economic growth by 0.052 and 0.011, respectively. FDI and domestic credit to the private sector are therefore said to promote economic growth in Nigeria. Comparing the results from equation (2b) with those from equation (2a), we find that when the measures of financial development used individually in equation (2a) were put together as an index, as done in (2b), financial development promotes economic growth such that FDV becomes significant and positively correlated with economic growth. Therefore, a percentage change in FDV will increase economic growth by 0.006%, which supports *a priori* expectations. This supports the study (Demetriades and Rewilak, 2020) that financial development improves economic growth when banks avoid the buildup of non-performing loans and use sound lending practices. Similar to the

Table 9. Threshold level of market capitalization (MKC) on economic growth (GDP).

Dependent Variable: LGDP **Threshold Variable: LMKC**		
Variables	**Regime 1** $LMKC < 1.996$	**Regime 2** $LMKC \geq 1.996$
C	7.697*** (0.150)	8.189*** (0.145)
LMKC	−0.039 (0.077)	−0.069 (0.042)
Observation	18	20
	Non-Threshold Variables	
FDI	−0.018 (0.014)	
LINF	−0.004 (0.019)	
TOP	−12.124*** (3.958)	
R-Squared	0.917	
Adjusted R-Squared	0.901	
F-Statistics (Prob)	57.242(0.000)	
Durbin–Watson	1.048	

Note: Numbers in () indicate the standard error. ***,**, and *denote 1%, 5%, and 10% levels of significance, respectively.

results from (2a), FDI improves GDP, while inflation hinders GDP in (2b). This supports the study (Yilmazkuday, 2011) that when inflation is high, it crowds out the positive effects of financial development on economic growth.

4.6. *Threshold regression*

The threshold regression results in Table 6 depict three regimes and two threshold values (2.546 and 3.061). In regimes 1 and 2, the effect of LBRM on GDP is positive and significant; however, in regime 3, LBRM exhibits a negative and significant relationship with GDP. This implies that in regime 1, when the value of LBRM is less than 2.546, LBRM promotes GDP by 0.431. Likewise in regime 2, when the value of LBRM is between 2.546 and 3.061, LBRM promotes GDP by 0.305%. But when the threshold value is equal to 3.061 or exceeds

Table 10. Threshold level of financial development index (FDV) on economic growth (GDP).

Dependent Variable: LGDP
Threshold Variable: FDV

Variables	Regime 1 $FDV < -0.570$	Regime 2 $-0.570 \leq FDV < 0.805$	Regime 3 $FDV \geq 0.805$
C	7.490***	6.648***	8.063***
	(0.091)	(0.644)	(0.078)
FDV	−0.028**	−1.956	−0.049**
	(0.024)	(1.169)	(0.022)
Observation	16	5	17
Non-Threshold Variables			
FDI		0.001	
FDI		(0.010)	
LINF		−0.003	
		(0.015)	
TOP		−9.521***	
		(3.155)	
R-Squared		0.955	
Adjusted R-Squared		0.943	
F-Statistics (Prob)		78.177(0.000)	
Durbin–Watson		1.976	

Note: Numbers in () indicate the standard error. ***,**, and *denote 1%, 5%, and 10% levels of significance, respectively.

it, it reduces GDP by 0.439%. In summary, broad money promotes economic growth when the threshold value is less than 2.546 or when it is between 2.546 and 3.061, but it retards growth when it is equal to or exceeds 3.061. The non-threshold variables are negative and significant, except for FDI, which is positively significant with respect to GDP.

The threshold regression results in Table 7 depict two regimes and one threshold value. The effect of LDCB in regime 1 is positive but negative in regime 2; it is non-significant in both regimes. This shows that in both regimes, LDCB does not significantly affect GDP in Nigeria. The non-threshold variables are not significant, except for TOP. Trade openness has a negative and significant relationship with

GDP such that when TOP increases by one percent, GDP reduces by 13.975 percent. Similarly, in Tables 8 and 9, the threshold variables LDCP and LMKC are not significant, and TOP is negative at 13.697 and 12.124, respectively.

The threshold regression results in Table 10 show three regimes with two threshold values (0.570 and 0.805). The effects of FDV on GDP in the three regimes are negative but only significant in regimes 1 and 3. This result contradicts *a priori* expectations, and this supports the finding (Ibrahim and Alagidede, 2018) that financial development may not improve economic growth depending on the simultaneous growth of the financial and real sectors. It also supports the study of Breitenlechner *et al.* (2015), which reported that financial development improves growth only in non-crisis periods but retards growth during crisis periods.

5. Conclusion and Recommendation

This research studied the nexus between financial development and economic growth in Nigeria between 1986 and 2023. The methods of estimation used in the study are threshold regression and GMM, as proposed by Arellano and Bover (1995) and Blundell and Bond (1998). The study first examined the descriptive statistics, the correlation matrix, unit root tests, and cointegration. Thereafter, it examined the trends in measures of financial development and also the GMM and threshold regression. The GMM results show that the financial development index promotes economic growth; however, when the measures of financial development are used separately, only domestic credit to the private sector is found to promote economic growth. For the threshold regression, broad money promotes growth only when the threshold value is between 2.546 and 3.061, while the financial development index does not significantly contribute to growth. Likewise, trade openness in the estimation of threshold regression is negatively associated with economic growth across all regimes. The study recommends that regulatory authorities ensure that the country derives greater benefits from trade openness and implement sound lending practices to improve financial development.

References

Ahmed, A. D. and Wahid, A. N. (2010). Financial structure and economic growth link in convergence: Theory and evidence. *Quarterly Journal of Economic Studies*, 38, 331–357.

Akintola, A. A., Oji-Okoro, I., and Itodo, I. A. (2020). Financial sector development and economic growth in Nigeria: An empirical re-examination. *Central Bank of Nigeria Economic and Financial Review*, 58(3), 59–84.

Aluko, O. A., Adeyeye, O. P., and Oladele, P. O. (2019). Finance-growth nexus in sub-Saharan Africa revisited: Evidence based on a new composite index. *Economic Change and Restructuring*, 1–23. https://doi.org/10.1007/s10644-019-09253-9.

Arellano, M. and Bover, O. (1995). Another look at the instrumental variable estimation of error components models. *Journal of Econometrics*, 68, 29–52.

Blundell, R. and Bond, S. (1998). Initial conditions and moment restrictions in dynamic panel data models. *Journal of Econometrics*, 87(1), 115–143.

Boulila, G. and Trabelsi, M. (2004). The causality issues in the finance and growth nexus: Empirical evidence from Middle East and North African countries. *Review of Middle East Economics and Finance*, 2, 123–138.

Breitenlechner, M., Gächter, M., and Sindermann, F. (2015). The finance-growth nexus in crisis. *Journal of Economics Letters*, 132, 31–33.

Demetriades, P. O. and Rewilak, J. M. (2020). Recovering the finance-growth nexus. *Economics Letters*, 196, 1–3.

Gurley, J. and Shaw, E. (1967). Financial structure and economic development. *Economic Development and Cultural Change*, 15, 257–268.

Hamdi, H., Hakimi, A., and Sbia, R. (2017). Finance and growth nexus: What role for institutions in developed and developing countries? *Journal of Economic Development*, 42(3), 1–22.

Ibrahim, M. and Alagidede, P. (2018). Effect of financial development on economic growth in Sub-Saharan Africa. *Journal of Policy Modeling*, 1–23. https://doi.org/10.1016/j.jpolmod.2018.08.001.

Ioannou, S. and Wojcik, D. (2020). Finance and growth nexus: An international analysis across cities. *Urban Studies Journal Limited*, 1–20. https://doi.org/10.1177/0042098019889244.

Khan, M. S. and Senhadji, A. S. (2003). Financial development and economic growth: A review and new evidence. *Journal of African Economies*, 12(2), 89–110.

McKinnon, R. (1973). Money and capital in economic development. *The Brooking Institutions*, Washington, DC.

Okafor, V., Bowale, E., Onabote, A., Afolabi, A., and Ejemeyovwi, J. (2021). Financial deepening and economic growth in Nigeria: A Johannsen and error correction model techniques. *International Journal of Financial Research*, 12(2), 263–273. https://doi.org/10.5430/ijfr.v12n2p263.

Olushola, O. A. and Uzoma, M. E. (2018). Financial sector development and economic growth in Nigeria: An econometric analysis, 1981–2017. *International Journal of Economics and Financial Management*, 3(3), 35–45.

Patrick, H. T. (1966). Financial development and economic growth in underdeveloped countries. *Economic Development and Cultural Change*, 14, 174–189.

Shaw, E. (1973). *Financial Deepening in Economic Development.* Oxford University Press, New York.

Stiglitz, J. (1994). The role of the state in financial markets. *Bank Conference on Development Economics*, 19–63.

Swamy, V. and Dharani, M. (2020). Thresholds in finance-growth nexus: Evidence from G-7 economies. *Australian Economic Papers*, March 2019, 1–40. https://doi.org/10.1111/1467-8454.12192.

Yilmazkuday, H. (2011). Thresholds in the finance-growth nexus: A cross-country analysis. *World Bank Economic Review Journal*, 1–18. https://doi.org/10.1093/wber/lhr011.

Younsi, M. and Bechtini, M. (2018). Economic growth, financial development and income inequality in Brics countries: Does Kuznets' inverted U-shaped curve exists? *Journal of the Knowledge Economy*, 1–22.

https://doi.org/10.1142/9789819823161_0018

Chapter 18

Sensitivity in the Cryptocurrency Market: Evidence from the Asian Countries

Ruchita Verma[*,§], **Shiney Sam**[†,¶], **and Dhanraj Sharma**[‡,||]

[*]*Department of Financial Administration, Central University of Punjab, Bathinda, Punjab, India*

[†]*School of Business & Management, Christ (Deemed to be University), Bengaluru, Karnataka, India*

[‡]*Department of Financial Administration, Central University of Punjab, Bathinda, Punjab, India*

[§]*ruchitaverma@cup.edu.in*

[¶]*sam.shiney13@gmail.com*

[||]*dhanrajsharma@cup.edu.in*

The present research aims to gauge the sensitive drivers of cryptocurrency prices, focusing on Asian countries, i.e., Japan, Korea, and India. The data for the present research study range from September 2015 to December 2021. The study reveals that cryptocurrency prices are distinctively sensitive to factors of respective countries. Cryptocurrency prices in Japan and Korea are observed to have positive sensitivity from GSIt, while GSIt negatively influences cryptocurrency in India. ΔGPRt is seen to positively impact Bitcoin price in Japan and India, whereas ΔGPRt does not influence cryptocurrency prices in Korea. The sensitivity of the factors on the Tether price is more or less insignificant in all the countries. The reason for such an oddity could be traced to the fact that Tether is a stable coin that mirrors the US dollar price and is not much affected by any other factor. The findings of this chapter are helpful to policymakers, academicians, and investors alike. It is helpful to understand how macroeconomic factors affect this nascent financial market and make better regulations for cryptocurrency, ensuring the safety of investors and stability of the economy. This chapter is helpful to financial scientists in further researching and estimating a sophisticated cryptocurrency returns prediction model.

Keywords: Sensitivity, Asian Countries, bitcoin, ethereum, tether and ripple.

1. Introduction

More than a decade after Bitcoin was set afloat, cryptocurrency appears to be the most profitable financial instrument for investors. The cryptocurrency was eye-catching, got exposure among investors as Bitcoin was the most traded cryptocurrency, and its price increased by 1700 percent in 2017 (Bleher and Dimplf, 2019). A Bloomberg Business report (January 2021) stated that "Bitcoin has emerged as the decades' best-performing asset with more than 9,000,000 percent profits". The intact growth in cryptocurrency grabs the attention of policymakers, researchers, governments, and investors. The various factors which affect the price fluctuation of cryptocurrency are social media sentiments (Abraham *et al.*, 2018; Shen *et al.*, 2018; Lamon *et al.*, 2017; Kim *et al.*, 2016), crude oil price, gold price, movement in major stock markets (Kapar and Olmo, 2019; Kjærland *et al.*, 2018; Das and Kannadhasan, 2018; Kristoufek, 2015), and other external and internal aspect such as interest rate, foreign exchange, demand and supply, economic factors, and geopolitical risk (Aysana, 2019; Sovbetov, 2018; Zhu *et al.*, 2017).

Cryptocurrency has also emerged as a safe haven, a diversifier, and a hedge in times of crisis based on economic conditions. Kliber *et al.* (2019) observe that Bitcoin can be treated as a safe haven or investment when traded in local currencies; however, in USD trade, it is a weak hedge. Further, Shahzad *et al.* (2019) reported that the global stock market considers Bitcoin as an alternative investment strategy to gold. Mamun *et al.* (2020) suggest that in times of worsened economic conditions, Bitcoin performs as well as gold and can act as a safe haven. Malladi (2022) says that cryptocurrencies are no substitute for gold as a safe haven. Boadu *et al.* (2022) reveal that cryptocurrencies can provide a safe haven, diversification, and hedge for the African stocks' investors. Also, Bouri *et al.* (2022) find that Bitcoin is a hedge against geopolitical risk.

Many countries have been caught off guard by the rapid development of cryptocurrencies. Cryptocurrency in Asia grew remarkably fast between July 2020 and June 2021, with Central and South Asian economies' transactions jumping by more than 700 percent and hitting $572 billion, or sharing 14 percent of the overall transactions of cryptocurrency globally. It is observed that Asian countries are not just paving the way for cryptocurrency but are also embracing and nurturing its underlying Blockchain technology. In this chapter, there are three different geographical economies, i.e., Japan, Korea and India, in whose local currencies cryptocurrencies are most traded in Asia. This chapter aims to gauge the sensitive drivers of cryptocurrency prices in the local currencies from their respective domestic factors, such as returns of stock indices, returns on gold, Google search intensity, change in economic and political uncertainty index, and geopolitical risk index.

2. Previous Studies

Cryptocurrencies are considered the riskiest financial instruments and remain a continuous focus of discussion among financial scholars, who have recently examined factors such as risk, volatility, and sensitivity in the cryptocurrency market (Aysan *et al.*, 2024; Liu *et al.*, 2024; Mba, 2024; Bruzgė *et al.*, 2023; Khalfaoui *et al.*, 2023; Ahmed, 2022; Yin *et al.*, 2022; Fakhfekh *et al.*, 2021). More than 20,000 cryptocurrencies are being traded daily on over 500 cryptocurrency exchanges across the globe. Liang *et al.* (2019) found that the fintech innovation of cryptocurrency (Bitcoin) has dynamics similar to those of stocks. Since it is traded like stocks and commodities, many studies have been conducted examining the characteristics/features of stocks in the cryptocurrency market. Studies are examining the relationship between cryptocurrency and varied traditional asset classes (Bianchi, 2018; Corelli, 2018; Eken and Baloglu, 2018; Trabelsi, 2018), determinants for the price fluctuation in cryptucurrencies (Kim *et al.*, 2016), volatility and spillover in Bitcoin from other assets such as gold, crude oil, major stock indices (Kristoufek, 2015), the impact of demand and supply on cryptocurrencies (Sovbetov, 2018), and much more. Dwyer (2014), Cheung *et al.* (2015), Carrick (2016), and Liang *et al.* (2019) observed that the nascent cryptocurrency market is much more volatile and fragile than other conventional markets. Because of the high volatility in cryptocurrency, it is more prone to speculative price bubbles than other tradable currencies (Grinberg, 2011). Between April 2013 and May 2017, El Bahrawy and Alessandretti (2017) studied the behaviour of 1469 cryptocurrencies. They discover that cryptocurrencies arise and regularly disappear, despite a dramatically rising market value.

Dirican and Canoz (2017) found a co-integrating relationship between Bitcoin and the leading stock markets of the US and China, but no relation between Bitcoin and the leading stock indices of Türkiye, the UK, and Japan. External and internal variables influencing cryptocurrency fluctuations are discussed by Poyser (2017), in which internal indicators include popularity and legality, whereas external indicators include interest rates, stock markets, and gold prices. Symitsi and Chalvatzis (2018) have observed that Bitcoin has low correlation with other assets such as gold, oil, and stocks, thus decreasing the overall portfolio risk. Teker *et al.* (2020) found that Tether, gold, and oil prices are co-integrated, but no cryptocurrency is yet a substitute for gold and oil as an investment portfolio.

Social media sentiments are the main driver behind the price movement and growth in cryptocurrency. Kristoufek (2013) initiated the research on this and found that Google search queries and the price of Bitcoin are connected asymmetrically. The findings of Sovbetov (2018) stated that the attractiveness of investors toward cryptocurrency affects the cryptocurrency price. Further, Smuts (2019) found that the Telegram group is a superior pointer for Bitcoin price movement than the trends of Google. Philippas *et al.* (2019) used the dual-process diffusion model and reported that Twitter- and Google-based information rationalizes sentimental thirst. Dastgir *et al.* (2019) also observed the bi-directional association between Bitcoin prices and Google trends while applying Granger Causality test. Aslandis *et al.* (2021) found that there is significant dependence between Google Trends and cryptocurrency return. Güler (2021) investigated Bitcoin returns and investor sentiment and found a positive impact on the FOMO behavior of investor sentiment.

The Economic Policy Uncertainty Index of Baker *et al.* (2016) and the Geo-Political Risk Index of Caldara and Iacoviello (2018) have also raised interest. In a similar direction, studies have observed the impact of these indices on the cryptocurrency market. Kombua *et al.* (2018) found interdependence between the EPU of the

US and cryptocurrencies, whereas Cheng and Chieh (2019a, 2019b) show that the EPU of China can predict Bitcoin returns as well as Bitcoin volatility. Also, Cheema *et al.* (2020) found that EPU predicts cryptocurrency returns, but over a short period and not over a long period. Papadamou *et al.* (2020) say that about half the cryptocurrencies traded in the market are connected to EPU during the bull market. Jiang *et al.* (2021) observed that cryptocurrency can hedge against the high EPU but not a low or moderate EPU. However, Haq *et al.* (2021) reveal that cryptocurrencies' connectedness to varied countries' EPU is a mixed pattern, and so the hedging against EPU is different across countries.

Further, Aysan *et al.* (2018), for the GPR index, observe that GPR has predictability regarding Bitcoin's returns and price volatility, and it may be considered as a risk mitigation device against global GPR. Al-Yahyaee *et al.* (2019) find that the GPR index is a factor that affects the Bitcoin volatility index. Al Mamun *et al.* (2020) find that geopolitical risk is the most substantial influencer of the risk premia and volatility of Bitcoin. Bauri *et al.* (2020) observed in their empirical study that Bitcoin jumps along with jumps in GPR and is a good hedge against the GPR. Kyriazis (2021) also found that GPR predicts Bitcoin returns and volatility the most among the other assets in the market.

Based on the reviewed literature, it is evident that the significant impact of economic variables on asset prices in both developing and developed economies has been one of the most prominent topics of interest among financial experts and researchers. Also, fluctuations in macroeconomic variables affect domestic investors' investment decisions. This postulate induces a researcher to examine the influence of macroeconomic variables on Bitcoin from the Indian market perspective. Thus, the present research aims to gauge the drivers to which cryptocurrency prices are sensitive.

3. Research Framework

The present study intends to gauge the sensitivity of macroeconomic drivers on cryptocurrency prices with a special focus on Asian countries, i.e., Japan, Korea, and India. According to Bitcointy.org, the top currencies in which Bitcoin (70 percent of market capitalization) is most traded in Asia are the Japanese yen, Korean Won, and Chinese Yuan. However, as cryptocurrency trading is banned in China and data on the Chinese Yuan are unavailable, China was excluded from the sample country list. India is included in the sample as it has the highest number of investors in the cryptocurrency market across the world. Thus, monthly data for the selected variables corresponding to the sample of three countries are collected. Further, the monthly price data (in the currency denomination of the three sample countries) of four cryptocurrencies, Bitcoin, Ethereum, Tether, and Ripple, with the highest market capitalization globally and longest availability of data, are also collected. The data for the present research study range from September 2015 to December 2021.

The present study gauges the impact of stock index and gold returns, Google Search Intensity (Standardized value of Google Trend Index), and change in Economic Policy Uncertainty (ΔEPU) and Geo-Political Risk (ΔGPR) Indexes, along with the lagged value of the respective cryptocurrency on the price of the sample cryptocurrency. Therefore, the dependent variable in the present study is cryptocurrency price and the independent variables are stock index returns, gold returns, Google search intensity, ΔEPU, and ΔGPR. A brief about the variables is given in Table 1.

The cryptocurrency price is defined as a function of the previous month's price, returns of stock indices of the current and previous month, gold returns of the current and previous month, GSI of the previous and current month, change in EPU of the previous and current month, and change in GPR of the current and previous month. Mathematically, it a function denoted as follows:

$$\int \mathrm{P} = (\mathrm{P}t - 1,\ \mathrm{Stockt},\ \mathrm{Stockt\text{-}1},\ \mathrm{Gold}t,\ \mathrm{Gold}t\text{-}1,\ \mathrm{GSI}t,\ \mathrm{GSI}t\text{-}1,\ \Delta\mathrm{EPU}t,\ \Delta\mathrm{EPU}t\text{-}1,\ \Delta\mathrm{GPR}t,\ \Delta\mathrm{GPR}t\text{-}1).$$

The equation to assess sensitivity in cryptocurrency prices is as follows:

$$\ln\Delta\mathrm{Pit} = \alpha + \beta 1^{*}\ln\Delta\mathrm{Pi}t\text{-}1 + \beta 2^{*}\ln\Delta\mathrm{STOCK}t + \beta 3^{*}\ \ln\Delta\ \mathrm{STOCK}t\text{-}1 + \beta 4^{*}\ \ln\Delta\ \mathrm{GOLD}t + \beta 5^{*}\ \ln\Delta\ \mathrm{GOLD}t\text{-}1 + \beta 6^{*}\mathrm{GSI}t + \beta 7^{*}\mathrm{GSI}t\text{-}1 + \beta 8^{*}\ \ln\Delta\ \mathrm{GPR}t + \beta 9^{*}\ \ln\Delta\ \mathrm{GPR}t\text{-}1 + \beta 10^{*}\ \ln\Delta\ \mathrm{EPU}t + \beta 11^{*}\ \ln\Delta\ \mathrm{EPU}t\text{-}1 + \varepsilon,$$

where

$\ln\Delta\mathrm{Pi}t$ = Natural logarithmic change in price of cryptocurrency i at time t month.

Table 1. Brief description of the explanatory variables.

Variable	Symbol	Operational Definition
Stock Index	STOCK	Monthly natural logarithmic returns of the stock index price are calculated as follows: rsi = lnSTOCKp, t − lnSTOCKp,t-1. The present study considers domestic stock index log returns of previous and current months to determine cryptocurrency price movement in the sample countries.
Gold	GOLD	Monthly natural logarithmic returns of the gold price are calculated as follows: rGi = lnGOLDp,t − lnGOLDp,t − 1. The present study considers gold log returns of previous and current months to determine cryptocurrency price movement in the sample countries.
Google Search Intensity	GSI	Monthly Google Search volume (GSV) is obtained for the search terms "Bitcoin", "Ethereum", "Tether", and "XRP", country-wise, and then standardized following Pries *et al.* (2013) to get GSI: $$GSI_t = \frac{GSV_t - \frac{1}{n}\sum_{i=1}^{n} GSV_i}{\sigma_{GSV}}$$ The standard deviation of the sample GSV data is scaled after the mean of the sample GSV data is subtracted from each observation for each coin. The present study considers the GSI of previous and current months to determine cryptocurrency price movement in the sample countries.
Economic Policy Uncertainty Index	ΔEPU	The EPU index captures uncertainty from news, policy, market, and economic indicators. (Al-Thaqeb and Algharabali, 2019). This index has been computed for major world economies on a monthly basis. The present study adopts a natural logarithmic change in the GPR index of previous and current months to determine cryptocurrency price movement in the sample countries.

(*Continued*)

Table 1. Brief description of the explanatory variables.

Variable	Symbol	Operational Definition
Geopolitical Risk Index	ΔGPR	The GPR index measures international tensions, cross-border tensions, military conflicts, terrorist acts, and war threats, as reported in the world's top newspapers monthly. The present study adopts a natural logarithmic change in the GPR index of previous and current months to determine cryptocurrency price movement in the sample countries.

$\ln\Delta\text{Pi},t{-}1$ = Natural logarithmic price of cryptocurrency i at time $t-1$ month.

$\ln\Delta$ STOCKt = Natural logarithmic returns of a stock index at time t month.

$\ln\Delta$ STOCK$t-1$ = Natural logarithmic returns of the stock index at time $t-1$ month.

$\ln\Delta$ GOLDt = Natural logarithmic returns of Gold at time t month.

$\ln\Delta$ GOLD$t-1$ = Natural logarithmic returns of Gold at time $t{-}1$ month.

GSIt = Google Search Intensity, standardized value of Google Trends Index at time t month.

GSI$t{-}1$ = Google Search Intensity, standardized value of Google Trends at time $t-1$ month.

$\ln\Delta$ GPRt = Natural logarithmic change in Geopolitical Risk Index at time t month.

$\ln\Delta$ GPR$t{-}1$ = Natural logarithmic change in Geopolitical Risk Index at time $t-1$ month.

$\ln\Delta$ EPUt = Natural logarithmic change in Economic Policy Uncertainty Index at time t month.

$\ln\Delta$ EPU$t{-}1$ = Natural logarithmic change in Economic Policy Uncertainty Index at time $t-1$ month.

4. Analysis and Discussion

This study gauges the drivers to which the cryptocurrency prices are sensitive, providing evidence from the Asian perspective, i.e., Japan,

Korea, and India. The data for the statistical analysis have been collected in the currency denomination of the sample countries. Table 2 presents descriptive statistics for all the study variables corresponding to the sample countries.

The present study has collected 76 observations for all the variables for all three sample countries. The maximum price recorded of cryptocurrencies during the study period in Japan is Bitcoin ¥6916405.66 and Ethereum ¥524062 in November 2021, in line with the Global Bitcoin highest price ever recorded, and Tether ¥123.19 in November 2015 and Ripple ¥259.23 in December 2017. Further, in India, the maximum price recorded for cryptocurrencies during the

Table 2. Descriptive statistics.

	Min	Max	Mean	Std Dev	Skewness	Kurtosis	Obsv
			JAPAN (Japanese Yen ¥)				
BTC	28218	6916405.66	1349532	1800850	1.86	2.308	76
ETH	88.53	524062	71045.35	118580.7	2.37	5.02	76
USDT	101.33	123.19	110.23	4.44	0.604	0.704	76
XRP	0.518	259.23	41.23	45.69	2.15	6.531	76
N^225	−0.141	0.142	0.005	0.051	−0.529	0.64	76
GOLD	−0.068	0.085	0.005	0.029	0.13	0.669	76
GSI(B)	4	100	18.26	15.65	3.194	12.61	76
GSI(E)	1	100	24.77	19.12	1.72	3.509	76
GSI(T)	5	100	19.23	16.41	2.414	7.763	76
GSI(R)	0.9	100	17.36	16.75	2.38	8.778	76
EPU	−0.623	0.581	−0.003	0.182	0.232	1.981	76
GPR	−1.247	1.307	0.011	0.531	0.321	−0.271	76
			KOREA (Korean Won ₩)				
BTC	279695.68	72025832	14280841	18710250	1.82	2.24	76
ETH	113.41	5728000	752452.8	1270112	2.37	5.04	76
USDT	1058.66	1229.04	1147.82	42.65	−0.09	−0.68	76
XRP	4.47	2760	432.57	485.52	2.18	6.72	76
KOSPI	−0.144	0.134	0.005	0.044	−0.32	2.13	76
GOLD	−0.091	0.136	0.006	0.041	0.41	0.84	76
GSI(B)	3	100	16.19	16.35	3.21	12.83	76
GSI(E)	0	100	20.26	17.37	1.99	5.68	76
GSI(T)	1	100	20.65	26.28	1.72	1.81	76
GSI(R)	0	100	21.42	22.13	1.63	2.72	76
EPU	−0.373	−1.369	0.0045	0.143	−0.19	0.56	76
GPR	0.341	1.44	0.0041	0.477	0.21	0.75	76

(Continued)

Table 2. (*Continued*)

	Min	Max	Mean	Std Dev	Skewness	Kurtosis	Obsv
			INDIA (Indian Rupees ₹)				
BTC	15276.93	4895166	911999.7	1252853	1.858	5.087	76
ETH	48.4	361032	48427.16	82886.11	2.35	7.716	76
USDT	60.21	75.80	69.67	3.81	−0.087	1.922	76
XRP	0.27	146.85	28.14	29.35	1.724	6.473	76
SENSEX	−0.276	0.108	0.01	0.052	−2.062	13.503	76
GOLD	−0.066	0.113	0.008	0.041	0.407	2.787	76
GSI(B)	1	100	13.22	15.07	3.169	14.27	76
GSI(E)	0.9	100	11.54	15.54	3.009	13.22	76
GSI(T)	6	100	17.53	18.8	2.918	8.821	76
GSI(R)	0	100	16.09	21.22	2.467	6.182	76
EPU	−0.803	1.13	−0.002	0.436	0.156	2.693	76
GPR	−0.98	1.4	0.011	0.543	0.257	2.508	76

study period is Bitcoin ₹4895166 in October 2021 (same as Korea), Ethereum ₹361032 in November 2021, Tether ₹75.80 in April 2020, and Ripple ₹146.85 in December 2017. It is important to note that Ripple is the least priced cryptocurrency in this study in all the sample countries. It is observed that Bitcoin was most searched in Japan and Korea during the study period, while Tether was most searched in India. The mean stock index returns and gold returns during the study period are maximum in India. The average change in EPU was negative for Japan and India during the study period, while GPR was positive for all three sample countries.

Further, the correlation has been computed among the cryptocurrencies of the selected countries to find out the direction of the relationship. Table 3(a–d) gives a correlation matrix of variables corresponding to Japan, Table 4(a–d) for Korea, and Table 5(a–d) for India.

Table 3(a–d) corresponds to Japan's data. In the matrix, Bitcoin, Ethereum, and Ripple have a significant and highly positive correlation to Google search intensity (GSI), but Tether has an insignificant and negative relation with GSI. Other variables of the study are seen to have an insignificant correlation with cryptocurrency. It is also pertinent to note that the correlation among the independent variables is very low and insignificant, thus implying the absence of multicollinearity.

Table 3. Correlation matrix: Japan.

	BTC	N^225	GOLD	GSI	EPU	GPR
BTC	1					
N^225	0.047	1				
GOLD	0.067	−0.182	1			
GSI(B)	0.24**	0.121	−0.039	1		
EPU	−0.057	−0.118	−0.102	−0.046	1	
GPR	0.013	0.038	0.082	−0.061	0.05	1

(a) *Bitcoin and Variables*

	ETH	N^225	GOLD	GSI	EPU	GPR
ETH	1					
N^225	−0.009	1				
GOLD	0.054	−0.182	1			
GSI	0.401*	0.042	−0.014	1		
EPU	−0.035	−0.118	−0.102	−0.046	1	
GPR	−0.028	0.038	0.082	−0.061	0.05	1

(b) *Ethereum and Variables*

	USDT	N^225	GOLD	GSI	EPU	GPR
USDT	1					
N^225	−0.052	1				
GOLD	−0.017	−0.182	1			
GSI	−0.173	0.064	−0.043	1		
EPU	0.133	−0.118	−0.102	−0.046	1	
GPR	0.116	0.038	0.082	−0.061	0.05	1

(c) *Tether and Variables*

	XRP	N^225	GOLD	GSI	EPU	GPR
XRP	1					
N^225	0.003	1				
GOLD	0.046	−0.182	1			
GSI	0.768*	0.082	0.034	1		
EPU	−0.004	−0.118	−0.102	−0.046	1	
GPR	−0.097	0.038	0.082	−0.061	0.05	1

(d) *Ripple and Variables*

Note: Level of Significance: *– 1 percent, **– 5 percent, and ***– 10 percent.

Table 4. Correlation matrix: Korea.

	BTC	KOSPI	GOLD	GSI	EPU	GPR
BTC	1					
KOSPI	0.861*	1				
GOLD	0.669*	0.487*	1			
GSI	0.352*	0.517*	0.065	1		
EPU	0.279*	−0.042	0.607*	−0.219***	1	
GPR	−0.256**	0.005	−0.420*	0.248**	−0.432*	1

(a) *Bitcoin and Variables*

	ETH	KOSPI	GOLD	GSI	EPU	GPR
ETH	1					
KOSPI	0.824*	1				
GOLD	0.554*	0.487*	1			
GSI	0.269*	0.459*	−0.109	1		
EPU	−0.042	−0.042	0.607*	−0.219***	1	
GPR	−0.420*	0.005	−0.420*	0.248**	−0.432*	1

(b) *Ethereum and Variables*

	USDT	KOSPI	GOLD	GSI	EPU	GPR
USDT	1					
KOSPI	−0.329*	1				
GOLD	0.378*	0.487*	1			
GSI	−0.153	0.799*	0.492*	1		
EPU	0.622*	−0.042	0.607*	−0.219***	1	
GPR	−0.424*	0.005	−0.420*	0.248**	−0.432*	1

(c) *Tether and Variables*

	XRP	KOSPI	GOLD	GSI	EPU	GPR
XRP	1					
KOSPI	0.671*	1				
GOLD	0.299*	0.487*	1			
GSI	0.695*	0.796*	0.456*	1		
EPU	0.011	−0.042	0.607*	−0.219***	1	
GPR	0.062	0.005	−0.420*	0.248**	−0.432*	1

(d) *Ripple and Variables*

Note: Level of significance: * – 1 percent, ** – 5 percent, and *** – 10 percent.

Table 5. Correlation matrix: India.

	BTC	SENSEX	GOLD	GSI	EPU	GPR
BTC	**1**					
SENSEX	0.112	**1**				
GOLD	−0.054	−0.093	**1**			
GSI	0.391*	0.066	−0.035	**1**		
EPU	−0.008	−0.172	0.108	−0.011	**1**	
GPR	−0.031	−0.019	−0.050	−0.096	−0.206***	**1**

(a) *Bitcoin and Variables*

	ETH	SENSEX	GOLD	GSI	EPU	GPR
ETH	**1**					
SENSEX	0.081	**1**				
GOLD	−0.039	−0.093	**1**			
GSI	0.644*	0.100	−0.021	**1**		
EPU	0.007	−0.172	0.108	−0.011	**1**	
GPR	−0.055	−0.019	−0.050	−0.096	−0.206***	**1**

(b) *Ethereum and Variables*

	USDT	SENSEX	GOLD	GSI	EPU	GPR
USDT	**1**					
SENSEX	−0.029	**1**				
GOLD	0.096	−0.093	**1**			
GSI	0.353*	0.023	−0.011	**1**		
EPU	0.051	−0.172	0.108	−0.011	**1**	
GPR	−0.049	−0.019	−0.050	−0.096	−0.206***	**1**

(c) *Tether and Variables*

	XRP	SENSEX	GOLD	GSI	EPU	GPR
XRP	**1**					
SENSEX	0.042	**1**				
GOLD	0.012	−0.093	**1**			
GSI	0.793*	0.079	0.044	**1**		
EPU	0.050	−0.172	0.108	−0.011	**1**	
GPR	−0.105	−0.019	−0.050	−0.096	−0.206***	**1**

(d) *Ripple and Variables*

Note: Level of significance: * – 1 percent, ** – 5 percent, and *** – 10 percent.

Table 6. Regression estimates: Japan.

	BTC	ETH	USDT	XRP
Constant	0.064*	0.094**	−0.000	0.075
	(0.00)	(0.02)	(0.84)	(0.14)
Cryptocurrency$_{t-1}$	0.058	0.048	−0.216	−0.256**
	(0.59)	(0.67)	(0.11)	(0.02)
N^225 Returns	0.809**	−0.337	0.024	−0.491
	(0.05)	(0.68)	(0.75)	(0.62)
N^225 Returns$_{t-1}$	0.083	−0.455	0.036	0.442
	0.083	−0.455	0.036	0.442
Gold Returns	−0.426	0.860	−0.063	0.056
	(0.52)	(0.56)	(0.61)	(0.97)
Gold Returns$_{t-1}$	−0.694	0.609	0.047	0.145
	(0.29)	(0.66)	(0.70)	(0.93)
GSI	0.212*	0.245*	−0.003	0.334*
	(0.00)	(0.00)	(0.47)	(0.00)
GSI$_{t-1}$	−0.203*	−0.275*	0.006	−0.349*
	(0.00)	(0.00)	(0.24)	(0.00)
GPR	0.103*	0.095	0.001	−0.101
	(0.01)	(0.25)	(0.85)	(0.32)
GPR$_{t-1}$	0.056	0.221*	−0.003	0.095
	(0.14)	(0.00)	(0.59)	(0.34)
EPU	−0.079	0.042	0.011	−0.012
	(0.43)	(0.84)	(0.53)	(0.96)
EPU$_{t-1}$	0.202***	−0.216	−0.002	−0.697**
	(0.07)	(0.37)	(0.89)	(0.02)
R^2	0.504	0.314	0.089	0.407
F-Stat	5.821*	2.625*	0.562	3.931*

Note: Level of significance: *− 1 percent, **− 5 percent, and ***− 10 percent.

The correlation matrix in Table 4(a–d) corresponds to Korea. Interestingly, the sample cryptocurrencies in Korea significantly correlate with the independent variables. Bitcoin in Korea is highly positively and significantly correlated to the stock Index KOSPI, gold, GSI, and Economic Policy Uncertainty (EPU), and negatively but significantly correlated to the Geo-Political Risk (GPR) index. Ethereum and Ripple are positively and significantly correlated to KOSPI, gold, and GSI. However, Ethereum negatively correlates to EPU (insignificant) and GPR (significant), whereas Ripple positively

Table 7. Regression estimates: Korea.

	BTC	ETH	USDT	XRP
Constant	0.918*	0.994*	1.156*	0.904*
	(0.00)	(0.00)	(0.00)	(0.00)
$\text{Cryptocurrency}_{t-1}$	0.086	0.012	−0.156	0.115
	0.086	0.012	−0.156	0.115
KOSPI Returns	0.007	0.039	−0.016***	0.099
	(0.83)	(0.87)	(0.06)	(0.81)
KOSPI Returns_{t-1}	0.073***	0.003	0.018***	0.093
	(0.06)	(0.98)	(0.07)	(0.82)
Gold Returns	0.010	0.663**	0.004	0.105
	(0.81)	(0.02)	(0.67)	(0.82)
Gold Returns_{t-1}	−0.106*	0.369	0.020**	0.063
	(0.00)	(0.17)	(0.04)	(0.88)
GSI	0.005**	0.013***	−0.000	0.026***
	(0.05)	(0.08)	(0.79)	(0.05)
GSI_{t-1}	−0.002	−0.008	−0.000	−0.029
	(0.42)	(0.59)	(0.53)	(0.28)
GPR	0.003	−0.016	−0.001	0.021
	(0.41)	(0.49)	(0.26)	(0.58)
GPR_{t-1}	0.005	0.034	−0.000	0.004
	(0.17)	(0.18)	(0.42)	(0.91)
EPU	−0.008	−0.137	0.006**	−0.133
	(0.52)	(0.10)	(0.02)	(0.32)
EPU_{t-1}	0.005	−0.132	0.009*	−0.005
	(0.64)	(0.11)	(0.00)	(0.96)
R^2	0.399	0.357	0.310	0.319
F-Stat	2.191**	1.878**	2.537*	1.923**

Note: Level of significance: * – 1 percent, ** – 5 percent, and *** – 10 percent.

but insignificantly correlates to both EPU and GPR. Tether in Korea significantly yet negatively correlates to KOSPI and GPR, whereas it significantly and positively correlates to Gold and EPU. Tether alone in Korea has an insignificant correlation to GSI. In Korea, too, the correlation among the independent variables is very low and insignificant, thus implying the absence of multicollinearity.

Table 5(a–d) corresponds to the correlation matrix of India. Like Japan, sample cryptocurrencies significantly and positively correlate with GSI only. Other variables are seen to have an insignificant correlation with other variables. Similarly, as seen in the table, the independent variables are insignificantly correlated to each other, implying non-multicollinearity. The overall gist of the correlation matrix depicts similar results in Japan and India to those in Korea.

Tables 6–8 give the results of the regression analysis. For all three sample countries, all the cryptocurrencies have a significant and positive relationship with their lagged term.

Regression Table 6 shows the OLS estimates. The results infer that the current month's return of the stock index of Japan N^225

Table 8. Regression estimates: India.

	BTC	**ETH**	**USDT**	**XRP**
Constant	0.066**	0.091**	0.001	0.086
	(0.02)	(0.06)	(0.68)	(0.12)
$\text{Cryptocurrency}_{t-1}$	0.089	0.179	−0.245***	−0.253**
	(0.49)	(0.16)	(0.08)	(0.03)
SENSEX Returns	−0.017	−0.469	−0.038	0.192
	(0.97)	(0.61)	(0.49)	(0.85)
SENSEX Returns_{t-1}	0.469	−0.163	0.035	0.294
	(0.36)	(0.85)	(0.51)	(0.77)
Gold Returns	−0.381	1.093	0.111	−1.316
	(0.55)	(0.32)	(0.11)	(0.29)
Gold Returns_{t-1}	−0.447	0.009	−0.027	−0.079
	(0.50)	(0.99)	(0.70)	(0.95)
GSI	−0.055***	−0.121***	0.005	−0.364*
	(0.18)	(0.05)	(0.12)	(0.00)
GSI_{t-1}	0.025	0.076	−0.002	0.364*
	(0.51)	(0.21)	(0.51)	(0.00)
GPR	0.114**	−0.126	−0.004	−0.051
	(0.03)	(0.16)	(0.41)	(0.63)
GPR_{t-1}	0.035	−0.081	0.002	−0.094
	(0.52)	(0.36)	(0.63)	(0.36)
EPU	0.019	−0.235**	−0.001	−0.118
	(0.77)	(0.04)	(0.90)	(0.36)
EPU_{t-1}	0.045	−0.154	0.004	−0.185
	(0.51)	(0.19)	(0.51)	(0.17)
R^2	0.392	0.308	0.166	0.351
F-Stat	3.89*	2.99*	1.118	3.100*

Note: Level of significance: * – 1 percent, ** – 5 percent, and *** – 10 percent.

has a significant and positive impact on the price of Bitcoin, i.e., a change of one standard deviation in the stock will result in a significant and direct change of 0.809 standard deviations in Japan's Bitcoin price. The GSI of the current month is seen to cause a significant and positive change of 0.212, 0.245, and 0.334 standard deviations on Bitcoin, Ethereum, and Ripple price changes, respectively. The current month's ΔGPR is observed to have a significant and positive influence on Bitcoin's price (0.103 std dev), while previous months' ΔGPR (0.221 std dev) has a positive and significant impact on the Ethereum prices in Japan. The previous month's ΔEPU has significantly impacted Bitcoin (positive) and Ripple (negative). The significance is at a p-value of less than 5 percent. R-Square helps to measure how well the independent variables predict cryptocurrency prices. The study's independent variables can account for the variation in Japan's Bitcoin prices by 50.4 percent, Ethereum by 31.4 percent, and Ripple by 40.7 percent, whereas the study's independent variables can explain only an 8.9 percent variance in Japan's Tether prices. The f-stats of all the regressions are significant, which implies model fit.

Regression Table 7 shows regression estimates of the Korean cryptocurrency market. The estimates show that the current month's stock index, KOSPI's returns, has an insignificant impact on the price of all the sample cryptocurrencies, but the previous month's return has a significant and positive impact on Bitcoin prices by 0.730 standard deviations. The current month's return of gold has a highly positive and significant impact on Ethereum (β: 6.630), and previous months' gold return has a significant impact on Bitcoin (negative; β: -1.06) and Tether (positive; β: 0.20). Further, the GSI of the current month (positive) is seen to impact the prices of Bitcoin, Ethereum, and Ripple significantly whereas previous months' GSI is insignificant on cryptocurrencies. ΔGPR is seen to have an insignificant impact on all cryptocurrencies in Korea. The current and previous months' ΔEPU is observed to impact Tether only significantly positively.

Regression Table 8's results are similar to Japan's. The results show that neither the current month's return nor the previous month's return of the stock index of India SENSEX has an insignificant impact on the price of any sample cryptocurrencies. The GSI of the current month is seen to significantly impact the price of Bitcoin, Ethereum, and Ripple, but negatively (Table 9). The GSI of the

Table 9. Sensitivity of variables on cryptocurrency: A summary.

		JAPAN	**KOREA**	**INDIA**
BITCOIN (BTC)	*BTC(-1)*	—	—	—
	STOCK	+ive*	—	—
	STOCK (-1)	—	+ive*	—
	GOLD	—	—	—
	GOLD(-1)	—	−ive*	—
	GSI	+ive*	+ive*	−ive*
	GSI(-1)	−ive*	—	—
	EPU	+ive*	—	+ive*
	EPU(-1)	—	—	—
	GPR	—	—	—
	GPR(-1)	+ive*	—	—
ETHEREUM (ETH)	*ETH(-1)*	—	—	—
	STOCK	—	—	—
	STOCK (-1)	—	—	—
	GOLD	—	+ive*	—
	GOLD(-1)	—	—	—
	GSI	+ive*	+ive*	−ive*
	GSI(-1)	−ive*	—	—
	EPU	—	—	—
	EPU(-1)	+ive*	—	—
	GPR	—	—	−ive*
	GPR(-1)	—	—	—
TETHER (USDT)	*USDT(-1)*	—	—	−ive*
	STOCK	—	−ive*	—
	STOCK (-1)	—	+ive*	—
	GOLD	—	—	—
	GOLD(-1)	—	+ive*	—
	GSI	—	—	—
	GSI(-1)	—	—	—
	EPU	—	—	—
	EPU(-1)	—	—	—
	GPR	—	+ive	—
	GPR(-1)	—	+ive	—
RIPPLE (XRP)	*XRP(-1)*	−ive*	—	−ive*
	STOCK	—	—	—
	STOCK (-1)	—	—	—
	GOLD	-	—	—
	GOLD(-1)	—	—	—
	GSI	+ive*	+ive*	−ive*
	GSI(-1)	−ive*	—	+ive*
	EPU	—	—	—
	EPU(-1)	—	—	—
	GPR	—	—	—
	GPR(-1)	−ive*	—	—

Note: −ive = Negative relation; *+ive* = Positive relation; *denotes to significance at 1%.

previous month has a positive and significant impact only on Ripple prices. The current month's GPR is seen to have a significant and positive impact on Bitcoin's price, while previous months' GPR has a negative and significant impact on the Ethereum price change in India. The significance is at a p-value of less than 5 percent. The geopolitical risk index significantly and positively impacts Bitcoin in Japan and India. Cheng and Yen (2020) reported that economic policy uncertainty of China affects Bitcoin returns. Thus, geopolitical tension between India and China and Japan supporting India against China would make Bitcoin prices sensitive to GPR in India and Japan. The f-stats (model fit) of all the regression models are significant.

5. Conclusion

The present research paper aims to gauge the sensitive drivers of cryptocurrency prices, focusing on Asian countries, i.e., Japan, Korea, and India. The four cryptocurrencies are Bitcoin, Ethereum, Tether, and Ripple, with the highest market capitalization globally. The data reveal that cryptocurrency prices are distinctively sensitive to factors of the respective countries. Where the current month's ΔGPR_t is seen to have a positive impact on Bitcoin price in Japan and India, the previous month's ΔGPR_{t-1} has a significant impact on Ethereum (positive) and Ripple (negative) in Japan and India, respectively. However, in Korea, ΔGPR and ΔGPR_{t-1} do not influence cryptocurrency prices. The influence of stock market returns, gold returns, ΔGPR, and ΔEPU, both of the current month and the previous month, on cryptocurrency prices is heterogeneous across the sample countries. However, the homogeneous significant influence (positive/negative) of Google search intensity is seen on the present cryptocurrency prices. Cryptocurrency prices in Japan and Korea are observed to have positive sensitivity from GSI_t, while GSI_t has a negative influence on cryptocurrency in India. Since Google search intensity can be proxied for investor attention, this implies that the magnitude of investor attention of a country has the predictive ability on the price movement of the cryptocurrency traded in that country (Aslandis *et al.*, 2022; Dastgir *et al.*, 2019; Nasir *et al.*, 2019; Sovbetov, 2018; Kristoufek, 2013). Another finding of this research shows that the sensitivity of the factors on the Tether price is identical in all the countries, i.e., the influence of the domestic factors of the sample countries on the Tether price is more or less insignificant. The reason for such an oddity could be traced to the fact that Tether is a stable coin that mirrors the US dollar price, which is now increasingly used as an inflation hedge. The value of Tether is guaranteed to be pegged to the US dollar. The findings of this study are helpful to countries' policymakers to understand how macroeconomic factors affect this nascent financial market and make better regulations for the cryptocurrency, ensuring the safety of investors and the stability of the economy. The study is helpful to financial scientists in further researching and estimating a sophisticated cryptocurrency returns prediction model.

References

Abraham, J., Higdon, D., Nelson, J., and Ibarra, J. (2021). Cryptocurrency price prediction using tweet volumes and sentiment analysis. *SMU Data Science Review*, 1(3).

Ahmed, W. M. (2022). Robust drivers of Bitcoin price movements: An extreme bounds analysis. *The North American Journal of Economics and Finance*, 62, 101728.

Al Mamun, M., Uddin, G. S., Suleman, M. T., and Kang, S. H. (2020). Geopolitical risk, uncertainty and Bitcoin investment. *Physica A: Statistical Mechanics and Its Applications*, 540, 123107.

Al-Yahyaee, K. H., Rehman, M. U., Mensi, W., and Al-Jarrah, I. M. W. (2019). Can uncertainty indices predict Bitcoin prices? A revisited analysis using partial and multivariate wavelet approaches. *The North American Journal of Economics and Finance*, 49, 47–56.

Aysan, A. F., Caporin, M., and Cepni, O. (2024). Not all words are equal: Sentiment and jumps in the cryptocurrency market. *Journal of International Financial Markets, Institutions and Money*, 91, 101920.

Aysan, A. F., Demir, E., Gozgor, G., and Lau, C. K. M. (2018). Effects of the geopolitical risks on Bitcoin returns and volatility. *Research in International Business and Finance*, 47, 511–518.

Baker, S. R., Bloom, N., and Davis, S. J. (2016). Measuring economic policy uncertainty. *The Quarterly Journal of Economics*, 131(4), 1593–1636.

Bianchi, D. (2018). Cryptocurrencies as an asset class? An empirical assessment. *The Journal of Alternative Investments*, 23(2), 162–179.

Bleher, J. and Dimpfl, T. (2019). Today I got a million, tomorrow, I don't know: On the predictability of cryptocurrencies by means of Google search volume. *International Review of Financial Analysis*, 63, 147–159.

Bouri, E., Gupta, R., and Vo, X. V. (2022). Jumps in geopolitical risk and the cryptocurrency market: The singularity of Bitcoin. *Defence and Peace Economics*, 33(2), 150–161.

Bruzgė, R., Černevičienė, J., Šapkauskienė, A., Mačerinskienė, A., Masteika, S., and Driaunys, K. (2023). Stylized facts, volatility dynamics and risk measures of cryptocurrencies. *Journal of Business Economics and Management*, 24(3), 527–550.

Caldara, D. and Iacoviello, M. (2018). Measuring geopolitical risk. *American Economic Review*, 112(4), 1194–1225.

Carrick, J. (2016). Bitcoin as a complement to emerging market currencies. *Emerging Markets Finance and Trade*, 52(10), 2321–2334.

Cheema, M. A., Szulczyk, K., and Bouri, E. (2020). Cryptocurrency returns and economic policy uncertainty: A multicountry analysis using linear and quantile-based models. Available at SSRN 3567635.

Cheung, A., Roca, E., and Su, J. J. (2015). Crypto-currency bubbles: An application of the Phillips–Shi–Yu (2013) methodology on Mt. Gox bitcoin prices. *Applied Economics*, 47(23), 2348–2358.

Das, D. and Kannadhasan, M. (2018). Do global factors impact bitcoin prices? Evidence from wavelet approach. *Journal of Economic Research*, 23, 227–264.

Dastgir, S., Demir, E., Downing, G., Gozgor, G., and Lau, C. K. M. (2019). The causal relationship between Bitcoin attention and Bitcoin returns: Evidence from the Copula-based Granger causality test. *Finance Research Letters*, 28, 160–164.

Dirican, C. and Canoz, I. (2017). The cointegration relationship between Bitcoin prices and major world stock indices: An analysis with ARDL model approach. *Journal of Economics Finance and Accounting*, 4(4), 377–392.

Dwyer, G. P. (2015). The economics of Bitcoin and similar private digital currencies. *Journal of Financial Stability*, 17, 81–91.

Eken, M. H. and Baloglu, E. (2018). Crypto currencies and their destinies in the future. *International Journal of Finance & Banking Studies*, 6(4). https://doi.org/10.20525/ijfbs.v6i3.810.

Fakhfekh, M., Jeribi, A., Ghorbel, A., and Hachicha, N. (2021). Hedging stock market prices with WTI, Gold, VIX and cryptocurrencies: A comparison between DCC, ADCC and GO-GARCH models. *International Journal of Emerging Markets*, 18(4), 978–1006.

Grinberg, R. (2011). Bitcoin: An innovative alternative digital currency. *Hastings Science & Technology Law Journal*, 4, 160.

Güler, D. (2023). The impact of investor sentiment on bitcoin returns and conditional volatilities during the era of Covid-19. *Journal of Behavioral Finance*, 24(3), 276–289.

Haq, I. U., Maneengam, A., Chupradit, S., Suksatan, W., and Huo, C. (2021). Economic policy uncertainty and cryptocurrency market as a risk management avenue: A systematic review. *Risks*, 9(9), 163.

Jiang, Y., Wu, L., Tian, G., and Nie, H. (2021). Do cryptocurrencies hedge against EPU and the equity market volatility during COVID-19?–New evidence from quantile coherency analysis. *Journal of International Financial Markets, Institutions and Money*, 72, 101324.

Kapar, B. and Olmo, J. (2019). An analysis of price discovery between Bitcoin futures and spot markets. *Economics Letters*, 174, 62–64.

Khalfaoui, R., Mefteh-Wali, S., Dogan, B., and Ghosh, S. (2023). Extreme spillover effect of COVID-19 pandemic-related news and cryptocurrencies on green bond markets: A quantile connectedness analysis. *International Review of Financial Analysis*, 86, 102496.

Kim, Y. B., Kim, J. G., Kim, W., Im, J. H., Kim, T. H., Kang, S. J., and Kim, C. H. (2016). Predicting fluctuations in cryptocurrency transactions based on user comments and replies. *PloS One*, 11(8), e0161197.

Kjærland, F., Khazal, A., Krogstad, E. A., Nordstrøm, F. B., and Oust, A. (2018). An analysis of bitcoin's price dynamics. *Journal of Risk and Financial Management*, 11(4), 63.

Kliber, A., Marszałek, P., Musiałkowska, I., and Świerczyńska, K. (2019). Bitcoin: Safe haven, hedge or diversifier? Perception of bitcoin in the context of a country's economic situation — A stochastic volatility approach. *Physica A: Statistical Mechanics and Its Applications*, 524, 246–257.

Kristoufek, L. (2013). BitCoin meets Google Trends and Wikipedia: Quantifying the relationship between phenomena of the Internet era. *Scientific Reports*, 3(1), 1–7.

Kristoufek, L. (2015). What are the main drivers of the Bitcoin price? Evidence from wavelet coherence analysis. *PLoS ONE*, 13(4), e0123923. https://doi.org/10.1371/journal.pone.0123923.

Kyriazis, N. A. (2021). A survey on volatility fluctuations in the decentralized cryptocurrency financial assets. *Journal of Risk and Financial Management*, 14(7), 293.

Lamon, C., Nielsen, E., and Redondo, E. (2017). Cryptocurrency price prediction using news and social media sentiment. *SMU Data Science Review*, 1(3), 1–22.

Liang, J., Li, L., Chen, W., and Zeng, D. (2019). Towards an understanding of cryptocurrency: A comparative analysis of cryptocurrency, foreign exchange, and stock. In *2019 IEEE International Conference on Intelligence and Security Informatics (ISI)*, 137–139. IEEE.

Liu, J., Wang, S., Xiang, L., Ma, S., and Xiao, Z. (2024). Unveiling hidden connections: Spillover among BRICS' cryptocurrency-implied exchange rate discounts and US financial markets. *The North American Journal of Economics and Finance*, 71, 102090.

Mba, J. C. (2024). Assessing portfolio vulnerability to systemic risk: A vine copula and APARCH-DCC approach. *Financial Innovation*, 10(1), 20.

Papadamou, S., Kyriazis, N. A., and Tzeremes, P. G. (2020). Non-linear causal linkages of EPU and gold with major cryptocurrencies during bull and bear markets. *The North American Journal of Economics and Finance*, 56, 101343.

Philippas, D., Rjiba, H., Guesmi, K., and Goutte, S. (2019). Media attention and Bitcoin prices. *Finance Research Letters*, 30, 37–43.

Poyser, O. (2017). Exploring the dynamics of Bitcoin's price: A Bayesian structural time series approach. *Eurasian Economic Review*, 9(1), 29–60.

Shahzad, S. J. H., Bouri, E., Roubaud, D., Kristoufek, L., and Lucey, B. (2019). Is Bitcoin a better safe-haven investment than gold and commodities? *International Review of Financial Analysis*, 63, 322–330.

Shen, D., Urquhart, A., and Wang, P. (2018). Does twitter predict Bitcoin? *Economics Letters*, 174, 118–122.

Smuts, N. (2019). What drives cryptocurrency prices? An investigation of google trends and telegram sentiment. *ACM SIGMETRICS Performance Evaluation Review*, 46(3), 131–134.

Sovbetov, Y. (2018). Factors influencing cryptocurrency prices: Evidence from bitcoin, ethereum, dash, litcoin, and monero. *Journal of Economics and Financial Analysis*, 2(2), 1–27.

Symitsi, E. and Chalvatzis, K. J. (2018). The economic value of Bitcoin: A portfolio analysis of currencies, gold, oil and stocks. *Research in International Business and Finance*, 48, 97–110.

Teker, D., Teker, S., and Ozyesil, M. (2020). Macroeconomic determinants of cryptocurrency volatility: Time series analysis. *Journal of Business and Economic Policy*, 7(1), 65–71.

Trabelsi, N. (2018). Are there any volatility spill-over effects among cryptocurrencies and widely traded asset classes? *Journal of Risk and Financial Management*, 11(4), 66.

Yin, W., Chen, Z., Luo, X., and Kirkulak-Uludag, B. (2022). Forecasting cryptocurrencies' price with the financial stress index: A graph neural network prediction strategy. *Applied Economics Letters*, 1–10.

Zhu, Y., Dickinson, D., and Li, J. (2017). Analysis on the influence factors of Bitcoin's price based on VEC model. *Financial Innovation*, 3(1), 1–13.

https://doi.org/10.1142/9789819823161_0019

Chapter 19

Assessing the Impact of Parliamentary Elections, Political Stability, and Government Effectiveness on Bank Risk in India: An Empirical Study

Tarika Singh Sikarwar[*,‡], **Surjeet Singh**[†,§], **and Sandeep Singh**[†,¶]

[*] *Management Department, Prestige Institute of Management & Research, Gwalior, Madhya Pradesh, India*

[†] *Management Department, Alumnus, Prestige Institute of Management & Research, Gwalior, Madhya Pradesh, India*

[‡] *singh.tarika@gmail.com, tarika.singh@prestigegwl.org*

[§] *surjeetsinghm51@gmail.com*

[¶] *sandeepsingh30081999@gmail.com*

This study investigates the intricate relationships between parliamentary elections, political stability, government effectiveness, and their collective impact on banking sector risk in India. Using a dataset spanning from 2009 to 2023, which includes four parliamentary election cycles, we employ a linear regression analysis after averaging the time series data to explore how these political factors influence bank risk, measured by restructured loans, priority sector lending, and non-performing loans. The findings reveal that while political events and government effectiveness are expected to significantly influence bank risk, the empirical results show a negligible and statistically insignificant relationship. This suggests that other variables may play a more crucial role in determining bank risk, necessitating further research into additional factors influencing the financial sector.

Keywords: Parliamentary elections, political stability, government effectiveness, bank, risk.

1. Introduction

Political stability or instability is one of the determinants of profitability in the banking sector. Since the 1990s, there has been a great deal of observation regarding the impact of political instability on economic studies. This is because it is unclear how the democracy variable affects macroeconomic performance, even though democracy is considered a political variable when looking for other variables besides economic ones to explain the differences in economic performance between developed and developing nations. Consensus on the conceptual definition of this type of instability was impeded by political instability arising from various causes in disparate countries. However, according to *Alesina and Perotti's (1996)* perspectives, two primary factors contribute to political instability: changes in constitutional or non-constitutional government, as well as social unrest and politics. The results of legislative elections have a big impact on political stability and government effectiveness. Free and fair elections ensure that the government reflects the views of the public and enables peaceful changes of power. Politically stable environments then enable effective government. Trustworthy governments have a higher likelihood of being rich and stable.

The financial sector depends heavily on banks to support many customers, including large multinational firms and individual consumers. Bank- and country-specific factors are not the only ones that impact bank performance. Politics and banks have a long-standing history together. It has been established in various contexts that political factors impact the performance of banks and financial institutions. According to Ghosh (2016), the Middle East and North African (MENA) countries saw the spread of political unrest known as the Arab Spring in the late 2010s, which affected the operational performance of banks in the region. Government or state-owned enterprises can raise capital to further their political goals when the ruling party runs them. For the government, state-owned banks assume risks and offer specialized services. Government ownership of banks is fairly common outside of the US. Research by La Porta *et al.* (2002) demonstrates that politicians use government-owned banks and that government bank ownership is associated with slower rates of economic growth in the future. Al-Bassam (2013) said that since effective and efficient administration within a democratic framework is linked to good governance, they are the foundation upon which social, political, and economic systems are built (Srivastava, 2009).

This relationship between political dynamics and financial markets has been the subject of extensive research, particularly in the context of developing economies like India. Political stability, government effectiveness, and electoral outcomes are significant factors that can influence financial institutions, including banks (Ullah *et al.*, 2024; Jagannath and Maitra, 2023; Mai *et al.*, 2023).

The literature suggests a significant relationship between political factors and bank risk in India. Parliamentary elections introduce uncertainty, which can increase bank risk. Political stability plays a crucial role in maintaining investor confidence and financial stability, while government effectiveness is essential in ensuring a robust regulatory environment that mitigates bank risk. This review underscores the importance of considering political factors in the analysis of bank risk, particularly in emerging markets like India, which is discussed in the section.

2. Review

2.1. *Impact of parliamentary elections on bank risk*

Parliamentary elections, in most cases, are considered large political events that create uncertainty in the financial markets. Elections raise uncertainty due to possible shifts in the economic policy, which, in turn, may affect the banks' performance (Kauppi and Saikkonen, 2008).

Electoral results themselves could potentially change investor perception, and therefore the risk of investing in banks in the context of India has been revealed (Bhaumik *et al.*, 2020). They pointed out that political risks create instability in banks' stocks due to people's expectations of a change in policies after an election. According to the suggestion given by Białkowski *et al.* (2015), the risk of banks can be affected by elections in corporate as well as institutional investment. In election years, most organizations cannot undertake crucial investments because of the uncertainty of what the winning political party is likely to do. Therefore, there exists an increased probability of additional reserves especially when it comes to loan losses or even an increased risk of a bank in the event of unfavorable outcomes of election.

In his study on the political influence of public banks, Dinc (2005) stressed on loan policies, and the study pointed out that public banks are most likely to extend their loan levels during the election year compared to private sector banking, based on a cross-section dataset. Contrary to this, Molyneux and Thornton (1992) found out that government ownership enhances the level of profitability among banks. On the other hand, Micco *et al.* (2007) found that public banks' performance is affected by business cycle factors, especially because their performance generally deteriorates during election years due to political influence.

Beltratti and Stulz (2012) have found that through their influence on the future potential economic policies, elections lead to market fluctuations. Chava, Purnanandam, and Amiyatosh (2014) explained that due to the volatility in the political environment and legislative changes, particularly during election moments in India, the risk in banks tends to be high. For instance, elections are certain to generate uncertainty about the new government's policies toward economic reforms, which in turn affects bank performance (Kauppi and Saikkonen, 2008).

2.2. *Impact of political stability and bank risk*

Another variable that has a bearing on the risk of banks is political risk. Political stability may be defined as the lack of social unrest or any events that are likely to culminate in sequences of a particular government. As established in this chapter, a stable political environment is conducive to banks' operations in terms of reduced overall risk levels. As concluded, the research initiated by Beck,

Demirgüç-Kunt, and Levine in 2006 proves the existence of a link between financial and political stability, where a high level of the former corresponds to the levels of the latter. This is so because a stable political environment enhances investment, which in turn boosts economic growth. Ghosh (2016) noted that political stability saw a decline in NPAs by banks, hence implying a decrease in the risk attached to the banks in the Indian setting.

Employing the cointegration technique, Moshirian, Nandha, and Pham (2008) analyzed the effect of political stability on the level of financial stability in emerging markets and argued that an increase in the level of political instability leads to growth in the level of financial instability and risk of banks. Laeven and Valencia (2012) also provided evidence to support this argument, as it was observed that political instability results in financial crises that are destructive to banks. The papers by Acharya, Kose, and Raghuram (2013) have stressed that political instability is likely to bring about adverse movements, including loss of investor confidence, increased capital outflows, and higher bank risk, mainly because of the tightening of the financial conditions.

2.3. *Impact of government effectiveness and bank risk*

Now, we take a look at the role that government effectiveness can have in the financial sustainability of the banking sectors in a given country. The quality of public services, policy formulation, enforcement of regulations, and government effectiveness are also defined. The government's effectiveness is measured by the capacity of the government to adopt the right policies and ensure the quality of regulations is highly connected with the stability of banks. Barth, Caprio, and Levine (2004) posited that sound governance lowers the risk of banks by placing sensible structures that provide a steady environment of supervision to the banking sector and enhancing sound framing of risk in banks. External shocks were defined by Demirgüç-Kunt and Detragiache (2002) as events that decrease the amount of financial resources available to the banks. In the same year, the two authors also pointed out that the government effectively reduces the impact of such shocks on the performance of the banks. According to Sharma and Seth (2020), government effectiveness, especially in the capacity to regulate banks, is important in India to ensure banks' stability in the event of a downturn.

Accounting for the elements of governance effectiveness and the quality of public services, as well as the formulation and implementation of policies, the role of the government factor is highly significant for bank risk. Policy efficiency coupled with good governance ensures safe implementation of policies, hence leading to the creation of a sound economic climate. The study conducted by La Porta *et al.* (1998) revealed that a strong financial system signifies a highly efficient government. Consequently, according to Roy and Singh (2018), in their research done in India, it is possible to link government efficiency to the ability to reduce Bank Risk by increasing the efficiency of regulatory mechanisms as well as eliminating possibilities of economically irresponsible actions.

Government effectiveness has come out strongly as a significant factor in banking stability, especially in the developing world, where a capable government is central in policy implementation. As a leading regulatory authority, the Reserve Bank of India (RBI) put into practice various codes meant for the elimination of hazardous microstructural threats to the banking structure. Thus, according to the provided sources, Dey and Ganguly (2021) maintained that less risk could be achieved if an efficient government puts into place policies that foster the monitoring of financial risks, eradicate corrupt practices, and enhance transparency to aid banking systems. The robustness of policies implemented by the Indian government, most especially in addressing issues touching on the application of banking regulations, explains the credit risk faced by banks (Gupta *et al.*, 2022).

In their theoretical study, Singh and Verma (2020) concluded that there is a possibility that problems of liquidity and solvency in banks are reduced when the government makes laws and ensures compliance with such laws. It was highlighted from their study that higher NPAs in Indian banks were often found in political turmoil or in an ineffective government phase. This finding is in line with cross-sectional research works that relate the emerging fortunes of financial markets and volatilities to government quality and political stability (Eichengreen and Gupta, 2020). As noted earlier, there are two ways that government efficacy impacts bank risk: policy consistency and regulatory openness.

As cited by Bhandari and Saxena (2023), the pressure is high in the banking sector in India for one main reason: the government's ineffective policies. For instance, when uncertainty is high due to a large number of governmental policy changes, then the banking industry may rely on high-risk lending procedures, which lead to an increase in the probability of default. In addition, according to Mishra and Jain (2021), government policies such as demonetization and the implementation of the GST increased the uncertainties in the financial market and increased the risks of banks in the short term. The causal component of the influence of government-led efforts on financial access is the final one. Schemes like Pradhan Mantri Jan Dhan Yojana (PMJDY) and Mudra loan schemes, as per the study of Desai and Rao (2022), have facilitated banking services among unserved people; yet, they have emerged as risky propositions for banks since they have shifted the financing to the vulnerable section of the population. This chapter does acknowledge that these hazards may be mitigated and contained with proper government intervention and regulation.

For causality between government effectiveness and bank risk in India, there are many empirical methods that have supported this fact.

Several empirical results have supported the causality between government effectiveness and risk in Indian banks. For example, in their study, Pandey and Roy (2022) applied a time series analysis in the consideration of how the variations in government policies affect banking risk. In their study, they proposed that with respect to risk standards, Indian banks experienced the lowest levels of risk during periods of high government efficiency, particularly after the banking sector reforms of the 1990s. On the other hand, during the uncertainty in the political and policy environment like the financial crisis in the financial year ending March 2013, NPAs and other risk parameters in banking also rose sharply.

The following case studies of particular commercial banks also support these findings. Saxena (2021) did a case analysis on SBI, and his analysis revealed that in response to the economic conditions, state activity became positive for the SBI banking sector when the government initiated new ideal reforms in the banking sector. However, where the government underperformed, delayed the process, or implemented reforms poorly, then the risk profile of the bank rose.

Lastly, a major proof of causality between government effectiveness and Bank Risk is articulated in the literature regarding Indian banks. Effective policies and coherent regulations in the sphere of banking activities can also be noted as reducing the probability of impact exposure. On the other hand, several government factors, such as government crises or lack of efficiency in operations, are likely to result in risks in the banking sector. The research underscores the importance of continuous government reform and policy consistency to maintain banking stability in India.

2.4. *Impact of political stability and bank risk*

Some of the past papers have examined the effect of political stability on bank risk with much focus on the link between political structures and banking structures. The stability of political systems is another factor that must be considered when explaining the conditions for economic activities and the level of risks in a country's banking system. This implies that political stability is normally accompanied by a relatively lower risk in the banking field due to the creation of favorable conditions for economic growth. On the other hand, political instabilities result in uncertainties, which reduce investor confidence, hence increasing the risk exposure among banks (Kumar and Singh, 2021).

The analytical techniques used to undertake research work for concluding that political stability and bank risk are causally related are as follows. A reason why time series studies are preferred is that the methods offer the researcher a convenient way of analyzing the nature of political events and their impact on financial variables through time. Likewise, panel data analyses enable one to establish the behavior of several banks in a variety of political settings. Further, econometric models have been applied in some studies to isolate the effect of political stability from other related factors.

The issue of interaction between political stability, economic development, government performance and governance remains under discussion (Man Li and Leung, 2015). There are two aspects to consider from these democratic trends in terms of economic impact; Milton Friedman believed that they lead to better economic returns. Some other similar studies, including those of Fidrmuc (2001), and

Peev and Murller (2012), support the inference that the democratic form of governance is good in the long run for the desired political economic performance (North, 1990, 1993; Olson, 2000) and for economic growth.

This study has aimed to examine the political stability and risk of banks, which has been a significant concern, especially in countries such as India, due to the speedy economic and regulatory changes. With regard to Alesina and Perotti's (1996) study on the factors affecting the banking sector's profitability, political stability is one of the aspects. The political instability has had a rather profound impact on economic studies after 1995. This is because, whereas democracy is considered a political factor, since there exist other factors other than economic ones that determine the differentiation of economic volatility between developed and developing countries, there is no clear understanding of how democracy influences the macroeconomy. Many types of political instabilities emerged from different sources in different countries, and hence there was no clear agreement on the conceptual definitions of this kind of instability. However, based on the outlined premises, it is possible to state that the ideas presented by Alesina and Perotti (1996) reflect two truths about political instability.

The extent of risk in banking has been seen as largely affected by the prospect of regulations, investors, and the overall economic environment. How? Well, election results, a government's stability, and efficiency all play roles in these aspects. It is pertinent to mention here that bank risk can be reduced with political stability and a sound political environment. Some of the differences in the effect on the risk of a bank will relate to the legal system of each of the countries involved.

It is also true that political stability and bank risk have an inverse relationship in the case of India, based on the findings of the following empirical studies. For instance, Sharma and Bhattacharya (2022) used time series analysis to analyze the effect of political variables on the banking sector in India. The result of the study, therefore, implies that banks are at higher risk during the period of political transition, as research showed that political instability, especially during the election period, causes high non-performing assets (NPAs) and low bank profitability.

The other study by Gupta and Saxena (2022) used panel data from several Indian banks to investigate the effect of changes in government policies on the probability of risk-taking by banks. As was revealed by the authors, political stability, identified as a predictable and consistent policy environment, reduces the level of risk in banking systems. They also pointed out how, during political stability, banks commonly use some “safe-and-sound” style of lending that minimizes credit risk.

Not all research works have associated political stability with bank risk and determinant causes exist, for instance, Mishra *et al.* (2023) who provided a qualitative analysis on the moderation effect of external variables, including international investment and global economic conditions, on the political stability–bank risk nexus. In their studies, they discovered that political stability is indeed the key to the banking sector risk, but due to external economic factors, the link tends to be masked and thus different from a simplistic model. In their study, Kumar and Singh (2021) employed the VAR model to examine the short- and long-term causality between political stability and bank risk; the authors reported a −0.5085 negative coefficient between political stability and bank risk.

3. Research Gaps

There are many works discussing the effects of political events and government stability on financial markets and banking systems; however, there are many gaps in the literature that analyze the transmission mechanisms that relate parliamentary elections, political environment, and overall government efficiency to banks’ risk-taking. This research gap includes the lack of studying not only the direct influence of political stability and elections on the banking risk, which might be reflected in changes in laws and policies, but also the depth and multiple channels through which the effects can be propagated over the financial sphere, including investors’ sentiment, the market confidence, and macroeconomic stability. Nevertheless, there is a lack of research that explores these relationships in detail across different countries, about the different political and economic aspects.

There is limited research on the topic that covers all the relationships and interdependencies that exist within parliamentary systems.

Although parliamentary elections also have an influence on the occurrence of uncertainty and change in the government's policy in the banking sector, it has been noted that they affect the risk profiles of banks. Other determinants that can influence the political stability and efficiency of the institutions of government include the regulatory environment and the ability of governments to respond to financial crises, thus translating to risk exposure among banks. It is easy, however, to see that these relations are intertwined, and as there is not much research on this topic, it is challenging to determine how exactly political stability, parliamentary elections, and government efficacy impact the risk inherent in the operation of banks. Penning in this knowledge vacuum could afford useful information to financial institutions and policymakers.

4. Proposed Model

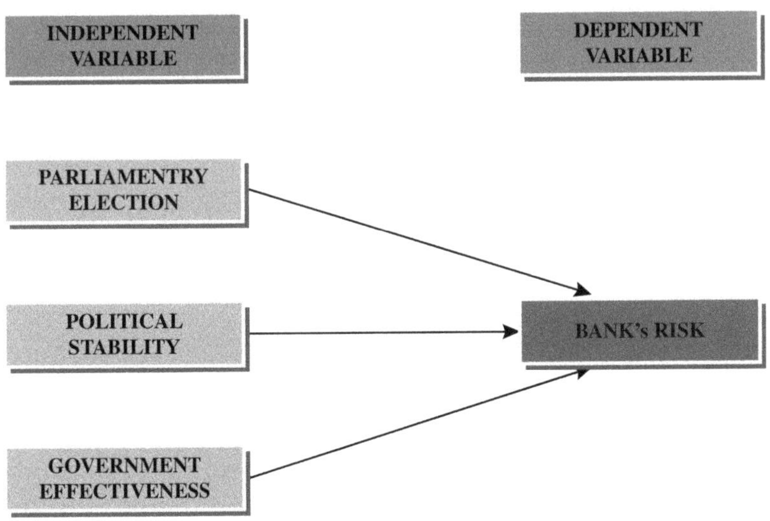

5. Hypotheses

- Ha1: There is a causal relationship between parliamentary elections and a bank's risk.
- Ha2: There is a causal relationship between political stability and a bank's risk.

- Ha3: There is a causal relationship between government effectiveness and a bank's risk.
- Ha4: There is a causal relationship between parliamentary elections, political stability, government effectiveness, and a bank's risk.

6. Research Objectives

- To establish whether or not the parliamentary elections — the independent variable — have a direct or indirect impact on banks' risk — the dependent variable.
- to identify the effect of the independent variable — political stability — on the dependent variable — the risk faced by banks.
- to identify the effect of government effectiveness as an independent variable and the risk of the bank as a dependent variable.
- to establish the impact of parliamentary elections, political stability, and government effectiveness as the independent variables on the risk as the dependent variable within the context of the bank involved.
- to compare public and private banks in terms of the impact of parliamentary elections, political stability, and government effectiveness as the independent variables on the risk as the dependent variable.

7. Research Methodology

The study is conducted on government-owned and private Indian banks, employing an exploratory design. A non-probability purposive sampling strategy was used to select the sample. The data were sourced from the Reserve Bank of India's (RBI) Database on Indian Economy (DBIE), which contains comprehensive information about scheduled Indian commercial banks. Further, the balance sheet and profitability figures of the state-owned and commercial banks from the beginning of the calendar year 2009 till 2023 were collected from the Prowess database of the Centre for Monitoring the Indian Economy (CMIE). The research period encompasses four parliamentary elections, one in 2009, the second in 2014, the third in 2019, and the last in 2023. Four measures were used to evaluate bank risk, including the amount of restructured loans, priority sector lending, and net and gross non-performing loans (NPLs). A linear regression approach was employed to establish causal relationships between the variables.

8. Discussion

8.1. *Linear regression private banks*

8.1.1. *Linear regression analysis with bank risk as dependent variable and parliamentary elections as independent variable*

The R Square value indicates that only 0.1% of the variation in bank risk is explained by the **Parliamentary Election**. This suggests that the **Parliamentary Election** is not a strong predictor of bank risk (Table 1).

***F*-statistic (0.029) and Significance (0.867):** The F-statistic is used to analyze whether the model in general is significant or not. Self-reported measures of job performance are valid out to two months before the date at which the performance appraisal was completed, while objectively measured measures of job performance are valid out to two years before the same date, based on non-parametric tests, t-tests, and ANOVA's test at the 5% significance level. However, there is valuable information in the rest of the sample; $p = 0.867$ suggests that the model is insignificant. This implies that change in the endogenous variable, **Parliamentary Election**, does not in any way shape the magnitude of bank risk (Table 2).

Regression Equation: Bank Risk = 6.579 − 0.2.933* Parliament Election.

Table 1. Summary statistics regression results.

***R*-Square**	***F***	**Sig.**
0.001	0.029	0.867

Table 2. Coefficient statistics regression results.

Model	Unstandardized Coefficients	Std. Error	Standardized Coefficients Beta
Dependent Variables: Constant and Bank Risk;	6.579	3.16	
Independent Variable: Constant, and Parliament Election	−2.933	17.293	−0.035

Intercept (6.579): This represents the expected value of bank risk when the **Parliamentary Election** is zero. In this context, if there were no parliamentary elections, the average bank risk would be 6.579.

The Coefficient for Parliamentary Election (−2.933): This indicates the effect of the **Parliamentary Election** on bank risk. A negative coefficient means that as the number or intensity of the **Parliamentary Election** increases by one unit, bank risk is expected to decrease by 2.933 units. However, it is important to note that the standard error is quite large (17.293), indicating that the estimate is not very precise.

The model suggests that **Parliamentary Election** has a negligible and statistically insignificant impact on bank risk. The negative coefficient might indicate a direction, but given the insignificance and low R Square, this result should not be used for making inferences or decisions. The high standard error of the coefficient for the **Parliamentary Election** further suggests that the relationship between the independent variable and bank risk is weak and uncertain.

8.1.2. *To determine the causal relationship between political stability as an independent variable and a bank's risk as a dependent variable, a linear regression test was used*

R Square (0.021): This value indicates that only 2.1% of the variance in bank risk can be explained by **Political Stability**. This suggests that **Political Stability** does not have a strong influence on bank risk (Table 3).

F-statistic (0.489) and p-value (0.491): The F-statistic is therefore used in the analysis of the overall significance of the regression model.

Table 3. Summary statistics regression results.

Model	*R* Square	*F*	Sig.
Dependent variable: Bank's Risk Independent variable: Political Stability	0.021	0.489	0.491

Table 4. Coefficient statistics regression results.

Model	Unstandardized Coefficients	Std. Error	Standardized Coefficients	*t*	Sig.
Dependent Variable: Constant, Bank's Risk;	7.997	2.858		2.798	0.01
Independent variable: Constant and Political Stability	−8.591	12.287	−0.144	−0.699	0.491

In this case, the *p*-value, also known as Sig., is equal to 0.491 and this is larger than the conventional level of significance of 0.05. This means that the model is statistically insignificant, and the results obtained suggest that there is no strong relationship between **Political Stability** and bank risk (Table 4).

The regression equation provided is
Bank Risk $= 7.997 + 0.591\times$ **Political Stability**.

Intercept (7.997): This is the expected value of bank risk when **Political Stability** is zero. Essentially, it is the baseline level of bank risk.

Intercept (7.997, $p = 0.01$): The intercept is statistically significant with a *p*-value of 0.01, suggesting that the baseline level of bank risk (when **Political Stability** is zero) is meaningful.

Political Stability coefficient (−8.591, $p = 0.491$): The coefficient for **Political Stability** is −8.591 with a *p*-value of 0.491. This suggests that **Political Stability** has a negative relationship with bank risk, but this relationship is not statistically significant (*p*-value > 0.05). The negative coefficient implies that as **Political Stability** increases, bank risk tends to decrease, but given the high *p*-value, this effect is likely due to random chance. The regression results suggest

Table 5. Summary statistics regression results.

Model	*R* Square	*F*	Sig.
Dependent Variable: Bank Risk; Independent Variable: Government Effectiveness	0.015	0.361	0.554

that **Political Stability** does not significantly predict bank risk. The model's overall explanatory power is low, and the relationship between the variables is weak and statistically insignificant.

8.1.3. *Determine the causal relationship between government effectiveness as an independent variable and the bank's risk as a dependent variable*

The results of this dummy regression analysis show that the multiple coefficient of determination, R Square (R^2) value, is 0.015 (Table 5). It can be seen as that the *Government effectiveness affects the bank's risk* only approximately by 1 percent. The results show that the independent variable, or predictor, of government effectiveness accounts for 5% of the variance in the dependent variable, bank risk. This is a very low percentage, and we can deduce that government effectiveness may not be a very good predictor of bank risk in this model.

Model Summary

- F-Statistics 0.361: The F-statistic is used to evaluate the quality of the general regression model, that is, all the considered independent variables. This value has a low F-value of 0. As seen from the coefficient of determination (R-squared) of 361, the model is non-significant.
- Significance (Sig.): The values are as follows: 554
  In this type of study, a cut-off p-value of 0.554 is above the limit of 500, which is used frequently to determine content similarity. 05. This therefore implies that "Government Effectiveness" does not cause "Bank Risk" as hypothesized, since the measures of the two independent and dependent variables are not strongly related.

Table 6. Coefficient statistics regression results.

	Unstandardized Coefficients	**Std. Error**	**Standardized Coefficients**
Dependent Variable: Constant, Bank Risk,	0.707	8.923	
Independent Variable: Government Effectiveness	26.957	44.847	.124

Regression Coefficients

The Unstandardized Coefficients (B): The value of the Constant (Intercept) is 0.707, and the Government Effectiveness Coefficient is 26.957.

The regression equation can be interpreted as

$$\text{Bank Risk} = 0.707 + 26.957 \times \text{Government Effectiveness.}$$

This means that a one-unit increase in government effectiveness increases the expected level of bank risk by 0.26 units.

- The standard error value is 8.923 for the intercept and 44.847 correlates with the coefficient of the Government Effectiveness Index (Table 6). The standard error shows the extent of deviation from the regression line of the observed values. If the variance value is larger, it means that the data are spread more in the given range.
- Standardized coefficients (Beta): 0.124. This value shows the degree/extent of the impact of government effectiveness on bank risk. A Beta of 0.124, which is a relatively low positive association, shows a weak positive correlation between the two variables.

In conclusion, the model accounts for a very small proportion of the variance in bank risk, i.e., 1.5%. Government effectiveness does not significantly predict bank risk ($p = 0.554$). The relationship between government effectiveness and bank risk is weak (Beta = 0.124). This model suggests that government effectiveness is not a significant predictor of bank risk, and the overall fit of the model is poor. Further investigation with additional variables or alternative models may be necessary to better understand the factors influencing bank risk.

8.1.4. *Linear regression analysis with bank risk as dependent variable and political stability, government effectiveness and parliament election as independent variable*

From Table 7, the Adjusted R Square is −0.100. This means that the model does not account for any of the variations in the dependent variable (Bank Risk). An adjusted R Square value below zero suggests that the model is performing worse than a model with no predictors at all. Essentially, this model does not fit the data well.

The F-value is 0.271. The F-statistic is used to test whether or not the general regression model is appropriate for evaluating the data. However, the F-value is rather small, which points toward the fact that the given model does not provide a significantly better prediction of the dependent variable than the model with no predictors.

The Sig. (p-value) is 0.845.

This p-value is very large, in other words, greater than 0.05; therefore, the overall model is not significant. Hence, it can be concluded that the predictors used in the model are unrelated to the dependent variable.

$$\text{Bank Risk} = 6.452 + .172 * \text{Government Effectiveness} + 16.465 * \text{Parliament Election} - 17.537 * \text{Political Stability}.$$

Coefficients

Here, the value of (Constant) B is 6.452, and Std. error is 12.724. The constant term is not statistically significant, as the standard error is quite large compared to the coefficient value.

Refer to Table 8, which indicates that for government effectiveness, B is 3.172, Std. Error is 57.827, and Beta is 0.015. This predictor has a very small standardized coefficient (Beta) and a large

Table 7. Summary statistics regression results.

Model	Adjusted R Square	F	Sig.
Dependent Variable: Bank Risk Independent Variable: government effectiveness, Parliament Election, and Political Stability	−0.100	0.271	0.845[a]

Table 8. Coefficient statistics regression results.

Dependent Variable: Bank Risk			
Model	**Unstandardized Coefficients**	**Std. Error**	**Standardized Coefficients**
(Constant)	6.452	12.724	
Government Effectiveness	3.172	57.827	0.015
Parliament Election	16.465	32.476	0.198
Political Stability	−17.537	25.759	−0.295

standard error, suggesting that it does not significantly contribute to the model. The Beta value close to zero further supports this.

Similarly, for parliament election, B is 16.465, Std. Error is 32.476, and Beta is 0.198. This predictor also has a large standard error and a relatively small Beta value. The predictor's contribution to the model is not statistically significant.

For political stability, B is -17.537, Std. Error is 25.759, and Beta is -0.295. Although this predictor has the largest Beta value among the three predictors, it is still not statistically significant, given the large standard error and non-significant p-value.

The regression model does not show significant relationships between the predictors (government effectiveness, parliament election, and political stability) and the dependent variable (bank risk). The model as a whole is not a good fit for the data, and none of the predictors significantly explain the variability in bank risk.

8.2. *Linear regression public banks*

8.2.1. *Linear regression public banks: The dependent variable is bank risk and the independent variables are political stability, government effectiveness, and parliament election*

The Adjusted R^2 takes into consideration the number of predictor variables in existence in the model. It is significant to note that, at 0.172, after deploying the number of predictors, the model predicts the percent of 17 (Table 9). Thus, the model accounts for a 2% variance in bank risk. As evident from the above-mentioned equation,

Table 9. Summary statistics regression results.

Model	Adjusted R-Square	F	Sig.
Dependent Variable: Bank Risk; Independent Variable: Political Stability, Government Effectiveness, Parliament Election	0.172	2.661	0.075

Table 10. Coefficient statistics regression results.

Model	Unstandardized Coefficients	Std. Error	Standardized Coefficients	t	Sig.
(Constant)	13.071	10.169		1.285	0.213
Government Effectiveness	−46.186	46.216	−0.231	−0.999	0.329
Parliament Election	69.219	25.956	0.905	2.667	0.014
Political Stability	−53.893	20.588	−0.982	−2.618	0.016

the value is lower than that of R^2 (0.275), which suggests that some of the predictors may not help in accounting for the variation of the dependent variable.

F-statistic: 2.661

- The F-statistic is used to analyze the general significance of the preferred model. It looks at the model without the predictors — intercept model — against the model with the predictors. An F-value of 2.66 statistically indicates that the model is not very significant.

p-value (Sig.): 0.075

- The p-value reflects the probability that the relationship found could have occurred by pure chance. Here, with the value of 0.075, the model cannot be said to be significantly different from zero, and therefore the model is not statistically significant at the conventional of 0.05 level, and hence the relationship is nearly significant, although at the 07 level the results were non-significant (Table 10).

Regression Equation

$$\text{BankRisk} = 13.071 - 46.186 * \text{Government Effectiveness} + 69.219 * \text{Parliament Election} - 53.893 * \text{Political Stability}.$$

Coefficients

- **(Constant):** 13.071 ($p = 0.213$)
  - The intercept value is 13.071, meaning that if all independent variables are zero, the bank risk is predicted to be 13.071. However, this is not statistically significant ($p > 0.05$).
- **GOVERNMENT_EFFECTIVENESS:** −46.186 ($p = 0.329$)
  - For every unit increase in government effectiveness, bank risk decreases by 46.186 units. However, this relationship is not statistically significant ($p > 0.05$).
- **PARLIAMENT_ELECTION:** 69.219 ($p = 0.014$)
  - For every unit increase in the parliament election, bank risk increases by 69.219 units. This is a statistically significant predictor ($p < 0.05$), indicating that election periods might increase bank risk.
- **POLITICAL_STABILITY:** −53.893 ($p = 0.016$)
  - For every unit increase in political stability, bank risk decreases by 53.893 units. This relationship is statistically significant ($p < 0.05$), suggesting that greater political stability reduces bank risk.

The linear regression model explains about 27.5% of the variance in bank risk, with parliament election and political stability being significant predictors. The model overall is not highly significant, but some of the predictors do show significant relationships with bank risk.

8.2.2. *Linear regression analysis for public banks with bank risk as dependent variable and government effectiveness as independent variable*

R-Square (R^2): 0.013: This value means that the model accounts for only 1.3% of the variation in the dependent variable, that is, bank

Table 11. Summary statistics regression results.

Model	*R* Square	*F*	Sig.
Dependent Variable: Bank Risk for Public Banks		0.295	0.592
Independent Variable: Government Effectiveness	0.013		

Table 12. Coefficient statistics regression results.

Model	Unstandardized Coefficients	Std. Error	Standardized Coefficients	*T*	Sig.
(Constant) Dependent Variable: Bank Risk for PUBLIC BANKS	−0.383	8.232		−0.047	0.963
GOVERNMENT_EFFECTIVENESS	22.478	41.373	0.113	0.543	0.592

risk (Table 11). This is a very low square of multiple coefficient of determination, which means that in this model, the efficiency of the government is not a good determinant of the risk of the bank.

***F*-Statistic**: 0.295: The F-statistic helps to determine whether the general regression equation is valid or not. In this case, the F value is equal to 0.295, which is low.

Significance (Sig.): 0.592: The p-value of the F-test statistic is 0.592, and hence, one can conclude that it is higher than the accepted value of 0.05 (Table 12). This means that the overall model is not statistically significant, thus we infer that government effectiveness does not affect bank risk in this model.

Coefficients

- **Constant (Intercept):**
  - **Unstandardized Coefficient (B):** −0.383
  - **Std. Error:** 8.232
  - ***t*-value:** −0.047
  - **Sig.:** 0.963

  - The constant term (intercept) is not significant (p-value = 0.963), indicating that when government effectiveness is zero, the predicted bank risk is −0.383, but this value is not statistically significant.

- **Government Effectiveness:**
  - **Unstandardized Coefficient (B):** 22.478
  - **Std. Error:** 41.373
  - **Standardized Coefficient (Beta):** 0.113
  - ***t*-value:** 0.543
  - **Sig.:** 0.592
  - The unstandardized coefficient for government effectiveness is 22.478, which means that for each one-unit increase in government effectiveness, bank risk increases by 22.478 units. However, the p-value (0.592) indicates that this relationship is not statistically significant.

The regression analysis suggests that government effectiveness does not have a statistically significant effect on bank risk. The model itself explains very little variance in bank risk (only 1.3%), and the coefficients are not significant. This implies that other factors may be more important in explaining variations in bank risk, and government effectiveness alone is not a strong predictor in this case.

8.2.3. *Linear regression analysis for public banks with bank risk as dependent variable and parliament election as independent variable*

R Square (R^2) = 0.23 (Table 13): This means that the model has the capability of accounting for about 23% of the variation in bank risk (i.e., by the independent variable **Parliament Election**). While this shows some degree of explanation, it is relatively low, implying that other factors not included in the model might explain the remaining 77% of the variance in bank risk.

Table 13. Summary statistics regression results.

Model	R Square	F	Sig.
Dependent Variable: Bank Risk; Independent Variable: Parliament Election	0.23	0.538	0.471

Table 14. Coefficient statistics regression results.

Model	Unstandardized Coefficients	Std. Error	Standardized Coefficients	t	Sig.
(Constant)	2.014	2.879		0.700	0.491
Dependent Variable: Bank Risk					
Parliament Election	11.559	15.757	0.151	0.734	0.471

***F*-statistic = 0.538 and Sig. (*p*-value) = 0.471:** The F-statistic tests if all regression slopes equal zero by comparing explained and residual variance. Here, the p-value is equal to <stem: 0.471, which is significantly greater than the common significance level (for example, 05), which means that the distances between observations and the model are statistically significant. This means that, overall, the independent variable (**Parliament Election**) does not significantly predict the dependent variable (Bank Risk).

Coefficients:

Constant (Intercept) = 2.014: This represents the predicted value of bank risk when all independent variables are zero. However, this value has limited interpretive value in this context.

- **Parliament Election (B = 11.559, p = 0.471)**

Unstandardized Coefficient ($B = 11.559$) (Table 14): From the analysis, it can be seen that for each unit change in the **Parliament Election** variable, the measure of bank risk is expected to change by 11. All other factors being equal, this implies that the total number of units will be 559 units.

- **Standardized Coefficient (Beta = 0.151):** This value represents the effect size of the independent variable in standard deviation units. The effect of the **Parliament Election** on bank risk is small (0.151 standard deviations) and not significant.

The regression model suggests that the variable **Parliament Election** has a positive but statistically insignificant relationship with bank risk. The low R^2 value and non-significant p-values indicate that the model does not provide strong evidence that **Parliament**

Table 15. Summary statistics regression results.

Model	***F***	**Sig.**	***R* Square**
Dependent Variable: Bank Risk; Independent Variable: Political Stability	0.664	0.424	0.28

Election is a meaningful predictor of bank risk. Other factors likely contribute more significantly to the variability in bank risk, and further analysis or additional variables might be needed to improve the model's explanatory power.

8.2.4. *Linear regression analysis with bank risk as dependent variable and political stability as independent variable*

***R* Square:** 0.28 (Table 15)

- This means that we have gotten to the extent at which political stability influences the dependent variable (Bank Risk), for which 28% of the variance is explained. The model demonstrated for a small degree of variance.
  F-value: 0.664
- The F-value is used to test the overall significance of the model, which means determining whether the overall model is significant. Here, the F-value is lesser, which shows that the model would not be a good fit to the data.
  Sig. (p-value for the F-test): 4240.0
- The p-value of 0.424 indicates that there is no statistically significant effect in the generated model. This indicates that the independent variable, political stability, does not affect bank risk in a significant manner.

Coefficients:

- **Constant (Intercept):** 6.153 (Table 16)
  - This is the predicted value of bank risk when **Political Stability** is zero.
- **Political Stability Coefficient (B):** −9.188

Table 16. Coefficient statistics regression results.

Model	Unstandardized Coefficients	Std. Error	Standardized Coefficients	t	Sig.
(Constant)	6.153	2.623		2.345	0.028
Dependent Variable: Bank Risk					
Political Stability	−9.188	11.277	−0.167	−0.815	0.424

- This negative coefficient suggests that holding all else constant, an increase in political stability is associated with a decrease in bank risk. However, the impact is not statistically significant.

- **Standard Error of Political Stability:** 11.277
  - This measures the accuracy of the coefficient. A larger standard error relative to the coefficient indicates less reliable estimates.
- **Standardized Coefficient Beta:** −0.167
  - The standardized coefficient indicates the relative importance of the independent variable in predicting the dependent variable. Here, it is a small negative value, indicating a weak inverse relationship.
- ***t*-value:** −0.815
  - The t-value tests the significance of the individual coefficients. A low t-value indicates that the coefficient is not statistically significant.
- **Sig. (*p*-value for Political Stability):** 0.424
  - The p-value for **Political Stability** is 0.424, which is greater than 0.05. This confirms that **Political Stability** is not a significant predictor of bank risk.

The regression model suggests that **Political Stability** does not have a statistically significant impact on bank risk. The model as a whole is also not statistically significant, and it explains only a small portion of the variance in bank risk. This means that other variables not included in the model might be more important in explaining the variation in bank risk.

Table 17. Comparative statistics results.

Variable	Public Bank Risk	Private Bank Risk
Constant (C)	13.071	6.452
Std. Error	10.169	12.724
t-Statistic	1.285	0.507
p-value	0.213	0.617
Government Effectiveness	−46.186	3.172
Std. Error	46.216	57.827
t-Statistic	−0.999	0.055
p-value	0.329	0.957
Parliament Election	69.219	16.465
Std. Error	25.956	32.476
t-Statistic	2.667	0.507
p-value	0.014	0.618
Political Stability	−53.893	−17.537
Std. Error	20.588	25.759
t-Statistic	−2.618	−0.681
p-value	0.016	0.503
R-squared	0.275	0.037
Adjusted R-squared	0.172	−0.100
S.E. of Regression	2.809	3.515
F-statistic	2.661	0.271
p-value (F-statistic)	0.075	0.845
Durbin–Watson statistic	1.143	0.208

8.3. *Time series analysis: Least squares regression*

To compare public and private banks in terms of the impact of parliamentary elections, political stability, and government effectiveness as the independent variables on risk as the dependent variable, Least Squares Regression using EViews software was applied.

Comparative assessment of causal association is done for public and private banks, and the results are summarized in the following:

The intercept coefficient for Public Bank Risk is 13.07108, accompanied by a p-value of 0.2127, indicating a lack of statistical significance. This suggests that when all other variables (Government Effectiveness, Parliament Election, and Political Stability) are zero, the baseline risk for public banks is estimated at 13.07108; however, this result lacks statistical reliability (Table 17).

For Private Bank Risk, the intercept is 6.452491 with a p-value of 0.6174, also not significant. This suggests a baseline risk of 6.452491 for private banks when all other factors are zero, but the estimate lacks statistical significance.

Government Effectiveness

The coefficient for Public Bank Risk is −46.18621, with a p-value of 0.3290, showing an inverse association between government effectiveness and public bank risk. Nevertheless, while the p-value is above 0.05, this link lacks statistical significance.

The coefficient for Private Bank Risk is 3.171725, with a p-value of 0.9568, indicating a positive yet exceedingly weak and non-significant correlation between government effectiveness and private bank risk.

Parliament Election

The coefficient for Public Bank Risk is 69.21866 (p-value = 0.0144), indicating statistical significance. This means that public bank risk rises significantly during parliamentary elections, by 69.21866 units, while other factors remain unchanged.

- The coefficient for Private Bank Risk is 16.46462 with a p-value of 0.6175, demonstrating a positive association but not statistically significant. This suggests that parliamentary elections have no meaningful impact on private bank risk.

Political Stability

The coefficient for Public Bank Risk is −53.89337 (p-value = 0.0161), indicating statistical significance. This suggests that better political stability is related to a large reduction in public bank risk of 53.89337 units, all other factors being equal.

- Private bank risk has a negative but non-significant association with political stability (coefficient = −17.53739, p-value = 0.5034).

Model Fit (R-squared, Adjusted R-squared)

The model accounts for 27.54% of the variability in public bank risk (R-squared = 0.275403).

After adjusting for the number of predictors, the adjusted R-squared of 0.171889 shows a modest fit, indicating that the model explains a significant fraction of the variation in public bank risk.

The R-squared value of 0.037296 indicates that the model only explains around 3.73% of the variability in private bank risk, which is a low level. The Adjusted R-squared score of -0.100233 reveals that the model may not adequately explain private bank risk. Adding more variables would not enhance the model.

F-statistic and Prob(F-statistic)

Public bank risk has an F-statistic of 2.660540 and a p-value of 0.074539, near the 0.05 threshold. This shows that the characteristics, taken together, may be substantial predictors of public bank risk, albeit on the borderline.

- Private bank risk is not significantly explained by the independent factors (F-statistic $= 0.271189$, p-value $= 0.845450$).

Durbin–Watson statistic

Public bank risk has a Durbin–Watson statistic of 1.142869, lower than the optimal value of roughly 2, indicating positive autocorrelation in residuals.

- The Durbin–Watson statistic for private bank risk is 0.207667, indicating a significant risk of positive autocorrelation in residuals. This may indicate serial correlation concerns in the model.

Hence, for public banks, the model demonstrates that political stability and parliamentary elections have a considerable impact on risk, with political stability lowering risk and elections increasing risk. However, the entire model explains a moderate portion of the variability in public bank risk, implying that other unaccounted-for factors may potentially be important.

For private banks, the model fails to explain private bank risk, with no variables having statistically significant impacts and very low explanatory power. This shows that the model's components are poor predictors of private bank risk, or that private bank risk is influenced by factors other than those in the model.

9. Conclusion

This study has explored the intricate relationship between parliamentary elections, political stability, and government effectiveness, and how these factors collectively influence bank risk in India. The findings reveal that while these political factors are expected to significantly affect bank risk, the actual impact is negligible and statistically insignificant. Specifically, the analysis showed that parliamentary elections, political stability, and government effectiveness explained a minimal portion of the variance in bank risk, and the coefficients for these variables were not statistically significant. This suggests that other macroeconomic or bank-specific factors, beyond political events, play a more crucial role in determining the risk exposure of banks in India.

10. Implications

The negligible effect of political factors on bank risk, as revealed by this study, underscores the need for banks and policymakers to broaden their focus when assessing risk. While political stability and government effectiveness are important for overall economic stability, their direct impact on bank risk appears to be limited. Financial institutions should place greater emphasis on other determinants of risk, such as market conditions, regulatory frameworks, and operational factors, to ensure resilience against financial volatility. Additionally, the findings suggest that further research is needed to investigate other potential influences on bank risk, including international economic conditions, sector-specific policies, and technological advancements. The study also calls for a deeper understanding of how external economic factors moderate the political stability–bank risk nexus in emerging markets like India.

References

Acharya, V., John, K., and Rajan, R. (2013). Political economy of government guarantees and bank risk-taking. *Journal of Financial Economics*, 107(3), 602–619. https://doi.org/10.1016/j.jfineco.2012.09.002.

Al-Bassam, B. A. (2013). The relationship between good governance and political instability. *Arab Journal of Administrative Sciences*, 20(2), 299–328.

Alesina, A. and Perotti, R. (1996). Income distribution, political instability, and investment. *European Economic Review*, 40(6), 1203–1228. https://doi.org/10.1016/0014-2921(95)00030-5.

Barth, J. R., Caprio, G., and Levine, R. (2004). Bank regulation and supervision: What works best? *Journal of Financial Intermediation*, 13(2), 205–248. https://doi.org/10.1016/j.jfi.2003.06.002.

Beck, T., Demirgüç-Kunt, A., and Levine, R. (2006). Bank concentration, competition, and crises: First results. *Journal of Banking & Finance*, 30(5), 1581–1603. https://doi.org/10.1016/j.jbankfin.2005.05.010.

Beltratti, A. and Stulz, R. M. (2012). The credit crisis around the globe: Why did some banks perform better? *Journal of Financial Economics*, 105(1), 1–17. https://doi.org/10.1016/j.jfineco.2011.12.005.

Bhandari, R. and Saxena, S. (2023). Government policies and risk in Indian banking sector: An analysis of the emerging challenges. *International Journal of Banking and Finance Studies*, 12(3), 145–160.

Bhaumik, S. K., Dang, V., and Kutan, A. M. (2020). Political connections and bank risk-taking: Evidence from India. *Journal of Corporate Finance*, 60, 101508. https://doi.org/10.1016/j.jcorpfin.2019.101508.

Białkowski, J., Gottschalk, K., and Wisniewski, T. P. (2015). Stock market volatility around national elections. *Journal of Banking & Finance*, 55, 1–11. https://doi.org/10.1016/j.jbankfin.2015.01.005.

Chava, S., Purnanandam, A., and Purushottam, A. (2014). The effect of banking crisis on bank-dependent borrowers. *Journal of Financial Economics*, 104(1), 208–223. https://doi.org/10.1016/j.jfineco.2012.01.002.

Demirgüç-Kunt, A. and Detragiache, E. (2002). Does deposit insurance increase banking system stability? An empirical investigation. *Journal of Monetary Economics*, 49(7), 1373–1406. https://doi.org/10.1016/S0304-3932(02)00171-X.

Desai, N. and Rao, K. (2022). Assessing the impact of government financial inclusion schemes on the banking sector: A case study of PMJDY and Mudra. *Finance & Development Journal*, 15(2), 189–203.

Dey, A. and Ganguly, A. (2021). The impact of government effectiveness on financial stability: The Indian context. *Journal of Financial Regulation and Compliance*, 29(3), 415–430.

Dinc, I. S. (2005). Politicians and banks: Political influences on government-owned banks in emerging markets. *Journal of Financial Economics*, 77(2), 453–479. https://doi.org/10.1016/j.jfineco.2004.06.011.

Eichengreen, B. and Gupta, P. (2020). Managing liquidity and solvency in developing economies: Government policies and their impact on banks. *Economic Policy Review*, 8(1), 65–88.

Fidrmuc, J. (2001). Economic reform, democracy and growth during post-communist transition. *European Journal of Political Economy*, 17(3), 585–604. https://doi.org/10.1016/S0176-2680(01)00041-5.

Ghosh, S. (2016). Political transition and bank performance: How important was the Arab Spring? *Journal of Comparative Economics*, 44(2), 372–382. https://doi.org/10.1016/j.jce.2016.01.002.

Gupta, R., Mishra, A., and Jain, P. (2022). The effects of regulatory frameworks on credit risk in Indian banks. *Journal of Risk and Financial Management*, 15(6), 305–320. https://doi.org/10.3390/jrfm15060305.

Gupta, S. and Saxena, P. (2022). Government policy changes and risk-taking behavior of Indian banks: A panel data analysis. *Journal of Banking and Financial Services*, 35(4), 67–79.

Jagannath, M. V. K. and Maitra, D. (2023). Do election cycles, political stability, and government effectiveness matter for the risk of banks? Evidence from Indian banks. *Journal of Behavioral and Experimental Finance*, 39, 100830. https://doi.org/10.1016/j.jbef.2023.100830.

Kauppi, H. and Saikkonen, P. (2008). Predicting U.S. recessions with dynamic binary response models. *The Review of Economics and Statistics*, 90(4), 777–791. https://doi.org/10.1162/rest.90.4.777.

Kumar, A. and Singh, R. (2021). The impact of political stability on bank risk in emerging economies: Evidence from the VAR model. *Emerging Markets Review*, 52, 100804. https://doi.org/10.1016/j.ememar.2021.100804.

La Porta, R., Lopez-de-Silanes, F., and Shleifer, A. (2002). Government ownership of banks. *Journal of Finance*, 57(1), 265–301. https://doi.org/10.1111/1540-6261.00422.

La Porta, R., Lopez-de-Silanes, F., Shleifer, A., and Vishny, R. W. (1998). Law and finance. *Journal of Political Economy*, 106(6), 1113–1155. https://doi.org/10.1086/250042.

Laeven, L. and Valencia, F. (2012). Systemic banking crises database: An update. *IMF Working Papers*, 12(163), 1–32. https://doi.org/10.5089/9781475505054.001.

Li, M. and Leung, M. K. (2015). Political stability and banking performance: Evidence from developing countries. *International Journal of Finance & Economics*, 20(4), 356–371. https://doi.org/10.1002/ijfe.1520.

Mai, A. N., Thi, T. M., and Nguyen, P. H. (2023). Political factors and bank risk in emerging markets: The case of India. *Journal of Financial Stability*, 68(1), 120–134. https://doi.org/10.1016/j.jfs.2023.120134.

Micco, A., Panizza, U., and Yañez, M. (2007). Bank ownership and performance: Does politics matter? *Journal of Banking & Finance*, 31(1), 219–241. https://doi.org/10.1016/j.jbankfin.2006.02.007.

Mishra, R. and Jain, D. (2021). Impact of demonetization and GST on banking risks in India. *Asian Journal of Economics and Banking*, 5(4), 312–329.

Mishra, R., Verma, S., and Jaiswal, A. (2023). The moderating role of external economic variables in the political stability and bank risk nexus: A qualitative approach. *International Journal of Banking*, 18(2), 198–214.

Molyneux, P. and Thornton, J. (1992). Determinants of European bank profitability: A note. *Journal of Banking & Finance*, 16(6), 1173–1178. https://doi.org/10.1016/0378-4266(92)90065-8.

Moshirian, F., Nandha, M., and Pham, T. (2008). Political risk and financial market integration: Implications for emerging markets. *Journal of International Financial Markets, Institutions and Money*, 18(2), 201–216. https://doi.org/10.1016/j.intfin.2006.09.001.

North, D. C. (1990). *Institutions, Institutional Change, and Economic Performance*. Cambridge: Cambridge University Press.

North, D. C. (1993). Economic performance through time. *American Economic Review*, 84(3), 359–368.

Olson, M. (2000). *Power and prosperity: Outgrowing Communist and Capitalist Dictatorships*. New York: Basic Books.

Pandey, M. and Roy, T. (2022). Government policy variations and banking risks: A time-series analysis. *Indian Journal of Economics and Banking*, 28(1), 75–89.

Peev, E. and Mueller, D. C. (2012). Democracy, economic freedom and growth in transition economies. *Kyklos*, 65(3), 371–407. https://doi.org/10.1111/j.1467-6435.2012.00540.x.

Roy, A. and Singh, N. (2018). Banking risk and governance in India: An empirical study. *Journal of Financial Stability*, 35(2), 49–60.

Saxena, P. (2021). State Bank of India and the role of government reforms: A case study. *Indian Journal of Finance*, 18(3), 105–121.

Sharma, A. and Seth, N. (2020). The importance of government effectiveness in regulating banks in India. *Journal of Banking and Financial Services*, 33(5), 231–248.

Sharma, K. and Bhattacharya, P. (2022). Political transitions and bank risk: Time series evidence from India. *Journal of Financial Risk Management*, 10(3), 205–218. https://doi.org/10.4236/jfrm.2022.103013.

Singh, K. and Verma, S. (2020). Political factors and their impact on Indian banking: A theoretical perspective. *Banking and Finance Research Journal*, 19(2), 87–103.

Srivastava, A. (2009). Good governance: Concept, meaning and features. *International Journal of Social Sciences*, 5(2), 100–108.

Ullah, W., Zubir, A. S., and Ariff, A. M. (2024). The impact of political instability on financial development, economic growth, economic growth volatility and financial stability in developing countries. *Theoretical and Practical Research in Economic Fields*, 15(2), 453. https://doi.org/10.14505/tpref.v15.2(30).22.

https://doi.org/10.1142/9789819823161_0020

Chapter 20

Return, Tracking Error, and Intraday Volatility under Asset Allocation: Evidence from ETFs in Iran

Meysam Kaviani[*,‡] **and Seyyed Ahmad Edalatpanah**[†,§]

[*]*Department of Management and Accounting*
Islamic Azad University, Karaj, Iran

[†]*Department of Applied Mathematics, Ayandegan Institute of Higher Education, Tonekabon, Iran*

[‡]*m_kaviani@iau.ac.ir*

[§]*s.a.edalatpanah@aihe.ac.ir*

This study examines the asset allocation performance of exchange-traded fund (ETF) managers, which can act as effective variables. We used four regression models to analyze asset allocation in ETFs and answer the question of how fund managers should allocate funds in a portfolio to outperform metrics such as a benchmark index or a simple portfolio. For this purpose, we use daily data from 2014 to 2023. Our overall results show that asset allocation is affected by the benchmark index trend, and asset allocation significantly affects the return and tracking errors of the Charism and Servat ETFs. Finally, the effect of asset allocation on intraday volatility is negative for Almas and Charism funds and positive for Servat and Firooze funds.

Keywords: Asset allocation, econometrics, ETF, intraday volatility, Iran, tracking error.

1. Introduction and Background

Today, ETFs or exchange-traded funds are very attractive because of their low fees, potential taxes, efficiency, and similar stock characteristics, as well as because of their easy trading hours and ability to provide innovative solutions for investors (Bansal and Somani, 2002; McGuire and Helmrich, 2008). In 1993, the first ETF, following the S&P 500 index, was launched and named Standard & Poor's Depository Receipts (SPDR). ETFs are continuously tradable throughout the day and are an option that allows investors to hold a set of assets at a low cost (Gastinho, 2010).

These funds significantly impact the characteristics of stocks in financial markets (Ben-David *et al.*, 2018), and research shows that funds' investment success is largely driven by asset allocation (Brinson *et al.*, 1991). Although asset allocation in the investment process refers to how investment funds are distributed among different types of assets — such as equities, debt instruments, derivatives, and other asset classes (Drobetz and Köhler, 2002; Laupodis, 2020) — it generally follows a common underlying principle (Amkter *et al.*, 2022). In the Tehran capital market, this principle allows portfolio managers to invest approximately 70% to 90% of their clients' assets in listed equities. Accordingly, the actual allocation decisions made by portfolio managers are typically guided by recommendations and constraints regarding the weighting of specific assets or asset classes within their portfolios (Ammann and Zimmermann, 2001). On the other hand, weight allocation is mainly retrospective and static and contradicts the dynamic nature of financial markets.

On the other hand, asset-weighting decisions are often dynamic and based on past information, which conflicts with the inherently dynamic nature of financial markets. Effective decision-making in such a dynamic environment requires greater adaptability, enabling the model to account for the factors that influence the long-term performance of the portfolio and, based on its interpretation of these factors, adjust the weight of each stock dynamically in response to current market conditions (Haratizadeh and Rezaee, 2023). Therefore, this study analyzes asset allocation (the percentage of shares invested in the fund) in the portfolio of ETFs in the Tehran Capital Market. Brinson *et al.* (1986) first conducted asset allocation analysis, and Drobetz and Kohler (2002) emphasized that investment managers in fund management should carry out activities such as determining asset allocation strategies and stock selection. In general, choosing stocks to build a portfolio is one of the most common issues faced by investors with different capital levels; at the same time, it is one of the most complex issues in the financial world (Kaviyani and Aghaee, 2023). However, choosing the best combination of financial assets to achieve maximum return and minimum portfolio risk is important (Peykani *et al.*, 2021).

In this case, asset allocation is the process of distributing capital among different asset classes and is widely regarded as one of the most important decisions of investors. The ultimate goal of this process is to build optimal portfolios based on predetermined goals (Brown *et al.*, 2010). This portfolio must be continuously monitored and adjusted, a dynamic and systematic process. Because it is a key factor in the investment performance of a portfolio, the investment process ultimately ends with evaluating portfolio performance (Laopodis, 2020). Since the price of financial assets fluctuates and the value of one asset in one portfolio can increase while another can decrease, such a situation leads to a change in the initial target allocation (Investment Company Institute (ICI), 2012).

In addition, many studies have shown that in the investment process, asset allocation is of more strategic importance than the selection of active securities (Emkter *et al.*, 2022). In addition, changes in allocation can increase risk or decrease returns (Investment Company Institute (ICI), 2012). In the last decade, with the dramatic change in the market for exchange-traded funds (ETFs) (Wang *et al.*, 2023), asset allocation strategies have been developed to help investors diversify their portfolios and reduce overall risk (Matthew and Matthew, 2016). In addition, considering that active versus passive investment plans, portfolio rebalancing, and weighting are intertwined concepts that lead to investors' decisions on how and where to allocate stock space, this decision is the key factor in future performance and, ultimately, the cumulative return of the investor (Stefanovska, 2020). Managers and investors may use the benchmark index to determine the quantity of risk and relate their portfolio behavior in terms of tracking error (TE) to their benchmark behavior (Buda and Kandrova, 2014).

Most academic studies agree on the importance of strategic asset allocation as a determining factor of return on investment. Brinson *et al.* (1986) claim in an article that strategic asset allocation decisions can explain 93.6% of performance changes. Their results show that strategic asset allocation is more important than market timing or securities selection. The results of Fish *et al.* (2019) research, which compared the portfolio's return against the Bloomberg Barclays commodity index, showed that the portfolio performed better than the model in terms of total return and Sharpe ratio. World (2017) shows that good portfolio performance can only be achieved through S&P 500 returns and rebalancing. Kim and Kang's (2014) research showed that tactical asset allocation generates significant surplus returns after adjusting for transaction risks and costs.

Basler *et al.* (2018) showed that industry-based asset allocation strategies could generate higher Sharpe, Omega, and Alpha ratios than country-based allocations. Aman and Zimmerman (2001) showed in a study that there is a relationship between tracking error criteria and asset allocation constraints, and this relationship has a significant practical relationship for analysts, investment strategists, and risk managers. In his research, Jemeron Watt (2020) concluded that stocks with higher ETFs show significantly higher volatility and arbitrage activity intensity, increasing the impact of ETFs on daily volatility due to incorrect stock prices. Schum *et al.* (2016) showed that end-of-day volatility is positively and significantly correlated with the ratio of potential rebalancing transactions to total trading volume. Considering these points, this study intends to answer the following questions using data related to the allocation of assets in the portfolios of four stock exchange-traded funds: What is the reaction of fund managers in asset allocation to changes in the benchmark index in their portfolios? How does asset allocation affect funds' returns and tracking errors? What is the intraday volatility in funds under asset allocations?

2. Models and Frameworks

2.1. *Benchmark index and asset allocation*

Kai and Hoff (2007) measured the effect of index changes on the long-term returns of mutual funds. In this case, the portfolio manager can create a portfolio with satisfactory performance by simply copying a good measure (Buda and Kandrova, 2014). Jacquier and Marcus (2001) showed that short-term volatility in market index volatility over time can be used to update portfolio positions. Therefore, using the benchmark index's effect on portfolio returns, fund managers change the composition of their investment portfolios with changes in the index. Therefore, ordinary least squares (OLS) regression analysis was used to determine (1):

$$\text{Allocation}_{i,t}^{\text{ETF}} = \alpha_i + \beta_i r_t^{\text{IND}} + \varepsilon_{it}. \tag{1}$$

According to the above-stated model, asset allocation is a portfolio because equity funds in Iran invest 70 to 90 percent of their clients' assets in the stocks of listed companies; therefore, the ratio of the percentage used in the asset allocation of the five stocks with the largest shares has been considered a criterion for measuring asset allocation. Additionally, r_t^{IND} is the return on the benchmark measure.

2.2. *Asset allocation and returns of ETFs*

If asset returns are predictable, optimal asset allocation depends on the investment horizon and predictor variables (Brennan *et al.*, 1997). Wahyudi *et al.* (2020) show that an asset allocation strategy positively affects investment portfolio performance. Fund managers always find the best strategy to combine capital growth and income (Hosseini Imeni and Najafi, 2013). Bharati and Gupta (1992) show that an active asset investment strategy outperforms passive strategies with a fixed mix of asset class weights and that superior portfolio performance is not just due to diversification. This shows that ETF asset allocation plays an important role in performance. In this study, the effect of asset allocation on returns based on the traded price was estimated using ordinary least squares (OLS) regression analysis in Model 2:

$$R_{i,t}^{\text{ETF}} = \alpha_i + \beta_i \text{ Allocation}_{i,t}^{\text{ETF}} + \varepsilon_{it}. \tag{2}$$

2.3. *Asset allocation and returns of ETFs*

The operational efficiency of ETFs is defined as their ability to replicate their underlying benchmarks fully. A negative deviation from the benchmark index is a tracking error and can be explained by factors

(Goel and Ahluwalia, 2021). There are several methods to measure tracking errors. The simplest is the difference between the returns of the ETF and the corresponding benchmark (total index) (Harper *et al.*, 2006), which we measure in this way. The second method is the absolute deviation between ETF and benchmark yields (Osterhoff and Kasserer, 2006). Milonas and Rompotis (2006) and Shin and Svidmir (2010) estimated the tracking error as the standard error caused by the regression of the fund's return on the index return.

Managers and investors use the benchmark index to quantify risk and relate the behavior of their constructed portfolios to their benchmark behavior in terms of a tracking error metric (Buda and Kandrova, 2014). Ammann and Zimmermann (2001) showed that tracking errors and correlation coefficients are very sensitive to tracking individual asset classes. Bajeux-Besnaino *et al.* (2013) state in their paper that active portfolio strategies aim to overcome the benchmark measure while maintaining tracking error within acceptable ranges. In addition, Bresnon (1991) shows that asset allocation is the main determinant of a highly diversified portfolio's risk balance and expected returns. All these studies show that asset allocation in the portfolio and determination of the weights of asset classes can affect the tracking error, which is analyzed in Model 3:

$$\mathrm{TE}_{it} = \alpha + \beta_1 \text{ Allocation}_{i,t}^{\mathrm{ETF}} + \beta_2 \text{ Market cap}_{it}^{\mathrm{ETF}} + \varepsilon_{it}. \quad (3)$$

In model 3, TEit shows the ETF tracking error on day t, which is the difference between the ETF return and its corresponding benchmark yield (Harper *et al.*, 2006) and MCAP represents the ETF's daily market capitalization on day t, which serves as a proxy for fund size and is therefore included as a control variable (Goel and Ahluwalia, 2021). ε denotes the error term.

2.4. *Asset allocation and intraday volatility*

Maintaining an asset allocation and rebalancing investment strategy in an ETF refers to adjusting its assets. Rebalancing refers to the return on the asset allocation value of a portfolio at defined levels. These levels match the investor's risk tolerance and willingness to reward. They are a tool for investors to adjust their portfolios by allocating the main objective of assets (Vashacamadz, 2012). Schum *et al.* (2016) show that portfolio rebalancing affects the intraday volatility of leveraged ETFs (Freitas and Barker, 2005). They showed that the decision to allocate a fund's investments between stocks, bonds, and cash significantly impacts the portfolio's risk profile. Therefore, according to Model 4, asset allocation is analyzed through portfolio rebalancing of intraday volatility:

$$\text{Inra}_{\text{Volatility}_{it}} = \alpha + \beta_1 \text{ Allocation}_{i,t}^{\text{ETF}} + \beta_2 \text{ Day trading}_{it}^{\text{ETF}} + \varepsilon_{it} \tag{4}$$

Since intraday volatility is affected by day trading (Kairolian, 2008), it is considered a control variable in the above-mentioned model. Day trading is calculated as the number of daily trades in funds. InraVolatilityt is the intraday volatility of an ETF and is calculated as follows:

$$\text{Inra}_{\text{Volatility}\,t} = \frac{\text{High}_t - \text{low}_t}{\text{close}_t} \tag{5}$$

3. Methodology and Data

The research used a positivist research philosophy, in which the goal is to discover relationships through data collection to test the hypotheses based on existing theories that have been confirmed. A deductive approach is used in which questions and hypotheses are generated from theories and then confirmed or disproved using data analysis (Crater and Lancaster, 2009). Four ETFs approved by the Tehran Stock Exchange were used as statistical samples. Daily data for the funds were extracted from the https://www.fipiran.com site since its data became available. This study used statistical and econometric tools and techniques to support the analysis and achieve the set goals.

4. Empirical Analysis

4.1. *Descriptive statistics*

Descriptive methods were used to describe the research data by presenting a table and using descriptive statistical tools, such as central measures and dispersion, to help clarify the issue. Table 1

Table 1. Descriptive statistics of research variables.

Symbol		DAY TRADING	INTRA	MARKET-CAP	ALLO-CATION	RETF	RIND	TE
Almas	Mean	65.26	0.029	47211	23.10	0.002	0.003	0.0005
	SD	124.54	0.044	124911.86	5.00	0.021	0.016	0.02
	No.	1142	1142	1142	1142	1142	1142	1142
Servat	Mean	45.12	0.018	63473	24.87	0.002	0.003	0.001
	SD	95.84	0.016	138622	4.52	0.017	0.016	0.021
	No.	1049	1049	1049	1049	1049	1049	1049
Firooze	Mean	182	0.02	197986	31.94	0.0019	0.002	3.5
	SD	416	0.03	801023	4.55	0.02	0.013	0.023
	No.	1733	1733	1733	1733	1733	1733	1733
Charism	Mean	350	0	1566000	35.75	0.003	0.003	0
	SD	549.13	0.04	2762827	8.84	0.02	0.02	0.02
	No.	1126	1126	1126	1126	1126	1126	1126

presents the descriptive statistics of the research variables for the four funds, presented in the form of means and standard deviations. As daily data were used to test the research questions, the frequency of observations for each box was different. In short, the average and standard deviation of the tracking error of the Servat fund were higher than those of other funds. In addition, the highest allocation to the five shares with the highest weight was related to the Charism fund, with a weight of 35.75%, which also had the highest number of transactions. Finally, the highest intraday volatility is related to Almas funds, which occur within the defined limited volatility range.

4.2. *Correlation of variables*

The Pearson correlation coefficient was used to investigate the correlation between the quantitative variables. According to Table 2, at the 95% confidence level for all funds, the correlation between the main variables in each model is low, preventing false results. According to these results, the correlation coefficient between the fund's return and the market return in the Charism fund, with a value of 36%, is the highest, indicating that this fund is more affected by the market index.

4.3. *Unit root test*

The reliability tests are among the most important for estimating regressions with reliable coefficients. Durability tests were used to

Table 2. Correlation matrix of research variables of selected funds.

Symbol	Variables	DAY TRADING	INTRA	MARKETCAP	ALLOCATION	RETF	RIND	TE
Almas	DAY TRADING	1						
	INTRA	0.39	1					
	MARKETCAP	0.41	0.19	1				
	ALLOCATION	0.19	0.24	0.0001	1			
	RETF	0.05	0.04	0.02	0.03	1		
	RIND	0.00	0.03	0.03	−0.02	0.21	1	
	TE	−0.04	−0.02	0.00	−0.04	−0.75	0.49	1
Servat	DAY TRADING	1						
	INTRA	0.44	1					
	MARKETCAP	0.46	0.29	1				
	ALLOCATION	−0.06	0.06	0.11	1			
	RETF	0.01	0.08	0.07	−0.05	1		
	RIND	0.04	0.07	0.0002	−0.08	0.09	1	
	TE	−0.01	−0.02	−0.06	−0.02	−0.66	0.66	1
Firooze	DAY TRADING	1						
	INTRA	0.56	1					
	MARKETCAP	0.48	0.33	1				
	ALLOCATION	−0.15	−0.07	−0.13	1			
	RETF	0.03	0.12	0.02	0.00	1		
	RIND	0.03	0.08	0.01	0.08	0.25	1	
	TE	−0.01	−0.07	−0.01	0.04	−0.83	0.32	1
Charism	DAY TRADING	1						
	INTRA	0.32	1					
	MARKETCAP	0.40	0.21	1				
	ALLOCATION	0.10	0.17	−0.08	1			
	RETF	0.04	0.04	0.01	−0.06	1		
	RIND	0.00	0.0001	−0.02	−0.07	0.36	1	
	TE	−0.04	−0.03	−0.02	0.00	−0.68	0.43	1

Table 3. Unit root test.

Symbol	TE	RIND	RETF	ALLO-CATION	MARKET-CAP	INTRA	DAY TRADING
Almas	−24.4***	−14.4***	−10.6***	−35.9***	−7.64***	−6.13***	−5.7***
Servat	−27.5***	−13.2***	−28.3***	−31.6***	−6.42***	−6.65***	−5.86***
Firooze	−18.8***	−16.8***	−31.5***	−3.81***	−8.8***	−6.5***	−3.09***
Charism	−16.9***	−14.9***	−16.6***	−34.4***	−8.02***	−10.2***	−4.27***
Result	I(0)	I(0)	I(0)	I(1)	I(0)	I(0)	I(0)

Table 4. Impact of benchmark index on asset allocation.

Symbol	α_i	β_i	F	Adj. R^2
Almas	89.29	21.28	970.28	0.94
	(0.00)	(0.00)	(0.00)	
Servat	71.09	3.88	3.03	0.79
	(0.00)	(0.052)	(0.04)	
Firooze	35.14	3.28	970.5	0.74
	(0.00)	(0.07)	(0.00)	
Charism	93.38	3.46	3220.85	0.89
	(0.00)	(0.03)	(0.00)	

prevent the estimation of dummy regression. In this study, the generalized Dickey–Fuller unit root test (ADF) was used to test the reliability of the variables. Table 3 test results show that all funds' main variables are at the I(0) level. Still, the ALLOCATION variable for all funds except the Firooze fund is type I(1) and has been manipulated with a one-time difference.

4.4. *Testing models*

4.4.1. *Benchmark index and asset allocation*

According to the results in Table 4, the effect of market index returns on asset allocation is positive and statistically significant for the Almas and Charism ETFs at the 95% confidence level and for the Firooze and Servat ETFs at the 90% confidence level. In other words, as market index returns increase, the allocation to the five largest-weighted stocks also rises. This indicates that fund managers adjust their portfolios in response to index growth, altering the weighted composition of their stock investments. Moreover, the adjusted R-squared values for these

Table 5. The effect of portfolio asset allocation on fund returns.

Symbol	α_i	β_i	F	Adj. R^2
Almas	0.0002	0.0005	3.48	0.01
	(0.00)	(0.53)	(0.00)	
Servat	0.02	−0.0006	6.76	0.02
	(0.00)	(0.40)	(0.00)	
Firooze	0.001	−0.0002	2.64	0.0004
	(0.13)	(0.86)	(0.00)	
Charism	0.02	−0.003	5.3	0.01
	(0.22)	(0.03)	(0.00)	

four funds are substantial, reflecting the explanatory power of the market index over asset allocation. Among them, the Almas ETF exhibits the highest explanatory power, with an adjusted R-squared of 94%.

4.4.2. *Asset allocation and ETF yield*

Table 5 shows the effects of asset allocation on fund returns. As is clear from Table 5, the effect of asset allocation on returns is negative and significant only for the Charism fund. The measures for evaluating the model's suitability for all ETFs, the F-statistic, were statistically significant and did not affect the other funds. These results show that the allocation of assets, despite being influenced by the model index (Table 5), has not been done well in funds and has not led to positive results in terms of the impact on returns, as the fund manager's asset allocation has led to a decrease in its returns.

4.4.3. *Asset allocation and tracking error*

Regression analysis is used in the third model to identify the effect of asset allocation on ETFs' tracking error. As is clear from the results in Table 6, the effect of portfolio asset allocation (coefficient $\beta(1)$) on Servat funds is positive and significant. These results suggest that if fund managers allocate their rights to their underlying assets, they can generate higher tracking errors. In other funds, asset allocation cannot change the tracked error, reflecting the portfolio's lack of proper asset allocation.

Table 6. The effect of asset allocation on tracking error.

Symbol	α_i	β_1	β_2	F	Adj. R^2
Almas	0.01	0.0003	−0.001	8.36	0.03
	(0.01)	(0.63)	(0.00)	(0.00)	
Servat	0.007	0.004	−0.0008	12.8	0.05
	(0.03)	(0.00)	(0.03)	(0.00)	
Firooze	0.005	−0.0003	−0.0005	4.9764	0.001
	(0.48)	(0.74)	(0.21)	(0.00)	
Charism	0.001	−0.0003	−0.00005	5.78	0.01
	(0.49)	(0.66)	(0.01)	(0.00)	

Table 7. The effect of rebalancing on intraday volatility.

Symbol	α_i	β_1	β_2	F	Adj. R^2
Almas	8.04	−0.001	0.0001	118.7	0.17
	(0.00)	(0.00)	(0.00)	(0.00)	
Servat	0.001	0.0005	0.0001	49.9	0.09
	(0.00)	(0.00)	(0.03)	(0.00)	
Firooze	−0.03	0.0006	−0.00003	376.5	0.30
	(0.30)	(0.00)	(0.21)	(0.30)	
Charism	0.03	−0.0003	0.00002	68.6	0.11
	(0.00)	(0.00)	(0.01)	(0.00)	

4.4.4. *Asset allocation and intraday volatility*

Table 7 shows the effect of portfolio asset allocation on the intraday volatility of ETFs. Therefore, according to the model of the effect of portfolio asset allocation on intraday volatility in equity funds, as shown in Table 6, it can be concluded that portfolio asset allocation reduces intraday volatility for Almas and Charism funds. However, it had a positive and significant effect on Servat and Firooze. The results of this model indicate that when managers allocate assets, investors track the investment of these funds and buy the shares of the funds that have a greater gap between the high and low prices in the two funds compared to the closing price, which somehow affects the behavior of investors in investment, the expected return of the funds, the behavior of market makers, and technical analysis. Also, the price trend of the underlying assets varies.

5. Conclusion

In the last decade, the development of investment fund markets in the Tehran capital market has provided a suitable ground for analyzing their performance. This study analyzes the allocation of funds' assets as one of the stages of the investment process, including benchmark index, return, tracking error, and intraday volatility. We found that the internal ETFs of the Indian markets outperformed their fund metrics. Because ETFs derive their characteristics from stocks and mutual funds, investing in ETFs is considered one of the best investment alternatives. When managed by professional experts, it is expected to provide higher returns than the benchmark index. ETF asset allocation refers to adjusting an ETF portfolio's assets to execute its desired investment strategy. This study answers these research questions by using weights related to asset allocation in five stocks with higher weights. The results indicate that the market index has a positive and significant effect on portfolio asset allocation. This suggests that fund managers, by taking into account changes in the index and confirming the persistence of an upward trend, adjust asset allocations within their portfolios. This behavior is somewhat analogous to the strategies employed by investors who attempt to time their trades. Moreover, these findings are consistent with Jacquier and Marcus (2001), who demonstrated that ETF asset allocation is influenced by overall market movements.

The results also showed that the effect of portfolio asset allocation on the return of ETFs was negative and significant only for the Charism fund, consistent with Brennan *et al.*'s (1997) findings. It can also be concluded that Charism fund managers have not been able to manage asset allocation better, and these results are inconsistent with the findings of Wahyudi *et al.* (2020). Considering the effect of asset allocation on tracking error, in a Servat fund portfolio, asset allocation positively affected tracking error. By comparing the results of this fund in the second model, it can be claimed that the positive effect of asset allocation not only created a positive return but also led to a positive tracking error. Finally, the results show that asset allocation hurts intraday volatility in Almas and Charism funds, and in Servat and Firooze funds, it has a positive effect. It appears that these results indicate that, in the two funds with negative effects, portfolio asset allocation decisions did not lead to significant intraday price fluctuations, and investors in these funds executed their investment decisions gradually. This behavior is clearly related to daily trading volume, as trading volume had a significant impact on intraday volatility across all funds and, except for the Firooze fund, this impact was positive in the remaining funds.

Based on the results of this study, it is suggested that fund managers who allocate their portfolio assets according to changes in the index take steps toward an optimal portfolio diversification strategy by considering the risk and return of each financial asset, which indicates a scientific approach to portfolio optimization. In addition, since the return of the fund's portfolio is affected by the allocation of the portfolio's assets, it is recommended that, in the case of creating a positive return, one should also consider the risk of the portfolio and consider the effective asset allocation strategy in such a way that a positive tracking error is created. Finally, it is suggested that fund managers optimally allocate portfolio assets to maintain the efficiency of funds' pricing through the net asset value, reducing intraday volatility.

References

Ammann, M. and Zimmermann, H. (2001). Tracking error and tactical asset allocation. *Financial Analysts Journal*, 57(2), 32–43.

Bajeux-Besnainou, I., Portait, R., and Tergny, G. (2013). Optimal portfolio allocations with tracking error volatility and stochastic hedging constraints. *Quantitative Finance*, 13(10), 1599–1612.

Bansal, V. K. and Somani, A. (2002). Exchange traded funds: Challenge to traditional mutual funds. *Review of Business*, 23(3), 40.

Ben-David, I., Franzoni, F., and Moussawi, R. (2018). Do ETFs increase volatility? *The Journal of Finance*, 73(6), 2471–2535.

Bessler, W., Taushanov, G., and Wolff, D. (2018). Optimal asset allocation strategies for international equity portfolios. *Journal of International Financial Markets, Institutions & Money*.

Bharati, R. and Gupta, M. (1992). Asset allocation and predictability of real estate returns. *Journal of Real Estate Research*, 7(4), 469–484.

Boďa, M. and Kanderová, M. (2014). Rebalancing issues in tracking error variance minimization.

Brennan, M. J., Schwartz, E. S., and Lagnado, R. (1997). Strategic asset allocation. *Journal of Economic Dynamics and Control*, 21(8–9), 1377–1403.

Brinson, G. P., Singer, B. D., and Beebower, G. L. (1991). Determinants of portfolio performance II: An update. *Financial Analyst Journal*, 47(3), 40–48.

Brown, K. C., Garlappi, L., and Tiu, C. (2010). Asset allocation and portfolio performance: Evidence from university endowment funds. *Journal of Financial Markets*, 13(2), 268–294.

Cai, J. and Houge, T. (2007). Index rebalancing and long-term portfolio performance. Available at SSRN 970839.

Crowther, D. and Lancaster, G. (2009). *Research Method: A Concise Introduction to Research in Management and Business Consultancy.* Butterworth-Heinemann, Oxford.

de Freitas, E. and Barker, C. (2005). ETFs—Tactical asset allocation tools. In *Exchange Traded Funds: Structure, Regulation and Application of a New Fund Class*, 85–94. Berlin, Heidelberg: Springer Berlin Heidelberg.

Drobetz, W. and Köhler, F. (2002). The contribution of asset allocation policy to portfolio performance. *Financial Markets and Portfolio Management*, 16(2), 219.

Emekter, R., Jirasakuldech, B., and Beaves, R. Efficient asset allocation for individual investors in the ETF world. *Financial Planning Research Journal*, 8(1), 79–98.

Fish, A. J. M., Patel, A., and Venkatraman, S. (2019). Optimal asset allocation for a portfolio of cointegrated commodity-ETF pairs. Available at SSRN 3487540.

Gill, J. and Johnson, P. (2010). *Research Methods for Managers.* Sage, Thousand Oaks.

Haratizadeh, S. and Rezaee, F. (2023). A novel machine learning approach for portfolio optimization. *Journal of Decisions and Operations Research*, 8(2), 527–539.

Hosseini Imeni, S. A. and Najafi, A. A. (2013). Fuzzy index tracking portfolio selection model based on value-at-risk. *International Journal of Research in Industrial Engineering*, 2(4), 41–57.

Investment Company Institute (ICI) (2000). 401(k) plan participants: Characteristics, contributions and account activity. Washington, DC, Spring 2000. Available at: http://www.ici.org/pdf/rpt_401k_planp.pdf.

Jacquier, E. and Marcus, A. J. (2001). Asset allocation models and market volatility. *Financial Analysts Journal*, 57(2), 16–30.

Jumroonwat, T. (2020). The impact of ETF mechanics and the bank of Japan intervention on the intraday volatility of the underlying stocks.

Kaviyani, M. and Aghaee, M. (2023). Analysis of the refinement fund's portfolio from start-up to sectorfund; comparison of theory with practice. *Financial and Banking Strategic Studies*, 1(3), 167–177.
Kim, S. H. and Kang, H. G. (2014). Tactical asset allocation using investors' sentiment. *Hitotsubashi Journal of Economics*, 56(2), 2016.
Kyröläinen, P. (2008). Day trading and stock price volatility. *Journal of Economics and Finance*, 32, 75–89.
Laopodis, N. T. (2020). *Understanding Investments: Theories and Strategies.* Routledge.
Mattei, M. D. and Mattei, N. (2016). Analysis of fixed and biased asset allocation rebalancing strategies. *Managerial Finance*, 42(1), 42–50.
McGuire, W. J. and Helmrich, R. F. (2008). The SEC's ETF rule proposal: Key issues for the future exchange traded products. *Investment Lawyer*, 15, 1–13.
Peykani, P., Nouri, M., Eshghi, F., Khamechian, M., and Farrokhi-Asl, M. (2021). A novel mathematical approach for fuzzy multi-period multi-objective portfolio optimization problem under uncertain environment and practical constraints. *Journal of Fuzzy Extension and Application*, 2(3), 191–203.
Rinson, G., Hood, L., and Beebower, G. (1986). Determinants of portfolio performance. *Financial Analyst Journal*, 39–48.
Shum, P., Hejazi, W., Haryanto, E., and Rodier, A. (2016). Intraday share price volatility and leveraged ETF rebalancing. *Review of Finance*, 20(6), 2379–2409.
Stefanovska, M. (2020). The effects of equal weighting and rebalancing on portfolio performance.
Vashakmadze, T. (2012). ETF portfolio rebalancing for retail investors. *Global Academic Society Journal: Social Science Insight*, 5(13), 13–22.
Vorlow, C. E. (2017). Simple tactical asset allocation strategies on the S&P 500 and the impact of VIX fluctuations. In *Handbook of Investors' Behavior during Financial Crises*, 383–400. Academic Press.
Wahyudi, S., Hasanudin, H., and Pangestutia, I. (2020). Asset allocation and strategies on investment portfolio performance: A study on the implementation of employee pension fund in Indonesia. *Accounting*, 6(5), 839–850.
Wang, G. J., Yao, C. Y., and Yelekenova, A. (2023). ETF rebalancing, hedge fund trades, and capital market. Available at SSRN 4324054.

https://doi.org/10.1142/9789819823161_0021

Chapter 21

Litigation Risk and Financial Performance of Banks: Do Internal Corporate Governance Mechanisms Matter?

Mohsen Imeni[*,‡] **and Seyyed Ahmad Edalatpanah**[†,§]

[*]*Department of Accounting, Ayandegan Institute of Higher Education, Tonekabon, Iran*

[†]*Department of Applied Mathematics, Ayandegan Institute of Higher Education, Tonekabon, Iran*

[‡]*imeni@aihe.ac.ir*

[§]*s.a.edalatpanah@aihe.ac.ir*

Examining the discussion of legal claims is fundamental due to the importance of damaging the image of banks and financial and credit institutions in the eyes of specific customers in this industry. Therefore, this study aims to investigate the litigation risk and the financial performance of banks with the role of moderator of internal corporate governance of banks listed on the Tehran Stock Exchange (TSE). This study, conducted from 2014 to 2023, involved 14 sample banks listed on the Tehran Stock Exchange. It was used to estimate the model using panel data. The results indicate that litigation risk has a negative and significant effect on the financial performance of banks. In addition, managerial ownership positively impacts the relationship between the litigation risk and the financial performance of banks, and other corporate governance variables, including board size and board independence, do not affect the relationship between the litigation risk and the financial performance of banks. Corporate governance mechanisms can reduce legal claims risk by improving transparency, increasing accountability, and reducing conflicts of interest. These mechanisms can also prevent fraud and financial violations, avoid legal claims, and, with better supervision, increase banks' financial performance.

Keywords: Litigation risk, bank financial performance, corporate governance.

1. Introduction

Most research on litigation risk has been conducted in developed economies, such as the US stock market, and the results of these studies cannot be generalized to other countries, especially civil rights countries with developing economies (Wu *et al.*, 2020). If a company is prosecuted due to a lawsuit by shareholders or others, it will face negative consequences (Alexander, 1990). Litigation damages the reputation of companies facing litigation, sends a risk signal to investors, creditors, independent auditors, and other stakeholders, and has a negative impact on the value and prospects of the company.

The Institute of Internal Auditors (IIA) defines risk as uncertainty about the occurrence of an event that could affect the achievement of goals (Imeni and Edalatpanah, 2023). The risk of litigation is significant for credit rating agencies and creditors because firms with a high risk of litigation are likely to have a lower credit rating and pay higher interest costs on loans, and the probability of lending to these firms is also lower (Arena, 2018; Diamond, 2004). The risk of litigation can also affect the company's other financing activities, such as IPOs. Qing Hao (2011) argues that the risk of litigation is a significant threat to companies planning to go public; in particular, companies with a high risk of litigation are more likely to cancel their IPOs. The cost of litigation is a heavy burden for companies, and companies that are sued face potential losses due to reduced customers and suppliers.

Performance is one of the important criteria for decision-makers (Bao and Motlagh, 2024). The risk of litigation can affect performance because the more the company is at risk of litigation, the more the value of the company may decrease. Users of financial reports evaluate a company's performance using a variety of measures (Bao and Motlagh, 2024). The relationship between litigation risk and firm performance is negative because litigation is often associated with a decrease in firm value (Lin *et al.*, 2013), destroys the firm's relationships with customers and suppliers, and affects the firm's operations (Lin *et al.*, 2013) .

Legal protection of shareholders' rights is essential to corporate governance (Shleifer and Vishny, 1997; Cheung *et al.*, 2010). It argues that corporate governance is critical in reducing agency conflicts between managers and shareholders. Countries transitioning from state control to market-based economies should strengthen their government laws and improve their investment and market environment. This topic makes it an appropriate environment to examine the impact of corporate governance, including internal controls and monitoring mechanisms, on the relationship between litigation risk and company performance.

Our study contributes to the literature on litigation risk, financial performance of banks, and internal corporate governance mechanisms in an emerging market such as Iran in several ways. First, while previous studies (Wu *et al.*, 2020; Malm *et al.*, 2023; Waheed *et al.*, 2024) have been conducted in the context of manufacturing firms, this study is conducted in financial services, i.e., banks. Therefore, the present study provides empirical evidence to better understand the relationship between litigation risk and banks' financial performance. Second, based on the results, it can be said that banks should have several corporate governance mechanisms in their structure to mitigate the adverse effects of litigation risk on firm performance.

Third, information transparency is essential for financial analysts and other information users. Information is vital for financial analysts to make decisions for investors in Iran; therefore, corporate governance as a regulatory mechanism can effectively mitigate the adverse effects of litigation risk on banks' performance. The remainder of this article is organized as follows. Section 2 presents the literature and develops the hypotheses. Section 3 explains the research method, including the statistical sample, the models, and the measurement of the variables. Section 4 presents the results, and Section 5 provides the discussion and interpretation.

2. Literature and Development of Hypotheses

2.1. *Risk of litigation and financial performance*

In today's business environment, companies face an increased risk of litigation due to their organizational complexity and responsibilities.

A lawsuit may arise from an error or fraud in the financial statements, a declaration of default or bankruptcy, or the resignation or dismissal of top managers (Alexander, 1990; Francis *et al.*, 1994). The literature shows that litigation risk affects firms' financial policies (Wu *et al.*, 2020; Bourveau *et al.*, 2018; Dash and Raithatha, 2018; Nguyen *et al.*, 2018; Zhang *et al.*, 2022). Firms under litigation pressure pay more to managers to protect shareholders' interests (Durongkadej *et al.*, 2021; Arena and Julio, 2015). However, empirical evidence linking litigation risk and performance in the context of emerging markets is scarce.

A study documents that stock prices react negatively to shareholder-initiated class actions (Gande and Lewis, 2009; Sharfman and Fernando, 2008). Another study hypothesizes that if firms can reduce the risk of litigation, their cost of capital is likely to decrease, leading to higher profit margins or economic performance. In other words, a higher cost of capital due to litigation has a negative impact on firms' operating performance. Empirically, litigation risk sends a negative signal about firms' future, thereby reducing their market value (Wu *et al.*, 2020). Financial institutions effectively monitor management with their financial expertise and market knowledge. The indirect costs of litigation are also significant. Litigation has a negative impact on the reputation of the firms involved and leads to a decline in their prestige (Engelmann and Cornell, 1988). The financial literature suggests that part of this decline in credit is due to reduced confidence in contractual terms with customers, suppliers of capital, and suppliers of goods (Karpoff and Lott Jr, 1993; Karpoff *et al.*, 2008).

Given the above-mentioned consequences associated with litigation, previous studies have examined their impact on firm behavior and financial policy. Firms facing litigation may be reluctant to pay cash dividends to preserve liquidity for prudential reasons (Malm and Kanuri, 2020; Arena and Julio, 2021). Litigation may induce firms to report earnings earlier than required (Field *et al.*, 2005).

When shareholders or others sue a company, it faces several negative consequences (Alexander, 1990). First, litigation damages the reputation of the companies involved. It sends a signal of risk to investors, creditors, external auditors, and other stakeholders that is negatively related to the value and prospects of the company (Godfrey *et al.*, 2009; Levy *et al.*, 2018). Second, litigation costs place a heavy burden on companies. One of the most expensive of these costs is settlement payments. Thirdly, companies involved in litigation may suffer material losses due to losing customers and suppliers. In addition, the loss of reputation caused by lawsuits may damage the public image, ultimately leading to a decline in the long-term operating performance of the companies involved in the litigation (Johnson *et al.*, 2014). In short, it is still unclear whether there is a relationship between the risk of litigation and the financial performance of banks. Based on this, the first hypothesis is explained as follows:

H1: The risk of litigation has a negative effect on the financial performance of banks.

2.2. *Interaction of corporate governance mechanisms*

Other research hypotheses have been explained based on the interactive effect of the presence of corporate governance mechanisms in banks. According to agency theory, firms with strong corporate governance are likely to perform better financially in uncertain environments because they have lower agency costs and more effective monitoring systems (Jensen and Meckling, 1976).

The recent wave of scandals involving the world's largest listed companies has made companies aware of the importance of improving corporate governance practices and increasing the transparency of accounting information (Mashyekh Pul and Fallah, 2021). Corporate governance is a global issue. Efficient corporate governance mechanisms are essential to ensure the proper functioning of the capital market and the economy as a whole, as well as to maintain public confidence, since corporate governance ensures the efficient use of capital by companies (Tseng *et al.*, 2024). Corporate governance reforms in developed economies have been essential in creating a favorable business environment (Bourveau *et al.*, 2018; Nguyen *et al.*, 2018). However, in developing economies, mechanisms related to citizens' rights, the judiciary, and the legal system are less developed (Arena and Ferris, 2018), and, as a result, companies in these economies face fewer lawsuits than their counterparts in developed economies (Arena and Ferris, 2018).

Other authors suggest that effective internal controls supported by active governance mechanisms reduce the likelihood of material misstatements in financial disclosures (Kinney and McDaniel, 1989; Rice and Weber, 2012; Guo *et al.*, 2015). This is because they provide reasonable assurance about the quality of financial reporting and minimize the detrimental effects of the agency problem. Companies with more robust internal governance have fewer governance deficiencies and, as a result, may face fewer lawsuits in the future. Weak corporate governance also leads to agency conflicts among corporate stakeholders, increasing the number of lawsuits in companies (Bourveau *et al.*, 2018; Nguyen *et al.*, 2018) .

Another study also examined the relationship between corporate governance and firm performance in the United States and found that firms with more robust internal governance had a higher return on equity (ROE), return on assets (ROA), and Q-Tobin's coefficient (Brown and Caylor, 2009). However, most of these studies focus on corporate governance in developed markets. Kaviani *et al.* (2024) indicate that there is no significant relationship between the cash ratio and profitability, while there is a positive and significant relationship between the CCC and profitability.

Furthermore, a recent study (Wu *et al.*, 2020) confirmed the moderating role of an index of internal corporate governance characteristics between litigation risk and performance. However, the role of external governance mechanisms needs to be explored, especially in the context of developing economies (Wu *et al.*, 2020). Agency theory suggests that financial institutions, with their financial expertise and market-based knowledge, provide a highly effective external regulatory governance mechanism that disciplines management (Liu *et al.*, 2018; Waheed and Malik, 2021). Based on the results and the existing literature, it is expected that more robust corporate governance mechanisms in banks can mitigate the potential adverse effects of litigation risk on firm performance. Therefore, the second, third, and fourth hypotheses are explained as follows:

H2: The size of the board of directors affects the relationship between the risk of litigation and the financial performance of banks.

H3: The independence of the board of directors affects the relationship between the risk of litigation and the financial performance of banks.

H4: Managerial ownership affects the relationship between the risk of litigation and bank financial performance.

3. Research Methodology

3.1. *Statistical sample*

The statistical population of the research includes the banks listed on the Tehran Stock Exchange for nine years from 2014 to 2023. The statistical sample is selected by systematic elimination, and the minimum restrictions for the selection of the sample are as follows:

(1) banks with a year-end.

(2) banks that were listed before 2014.

(3) the required data are available.

According to the restrictions applied, 14 banks from the Tehran Stock Exchange were sampled.

3.2. *Variables and research model*

To test the research hypotheses, the multivariate regression method based on panel data is used. Model 1 is used to test the first hypothesis of the research:

$$\text{ROA}_{it}/\text{ROE}_{it} = \beta_0 + \beta_1 \text{ litigation Risk}_{it} + \beta_1 \text{ Controls}_{it} + \varepsilon_{it} \quad (1)$$

Model 2 is also used to test the second to fourth hypotheses:

$$\begin{aligned}\text{ROA}_{it}/\text{ROE}_{it} = \beta_0 &+ \beta_1 \text{ Litigation Risk}_{it} + \beta_2 \text{ CGl}_{i,t} \\ &+ \beta_3 \text{ Litigation Risk}_{i,t} \times \text{CGl}_{i,t} + \beta_J \text{ Controls}_{it} + \varepsilon_{it}\end{aligned} \quad (2)$$

The following are applicable for the current models:

Dependent variables

In this study, two financial performance indicators (i.e., return on assets and return on equity) were used. The following is how they are calculated:

(ROA): net profit divided by total assets.

(ROE): net profit divided by the number of shares of stockholders' equity.

Independent variable

Litigation risk: Previous theoretical and empirical research (Simunic, 1980; Pratt and Stice, 1994) has found that audit pricing is significantly influenced by the auditor's assessment of the client's business risk. Therefore, consistent with previous research (Badertscher *et al.*, 2014; Drake *et al.*, 2018), we use audit fees as a proxy for litigation risk, calculated as the natural logarithm of the bank's total audit fees (Shemshad and Karim, 2023; Shemshad, 2023).

Control variables

Operating income growth: From the difference in operating income between the current and previous years, divide the resulting figure by the operating income in the last year.

Size: the natural logarithm of the total book value of the bank's assets.

Cash flow: the natural logarithm of the cash flow from operating activities.

Turnover: total sales and services divided by total assets for the year.

Operating expenses: operating expenses divided by total sales for the current year.

Salary: the natural logarithm of executive directors' remuneration (bonus).

BtM: the ratio of book value to market value.

Modifier variables

Independent director: If the percentage of non-dependent directors in the total board exceeds the sample average, the value is one. Otherwise, it is zero.

Director size: If the log of the number of directors is greater than the sample mean, the value is one. Otherwise, it is zero.

Managerial ownership: If the percentage of managerial ownership is more significant than the sample mean, the value is one. Otherwise, it is zero.

4. Research Findings

4.1. *Descriptive statistics*

This section first discusses the descriptive statistics indicators, the results of which are shown in Table 1. Table 2 shows dummy variables.

Table 1. Descriptive statistics of variables.

Variable	Variable Symbol	Mean	Median	Max	Min	S.D.
Return of Assets	ROA	0.004	0.009	0.062	−0.317	0.051
Return of Equity	ROE	0.167	0.167	3.202	−4.19	0.559
Litigation risk	LITIGATION	0.096	0.03	0.859	0.0006	0.152
Operating income growth	OPINGROW	0.038	0.19	0.831	−3.984	0.906
Firm size	SIZE	19.485	19.53	22.75	15.14	1.456
Cash Flow	CASHFLOW	0.016	0.014	0.234	−0.369	0.084
Turnover	SALE	0.066	0.049	0.156	0.004	0.044
Operating costs	EXPEN	0.349	0337	0.843	0.057	0.211
Bonus	SALARY	9.102	9.186	10.903	6.11	1.096
The ratio of book value to market value of equity	BtM	0.715	0.807	1.84	−3.484	0.736

Table 2. Dummy variables.

Variable	Symbol		Number	Percentage
Independence of the board	INDEP	(0)	68	48.57
		(1)	72	51.43
Board size	DISIZE	(0)	124	88.57
		(1)	16	11.43
Management ownership	MO	(0)	68	4857
		(1)	72	51.43

4.2. *Results of research*

4.2.1. *Estimation of the first hypothesis*

The results of the first hypothesis test (dependent variables ROA and ROE) are presented in Tables 3 and 4. According to Table 3, the significance level between two variables is equal to 0.0464, which is lower than the significance level considered in the current research

Table 3. The result of the Hl test (Independent variable: ROA).

Variable Name	Coeff.	*t*-stat.	Sig.
C	0.11	0.805	0.4237
LITIGATION	−0.005	−2.004	0.0464
OPINGROW	0.0004	0.09	0.9278
SIZE	−0.006	−0.937	0.3518
CASHFLOW	0.22	4.167	0.0001
SALE	−0.239	−1.665	0.1005
EXPEN	−0.046	−1.832	0.0714
SALARY	0.002	0.573	0.5685
BtM	0.033	6.02	0.0000
R^2	0.763	F-stat	10.139
Adjusted R^2	0.688	Sig.	0.0000
Durbin–Watson	1.544		

Table 4. The result of the Hl test (Independent variable: ROE).

Variable Name	Coeff.	*t*-stat.	Sig.
C	−0.37	−0.22	0.824
LITIGATION	−0.8	−2.3	0.0246
OPINGROW	−0.073	−1.328	0.1886
SIZE	0.046	0.566	0.5733
CASHFLOW	−0.327	−0.501	0.6178
SALE	1.564	0.879	0.3822
EXPEN	0.36	1.156	0.2516
SALARY	−0.059	−2.053	0.0106
BtM	−0.112	−3.639	0.0058
R^2	0.726	F-stat	11.52
Adjusted R^2	0.611	Sig.	0.0000
Durbin–Watson	2.312		

(5%), as well as the absolute statistical value of t, which is equal to 2.004 from 1.96, which is equivalent to the distribution. The normal standard is 0.95, which is more significant; therefore, at the 95% confidence level, the null hypothesis that the risk of litigation does not have a negative effect on the financial performance of banks (return on assets) is not confirmed, and the leading hypothesis is confirmed. In other words, litigation risk has a negative effect on banks' financial performance (return on assets). According to Table 4, the significance level between the two variables is 0.0246, which is lower than the significance level considered in this research (5%). Therefore, at 95% confidence level, litigation risk has a negative effect on banks' financial performance (return on equity).

4.2.2. *Estimation of the second hypothesis*

In this research, three criteria were considered for internal corporate governance mechanisms: (1) the size of the board of directors, (2) the independence of the board of directors, and (3) the ownership of the management.

Table 5 shows the results of the test of the second hypothesis that the size of the board of directors affects the relationship between the risk of litigation and the financial performance of banks.

Table 5. The result of the H2 test (Independent variable: ROA).

Variable Name	Coeff.	*t*-stat.	Sig.
C	0.11	0.78	0.4325
LITIGATION	−.0006	−0.241	0.8098
DISIZE	0.01	0.405	0.6843
LITIGATION*DISIZE	−0.047	−0.389	0.6984
OPINGROW	0.0003	2.081	0.0352
SIZE	−0.006	−0.956	0.3423
CASHFLOW	0.216	3.96	0.0002
SALE	−0.219	−1.425	0.159
EXPEN	−0.043	−1.425	0.112
SALARY	0.002	2.659	0.0122
BtM	0.033	5.92	0.0000
R^2	0.764	*F*-stat	9.013
Adjusted R^2	0.679	Sig.	0.0000
Durbin–Watson	1.566		

Table 6. The result of the H2 test (Independent variable: ROE).

Variable Name	Coeff.	t-stat.	Sig.
C	−0.422	−0.246	0.8063
LITIGATION	0.752	2.131	0.0369
DISIZE	−0.387	−1.195	0.2363
LITIGATION*DISIZE	1.547	1.039	0.3025
OPINGROW	−0.072	1.294	0.2
SIZE	0.063	0.75	0.4556
CASHFLOW	−0.175	−0.262	0.7937
SALE	0.837	0.445	0.6576
EXPEN	0.252	0.768	0.4451
SALARY	−0.077	−1.647	0.1044
BtM	−0.128	−1.833	0.0714
R^2	0.642	F-stat	31.47
Adjusted R^2	0.505	Sig.	0.0000
Durbin–Watson	2.342		

According to Table 5, the level of significance between two variables is equal to 0.6984, which shows that the size of the board of directors has no effect on the relationship between the risk of litigation and the financial performance of banks (profitability). According to Table 6, the level of significance between the two variables is equal to 0.3025, which means that the size of the board of directors cannot moderate the relationship between the risk of litigation and the financial performance of banks (with the return on equity index).

4.2.3. *Estimation of the third hypothesis*

According to Table 7, the significance level between the two variables is equal to 0.1218, which shows that the board of directors' independence has no effect on the relationship between the risk of litigation and the financial performance of banks (profitability). Also, the significant level of the interaction effect between the two variables is equal to 0.2301; based on the results of Table 8, it can be said that the independence of the board of directors has no effect on the relationship between the risk of litigation and the financial performance of banks (return on equity).

Table 7. The result of the H3 test (Independent variable: ROA).

Variable Name	Coeff.	*t*-stat.	Sig.
C	0.131	0.966	0.3376
LITIGATION	−0.045	−1.014	0.3142
INDEP	−0.021	−3.816	0.0039
LITIGATION*INDEP	0.067	1.482	0.1218
OPINGROW	−0.0005	−0.115	0.908
SIZE	−0.006	−1.057	0.2944
CASHFLOW	0.224	4.286	0.0001
SALE	−0.21	−1.471	0.1459
EXPEN	−0.037	−1.457	1497/0
SALARY	0.001	0.557	0.5793
BtM	0.034	6.232	0.0000
R^2	0.775	F-stat	9.614
Adjusted R^2	0.694	Sig.	0.0000
Durbin–Watson	1.55		

Table 8. The result of the H3 test (Independent variable: ROE).

Variable Name	Coeff.	*t*-stat.	Sig.
C	−0.212	−0.226	0.3376
LITIGATION	−0.148	−3.381	0.3142
INDEP	−0.163	−1.527	0.0039
LITIGATION*INDEP	0.893	1.211	0.1218
OPINGROW	−0.078	−1.166	0.908
SIZE	0.037	0.88	0.2944
CASHFLOW	−0.307	−0.638	0.0001
SALE	1.882	4.039	0.1459
EXPEN	0.449	2.847	1497/0
SALARY	−0.054	−1.261	0.5793
BtM	−0.105	−2.899	0.0000
R^2	0.64	F-stat	21.49
Adjusted R^2	0.515	Sig.	0.0008
Durbin–Watson	2.072		

4.2.4. *Estimation of the fourth hypothesis*

According to Tables 9 and 10, managerial ownership affects the relationship between litigation risk and banks' financial performance (return on equity and return on assets).

Table 9. The result of the H4 test (Independent variable: ROA).

Variable Name	Coeff.	t-stat.	Sig.
C	0.096	0.696	0.4886
LITIGATION	−0.015	−0.357	0.722
MO	0.004	3.383	0.0023
LITIGATION*MO	0.046	2.879	0.0123
OPINGROW	0.001	0.331	0.7414
SIZE	−0.005	−0.861	0.3924
CASHFLOW	0.224	2.4	0.0001
SALE	−0.27	−1.83	0.0707
EXPEN	0/046	−1.788	0.0784
SALARY	0.002	0.648	0.519
BtM	0.034	5.93	0.0000
R^2	0.772	F-stat	9.43
Adjusted R^2	0.69	Sig.	0.0000
Durbin–Watson	1.54		

Table 10. The result of the H4 test (Independent variable: ROE).

Variable Name	Coeff.	t-stat.	Sig.
C	−0.97	−0.577	0.5658
LITIGATION	0.017	0.033	0.9735
INDEP	−0.172	−3.103	0.0053
LITIGATION*INDEP	1.367	2.13	0.037
OPINGROW	−0.077	−1.381	0.172
SIZE	0.068	0848	0.3992
CASHFLOW	−0.109	−0.167	0.8674
SALE	1.695	0.948	0.3464
EXPEN	0.481	1.524	0.1324
SALARY	−0.034	−0.77	0.4427
BtM.	−.0132	−1.998	0.0408
R^2	0.67	F-stat	21.64
Adjusted R^2	0.546	Sig.	0.0001
Durbin–Watson	2.282		

5. Conclusions and Suggestions

The results obtained from the first hypothesis of the research show that the risk of litigation affects banks' financial performance (return on assets and return on equity). Due to the negativity of the variable coefficient of litigation risk in both models of return on assets and return on equity, (−0.005) and (−0.8), respectively, the risk of litigation negatively affects banks' financial performance. The risk of litigation is a major threat to companies that intend to go public; in particular, companies with a high risk of litigation are more likely to cancel their IPOs. The cost of litigation is a heavy burden for companies, and companies that are sued face potential losses due to losing customers and suppliers. Therefore, litigation can often lead to a decrease in the company's value, damage relationships with customers and suppliers, and affect its business activities. The findings of the present study (testing the first hypothesis) are consistent with the results of other studies (Lin *et al.*, 2013; Koh *et al.*, 2014).

The results of the second hypothesis of the research show that the size of the board of directors does not affect the relationship between the risk of litigation and the financial performance of banks. In our country, despite the compilation of corporate governance principles and the need to implement them, companies are not yet required to present them to the public, even voluntarily. Therefore, given the weakness of the control environment in Iranian banks and the constant number of board members (five on average), board size cannot effectively moderate the relationship between litigation risk and bank performance. This finding indicates that board effectiveness is more closely related to the quality of supervision, the corporate governance structure, and member independence than to board size. In this regard, the results of the second hypothesis test are inconsistent with and do not support the findings of Wu *et al.* (2020); an issue that could be due to differences in the institutional and regulatory environments and the level of corporate governance maturity in Iran compared to those studied in previous studies.

The results of the third hypothesis of the research show that managerial ownership affects the relationship between litigation risk and the financial performance of banks. Given the positive coefficients in the models of return on assets and return on equity, managerial ownership plays an important role in corporate governance by reducing the representation conflict between managers and shareholders. Countries transitioning from state control to market-based economies should strengthen government laws and improve their investment and market environment. This issue makes managerial ownership, including internal controls and monitoring mechanisms on the relationship between litigation risk, positively impact legal and bank performance. The results of the fourth hypothesis test are consistent with and supported by research findings (Wu *et al.*, 2020; Agnes Cheng *et al.*, 2010).

According to the research results, the following is suggested:

1. Due to the negative impact of litigation risk on bank performance, it is recommended that bank management focus more on litigation risk management to improve bank performance and asset returns.
2. It is recommended that bank management pay more attention to cases that increase potential debt or litigation.
3. Corporate governance is a concept that has been proposed in recent years to address issues such as accountability and improving the quality of information. Given the weakness of corporate governance in some Asian countries, as well as the lack of solid foundations of corporate governance in the public and private sectors, this can lead to many financial crises. Therefore, it is suggested that the Stock Exchange Organization closely monitor managers' activities and performance, as well as the publication of information and reports by banks.

References

Agnes Cheng, C. S., He Huang, H., Li, Y., and Lobo, G. (2010). Institutional monitoring through shareholder litigation. *Journal of Financial Economics*, 95(3), 356–383. https://doi.org/10.1016/j. jfineco.2009.11.006.

Alexander, J. C. (1990). Do the merits matter: A study of settlements in securities class actions. *Stan. L. Rev*, 43, 497.

Arena, M. P. (2018). Corporate litigation and debt. *Journal of Banking and Finance*, 87, 202–215. https://doi.org/10.1016/j.jbankfin. 2017.10.005.

Arena, M. P. and Ferris, S. P. (2018). A global analysis of corporate litigation risk and costs. *International Review of Law and Economics*, 56, 28–41. https://doi.org/10.1016/j.irle.2018.05.003.

Arena, M. P. and Julio, B. (2021). Litigation risk management through corporate payout policy. *Journal of Financial and Quantitative Analysis*, 58(1), 148–174. https://doi.org/10.1017/S002210902200076X.

Arena, M. and Julio, B. (2015). The effects of securities class action litigation on corporate liquidity and investment policy. *Journal of Financial and Quantitative Analysis*, 50(1–2), 251–275. https://doi.org/10.1017/ S0022109015000010.

Badertscher, B., Jorgensen, B., Katz, S., and Kinney, W. (2014). Public equity and audit pricing in the United States. *Journal of Accounting Research*, 52(2), 303–339. https://doi.org/10.1111/1475-679X.12041.

Bao, Z. and Motlagh, B. P. (2024). How investment efficiency affects firms performance? *Accounting and Auditing with Applications*, 1(1), 17–26.

Bourveau, T., Lou, Y., and Wang, R. (2018). Shareholder litigation and corporate disclosure: Evidence from derivative lawsuits. *Journal of Accounting Research*, 56(3), 797–842. https://doi.org/10.1111/1475-679X.12191.

Brown, L. D. and Caylor, M. L. (2009). Corporate governance and firm operating performance. *Review of Quantitative Finance and Accounting*, 32, 129–144.

Cheung, Y. L., Jiang, P., Limpaphayom, P., and Lu, T. (2010). Corporate governance in China: A step forward. *European Financial Management*, 16(1), 94–123. https://doi.org/10.1111/j.1468-036X.2008.00446.x.

Dash, S. R. and Raithatha, M. (2018). Impact of disputed tax litigation risk on firm performance: Evidence from India. *Accounting Research Journal*, 31(3), 458–478. https://doi.org/10.1108/ARJ-07-2016-0095.

Diamond, D. W. (2004). Presidential address, committing to commit: Short-term debt when enforcement is costly. *Journal of Finance*, 59(4), 1447–1479. https://doi.org/10.1111/j.1540-6261.2004.00669.x.

Drake, M. S., Cassell, C. A., and Dyer, T. A. (2018). Auditor litigation risk and the number of institutional investors. *Auditing*, 37(3), 71–90. https://doi.org/10.2308/ajpt-51832.

Durongkadej, I., Wei, S., and Rao, R. (2021). Shareholder litigation and the risk incentive effect of executive compensation: A re-examination. *Finance Research Letters*, 41. https://doi.org/10.1016/j.frl.2020.101790.

Engelmann, K. and Cornell, B. (1988). Measuring the cost of corporate litigation: Five case studies. *The Journal of Legal Studies*, 17(2), 377–399. https://doi.org/10.1086/468134.

Field, L., Lowry, M., and Shu, S. (2005). Does disclosure deter or trigger litigation? *Journal of Accounting and Economics*, 39(3), 487–507. https://doi.org/10.1016/j.jacceco.2005.04.004.

Francis, J., Philbrick, D., and Schipper, K. (1994). Shareholder litigation and corporate disclosures. *Journal of Accounting Research*, 32(2), 137. https://doi.org/10.2307/2491279.

Gande, A. and Lewis, C. M. (2009). Shareholder-initiated class action lawsuits: Shareholder wealth effects and industry spillovers. *Journal of Financial and Quantitative Analysis*, 44(4), 823–850. https://doi.org/10.1017/S0022109009990202.

Godfrey, P. C., Merrill, C. B., and Hansen, J. M. (2009). The relationship between corporate social responsibility and shareholder value: An empirical test of the risk management hypothesis. *Strategic Management Journal*, 30(4), 425–445. https://doi.org/10.1002/smj.750.

Guo, J., Huang, P., Zhang, Y., and Zhou, N. (2015). The effect of employee treatment policies on internal control weaknesses and financial restatements. *Accounting Review*, 91(4), 1167–1194. https://doi.org/10.2308/accr-51269.

Hao, G. Q. (2011). Securities litigation, withdrawal risk and initial public offerings. *Journal of Corporate Finance*, 17(3), 438–456. https://doi.org/10.1016/j.jcorpfin.2010.12.005.

Imeni, M. and Edalatpanah, S. A. (2023). Resilience: Business sustainability based on risk management. *Industrial and Applied Mathematics*, Part F2111, 199–213. https://doi.org/10.1007/978-981-19-9909-3_9.

Jensen, M. C. and Meckling, W. H. (1976). Theory of the firm: Managerial behavior, agency costs, and ownership structure. *Journal of Financial Economics*, 3, 305–360. https://doi.org/10.1016/0304-405X(76)90026-X.

Johnson, W. C., Xie, W., and Yi, S. (2014). Corporate fraud and the value of reputations in the product market. *Journal of Corporate Finance*, 25, 16–39. https://doi.org/10.1016/j.jcorpfin.2013.10.005.

Karpoff, J. M. and Lott, J. R. (1993). The reputational penalty firms bear from committing criminal fraud. *The Journal of Law and Economics*, 36(2), 757–802.

Karpoff, J. M., Lee, D. S., and Martin, G. S. (2008). The cost to firms of cooking the books. *Journal of Financial and Quantitative Analysis*, 43(3), 581–611. https://doi.org/10.1017/S0022109000004221.

Kaviani, M., Kaviani, K., and Kaviani, M. (2024). Working capital management and profitability of banks: Evidence from the Iranian capital market. *Transactions on Quantitative Finance and Beyond*, 1(1), 29–34. https://tqfb.reapress.com/journal/article/view/18.

Kinney, W. R. and McDaniel, L. S. (1989). Characteristics of firms correcting previously reported quarterly earnings. *Journal of Accounting and Economics*, 11(1), 71–93. https://doi.org/10.1016/0165-4101(89)90014-1.

Koh, P. S., Qian, C., and Wang, H. (2014). Firm litigation risk and the insurance value of corporate social performance. *Strategic Management Journal*, 35(10), 1464–1482. https://doi.org/10.1002/smj.2171.

Levy, H., Shalev, R., and Zur, E. (2018). The effect of CFO personal litigation risk on firms' disclosure and accounting choices. *Contemporary Accounting Research*, 35(1), 434–463. https://doi.org/10.1111/1911-3846.12378.

Lin, B., Zhou, M., Shu, W., and Liu, C. (2013). Internal control, litigation risk and firm valuation. *China Accounting Review*, 11, 431–456.

Liu, N., Laing, E., Cao, Y., and Zhang, X. (2018). Institutional ownership and corporate transparency in China. *Finance Research Letters*, 24, 199–220. https://doi.org/10.1016/j.frl.2017.12.001.

Malm, J. and Kanuri, S. (2020). Litigation risk and payout policy. *Managerial Finance*, 46(11), 1391–1406. https://doi.org/10.1108/MF-09-2019-0485.

Malm, J., Soyeh, K. W., and Kanuri, S. (2023). Litigation risk and corporate performance. *Journal of Behavioral and Experimental Finance*, 37. https://doi.org/10.1016/j.jbef.2022.100725.

Mashyekh Pul, Z. and Fallah, R. (2021). The effect of auditing fees on the relationship between auditor time pressure and profit quality. *Big Data and Computing Visions*, 1(4), 179–191. https://doi.org/10.22105/bdcv.2021.142088.

Nguyen, H. T., Phan, H. V., and Sun, L. (2018). Shareholder litigation rights and corporate cash holdings: Evidence from universal demand laws. *Journal of Corporate Finance*, 52, 192–213. https://doi.org/10.1016/j.jcorpfin.2018.08.002.

Pratt, J. and Stice, J. D. (1994). The effects of client characteristics on auditor litigation risk judgments, required audit evidence, and recommended audit fees. *The Accounting Review*, 69(4), 639–656.

Rice, S. C. and Weber, D. P. (2012). How effective is internal control reporting under SOX 404? Determinants of the (non-)disclosure of existing material weaknesses. *Journal of Accounting Research*, 50(3), 811–843. https://doi.org/10.1111/j.1475-679X.2011.00434.x.

Sharfman, M. P. and Fernando, C. S. (2008). Environmental risk management and the cost of capital. *Strategic Management Journal*, 29(6), 569–592. https://doi.org/10.1002/smj.678.

Shemshad, A. (2023). Financial distress and audit fees: New evidence of the role of firm size. *Innovation Management and Operational Strategies*, 4(4), 355–368.

Shemshad, A. and Karim, R. G. (2023). The effect of managerial ability on the timeliness of financial reporting: The role of audit firm and company size. *Journal of Operational and Strategic Analytics*, 1(1), 34–41. https://doi.org/10.56578/josa010105.

Shleifer, A. and Vishny, R. W. (1997). A survey of corporate governance. *Journal of Finance*, 52(2), 737–783. https://doi.org/10.1111/j.1540-6261.1997.tb04820.x.

Simunic, D. A. (1980). The pricing of audit services: Theory and evidence. *Journal of Accounting Research*, 18(1), 161. https://doi.org/10.2307/2490397.

Tseng, H. Y., Salam, N. A., Kazemi, M., Nadiheidari, H., and Mehlabani, E. G. (2024). Reevaluating the impact of corporate governance mechanisms on investment management, financing strategies, and corporate performance. *Management Analytics and Social Insights*, 1(1), 1–16. https://masi.reapress.com/journal/article/view/18.

Waheed, A. and Malik, Q. A. (2021). Institutional ownership board characteristics and firm performance: A contingent theoretical approach. *International Journal of Asian Business and Information Management*, 12(2), 1–15. https://doi.org/10.4018/IJABIM. 20210401.oa1.

Waheed, A., Mahmood, H., and Wen, J. (2024). Corporate governance, litigation risk and firm performance: A mediation moderating model. *International Journal of Emerging Markets*, 19(3), 665–678. https://doi.org/10.1108/IJOEM-02-2022-0320.

Wu, W., Peng, F., Shan, Y. G., and Zhang, L. (2020). Litigation risk and firm performance: The effect of internal and external corporate governance. *Corporate Governance: An International Review*, 28(4), 210–239. https://doi.org/10.1111/corg.12319.

Zhang, H., Zou, Y., Zhang, L., Xiong, H., and Xie, Z. (2022). Absence of controlling shareholders and litigation risk: Evidence from China. *Emerging Markets Finance and Trade*, 58(4), 1176–1190. https://doi.org/10.1080/1540496X.2021.1973422.

https://doi.org/10.1142/9789819823161_bmatter

Index

E

F

O

P

Q

R

S

T

U

V

www.ingramcontent.com/pod-product-compliance
Lightning Source LLC
LaVergne TN
LVHW070907300926
849162LV00010B/1842
9789819823154